RECENTIORES: LATER LATIN TEXTS
AND CONTEXTS

Parody in the Middle Ages

"A picture of Nobody, since Nobody is depicted in it." An illustration from a book printed between 1505 and 1510, now Augsburg, Staats- und Stadtbibliothek rar 58, p. 152r. A modern classification number has been blocked out of the picture.

PARODY IN THE MIDDLE AGES

The Latin Tradition

Martha Bayless

Ann Arbor

THE UNIVERSITY OF MICHIGAN PRESS

Copyright © by the University of Michigan 1996
All rights reserved
Published in the United States of America by
The University of Michigan Press
Manufactured in the United States of America
⊗ Printed on acid-free paper

1999   1998   1997   1996   4   3   2   1

*A CIP catalog record for this book is available from the British
Library.*

Library of Congress Cataloging-in-Publication Data

Bayless, Martha, 1958–
     Parody in the Middle Ages : the Latin tradition / Martha Bayless.
          p.   cm. — (Recentiores : later Latin texts and contexts)
     Includes bibliographical references and indexes.
     ISBN 0-472-10649-X (alk. paper)
     1. Parodies, Latin (Medieval and modern)—History and criticism.
2. Middle Ages. 3. Parody.   I. Title.   II. Series: Recentiores.
PA8030.P35B39   1996
877′.0309—dc20   96-19030
                                                              CIP

The frontispiece is reproduced with the permission of the Staats- und
Stadtbibliothek, Augsburg.

To ignore or to underestimate the laughing people of the Middle Ages . . . distorts the picture of European culture's historic development.

—Mikhail Bakhtin, *Rabelais and His World*

Acknowledgments

For valuable help and suggestions in a wide range of fields I would like to thank Michael Lapidge, Peter Dronke, and my doctoral examiners, Douglas Gray and James Simpson. I also owe a debt of gratitude to many people who made comments, observations, and suggestions both analytical and paleographical. Foremost among these is Neil Wright, whose help with many points of Latin was invaluable. I am also grateful to Mary Garrison, who lent me her essay on centos and who served as an invaluable critic on the style and content of several chapters. Oliver Padel also gave advice on matters of style and helped with a number of thorny problems of transcription. Isabel Henderson was of enormous help as my graduate tutor at Newnham College. In addition the comments of Peter Jackson, Catherine Byfield, Debby Banham, Julia Crick, Jim Simpson, and Augustine Thompson illuminated many points and saved me from a number of errors. Catherine Byfield and Roger Calnan served as excellent typists, and Steven Shurtleff helped a great deal in the final stages of manuscript preparation. I am very grateful for the financial assistance provided by Newnham College, in the form of Clothworkers' Studentships in 1985–86 and 1986–87, and by the trustees of the Chadwick Fund, in the form of grants in the same years. Finally, I benefited considerably from the comments of the anonymous readers for the University of Michigan Press.

Contents

Abbreviations

Some of the works cited in this book are abbreviated as follows.

Acta Sanctorum	*Acta Sanctorum quotquot toto orbe coluntur.* Ed. Jean Bolland *et al.* Antwerp and Brussels, 1643–.
CSEL	*Corpus Scriptorum Ecclesiasticorum Latinorum.* Vienna, 1866–.
Lehmann	Paul Lehmann. *Die Parodie im Mittelalter.* 2d ed. Stuttgart, 1963.
MGH	*Monumenta Germaniae Historica.* Hanover, 1826–.
MGH, Poetae	*Poetae Latini Aevi Carolini.* Berlin, 1923.
Migne, *PL*	J.-P. Migne, ed. *Patrologiae [Latinae] Cursus Completus.* 221 vols. Paris, 1844–64.
Walther, *Initia*	Hans Walther. *Initia carminum ac versuum medii aevi posterioris Latinorum: Alphabetisches Verzeichnis der Versanfänge mittellateinischer Dichtungen.* Carmina medii aevi posterioris Latina 1. Göttingen, 1959.
Walther, *Proverbia*	Hans Walther. *Proverbia sententiaeque Latinitatis medii aevi: Lateinische Sprichwörter und Sentenzen des Mittelalters in alphabetischer Anordnung.* 9 vols. Carmina medii aevi posterioris Latina 2. Göttingen, 1963–86.

Biblical abbreviations conform to those used in the concordance to the Vulgate: *Novae Concordantiae Bibliorum Sacrorum iuxta Vulgatam Versionem Critice Editam,* ed. B. Fischer, 5 vols. (Stuttgart, 1977).

I have reproduced verbatim the spelling of both printed editions and works in manuscript. Thus passages quoted from nineteenth-century printed editions of Latin texts retain the *j* and *v* of the edition, as do my editions of sixteenth- and seventeenth-century manuscripts which spelled Latin with these letters. Many scribes of the late Middle Ages also mixed arabic and roman numerals randomly; I have retained this variation as it appears in manuscript.

Translations of biblical passages usually follow the Douay-Rheims version, although when the wording of the King James version is well known, as in such phrases as "Get thee behind me, Satan," I have used the King James version to retain a sense of familiarity. Where neither version allowed for puns made on the Latin, I have supplied my own translation.

For most of these texts it is impossible to give a smooth English translation that conveys much sense of the Latin wordplay, so I have striven to provide an accurate literal translation, however flat-footed the result. The reader should keep in mind, however, that the English is a poor substitute for the complexities of the original.

Note

Nothing demonstrates the popularity of medieval parody more than sheer numbers of manuscripts. When I began this project, so many remained unpublished that at one point I was finding new texts on a daily basis. It was to be predicted, then, that even as this book was going into press, new texts would turn up—far too late, unfortunately, to incorporate them into the body of the narrative. In an effort to be as complete as possible, I will mention them here. They are: the Short *Nemo* and a nonsense-cento, *Ex nihilo nihil fit,* in Ottobeuren, Benediktinerabtei MS 0.54; and the Long *Nemo* and a version of *Invicem* in Cologne, Historisches Archiv MS G.B. oct. 61. Though I will devote further scholarship to these texts, nothing in these discoveries alters the accounts given in this book in any significant way.

Without question many more texts remain undiscovered, and I would be grateful to hear of other new versions or manuscripts.

Martha Bayless
Department of English
University of Oregon
Eugene, Oregon 97403
U.S.A.

CHAPTER 1

Introduction

Serious medieval literature, and the culture from which it sprang, have been the objects of scholarly study for more than a century, but only lately have scholars been able to look the medieval sense of humor full in the face. Johan Huizinga's influential study *The Waning of the Middle Ages,* published in 1924, exemplifies the attitude of generations of critics: "What are we to say, lastly," he asks, "of the curious levity of the authors of the close of the Middle Ages, which often impresses us as an absolute lack of mental power?"[1]

In recent years, however, scholars have begun to pay serious attention to humorous texts, and studies of such works as medieval Latin satire, the Old French fabliaux, and the works of Boccaccio and Chaucer have demonstrated that medieval humor need not be intellectually unsophisticated, though it may still alarm those who, like Chaucer's Absolon, are "squeamish of farting." In sum, however, scholars have come to recognize that medieval culture was neither as monolithically serious nor as unremittingly grim as it has often been portrayed. Indeed, the more closely we study the Middle Ages, and the wider the range of sources we use in that study, the more the complexity of medieval culture becomes, like Alonzo in the sea, very rich and strange. In the realm of humor, modern scholars have increasingly come to depict this strange complexity as a polarity between two worlds: the "official" world of the Church and the "unofficial," carnivalesque world of the street. With increasing scholarly attention to medieval popular culture, moreover, many have come to see the contention between the serious and the carnivalesque as one of the defining aspects of the Middle Ages.

My purpose in the present work is to catalog, describe, and elucidate one variety of medieval carnivalesque literature, the parody of what we might now call nonfiction: hymns, prayers, Masses, saints' lives, biblical narrative, and so forth. It is unfortunate that these little pieces have languished in obscurity so long: they have close affinities with works in most of the medieval European

---

1. Johan Huizinga, *The Waning of the Middle Ages,* trans. F. Hopman (1924; reprint, Harmondsworth, 1975), 226.

vernaculars, they expand our understanding of the range of medieval literature significantly, and many of them are complex and entertaining works in their own right. But apart from the literary value of parodies, the very existence of the genre throws a cat among the pigeons of traditional assumptions about medieval culture. Medieval Latin parody confounds the polarity between the official and unofficial cultures: these carnivalesque texts, many lampooning religious forms and ideas, were written by and for members of what has been considered the bastion of medieval seriousness, the Church. In short, the complexities of the genre call into question many of the standard assumptions about the conflict between humorous literature and religious culture.

Before we can undertake a new assessment of such assumptions, however, we must be grounded in a detailed knowledge of the texts. The body of this work attempts this, outlining the historical and social context of Latin parody, exploring literary issues, and tracing the development of new forms and versions. The final chapter then discusses the implications of the form and its place in medieval culture. I hope, then, that this study will demonstrate two things: first, that medieval Latin parody was a widespread, uncontroversial, and often sophisticated literary form; and, second, that medieval culture consisted not of two worlds, diametrically opposed, but of a single world, varied and complex, with humor one of its most universal pleasures.

Parody: Definitions and Considerations

Before embarking on the study of medieval Latin parody specifically, it is important to define my terms and clarify the scope of the investigation. This chapter, then, will be taken up with first principles: an explanation of what, for the purposes of this study, constitutes parody, and the ways in which it relates to its model; an outline of the historical and literary scope of the study; a general description of the character of medieval Latin parody; and, finally, an overview of previous scholarship on the topic.

Parody is a particularly elusive literary term, and few critics have agreed on its precise definition. Historically the word is derived from the Greek παρωδία—a combination of παρ(ά), "beside, subsidiary, mock-," and ᾠδή, "song, poem"—a term used to describe humorous imitations as early as the fourth century B.C.[2] The modern usage is considerably less exact than the

---

2. The various aspects of the definition of parody have been discussed by F. W. Householder, Jr., in "Parodia," *Classical Philology* 39 (1944): 1–9; F. J. Lelièvre in "The Basis of Ancient Parody," *Greece and Rome,* 2d ser., 1 (1954): 66–81; Hermann Koller in "Die Parodie," *Glotta* 35 (1956): 17–32; Wido Hempel in "Parodie, Travestie und Pastiche: Zur Geschichte von Wort und

ancient, and each scholar of the subject must specify his or her definition at the outset. Throughout this study, therefore, I define a parody as an intentionally humorous literary (written) text that achieves its effect by (1) imitating and distorting the distinguishing characteristics of literary genres, styles, authors, or specific texts (*textual parody*); or (2) imitating, with or without distortion, literary genres, styles, authors, or texts while in addition satirizing or focusing on nonliterary customs, events, or persons (*social parody*).

An example may serve to make this distinction between textual and social parody clearer. (I shall use modern illustrations, in this instance, to make the explanation as clear as possible.) Henry Wadsworth Longfellow's poem "The Song of Hiawatha" has provided fruitful material for the parodist. The style of the original is clear from this excerpt.

> He had mittens, Minjekahwuru,
> Magic mittens made of deer-skin;
> When upon his hands he wore them,
> He could smite the rocks asunder,
> He could grind them into powder.
> He had moccasins enchanted,
> Magic moccasins of deer-skin;
> When he bound them round his ankles,
> When upon his feet he tied them,
> At each stride a mile he measured![3]

G. A. Strong's textual parody of the poem, "Hiawatha Revisited," simply imitates and exaggerates the excesses of this style.

> When he killed the Mudjokivis,
> Of the skin he made him mittens,
> Made them with the fur side inside,
> Made them with the skin side outside,
> He, to get the warm side inside,
> Put the inside skin side outside;
> He, to get the cold side outside,
> Put the warm side fur side inside.

Sache," *Germanisch-romanische Monatsschrift,* 46 N. F. 15 (1965): 150–76; and in the *Oxford Classical Dictionary,* ed. N. G. L. Hammond and H. H. Scullard, 2d ed. (Oxford, 1970), s.v. "Parody, Greek."

3. *The Poetical Works of Henry Wadsworth Longfellow,* 6 vols. (New York, 1966), 2:139, bk. 4.

That's why he put the fur side inside,
Why he put the skin side outside,
Why he turned them inside outside.[4]

By contrast, Lewis Carroll's "Hiawatha's Photographing" both parodies Long-fellow's rhythms and satirizes a cultural convention, the pomposity of Victorian portrait photography. This representative passage describes the father's session with the photographer.

First the Governor, the Father:
He suggested velvet curtains
Looped about a massy pillar;
And the corner of a table,
Of a rosewood dining table.
He would hold a scroll of something,
Hold it firmly in his left-hand;
He would keep his right-hand buried
(Like Napoleon) in his waistcoat;
He would contemplate the distance
With a look of pensive meaning,
As of ducks that die in tempests.
    Grand, heroic was the notion:
Yet the picture failed entirely;
Failed, because he moved a little,
Moved, because he couldn't help it.[5]

Here Longfellow's rhythms serve primarily as a vehicle for the satire of Victorian aesthetics. In short, social parody satirizes something other than the literary text it parodies. This dimension of social satire is undertaken in addition to, rather than as an alternative to, the textual parody practiced in the work.

In including social parody in my definition of parody I depart from the practice of most scholars, who often see engagement with extraliterary social issues as outside the strict compass of true parody. To a great extent the definition of parody has been determined by the character of the texts prevalent in each era: thus the modern restriction of the term *parody* to textual parody results from the preponderance of exclusively textual parody in the modern

---

4. William Zaranka, *Brand-X Poetry: A Parady* [sic] *Anthology* (London, 1984), 203.
5. *The Penguin Complete Lewis Carroll,* ed. Alexander Woollcott (Harmondsworth, 1982), 769.

period.[6] In the later medieval period, however, social parody was by far the more popular category of the genre and served as the vehicle for a significant proportion of medieval satire. Parodies went under the guise of the most familiar literature of the day—the Bible, liturgy, sermons, decrees—but the ridicule was often directed at illicit drinking, gambling, gluttony, ecclesiastical corruption, or the vileness of the peasantry. Rather than being restricted to a form of intertextual commentary, parody was pressed to the service of larger social issues. Scholars of twentieth-century literature may be justified in excluding from their discussion of parody a category insignificant in the modern period, but its prevalence in the Middle Ages means that no scholar of medieval parody can afford to omit discussion of the social dimension of the genre.

With regard to satire, I shall define it simply as any form of literature, in verse or prose, which ridicules vice or folly. As parody is a ridiculing composition of a particular type, it can justly be considered a subgenre of satire.

Parody and Criticism of the Model Text

As in the demarcation of terms, the discussion of theoretical issues must be influenced by the particular character of medieval parody. Chief among these issues is that of the attitude of the parodist toward his literary model, the literary form he mimics. The minority view is summed up by the turn-of-the-century critic Arthur Symons, who claimed that admiration for the model was "the very essence of the act or art of parody."[7] Much modern critical theory, on the other hand, maintains that parody is intrinsically critical of its model. This critical nature, in this view, determines the types of text most likely to be parodied: the most popular targets are the avant-garde, with its conspicuous peculiarities, and more mainstream authors of a marked individuality, whose stylistic mannerisms are easily mimicked and recognized. In such cases parody has the effect of safeguarding literary convention and resisting innovation.[8] Other critics, however, feel that modern parody has now transcended that function and developed into a more independent art form, a type of self-

---

6. That critics often arrive at a definition of parody by studying texts of a limited historical period is discussed by Joseph A. Dane in *Parody: Critical Concepts versus Literary Practices, Aristophanes to Sterne* (Norman, Okla., and London, 1988), 175–84 (chap. 10, "Paul Lehmann"). Dane attempts to show that Lehmann's definition of parody in *Die Parodie im Mittelalter* suffers from an inadequate historical perspective.

7. Arthur Symons, ed., *A Book of Parodies* (London, n.d. [*c.* 1908]), v. On nineteenth-century views on this question see Christopher Stone, *Parody* (London, 1915), 12–14.

8. Among the many critics espousing this view are J. G. Riewald, in "Parody as Criticism," *Neophilologus* 50 (1966): 125–48; and Margaret Rose, in *Parody/Meta-Fiction: An Analysis of Parody as a Critical Mirror to the Writing and Reception of Fiction* (London, 1979).

consciously referential art. This view of the modern successor to conventional parody amounts to a redefinition of the term, a redefinition which has been adopted in some other recent discussions of parody.[9]

In most cases we find that the modern critics' assessment, based on the character of modern parody, is unsatisfactory for the analysis of medieval examples. Medieval parody, for instance, imitates a much different kind of text than those discussed in modern studies. Instead of relying on the eccentricities of highly individualistic texts to ensure reader recognition, medieval parodists took as their models the most widely known texts, the Bible foremost among them. In short, the Middle Ages parodied the classic and the conventional rather than the idiosyncractic and the avant-garde. Anthony Marks, in his survey of sixteenth- and seventeenth-century parody, recognized the canonical status of many medieval model texts, stating, ". . . the humorous effect (and satirical effectiveness) of such parodies often depends on the reader's reverence for the model, without which the implied contrast would be seriously impaired."[10] Marks assigns the birth of parody as an invariably critical force to the nineteenth century, citing a trial early in the century in which the idea was successfully refuted.[11]

Whenever the ascendancy of parody as the tool of conservative critical forces came about, it is certain that it had not yet occurred in the Middle Ages. This is true of both textual and social parody's treatment of the model text and is easily demonstrated by examining the types of parody produced during the period. There is, for example, a sizable proportion of religious parody which amuses its audience through the humorous imitation of religious literature without ridiculing religion per se. Such biblical parodies as the *Cena Cypriani*

---

9. The critical literature on this view of parody is summed up by Linda Hutcheon in "Authorized Transgression: The Paradox of Parody," in *Le singe à la porte: Vers une théorie de la parodie* (New York, 1984), 13–26. See also Linda Hutcheon, *A Theory of Parody: The Teachings of Twentieth-Century Art Forms* (New York and London, 1985); Rosemary Freeman, "Parody as a Literary Form: George Herbert and Wilfred Owen," *Essays in Criticism* 13 (1963): 307–22; G. D. Kiremidjian, *A Study of Modern Parody: James Joyce's* Ulysses, *Thomas Mann's* Doktor Faustus (New York and London, 1985); Clive Thomson and Alain Pagès, eds., *Dire la Parodie: Colloque de Cerisy,* American University Studies, ser. 2, Romance Languages and Literature 91 (New York, 1989); and Margaret Rose, *Parody: Ancient, Modern, and Post-Modern* (Cambridge and New York, 1993).

10. Anthony Marks, "The Parody of Liturgical and Biblical Texts in Germany in the Sixteenth and Seventeenth Centuries." (Ph.D. diss., University of Cambridge, 1970), 9, 10–11.

11. *Ibid.,* 10–11. William Hone, a London publisher and bookseller tried in 1817 for selling parodies of religious texts, successfully employed the defense that the objects of parody had been chosen solely on account of their familiarity and not out of disrespect. See William Hone, *The Three Trials of William Hone,* with introduction and notes by W. Tegg (London, 1876), 19, 119, 162.

(Cyprian's feast) served as teaching tools as well as humorous narratives, a function incompatible with any ridicule of the Bible. In such social parodies as drinkers' Masses, the ludicrous prayers and invocations of the parody contrast with the solemnity of the original, but this does not mean that the parody is actually critical of that solemnity; rather, tavern literature serves to point up the folly of those who have made wine their god.

Further, social parody is not invariably critical, even of the subjects it satirizes. To cite one instance, medieval satire on drinking and gluttony often regards these vices affectionately, with explicit or implicit indications that the satirists are drinkers and gluttons themselves. That medieval parody is not necessarily a critical force, however, does not mean that it never expresses criticism of its model or of social issues. But on the whole—and there are some important exceptions—medieval parody is not the tool of the reformer, literary or social. It is more often entertainment than polemic.

The Scope of the Investigation

The term *parody,* in its range of definitions, has often been applied uncritically to the satirical, the imitative, and the eccentric texts of the Middle Ages. This wealth of potential material makes it all the more important to limit the scope of this investigation and to explain these limitations in some detail. This explanation will, I hope, make unnecessary further discussion of the omission of certain texts that other scholars may have considered parody.

Briefly, this study is concerned with autonomous Latin parodies of non-imaginative literature (or, in modern terminology, nonfiction) current in the period from roughly A.D. 500 to 1500. By stipulating that the parodies under investigation be autonomous I mean to exclude all works of which only a portion is actually parodic (such as poems with isolated parodic lines) and parodies, however complete in themselves, which make up only part of a nonparodic work (such as parodic speeches in plays).

The parody of nonimaginative literature forms a coherent subcategory and confines the issues to those which can be adequately examined in a study of this length. The Middle Ages produced an abundance of parodic fiction—mock epic, beast epic, narrative poems, and both substantial and brief prose works with parodic components—as well as parodic lyric poetry. These form an important body of literature, and I would emphasize that I do not question their status as parody. They are omitted from this study simply to narrow the topic enough to make a detailed study possible.

The survey is confined to Latin texts, excluding both vernacular and mac-aronic works. The quantity of vernacular material from the later medieval period is immense, and scholarship in the field remains for the most part as elementary as that concerning Latin parody. At least as important as the vol-ume of material is the context in which Latin parody may most fruitfully be examined. Medieval Latin satire has long been recognized as a distinct genre and has been examined in several recent studies. To restrict the investigation to Latin parody, produced in a similar milieu and geared to the same restricted audience of clerics and learned men, facilitates comparison with this tradition. The exclusion of vernacular texts is possible by virtue of the peculiar relation-ship of Latin and vernacular parody: the direction of influence is almost ex-clusively from Latin to the vernacular. It is thus possible to undertake an assessment of the genre without detailed reference to vernacular parody.

The choice of A.D. 500 as the starting date is necessarily approximate, as none of the early medieval Latin parodies can be assigned a definite date of origin. The only text under investigation to have been composed before this date is the mock-biblical narrative known as the *Cena Cypriani,* which may have originated as early as the fifth century.[12] Though this was a very early production, the *Cena Cypriani* was widely known and imitated throughout the Middle Ages and thus qualifies as a genuine participant in the medieval tradi-tion. At the other end of the period, several factors make the date of 1500 similarly approximate. In the first place, several texts survive only in postmedieval collections but show good reason to be dated to the fifteenth century or earlier. Second, certain kinds of parody remained popular beyond the medieval period, and the production of new examples of traditional forms showed no significant break between the Middle Ages and the Renaissance. In these cases I shall discuss those traditions in which a specific text, rather than a broad category, has experienced continued development. So, for instance, the sixteenth-century elaborations of drinkers' Masses come under investigation, but there is no mention of postmedieval parodic centos, these having no rela-tion in content to their medieval forebears.

Three additional types of imitation are specifically excluded from this study. The first is the "Devil's Letter," a sarcastic commendation of sins purporting to be a letter from the Devil. I consider the Devil's Letter to be polemic rather than humor, and thus not parody but another distinctive form of satire. The second category is the political *passio,* a narrative describing political events in the

---

12. All references to printed editions are in the handlist of Medieval Latin parody, in App. 1.

style and phrasing of the story of Christ's passion. These *passiones* are primarily propagandistic and often have no humorous component whatsoever. The third type of imitation borrows the contents, rather than the form, of another type of literature: an example would be a poem that uses a grammatical conceit but does not have the form of a grammar. I have not included such works in this study.

Last, there remains a class of text with unusual features, characteristics which have led some critics to propose that the works are mockeries rather than serious examples of their genre. These texts range from relatively conventional medieval works, such as Geoffrey of Monmouth's *Historia regum Britanniae*,[13] to the peculiar seventh-century grammars of Virgilius Maro Grammaticus, the *Epitomae* and *Epistolae*.[14] I have considered the likely candidates for inclusion in this study and have rejected several on the grounds that there is insufficient proof to call them parody. To go into the details of these decisions for every text is, unfortunately, beyond the scope of this investigation.

The complete schema of classification used in this study is set out in the handlist of medieval Latin parody in appendix 1. In other histories of the subject (see "History of Scholarship" later in this chapter), parodies have been classified by theme or by intent; but these classifications obscure the modus operandi of parody, which is the imitation of form. In appendix 1, therefore, and throughout this study, parodies are grouped according to the form of the text they imitate. In some instances, as in the case of drinkers' Masses, form and theme fall together to constitute subcategories; in other cases theme is discussed where appropriate.

My object has been to supply a basic reference work on medieval Latin parody. The immensity of the field, however, has meant that only a limited number of parodic traditions can be treated in any detail in a single volume. In this volume I have concentrated on the most widespread and prolific traditions of religious parody: biblical parody, mock saints' lives, liturgical parody, and humorous centos of religious texts. I hope to follow this study with another treating the principal secular traditions. In the interests of comprehensiveness,

---

13. The standard edition, though not entirely satisfactory, is *The* Historia regum Britanniae *of Geoffrey of Monmouth,* ed. Acton Griscom (London and New York, 1929). On this work as a parody, see Valerie I. J. Flint, "The *Historia Regum Britanniae* of Geoffrey of Monmouth: Parody and Its Purpose. A Suggestion," *Speculum* 54 (1979): 447–68.

14. *Virgilio Marone Grammatico: Epitomi ed Epistole,* ed. G. Polara, trans. L. Caruso, Nuovo Medioevo 9 (Naples, 1979). Critics who have called these texts parody include Paul Lehmann, in Lehmann 9–10; Mikhail Bakhtin, in *Rabelais and His World,* trans. Helene Iswolsky (Cambridge, Mass., 1968), 14; and R. A. S. MacAlister, in *The Secret Languages of Ireland* (Cambridge, 1937), 83–87.

however, appendix 1 provides full references for every parody known to me, including a number I have not been able to mention in the body of this book. Full references are given for those who wish to explore these small unexplored worlds. The necessary groundwork would be incomplete if the parodies themselves remained inaccessible: accordingly, in appendix 2 I have edited a number of texts, most of them previously unavailable in critical editions.

The Character of Medieval Latin Parody: An Overview

We are concerned, then, with a specific type of humorous imitation current in the Middle Ages: works that are self-contained parodic texts rather than components in larger, nonparodic works (such as, for example, parodic speeches in plays); they are wholly parodic, rather than containing isolated parodic lines or sections; and the survey is limited to Latin parodies of nonimaginative literature. Henceforth when I discuss medieval parody and its characteristics I shall be referring to this category of parody; my remarks should not be understood to apply to examples of parody outside this category.

The greater part of the remaining chapters of this study are taken up with selected strands of this genre: the parody of biblical narrative, of liturgy, and of saints' lives. Before looking at specific texts in detail, however, it may be helpful to outline the larger field of medieval Latin parody.

Parody was a popular form in all senses of the word: in its quotidian concerns, continuously adapted versions, and low status in the literary hierarchy; and in its widespread appeal to audiences. From the period 500 to 1500 there survive more than seventy Latin parodies of the type specified above; but this number, taken at face value, is misleadingly low. In practice continual rewriting took place, so that many redactions of old works are virtually new creations; when we count these variants as independent texts the number rises to more than two hundred. In addition several parodies with a relatively unchanging content survive in multiple copies, the most numerous being the *Apocalypsis Goliae* (The apocalypse of Golias), with sixty-eight manuscripts extant, and the *Cena Cypriani,* with fifty-four. Thus the quantity of surviving parody is considerably greater than the handlist of medieval Latin parody in appendix 1 might suggest. In assessing the popularity of the genre in the Middle Ages it is also necessary to take into account the probable low survival rate of such a low-status form. Even so, the number of parodies surviving allows us to assign parody a significant position in the satirical output of the Middle Ages.

Although parodies survive from every period of the Middle Ages, the character of parody did not remain static throughout that time. The texts of the early period (roughly 500–1100) are by and large amusing, noncritical works, often genuinely instructive. They are also principally textual, rather than social, parodies. The giant of the era was the *Cena Cypriani,* a tale told in biblical quotations and allusions, about a number of Old and New Testament characters attending a feast and ludicrously reenacting their biblical roles. The original text, which falsely went under the name of the third-century bishop St. Cyprian, was rewritten four times in the early medieval period: all versions combine humor with clear allegorical and didactic aims.

The few other parodies which survive from the early Middle Ages are gentle and amusing. The only potentially early caustic parody is *Salomon et Marcolfus,* a dialogue in which the fool Marcolf cruelly parodies Solomon's wise proverbs. The age of this piece is in question: although problematic references to it date from the sixth and tenth centuries, there is no certain allusion to the piece until the thirteenth century, and the earliest surviving manuscripts were written a century after that. Its uncertain date makes it difficult to say whether *Salomon et Marcolfus* gives genuine testimony to a more barbed early medieval wit.[15]

Mild literary parody remained popular throughout the later Middle Ages: early medieval parodies often retained their popularity and were joined by others, such as the legends of the fictional saints Nemo and Invicem. Nonsense prose also made its appearance at this time.

But it was in the later period (1100–1500) that a sharper, more satirical dimension appeared in parody. A new set of concerns also came to the fore, subjects which also occupied the goliard poets: the celebration of vices such as drinking, gluttony, and gambling. A favorite expression of these was the parody Mass, in which the worshipers paid homage to such figures as Bacchus and Decius. The popularity of this conceit spawned drinkers' gospels, sermons, prayers, epistles, and decrees, as well as liturgy. A similar goliardic impetus lay behind such productions as a thirteenth-century litany to the bad food served in taverns, and mock decrees from the archbishop of wandering scholars and the Lord of Misrule at Oxford University. These are social parodies of the mildest type. The ridicule grew stronger when it was directed at groups of which the author was presumably not a member. In mock genealogies the invective may be directed against the pope; in the mock recipe *Receptum pro stomacho*

---

15. On the dating of *Salomon et Marcolfus* see Robert J. Menner, *The Poetical Dialogues of Solomon and Saturn,* Modern Language Association of America Monograph Series 13 (New York and London, 1941).

S. Petri (Recipe for the stomach of St. Peter), against corrupt clergy; in an anti-Hussite Mass, against other sects. Thus, though humorous nonsatirical parodies persisted into the late Middle Ages, they were joined by a new breed of social parody extending across the spectrum from satirical to polemic.

To a great extent the rise in satirical parody paralleled the reemergence of other modes of satire in the twelfth century.[16] What status parody obtained as a genre was a reflection of the status enjoyed by satire, which had both prestigious Classical precursors and a position in the canons of formal rhetoric, advantages of which parody could not boast.

Whether chiefly amusing or chiefly polemical, medieval parody is rarely aesthetically sophisticated; it is popular rather than refined. The concerns of parody rarely intrude on those of more sophisticated literary genres, whether these were love and *courtoisie* or doctrine and scholarship. The forms and subjects involved reflect the everyday interests and preoccupations of clerics, students, and educated men, free from the constraints of religious and literary propriety. The most familiar passages of the Bible and liturgy, sermons, homilies, hagiography, grammars, and bad Latin are the stuff of parody. Though medieval parody is frequently clever, it is, above all, popular literature, written for simple entertainment as much as for artistry.

The predominance of ecclesiastical parody reflects the preeminence of the Church in medieval life and in particular the position of religious texts as the formal literature most familiar to the medieval audience of these works. Only about a tenth of the parodies surviving have no connection with the Bible or the Church. In religious parodies the most conspicuous target of satire is the corruption and avarice of the organized Church, followed by the ridicule of monks. The latter, for example, come under attack in a pair of mock homilies on adulterous monks; the *Metra de monachis carnalibus* (Verse on lustful monks), a satirical cento on monks; *Monachus ethymologyce* (The etymology of *monk*), a satirical acrostic; *De monachis* (On monks), a vicious mock grammar vilifying monks; and *Quondam fuit factus festus* (Once there was a feast made), a pidgin Latin satire of the higher clergy from the point of view of an upstart monk. By contrast, there is almost no mention of wandering scholars, traditionally assumed to be the retailers of such works. It may be, of course, that wandering scholars wrote these pieces and that they particularly wished to ridicule their more stolid brothers. But evidence for the *Metra de monachis*

---

16. On this reemergence see Rodney M. Thomson, "The Origins of Latin Satire in Twelfth Century Europe," *Mittellateinisches Jahrbuch* 13 (1978): 73–83.

carnalibus suggests that a good proportion of the manuscripts came from monastic houses—in short, that the monks were ridiculing themselves.

As is the case for other Latin satire of the Middle Ages, most Latin parody was the product of the clergy. The fascination with Church matters, with monks, and with the grades and ranks of the ecclesiastical hierarchy suggest that such criticism comes from within the system. The Church's monopoly on Latin satire was not absolute, however: we might keep in mind the example of the political *passiones,* which, as Paul Lehmann notes, may often be products of a secular milieu.

Medieval parody rarely offers any sophisticated analysis of its target: even at its most critical its aim is not to direct reform but to humiliate the victim. Its sugarcoated, uncomplicated satire made it an amusement for the widest Latin-educated audience. This is not to say that every parody was without literary merit. At least one example can be called a tour de force: the *Garcineida,* a celebration of the relics of the pseudosaints Albinus (Silver) and Rufinus (Gold), modeled on Terence. This formidable piece, the late-eleventh-century work of a churchman of Toledo, surpasses most medieval satire in a superb parody of the Church's flights of bombastic rhetoric. But although parody rarely reaches this height, it is often at least witty. Particularly notable are the *Cena Hrabani* (Hrabanus's feast) and Arras *Cena;* the legends of St. Nemo, lengthy mock sermons constructed on a framework of biblical puns; the *Apocalypsis Goliae,* an antimonastic parody of Revelations; and the *Sermo contra abstinentiam* (Sermon against fasting), a fifteenth-century parody of logic and philosophy which proves, by deduction from the writings of Aristotle and Boethius, that gluttony rather than fasting constitutes the greatest good.

The main run of parodies fall between the artistry of sophisticated literature and the crudity of the lowest classes of written works, such as ribald anecdotes. Although a measure of license is necessary for satire, parody rarely descends into obscenity or scatology. Sex is confined to the two tales of the adulterous monk, the *Passio cuiusdam nigri monachi secundum luxuriam* (Passion of a black monk according to excess) and *De cuiusdam claustralis dissolucione et castracionis eventu* (The downfall and castration of a certain monk), which told essentially the same story; to a few suggestive lines common to several texts; and to the scurrilous dialogue *Salomon et Marcolfus.* Scatology is restricted to even fewer works.

Parodies were also popular in the degree to which their audiences were involved with them: in composition as well as reception they were within reach of the average person with some knowledge of Latin. This means that parodies were subject to continual alteration, amplification, and pillaging of phrases and sections from one text to another. Frequently the variations from one copy to the next are due not to scribal corruption but to this deliberate and often wholesale revision. Few texts achieved a "canonical" status from which deviation was considered undesirable. In most cases, to produce a critical edition of a parody is merely to establish the starting point of a long history of elaborations: subsequent rewritings of the text were often as innovative as the original and were often better known to the medieval audience.

No category of parody escaped this repeated reworking. The *Cena Cypriani* was entirely rewritten four times, twice into verse. The *Evangelium secundum marcas argenti* (Gospel according to the mark of silver), a biblical cento about papal avarice, appears to have been reworked at nearly every copying, so that each of its sixteen manuscripts contains different jokes and quotations. *Quondam fuit factus festus,* a poem about a monastic dispute in deliberately laughable Latin, offered each of its eleven redactors the opportunity to rearrange both the plot and the grammar, and the length of the poem varies from eleven to sixty-two verses. These instances exemplify the medieval attitude toward these works as "participation texts" rather than as canonical works to be transmitted verbatim. Every copyist was a potential redactor. The number of variant versions of these texts shows a greater creativity on the part of scribes than might be supposed and reveals in addition a remarkable enthusiasm on the part of the average cleric, not only for literary creativity, but for humor and frivolity.

History of Scholarship

The popularity and composition of these parodies did not wane with the Middle Ages, though inevitable changes in style and theme gradually modified the nature of the genre. Throughout the sixteenth century we find medieval parodies copied and imitated: in the most conspicuous case, that of St. Nemo, the fictional saint becomes the subject of a succession of florid and self-consciously literary poems in both Latin and the vernaculars. Postmedieval parodic liturgy similarly continued to develop. In a sense, then, the first scholars of medieval parody were the satirists and littérateurs of the sixteenth century, who mined the medieval corpus to supplement and inspire their own prolific production of parody and satire. This was the role of such editors as Caelius Secundus Curio (1503–69), whose satirical compendium *Pasquillorum tomi duo* (1544) contained both genuinely medieval texts and postmedieval parodies in traditional styles. A more purely antiquarian interest may have lain behind the parody collection in Munich, Bayerische

Staatsbibliothek MS clm. 10751, a compilation assembled by the Benedictine monk Anton Husemann in 1575. Husemann wrote that he acquired his pieces "partim ex vetustis manuscriptis codicibus, partim ex familiaribus bonorum virorum et amicorum colloquiis"; both these sources evidently produced traditional material, for the greater part of the parodies in the collection are demonstrably medieval products. With changes in literary taste, however, and particularly with the growing domination of the vernacular, Latin parodies of the medieval type finally passed out of circulation, and there is markedly less interest from seventeenth-century writers and antiquarians.

The German scholars of the nineteenth century were the first to show a renewed interest in medieval Latin parody. The *Anzeiger für Kunde der deutschen Vorzeit* published notices of newly discovered parodies from the 1830s through the 1870s, providing a forum for Wilhelm Wattenbach's systematic publication of the parodies from Anton Husemann's 1575 collection. With new texts in print, it became possible to trace the development of individual parodies through time. Studies of the legends of St. Nemo appeared in 1876 and 1888, describing and analyzing the relationships of all the texts known at that time, and a number of scholars turned their attention to the *Cena Cypriani*.

The first general study of medieval Latin parody, Francesco Novati's long essay "La parodia sacra nelle letterature moderne," appeared in 1889.[17] Novati discussed only religious parody, both in Latin and in the vernacular, with a concentration on the medieval period. Although in principle his range of texts was restricted, in practice such a great proportion of medieval parody is religious that his survey of the field is more thorough than his title might suggest. Novati also edited four texts in an appendix: of these his *Neglectio epistolae beati Paulisper* remains the standard edition. Though the wide range of material makes his account somewhat chaotic, Novati was the first to analyze and collate, on a large scale, the information brought to light by texts already in print. His work also has the virtue of clear and accurate references.

Paul Lehmann's *Die Parodie im Mittelalter* first appeared in 1922 and has remained the classic work in medieval Latin parody, not least because no survey of the field has been attempted since that time.[18] Restricted to Latin works, Lehmann's survey aims to study a smaller range of texts than Novati's, although this virtue is outweighed by its lengthy digressions on nonparodic

---

17. Francesco Novati, "La parodia sacra nelle letterature moderne," in *Studi critici e letterari* (Turin, 1889), 177–310.

18. Paul Lehmann, *Die Parodie im Mittelalter* (1st ed.: Munich, 1922; 2d ed., Stuttgart, 1963). The appendix of the second edition was first printed separately as *Parodistische Texte* (Munich, 1923). All references are to the second edition.

satire. One of the most important accomplishments of *Die Parodie im Mittelalter* is its appendix, in which Lehmann assembled and edited twenty-two parodies; five more appeared in the second edition.

Lehmann was the first to discuss the complete range of medieval Latin parody, an achievement of considerable value; but in many ways his book is seriously flawed. Its first shortcoming is Lehmann's failure to distinguish in practice between parody and satire, so that his discussion of parodic tradition is often confused by the inclusion of wholly nonparodic satires on similar themes. The second shortcoming of *Die Parodie im Mittelalter* weakens the book almost irreparably: Lehmann's references are frequently both inadequate and unreliable. A number of parodies are mentioned without references either to printed editions or to manuscript sources; references to secondary sources and modern scholarship are rarely given, and when given they are often incorrect; at several points only the German translation of a text is printed, and in some cases these texts are otherwise unpublished and hence the original Latin is in effect unobtainable.

At times Lehmann's carelessness and slipshod references have more serious consequences. A single example will suffice. As the first text in his appendix, Lehmann edits the *Evangelium secundum marcas argenti,* a Money-Gospel best known to modern scholars by virtue of its inclusion in the *Carmina Burana.* Lehmann lists eighteen manuscripts of the text, which he edits in three groups. These consist of the "oldest" version (the thirteenth-century *Carmina Burana* text alone); a "youngest" (latest) version (a single fifteenth-century text, with a reference to another manuscript, which is in fact a copy of the intermediate version); and an intermediate version. The intermediate version as edited by Lehmann has been reconstructed from only eleven of the fifteen unedited manuscripts; and though the individual manuscripts contain significant differences—some are almost twice as long as others—Lehmann makes no indication of this and prints no apparatus. Lehmann classifies with this intermediate version the four manuscripts not used in the edition, and he apparently does so at random, never having examined the manuscripts. Of the four, one is a different parody altogether. The notes to these editions are so chaotic that the deficiencies of Lehmann's editing process are not clear without considerable study, and the lack of apparatus makes it difficult to recognize, even with the original manuscript in hand, that his transcriptions are inaccurate.

The second edition of *Die Parodie im Mittelalter,* which appeared in 1963, confirms, rather than remedies, Lehmann's failings. In particular the book makes almost no use of scholarship which had appeared since 1922. To cite a single instance, Lehmann did not note the new editions, based on newly discovered manuscripts, of *Rusticus que pars* and *Preces famulae sacerdotis*, two parodies printed in his first edition (one only in a German translation), though these new editions appeared in *Studi medievali* as early as 1931. He failed to make use of a number of other discoveries, even neglecting to consult Hans Walther's *Initia carminum* (1959), which lists additional manuscripts of several of the parodies in Lehmann's appendix. Although the second edition adds five texts to the appendix, Lehmann does not reedit any of the original texts in the cases in which he does note new manuscripts. Neither does he correct errors: in one place, for example, he continues to refer to Munich clm. 10751 as Munich 17501 (1st ed., p. 203; 2d ed., p. 147). The second edition has no bibliography, no table of abbreviations, no general index, and an incomplete index of parodies. In short, Lehmann's catholic reading and valuable knowledge of manuscript material are unfortunately offset by the inadequacy of his presentation. The mere difficulty of using the book may have acted as a deterrent to later would-be scholars of parody.[19]

Aside from *Die Parodie im Mittelalter*, twentieth-century scholarship in the field has been confined to the analysis of single texts, most notably the *Cena Cypriani*. Although significant advances have been made in the study of medieval satire,[20] there has been no further attempt to assess medieval Latin parody as a whole. The absence of a reliable handlist of texts, coupled with the lack of groundwork in the analysis of literary relationships and genre development, have meant that, despite Lehmann's encyclopedic aims, work in the field must still begin with the most elementary questions.

---

19. Further observations on Lehmann's deficiencies and on medieval Latin parody in general are provided by Fidel Rädle, "Zu den Bedingungen der Parodie in der lateinischen Literatur des hohen Mittelalters," in *Literaturparodie in Antike und Mittelalter*, ed. Wolfram Ax and Reinhold F. Glei (Trier, 1993): 171–85.

20. Important general studies include Thomson, "Origins"; John A. Yunck, *The Lineage of Lady Meed: The Development of Mediaeval Venality Satire*, University of Notre Dame Publications in Mediaeval Studies 17 (Notre Dame, Ind., 1963); Josef Benzinger, *Invectiva in Romam: Romkritik im Mittelalter vom 9. bis 12. Jahrhundert*, Historische Studien 404 (Lübeck and Hamburg, 1968); and Helga Schüppert, *Kirchenkritik in der lateinischen Lyrik des 12. und 13. Jahrhunderts*, Medium Aevum, Philologische Studien 23 (Munich, 1972).

CHAPTER 2

The Biblical Feast and Allegorical Parody

The *Cena Cypriani*

The *Cena Cypriani* may be the most popular parody known to the Middle Ages; it was also one of the most extraordinary. Cast in the form of a parable or an episode in Scripture, it is an allegorical concatenation of biblical characters and incident jumbled together at a peculiar feast. The success of this unprecedented literary endeavor was great enough to inspire four medieval imitations and a learned exegetical commentary, and the tradition as a whole does much to illuminate the relationship of humor and religion in the Middle Ages.

The *Cena Cypriani* is a short text, in prose, of some fifteen hundred words.[1] Ostensibly in the form of a story or parable, it nevertheless has a disjointed and seemingly pointless plot. The tale is set at a wedding feast given by a certain Joel, king of Cana, and revolves around the progress of the banquet and the behavior of the king and his guests. But although the substance of the tale is unusual, the focus of the story is the inventories of characters and their actions, each action or attribute drawn from the character's role in the Bible. The description of the seating at the banquet illustrates the narrative method.

Primus itaque omnium sedit
    Adam in medio, Eva super folia,
    Cain super aratrum, Abel super mulgarium,
    Noe super arcam, Iafeth super lateres,
    Abraham sub arbore, Isaac super aram . . .
    Iesus super puteum, Zachaeus super arborem,
    Matthaeus super scamnum, Rebecca super hydriam,
    Raab super stuppam, Ruth super stipulam,
    Thecla super fenestram, Susanna in horto,

---

1. It is edited in Karl Strecker, "Iohannis Diaconi versiculi de cena Cypriani," *MGH, Poetae,* 4.2: 857–900 (at 872–98); and in Christine Modesto, *Studien zur Cena Cypriani und zu deren Rezeption,* Classica Monacensia 3 (Tübingen, 1992), 14–34. Modesto's study was published too late to be incorporated into this chapter.

Abessalon in frondibus, Iudas super loculum,
Petrus super cathedram, Iacobus super retem,
Samson super columnam, Heli super sellam,
Rachel super sarcinam. . . .

(*CC* 8–12, 19–26)

[And so first of all sat
    Adam in the middle, Eve on a leaf,
    Cain on a plough, Abel on a milk pail,
    Noah on an ark, Japheth on bricks,
    Abraham under a tree, Isaac on an altar, . . .
    Jesus on a well, Zachaeus on a tree,
    Matthew on a bench, Rebecca on a jug,
    Rahab on tow, Ruth on a stalk,
    Thecla on a window, Susanna in the garden,
    Absolon on foliage, Judas on a money box,
    Peter on a seat, James on a net,
    Samson on a column, Eli on a stool,
    Rachel on a bundle . . .]

Every action is accompanied by a similar list of characters. The text is, in effect, an animated catalog of symbols and correspondences, and, in its attention to detail, similar to the meticulousness of medieval exegesis; in its association of biblical characters with representative items, furthermore, it anticipates medieval religious iconography.

The plot too is singular, highly episodic and seemingly disjointed. A king called Joel invites a multitude of guests to a wedding in Cana. The guests bathe in the Jordan before arriving, and then they assemble for the wedding feast. The description of the feast is composed of numerous inventories of the guests' choice of seats, offerings, food, and so forth. At one point the guests seem to fall asleep, though it is unclear whether this represents an entire night's rest or merely a siesta. When they awake the king commands the guests to assume new clothes and prepare to return home. In response they offer parting gifts, whereupon certain items are found to be missing. Though all the guests are implicated in wrongdoing, Achar alone is condemned as a thief and sentenced to death by the king. At the king's behest, the guests kill Achar, bury him, and set off on the journey home.

The origins of this remarkable text are almost totally obscure, and little work has been done on the question since the turn of the century. Consequently nearly all the questions concerning the origin of the *Cena Cypriani* are matters of debate: scholars have reached no consensus on the text's date, place of origin, or authorship, or even on its purpose.

There is universal agreement that, on linguistic grounds, the *Cena* cannot genuinely be the work of St. Cyprian, the third-century bishop of Carthage and a martyr, to whom it is attributed in manuscript. In 1899 Adolf Harnack, one of the earliest scholars to study the piece, inaugurated one school of opinion on its authorship when he assigned it to another Cyprian, a poet who wrote in southern Gaul or northern Italy in the first half of the fifth century.[2] Harnack's attribution rests on his assertion that the author of the *Cena* knew the Apocryphal *Acta Pauli* and on the fact that a poet named Cyprian was active in one of the areas in which the *Acta Pauli* circulated. Nothing is known of this Cyprian beyond the fact that he was the author of the *Heptateuchos,* a Latin version of the Heptateuch in hexameters;[3] Harnack also credits him with another text attributed in manuscript to St. Cyprian, the *Oratio Cypriani.* By contrast, Hass disagrees that the *Heptateuchos* and the *Cena Cypriani* can be attributed to the same man, on the grounds that the two works use different versions of the Bible.[4] In favor of the Gaulish Cyprian's authorship is the fact that a man who had turned the Heptateuch into verse would have possessed the detailed knowledge of the Bible necessary to compose the *Cena;* but the systematic comparison of the *Heptateuchos* and the *Cena* needed to confirm this attribution has never been attempted.

Brewer, writing in 1904, agreed with Harnack in identifying the author of the *Cena* with that of the versified Heptateuch, but he disagreed on the circumstances of the poet. He attempted to show that Harnack's dating of the *Cena* rested on doubtful evidence, and he instead ascribed both pieces to a different Cyprian, a priest who corresponded with Jerome in 418.[5]

In 1912 Karl Strecker attempted to identify the version of the Bible used in the *Cena,* one of the key diagnostic elements in the search for the text's date and place of origin.[6] Strecker's preliminary opinion was that the author of the

---

2. Adolf Harnack, "Drei wenig beachtete Cyprianische Schriften und die 'Acta Pauli,'" *Texte und Untersuchungen zur Geschichte der altchristlichen Literatur,* N. F. 4, 3b (Leipzig, 1899).

3. This is edited in Leo Rudolf Peiper, *Cypriani Galli Poetae Heptateuchos,* in *CSEL* (1891) vol. 23.

4. W. Hass, *Studien zum Heptateuchendichter Cyprian mit Beiträgen zu den vorhieronymianischen Bibelübersetzungen* (Berlin, 1912).

5. H. Brewer, "Über den Heptateuchdichter Cyprian und die Caena Cypriani," *Zeitschrift für katholische Theologie* 28 (1904): 92–115.

6. Karl Strecker, "Die *Cena Cypriani* und ihr Bibeltext," *Zeitschrift für wissenschaftliche Theologie,* 54 (N. F. 19) (1912): 61–78.

Cena used the Codex Lugdunensis. The issue of the source of the *Cena*'s biblical references was taken up, along with other issues, by Arthur Lapôtre in a reply to Strecker's article in the same year.[7] Lapôtre disputed Strecker's suggestion that the author of the *Cena* knew the Codex Lugdunensis, and he argued instead that the piece was based directly on the Septuagint, with no Latin intermediary. Lapôtre also became the first scholar to devote attention to the literary aspects of the *Cena,* and he located complex symbolism and puns in its biblical references. In the most controversial part of his study, he analyzed the arrangement of objects in the banquet hall—the plough on which Cain sits, Abel's milk pail, Noah's chest, and so forth—and attempted to identify a place and period in which such an arrangement would have been found. He combined this evidence with other features of the banquet, such as the sequence of the courses and the presence of a siesta, in an effort to establish the social conventions of the milieu in which the *Cena* was produced. To this he added his interpretation of complexities in the text, concluding finally that the *Cena* was composed in Antioch in 362–63 and intended as a satire on the religious views of Julian the Apostate. He attributed authorship of this satire to a Spanish poet, Bachiarius, who is thought to be the author of a number of religious works, among them two poems also erroneously attributed to St. Cyprian, *Sodoma* and *De Iona.*

Lapôtre's conclusions have not found general favor among later scholars. They were first disputed in 1913 by Morin, who felt the *Cena* was too profane to be the work of an orthodox poet such as Bachiarius.[8] Instead Morin suggested that the *Cena* came from a milieu such as fifth-century Gaul, where there is evidence of a partially Christianized society in which non-Christians might have been familiar with the Christian tradition without social or legal compulsion to be reverent toward it.

The assumption that the *Cena* must have been irreverent informs many scholars' views, and critics have not hesitated to denounce the vulgarity of the text. Lapôtre, for example, asserts:

> il ne pouvait y avoir qu'une seule conclusion à tirer de la platitude manifeste ou de l'extravagante ineptie de la plupart de ses inventions: c'est qu'elles étaient sorties de la cervelle d'un pitoyable écrivain, muni sans doute d'une certaine érudition biblique, mais totalement dépourvu

---

7. Arthur Lapôtre, "La 'Cena Cypriani' et ses énigmes," *Recherches de science religieuse* 3 (1912): 497–596.

8. G. Morin, review of "La 'Cena Cypriani,'" by Arthur Lapôtre, *Revue Bénédictine* 30 (1913): 472–73.

de talent et de goût. . . . ne devait-on pas conclure logiquement qu'il
était animé d'intentions malveillantes à l'égard des livres saints du
christianisme?[9]

[there is only one conclusion to be drawn from the obvious vacuity or the
extravagant ineptness of most of his inventions: that they are the products of the brain of a miserable writer, armed, to be sure, with a certain
amount of biblical learning, but totally devoid of talent and of taste. . . .
mustn't one conclude logically that he was prompted by evil intentions
toward the holy scriptures of the Christian religion?]

Other critics have resolved the same uneasiness about the author's intentions
by disregarding the humor of the text. Brewer, for example, interpreted the
Cena as a reworking of a sermon of Zeno of Verona, intended, despite its
sensational elements, as a didactic story to impress the literal details of the
Bible on its audience.[10]

Scholars familiar with medieval parody have been more willing to consider
the possibility that the text might be both humorous and allegorical. Francesco
Novati recognized the comedy in the *Cena,* calling the piece a "bizarra face-
zia," but he also found a didactic intent, claiming that it combined "l'utile ed il
dilettevole."[11] In 1897 Ernesto Monaci suggested that although the piece may
have been composed as a purely didactic work, its peculiarities meant that it
was understood as parody later in its history.[12] In *Parodies des thèmes pieux*
Eero Ilvonen suggested that the *Cena* was an allegorical parody of the heavenly
feast, based on Matthew 22.1–14; he referred to it as "une facétie . . . irré-
vérencieuse."[13] Paul Lehmann thought it could well be either a serious or a
parodic imitation of the sermon of Zeno of Verona.[14] In his detailed study of
works derived from the *Cena,* Giovanni Orlandi regarded the piece as parody
pure and simple.[15]

The suggestion that the *Cena Cypriani* might be both parody and allegory is
perhaps the most foreign to modern views of religious literature, yet the piece

---

9. Ibid., 499.

10. Brewer, "Heptateuchdichter," 100–102.

11. Novati, "La parodia," 178, 181.

12. Ernesto Monaci, "Per la storia della *Schola cantorum* lateranense," *Archivio della R.
Società Romana di storia patria* 20 (1897): 451–63.

13. *Parodies des thèmes pieux dans la poésie française du moyen âge* (Paris, 1914), 2.

14. Lehmann 13–14.

15. Giovanni Orlandi, *Rielaborazioni medievali della "Cena Cypriani,"* Centro di Studi sul
Teatro medioevale e rinascimentale (Rome, 1978), 4 and passim.

can lay strong claims to an allegorical foundation. It would be well to examine this foundation before considering the more absurd aspects of the text's construction.

The *Cena Cypriani* as Allegory

The wedding feast as an image of the Kingdom of God has authority from both the Old and the New Testaments. Underlying this image are two separate traditions: first, the feast as an image of heaven; and, second, marriage as an image of Christ's relationship to the Church.[16]

One of the earliest images of the eschatological banquet—the banquet to take place in heaven at the end of time—occurs in Isaiah.

> Et faciet Dominus exercituum omnibus populis in monte hoc convivium pinguium, convivium vindemiae; pinguium medullatorum, vindemiae defecatae. (Is 25.6)

> [And the Lord of hosts shall make unto all people, in this mountain, a feast of fat things, a feast of wine, of fat things full of marrow, of wine purified from the lees.]

It also occurs in the cup that runneth over in the Psalms (Vulgate Ps 22.5) and in the New Testament, most notably in the words of Jesus to the apostles about the Kingdom of God.

> Et ego dispono vobis sicut disposuit mihi Pater meus regnum, ut edatis et bibatis super mensam meam in regno . . . (Lc 22.29–30)

> [And I dispose to you, as my Father hath disposed to me, a kingdom: that you may eat and drink at my table, in my kingdom . . .]

> Dico autem vobis, quod multi ab oriente et occidente venient et recumbent cum Abraham et Isaac et Iacob in regno caelorum. (Mt 8.11; cf. Lc 13.28–29)

> [And I say to you that many shall come from the east and the west, and shall sit down at table with Abraham and Isaac and Jacob in the kingdom of heaven.]

---

16. These themes are discussed further by Jean Daniélou, "Les repas de la Bible et leur signification," *La Maison-Dieu* 18 (1949): 7–33.

Further examples are found at Luke 22.15–18, Deuteronomy 12.5–7 and 12.17–18, Isaiah 55.1–2, and Revelation 3.20.

The image of the Messiah as bridegroom is also common. This was the standard interpretation of the Song of Solomon[17] and is reiterated at Revelation 21.2, 9; 2 Corinthians 11.2; Matthew 25.1; John 3.29; and Ephesians 5.25.

The image of the wedding feast of Christ is derived from these two metaphors. It is used in Matthew, for example.

> Et respondens Iesus dixit iterum in parabolis eis, dicens: "Simile factum est regnum caelorum homini regi qui fecit nuptias filio suo. Et misit servos suos vocare invitatos ad nuptias, et nolebant venire. . . . Et egressi servi eius in vias, congregaverunt omnes quos invenerunt, malos et bonos, et impletae sunt nuptiae discumbentium." (Mt 22.1–3, 10; cf. Lc 14.15–24)

> [And Jesus, answering, spoke again in parables to them saying: "The kingdom of heaven is likened to a king who made a marriage for his son. And he sent his servants to call them that were invited to the marriage and they would not come. . . . And his servants going forth into the ways, gathered together all that they found, both bad and good, and the marriage was filled with guests at table.]

Similar images occur at Revelation 19.7, 9; Revelation 22.17; Mark 2.19–20; Matthew 9.14–15; and Luke 5.33–36.

The *Cena Cypriani* is a detailed narrative of this feast, attended by Abraham, Isaac, Jacob, and other characters of the Bible, "mali et boni" [good and bad] (Mt 22.10), at the marriage of Christ the bridegroom to the Church in the Kingdom of God. The story is set in Cana, the site of the wedding feast at which Jesus performed his first miracle when he provided wine for the guests—that feast itself a prefiguration of the mystical wedding feast of God. The king, Joel, is a type of God; the guests reenact their biblical roles because participation in the life of the Old or New Testament is also participation in the figurative banquet offered by God. What takes thousands of years in historical time is telescoped into a single event, conforming with the statement in 2 Peter

---

17. See Claude Chavasse, *The Bride of Christ: An Enquiry into the Nuptial Element in Early Christianity* (London, 1940). On the interpretation of the Song of Songs see P. Vuillard, *Le Cantique des Cantiques d'après la tradition juive* (Paris, 1925); F. Ohly, *Hohelied-Studien* (Wiesbaden, 1958); and David Lerch, "Zur Geschichte der Auslegung des Hoheliedes," *Zeitschrift für Theologie und Kirche* 54 (1957): 257–77.

3.8: "unus dies apud Dominum sicut mille anni et mille anni sicut dies unus" [one day with the Lord is as a thousand years and a thousand years as one day].

Understanding the *Cena* as an allegory of life in the kingdom of God accounts for the story's lack of coherent incident, forward propulsion, or narrative structure. It also explains the sequence of crime and punishment at the end of the feast, a series of events otherwise oddly placed in a story of celebration and merriment. The sequence contains the significant elements of Christ's crucifixion: all the guests are guilty of sin, but only one takes on the burden of punishment. The sacrificial victim, Achar (also called Achan in Joshua), clearly prefigures Christ in the biblical account of his crime and death.

> Filii autem Israhel praevaricati sunt mandatum, et usurpaverunt de anathemate. Nam Achan filius Charmi . . . tulit aliquid de anathemate, iratusque est Dominus contra filios Israhel. . . .
>
> Dixitque Dominus ad Iosue, "Surge, cur iaces pronus in terra? Peccavit Israhel, et praevaricatus est pactum meum: tuleruntque de anathemate, et furati sunt atque mentiti, et absconderunt inter vasa sua. . . . Anathema in medio tui est Israhel: non poteris stare coram hostibus tuis, donec deleatur ex te qui hoc contaminatus est scelere. . . . Et quicumque ille in hoc facinore fuerit deprehensus, conburetur igni cum omni substantia sua, quoniam praevaricatus est pactum Domini, et fecit nefas in Israhel. (Jos 7.1, 10–11, 13, 15)

> [But the children of Israel transgressed the commandment, and took to their own use of the anathema. For Achan the son of Charmi . . . took something of the anathema. And the Lord was angry against the children of Israel. . . .
>
> And the Lord said to Joshua: "Arise, why liest thou flat on the ground? Israel hath sinned, and transgressed my covenant: and they have taken of the anathema, and have stolen and lied, and have hidden it among their goods. . . . The anathema is in the midst of these, O Israel: thou canst not stand before thy enemies, till he be destroyed out of thee that is defiled with this wickedness. . . . And whosoever he be that shall be found guilty of this fact, he shall be burnt with fire with all his substance, because he hath transgressed the covenant of the Lord, and hath done wickedness in Israel."]

Joshua accuses Achan of the crime.

Responditque Achan Iosue, et dixit ei: "Vere ego peccavi Domino Deo Israhel, et sic et sic feci." . . . ubi dixit Iosue, "Quia turbasti nos, exturbet te Dominus in die hac." Lapidavitque eum omnis Israhel: et cuncta quae illius erant, igne consumpta sunt. Congregaverunt quoque super eum acervum magnum lapidum . . . (Jos 7.20, 25–26)

[And Achan answered Joshua, and said to him: "Indeed I have sinned against the Lord the God of Israel, and thus and thus have I done. . . . Where Joshua said: "Because thou has troubled us, the Lord trouble thee this day." And all Israel stoned him: and all things that were his, were consumed with fire. And they gathered together upon him a great heap of stones . . .]

The parallel incident in the *Cena Cypriani* follows.

et posteaquam probatum est regi, quod Achar filius Charmi solus esset reus furti, iussit eum mori donavitque eum omnibus. Tum occasione accepta
   primus omnium calce eum percussit Moyses, abiit in complexum
      Iacob,
   vestem detraxit Thecla, ad terram elisit Danihel,
   lapide percussit David, virga Aaron,
   flagello Iesus, medium aperuit Iudas,
   lancea transfixit Eliezer.
Tunc iussit rex, uti qui mortuus erat sepeliretur. (*CC* 258–65)

[And after it was shown to the king that Achar son of Charmi alone was guilty of theft, he ordered that he should die and gave him to them all. Then, taking the opportunity,
   first of all, Moses hit him with a rock, Jacob grappled him,
   Thecla took off his vest, Daniel struck him to the ground,
   David hit him with a stone, Aaron with a rod,
   Jesus with a whip, Judas opened his innards,
   Eliezer pierced him with a lance.
Then the king ordered that he who was dead should be buried.]

Thus Achan's biblical role as a type of Christ is transposed directly into the narrative of the *Cena Cypriani*. The *Cena* uses the image of the feast of God as a framework, both elaborating those incidents natural to a banquet and supplying others which make the allegorical substructure more coherent.

Employing these images, the *Cena Cypriani* forms a serious allegory on a conventional biblical topic. Its status as a learned allegory has independent witnesses. The most substantial is a commentary on the text (similar to a conventional biblical commentary) written in the twelfth century. The author, Herveus of Bourg-Dieu (also called Herveus Dolensis or Hervaeus Burgidolensis), was a Benedictine monk and exegete from the French monastery of Bourg-Dieu (also called Bourg-Déols; the town is now known as Déols). Born in 1080, Herveus entered the monastery around the age of twenty and, in the fifty years before his death in 1149 or 1150, wrote a number of learned studies, chiefly commentaries on the Bible. These include works on Genesis, Deuteronomy, Ruth, Tobit, Proverbs, Isaiah, the minor prophets, and the Pauline Epistles, and on the chapters of Ezekiel not treated by the commentary of Gregory the Great. In addition Herveus composed a collection of homilies on passages from the Gospels, an account of the miracles of the Virgin in Bourg-Dieu, and a commentary on the *Hierarchia caelestis* of Pseudo-Dionysius the Areopagite.[18] Among the most original of his works was the *De correctione quarundam lectionum,* an attempt to rationalize and emend the text of the missal, an undertaking which required a critical and analytical approach to religious texts.[19] His experience as an exegete meant that he must have dealt with much of the material used in the *Cena* in the normal course of his reading.

Herveus's last work was his commentary on the *Cena Cypriani,* a work which he was still waiting to complete when he died. The piece was apparently commissioned by the abbot of Bourg-Dieu, with the support of the monks, as a brief pastime to fill Herveus's declining days. The death roll of the monastery describes this commission.

Demum, quamvis propinquum finis sui terminum paulatim vigore deficiente sensisset, tamen sine consueto scribendi opere esse non poterat. Et rogatus a nonnullis, ut qui omnes Scripturas supra cunctos memoriter retinebat, *De Coena Sancti Cypriani Caecilii Carthaginensis Episcopi,* fere de omnibus libris Canonicis aggregata, quae quid intimaret, eatenus apud nos incognitum erat, edoceret. . . . adquievit rogantibus dicens, dum scriberet, se fortassis cum ista praesentam vitam finire. . . . Sicque

---

18. For further references see the *Lexikon für Theologie und Kirche,* ed. Josef Hofer and Karl Rahner, 2d ed., 10 vols. (Freiburg, 1957–67), 5:283; and for the biblical commentaries see Friedrich Stegmüller, *Repertorium Biblicum Medii Aevi,* 11 vols. (Madrid, 1940–80), 3: nos. 3251–89.

19. The work is edited and discussed by G. Morin in "Un critique en liturgie au XIIe siècle. Le traité inédit d'Hervé de Bourgdieu. *De correctione quarundam lectionum,*" *Revue Bénédictine* 24 (1907): 36–61.

contigit. Namque cum eandem *Coenam* usque ad illum locum ex-
posuisset, quo dicitur: *Confundebatur Elizabeth, stupebat Maria, ridebat
de facto Sara:* quo loco videlicet apud nos terminabatur, arbitrabatur
autem de ea non nimiam abesse partem, tam ipse quam dominus Abbas
Girbertus, qui hoc ei tanquam monacho suo et filio mandaverat, eamque,
quae deerat partem, ab abbate Sancti Savini, qui se eam habere dicebat et
mittendam eis promiserat, exspectabant: multa siquidem in ea vel
dempturus fortasse vel additurus, illam sicut erat in abolitione reliquit.[20]

[At length, although he sensed the nearness of his end, his strength
waning bit by bit, nevertheless he was not able to live without his
accustomed work of composition. And, entreated by many that he, who
knew all the Scripture by heart above all others, should give instruction
on the *Feast of St. Cyprian Cecilius, bishop of Carthage,* gathered together from nearly all the canonical books, the meaning of which had
until that time remained unknown to us. . . . he came to a stop, saying to
those who asked as he wrote that perhaps he was finished with this
present life. . . . And so it happened. For when he had expounded the
Cena up to the point in which it says *Elizabeth was confounded, Mary
was amazed, Sarah laughed at it,* at which place the text ended in our
copy, he judged that not too much was lacking, as did the lord abbot
Girbertus, who requested this of him like a monk and his own son. And
they awaited the missing part from the abbey of St. Savinus, which said it
possessed it and promised to send it to them. If indeed there were many
things to be deleted or added to it, he left it abandoned, just as it was.]

Although the abrupt ending of their text led Herveus and his colleagues to
believe that their text of the *Cena* was faulty, in fact there is only a single
sentence after the line "ridebat de facto Sarra," and thus Herveus's death left
the work less incomplete than his companions thought.

Herveus's commentary on the *Cena* is entirely a serious work of exegesis.
Herveus begins with a short preface describing the techniques of the *Cena.*

Tetigit, inquam, breuibus uersiculis, non metricis, gesta singulorum, so-
ciando fere semper duas sententias similes. Nec seruauit ordinem historie, sed similes sensus aliis similiter iunxit. Et aliquoties historie uerba

---

20. The death roll is printed in Léopold Delisle, *Rouleaux des morts du IXe au XVe siècle*
(Paris, 1866), 355–59; and in Magnoald Ziegelbauer, *Historia rei litterariae ordinis S. Benedicti,* 4
vols. (1754; reprint, Farnborough, 1967), 3:131–32.

posuit, aliquoties sensum quem ab his enigmatice sumpsit. Propter quod et explanatio facienda erit: nunc historialiter, nunc figuraliter. Nec solum de iustis hic agitur, sed et de prauis, ut recogitemus et premia bonorum et penas malorum.[21]

[It concerned, I say, in short little verses without meter, the deeds of individual people, almost always by associating two similar meanings; and it did not follow the order of history but juxtaposed similarly like senses to others. And sometimes it set forth the literal word of history, sometimes the sense which it took from these things in a riddling fashion. The explanation should also follow this manner: now historical, now figurative. And it treats not only of the just but also of the iniquitous, so that we may see both the rewards of the good and the punishment of the evil.]

He interprets the allegory explicitly in the main section, identifying Joel as God and the wedding as that of the Word with the Church.

Illud ergo uerbum quod non habuit inicium, sed semper equale natum est de patre, propter incomprehensibilitatem tante celsitudinis dicitur *quidam rex. Rex,* inquit, *nomine Iohel. Iohel* interpretatur *deus,* est enim dei uerbum, de se ipso dicens ad Moisen: *Ego sum qui sum,* sic dicens filiis Israhel, *qui est misit me ad uos* [Ex 3.14]. Idem etiam deus est, Paulo attestante, qui ait de eo: *quorum patres et ex quibus Christus secundum carnem, qui est semper omnia deus benedictus in secula* [Rm 9.5]. Qui faciebat nuptias, quia tanquam sponsus procedens de thalamo suo sanctam sibi copulauit ecclesiam. Has autem nuptias faciebat in regione orientis, ubi primo lux cernitur, hoc est in Iudea, unde processit origo Christiane fidei, in Chana Galilee, hoc est in zelo perpetrate trans-migrationis. Quia qui de uiciis ad uirtutes transmigrationem fecerunt, et zelo dei succensi sunt, in his nuptiales fiunt. Rex iste inuitauit plures ut eius cenam eius conuiuii frequentarent, quia missis predicatoribus con-uocauit orbem. Qui temperius, id est citius, loti in Iordane, hoc est in baptismo, adfuerunt . . .[22]

---

21. André Wilmart, "Le prologue d'Hervé de Bourgdieu pour son commentaire de la *Cena Cypriani," Revue Bénédictine* 35 (1923): 255–63 (at 257).

22. Tours, Bibliothèque Municipale MS 257, fol. 137ra–137rb; and Troyes, Bibliothèque Municipale MS 4417, fols. 87vb–88rb. Variants not noted.

[That word which has no beginning but was born forever equal from the father, is called, because of the incomprehensibility of such loftiness, *a certain king. A king,* he says, *by the name of Joel. Joel* means *God,* that is, the word of God, who said to Moses of himself: *I am that I am,* thus saying to the sons of Israel, *who hath sent me unto you.* That one is God, as Paul witnesses, who says of him: *whose are the fathers, and of whom is Christ, according to the flesh, who is over all things, God blessed for ever.* He held a wedding, for like a bridegroom coming from his chamber he wed the Holy Church to himself. He held this wedding in the land of the East, where the light is first discerned, that is, in Judea, where the origin of the Christian faith emerged, in Cana Galilee, that is, in the desire for the completed crossing. For those who make the crossing from vices to virtues and are kindled with the ardor of God are wed in these things. This king invited many to come to the feast of his banquet, for, sending out messengers, he summoned the globe. And these, at the proper time, that is, quickly, having washed in the Jordan, that is, in baptism, arrived . . .]

The rest of his analysis is similarly sober, chiefly explaining the historical allusions in the *Cena.* He explains that Mary's amazement ("stupebat Maria"), for instance, comes "de magnitudine tante nouitatis, quod scilicet uirgo peperisset, quod creatura creatorem, femina deum genuisset" [from the greatness of such tidings, that a virgin should give birth, that a creature should bring forth the creator, a woman should bring forth God] (Wilmart, "Le prologue," 262 n. 4). In this explanation Mary's action is related directly to her biblical role. In other instances Herveus's exposition eschews any historical associations. In the *Cena* itself Abel is associated with a milk pail because of the passage at Genesis 4.2 describing him as a keeper of sheep. Herveus gives the milk pail a Christological interpretation: "*super mulgarium* quia sustentatus est cibo innocentie de mundis animalibus et innocentiam uel passionem Christi presignauit" [*on a milk pail* because he is sustained on the food of innocence from clean animals and prefigures the innocence or suffering of Christ] (Wilmart, "Le prologue," 262 n. 4). In short, he treats the *Cena* not as a derivative text but as a reformulation of the Bible itself, capable of yielding religious truth on a par with Holy Scripture.

This attitude toward the *Cena* might at first seem to indicate that Herveus regarded the text as a wholly serious piece of work, composed as earnestly as Herveus analyzes it. But because Herveus sees the *Cena* as a store of religious truth does not necessarily indicate that he was immune to its humor. Indeed, the

circumstances of the commentary's composition may reveal something about
the way in which the *Cena* was regarded by the monastic community at Bourg-
Dieu. It looks as if, once Herveus's ability to compose substantial biblical
commentaries had waned, he was asked to apply his talents to a text valuable to
the community in a different way—a text they liked, rather than one they
revered. Herveus chose to elucidate the allegorical aspects of the text, the
features of the text which require the most learning to appreciate; the humorous
aspects speak for themselves. Nothing about Herveus's efforts presupposes
that the *Cena* cannot be considered as humor. On the contrary, Herveus's
treatise makes it clear that humor in a text need not preclude religious truth.

The *Cena Cypriani* as Parody

The humor of the *Cena Cypriani* lies in the ridiculous effect of juxtaposing
diverse biblical characters in a series of ludicrous situations. The most obvious
of these involve a pun, such as Noah sitting on an ark (*CC* 11) or John the
Baptist eating a *locusta,* a lobster (*CC* 124). Other allusions are humorous
because of their triviality. It is straightforward enough to identify Abel as a
shepherd, for example, but to symbolize this association by means of a milk
pail is to invite laughter. There is similar humor throughout the seating sequence. Even in those descriptions in which the association of character and
object is commonplace, the notion of the character actually sitting on the
object—or eating or drinking it, or employing it in other mundane ways—
trivializes the association: the great symbols of the Bible are reduced to vernacular objects in a household. Isaac's association with an altar, for instance,
recalls Genesis 22.9, in which he nearly met death at his father's hand, at the
command of the Lord; but the altar becomes ludicrous when we imagine Isaac
perched atop it, eating dinner. However grand in conception the allegory of the
feast of the Kingdom of God, its execution becomes laughable when the reader
is encouraged to visualize the details of the arrangements. A scene in which
Cain is sitting on a plough (*CC* 10), Tobit on a bed (15), Rebecca on a jug (20),
Jesus on a well (19), and Samson on a column (25) looks less like an allegory
and more like a circus. The author brings this sequence to a climax of absurdity
by transposing Job's biblical lamentation to a matter of grousing about the
seating allotment.

> Patiens stabat Paulus, et murmurabat Esau,
> et dolebat Iob, quod solus sedebat in stercore.
>
> (*CC* 27–28)

[Paul stood patient, and Esau murmured,

and Job wailed, because he was the only one sitting on dung.]

Not only the juxtaposition of biblical allusions but also the pace of the narrative make the story ludicrous. The practice may have sound Scriptural backing—that "a thousand years with the Lord are as a single day"—but to visualize the literal enactment of this is essentially to put biblical characters through their paces at double time—like an allegory performed by the Keystone Kops.

These ludicrous effects are the result of the deliberate exaggeration of conventional methods of biblical interpretation. The author parodies three kinds of exegetical pedantry in his depiction of the ridiculous feast. First, the *Cena* satirizes the use of earthly terms to convey the realities of a divine state. As such it can be said to parody religious allegoresis in general and allegories of the feast of God in particular. While in an allegorical sense feasting symbolized sharing in the community of God, there was always a danger that such metaphors might take on too many of the qualities of gluttony and earthliness associated with food in the human world. In a sense, feasting was only safe when free of earthly taint, when expressed in a purely ethereal sense. To specify which joints of meat the citizens of heaven take, and how they cook them, is to degrade the image.

The *Cena* parodies two additional exegetical techniques. The first is the practice of assembling objects from different biblical passages and contexts. The association of parallel events, particularly between the Old and New Testaments, was of course the essence of typology and a key to the interpretation of biblical history. The ludicrous juxtapositions of the *Cena Cypriani* reflect the medieval passion for assembling such lists and for assuming that any action, such as donning clothes, must have a constant meaning throughout the Bible. Such assumptions gave rise to dictionaries of biblical symbolism such as the *Allegoriae in universam sacram scripturam*[23] which assumed that parallel actions in the Bible had a single uniform meaning. To juxtapose several of these lists would produce a text much like the *Cena Cypriani*.

A rudimentary plot appears in a second type of exegetical commentary. Short narratives grew out of the belief that all the events of the Bible were linked and that their associations could be understood on an allegorical level as the unfolding of God's plan. In such a narrative the commentator assembles a

---

23. The *Allegoriae* is edited in Migne, *PL* 112: cols. 849–1088. The text was formerly attributed to Hrabanus Maurus; current scholarship suggests that instead it may be the work of Garner or Warner of Rochefort, who died sometime after 1225.

series of appropriate allegorical images from different parts of the Bible into a story; the dialogue is composed of direct quotations from Scripture. Ambrose, in his *De Mysteriis,* makes the image of the newly baptized person entering the Christian life into a brief narrative.

> . . . depositis enim inveterati erroris exuviis, renovata in aquilae juventute, coeleste illud festinat adire convivium. Venit igitur, et videns sacrosanctum altare compositum, exclamans ait: *Parasti in conspectu meo mensam* [Ps 22.5]. Hanc loquentem inducit David dicens: *Dominus pascit me, et nihil mihi deerit: in loco pascuae ibi me collocavit. Super aquam refectionis educavit me* [Ps 22.1–2].[24]

> [. . . having laid aside the robes of long error, renewed in youth like an eagle, he hastens to go to the feast. He comes, therefore, and seeing the most holy altar prepared, exclaims: *Thou preparest a table before me.* David brings in these words: *The Lord is my shepherd; I shall not want. He maketh me to lie down in green pastures. He leadeth me beside the waters of refreshment.*]

Ambrose's characterization of the heavenly feast is more a metaphor than a sustained allegory. Allegories on the same principle were also composed at greater length, so that they almost become self-sufficient narratives. Origen, for example, composed one on the theme of the heavenly banquet, in which he assembles a number of disparate biblical images into a coherent sequence of events. In particular it anticipates the *Cena Cypriani* in expanding on the parable of Isaac, Abraham, and Jacob together at the divine feast, as found in Matthew 8.11 and Luke 13.28–29, by bringing in other biblical characters as well. The fable appears in Origen's commentary on the Song of Songs, which was widely available in a Latin translation by Rufinus throughout the Middle Ages.

> *Introducite me in domum vini.* Sponsae adhuc verba sunt, sed ad amicos et familiares sponsi, ut arbitror, diriguntur, a quibus videtur exposcere, ut introducant eam in domum laetitiae, ubi vinum bibitur et epulae parantur. Quae enim iam viderat cubiculum regium, desiderat etiam nunc regale introire convivium et frui vino laetitiae. Supra iam diximus amicos sponsi prophetas et omnes, qui ministraverunt Verbum Dei ab initio saeculi, intelligendos, ad quos recte vel ecclesia Christi vel anima Verbo

---

24. Ambrose, *De mysteriis liber unus,* in Migne, *PL* 16: cols. 389–410 (at chap. 8, col. 403).

Dei adhaerens dicat, ut se introducant in domum vini, id est ubi sapientia miscuit in cratere vinum suum, et deprecatur per servos suos omnem insipientem et egentem sensu dicens: *Venite, manducate panes meos, et bibite vinum, quod miscui vobis* [Prv 9.5]. Ista est domus vini domusque convivii, in quo convivio omnes, qui veniunt ab oriente et occidente recumbent cum Abraham et Isaac et Iacob in regno Dei. . . . Istud est vinum ex illa vite vindemiatum quae dicit: *ego sum vitis vera* [Jo 15.1], quod expressit pater caelestis agricola. . . . Ad hanc ergo domum vini ecclesia vel anima unaquaeque, desiderans quae perfecta sunt, festinat intrare . . .[25]

[*Lead me into the house of wine.* These are the words of the bride, but they are directed to the friends and the household of the bridegroom, as I believe, whom she seems to entreat to lead her into the house of joy, where wine is drunk and sumptuous dishes prepared. When she had seen the royal bedchamber, she desired to come in to the royal banquet and to enjoy the wine of delight. We said above that the friends of the bridegroom should be understood as the prophets and all who have sown the word of God since the beginning of the world. To these the Church of Christ or the soul adhering to the word of God may say, rightly, that they should lead them into the house of wine, where wisdom mixed wine in her drinking cup and prays for the poor and the needy through her servants, saying, in effect: *Come, eat my bread, and drink the wine which I have mingled for you.* That is the house of wine and the house of feasting where all who come from east and west sit down with Abraham and Isaac and Jacob in the Kingdom of God. This is the wine from the vine of the vineyards which says *I am the true vine,* which the husbandman, the father of heaven, presses out. . . . The Church or the soul, wanting to be made perfect, therefore hastens to enter this house of wine.]

The *Cena Cypriani* is a ludicrous combination of two practices. An allegorical narrative is constructed, but after every action takes place an entire list of parallel actions, culled from the Bible, is introduced before the narrative can progress. To be coherent and convincing, medieval reminiscence exegesis employs one or the other of these techniques of association. The *Cena Cypriani* employs the two simultaneously. In sum, these three types of exegesis—the

---

25. *Origenes Werke,* ed. W. A. Baehrens, Die griechischen christlichen Schriftsteller der ersten drei Jahrhunderte 8 (Leipzig, 1925).

casting of eschatological ideas in earthly terms, the juxtaposition of similar events and items from diverse biblical passages, and the framing of a sequence of allegorical images into a narrative—produced the *Cena Cypriani.*

Within the text, as well, puns serve both a humorous and an allegorical function. When the guests robe themselves to return home, Peter dresses as a *retiarius,* a net-bearing gladiator—a symbolic representation of his role as a fisher of men, as recounted in Mark 1.16 and Luke 3.20. In contrast, Pharaoh is garbed as a *secutor,* the sword-bearing gladiator who pursues the *retiarius,* a symbol of the unbeliever's persecution of the chosen people, as recorded in Exodus 14. We see these two together, Peter first and then Pharoah as if in pursuit: "in retiario Petrus, in secutore Pharao" (*CC* 179). Adam's gardener's costume is elementary symbolism, but Eve's costume is more ingenious: she is dressed "in exodiario," as a player in a Roman *exodium,* a comic play (*CC* 181). Her appearance "in exodiario" recalls her role in bringing about the exodus from the Garden of Eden, but she assumes that costume as a part of the spectacle of the *Cena Cypriani,* another sort of comic play.

The feast of fish, a repository of specialist vocabulary based ultimately on Pliny, is particularly acute in using puns in symbolic associations. John the Baptist chooses a *locusta,* a lobster, as he feasted on locusts in the desert (Mt 3.4; Mc 1.6; *CC* 124); Cain a *gladium,* a swordfish, recalling his murder of his brother Abel (Gn 4.8; *CC* 124). Lazarus, who rose from the dead (Jo 11.38–44), takes an *umbra,* a type of fish, recalling the *umbra mortis* of Psalm 22 (*CC* 129). There are similarly well-realized symbolic puns throughout the *Cena Cypriani.*

Possible Model Texts for the *Cena Cypriani*

The *Cena Cypriani* copied the kinds of exegesis described in this chapter for its ludicrous effects. In addition, scholars have identified two specific texts which may have served as models for the *Cena.*

In 1739 the brothers P. and J. Ballerini, editors of Cyprian's works, first suggested that the *Cena Cypriani* was inspired by a sermon of Zeno of Verona, a bishop who died around 380. The sermon is known as "Post traditum baptisma"; it is very short, less than three hundred words long, and exhorts neophytes to behave with dignity at the feast following their baptism.[26] To this end Zeno provides his audience with fourteen examples of food and drink found in the Bible. Though the passage does bear some resemblence to the *Cena,* there are no significant parallels of vocabulary or phrasing between the two, and

---

26. The sermon is edited in *Zenonis Veronensis Tractatus,* ed. B. Löfstedt, Corpus Christianorum, Series Latina 22 (Turnhout, 1971), 71–72.

none of the associations of characters and food point to borrowing between the texts. But the structure of the sermon is indeed very close to that of the *Cena Cypriani:* if the list of biblical characters were framed by a more fully developed metaphor of the heavenly feast, the result would be a piece very much like the *Cena.* Though it is possible that the author of the *Cena Cypriani* knew the sermon, he could easily have written the *Cena* without Zeno's example; both are based on ideas widely current throughout Western Christendom at the time.

The second possible source for the *Cena Cypriani* is a debate poem of the Late Latin era, the "Iudicium coci et pistoris" (Debate between the cook and the baker) by an otherwise unknown poet named Vespa. The piece was probably composed between the end of the third and the middle of the fifth century, and it now survives only in the Codex Salmasianus, a collection of material first assembled in the sixth century.[27] The poem consists of ninety-nine hexameters of debate between a cook and a baker, each claiming greater merit for his craft. The cook's grandiose claims lead him to describe a banquet suitable for the gods.

> Partes quisque suas tollet qui cenat apud me:
> ungellam Oedipodi, sycotum pono Promethei,
> Pentheo pono caput, ficatum do Tityoni,
> siccus aqualiculum reddi sibi Tantalus orat.
> cervinam Actaeon tollit, Meleager aprinam.
> agninam Pelias, taurinam longulus Aiax,
> Orpheu, tu tolles chordas, Leandre, lacertos,
> me sterilem Niobe, linguam Philomela rogant me,
> pinna Philoctetam meruit, rogat Icarus alas,
> bubula Passiphae, Europe bubula poscit,
> auratam Danaae, cygnum bene condio Ledae.
>
> ("Iudicium" 83–93)

> [Each one that dines with me shall get his appropriate portions.
> I serve trotters to Oedipus, fois gras to Prometheus,
> head to Pentheus, fois gras again to Tityo.
> Thirsty Tantalus begs to be given a paunch.
> Actaeon gets venison, Meleager boar,
> Pelias lamb, tall Ajax bull-beef.

---

27. The "Iudicium coci et pistoris iudice Vulcano" is edited in D. R. Shackleton Bailey, ed., *Anthologia Latina* (Stuttgart, 1982*N*), 1: no. 190, pp. 135–39.

Orpheus, you will get gut, you, Leander, mussels.
Niobe asks me for a sterile matrix, Philomena for tongue,
a sea-pen got Philoctetes, Icarus asks for wings,
Pasiphaë and Europa both want beef,
for Danaë I season a gilt-bream nicely, for Leda a swan.[28]]

The similarities between this passage and the *Cena Cypriani* were first noted by Karl Weymann and have since been elaborated by Giovanni Orlandi, who finds verbal similarities as well as the obvious similarities of content.[29] The relevant section of the *Cena* describes the meat eaten by the guests.

Tunc ceteri partes suas tenebant, quas ex variis venationibus acceperant:
Abraham vitulinam, Esau cervinam,
Abel agninam, Noe arietinam,
Samson leoninam, Helisaeus ursinam,
maiorem partem tenebat Beniamin.

(*CC* 98–102)

[Then the rest laid hold of their pieces, which they had taken from the various animals.
Abraham veal, Esau venison,
Abel lamb, Noah ram,
Samson lion, Helisaeus bear,
Benjamin took the largest piece.]

Orlandi points out that the texts share the phrase *partes suas* and a number of words ending in *ina* (*cervina, aprina, agnina,* and *taurina* in Vespa; *vitulina, cervina, agnina, leonina,* and *ursina* in the *Cena*). The similarity of the joke is indeed notable; however, the same conceit might have arisen naturally from the conventions of exegetical narrative.

The *Cena nuptialis* of Hrabanus Maurus

The first rewriting of the *Cena Cypriani* was undertaken by Hrabanus Maurus, abbot of Fulda and, later, archbishop of Mainz. Hrabanus, who was born

---

28. Translation by D. R. Shackleton-Bailey, from "Three Pieces from the 'Latin Anthology,'" *Harvard Studies in Classical Philology* 84 (1980): 177–217.

29. Weymann noted the resemblances in his *Beiträge zur Geschichte der christlich-lateinischen Poesie* (Munich, 1926), 22. Orlandi discusses the "Iudicium" in *Rielaborazioni,* 5–6.

around 780–84 and died in February 856, was the author of both exegetical and pastoral works and assembled several encyclopedic compilations. Like Herveus's commentary, Hrabanus's *Cena nuptialis* was a work composed in its author's old age. It is dedicated to Lothar II, king of Lotharingia and grandson of Louis the Pious, who ruled from 855 to 869. Thus it cannot have been written earlier than 855 and was certainly complete by Hrabanus's death in February 856. The *Cena nuptialis* survives in eighteen manuscripts.[30]

Hrabanus has made a number of changes to the *Cena Cypriani,* most with a view to making the allegory clearer and the narrative more rapid and coherent.[31] The entire sequence of events takes place in a single day, in contrast to the two days covered in the *Cena Cypriani.* In the original *Cena,* too, the meal is interrupted by the king's offer of new clothing and by further preparation of food, and after the meal the king gives the guests yet another change of costume. Hrabanus has rationalized this repetitive set of incidents: the feast takes place without interruption, and the change of clothing takes place in a single episode after the meal is finished.

Other dramatic alterations have been made to the allegory. The king is called not Joel but Abbatheos (God the Father), while his son, whose name is never explicitly mentioned in the original, is called Bartheos (God the Son). The final episode of sin and punishment has likewise been made much more explicitly allegorical. In the *Cena Cypriani* the sin is entirely the fault of Achar, who, as in the biblical account, represents an entire people. In Hrabanus's *Cena nuptialis* the sin is more closely analogous to original sin: everyone at the feast is guilty and was guilty even before the feast began. When an investigation is undertaken, the serpent is identified as the first sinner. There follows a list of the sins of each guest, corresponding to their wrongdoings in Scripture. Abbatheos begins to punish the sinners for their crimes but comes to realize that such a solution is too harsh and that his son must die in their place. The son is crucified and buried by the guests.

In trying to make his version a more coherent allegory, Hrabanus has compounded one of the illogicalities of the original *Cena,* the presence of both an allegorical character representing Jesus and Jesus himself. In the *Cena Cypriani,* Achar's atonement prefigures the crucifixion. In Hrabanus's *Cena*

---

30. The *Cena Hrabani* is edited in Modesto, *Studien,* 132–56. It is also found in three manuscripts unremarked by Modesto: Paris, Bibliothèque Nationale MS lat. 3549, fols. 18r–22r; Oxford, Trinity College MS 39, fols. 138r–144v; and Grenoble, Bibliothèque Municipale MS 265, fols. 136r–138v.

31. These changes have also been discussed, in greater detail, in Orlandi, *Rielaborazioni,* 6–12.

Bartheos, the son, is crucified, making the presence of the literal Jesus at the feast seem doubly extraneous. The problem worried at least one medieval reader, who changed the text to replace Bartheos with Jesus in the crucifixion scene.[32]

This is Hrabanus's only failing in a narrative which is otherwise much clearer and more accessible than the previous *Cena*. Many of the Apocryphal characters, who would no longer be familiar to listeners in the ninth century, have been excised or replaced with more orthodox figures. Orlandi has also noted a number of substitutions in characters' actions and associations to reconcile the story with the Vulgate and to make the references more intelligible.[33] In many instances Hrabanus has also reordered the lists of characters to conform with the order in which they appear in the Bible, an alteration which makes clearer the *Cena*'s role of telescoping biblical history into a single event.

In his dedication to Lothar II Hrabanus makes it clear that he regards the *Cena* as both amusement and edification and outlines some of his allegorical aims.[34]

The *Cena Iohannis* of John Hymmonides

The ninth century saw a second imitation of the *Cena Cypriani,* a verse adaptation by the Roman deacon and hagiographer John Hymmonides.[35] Iohannes Hymmonides—also referred to as Iohannes Diaconus—was born around 825 and died in or before 882. Nothing certain is known of his particulars until the last decade of his life, when he appears in Rome in the pontificate of John VIII (872–82). He may have been a monk of Monte Cassino and a member of the court of Charles the Bald, possibly later assuming the position of papal secretary. In addition to his adaptation of the *Cena,* Hymmonides composed a vita of Gregory the Great and may have been the author of a commentary on the Pentateuch.[36]

---

32. Munich, Bayerische Staatsbibliothek MS clm. 8437, fol. 182r. The text as a whole has been shortened and rewritten in this manuscript.

33. Orlandi, *Rielaborazioni,* 6–12. Work on Hrabanus's text and references has also been done by Hermann Rönsch, "Einiges zur Erläuterung der Caena Hrabani Mauri," *Zeitschrift für wissenschaftliche Theologie* 27 (1883): 344–49.

34. The letter of dedication is edited by E. Dümmler in *MGH, Epistolae,* 3:506; and in Modesto, *Studien,* 133–32.

35. The *Cena Iohannis* is edited in Strecker, "Iohannis Diaconi," 872–98. Strecker's edition is reprinted in Modesto, *Studien,* 178–200.

36. On Hymmonides's life see Arthur Lapôtre, "Le Souper de Jean Diacre," *Mélanges d'archéologie et d'histoire* 21 (1901): 305–85; Max Manitius, *Geschichte der lateinischen Literatur des*

The *Cena Iohannis* (Feast of John) comprises 324 rhythmical lines of fifteen syllables each, with frequent rhyme and assonance at the half line and line end. Unlike Hrabanus Maurus—whose rewriting of the *Cena Cypriani* was apparently unknown to him—John made no radical changes to the original. His adaptation follows the original *Cena* virtually phrase for phrase, expanding the description or altering the sequence only to accommodate the demands of the verse form. Most of these changes have been described and analyzed by Giovanni Orlandi, who demonstrates that the author used considerable literary skill to make his composition both humorous and scripturally meaningful. Orlandi also concludes that John attempted to provide a greater sense of cause and effect in his poem and took care to emphasize the spectacle and the sense of the miraculous.

John provides evidence of his intent in three poems which accompany the *Cena Iohannis:* a prologue, an epilogue, and a dedicatory poem to Pope John VIII. In these the poet states clearly that the piece was composed as both entertainment and pious instruction. The first stanza of the preface shows this explicitly.

Quique cupitis saltantem   me Iohannem cernere,
Nunc cantantem auditote,   iocantem attendite:
Satiram ludam percurrens: divino sub plasmate,
Quo Codri findatur venter.   Vos, amici, plaudite.
        (Strecker, "Iohannis Diaconi," 870, stanza 1, lines 1–4)

[Who wants to see me, John, performing,
Now listen to the song, attend to the merrymaking:
I shall play, going through the verse in divine form,
Which would make Codrus's belly burst [from laughing].
        Applaud, friends.]

John also prescribes an allegorical interpretation of his wedding-poem by alluding to another wedding allegory, Martianus Capella's *De nuptiis Philologiae et Mercurii* (Strecker, "Iohannis Diaconi," 870, stanza 2, lines 1–2). Elsewhere he calls the story of the *Cena* an "imperialis iocus" [a royal jest] (Strecker, "Iohannis Diaconi," 871, stanza 4, line 4); yet he also emphasizes the sanctity of the events in the poem:

Mittelalters, 3 vols. (1911–31; reprint, Munich, 1965–73), 1:689–95; and G. Arnaldi, "Giovanni Immonide e la cultura a Roma al tempo di Giovanni VIII," *Bulletino dell'Istituto storico italiano per il medio evo e Archivio Muratoriano* 68 (1956): 33–89.

Ad cenam venite cuncti . . .
Quam sophista verax lusit   divinis miraculis,
Non satiricis commentis,   non comoedi fabulis.
                (Strecker, "Iohannis Diaconi," 871, stanza 6, lines 1, 3–4)

[Come to the feast, everyone, . . .
Which the true scholar performs with divine miracles,
Not with invented satires nor comedian's fables.]

Here he implies that the "game" of the *Cena* is more valuable than the fictions of the satirists or storytellers precisely because it concerns religious truth. By implication other comedy is objectionable not because it is frivolous but because it is secular. The triumph of the *Cena* is to bring religious mysteries even into the realm of laughter.

The dedicatory letter to the pope again advertises the humor of the text.

Ludere me libuit; ludentem papa Iohannes
    Accipe; ridere, si placet, ipse potes . . .
(Strecker, "Iohannis Diaconi," 900, lines 1–2)

[It pleased me to play; take this amusement, Pope John;
    It may make you laugh, if it's pleasing . . .]

Of this humor John comments, "Qui risum poterit stringere, marmor erit" [He who can keep from laughing is made of marble] (line 10). The poem closes with a benediction, an affirmation of the blessings of religious laughter: "Nunc hilarem populum musa iocosa beat" [Now let the jesting muse bless the merry people] (line 12).

The accompanying poems also provide evidence for the performance of the piece in ninth-century Rome. Unfortunately the descriptions are ambiguous, so much so that they have given rise to a great deal of unresolved scholarly debate. The preface seems to indicate that the piece was performed at the Roman festival of Cornomannia, a celebration that took place at Easter time, and the epilogue recounts another performance at the imperial coronation of Charles the Bald, held in Rome on 25 December 875. There are, however, a number of questions about these performances; critics have disagreed on whether the poet is foretelling or recalling the occasions and on whether it was the *Cena Iohannis* or actually the original *Cena Cypriani* which was performed in each instance.[37]

Despite the difficulties of the evidence, many scholars have been eager to claim the poem as an important example of early medieval drama. Orlandi notes that the prologue resembles that of a Classical comedy, with an *abba* stanza structure and the formulas "vos, amici, plaudite" and "attendite."[38] He disputes the idea, however, that it was part of a limited revival of Classical literature in ninth-century Rome, noting that of Classical dramatists only Terence appears to have been known at the time. Instead, he proposes, the performance of the *Cena Iohannis* may have formed part of an enduring popular tradition of drama, perhaps being sung and mimed simultaneously. Vincenzo de Bartholomaeis has no doubt that the *Cena Iohannis* was performed to mime and understands the poem as a libretto for a troupe of mimes.[39] He suggests that King Joel was played by a professional mime, directing the entrances and exits of the other characters. In support of this thesis Orlandi notes that the prologue suggests a visual delivery of the poem with such phrases as "Hanc exhibeat" [Let him show] and "Quique cupitis saltantem me Iohannem cernere" [Who wants to see me, John, performing]. There may also be a suggestion that the poem was sung rather than recited in the phrase "cantantem auditote" [listen to the song]. In sum, Orlandi concludes that such a long poem, consisting principally of lists of characters, would be wearisome to the audience without some form of visual presentation: the costumes of the players would add color and variety to the performance, and such a large number of characters would be manageable because most characters appear only briefly.

A number of objections can be raised to this proposal. Many of the jokes simply could not be adequately represented in mime: a case in point is the variety of fish chosen by the banqueters. The stage would have to be crowded with characters because, although each has only a small role, each is "onstage" at table throughout the feast. Further, when John says, "Quique cupitis saltantem me Iohannem cernere," he is referring only to himself; whether he is

---

37. On these questions see Arnaldi, "Giovanni Immonide"; Lapôtre, "Le Souper"; and Paul Devos, "Le mystérieux épisode finale de la *Vita Gregorii* de Jean Diacre: Formose et sa fuite de Rome," *Analectia Bolandiana* 82 (1964): 355–81 (at 375 n. 3).

38. Orlandi, *Rielaborazioni*, 24–25.

39. Vincenzo de Bartholomaeis, *Origini della poesia drammatica italiana,* 2d ed., Nuova biblioteca Italiana 7 (Turin, 1952), 151–67. Agreeing with him are Antonio Viscardi, *Le origini,* Storia letteraria d'Italia 1 (Milan, 1939; I have not seen the second edition of this book, published in Milan in 1950); and Ezio Franceschini, "Il teatro postcarolingio," in *I problemi comuni dell'Europa post-carolingia* (Spoleto, 1955), 295–312.

acting out the text or merely reciting or singing it, his actions do not imply that a troupe of actors is accompanying him. The jester Crescentius seems to have trouble with the names (Strecker, "Iohannis Diaconis," 871, line 5.4). This appears to imply that he is pronouncing these names for the first time, perhaps repeating them while Gaudericus laughs and Anastasius explains the allusions (Strecker, "Iohannis Diaconis," 899, stanza 3, lines 3–4). In any case, he is surely not the speaker, who would have rehearsed beforehand, and he is certainly not a mime, who would not have pronounced the names at all.

To suggest that mimes are required is to assume that the poem itself is not funny enough to warrant a recital without accompaniment; but it is difficult to see why the piece would be recited or performed at all—particularly at such an important occasion as an imperial coronation—if the basic text were so unpromising. Instead, the piece was most likely performed for the same reason that the various versions of the *Cena* were so popular: the humor of the text is clever, unusual, challenging, and religious. Mimes or actors would be beside the point of this textually based humor; indeed, they would more likely serve as a distraction.

The *Cena Azelini* of Azelinus of Reims

Yet a third imitation of the *Cena Cypriani* was composed by the monk Azelinus of Reims, most likely in the eleventh century.[40] The only source of information on Azelinus is the title of the poem itself: *Cena Azelini, Remensis monachus, quam condidit ad Henricum imperatorem, imitatus Cyprianum, episcopum Cartageninsem* (The feast of Azelinus, monk of Rheims, which he composed for the emperor Henry, in imitation of Cyprian, bishop of Carthage). This title and two stanzas from the poem were copied from a manuscript (now lost) by Claude de Saumaise in 1620.[41] Francesco Novati argued that the emperor referred to here was Henry III of Germany, who ruled from 1039 to 1056, thus placing the text in the middle of the eleventh century.[42] These two stanzas, in octosyllabic four-line stanzas, resemble those in another fragmentary poem in a Paris manuscript.[43] This fragmentary poem consists of the first fifty-four stanzas of a versified version of the *Cena,* clearly incomplete, as the poem

---

40. The *Cena Azelini* is edited in Modesto, *Studien,* 220–30.

41. Claude de Saumaise, *Historiae Augustae Scriptores IV* (Paris, 1620), 399, 410. The verses are reprinted in Édélestand du Méril, *Poésies populaires latines du moyen âge* (Paris, 1847), 93 n. 2.

42. Novati, "La parodia," 327.

43. This was noted by Édélestand du Méril in his edition of the Paris poem, in *Poésies populaires latines,* 93–102.

breaks off in midstrophe. The two verses cited by Saumaise have no counterpart in the Paris manuscript, but there is little doubt that Saumaise's two verses and du Méril's fifty-four come from the same poem. There is no other record of either Azelinus or the poem, with one exception: the *Cena Azelini* was known to the author of the Arras *Cena* (discussed in the next section of this chapter), who mentions him explicitly: thus the *Cena Azelini* was certainly in existence in or before 1200.

Though more prolix than its predecessors, the *Cena Azelini* retains the story and framework of the *Cena Cypriani*. The poem as printed is 218 lines long, but when it breaks off after fifty-four verses the author has not yet finished cataloging the seating arrangement of the guests; thus very little of the plot survives. The additional verses printed by Saumaise show biblical characters eating and dressing, suggesting that the poem continued to follow the outline of the original *Cena*.

The comic features of the poem are weakened in Azelinus's hands. An entire four-line stanza is usually devoted to each character: this discursive style means that even the lengthy series of allusions becomes a narrative rather than a catalog, making the juxtaposition of characters less ridiculous. In addition Azelinus's associations are less recondite, so that characters are far less often represented by trivial objects of association. In the *Cena Cypriani* Jacob is seated "super petram" [on a rock] (*CC* 13), a reference to the stone he used as a pillow when he dreamed about the ladder stretching to heaven and which he later set up as a pillar at Bethel (Gn 28.11 and 28.18). Azelinus not only explains the allusion to the stone but brings the ladder into the banquet.

> Duas sedes Jacob habet,
> petram scalamque possidet;
> super petram tamen sedet,
> Deum qui vidit in Bethel.
>
> (du Méril, *Poésies populaires latines,* 96)

> [Jacob has two seats,
> he possesses a rock and a ladder;
> nevertheless he sits upon the rock,
> he who saw God in Bethel.]

This is laboring the joke. Similar reworking occurs throughout.

Azelinus has also imposed a new system on the selection of characters, abandoning the random order present in the *Cena Cypriani*. He follows the

Cena Cypriani's sequence of characters through the baptism, but from the beginning of the banquet he moves in sequential order through the New Testament. Thus the first twenty-four verses of the banquet enumerate characters from Genesis, paralleling the *Cena Cypriani*'s first five characters, but choosing Abraham where the *Cena Cypriani* specifies Iafeth. This allows the introduction of eleven figures from Genesis not paralleled in the *Cena Cypriani*. Azelinus then covers Exodus in three verses, Joshua in the same number, Ruth in two, and the four books of Kings (in roughly sequential order) in fifteen. The last verse fragment refers to Tobit. It is curious in this regard that the first of the additional verses quoted by Saumaise is derived from Genesis, which disrupts the chronological sequence. (The second, from Daniel, is in accordance with biblical chronology.)

Azelinus thus worked to remedy the faults of the *Cena Cypriani* in a number of ways. He attempted to make each character's allusion more truly representative of his biblical role; to place the characters in a systematic sequence; to add a number of important characters from the Bible; and to expand the description of each to make the allusions less of a guessing game and more of a teaching tool. The description of Noah is particularly representative of Azelinus's overriding didacticism. Noah sits "super archam diluvii" [on the ark of the flood], a description spoiling the *Cena Cypriani*'s pun on *arca* with its double meaning of "box" and "vessel of the flood." Finally, a later verse is marked with musical notes, suggesting that the poem was meant to be sung or chanted—possibly further confirmation that the piece was rewritten in the interests of pedagogy.

The Arras *Cena*

A fourth rewriting of the *Cena Cypriani* took place around the year 1200.[44] The only known manuscript of this was written at Arras, and it is possible that the poem may have formed an early part of the great burgeoning of literature in Arras in the thirteenth century.[45] The author's changes to the original *Cena* show concern for both the allegorical and the literary aspects of the piece, and for the humor of the text as well as for its more serious qualities.

The poem is in rhymed stanzas of four octosyllabic lines each. It is incomplete as we have it: the preface states that the story takes place over a period of three days, with a book of the poem corresponding to each, but the

---

44. The Arras *Cena* is edited in appendix 2, no. 1 and in Modesto, *Studien,* 244–78.

45. This has been described by Marie Ungureanu, in *La bourgeoisie naissante: Société et littérature bourgeoises d'Arras aux XIIe et XIIIe siècles,* Memoires de la Commission des Monuments Historiques du Pas-de-Calais 8¹ (Arras, 1955).

text breaks off in the middle of the second book, with the remainder of the page left blank. This is not, however, an autograph copy of the poem, as the presence of scribal error demonstrates. In its incomplete form it has 160 stanzas. In the poem as it stands, King Joel prepares a feast but Eve violates the law by sampling the soup too early, and the king casts all the guests out to labor for their food. After the flood, Abraham and Sarah produce a son and Abraham prepares a new feast; in this setting the king laments Job's afflictions and the guests take vengeance on Job's attackers. There follows a great deal more eating, enumeration of gifts and sacrifices, and various activities, including brief episodes of seduction, debauchery, the use of latrines, and the theft and recovery of a cup. Soon thereafter the poem breaks off.

The Arras *Cena* is a much more sophisticated work than its predecessors. The allegory has been restructured and rationalized so that the feast corresponds to the chronology of biblical history. In this it is much more an ecclesiological allegory than an eschatological one: in other versions of the *Cena,* the characters reenact their biblical roles; in this version, their actions throughout history are presented as literal participation in the feast of God. In short, the feast does not symbolize biblical history; it is identical with biblical history. Further, where previous versions have structured the feast as a series of allegorical incidents in more or less random order, the Arras *Cena* recounts biblical history as a coherent narrative in which the characters respond rationally to events and to each other. The sophistication of this narrative method raises the piece from an allegorical curiosity, like the previous versions, to a work of genuine literary merit.

The author's concern for the clarity of his symbolism prompts him to spell out the meaning of the text in his verse preface, where he specifies that the feast will be divided into three parts, to correspond to the three ages of biblical history. These refer to the time before the gift of the law to Moses, that after it, and the time since Christ and the new dispensation—"ante legem et sub ea / et sub moderna gratia" [before the law, under it, and in the modern period of grace] (5.3–4). He also instructs us explicitly to understand King Joel as Christ (a variant on previous texts, in which the son of the king had the role of Christ) and Joel's bride as the Church, and he lays out the terms of the allegory with an example of a type.

> Tobiam namque sequimur
> Priuantem se complexibus
> Tribus diebus, coniugem
> Dum uirgo seruat uirginem.

Quod ille fecit typice
Canamus nos ueridice,
Dantes diem pro tempore
Res possit ut subsistere.

(Arras *Cena* 7–8)

[We may follow the example of Tobias,
Depriving himself of embraces
For three days
While he, a virgin, preserves his bride as a virgin.

What he did as a type
Let us present as actual deeds,
Using a single day to represent each period
So that the thing may have a firm basis.]

The example of Tobias is especially apt in this context. Like Christ in the allegory of the wedding feast, Tobias retained the status of bridegroom for three days. The three days correspond to the three ages of biblical history, and at the end of this period comes the consummation, whether of the marriage or of secular and divine history. When the Arras author writes "quod ille fecit typice / canamus nos ueridice," he indicates that he is describing the real events of biblical history, albeit by encoding them into a symbolic narrative.

Every detail of the poem has been similarly devised to conform to the allegorical framework. The feast takes place in a remote setting, unknown to everyone thereafter. The first trespass is committed when one of the guests samples the food illicitly before the feast has begun. This incident is in fact a good example of the ingenious combination of symbolism and humor in the text.

Necdum erat conuiuium
Per ordinem dispositum
Cum fauce furtim auida
Ius cene uirgo uiolat.

(Arras *Cena* 14)

[And not yet had the feast been arranged
In order when secretly,
With eager jaws,
The virgin assaults the soup [law] of the meal.]

By tasting the soup, *ius,* too soon, the virgin has violated a propriety, *ius,* of the feast, as well as the law (again *ius*) given by God. The term *uirgo* carries a double meaning with a more typological sense: here, unusually, it refers to Eve, whose innocence was destroyed when she committed the first sin; but it also anticipates the virgin Mary, the typological successor to Eve who helped to atone for her predecessor's guilt.

After this incident, the guilt-ridden guests leave the feast, an event clearly corresponding to the expulsion from Eden: the king continues to provide food, but the guests must earn it with toil. Partial redemption comes from Abraham and his faith in the Lord, and the feast Abraham prepares after the weaning of Isaac prompts the resumption of the allegorical feast. The contributions brought by the guests to this feast are not the random associations used in previous versions of the *Cena* but cogent contributions to the story. Rather than altering the characters' relationship to the objects traditionally associated with them, the author has simply telescoped biblical history into the space of a single meal. As part of this, for instance, we see Isaac serving Abimelech and Philcol from the wells he has discovered, as in Genesis 26.26–33; Reuben producing mandrakes, as he does in Genesis 30.14–16, with the same strife between Rachel and Leah; and, as a contribution to the festivities, Pharaoh giving a birthday party as he does in Genesis 40.20–22, complete with the hanging of the baker. The first day comes to an end with the crossing of the Red Sea as a symbolic baptism.

As promised in the poem's preface, the second book concerns the period after Moses' acceptance of the law; and to symbolize this it is Moses himself who reconvenes the feast and presides over its arrangement. An allegorical incident new to this version involves Job, unjustly afflicted by his enemies. When the Lord of the feast grants the guests the power to defy this enemy, the guests take up the weapons appropriate to them and set out to avenge Job. In the resulting melee the human enemies of God are routed, elevating the incident to a symbolic victory of the righteous over the forces of evil. The feast proper follows this victory. It is not solely a feast of the good things accompanying participation in the biblical world: the first thing served is the apple, which the first waiter, the serpent, offers to Adam and Eve. While some partake of food, as they do in the Bible, others bring and offer sacrifices: these offerings are made up of the sacrifices of animals performed in the Old Testament.

When the food and wine are finished the story turns into a compendium of biblical incident, and here the narrative technique undergoes another twist. Previously the actions of the characters constituted single elements of a developing story; in the last section the narrative force takes over, as it were, so that several characters contribute to a single action. In the following passage, for instance, seduction and pregnancy take place as if independent of the characters, each of whom only appears for the instant justified by his or her biblical role.

> In Ioseph ardet domina,
> Annon accumbens constuprat,
> Pregnans Agar intumuit,
> Gemens Rebecca parcurit.

(Arras Cena 153)

> [The mistress is ardent for Joseph;
> Annon, lying down, debauches.
> Pregnant Agar swells up;
> Groaning Rebecca gives birth.]

This kind of interaction is common in the text. It champions typological perspective over the literal, even taking it to extremes, effacing all differences of chronology and individuality among biblical characters.

To structure the retelling of biblical history in this way is almost to make a pun of biblical incident—to give it two meanings, each coherent in a different context. The author supplements this allegorical double meaning with lexical double meaning, frequent puns and transpositions of biblical quotations. He begins his outline of the narrative with the word *prelibo,* "I shall take a foretaste," as if we, too, are participating in the feast. This idea is further implied later in the preface, when he gives the impression that while he describes the poem the entire banquet itself is waiting for us. Defending himself against complaints that the guests may not be arranged in a suitable order, he says:

> Nam ad regales epulas
> Si cunctas sedes ordinas
> Cum temporis dispendio,
> Ciborum fit perditio.

(Arras Cena 10)

> [For if you order all the seats
> At the royal feasts,
> With a corresponding waste of time,
> It makes a ruin of the food.]

The impression that the banquet is merely waiting for the listeners is powerful, and the humor is enriched by the idea that if we insist the poet take the time to order the characters correctly, "ciborum fit perditio": to make the heavenly banquet wait plays hell with the food.

The overliteral interpretation of eschatological prophecy also contributes to the humor. In one instance, the author uses Jesus' words that "multi erunt primi novissimi et novissimi, primi" (Mt 19.30) to justify the nonchronological appearance of the guests at the feast.

> Et ne causeris ordinem
> Non imitantem seriem,
> Erunt primi nouissimi,
> Nouissimi primarii.

> (Arras *Cena* 9)

> [And lest you object that the arrangement
> Does not follow the correct order,
> "The first shall be last,
> The last first."]

In general the characters' biblical actions are easily integrated into a feast, but the author also finds humor in the integration of some unlikely biblical events. For instance, when Abraham renews the feast, the conflagration of the Cities of the Plain serves as the barbecue, and Lot's wife as a saltcellar.

> At cetera cibaria
> Ne prepediret tarditas,
> Pentapolis succenditur,
> Loth uxor sal efficitur.

> (Arras *Cena* 31)

> [And lest lateness spoil
> The rest of the food,
> Pentapolis is set on fire,
> Lot's wife is made into salt.]

The Arras *Cena* is certainly the most sophisticated literary achievement in the long history of the *Cena* form. Its allegorical underpinning is both complex and coherent, and the marriage of humor and allegory is deftly accomplished.

"Heriger" and Later Descendants of the Heavenly Banquet

Religious parody underwent a renaissance in the twelfth century, and this period witnessed a shift in parodists' attitudes toward the use of biblical characters in humor. The *Cena Cypriani* had enjoyed the acceptance of humor accompanied by a serious religious stance. In the later medieval period poets made use of similar themes without this backbone of serious moral purpose. The divine feast itself became the object of parody.

One early work mocking the tradition of the heavenly banquet is a piece from the Cambridge Songs, "Heriger, urbis Maguntiacensis" (Heriger, of the city of Mainz).[46] The poem can be dated by the archbishopric of Heriger, archbishop of Mainz, the central character, whose tenure lasted from 913 to 927. The narrative takes the form of a poetic dialogue between a man who falsely claims he has had a vision of heaven and hell, and the archbishop, who counters the liar's claims with wry comments. The association of the poem with the *Cena Cypriani* lies in the man's depiction of heaven as a place of eating and drinking and of the figures of heaven as the attendants in a sort of celestial tavern. It is the vulgar interpretation of the heavenly feast: the marriage, sin, redemption, and other allegorical elements are gone, and only the earthly expression of religious ideas remains. The archbishop never overtly challenges these views, but ridicules the man in his own terms.

> Vir ait falsus, "Fui translatus
> in templum celi Christumque vidi
> letum sedentem et comedentem.
>
> Johannes baptista erat pincerna
> atque preclari pocula vini
> porrexit cunctis vocatis sanctis."
>
> Heriger ait: "Prudenter egit
> Christus, Johannem ponens pincernam
> quoniam vinum non bibit unquam."
>
> (Strecker, *Die Cambridger Lieder,* 65–66)

> [The lying man said, "I was taken
> to the temple of heaven, and I saw Christ

---

46. The poem is edited in Karl Strecker, *Die Cambridger Lieder, MGH, Scriptores rerum Germanicarum* 40 (Berlin, 1926), no. 24, pp. 65–66.

happily sitting and eating.

John the Baptist was the bartender
and poured a cup of clear wine
for all the saints called there."

Heriger said: "Christ acted prudently
when he made John the bartender,
since he never touched wine."]

The next verse is missing, but the archbishop's reply shows the false man to
have been claiming that Peter served as chief cook.

"Mendax probaris, cum Petrum dicis
illic magistrum esse cocorum,
est quia summi ianitor celi."

(Strecker, Die Cambridger Lieder, 66)

["You show yourself a liar when you say Peter
was the chief cook there,
because he is the doorkeeper of highest heaven."]

In the end the false visionary is thrown out on his ear. Despite this moralistic
conclusion, the poem is an amusement rather than a serious diatribe against an
overliteral understanding of religion. It may remind the reader that images of
the divine cannot be interpreted superficially, but it does so in good humor.

The two remaining pieces in the tradition of the heavenly banquet have no
such moral underpinning: they are pure doggerel. It is difficult to assign a date
to these poems. The more coherent of the two, "O Deus, O Christe," is un-
dated.[47] Fragments of "O Deus" are found in the second poem, "In viridi
campo," but the finished product has suffered more corruption. "In viridi

---

47. The poem is printed in C. Hofmann, "Ueber die lateinischen Sequenzen," *Sitzungsberichte
der philosophisch-philologischen und historischen Classe der k. b. Akademie der Wissenschaften
zu München* 2 (1872): 454–60 (at 460). Hofmann notes that he has reprinted the poem from an
article by W. Wattenbach in the "Anzeiger des Germanischen Museums, (Sp. 190)." By this I
assume he must mean the *Anzeiger für Kunde der deutschen Vorzeit* (Organ des Germanischen
Museums), Wattenbach's usual forum; but I have searched this journal page by page for the period
1864–72 and have not located it. Hofmann draws attention to the similarity between "O Deus" and
the *Cena Cypriani* on his p. 459.

campo" has been incorporated into a patchwork of verses from different sources preserved in a sixteenth-century manuscript.[48]

The poems are only very distantly related to the tradition of the *Cena Cypriani* proper, but they share the theme of a collection of biblical characters concerned with food. All symbols and allusions have vanished, and instead of being participants in a divine community, the characters are absorbed in bickering over the food. The first of the poems reads:

"O Deus, O Christe, quid portat rusticus iste?"
"Saccum cum pomis." "Si vellet vendere nobis?"
"Vendere volo tibi, quia melius acquisivi."
Tunc dixit Peter: "Nolo peccare, magister.
Peccare nolo, poma comedere volo."
Omnipotens Deus et sanctus Bartholomaeus
Emerunt saccum pro tribus marcam et unum.
Tunc voluit Christus saccum comedere solus.
Tunc dixit Jacop: "Non facies, per meum calcop [Kahlkopf]."
Accept baculum, voluit percutere Christum.
Christus clamavit, omnes sanctos invocavit.
Omnes venerunt qui in throno fuerunt,
Praeter unus homo qui natus fuit sine talo,
Talum non habuit, currere non potuit.
Johannes Baptista venit cum sua balista.
Imposuit telum, voluit sagittare Jacobum.
Thomas in fornace clamavit: "Sitis in pace."

["Oh God, oh Christ, what is this peasant carrying?"
"A sack of apples." "Does he want to sell us any?"
"I want to sell to you because I've gotten better ones."
Then Peter said: "I don't want to sin, master.
I don't want to sin, I want to eat an apple."
Almighty God and Saint Bartholomew
Bought a sack for four marks.
Then Christ wanted to eat the sackful alone.
Then Jacob said: "You shall not, by my bald head."
He took a stick, he wanted to beat Christ.
Christ cried out, he called on all the saints.

---

48. The poem is printed in Thomas Wright and James Orchard Halliwell, *Reliquiae Antiquae*, 2 vols. (London, 1841–43), 1:290.

All the saints who were on their thrones came
Except one man who was born without an ankle;
He had no ankle, he couldn't run.
John the Baptist came with his ballista,
He loaded an arrow; he wanted to shoot Jacob.
Thomas in the furnace cried, "Go in peace."]

Here the heavenly feast has been transformed into a heavenly melee. The form is no longer that of a parable but of the kind of debate poem instigated by asking a question of a person on the road.[49] Again the humor arises from the description of the saints acting in vulgar and corporeal ways, as when the first speaker addresses Christ rhetorically in his swearing, and Christ actually answers the question; and again when Christ calls on all the saints and they come running physically into the scene.

The second version reads:

In viridi campo steterunt principes ambo.
Unus erat Jesus, alter fuit Bartholomeus:
Emerunt vagam propter dimidium marcum.
Tunc dixit Jhesus: "Volo comedere solus."
Respondit Abraham: "Non sic facis, per meam barbam."
Accepit baculum, vellet percutere Jhesum;
Jhesus calamabat Petrum, Paulum qui vocabat,
Ambo venerunt, Habraham bene verbaverunt.
Tunc dixit Jhesus: "Ego sum hic timide solus;
Adiuva me modo vagam, grossum vobis dabo."
Tunc dixit Abraham: "Hewe, hev, quod huc veni unquam,
Si non venissem, nunquam bene verberavisse⟨m⟩."

[In a green field stood two princes.
One was Jesus, the other was Bartholomew:
They bought from a tramp for half a mark.
Then Jesus said: "I want to eat alone."
Abraham answered, "You shall not do that, by my beard."
He took a stick, he wanted to hit Jesus;

---

49. This type of poem is discussed by Hans Walther in *Das Streitgedicht in der lateinischen Literatur des Mittelalters,* Quellen und Untersuchungen zur lateinischen Philologie des Mittelalters 2 (Munich, 1920), 9–10 n. 2, in which he cites several poems that begin by addressing a "rusticus."

Jesus cried out to Peter, who called Paul,
The two of them came, they thrashed Abraham soundly.
Then Jesus said, "I am here alone, fearful;
Help me, a tramp, now: I'll give you a groat."
Then Abraham said: "Alas, alas that I ever came here,
If I hadn't come, I never would have been beaten."]

If the *Cena Cypriani* was an allegory as performed by the Keystone Kops, these final versions are the Keystone Kops without the allegory.

CHAPTER 3

Mock Saints' Lives

The cult of the saints formed one of the most distinctive features of medieval religious culture, and tales of holy men and women enjoyed an enormous popularity. Certainly these stories were better known to most people, both ecclesiastics and laymen, than more recondite doctrinal theology; but familiarity breeds parody, and the legends of the saints were no exception. The later Middle Ages saw a proliferation of parodic saints' lives, spearheaded by Latin sermons on two mock saints: Nemo and Invicem. These elaborate instances of wordplay reflect both learned and popular traditions of religious understanding: some display an awareness of theological and exegetical issues, others no more than an uncomplicated desire to mock the self-importance of the literature and cult of the saints.

St. Nemo

Sermons on the fictitious St. Nemo appear to have been among the most popular literary jokes of the Middle Ages. In combinations of mock exegesis and exhortation, the sermons and vitae on Nemo construct an elaborate account of the life and deeds of a saint of that name, basing their humor on the deliberate misunderstanding of the word *nemo* in the Bible. Thus, for example, the saint is credited with the powers of prophecy on the basis of the biblical passage "Nemo propheta acceptus est in patria sua" [Nobody is accepted as a prophet in his own country] (Lc 4.24). Mock sermons on Nemo survive in five main versions, comprising a total of nineteen manuscripts; the diversity among the versions, and even between different copies of the same version, demonstrates the enthusiasm medieval ecclesiastics must have felt for such displays of theological levity.

The earliest *Nemo* tract, now lost, was most probably composed in the second half of the thirteenth century. Because the contents of this text are described by a contemporary, we can ascertain that it was a lengthy and ornate version of the sermon, and I call it the Long *Nemo*. This Long *Nemo* was subject to considerable alteration and paraphrase, giving rise to several derivative sermons in the course of the next three hundred years. In the fourteenth or fifteenth century these were joined by the Short *Nemo,* written in simpler and more succinct Latin and marshaling a different set of biblical quotations. The marriage of these two then produced the Combined *Nemo,* apparently of the fifteenth century, which retained many features of the old sermons while adding new jokes and allusions. Finally, the fifteenth century also saw two more or less sophisticated elaborations of the basic premise: the rhetorically ornate Cambridge *Nemo;* and the Zurich *Nemo,* which recasts the text into a dispassionate and reasoned argument for the veneration of the saint.

The Long *Nemo*

The first appearance of Nemo took place in the long version of the sermon, which took form most likely in the late thirteenth century and continued to evolve until the Renaissance. The date and circumstances of the Long *Nemo*'s composition are problematic; I will take up these issues in this chapter after an appraisal of the Long *Nemo*'s contents.

The Long *Nemo* uses an arsenal of biblical quotations to outline the deeds and virtues of this fictional saint. It begins with a quotation from the Epistle to the Hebrews, a phrase often pressed into service to introduce medieval sermons.[1] The Biblical original reads:

> Multifarie multisque modis olim deus loquens patribus in prophetis; novissime diebus istis locutus est nobis in filio, quem constituit heredem universorum, per quem fecit et saecula. (Hbr 1.1–2)

> [God, who, at sundry times and in divers manners, spoke in times past to the fathers by the prophets, last of all, in these days, hath spoken to us by his Son, whom he hath appointed heir of all things, by whom also he made the world.]

The author of *Nemo* has combined this with other biblical and liturgical quotations, such as the phrase from Luke 1.79: "his qui in tenebris et in umbra mortis sedent" [them that sit in darkness and in the shadow of death]. The resulting parody begins:

---

1. The popularity of the opening can be verified by consulting the index of incipits of manuscript catalogs. To take a sample, the collection of incipits compiled by Hauréau lists ten sermons with this opening (B. Hauréau, *Initia Operum Scriptorum Latinorum Medii Potissimum Aevi,* 8 vols. [Turnhout, n.d.], 4:114); the manuscript catalog of the Bibliothèque Nationale in Paris lists seven, of which one is the sermon on Nemo itself (*Bibliothèque Nationale: Catalogue général des manuscrits latins,* vol. 2, *Tables des Tomes III à VI,* pt. 1, *Table des Incipit A-M* [Paris, 1983], 575).

Multifarie multisque modis, karissimi, loquebatur olim deus per prophetas, qui, velut in enigmate et quasi sub nebulosa voce, unigenitum dei
filium, pro redimendis laborantibus in tenebris et in umbra mortis sedentibus, preconizarunt venturum. (Long *Nemo* 2–5)

[At sundry times and in divers manners, dearly beloved, God spoke in
times past through the prophets, who, as if in riddles and an obscure
voice, foretold the coming of the only-begotten son of God for the
redemption of those who labor in darkness and sit in the shadow of
death.]

The emphasis on the obscurity of the ancient prophets' message throws into
relief the contrasting straightforwardness of the new communication from
God. But here the enigmatic prophets of the Old Testament are succeeded not
by the coming of Christ but by the coming of St. Nemo.

Novissimis autem diebus per suam sanctam scripturam palam loquitur, et
beatissimum et gloriosissimum Neminem ut sibi comparem, ante secula
genitum, humano tamen generi hactenus (peccatis exigentibus) incognitum fore predicat, enucleat et testatur. Sed ipsemet salvator noster et
dominus, cui semper proprium est misereri et qui suos nunquam deserit
inadiutos, suo sanguine proprio redempti populi misertus est, et ab oculis
nostris remota penitus vetusta caligine thesaurum huius gloriosissimi
Neminis tam celebrem nobis dignatus est aperire . . . (Long *Nemo* 5–12)

[In the last days, however, he speaks openly through his holy Scripture,
and foretells, explicates, and bears witness to the most blessed and glorious Nobody as similar to himself, begotten before the ages, yet unknown
to humankind until now by reason of our sins. But our own savior and
lord himself, who is always merciful, and who never leaves his own
helpless, showed pity to the people redeemed by his own blood, and with
the ancient darkness wholly removed from our eyes, he has deigned to
reveal to us the treasure, so renowned, of this most glorious Nobody . . .]

St. Nemo is later compared explicitly to Christ.

Beatus igitur Nemo iste contemporaneus dei patris et in essentia precipue
consimilis filio, velut nec creatus nec genitus sed procedens in sacra
pagina reperitur, in qua plene dictum est per psalmistam dicentem: *Dies
formabuntur et Nemo in eis* [Ps 138.16]. (Long *Nemo* 14–17)

[This blessed Nobody, therefore, is found to be contemporaneous with
God the Father, and in essence particularly like the Son, as he was neither
created nor begotten but proceeds forth in Holy Scripture, in which it is
set forth fully by the psalmist, who says: *Days shall be formed, and
Nobody in them.*]

Like Christ, Nemo is the product neither of divine creation nor of earthly
propagation, but proceeds forth. Unlike Christ, however, he proceeds forth
solely from the phrasing of Scripture.

Similar quotations provide authority for Nemo's other abilities and exploits.
The author cites proof of his power to defy God ("Deus claudit et Nemo aperit,
deus aperit et Nemo claudit" [God shutteth and Nobody openeth, God openeth
and Nobody shutteth], from Apc 3.7); his distinguished lineage ("Nemo enim
ex regibus aliud nativitatis habet initium," [For Nobody has his birth from
kings], from Sap 7.5); and of the privileges granted to him by both secular and
heavenly authorities ("Nemini permittitur binas habere uxores" [Nobody is
permitted to have two wives], from Mt 6.24); "Nemo potest duobus dominis
servire" [Nobody can serve two masters], from Lc 16.13).

The prophets and the evangelists often praise Nemo directly, but we also
observe reverence for the saint enacted within the Bible itself. Nicodemus, for
instance, testifies to the saint's special powers.

Princeps autem Iudeorum, Nichodemus nomine, potentiam istius
gloriosissimi Neminis referens, ait: *Rabi, Nemo potest hec signa facere
que tu facis* [Jo 3.2]. (Long *Nemo* 31–32)

[The ruler of the Jews, moreover, Nicodemus by name, referring to the
power of this most glorious Nobody, said: *Rabbi, Nobody can do these
signs that thou dost.*]

In other instances Christ himself shows Nemo special favor.

Cum ipse cui omnia vivunt et quem laudant archangeli istum sanctum
Neminem benedictum per secula adeo puro dilexit amore, ita quod dum
suos per mundum misisset apostolos, precepit eis ut cum Nemine beatissimo obviarent, ipsum salutarent et eidem visiones et secreta eius
tanquam suo secretario fiducius aperirent, sicut scriptum est: *Neminem
per viam salutaveritis* [Lc 10.4], et alibi: *Visionem quam vidistis Nemini
dixeritis* [Mt 17.9]. (Long *Nemo* 103–9)

[Since he for whom all things live, and whom the archangels praise, loved this holy Nobody, blessed throughout the ages, with such a pure love that when he sent his apostles through the world, he commanded them that when they met the most blessed Nobody along the way they should greet him and reveal to him the visions and secret things just as if to their secretary, with great confidence, as it is written: *Salute Nobody by the way,* and elsewhere: *Tell the vision which you have seen to Nobody.*]

At one point Jesus even defers to the saint.

Nam dum Iudei in verbis dominum capere cuperent, et mulierem in adulterio deprehensam coram eo adducerent, ipse, cui nihil absconditum est, discretionem, scientiam et valorem dilecti sui Neminis agnoscens, plenarie in beati Neminis reverentia et honore dictam mulierem accusatam per eum renuit iudicare, dicens: *Mulier, ubi sunt qui te accusant? Nemo te condemnavit?* Que respondit: *Nemo, domine.* Audiens hoc dominus, nolens falcem mittere in messem alienam, dictam mulierem remisit ad sanctum Neminem, dicens: *Nec ego te condempnabo* [Jo 8.10–11]. (Long *Nemo* 112–19)

[For when the Jews wished to ensnare the Lord in words, and brought the woman taken in adultery before him, he to whom nothing is hidden, recognizing the discernment, wisdom, and valor of his beloved Nobody, refused to judge the aforesaid woman accused by him, full of reverence and honor for the blessed Nobody, saying: *Woman, where are they who hath accused thee? Hath Nobody condemned thee?* She replied: *Nobody, Lord.* Hearing this, the Lord, not wanting to ply his sickle in another man's field, conceded the aforesaid woman to the holy Nobody, saying: *Neither will I condemn thee.*]

Where conventional hagiographies are modeled on the Bible, the sermon on Nemo reinterprets the events of the Bible itself. The concern of Scripture is no longer to instruct us on the sanctity of Christ: instead Christ is relegated to a secondary role in the larger scheme of demonstrating the sanctity of Nemo.

Biblical quotations are also adduced to outline the saint's expertise at a variety of professions: he is a soldier; a scholar proficient in arithmetic, grammar, and astronomy; and a man diligent in both the active and the contemplative realms. In short, he excels in both secular and religious life. Where traditional hagiography claims for the saint a particular conventional set of virtues, St. Nemo is perfect in every way. He not only rivals the perfection of individual saints but encompasses all possible perfection: as the text says, "Nemo sine crimine vivit" [Nobody lives without guilt] (from *Disticha Catonis* 1.5) and "Nemo ex omni parte beatus" [Nobody is blessed in every way]. In these assertions the author satirizes the demands of sanctity, which call for perfection beyond the capacity of humans. Though Christ instructs the faithful, "Estote ergo vos perfecti, sicut et Pater vester caelestis perfectus est" [Be ye therefore perfect, as also your heavenly father is perfect] (Mt 5.48), the human race by nature is incapable of such perfection. The author emphasizes man's essential incapacity by ascribing flawless virtue to the only saint capable of achieving this perfection: one who is imaginary by definition.

The Long *Nemo* contains between fifty and sixty-five of these biblical testimonies to the perfection of St. Nemo. The muster of scriptural authority is supplemented by Classical and Late Latin authors (Horace, Priscian, the *Disticha Catonis*), the Church fathers (Augustine, Gregory), and monastic rules, canon law, and the formulas of papal decrees.

In the Long *Nemo* in particular, the essence of the joke is the overliteral interpretation of Scripture, a method of reading that inverts the conventional process of interpretation. By invoking authority to such an extent—all of the hagiographer's claims about St. Nemo are underpinned by passages from authority—the sermon affirms that the improper use of authority can lead to false belief. The author plays on the conventions of biblical exegesis in his metaphors of blindness and concealment.

> . . . et ab oculis nostris remota penitus vetusta caligine thesaurum huius gloriosissimi Neminis tam celebrem nobis dignatus est aperire, ut ipsum usque nunc damnifere nobis absconditum intueri deinceps oculata fide salubrius valeamus. (Long *Nemo* 10–13)

> [. . . and with the ancient darkness wholly removed from our eyes, he has deigned to reveal to us the treasure, so renowned, of this most glorious Nobody, that we may be able to see him (hidden to us, damnably, until now) more soundly thereafter, with the eye of faith.]

In this view of the Bible, the metaphorical meaning has always been evident; it is the literal meaning which has been concealed. That St. Nemo's existence comes solely from the phrasing of Scripture is emphasized many times in the author's invocations of authority, as when he writes that Nemo is "nec creatus nec genitus sed procedens *in sacra pagina*" [neither created nor begotten, but proceeds forth *in Holy Scripture*] (Long *Nemo* 15; my emphasis). The joke on authority is repeated with each assertion, every quotation being prefaced by such a phrase as *sicut legitur, ubi dicitur,* or *ut dictum est.*

> Qui, dum celum ascenderet, ut dictum est, deitatem puram et integram et insimul trinitatem vidit ibidem sanctissimus Nemo, sicut legitur: *Nemo deum vidit* [Jo 1.18]. (Long *Nemo* 21–23)

> [When this most holy Nobody ascended into heaven, as it is said, he saw the pure and complete and at the same time threefold Godhead himself, as it is read: *Nobody hath seen God.*]

In the most literal sense, then, the saint was spoken into being: Nemo has come to fulfill the words of the prophets.

Five versions of the Long *Nemo* survive. The oldest, which I shall call the First Recension, is found in two manuscripts, the earliest dating from the late fourteenth century. That the First Recension was in existence a century before that, however, is attested by an anti-*Nemo* tract composed in 1290 by a certain Stephanus. This tract is entitled the *Reprobatio nefandi sermonis editi per Radulphum de quodam Nemine heretico et dampnato, secundum Stephanum de Sancto Georgio christiane fidei defensorem* [The refutation of the abominable sermon put forth by Radulphus, about a certain Nobody, heretic and damned].[2] The author and the circumstances of its production are obscure. Stephanus apparently intended to refute the claims of the sermon on Nemo, and to do this he goes through the sermon systematically, citing each of the quotations from authority in order of their appearance. This allows us to reconstruct the text of the sermon available in Rome around 1290.

A comparison of the two texts makes it clear that it is likely that neither the oldest extant manuscript, dating from the late fourteenth century, nor the text available to Stephanus represents the incorrupt text of the first *Nemo,* though both may be very close to it.[3] Moreover, we cannot be sure that the lost *Nemo*

---

2. The *Reprobatio* is edited in Heinrich Denifle, "Ursprung der Historia des Nemo," *Archiv für Literatur- und Kirchen-Geschichte des Mittelalters* 4 (1888): 330–48 (at 340–48).

3. The earliest manuscript (Oxford, Bodleian Library MS Selden supra 74; hereafter referred to as O) and Stephanus's lost exemplar were closely related, agreeing more closely in both the order and wording of quotations than O does with the other text of the First Recension, M. (For manuscript references, see the edition of the Long *Nemo* in appendix 2, no. 2.) The shared readings of O and the *Reprobatio* extend to the biblical misquotation "Vide, Nemini dixeris" (line 109)

of 1290 was actually the first *Nemo* tract ever composed.[4] Stephanus merely refers to the text as "editus per Radulphum," which leaves the role of Radulphus ambiguous. It may be that Radulphus served merely as the redactor of an existing text and that Stephanus erroneously supposed that Radulphus had actually composed it; or it may be that the actual author was unknown to Stephanus.

Two later rewritings of the Long *Nemo* clearly used the First Recension as their foundation. The first is found in a single manuscript of the fifteenth century. Although the text has been rephrased and the sections have been ordered differently, in essentials it remains very similar to the standard version.[5] A late derivative of the Long *Nemo* appears in the sixteenth-century collection of satire and poetry assembled by the Benedictine Anton Husemann.[6] This *Sermo de sancto Nemine* retains the framework of previous versions, but the text has been abbreviated and rewritten in the elegant neo-Latin of the Renaissance humanists. To give a brief example, in the earliest manuscript of the Long *Nemo* (O), Jesus' words to the leper claim only a single sentence: "Curato etiam de lepra in evangelio dixit illi: *Vide Nemini dixeris*" [To the one cured of leprosy in the gospel, he said: *See thou tell Nobody*] (Long *Nemo,* apparatus to line 109). The Abbreviated Long *Nemo* is considerably more elaborate.

> Omnipotens deus qui occultorum est cognitor, cordium et cogitationum rimator, et quem nullum latet secretum, cum magni aliquid egit in carne mortali constitutus, ilico voluit quo illud Nemini intimaretur, unde cum leprosum pristine reddidisset sanitati, *Vade,* ait, *Nemini dixeris* [Mc 1.44]. (Abbreviated Long *Nemo* 78–82)

where all other manuscripts have the correct reading, "Vade, Nemini dixeris." However, O is not an entirely trustworthy witness to the urtext of *Nemo.* In the section in which Nemo is said to serve two masters, O lacks the actual quotation "Nemo potest duobus dominis servire," though it retains the versified repetition of the joke, "Utiliter servit Nemo duobus heris" (lines 39–40). The quotations in the *Reprobatio* too show that Stephanus's exemplar differed from all other witnesses of the tradition in at least two places: it apparently omitted the quotations "Nemo tenetur propriis stipendiis militare" and "Nemo nos conduxit" (lines 61 and 144 in the Long *Nemo*), which are found in all other manuscripts. Either these were added to a later copy, from which all other extant manuscripts are descended, or Stephanus's exemplar was itself an incomplete copy of an earlier *Nemo* text.

4. Work being done by Nicole Bériou, of the Sorbonne, suggests that the text may also have circulated in Paris at a similar date.

5. The parts of this manuscript (P) which vary significantly from other manuscripts of the Long *Nemo* are printed separately as the third appendix to the Long *Nemo* in appendix 2, no. 2.

6. The text of this late derivative is printed in appendix 2, as no. 3, "The Abbreviated Long *Nemo.*"

[When the omnipotent God who knows all hidden things, investigator of hearts and thoughts, from whom no secret is concealed, performed any worthy thing while enveloped in the mortal flesh, he wished it to be made known to Nobody straightaway; so that when he had restored the leper to his former health, *Go,* he said, *tell Nobody.*]

Several of the texts preserved in Anton Husemann's satirical commonplace book appear in this rhetorically sophisticated style, and it is not unreasonable to suppose that he may have rewritten them himself.

The Second Recension of the Long *Nemo*—in existence by the late fourteenth century—is especially interesting for the clerical and monastic bias of its additions. In the framework of the First Recension the author incorporates new quotations from Augustine, Gregory, and the penitentials. His scholarly tendencies are also revealed in annotations to the eleven new biblical quotations, for which he is careful to cite book and chapter. He also denounces the worldliness of both soldiers and clerics. Money-grasping soldiers, he asserts, are no better than fresh herring[7]—for sale to anyone.

Sua vero militia, ut moderni milites, non est usus, qui, ad modum allecium recentium pro quibus habendis a venditoribus prius solvitur precium, sunt venales . . . (Long *Nemo* 55–57)

[He did not profit by his military service in the way of modern soldiers, who, like fresh herring for which the price must be paid before it can be obtained from the fishmonger, are up for sale . . .]

Criticism of secular mercenaries is conventional for a man of the cloth, but the author condemns the clergy as well.

Prophetiam autem suam et suum dogma generale, quod multis vigiliis acquisivit, ut moderni clerici non consumpsit, qui ob aliud non curant addiscere, nisi ut solum pecuniam cumulent pecunie et pinguibus ditentur prebendis, et ob hoc, omissis liberalibus scientiis, solummodo facultates petunt lucrativas, sed prorsus quibuslibet sumptibus contagiis solus

---

7. The analogy between clerics and herring may appear extraordinary, but it is in fact found in another medieval sermon printed in Frederic C. Tubach, *Index exemplorum: A Handbook of Medieval Religious Tales,* FF Communications 86, no. 204 (Helsinki, 1969), no. 2586: "Just as herrings are sold at 1000 a penny for lack of salt, so, when good prelates are lacking, the devil obtains souls cheaply." Tubach's source is J. A. Herbert, *Catalogue of Romances in the Department of Manuscripts in the British Museum* (London, 1910), 3:560, no. 7.

iste Nemo sanctissimus celestia contemplatus est, sicut legitur: *Nemo sine crimine vivit* [*Disticha Catonis* 1.5], et alibi: *Nemo ex omni parte beatus* [Walther, *Proverbia,* no. 16343]. (Long *Nemo* 65–71)

[But he did not squander his powers of prophecy and his wide learning, which he acquired through much study, in the manner of modern clerics, who, in pursuit of a certain other thing, do not care to increase their learning unless they can add money to money and be enriched by hefty allowances; and because of that, disregarding the liberal arts, they pursue only the lucrative faculties. But as they have taken on all manner of impurities, this most holy Nobody alone has regarded the heavenly things, as it is read: *Nobody lives without fault,* and elsewhere: *Nobody is blessed in every way.*]

Though the criticism of contemporary churchmen is pointed, it need not imply that the sermon on Nemo was the work of someone outside the clergy. The intimate familiarity with Scripture, the exegetical satire, and the use of sermon formulas strongly suggest clerical authorship. The venality of the clergy was a satirical commonplace among ecclesiastical writers and functioned less as criticism of one's own kind than as complaint on the corruption of the modern world.[8] The context, moreover, is inappropriate to a serious condemnation of ecclesiastical avarice. The passage functions to throw the virtues of Nemo into relief, but the author is not urging the listener to emulate the saint: this particular saint can inspire veneration but never imitation.

This passage alone, then, by no means contradicts the theory of clerical authorship. In addition, the author encourages his audience to consider Nemo their patron saint, "patronus noster," an epithet which may suggest that the audience shares the calling of the preacher ostensibly giving the sermon. In a series of conventional anathemas, the author exhorts his audience to defend the honor of their patron.

Fugiat ergo omnis hostis iniquus beatissimi et gloriosissimi Neminis patroni nostri, et deleatur de libro viventium et cum iustis non scribatur, nec sit ulterius eius memoria super terram, qui glorioso operi nostro recalcitrare nititur, et corda fidelium nostrorum suis falsis suggestionibus nuperime credidit subornare. . . .

---

8. On satire of clerical avarice in general, as opposed to that of the pope and the papal curia, see Yunck, *Lady Meed,* 117–27 ("Satire on the Venality of Bishops and the Lesser Clergy").

Estote igitur viri fortes in agone, velut doctor noster Nemo, et robusti. Et certamen illius qui nullis falsis probationibus nec scripturis subsistit non recusetis subire. Reservamus etiam in nostri pectoris scrinio ad laudem et gloriam patroni nostri beatissimi Neminis et suorum tot et tantas auctoritates tam divinas canonicasve quam civiles cum infinitis sanctorum sanctionibus patrum, philosophicis insuper et naturalibus argumentis. (Long *Nemo* 193–97, 202–7)

[Therefore let every wicked enemy of our patron, the most blessed and glorious Nobody, take flight, and let him be blotted out from the Book of the Living and not be inscribed among the just; nor let his memory remain on earth who strives to reject our glorious work, and who not long ago thought to seduce the hearts of our faithful with deceitful promptings. . . .

Therefore be brave men in the fight, like our teacher Nobody, and strong. And may you not refuse to enter into the struggle of him who stands firm through no false proof or scripture. Let us lay up in the coffer of our heart, for the praise and glory of our patron, the most blessed Nobody, the testimony of so many and such great authorities, divine and canonical as well as civil, with unending confirmation from the holy Fathers, and, what is more, with arguments from philosophy and nature.]

This last passage urges the listener to expand the scope of his or her misinterpretation: by seeking out the word *nemo* in other texts, the scholar can find the saint witnessed in every type of literature. Thus the sermon on Nemo champions two methods of manipulating authority. First, the author implies, any argument can be proven by citing authority (albeit misinterpreted) as he does in this sermon; second, he argues, readers can concoct authority at will by applying their ready-made misinterpretations to any text.

The quantity and magnificence of Nemo's virtues finally send the author into a frenzy of praise.

Certe nec penna nec calamus cum ambabus manibus illius scribe velociter scribentis . . . ad laudem et gloriam patroni nostri beatissimi et gloriosissimi Neminis non competent lucidandam . . . (Long *Nemo* 189–91)

[Certainly neither the quill nor the reed pen, with both hands of the scribe writing furiously . . . are sufficient to express the excellence and glory of our patron, the most blessed and most glorious Nobody . . .]

Exuberance is the hallmark of the many copies of the Second Recension: as each scribe inherited the text, he added more jokes, more involved metaphors, and more fulsome praise of Nemo. This is typified in the final summing-up of Nemo's virtues. The earliest First Recension text reads:

> Similiter ergo, karissimi, predicta in parte plane videre potestis essenciam, potenciam, audaciam, incarnacionem, genus, scienciam, bonitatem, honorem, humilitatem et caritatem istius gloriosissimi Neminis . . .[9]

> [Therefore in a similar manner, dearly beloved, you can see distinctly to some extent the essence, power, daring, incarnation, nature, knowledge, goodness, honor, humility, and charity of this most glorious Nobody . . .]

By the time the tradition reaches the earliest manuscript of the Second Recension (V, of the late fourteenth century), the ten virtues have ballooned to thirty-one. In the latest manuscripts (A and L, of the fifteenth century), the list has grown to the extravagant proportions of forty virtues.

> Per predicta igitur, karissimi, in parte plane videre potestis formacionem, essenciam, potentiam, audaciam, securitatem, nobilitatem, miliciam, probitatem, doctrinam, scienciam, dignitatem, sanctitatem, gloriositatem, virtuositam, laudem, honorem, reverenciam, verecundiam, castatitem, providentiam, beatitudinem, felicitatem, compassionem, obedienciam, pacienciam, prudenciam, iusticiam, fortitudinem, temporanciam, largitatem, coeternitatem, sempiternam, perpetualitatem, stabilitatem, immobilitatem, humilitatem, corroboracionem, fidem, spem et caritatem istius gloriosissimi Neminis . . .[10]

> [By the above, dearly beloved, you can see distinctly to some extent the form, essence, power, daring, security, nobility, military valor, honesty, teaching, knowledge, dignity, holiness, glory, virtue, fame, honor, reverence, modesty, chastity, foresight, blessedness, felicity, compassion, obedience, patience, prudence, good judgment, fortitude, moderation, generosity, coeternality, imperishability, everlastingness, stability, fix-

---

9. The reading of O is found in the apparatus to lines 149–55 of the Long *Nemo* in app. 2 and on p. 319 of the edition of O in Anatole de Montaiglon and James de Rothschild, eds., *Recueil de poésies françoises,* 13 vols. (Paris, 1855–78), 11:314–20.

10. For this reading in A and L see the Long *Nemo* in app. 2, lines 150–56 and apparatus to line 150.

ity, humility, strength, faith, hope, and charity of this most glorious
Nobody . . .]

The scribes here have recognized the hyperbole of the claims about Nemo and
have taken these to their logical extreme, crediting the saint with every virtue
under the sun. A further version of the sermon on Nemo is derived from the
Long *Nemo*'s Second Recension. This is a truncated copy of the Second Recension, which omits some parts and summarizes others; in all it is roughly two-
fifths the length of the full Second Recension and introduces no new
elements.[11]

The dedication of another redactor, working in Heidelberg sometime between 1443 and 1447, is evident in one manuscript of the Long *Nemo*. It was
not unusual for scribes to add new biblical quotations to the text as they copied
it, but the scribe of the Heidelberg manuscript combed Cicero for *nemo* quotations and added them as well, testifying to the scholarly character of at least
one of Nemo's disciples.[12]

The Cambridge *Nemo*

The Cambridge *Nemo* appears in a single manuscript written at St. Albans in
the fifteenth century.[13] The author has clearly based his text on the Long *Nemo*,
retaining most of the quotations in a nearly identical order but rewriting the
connecting material entirely. Although the style of the piece is garrulous and
discursive, the text breaks off suddenly, with no closing formulas. This abrupt
ending suggests that the piece was unfinished or at least that the text in the
single surviving manuscript is incomplete. The text's affinities with the Long
Nemo bear this out: the Cambridge *Nemo* appears to be developing an argument along lines similar to the Long *Nemo* but then concludes abruptly where
the Long *Nemo* continues.

In other aspects the Cambridge *Nemo* is more original. The author discards
the Long *Nemo*'s conceit of literal and allegorical exegesis; instead he adopts a
stern pastoral tone. The sermon begins with a mock condemnation of worldly
frivolity and purports throughout to be intended solely as sober edification.
This didactic guise is reinforced by scholarly tags, conveying an impression of

---

11. The text is found in Hamburg, Staats- und Universitätsbibliothek MS Petri 22 (G), of
1435; it is edited in appendix II below as no. 2, where it is collated as part of the Long *Nemo* as far
as line 50; the remaining text of G forms the second appendix to the Long *Nemo* in app. 2.

12. The Ciceronian quotations from the Heidelberg manuscript (H) are edited separately in
appendix 2, no. 2, as the first appendix to the Long *Nemo*.

13. Cambridge, Gonville and Caius College MS 230/116, pp. 73–77 (old foliation 34r–36r).
This *Nemo* text has not been edited.

scrupulous precision of expression: *si dici fas sit,* "if it can be stated"; *studebo declarare,* "I shall take care to proclaim." The care apparently taken to use vocabulary accurately makes it all the more ironic that the entire sermon is founded on the misuse of vocabulary.

The tone of seriousness and solemn didacticism is apparent in the opening of the sermon.

Recolendi patres et domini, scriptura teste ociositas summe inimicatur anime, nec valet absque egestate vivere, qui totaliter noscitur ociositati deservire. Idcirco ne hec dies, que iam ex magna parte transiit, inanis consumetur et vacua, in illo iam exiguo quod restat verbo exhortationis vestra cum patientia studebo pro posse universos relevare.

Fuit, dilectissimi, diebus regis Emanuelis, Iherusalum triumphantis, quidam vir prepotens meritis Nemo a suis vocitatus, qui ipsi deo contemporaneus per omnia potentia et virtute, si dici fas sit, factus est equalis. Nam eius filio maxime consimilis in creatione substantie mundialis affuit, nec creatus nec genitus sed procedens, ipsius ma[ca]crocosmi mi[ca]crocosmique formationem cum eis discrete disponens atque consummans, testante propheta, qui ait: *Dies formabuntur et Nemo in eis* [Ps 138.16]. (Cambridge, Gonville and Caius College MS 230/116, p. 73)

[Honorable fathers and lords, by the testimony of Scripture, idleness is the enemy of the soul in the highest degree, nor can he who is known to serve idleness wholly live without need. Therefore, lest this day, which now has passed over for the greatest part, should be taken up with vain and empty things, in the little space that now remains, with your patience, I shall take care to reveal the things of the universe, with a word of exhortation, as far as it is possible.

There was, dearly beloved, in the days of King Emmanuel, conqueror of Jerusalem, a man, very powerful through his merits, called Nobody by his own people, coexisting through every power and virtue, who, if it is right to say, was made equal to God himself. For he, like the Son of God, was present at the creation of the world's substance with them, neither created nor begotten but proceeding forth, ordering and perfecting the formation of the macrocosm and microcosm, with the prophet as witness, who said: *The days will be formed and Nobody in them.*]

Otherwise the text presents many of the *Nemo* jokes familiar from other versions. The only sustained piece of invention appears in a coruscating

diatribe on the venality of clerics, who, the author charges, fleece their par-
ishoners like so many sheep. This fulmination against clerical avarice seems
out of place in such a context. The author's outcry against clerical greed seems
genuinely impassioned, but in the next breath he champions the moral purity of
a mock saint. To cite Nemo's selflessness as a counterpoint to the avarice of
corrupt clerics is to undercut more sober calls for reform.

The Short *Nemo*

The short version of the sermon on Nemo seems to have rivaled the Long *Nemo*
in popularity. It now survives in seven manuscripts, the earliest from the
beginning of the fifteenth century. All seven are now in collections from
Germany or central Europe (in Augsburg, Brno, St. Florian, Berlin, Munich,
Salzburg, and Vienna), which suggests that the text originated and circulated in
these areas.

The text of the Short *Nemo* is much briefer and simpler than that of the Long
Nemo. There is very little connecting material between the biblical citations,
and all nonbiblical authorities have been excised from the text. The author
classifies Nemo's qualities into six categories, with a short exposition of each.
These virtues are spelled out in the opening of the sermon.

> Vir erat in oriente nomine Nemo, et erat vir ille ut alter Iob inter omnes
> orientales. Magnus namque erat sanctus iste Nemo in genere et prosapia,
> magnus in potentia, magnus in scientia, magnus in clementia et in com-
> passione, magnus in honore et reverentia, et magnus in audacia. Et hec
> omnia per sacram scripturam comprobantur.
>
> Primo dico quod magnus fuit iste sanctus Nemo in genere et prosapia,
> similis Ade, qui nec creatus nec genitus sed formatus, secundum quod
> habetur per prophetam dicentem: *Dies formabuntur et Nemo in eis* [Ps
> 138.16]. (Short *Nemo* 2–9)

> [There was a man in the East named Nobody, and that man was like
> another Job among all the people of the East. For this holy Nobody was
> great in race and lineage, great in power, great in knowledge, great in
> mercy and compassion, great in honor and reverence, and great in daring.
> And all of these things are confirmed in Holy Scripture.
>
> First, I say that this holy Nobody was great in race and lineage, like
> Adam, who was neither created nor begotten but formed, as it is said by
> the prophet: *The days will be formed and Nobody in them.*]

The simpler, sparer style of the Short *Nemo* is clear immediately. However, the text is not entirely without sophistication. The first two lines parody Job 1.1–3, which reads:

> Vir erat in terra Hus nomine Iob, et erat vir ille simplex et rectus et timens Deum. . . . et fuit possessio eius septem milia ovium et tria milia camelorum . . . ac familia multa nimis eratque vir ille magnus inter omnes Orientales.

> [There was a man in the land of Hus, whose name was Job, and that man was simple and upright, and fearing God. . . . And his possession was seven thousand sheep and three thousand camels . . . and a family exceeding great, and this man was great among all the people of the East.]

Each of the qualities enumerated in the opening paragraph of the Short *Nemo* corresponds to a paragraph on that virtue in the body of the text. This repetition becomes formulaic: "Primo dico quod magnus fuit iste sanctus Nemo in genere et prosapia" [First I say this holy Nemo was great in race and lineage]; "Secundo iste Nemo fuit magnus in potentia" [Second, this Nobody was great in power]; "Tertio iste Nemo fuit magnus in scientia" [Third, this Nobody was great in knowledge]; "Item fuit magnus in clementia et compassione" [He was also great in mercy and compassion]; and so on. Sometime, too, after the text was first composed, a redactor added a section between the fourth and the fifth sections, describing Nemo's valor in the active and contemplative lives: this "extra" virtue is present in every extant manuscript. Remarkably, this additional virtue was never added to the list of qualities given in the introduction to the text; moreover, the virtues outlined in the introduction never correspond accurately with those later described in the body of the text. These inconsistencies are particularly surprising in view of the fact that scribes evidently felt free to modify and rewrite parodic texts as they saw fit. Evidently their zeal to rewrite was more creative than methodical.

The humor of the Short *Nemo* is much simpler and more straightforward than that of the Long *Nemo,* uncomplicated by secondary exegetical or satirical conceits. Only two of the quotations are new to this version.

> Item filio prodigo compassus fuit, qui cupiebat ventrem suum saturare de siliquis quas porci manducabant, et *Nemo illi dabat* [Lc 15.16]. Fuit etiam pauperum consolator, unde Ecclesiastae decimo: *Verti me ad alia et vidi calumpnias que sub sole geruntur, et consolatorem Neminem inveni* [Ecl 4.1]. (Short *Nemo* 43–47)

[He was also merciful to the prodigal son, who wanted to fill his stomach with the husks that the swine ate, and *Nobody gave unto him.* He was also the comfort of the poor, whence Ecclesiastes 11: *I turned myself to other things, and I saw the oppressions that are done under the sun, and I found Nobody a comforter.*]

The Salzburg manuscript (S) is unusual in adding three new quotations: two of these cite canon law and the third (quoted unfortunately without an accompanying explanation) implies another personage named Nullus: "Nullus et Nemo mordent se in sacco" [No one and Nobody bite themselves in the balls].[14]

Some of the scribal annotations to the Short *Nemo* are also worthy of note. The scribe of the Salzburg manuscript (S) was apparently worried about the reader's naïveté; he warns the unwary, "Illa relatio est scripta propter solacium, non propter veritatem" [This account is written for amusement, not for truth]. By contrast, the Brno manuscript (B) defies the reader to question its account: the scribe invokes the foolishness of Doubting Thomas, ironically challenging the skeptic, "Si non credis, tunc palpa" [If you do not believe, then touch]. The most extravagant joke belongs to the early printed version of the Short *Nemo* (A), in which the sixteenth-century editor has provided an illustration on the opening page. This consists of a large square with nothing in it, accompanied by the rubric "Figura Neminis, quia Nemo in ea depictus" [A picture of Nobody, for Nobody is depicted in it]. (The illustration is reproduced as the frontispiece to this book.)

The Combined *Nemo*

The Short *Nemo* spawned two variants, the Combined *Nemo* and the Zurich *Nemo*. The first, the Combined *Nemo,* is found in the Sterzing Miscellany, a collection of texts assembled in the fifteenth century. The framework of the Short *Nemo* is discernible in the text, but the author has added a number of quotations from the Long *Nemo,* as well as a few of his own.

The basic structure of the Combined *Nemo* follows that of the Short *Nemo* in setting out the saint's virtues in an opening paragraph, to be illustrated in later sections.

Fuit vir in oriente nomine Nemo, et fuit vir ille ut alter Iob magnus inter omnes orientales. Magnus fuit namque in genere et prosapia, magnus in potentia, magnus in scientia, magnus in compassione et clementia, mag-

---

14. I have been unable to find a source for this quotation.

nus in perfectione multimoda, magnus ⟨in⟩ honore et reverentia, magnus in audacia, magnus ⟨in⟩ gloria e⟨t⟩ felicitate. Hec omnia probantur per sacram scripturam.

Primo sanctus iste Nemo fuit magnus in genere et prosapia. Fuit Nemo de genere militari, secundum epistolam ad Ephesios: *Nemo militans deo* [2 Tm 2.4]. (Combined *Nemo* 1–7)

[There was a man in the East named Nobody, and that man was like another Job, great among all the people of the East. For he was great in race and lineage, great in power, great in knowledge, great in compassion and mercy, great in mainfold perfection, great in honor and reverence, great in daring, great in glory and felicity. All these things are shown in Holy Scripture.

First, this holy Nobody was great in race and lineage. Nobody was of a military lineage, according to the epistle to the Ephesians: *Nobody being a soldier to God.*]

The text preserves the "extra" section on the active and the contemplative life, classifying these qualities as "perfectio multimoda." The author also introduces biblical quotations without the word *nemo* in them, rounding off each section with a quotation of this sort. As he says about Nemo's manifold perfection:

Quinto iste sanctus Nemo fuit magnus in perfectione multimoda. Fuit Nemo activus ut Martha manum ad aratrum mittendo, iuxta ewangelium: *Nemo mittens manum ad aratrum* [Lc 9.62]. Et non solum fuit activus ad aratrum mittendo, unde et otiosos ad laborem conducendo ut in Matheo: *Nemo nos conduxit* [Mt 20.7]. Fuit etiam contemplativus ut Maria officium sacriste faciendo, iuxta illud: *Nemo lucernam accendat* [Lc 11.33]. Et propter hanc perfectionem multimodam, potest dici de eo quod dicitur de I[a]saac, Genesis: *Ibat proficiens et succrescens et vehementer effectus est magnus* [Gn 26.13]. (Combined *Nemo* 58–65)

[Fifth, this holy Nobody was great in manifold perfection. Nobody was active, like Martha, in putting his hand to the plough, according to the Gospel: *Nobody putteth his hand to the plough.* And he was not active merely in putting his hand to the plough, but also in leading the idle to labor, as in Matthew: *Nobody hath hired us.* He was also a contemplative, like Mary, in performing the office of sacristan, according to the

passage: *Nobody lighteth a lamp.* And because of this manifold perfection, it can be said of him as it was said of Isaac in Genesis: *He prospered
and grew successful and became exceedingly great.*]

There are nine of these supporting quotations; eight of them contain the word
magnus, "great." The author has extended his practice of understanding all
parts of the Bible as potential references to the saint. Since he calls Nemo
"magnus" in the introduction to the text, all quotations containing the word
magnus are consequently adduced as references to the saint as well. Nemo has
progressed from being mentioned in the Bible to being prefigured in it.

Ingenuity is the hallmark of the Combined *Nemo.* In addition to ending each
section with a quotation on *magnus,* the author introduces several absurd new
nemo quotations, such as "Nemo nudus debeat contendere et inermis hostis
obviare" [Let Nobody have to fight naked and withstand the enemies unarmed]
(Combined *Nemo* 91–92). This feat is justifiably attributed to Nemo's "audacia"; the author commends Nemo's skill with the remark "Et propter hec
potest dici sanctus iste *magnus coram domino*" [And because of these things
the saint could be said to be *great before the Lord*] (Combined *Nemo* 92–93).
The author also adds a joke of a new sort. At a number of places in the text he
refers to St. Nemo as "N," following the usage common in legal papers,
circulating letters, and similar documents, in which "N" stands for *nomen,*
"name," where individual names can be specified. In referring to Nemo as "N"
the author expands the joke of interpreting an abstract identity as an actual
person: here "N" refers not to an undesignated person who exists but to a
specific person who does not exist.

The Zurich *Nemo*

More dramatic alterations take place in a second elaboration of the Short
Nemo, found in an interesting compendium from St. Gall which once also
contained a parody Mass.[15] The manuscript is typical of the miscellanies in
which parodies are often found: the collection is a hodgepodge of interesting
material of many types and is written so informally as to be nearly illegible.
Although in structure the Zurich *Nemo* bears more resemblance to the Short
Nemo than to any other version, the text is most notable for its originality. The
familiar *nemo* quotations are brought forward in support of the sermon's thesis,

---

15. The Zurich *Nemo,* which is both difficult to read and corrupt in several places, has never
been edited. The manuscript (Zurich, Zentralbibliothek MS C.101) is described by Jakob Werner
in *Beiträge zur Kunde der lateinischen Literatur des Mittelalters aus Handschriften gesammelt,* 2d
ed. (Aarau, 1905), 152–83.

but the author has employed a different theological model as a basis for his argument. Whereas in other versions biblical quotations are assembled in a more or less random order, here the author is careful to establish a strictly logical line of reasoning to support his point. He begins by stating his theme—that Nemo's powers eclipse those of all other saints—and outlines seven categories of virtues by which the saint is distinguished.

> Benedictionem omnium gentium dedit illi †sapientie† beatissimus Nemo ad cuius recommendacionem verba ista dicta sunt. Percepit pre ceteris sanctis, [?] dictum est [*illegible word crossed out*], benedictionem omnium gentium: hoc est quod ceteris sanctis per partes data est [*sic*], hec huic sancto Nemini plenissime donata sunt. . . . Hoc probatur per illud quia inter natos mulierum habetur Nemo maior, unde excellit et precellit sanctum Iohannem baptistam et omnes sanctos, quia ab ipso deo formatus est ante primos parentes, videlicet Adam et Evam. Hoc probat auctoritate Davit propheta cum dicit: *Dies formabuntur et Nemo in eis* [Ps 138.16]. Quo merito hic sanctus Nemo nobis propter multa recommendandus est [propter multa *written again and deleted*] que refulgent in eo, quia usque vel quasi in infinitum gratia sit a deo preventus etc., unde specialiter septem sunt que in eo privilegia resultant.
>
> Primo eius nobilitatis ingenuitas et iusta dignitas. Secundo noscuntur eius scientia et doctrina. Tertio dicere de eius sublimi promocione. Quarto de eius caritate et prestantia. Quinto de eius misericordia et honore. Sexto de eius fortitudine et triumpho. Septimo de eius maiestate et potestate. (Zurich, Zentralbibliothek MS C.101, fol. 166v)

[The most blessed Nobody gave the benediction of all peoples to that wise one on whose recommendation these words are set forth. He received, before the rest of the saints . . . it is said, the benediction of all peoples: that is, that which is given to other saints in part, these things are given to this holy Nobody most fully. . . . This is shown by the fact that Nobody is held to be greatest among the sons of women, and so he excels and surpasses St. John the Baptist and all the saints. For he was formed by God himself before the first parents, that is, Adam and Eve. This the prophet David shows with authority when he says: *Days shall be formed, and Nobody in them.* By this excellence the holy Nobody is to be commended to us, by virtue of many things that shine forth in him. For his grace may be foreseen by God as far as or even until infinity, etc., and seven special virtues arise from this.

First, his demeanor of nobility and his just dignity. Second, his wisdom and doctrine are recognized. Third, to tell of his sublime advancement. Fourth, of his charity and preeminence. Fifth, of his mercy and honor. Sixth, of his strength and victory. Seventh, of his majesty and power.]

The need for proof provides a structure for the piece.

Primo beatus Nemo fuit de nobilissima origine et prosapia gradatim, unde noscere debemus quod fuit de illustrissimis regum ramis procreatus. Hoc probat sapiens Ecclesiasticus 5: *Nemo ex regalibus sedibus venit* [Sap 7.5]. Ideo honorandus tanquam rex. . . . Nullus potest esse rex nisi prius fuerit miles in armis. Hoc probat apostolus eum fuisse militem dei, scribens ad Thymoteum: *Nemo militans deo* [2 Tm 2.4]. (Zurich, Zentralbibliothek MS C.101, fol. 166)

[First, the blessed Nobody was descended, step by step, from the most noble beginnings and lineage, and so we may know that he was brought forth from the most distinguished family of kings. This the wise man shows in Ecclesiasticus 5: *Nobody comes from the seats of kings.* Therefore he is to be honored as a king. . . . No one can be a king unless he is first a soldier in arms. The apostle shows that he was a soldier of God, writing to Timothy: *Nobody being a soldier to God.*]

This passage exemplifies the author's technique of intimating that the saint's virtues are connected in a meaningful and preordained fashion. He accomplishes this by setting up false contingencies: a true saint, he implies, has royal blood; but every true king must also be a soldier. Having specified these interrelated criteria for sanctity, he sets out his ersatz proof, and Nemo's triple merit as soldier, king, and saint falls into place.

The evidence that Nemo has powers to rival those of God is taken to mean not that he can oppose God, as in other versions, but that God has willingly granted the saint a status similar to his own. From this the author constructs a logical chain of argument which begins with Nemo's ability to open the gates of heaven and culminates in his powers to rescue the dead from hell.

Nec hoc sufficiebat meritis sancti Neminis, non etiam ad honorem et potestatem applicatis dignitatis eligeretur, cui deus voluit dare clavium celestium auctoritatem, unde canit Ecclesiasticus: *Quod deus claudit,*

Nemo aperit, et quod deus aperit, Nemo claudit [Apc 3.7]. Quarto videre debemus quod hic beatus Nemo in caritate dei aput deum et homines precellebat, per quem in infinitum meruit, quod probatur Iohanne: *Maiorem caritatem Nemo habet* [Jo 15.13]. Unde ex virtute caritatis, que est omnium virtutum maior, pervenit ad presbiterium [presbiteriam *MS*]. . . . Poterat discernere utrum homo electus vel reprobus sit, quod evangelista probat, dicens: *Nemo scit utrum homo amore vel odio dignus sit* [Ecl 9.1]. Ipse enim animas de inferno, quando vult, potest eripere et de manu ire dei. Hoc probat beatus Iob, dicens: *Cum sit Nemo qui de manu tua possit eruere* [Jb 10.7]. Unde implorandus est potissime pro defunctis fidelibus. (Zurich, Zentralbibliothek MS C.101, fol. 167r)

[Nor has this been sufficient to reveal the merits of the holy Nobody, to whom God wanted to grant the authority of the keys of heaven, so that Ecclesiasticus sang: *What God closes, Nobody opens, and what God opens, Nobody closes.* Fourth, we should know that this blessed Nobody was foremost in the love of God among God and men, by which he deserved unending reward, as is shown by John: *Greater love Nobody hath.* Whence from the virtue of his charity, which is the greatest of all virtues, he ascended to the priesthood. . . . He could discern whether a man was chosen or condemned, as the evangelist shows when he says: *Nobody knoweth whether a man be worthy of love or hatred.* Indeed, he could snatch souls from hell and from the hand of the wrath of God, if he chose. The blessed Job proves this when he says: *Whereas there is Nobody who can deliver out of thy hand.* Because of this, he ought to be prayed to most fervently for the faithful dead.

Logical deduction and biblical authority are combined to make the author's statements on Nemo's sanctity seem inevitable. Rather than merely culling tractable biblical quotations to illustrate the powers of the saint, the author mimics the techniques of deductive theology, in which knowledge of theological truth can be expanded by logical methods. In such a scheme the culmination of the saint's career—"Nemo ascendit in celum" [Nobody ascended into heaven]—is presented both as further evidence of Nemo's sanctity and as the only logical conclusion to the argument of his previous actions.

Puns on the word *nobody* are at least as old as Homer[16] and require no scholarly training to make or to appreciate. But the sophisticated elaboration of

---

16. The "Nobody" joke occurs in the *Odyssey,* book 9, line 366. A medieval *nemo* joke, in a somewhat garbled form, appears in the *Fasciculus morum* III.xxiii.14–19; see Siegfried Wenzel,

the joke into a mock sermon took place against a background of newly invigo-rated scholasticism. The sermon parodies the scholarly and exegetical methods characteristic of scholasticism: concern with textual details, the rational order-ing of the argument, and an explicitly declared interest in discerning the truth through the correct interpretation of the allegorical and literal senses of the Bible. Disguised as objective exegesis, the sermon on Nemo satirizes the excessively literal interpretation of abstract statements. The tendency to con-centrate on the object at the expense of the thing it symbolized—to lose sight of the sense of Scripture through overattention to questions of detail about the literal—was always a danger when exegetes expounded on biblical minutiae, and the *Nemo* sermons take this tendency to its extreme. In particular, these parodies exploit medieval fascination with the opening words of the Gospel of John, which characterizes Christ as a Word: "In principio erat Verbum, et Verbum erat apud Deum, et Deus erat Verbum" [In the beginning was the Word, and the Word was with God, and the Word was God] (Jo 1.1). The world of *Nemo* takes such statements at face value: while in the Bible a person appears as a Word, in *Nemo* a word appears as a person. St. Nemo, then, is the literal result of a Word made flesh.

Like the *Verbum* described by John, the word-saint Nemo is repeatedly equated with Christ. The sermon on Nemo arrives at the idea that Nemo and Christ are identical by engaging in a common exegetical practice, the practice of interrogating metaphorical images in the Bible with questions of concrete detail. In this overliteral questioning of Scripture, the metaphorical statement "Deus erat Verbum" should be analyzed by asking exactly *which* word was God. The sermon specifies the answer: the word was *nemo*.

The *Nemo* tracts, moreover, take the form of sermons in celebration of the saint. Parts of a saint's vita would be read out in church on that saint's feast day; the sermons on *Nemo* are similar but grander in scale than these readings. The saint is presented as an entirely new figure who supplants the traditional pantheon of saints, with the fanfare of praise appropriate to a newly invented object of veneration. In keeping with this presentation, the sermon satirizes the methods by which hagiographers and theologians sought to ascertain and prove the sanctity of such newfound saints, and as a result it shows the in-stability of the entire apparatus of authority. In any search for truth the ultimate source of *auctoritas* was Holy Scripture, and the elucidation of the truth inher-ent in the Bible was the responsibility of biblical exegesis. It is precisely this

---

ed. and trans., *Fasciculus morum: A Fourteenth-Century Preacher's Handbook* (University Park, Pa., and London, 1989), 298–99. Wenzel identifies it as a *nemo* joke in "The Joyous Art of Preaching; or, The Preacher and the Fabliau," *Anglia* 97 (1979): 304–25 (at 319).

interest in the multiple meanings inherent in the Bible that makes *Nemo* possible. The violence of *Nemo*'s misinterpretation transforms literal sense into the typological: as with the Old Testament figures of Christ, the text understood in one way is merely historical; understood in another, it prefigures a person.

By understanding the Bible as the source of all meaningful examples and prototypes, the wise were able to establish the religious implications of later history. But there remained the problem of establishing exactly which lives and events were worthy of being endowed with religious truth: what kinds of similarity to biblical events were required to invoke comparisons with Scripture? The hagiographer's task was to present his audience with a clear picture of the saint's merit by citing similarities of a convincing quantity and character. The citations of authority in *Nemo* bring into focus a paradox inherent in the hagiographer's attempts to convey the merit of his subject. God reveals the worth of the saints in their ability to perform miracles, by definition extraordinary and otherwise unbelievable events. This basis for authority raises the problem of having to establish truth by reference to the incredible—the unbelievable was a necessary criterion for the credibility of the story. The authority of Nemo springs from this paradox. If a saint is defined by his ability to perform the impossible, Nemo is inherently endowed with powers beyond those of all other saints: by definition, if a thing is impossible, Nemo can do it.

If no account of a saint's life can be evaluated by the inherent probability of its events, the character of the saint's miracles becomes the sole criterion for sanctity: his power and efficacy are confirmed by his ability to reenact Holy Scripture. By these standards Nemo again surpasses all other saints: he does not merely resemble Scripture; he is constituted from Scripture itself.

The more a saint's miracles resembled those of Jesus, the more venerable the saint; but a saint whose life conformed too closely to Scripture lacked the individuality by which he might attract adherents. By contrast, those whose miracles and sanctity were distinctive and extraordinary commanded special reverence. Nemo can claim distinctive powers in the competition for spectacular accomplishments, but even so his miracles are rivaled by those claimed for many real saints. To cite only a few instances, a number of saints, among them St. Paul and St. Denis, continued to speak after their heads were cut off.[17] St. Rumwold, the eighth-century Anglo-Saxon saint, lived a life of only three days, preaching to the surrounding company.[18] Thirteenth-century France saw

---

17. For accounts of these saints see Edmund Colledge and J. C. Marler, "Céphalogie, a Recurring Theme in Classical and Medieval Lore," *Traditio* 37 (1981): 411–26.

18. Rumwold's vita is edited in *Acta Sanctorum,* Nov. I (1887), 682–90.

the cult of St. Guinefort, who was thought to be a greyhound.[19] For new saints to command attention, their hagiographers were tempted to describe miracles of a similarly remarkable character. This absurd competition for sanctity is satirized in the texts' claims that Nemo surpasses not only all other saints but finally even God himself. This extraordinary boast is the logical conclusion of the increasingly inflated claims needed to establish a saint's reputation.

The Modern and Medieval Reception of the Sermon on Nemo

To sum up, then, the legend of St. Nemo is found in five guises—the long, short, combined, Cambridge, and Zurich versions—each version and each manuscript showing evidence of creativity and scholarly invention on the part of the text's redactors. In this we can see some indication of the text's appeal to those who could understand Latin in the Middle Ages.

The piece has not always enjoyed a similarly favorable reception among modern scholars. In 1888, when Heinrich Denifle attempted a complete history of the legend of Nemo, he took it for granted that the author of the first sermon on Nemo was a gullible and overliteral ignoramus who actually believed that the word *nemo* referred to a person.[20] G. G. Coulton, in his *From St. Francis to Dante,* had no greater respect for the intelligence of the author.

> A certain Radulphus, about 1290, got it into his head that whenever the word *nemo* (*no man*) occurred in Latin writings, it was no mere negation, but referred to a person of that name, whom he proved to be identical with the Son in the Holy Trinity. His own reading (as may well be believed) was small: but he paid monks and clerks to make a collection of such passages, mainly from the Bible, from which he composed a "Sermon upon Nemo." . . . One might be tempted to take it all for an elaborate hoax but for the abundant medieval evidence of the same sort, and for the fact that [the *Reprobatio*] is solemnly filed among the Vatican archives.[21]

This attitude of offended incredulity persisted beyond the turn of the century. G. R. Owst, in *Literature and Pulpit in Medieval England,* fumed:

---

19. On Guinefort see J.-C. Schmitt, *The Holy Greyhound: Guinefort, Healer of Children since the Thirteenth Century,* trans. M. Thom (Cambridge, 1982).

20. Denifle, "Ursprung." Preliminary work on the subject on Nemo had already been done by P. Meyer in Montaiglon and Rothschild, *Recueil,* vol. 11, which contains the Oxford manuscript (O) of the Long *Nemo* on pp. 314–20.

21. G. G. Coulton, *From St. Francis to Dante: Translations from the Chronicle of the Franciscan Salimbene (1221–88),* 2d ed. (1907; reprint, Philadelphia, 1972), 407–8.

Absurdity reaches its monstrous climax with the better-known *Nemo*
sermons, apparently an invention late in the thirteenth century. It is an
absurdity which does not seem to stop short of blasphemy at times. The
homilist, with an industry that far outshines his good taste, collects from
a concordance every manageable text of Scripture that he can find containing the word "Nemo," and treats the latter as though it were the
proper name of a person.[22]

Needless to say, there is no evidence that the author was so ignorant that he was
forced to pay clerics to collect suitable passages. The comments of modern
critics betray a horror of religious whimsy strong enough to obscure their
understanding of the text—a horror which, to judge from the relish with which
the sermon on Nemo was copied and embellished, many medieval clerics did
not share.

To the good-natured humor of St. Nemo we encounter only one medieval
opponent—but that opponent offers a curious and problematic argument. His
objections are spelled out in the *Reprobatio* of 1290, an extraordinary document seemingly intended to disprove and condemn Radulphus's "Sermo de
Nemine." The *Reprobatio* is addressed to Cardinal-deacon Benedetto Caetani,
who was to become Pope Boniface VIII two years later, in 1292. This appeal
might be taken as evidence that such a text would be roundly condemned by
ecclesiastical authorities, but for two facts: first, Stephanus reports that the
"Sermo de Nemine" had itself been presented to Cardinal-deacon Caetani;
second, from contemporary accounts of Caetani—even discounting the most
critical and problematic—it is clear that he was a man much given to witty
irreverence and more likely to appreciate *Nemo* than to condemn it.[23]

The tone of the refutation is vituperative in the extreme, as is shown in
Stephanus's declaration of his aims and situation.

Set ut cum Symone mago hereticoque dampnato idem profanus Nemo
cum suo amente dampnetur auctore et in puteum perditionis precipitetur
uterque, auctoritates divine pagine, quas idem Radulphus eidem Nemini
mendaciter appropriare presumit et quas idem Radulphus reverendo patri
et domino, domino B. Sancti Nicolai in Carcere Tulliano diacono Car-

---

22. G. R. Owst, *Literature and Pulpit in Medieval England,* 2d ed. (1933; reprint Oxford,
1961), 63.

23. The standard biography of Boniface VIII is T. S. R. Boase, *Boniface VIII* (London, 1933).
For references to modern assessments of the worst accusations against Boniface, see Robert
Brentano, *Rome Before Avignon: A Social History of Thirteenth-Century Rome* (Berkeley and Los
Angeles, 1990), 314–15 n. 38.

dinali presentasse dicitur tanquam hereticus comburendus, nunc in caput eiusdem Neminis retorquere veraciter, nunc contra ipsum assistente nobis sapientia Dei Patris exponendo pariter et glosando confutare curabimus . . . (Denifle, "Ursprung," 340–41)

[But so that, like Simon Magus, heretic and accursed, the same impious Nobody may be damned, along with his insane author, and that both of them may be thrown into the pit of perdition, we, the authorities on Holy Scripture (which this same Radulphus deceitfully presumes to appropriate to this Nobody, and which this Radulphus, who deserves to be burnt as a heretic, is said to have presented to the reverend father and lord, the lord cardinal-deacon of the blessed St. Nicholas in Carcere Tulliano), will take care to overturn this Nobody truly, to confute him, with the wisdom of God aiding us, by explanation and commentary . . .]

Yet there is something peculiar about the *Reprobatio;* its objections are not what we would expect of a medieval Coulton or Owst. Stephanus shows little concern for the text's absurdity or bad taste; his emphasis is chiefly on the character of Nemo himself.

He first argues that the word *Nemo* does not refer to an actual person, citing as proof the derivation of the word from *ne-homo,* as explained in Isidore's *Etymologiae.* He concludes, "fantasticus iste Nemo" [this Nobody is a fantasy] (Denifle, "Ursprung," 341). In view of this reasonable line of argument the analysis that follows is even more surprising. Having just disproved the existence of Nemo, Stephanus goes on to condemn the saint exactly as if he did exist. His grounds for condemnation are not that Nemo is a fiction, but that his virtues and sanctity are fraudulent—that he is actually an outrageous and heretical imposter. As evidence Stephanus goes through the quotations used in the sermon one by one, never questioning that each one refers to a real person, and explaining that each actually illustrates Nemo's impiety and blasphemy. Many of the arguments presented in this way are not so much logical analysis as sheer abuse.

Maiorem caritatem Nemo habet. Glosa: Cum ordinata caritas incipiat a se ipsa, quomodo invidus Nemo iste sibi attribuit caritatem cum sibi odiosus existat, cum legatur: "Nemo carnem suam odio habuit"? Revera qui odium portat, caritatem non habet; cum subintrat vitium, virtus abit. (Denifle, "Ursprung," 344)

[*Greater love than this Nobody hath.* Interpretation: Since ordered love begins from love itself, how did that envious Nobody attribute love to himself when he is hateful to himself, since it is read: "Nobody hates his own flesh"? In truth, he who bears hate has no love; when vice enters, virtue departs.]

This is a good example of the way in which Stephanus proffers his own *Nemo* quotations in support of his argument. He also builds on the points he has made previously. For instance, he uses Nemo's lack of *caritas* to condemn the saint on further counts.

Viri iusti tolluntur et Nemo considerat. Audite iterum versutiam huius Neminis demonis incarnati. Considerat ut pervertat, et in volutabro sui erroris iustos involvat, cum nullam, sicut probatum est, habeat caritatem. (Denifle, "Ursprung," 344)

[*Just men are destroyed and Nobody takes heed.* Listen to the wiles of this Nobody, demon incarnate. He takes heed so that he can pervert and enmire the just in the wallow of his error. For, as it is shown, he has no charity.]

The author also implies that the quotations in support of Nemo are only half-truths.

Nemo accendit lucernam. Audite quod sequitur: *et ponit sub modio,* ut cecus iste Nemo veritatem non videat que est Christus, set remaneat dampnandus eternaliter in tenebris sui erroris. (Denifle, "Ursprung," 346)

[*Nobody lighteth a lamp.* Listen to what follows: *and putteth it in a hidden place,* so that this blind Nobody does not see the truth that is Christ, but remains eternally damnable in the darkness of his error.]

Nemo duraturus. Glosa: in penis eternis.
Nemo est qui semper vivat. Verum est, in cruciatibus et tormentis. (Denifle, "Ursprung," 346)

[*Nobody will endure.* Interpretation: in eternal punishment.
Nobody lives forever. This is true: in torture and torment.]

He also attempts to discredit the authority by which Nemo is commended.

Neminem inveni socium. Glosa: Verum dicit, Priscianus enim hereticus hereticum invenit hunc Neminem, quia simile applaudit suo simili. Socii ergo dampnationis fiant, socii tormentorum. (Denifle, "Ursprung," 344)

[*I found Nobody my friend.* Interpretation: He speaks the truth, for the heretic Priscian found this heretic Nobody, because like meets like. May they be, therefore, friends of damnation, friends of torment.]

Other objections evince a certain odd humor.

Nemo observat lunam. Glosa: Ergo lunaticus est Nemo iste morbosus et augur, quod est prohibitum in divinis. (Denifle, "Ursprung," 345)

[*Nobody looks at the moon.* Interpretation: Therefore this diseased Nobody is moonstruck and a soothsayer, which is prohibited in divine scripture.]

Elsewhere we read "Nemo vos seducat" [Let Nobody lead you astray] (344), "Nemo in peccatis positus" [Nobody is enmired in sin], and "Neminem reliquit Deus de omnibus" [God abandoned Nobody out of all of them] (347). Stephanus concludes by urging that the Antichrist Nemo be burnt to death along with his disciples.

One of the most peculiar features of the text is the way in which Stephanus discusses Nemo not as if he were an outlandish fiction devised by Radulphus but as if he, too, has an informed knowledge of the saint: he concocts stories about him as readily as does Radulphus. Though Stephanus demonstrates that he knows the word *nemo* does not refer to a person, he plays Radulphus's game of make-believe without hesitation, even to the point of basing his arguments on authority in a similar way. Is the *Reprobatio,* then, not a serious tract but parody denunciation or mock exegesis? If so, it is surprisingly polemical, even vicious, in its zeal. It is also inept, explaining away the joke by exposing "Nemo" as an invention even before the humor gets underway, and it wearies the reader with an argument several times longer than the *Nemo* text itself. The most that can be said at this point is that the *Reprobatio* is the work of either a misguided zealot or a clumsy satirist. It may indeed be a serious text, but if so it is a very peculiar one, and its disapproval of St. Nemo is far removed in kind from the objections of modern critics.

The end of the Middle Ages did not mean the death of St. Nemo. Around 1512 the humanist and satirist Ulrich von Hutten confected a Latin poem about Nemo in sixty-eight distichs, and in 1516 he published an expanded version. In 1579 Vincent Cossard, a lawyer in Paris, composed a new prose vita of Nemo by adding Classical quotations to the Long *Nemo*,[24] and in 1579 Théodore Marcile composed seventy-six Latin distichs on the saint.

The legend spread not only throughout Latin Europe but into the vernaculars. In France the dramatist Jehan d'Abundance composed "Les grans et merveilleux Faictz du Seigneur Nemo" (ca. 1530), while the Germans and Dutch described the exploits of Niemand, and the English the doings of Nobody. An English play dating from 1606, *No-body and Some-body,* bore a frontispiece of a man with no body, apparently inspiring the jester Trinculo's remark in Shakespeare's *Tempest:* "This is the tune of our catch, play'd by the picture of Nobody."[25] Even as late as 1679 a work appeared in London entitled "A Letter from Nobody in the City to Nobody in the Country. Printed by Somebody."[26] In the wake of these came accounts of a whole host of fictional characters, until the practice became almost a humorous counterpart to personification allegory. The outstanding examples of these were the French *sermons joyeux,* which concerned not only St. Nemo but such personages as St. Hereng, St. Oignon, and St. Andouille.[27]

---

24. The text, which is unedited, is found in Paris, Bibliothèque Nationale MS franç. 928, fols. 202v–206v, entitled the *Sermo de vita et rebus gestis viri admirandi Neminis.* Cossard's exemplar was the Paris manuscript of the Long *Nemo* (P), as shared readings clearly demonstrate.

25. *The Tempest,* act 3, scene 2, line 127. The "Nobody" reference is detailed by Irving Ribner and George Lyman Kittredge, *The Complete Works of Shakespeare* (Waltham, Mass., and Toronto, 1971), under line 121.

26. P. Meyer gives references to this and enumerates other German, English, and French examples, in Montaiglon and Rothschild, *Recueil.* Johannes Bolte prints a sixteenth-century German "Niemand" text and cites a great many more versions, principally in German, in "Die Legende vom heiligen Niemand," *Alemannia* 16 (1888): 193–201. He adds to this list in "Von S. Niemand," *Alemannia* 17 (1889): 151; and he edits a Dutch poem of the sixteenth century in "Vom heiligen Niemand," *Alemannia* 18 (1890), 131–34. Further references to German versions are given by Sander L. Gilman, *The Parodic Sermon in European Perspective* (Wiesbaden, 1974), 13.

27. Sources of information on mock saints and *sermons joyeux* include Jelle Koopmans, *Quatre sermons joyeux* (Geneva, 1984) and *Recueil de sermons joyeux,* Textes littéraires français 362 (Geneva, 1988); Jelle Koopmans and Paul Verhuyck, "Quelques sources et parallèles des sermons joyeux français des XVe et XVIe siècles," *Neophilologus* 70 (1986): 168–84, and *Sermon joyeux et truanderie (Villon—Nemo—Ulespiègle),* Faux Titre 29 (Amsterdam, 1987); Dick Kaijser, "Het laatmiddeleeuwse spotsermoen," *Spektator* 13 (1983–84): 105–27; Rita Lejeune, "Hagiographie et grivoiserie: À propos d'un Dit de Gautier le Leu," *Romance Philology* 12 (1958): 355–65; and Émile Picot, "Le monologue dramatique dans l'ancien théâtre français," *Romania* 15 (1886): 358–422. A useful survey of the entire tradition will be provided by Jacques E. Merceron, *Dictionnaire des saints burlesques et imaginaires français* (Paris, forthcoming).

The Legend of Invicem

The Latin *Nemo* also inspired the creation of one similar medieval Latin character, Invicem, whose story is based on biblical instances of the word *invicem* (one another). The person of Invicem is depicted as a follower of St. Paul, and the legend details Paul's unstinting efforts to settle his disciple in a monastery. Like a slapstick comedy, countless things go wrong with the plan, and Paul is forced to intervene again and again to defend his hapless follower from the bad temper of the monks. One conceit of the text is that Paul's instructions to the brothers on Invicem are recorded as the Pauline Epistles.

The sermon on Invicem exists in three recensions, each recounting essentially the same story. The earliest of these is found in a manuscript of 1435, a collection which incidentally also contains both the Long *Nemo* and a nonsense-sermon.[28] A related copy of the text is found in the Besançon collection, a manuscript of the mid–fifteenth century that contains six parodies.[29] Together these versions can be considered to constitute the Short *Invicem.* The two copies exemplify the enormous creativity of medieval scribes: though the two have a nearly identical plot, not a single sentence, and in parts scarcely a single word, of one copy agrees with the other.

The Long *Invicem* occurs in one manuscript, Anton Husemann's collection of Renaissance satire, which also contains the Abbreviated Long *Nemo.*[30] The text of this later *Invicem* is longer, the prose style is more elaborate, and the piece contains many more quotations than either of the other manuscripts. Again the plot is the same.

The sermon on Invicem is a narrative rather than a celebration of the saint in the manner of the *Nemo* texts. Its chief religious connection lies in the person of Paul; only in the title of one manuscript is Invicem himself advertised as a

---

28. The *Invicem* text from this manuscript is printed in appendix 2, no. 7, as "The Short *Invicem:* The Hamburg Recension." The manuscript also contains version G of the Long *Nemo* and the cento-sermon *Fratres mei dilectissimi,* both edited in appendix 2.

29. The Besançon *Invicem* has never been edited. For a list of the contents of the manuscript (Besançon, Bibliothèque Municipale MS 592), see Auguste Castan, *Catalogue général des manuscrits des bibliothèques publiques de France: Départements,* 32 (Paris, 1897), 350–52. The Besançon *Invicem* is found on fols. 7v–9r.

30. The Long *Invicem* is edited separately in appendix 2 as no. 6. Two additional manuscripts of *Invicem* have proven impossible to locate. W. Wattenbach, "Geistliche Scherze des Mittelalters III," *Anzeiger für Kunde der deutschen Vorzeit,* N. F. 15 (1868): col. 38, cites another copy of *Invicem* "im Wiener Cod. 578" which does not now appear in the manuscript of that number, and the staff of the Österreichische Nationalbibliothek in Vienna inform me that they have no way of determining which manuscript Wattenbach may have been describing. Lehmann 178 refers to a seventeenth-century *Invicem* text in Cologne, Historisches Archiv MS G. B. 8° 61, which has proven impossible to locate. (But see "Note" on page xii.)

saint, and he is never credited with special powers. Since the pathetic Invicem has few qualities worth commending, his story is not a miracle tale but a failed *passio*. Incapable of wonders, the would-be holy man undergoes a kind of watered-down martyrdom: instead of suffering a glorious death at the hands of unbelievers, he is merely ingloriously needled by a monastery full of temperamental monks. The conceit of the sermon transforms much of the New Testament—heretofore considered an account of Christ and the deeds of the Apostles—into the record of a hapless little man too feeble to command influence and too ridiculous to be martyred.

In the Short *Invicem* the account of his sufferings begins as follows:

Suscipite Invicem [Rm 15.7]. Romanos xvº. Notandum est quod beatus Paulus habuit quendam discipulum discretum quem ponere voluit in religione, ut ibi deo ministraret et a mundi naufragio solveretur, qui vocabatur Invicem. Considerantes autem fratres monasterii quod intrare proponebat, modum et gestum predicti Invicem dissuaserunt Paulo, dicentes illud Mathei xviiii: *Odio habebunt Invicem et Invicem tradent* [Mt 24.10]. (Besançon, Bibliothèque Municipale MS 592, fol. 7v.)[31]

[*Receive One-Another.* Romans 15. It is worthy of note that the blessed Paul had a certain distinguished disciple whom he wished to place in the religious life, so that there he might serve God and be freed from the shipwreck of this world, who was called One-Another. But the monastic brothers, contemplating the fact that he proposed to enter, argued to Paul against the ways and deeds of the aforesaid One-Another, citing Matthew 19: *They shall hate One-Another and betray One-Another.*]

Having introduced his disciple to the monastery, Paul gives the brothers a set of instructions on how he should be treated, such as "Consolamini Invicem et edificate" [Comfort and edify One-Another] (1 Th 5.11), "Orate pro Invicem" [Pray for One-Another] (Jac 5.16), and "Munera mittite Invicem" [Send gifts to One-Another] (Apc 11.10). The monks despise the unfortunate Invicem and accuse him of scheming, dalliance ("Mulieres loquebatur ad Invicem" [The women spoke to One-Another], Mc 16.3), and finally murder ("Ad Invicem dicebant: 'Utique homicida est homo hic'" [They said to One-

---

31. Since the Hamburg Recension of the Short *Invicem* is printed in appendix 2, I quote the Besançon Recension (similar in essentials) in this chapter to give some impression of the nature of the text.

Another, 'Undoubtedly this man is a murderer' "], Act 28.4). The monastery
rises against the persecuted Invicem.

Videntes autem quod nihil proficerent adversus eum, nec sic possent eum
deprimere, voluerant eum occulte occidere, Mathei vii°: *Dixerunt ad
Invicem: "Venite occidamus eum"* [Mc 12.7]. Deus autem eripuit eum de
manibus eorum, sciens quod per invidiam tradidissent eum, propter quod
*dixerunt ad Invicem: "Merito hec patimur, quia peccavimus in fratrem
nostrum,"* Genesis xlii° [Gn 42.21]. Item accusavit eum alius pro prodicione, Iohannis xiii°: *"Unus ex vobis me tradet." Et respiciebant ad
Invicem* [Jo 13.21–22]. (Besançon, Bibliothèque Municipale MS 592,
fol. 8rv).

[But seeing that they prevailed against him not at all, nor were they able
to oppress him, they desired to kill him in secret, Matthew 7: *They said to
One-Another: "Come, let us kill him."* But God snatched him from their
hands, knowing that they had betrayed him through jealousy, according
to which *they said to One-Another: "We deserve to suffer these things,
because we have sinned against our brother"* (Genesis 42). Likewise
another accused him of treachery, John 13: *"One of you shall betray
me." And they looked at One-Another.*]

To justify their dislike the monks complain to Paul that the new brother is
always late for meals. This gives rise to one of the most ingenious set pieces in
the narrative, an account of the conflict over the dinner arrangements which
culminates in the new commandment given by Christ. The episode is set in
motion by Paul's exhortation to serve Invicem.

Et dixit etiam eis quod tenebantur ei servire in caritate, Galatas v°: *Per
caritatem spiritus servite Invicem* [Gal 5.13]. Quid autem volentes se
iustificare et ipsum condempnare, dixerunt quod non poterant ei bene
servire quia semper veniebat ultimus ad mensam. Quibus dixit Paulus
illud ii ad Corinthios: *Venientes ad manducandum, Invicem expectate* [1
Cor 11.33]. Quid autem volentes eum excusare, dixerunt quod infirmus
erat, et ideo venire non poterat tempestive. Quibus ille dixit quod debe-
bant eum portare sive supportare, iuxta illud Ephesios iiii°: *Supportantes
Invicem in caritate* [Eph 4.2]. Hiis itaque gestis fecit Paulus districtum
preceptum et precepit fratribus ut eum diligerent, Iohannis v°: *Hoc est*

preceptum meum, ut diligatis Invicem [Jo 13.34]. (Besançon, Bibliothèque Municipale MS 592, fol. 8v)

[And he also told them that they were required to serve him in charity,
Galatians 5: *By charity of the spirit serve One-Another.* But they, wanting
to justify themselves and condemn him, said that they were not able to
serve him well because he always came to the table last. To these Paul
spoke the words of 2 Corinthians: *When you come together to eat, wait
for One-Another.* But they, wanting to disregard him, said that he was
feeble, and therefore he could not come on time. To these Paul said that
they should carry or support him, according to Ephesians 4: *Supporting
One-Another in charity.* And so, these things done, Paul set out a strict
injunction and commanded the brothers to love him, John 5: *This is my
commandment, that you love One-Another.*]

The story ends with a new set of commandments on the treatment of the monk
and a final admonition from Paul: "In hoc cognoscent omnes quia mei estis
discipuli, si dilectionem habueritis ad Invicem" [By this shall all men know
that you are my disciples, if you have love for One-Another] (Jo 13.35).

The sermons on Invicem display considerable invention, but ultimately the
humor is more pedestrian than that of the *Nemo* texts. In the first place, the
possibilities of wordplay involving *invicem* are more restricted than puns on
nemo. This results from the fact that there is a less extreme contrast between
the correct meaning of the word and the new meaning: the fact that understanding the word *nemo* as a person is in direct opposition to its true meaning
enables the text to set up ironies which cannot exist for *invicem.* The author
must be content with a weaker irony: that the word *invicem* should properly
convey mutuality, but its new meaning contradicts this by restricting it to refer
to a single person. The word *invicem* also suffers from a disadvantage in that it
must always be used in an oblique case. The biblical quotations detailing
Invicem's activities, therefore, must always show him in a passive role, never
as the subject of the sentence. This necessarily limits the role of the character in
the story.

The author or authors have nevertheless exercised considerable imagination
within the necessary restrictions of the subject. Unlike the *Nemo* texts, the
piece is a continuous coherent story, and the biblical quotations are incorporated much more naturally within the narrative. In the *Nemo* tracts, the biblical
quotations were brought in to support the claims of the text, and the sermon
masqueraded as an exercise in exegesis. In the *Invicem* stories the plot explains

how the quotations came into being, implying that the story of Invicem is self-evident. Although the text implies that Invicem has biblical authority, it never goes so far as to demand an entirely new mode of scriptural interpretation.

The heart of the joke in both cases is an overliteral interpretation of Scripture. The sermon on Invicem achieves this by altering the context of biblical injunctions so that the most general of them, such as "Munera mittite Invicem," are understood to apply to a single person on a single occasion. This operation can be seen at work not only in the text's understanding of Scripture but with the characters' understanding of the text: thus one of the monks understands Paul's instruction "Per caritatem spiritus servite Invicem" as referring to serving the man at table—and he is right, for then Invicem, Paul, and the monks fall to quibbling about the dinner arrangements. One of the virtues of the text is the way it uses linguistic ambiguity to surprise the reader in this way. Scriptural quotation is thus reduced from the general to the specific on every level: first, in using a general injunction meant to apply to everyone to refer to a single person on one occasion; second, on the semantic level of the word *servite,* in using this specific injunction in the most specialized sense.

Although Nemo and Invicem appear to have been the only parody saints found in Latin, the urge to personify the abstract found many forms of expression in the Middle Ages, both serious and humorous. A genuine misinterpretation of the kind championed by *Nemo* and *Invicem* occurred in the twelfth century, when a Breton named Eon or Eun set himself up as a messiah, claiming to be the one referred to in the phrases "per *eun*dem dominum nostrum Iesum Christum" and "per *eum* qui venturus est iudicare vivos et mortuos et seculum per ignem."[32] A number of false saints arose from misunderstandings of inscriptions or other evidence: a St. Galla, for instance, was enrolled in the Clermont-Ferrand roll of saints through a misinterpretation of the inscription "sanctae memoriae Gallae" and similar blunders occurred in many places.[33] Intentionally humorous examples appeared in guises as diverse as the French fabliau "Estula," in which a dog's name is misinterpreted as the

---

32. The story of Eon is related by Norman R. C. Cohn in *The Pursuit of the Millennium: Revolutionary Millenarians and Mystical Anarchists of the Middle Ages,* rev. ed. (London, 1970), 44–46, with references to the primary sources on p. 335. I am grateful to Jill Mann for pointing out this parallel.

33. The instance of Galla is described by Gustave Bardy in "Remarques critiques sur une liste des saints de France," *Revue d'histoire de l'église de France* 31 (1945): 219–36 (at 225–26). The phenomenon as a whole is outlined by Louis Reau in "Du role des mots et des images dans la formation des légendes hagiographiques," *Mémoires de la Société Nationale des Antiquaires de France,* 8th ser., 8 (1934): 145–68. I am grateful to Jacques Merceron for a number of references to the literature on imaginary saints.

demand "Es tu là?" and Robert Henryson's fable of the *nekhering,* in which a
wolf pursues a *nekhering,* (a blow on the neck) in the belief that the word refers
to a large fish.[34] A peasant woman in the twelfth-century *Ysengrimus* calls on
Saints Hosanna, Alleluia, Excelsis, and Celebrant, all liturgical words which
she has misinterpreted as referring to persons.[35] A similar joke with a biblical
foundation appears in a late version of the *Ioca monachorum,* a catechism of
Biblical riddles, in which the name of Tobit's dog is specified as Quippe:
"Quomodo vocabatur canis Tobiae? 'Quippe': Quippe movebat caudam suam"
[What was Tobit's dog called? "Certainly": Certainly he wagged his tail].[36]
The stories of *Nemo* and *Invicem* show a particularly literary and clerical bias,
but the basic impulse need not presuppose a clerical or scholastic background.
The texts do prove, however, that scholars and clerics were both able and eager
to elaborate wordplay into sophisticated mock-religious amusements.

---

34. "Estula" is printed in Willem Noomen and Nico van den Boogaard, *Nouveau Receuil complet des fabliaux* (Assen, 1983–), 4:345–61. Henryson's "The Fox, the Wolf, and the Cadger" is edited in *The Poems of Robert Henryson,* ed. Denton Fox (Oxford, 1981), 76–91.

35. *Ysengrimus: Text with Translation, Commentary, and Introduction,* ed. Jill Mann, Mittellateinische Studien und Texte 12 (Leiden and New York, 1987), 2.61–69 (pp. 264–66).

36. From a three-question version of the *Ioca monachorum* found in a seventeenth-century manuscript (Ghent, Bibl. Univers. MS 456), printed in *Anzeiger für Kunde der deutschen Vorzeit* 7 (1838): col. 50.

CHAPTER 4

Liturgical Parody

The centrality of the divine office to Christian worship made it a natural subject for the parodist—most involved in the religious life must have known the Mass by heart. Of course, only those with Latin training could understand the meaning of the phrases, and so for the composition and appreciation of liturgical parody, as for other Latin religious parody, we must restrict the circle of participants to those with a clerical education. The audience need be narrowed no further, however. Such parody was available to a clerics of every station, and by the evidence of these and other examples of goliardic tomfoolery, we can see that such mischief was embraced as often as it was denounced.

Liturgical parody is social parody of the mildest type, and although by implication it reproves the iniquitous, its condemnation is much like commendation. This is particularly true of the most popular example of the form, the drinkers' Masses. More earnest censure lay behind an unusual example of liturgical parody, the anti-Hussite Mass, which lambastes Protestant reformers and their diabolical patron; but even here the satirist has taken care to make the text entertaining. Clearly if the writer had meant to challenge the sect rather than mock it, he would have written not a parody but a serious tract setting out his arguments. The same holds true for the derision heaped on the irritants of clerics' lives, annoyances which ranged from obstreperous peasants to atrocious tavern food. The parodist condemns such things, but he does so affectionately, and by couching his scorn in liturgical diction he also ridicules himself for taking petty irritations so seriously. In all, liturgical parody is too mild to amount to blasphemy—almost too mild even to amount to a call for reform.

Drinkers' and Gamblers' Masses

If we were to rely solely on the evidence of goliardic literature, it would appear that drinking was the chief preoccupation of the clergy: certainly it formed a seemingly inexhaustible source of clerical amusement. A number of elements made drinking such a promising subject for narrative humor. First, illicit clerical drinking seems to have been genuinely prevalent in medieval Europe, and thus the topic was immediate to contemporary audiences. Second, drinking is an ideal vice for literary purposes because—unlike more prosaic sins, such as sloth—it involves an appealing array of practices and conventions. The sinner can be described with a host of iconographical objects: cups, wine, dice, taverns, tavern keepers, and fellow drunkards. The vice is, moreover, rich with potential forms of comic degradation: beguilement by tricksters and women of dubious reputation, vomiting, urinating in public, falling into dung-hills. Since dicing often accompanied tavern-going, the hapless drinker was also in danger of gambling away his clothes and having to return home naked.[1] These attendant features provided a fertile stock of comic images and narrative possibilities.

Latin drinkers'-texts forged the stock comic elements of tavern going into sophisticated parodies of religious rite. As money-centos projected a money world, drinkers' texts implied a drink-world, a world in which the Christian God had lost his place to the god of wine. Such texts are the comic cousins of more serious condemnations of drink; both sermons and moral satire often depicted the tavern as the "Devil's chapel," populated by sinners and by the personified vices, where drinking songs took the place of hymns and sinners fell to their knees in inebriation.[2] The tavern was hence a standard literary convention both for the depiction of irreligious practices and for humor. It inevitably became the locus classicus of comic impiety.

Drinkers' Masses form the genial side of such satire, emphasizing puns and buffoonery over the moral aspects of such a depiction. Drink was deified, most often as Bacchus, less frequently as Lieus, a term for wine which had the virtue of punning on *Deus*. The satirists also devised alternatives for the various epithets of God: *Pater noster* (Our father) became *Potus noster* (Our drink), *Verbum* (The Word) became *Vinum* (The Wine). An entire mock religion was constructed around this god, incorporating into the holy rites the stock elements of inebriation, debts, loss of clothes, vomiting, shrewd tavern keepers, and, above all, the drunkard's fervent devotion to his lord.

---

1. Further examples of the medieval fondness for nudity as a staple of humor are cited by Ernst Robert Curtius in *European Literature and the Latin Middle Ages,* trans. Willard R. Trask (1953; reprint, London, 1979), 431–35 ("Kitchen Humor and Other *Ridicula*").

2. The tavern is often portrayed as the "Devil's chapel" in English sermon literature; for examples see Owst, *Literature,* 439–41. Perhaps the most elaborate depiction of the theme is found in *Piers Plowman* (William Langland, *Piers Plowman: The B Version,* ed. George Kane and E. Talbot Donaldson [London, 1975]), Passus V, pp. 296–318; the imagery of the passage is discussed by Nick Gray, "The Clemency of Cobblers: A Reading of 'Glutton's Confession' in *Piers Plowman," Leeds Studies in English,* n.s., 17 (1986): 61–75.

The motifs of the drink world circulated in a variety of forms. They appear, for example, in drinking songs, such as the *Carmina Burana*'s "In taberna quando summus."

Quidam ludunt, quidam bibunt,
quidam indiscrete vivunt.
sed in ludo qui morantur,
ex his quidam denudantur,
quidam ibi vestiuntur,
quidam saccis induuntur.[3]

[Some gamble, some drink,
some live indiscreetly.
But of those who loiter at the gaming,
some are stripped,
some are clothed there,
some are clad in sacks.]

This poem uses religious metaphors to form a drinking-litany in which the poet proposes toasts to a succession of worthies and miscreants and, finally, in an imprecation against his critics, invokes a scriptural anathema: "Qui nos rodunt, confundantur / et cum iustis non scribantur" [May our critics be confounded / and not enrolled among the just] (from Ps 68.29). A second example from the *Carmina Burana* is narrated by a personified abbot of wine.

Ego sum abbas Cucaniensis
et consilium meum est cum bibulis
et in secta Decii voluntas mea est,
et qui mane me quesierit in taberna,
post vesperam nudus egredietur . . .[4]

[I am the abbot of Cockagne
and my council is with the drinkers
and my affection with the sect of the Die,
and who shall seek me in the tavern in the morning,
he shall leave naked at the end of the evening . . .]

---

3. Alfons Hilka, Otto Schumann, et al., eds., *Carmina Burana,* 3 vols. (Heidelberg, 1930–71), vol. 1, pt. 3, no. 196, pp. 35–36.

4. Ibid., vol. 1, pt. 3, no. 222, pp. 81–82.

In his "Confessio Goliae," the Archpoet also characterizes his dedication to drink as a type of religion, drawing parallels between the wine of the tavern and the communion wine.

Poculis accenditur animi lucerna;
cor inbutum nectare volat ad superna.
mihi sapit dulcius vinum de taberna
quam quod aqua miscuit presulis pincerna.[5]

[The lamp of the soul is lit by cups of wine;
the heart filled with nectar soars on high.
The wine of the tavern tastes sweeter to me
than that which the bishop's butler mixed with water.]

His equation of religion and insobriety was so like the conceit behind drinkers' Masses that verses from the "Confessio" often appeared as parody hymns.

If drinking transformed a man into a fool, the comic value was even greater if the fool was a cleric: drinking had the thrill of being improper, and the degradation was greater when drunkenness brought down the supposedly dignified man of God. Accordingly, medieval satirists took delight in depicting the clergy drunk, with attendent horrors and mishaps. One poem in pidgin Latin, for instance, describes with loving elaboration the altercation at a monastic feast when the abbot and prior drink too much and begin to brawl with each other.[6] A lowly and comparatively sober cleric details his superiors' descent into inebriation. (In defense of the grammar of these passages, it should be noted that the Latin of the poem is deliberately bungled.)

Habet tantum de hic potus,
Quod conventus bibit totus,
Et cognatus et ignotus,
   de aegris servisia.

Abbas vomit et prioris;
Vomis cadit super floris;

---

5. Edited in Heinrich Watenphul and Heinrich Krefeld, *Die Gedichte des Archipoeta* (Heidelberg, 1958), no. 10, pp. 73–76 (at 75).

6. The poem, "Quondam fuit factus festus," appears in a multitude of versions; for references see the handlist of medieval Latin parody in appendix 1.

Ego pauper steti foris,
  et non sum laetitia.[7]

[He had so much of this drink,
Which the whole monastery drank,
Both the well-known man and the obscure one,
  of this queasy beer.

The abbot vomited and the prior;
The vomit fell on the floor [*sic*];
I, a poor man, stood outside,
  and I was not happy.]

This poem combines several of the favorite low-life themes of medieval comedy: clerics of high status, drinking, and vomiting. Another version of the poem presumably intensifies the fun by bringing in a greater variety of drinking degradation.

Postquam crastin surrexebant,
Omnes caput doluebant,
Et nullus horum recordebant
  De factis heristernia.

Abbas mingit suum stratum,
Prior merdans ad cellatum,
Cocus vomit in ollatum
  De turpis materia.[8]

[The next day, after everyone rose,
Every head ached,
And none of them remembered
  The doings of the day before.

The abbot wets his bed,
The prior craps his cell,

---

7. This version of the poem, from London, British Library Harley MS 913, is printed in Wright and Halliwell, *Reliquiae Antiquae,* 1:140–44.

8. This version of "Quondam fuit," from a Basel manuscript, is printed in W. Wattenbach, "Das Fest des Abts von Gloucester," *Anzeiger für Kunde der deutschen Vorzeit,* N. F. 28 (1881): cols. 121–28 (as Wattenbach's manuscript A); the verses quoted above are nos. 39–40.

> The cook vomits in the pot
>   A nasty substance.]

The image of an entire monastery stupefied with drink was obviously rich with comic potential. Drinkers' Masses exploit the same vein of humor, suggesting not only a collection of drunken fools but a roisterous congregation of drunken *clerical* fools.

Liturgical parody promulgates an especially elaborate version of the drink-world, in which the iconography of drink-comedy replaces the iconography of Christianity. The worshipers pay homage to their god, Bacchus, in a ceremony in the temple of drink, the tavern. Rather than donning special garments for the ritual, they often lose theirs during the course of it. The human intermediary of the divine is the *pincerna* or *tabernarius* (tavern keeper), and the ceremony itself is centered around what the *pincerna* alone has the authority to provide, the physical presence of the god in the form of wine. Finally, the earthly tavern is merely the antechamber to the heavenly sanctuary, the hope of every earnest drinker, where those whose earthly life was devout will be allowed to worship their god in eternal bliss.

The drunkards' Mass is structured to call attention to the humor of the drink-world; accordingly, drinkers' Masses do not follow the literal structure of the Catholic Mass part for part but use only those which can be parodied most profitably. Even the most complete parodies are abbreviated versions of the genuine Mass. Some truncated versions maintain the pretense of being complete Masses; in other instances disparate parts of the mock liturgy appear in random order. Some of these partial versions may be excerpts from more complete Masses, but the number of fragments circulating (particularly of mock hymns, which occur much more frequently alone than in conjunction with other parts of parody Masses) suggests that there was considerable trade in drinkers' prayers, hymns, and Gospels independent of the full apparatus of the mock liturgy.

Four drinkers' Masses appear in complete form, comprising eight manuscripts in all: the number rises to nine if we include the gamblers' Mass found in the *Carmina Burana*. The four complete Masses are, from the fifteenth century, *Leccio actuum potatorum ad ebrios fratres* [The reading of the acts of the drinkers to the drunken brethren] (one manuscript)[9] and *Confitemini Bacho* [We confess to Bacchus] (four manuscripts);[10] and, from the sixteenth century,

---

9. This is edited in Lehmann 241–47.

10. Three manuscripts of *Confitemini Bacho* are edited in Lehmann 233–41; a fourth is edited as *Missa potatorum* in appendix 2, no. 10.

Missa de potatoribus [The Mass of the drinkers] (two manuscripts)[11] and *Confitemini Dolio* [We confess to the cask] (one manuscript).[12] These represent the fullest development of the form and appear comparatively late in the history of liturgical parody. The single gamblers' Mass, *Officium lusorum* (The office of the gamblers), dates from the thirteenth century, and as many as five fragments of drinkers' Masses were known in the thirteenth and fourteenth centuries.[13] All complete Masses and fragments are related, although some more closely so than others; the only truly anomalous version is the gamblers' Mass, in which familiar material and techniques are applied to a different theme. As is the case with much other medieval Latin parody, the repeated recombination of phrases, puns, and images in disparate versions implies a huge circulation of the form.

The Drinkers' Mass and the Catholic Mass

A familiarity with the exact form and wording of the model is vital to the appreciation of liturgical parody. Since such detailed knowledge is rare in the modern world, I shall take some time to compare a single parody Mass, *Confitemini Dolio,* to the genuine Mass. By examining a single example in exhaustive detail I hope both to indicate what is typical and what is unusual in this specific text and to illuminate the strategies of the genre as a whole.

Confitemini Dolio (edited in app. 2) is a late example of liturgical parody, surviving only in a manuscript of the sixteenth century, but its form and some of its contents are identical to those of earlier Masses. Unusually, we have information about the provenance of the text. The scribe records:

> Een Boeck gevonden in Engelant in een Abdie tussen Norwits en Londen in den Jaere 1535 also Conick Hendrick de achste alle de Cloosters ruyneerde ende alle de Monicken ende Bagynen ten Lande uytdreef, waermede de vorsehen Monicken der Abdye op feestdaegen haere recreatie mede Hielden.

---

11. The *Missa de potatoribus* is edited in Lehmann 233–41, from three manuscripts. One of these, which is only distantly related to the others, might better be considered an independent fragment, and it is printed in its full form (including parts which Lehmann omitted) as *Exhortatio ad potandum perutilis* in appendix 2, no. 12.2, "Fragments of Drinkers' Masses."

12. Edited in appendix 2, no. 11 ("A Drinkers' Mass: *Confitemini Dolio*").

13. The *Officium lusorum* is edited in Lehmann 247–49 and in Hilka, Schumann, et al., *Carmina Burana,* 1: no. 215, pp. 64–65. Full references for drinkers' fragments appear in the handlist of Medieval latin parody in appendix 1.

[A book found in England in an abbey between Norwich and London in the year 1535, when King Henry VIII destroyed all the monasteries and drove all the monks and Beguines out of the country, which the aforementioned monks of the abbey used for their recreation on feast days.]

We may also have some indication of the monks' method of performance. Uniquely among liturgical parody, *Confitemini Dolio* assigns its sections to interlocutors, a priest and a deacon. There is no congregation, the response passages being delegated to the deacon, and hence these may be indications of stage roles assigned to a priest and a deacon for a mock performance.[14]

The mock Mass begins with a parody of the Psalm verse which serves as an introduction to the Confiteor. The original Catholic Mass, divided between the celebrant and the congregation, reads:

Confitemini Domino quoniam bonus,
Quoniam in aeternum misericordia eius [Ps 105.1, 135.1].[15]

[We confess to the Lord because he is good,
Because his mercy endureth forever.]

The drinkers' version is similar.

Sacerdos: Confitemini Dolio quoniam bonum.
Diaconus: Quoniam in taberna misericordia eius.

(*Confitemini Dolio*)

[*Priest:* We confess to the Cask because he is good.
Deacon: Because his mercy is in the tavern.]

This is followed by the confiteor itself, which in the Catholic Mass reads:

Confiteor Deo omnipotenti, beatae Mariae semper virginis, beato Michaeli archangelo, beato Joanni Baptistae, sanctis apostolis Petro et Paulo, et omnibus sanctis, quia peccavi nimis cogitatione verbo et opere: mea culpa, mea culpa, mea maxima culpa. Ideo precor beatam Mariam semper virginem, beatum Michaelem archangelum, beatum Joannum Bap-

---

14. This is noted by Marks in "Parody," 320.
15. Passages from the Mass have been taken from the modern text of the Catholic Missal, which is very similar to the medieval Missal, and from the Vulgate.

tistam, sanctos apostolos Petrum et Paulum, et omnes sanctos, orare pro me ad Dominum Deum nostrum.

[I confess to almighty God, to blessed Mary ever a virgin, to blessed Michael the archangel, to blessed John the Baptist, to the holy apostles Peter and Paul, and to all the saints, that I have sinned exceedingly in thought, word, and deed, through my fault, through my fault, through my most grievous fault. Therefore I beseech the blessed Mary, ever a virgin, blessed Michael the archangel, blessed John the Baptist, the holy apostles Peter and Paul, and all the saints, to pray to the Lord our God for me.]

As much as the conventional Mass-goer has sinned, the parody *potator* (drinker) has drunk, and he entreats intercession from the drinkers and gluttons whose capacity he venerates.

Confiteor Dolio, regi Baccho et omnibus schyphis eius a nobis acceptis, quia ego potator potavi nimis instando, sedendo, videndo, vigilando, ludendo, et ad schyphum inclinando, vestimentaque mea perdendo: mea crapula, mea crapula, mea maxima crapula. Ideo precor vos, solemnes potatores et manducatores, devote orare pro me. (*Confitemini Dolio*)

[I confess to the Cask, to King Bacchus and to all his cups taken up by us, that I, a drinker, have drunk exceedingly while standing, sitting, watching, waking, gambling, and inclining toward the cup, and in losing my clothes, through my drunkenness, through my drunkenness, though my most extreme drunkenness. Therefore I beseech you, solemn drinkers and diners, to pray devotedly for me.]

This marks the introduction of the stock motif of the drinkers' loss of clothes. Another version plays on the drinkers' nausea, addressing Bacchus not as *deus,* "God," but as *reus,* "culprit," as well as by the ingenious epithet *omnepotans,* "all-drinking."

Confiteor reo Bacho omnepotanti et reo vino coloris rubei et omnibus ciphis eius et vobis potatoribus me nimis gulose potasse per nimiam nauseam rei Bachi, Dei mei.[16]

[I confess to the sinner Bacchus the all-drinking and to the culprit wine, the color of red, and to all his cups, and to you, drinkers, that I have

---

16. From "Introibo ad altare Bachi," in Lehmann 233.

drunken most greedily through the very great queasiness of the culprit Bacchus, my Lord.]

Exuberant puns are a hallmark of liturgical parody. In *Confitemini Dolio* the deity is often praised as *ventripotens,* "stomach-potent"; in other parody Masses he appears as *ciphipotens,* "cup-potent," *vinipotens,* "wine-potent," and *bellipotens,* "battle-potent." Instead of closing prayers with "Amen," the drinkers say, "Stramen" [Straw]; instead of "Alleluia," "Allernebria" or "Allecia" [Herring]; and instead of "Oremus" [Let us pray], "Ornemus" [Let us adorn], "Ploremus" [Let us wail], or "Potemus" [Let's drink]. Two formulas are particularly common: in place of the invocation "Dominus vobiscum / Et cum spiritu tuo" [The Lord be with you / And with thy spirit], the Masses substitute "Dolus vobiscum / Et cum gemitu tuo" [Fraud be with you / And with thy groaning], and instead of the collocation "per omnia secula seculorum" [world without end] liturgical parody substitutes "per omnia pocula poculorum" [cups without end]. The medieval Christian was exhorted to understand the spiritual meaning of events as well as the literal one, but in the debased drink-world the abject *peccator* (sinner) is replaced by a *potator* who, in his drunkenness, mistakes the letter as well as the spirit.

The confiteor is followed by the absolution, which normally takes the following form: "Misereatur vestri omnipotens Deus, et, dimissis peccatis vestris, perducat vos ad vitam aeternam" [May almighty God have mercy upon you, forgive you your sins, and bring you to life everlasting]. In the parody we get the first sense of the tavern as heavenly sanctuary, as the ultimate *locus amoenus.* Having discarded their earthly encumbrances, the sanctified will be able to proceed to their reward, a tavern teeming with drinkers. Thus in the parody form the absolution reads: "Misereatur vestri ventripotens Bacchus. Et permittat te perdere omnia vestimenta et sensum, liberetque te ab oculis et dentibus tuis, et perducat te ad plenam tabernam" [May stomach-potent Bacchus have mercy on you. And allow thee to lose thy clothes and thy sense, and free thee from thine eyes and teeth, and bring thee into the full tavern].

The introit introduces another theme common to drinking satires: that the drinkers, although dedicated to their vice and longing for the tavern, never derive actual happiness from their mock religion. This is primarily a result of their inability to shun the dice, the embodiment of diabolical bad fortune. Like sinners in the real world, the inhabitants of the drink-world are constantly tempted, and much misery ensues as a result; but whereas in the Christian world God strengthens sinners against temptation, in the drink-world Bacchus weakens their virtuous resolve. Thus the introit of the genuine Mass, a call for rejoicing, is inverted in the drink-world and becomes a call for lamentation. The mock introit of *Confitemini Dolio* parodies the real introit for the Feast of All Saints, which reads:

> Gaudeamus omnes in Domino, diem festum celebrantes sub honore sanctorum omnium: de quorum solemnitate gaudent angeli . . .

> [Let us all rejoice in the Lord, celebrating a festival day in honor of all the saints: at whose solemnity the angels rejoice . . .]

The parody counterpart takes the following form:

> Lugeamus omnes in Dolio, diem maestum ululantes sub honore quadrato Decii, de cuius potatione gaudent miseri. (*Confitemini Dolio*)

> [Let us all lament in the Cask, bewailing a mournful day in four-square honor of the Die, at whose drinking the wretched rejoice.]

The collect sustains the image of the drinkers' clothes as an earthly burden from which tavern worship will free them. We are also reminded of God's infinite care for the tiniest details of the world, even to something as minute as the spots on the die. In a form typical to the collect, the serious collect proper to Pentecost reads:

> Oremus. Deus qui hodierna die corda fidelium Sancti Spiritus illustratione docuisti: da nobis in eodem Spiritu recta sapere; et de eius semper consolatione gaudere.

> [Let us pray. O God, who on this day didst instruct the hearts of the faithful by the light of the Holy Ghost: grant that by the same Spirit we may relish what is right, and ever rejoice in his consolation.]

The collect of *Confitemini Dolio* appears as follows:

> Ploremus. Ventripotens deus qui tres quadratos decios sexaginta tribus oculis mirabiliter illuminasti, concede propitius ut omnes qui vestimentorum suorum pondere pergravantur quadrati Decii iactatione liberentur, tu qui incessanter bibis et potas, per omnia pocula poculorum. (*Confitemini Dolio*)

[Let us wail. Stomach-potent God who didst wondrously adorn three four-square dice with sixty-three spots, grant most favorably that all who are burdened by the weight of their clothes shall be set free by the tossing of the four-square Die, thou who drinkest and imbibest without ceasing, cups without end.]

This is followed by a reading from the Bible, but the Epistle read is addressed not *ad Hebraeos* (to the Hebrews) but *ad Ebrios* (to the Inebriates)—to the chosen people who have continued to worship their god despite countless tribulations. The reading itself is assembled of passages from Isaiah, Luke, and Matthew.

O vos omnes sitientes, venite ad aquas et qui non habetis argentum, properate emite et comedite. Venite, emite absque argento et absque ulla commutatione vinum et lac. (Is 55.1)

[All you that thirst, come to the waters: and you that have no money, make haste, buy and eat. Come ye, buy wine and milk without money and without any price.]

Omnia quaecumque habes, vende et da pauperibus, et habebis thesaurum in caelo. (Lc 18.22)

[Sell all whatever thou hast and give to the poor: and thou shalt have treasure in heaven.]

. . . qui perdiderit animam suam propter me, inveniet eam.
(Mt 10.39)

[. . . and he that shall lose his life for me shall find it.]

In the heavenly kingdom, the beloved of God are free to partake of spiritual nourishment, and their poverty wins them riches in the afterlife. In the drink-world, by contrast, they relinquish their possessions for earthly goods, and their only reward is illusory.

In diebus illis: Dixit tabernarius ad potatores: "Omnes sitientes venite ad tabernas, et qui non habetis argentum, properate et vendite vestimenta vestra, ac date tabernario et vos habebitis thesaurum in schyphis, nam qui perdit in taberna vestimenta sua, in somnis inveniet ea." (*Confitemini Dolio*)

[In those days: The tavern keeper said to the drinkers: "All you that thirst, come to the tavern, and you that have no money, make haste and sell your clothes, and give to the tavern keeper, and you shall have treasure in the cups, for he that loses his clothes in the tavern shall find them in his dreams."]

The gradual and alleluiah reiterate these themes (parodying Ps 54.23 and 127.3), culminating in a further equation of the tavern as the heavenly sanctuary. The original passage, from Acts 7.55, reads: "Video caelos apertos et filium hominis stantem a dextris Dei" [I see the heavens opened and the Son of man standing on the right hand of God]. The drinker imagines his heaven: "Video tabernam apertam et schyphum positum a dextris Dolii" [I see the tavern open and the goblet set on the right hand of the Cask]. This gives rise to a chorus of drunken jubilation, the drinkers' hymn.

Drinkers' Hymns

The medieval hymn, an outpouring of religious devotion, had its counterpart in the drinking song, as suitable for the tavern as the hymn was for the divine office. Two parodic drinkers' hymns were in common circulation in the medieval period: the first was an imitation of a hymn to the Virgin, "Vinum bonum et suave"; the other, less common, was derived from the drinking-poem of the Archpoet. *Confitemini Dolio* uses the second of these, a collection of verses in goliardic meter derived from the "Confessio Goliae." The original poem, the work of the anonymous Archpoet (d. ca. 1165), is a sophisticated mock confession and hymn to drink which employs the iconography of tavern-religion to deprecate the poet's own devotion to his false god.[17] The combination of religious imagery and drinking made it singularly suitable to drinkers' Masses, though the two verses found in parody Masses also appear independently.[18]

---

17. Edited in Watenphul and Krefeld, *Die Gedichte*. The poem is also known as the Archpoet's Confession or, from its incipit, "Estuans intrinsecus."

18. The range of versions of parodies of the "Confession" is discussed by Lehmann (164–67). For a complete list of versions, the poems cited by Lehmann should be supplemented by Walther, *Initia*, no. 10989, "Meum est propositum in taberna mori" (seven examples); no. 11004, "Mihi est propositum . . . " (one example); no. 10990, "Meum est propositum ire ad tabernam" (one example); no. 5274, "Ego super omnia diligo tabernam" (one example); and no. 20380, "Vinum super omnia semper diligamus" (one example).

These verses, appropriately, are those which best exemplify the poet's drink-
religion. In the original poem they read:

> Tercio capitulo memoro tabernam.
> illam nullo tempore sprevi neque spernam,
> donec sanctos angelos venientes cernam
> cantantes pro mortuis "Requiem eternam."
>
> Meum est propositum in taberna mori
> ut sint vina proxima morientis ori.
> tunc cantabunt letius angelorum chori:
> "sit deus propitius huic potatori."
> (Watenphul and Krefeld, *Die Gedichte,* 74–75)
>
> [The third chapter: I speak of the tavern.
> At no time have I spurned it, nor shall I,
> until I see the holy angels approaching
> singing "Eternal Rest" for the dead.
>
> It is my intention to die in the tavern
> so the wines will be near the mouth of the dying.
> Then a chorus of angels will sing joyfully:
> "God be merciful to this drinker."]

Confitemini Dolio has altered the first verse to emphasize the dichotomy between the church and the tavern, and to bring in an image of the Greyfriars as
the drunken equivalent of angels.

> Magis quam ecclesiam diligo tabernam:
> Illam nullo tempore sprevi neque spernam
> Donec fratres grisei veniant Falernam,
> Ut cantent cum ebriis requiem aeternam.
> (*Confitemini Dolio*)
>
> [More than the church, I love the tavern:
> At no time have I spurned it, nor shall I
> Until the Greyfriars come with Falernian wine
> To sing eternal rest with the drunkards.]

A different elaboration of the original occurs in a seventeenth-century manuscript copy of drinkers' material. In the Archpoet's original, the "angelorum

chori," a chorus of angels, will appear to entreat mercy for the "potator," a play on the liturgical "peccator." The drinkers' parody seconds this exchange by altering the "angelorum chori" to an "ebriorum chori," a chorus of drunkards:

> Meum est propositum in taberna mori
> Et vinum appositum sicienti ori
> Ut dicant cum venerint ebriorum chori,
> "Deus sit propitius huic potatori."
>
> (*Potator quidem egregius*)[19]

> [It is my intention to die in the tavern
> And to put wine near the mouth of the thirsty
> So that when the chorus of drunkards comes, they will say,
> "God be merciful to this drinker."]

The substitution of drunken messengers for heavenly denizens is one of the most popular changes perpetrated on the original "Confessio." The helpless drunkard, in need of heavenly intercession, also replaces the dead as an object of prayer. The original line, "cantantes pro mortuis 'Requiem eternam,'" hence becomes "Cantantes pro ebriis requiem eternam,"[20] "cantantes pro ebriis pulchram cantilenam,"[21] or "Cantantes pro bibulo requiem eternam."[22] Other alterations transformed the Archpoet's solitary lamentation into a communal profession of vice.

> Nostrum est propositum in thaberna mori,
> ubi potus non deest sitienti ori,
> ubi sonant cithare et resonant chori
> decantantes dulcia mihi potatori.[23]

> [It is our intention to die in the tavern,
> where a drink will not fail the mouth of the thirsty,
> where citherns will resound and choruses sound out
> singing sweet things to me, a drinker.]

---

19. From *Potator quidam egregius,* edited in appendix 2, no. 12.3, "Fragments of Drinkers' Masses."

20. From a fifteenth-century version of the drinking hymn printed in Thomas Wright, *The Latin Poems Commonly Attributed to Walter Mapes* (London, 1841), xlv.

21. From the seventeenth-century version, *Potator quidam egregius.*

22. Quoted in Lehmann 165.

23. From a fifteenth-century version, quoted in Lehmann 165.

Typically these borrowed verses form part of a longer drinking-hymn, the rest of which is composed without any specific hymn as a model. In some versions these extra verses glorify the miraculous powers of drink, which, like God, can bring about extraordinary transformations. The most satisfactory version of the *vini mirabilia* is preserved among the seventeenth-century drinkers' material.

> Vini mirabilia nolo pertransire:
> Vinum facit vetulas leviter salire,
> Ditescit et pauperes, claudos facit ire,
> Mutis dat eloquium et surdis audire.
>
> (*Potator quidam egregius*)[24]

> [The miracles of wine I shall not overlook:
> Wine makes old women leap lightly
> And enriches paupers, makes the lame walk,
> Gives eloquence to the dumb and hearing to the deaf.]

In money satires, as discussed in Chapter 5, the author implies that such vice could flourish only in a *monde renversé* in which men's values have been perverted. But the *monde renversé* of the drink-world brings its subjects benefit, however temporary or illusory. It even improves clerics' command of Latin.

> Fertur in conviviis vinus, vina, vinum.
> Masculinum displicet, placet faemininum,
> Sed in neutro genere vinum est amoenum:
> Loqui facit clericos optimum latinum.
>
> (*Potator quidam egregius*)[25]

---

24. From *Potator quidam egregius*. Where this copy reads "Mutis dat eloquium," the version in *Confitemini Dolio* reads "Mutos ad facundiam."

25. This version, from *Potator quidam egregius,* was copied between 1609 and 1616, but the poem can be found as far back as the thirteenth century; it appears as a single verse in the chronicle of Salimbene de Adam, who wrote in 1283.

> Fertur in convivio   vinus, vina, vinum:
> masculinum displicet   atque femininum;
> in neutro genere   ipsum est divinum,
> loquens linguis variis   optimum latinum.

It is printed in *Salimbene de Adam Cronica,* ed. Giuseppe Scalia, 2 vols. (Bari, 1966), 1:119.

[In to the guests is brought masculine, feminine, neuter wine.
The masculine is distasteful, the feminine pleasing,
But in the neuter gender wine is delightful:
It makes clerics speak the best Latin.]

The changes effected in the drunken clerics' Latin by implication give rise to
the drinkers' Mass, a more accurate description of the clerics' object of worship than the true Mass. When wine gives clerics the power to speak accurate
Latin, *pater* becomes *potus* and *deus* gives way to *Lieus*.

The hymn parody most common to drinkers' Masses was an imitation of a
six-stanza hymn to the Virgin, "Verbum bonum et suave." Drinking-versions of
this piece were probably the single most popular parody composed in the
Middle Ages. They took a number of forms, most often commencing with the
line "Vinum bonum et suave"[26] or parodying the third and fourth verses of the
original with "Ave, color vini clari."[27] The original began:

Verbum bonum et suave
Personemus, illud *Ave,*
Per quod Christi fit conclave
    Virgo, mater, filia.

("Verbum bonum et suave")[28]

[Let us proclaim that word,
Good and sweet, that "Hail"
By which she became the vessel of Christ,
    The virgin, mother, daughter.]

This became, for instance:

Vinum bonum cum sapore
Bibit abbas cum priore

---

26. For "Vinum bonum et suave" see Walther, *Initia,* no. 20366 (nineteen examples). Related
forms occur as "Vinum bonum cum sapore," no. 20365 (six examples); and "Bonum vinum cum
sapore," no. 2225 (three examples).

27. For "Ave, color vini clari, / Ave, sapor sine pari," see Walther, *Initia* no. 1901 (twelve
examples); for "Ave, color vini clari, / Dulcis potus, non amari," no. 1902 (four examples). There is
a further example unknown to Walther in Paris, Bibliothèque Nationale MS lat. 3528, fol. 119r
(unpublished), accompanied by a drinkers' prayer (noted in the handlist of medieval Latin parody
in app. 1 as *Pour les buveurs*).

28. In G. M. Dreves, ed., *Analecta Hymnica Medii Aevi,* 58 vols. in 30 (Leipzig, 1886–72), 54:
no. 218, p. 343.

Et conventus de peiore
  Bibit cum tristicia.

(*Missa potatorum*)[29]

[Good wine with savor
The abbot drinks with the prior,
And the monastery from the worse wine
  Drinks with sadness.]

Other stanzas of the original also found parodies.

Ave, solem genuisti,
Ave, prolem protulisti,
Mundo lapso contulisti
  Vitam et imperium.

("Verbum bonum et suave")

[Hail, you have borne the sun,
Hail, you have brought forth a son,
You have given the fallen world
  Life and dominion.]

Ave, color vini clari,
Ave, sapor sine pa⟨ri⟩,
Tua nos letificari
  Dignetur potencia.[30]

[Hail, color of clear wine,
Hail, flavor without equal,
May your power deem us worthy
  To be merry.]

The final supplication was also mimicked.

Supplicamus, nos emenda,
Emendatos nos commenda

---

29. Edited as *Missa potatorum* in appendix 2, no. 10.
30. From a fragmentary thirteenth-century drinkers' Mass, edited in appendix 2, no. 12.1, "Fragments of Drinkers' Masses."

Tuo nato ab habenda
   Sempiterna gaudia.

("Verbum bonum et suave")

[We entreat: help reform us,
Commend us, reformed,
To your son, so that we may obtain
   Eternal joy.]

Supplicamus: hic abunda.
Omnis turba sit fecunda.
Sit cum voce non iucunda
   Personemus gaudia.

(*Missa potatorum*)

[We entreat: be overflowing here.
May every crowd be fruitful.
Let us proclaim joy
   With a cheerless voice.]

These drinking-hymns mimic hymns to the Virgin in several aspects in addition to metrical form. These include the sensual description of the subject's appearance and fragrance, two typical attributes of feminine beauty, which in the parody are joined by the incongruous addition of taste. The image of Christ within Mary, moreover, is transmuted into an image of corporeal ingestion, as in the following words to the wine:

Felix venter quem intrabis,
Felix guttur quod rigabis,
Felix os quod tu lavabis,
   O beata labia.[31]

[Happy stomach which you enter,
Happy throat which you wet,
Happy mouth which you bathe,
   O blessed lips.]

Here the praise of the belly is followed by a paean to the throat and lips, tracing the path of the wine into the drinker: instead of concentrating on the venerable

---

31. Ibid.

word *Ave,* which heralded the earthly inception of Jesus within the womb of the Virgin, we are confronted with the physical details of the wine's journey into the subject's stomach, a gross contrast of the ineffable with the corporeal.

The Remainder of the Mass

We should now return to *Confitemini Dolio,* which has provided a parody of the "Confessio Goliae" and a version of "Vini mirabilia" as its hymn. The most extended piece of prose in the latter part of the Mass is the Gospel reading, an opportunity for narrative which proved fruitful for the parodist. The Gospel of *Confitemini Dolio* parodies the passage read on the second Mass at Christmas, in which the simple shepherds go to find the Christ child:

> In illo tempore: Pastores loquebantur ad invicem: "Transeamus usque Bethleem, et videamus hoc verbum quod factum est, quod fecit Dominus et ostendit nobis." Et venerunt festinantes et invenerunt Mariam et Joseph, et infantem positum in praesepio. Videntes autem cognoverunt de verbo quod dictum est illis de puero hoc. Et omnes qui audierunt mirati sunt, et de his quae dicta erant a pastoribus ad ipsos. Maria autem conservabat omnia verba haec conferens in corde suo. Et reversi sunt pastores glorificantes et laudantes Deum in omnibus quae audierant et viderant. (Lc 2.15–20)

> [In those days: The shepherds said to one another: "Let us go over to Bethlehem, and let us see this word that is come to pass, which the Lord hath shewed to us." And they came with haste, and they found Mary and Joseph and the infant lying in the manger. And seeing, they understood of the word that had been spoken to them concerning this child. And all that heard wondered, and at those things that were told them by the shepherds. But Mary kept all these words, pondering them in her heart. And the shepherds returned, glorifying and praising God for all the things they had heard and seen.]

The simple drinkers also seek out their god.

> In illo tempore: Potatores loquebantur ad invicem, dicentes: "Transeamus usque ad tabernam, et videamus si verum sit quod dictum est a Dolio illo." Et festinantes venerunt et invenerunt tabernam apertam ac mensam ornatam et Decios appositos super mensam. Cum autem intrassent, de claro cognoverunt verum esse quod dictum erat de Dolio. Et

tabernarius cogitabat in corde suo eorum vestes nihil valere. Potatores vero diviserunt vestimenta sua, glorificantes Dolium et maledicentes Decios. (*Confitemini Dolio*)

[In that time: The drinkers spoke to one another, saying: "Let us go over to the tavern, and let us see if it is true which is said of that Cask." And they came with haste and they found the tavern open, and the table laid, and Dice set on the table. And when they came in, they knew clearly that what was said of the Cask was true. And the tavern keeper pondered in his heart that their clothes were worth nothing. But the drinkers divided their garments, glorifying the Cask and cursing the Dice.]

Then follows the offertory (here with a parody of the Antiphon) and the preface and Sanctus. This last section parodies the preface for the Ascension, though here it is not Christ but drinking cups that are raised on high. The author displays particular ingenuity in transforming even transitional words into mockery; thus *ideo* (therefore) becomes *rideo* (I laugh). The Catholic Mass reads:

Vere dignum et justum est, aequum et salutare, nos tibi semper et ubique gratias agere: Domine sancto, Pater omnipotens, aeterne Deus: per Christum, Dominum nostrum. Qui post resurrectionem suam omnibus discipulis suis manifestus apparuit et, ipsis cernentibus, est elevatus in coelum, ut nos divinitatis suae tribueret esse participes. Et ideo:

Sanctus, Sanctus, Sanctus, Dominus, Deus Sabaoth. Pleni sunt coeli et terra gloria tua. . . . Benedictus qui venit in nomine Domini.

[It is truly meet and just, right and availing unto salvation, that we should at all times and in all places give thanks unto thee, O holy Lord, Father almighty, everlasting God: through Christ our Lord. Who after his resurrection appeared and showed himself to all his disciples and, while they beheld him, was lifted up into heaven, so that he might make us partakers of his Godhead. And therefore,

Holy, Holy, Holy, Lord God of hosts. Heaven and earth are full of thy glory. . . . Blessed is he that cometh in the name of the Lord.]

The parody version proceeds as follows:

Vinum et mustum iniquum est damnare Bacchoque iustum est gratias agere, qui est inferni ventripotens patronus per vinum et Dolium nostrum, qui propter vini donationem bibentibus clarus apparuit et, ipsis potantibus, est elevatus in schyphis, ut nos ebrietatis suae tribuerit participes. Et rideo cum miseris, nudis, miserrimisque potatoribus impietate ludentibus vinumque sine fine bibentibus:

Planctus, planctus, planctus, decies, Decius Astaroth. Pleni sunt schyphi et patera tua. Maledictus qui venit in nomine Decii, perditio quoque in Deciis per omnia pocula poculorum. (*Confitemini Dolio*)

[It is wicked wine and must to condemn and just to give thanks unto Bacchus, who is the stomach-potent defender of the infernal depths through wine and our Cask; who, on account of the bringing of the wine, appeared clear to the drinkers and, as they drank, was lifted up in goblets, so that he might make us partakers of his drunkenness. And I laugh with the wretched, the unclothed, and the most wretched drinkers, with impiety in gaming and imbibing wine without end:

Moaning, moaning, moaning, times ten, Die of Astaroth. Full are thy cups and thy vessel. Accursed is he that cometh in the name of the Die, and perdition in the Dice, cups without end.]

The preface is followed by the Lord's Prayer, of which the parody in *Confitemini Dolio* is relatively tame. The Latin of the Catholic Mass reads:

Pater noster, qui es in caelis, sanctificetur nomen tuum. Adveniat regnum tuum. Fiat voluntas tua sicut in caelo et in terra. Panem nostrum quotidianum da nobis hodie. Et dimitte nobis debita nostra, sicut et nos dimittimus debitoribus nostris. Et ne nos inducas in tentantionem: sed libera nos a malo.

[Our Father, who art in heaven, hallowed be thy name. Thy kingdom come. Thy will be done on earth as it is in heaven. Give us this day our daily bread. And forgive us our trespasses, as we forgive those who trespass against us. And lead us not into temptation, but deliver us from evil.]

And the parody reads:

Pater Bacche qui es in schyphis, sanctificetur bonum vinum. Adveniat damnum tuum. Fiat tempestas tua sicut in schypho sic etiam in taberna. Potum nostrum da nobis hodie. Et dimitte nobis pocula nostra, sicut et nos dimittimus compotatoribus nostris. Et sic nos inducas in ebrietatem, sed ne libera nos a vino. (*Confitemini Dolio*)

[Father Bacchus who art in cups, hallowed be good wine. Thy ruination come. Thy turmoil be done in the cup as it is in the tavern. Give us this day our daily drink. And send forth our cups to us as we send forth to our fellow drinkers. And lead us not into drunkenness, but do not deliver us from wine.]

The entreaty to be preserved from drunkenness is at variance with the general tone of the drinkers' Mass, and other Masses evince less sobriety.

Pater Bache qui es in ciphis, multiplicetur vinum tuum. Fiat tempestas tua sicut in Decio et in taberna. Vinum bonum ad bibendum da nobis hodie, et dimitte nobis pocula nostra sicut et nos dimittimus potatoribus nostris. Et ne nos inducas in sobrietatem, sed libera nos a vomitu. (*Missa potatorum*)

[Father Bacchus who art in cups, increased be thy wine. Thy turmoil be done in the Die as it is in the tavern. Give us this day good wine to drink, and send forth our cups to us as we send forth to our fellow drinkers. And lead us not into sobriety, but deliver us from vomit.]

Others ask to be liberated from their clothes or for peasants to be kept away from wine.[32]

The Agnus Dei is followed by a communion verse, though *Confitemini Dolio* does not include an imitation of Communion itself. The original verse from the Catholic Mass consists of a passage from Matthew, used as the Communion verse on the feasts of the apostles.

. . . vos qui secuti estis me in regeneratione cum sederit Filius hominis in sede maiestatis suae, sedebitis et vos super sedes duodecim, iudicantes duodecim tribus Israhel. (Mt 19.28)

[. . . you, who have followed me, in the regeneration when the Son of man shall sit on the seat of majesty, you also shall sit on twelve seats judging the twelve tribes of Israel.]

---

32. For the loss of clothes see *Introibo ad altare Bachi,* in Lehmann 240, col. 1; for peasants see *Leccio actuum potatorum,* in Lehmann 247 (related to the Pater Noster of *Confitemini Bacho,* in Lehmann 240, col. 2).

The image of being seated in the kingdom of heaven leads the parodist to envision a mock heavenly feast.

Vos qui secuti estis Decium, sedebitis super duodecim sedes gustantes lagenas vini, dicit Decius. (*Confitemini Dolio*)

[You who have followed the Die, you shall sit on twelve seats tasting tankards of wine, saith the Die.]

The closing prayer illustrates another motif of monastic parody, the clerical antipathy toward peasants and joy in profiting from their labors and wives. The passage does not parody any prayer in specific but assumes a typical form.

Ploremus. Deus qui multitudinem laicorum ad congregationem spiritualium vino madidorum pervenire fecisti, concede propitius ut de eorum laboribus vivamus in terris, et de eorum uxoribus, filiabus ac domicellis ad cordis oblectationem diu perfrui mereamur, per ipsum Dolium nostrum. (*Confitemini Dolio*)

[Let us wail. God who hast brought a multitude of laymen to the congregation of drunkards inspirited with wine, graciously grant that we may live off the labors of those who work the soil, and off their wives, and may we be worthy to enjoy their daughters and servant girls to the full, to the delight of the heart, through him our Cask.]

Variants of this passage are found in a number of parodies; most acknowledge clerical-peasant antagonism explicitly, opening with, "Deus qui perpetuam discordiam inter clerum et rusticum seminasti" [God who hast sown perpetual discord between clerics and peasants].[33] Others find occasion to subject peasants to slapstick indignities, as in this offertory from *Leccio actuum potatorum:*

Sanctificavit Decius altare offerens super illud quadratum rusticum, extractis capillis capitis sui, proiecerunt eum in merdatorium monachorum in conspectu omnium potatorum. (Lehmann 246)

---

33. *Confitemini Bacho,* in Lehmann 240, col. 2 (Halberstadt and Vatican MSS; also in the version edited in app. 2 as *Missa potatorum*). Other versions of the passage occur in *Introibo ad altare Bachi,* in Lehmann 235, col. 1 (the two London MSS only); *Leccio actuum potatorum,* in Lehmann 247; in a prayer appended to the *Officium lusorum* (for references see the handlist of medieval Latin parody in app. 1; the prayer is printed in Hilka, Schumann, et al., *Carmina Burana,* 3:67); and in the mock litany *Preces famulae sacerdotis* (discussed in chap. 5).

[The Die sanctified the altar, offering upon it a sturdy peasant, having
pulled out the hair of his head, and threw him on the dunghill of the
monks in view of all the drinkers.]

Pedants might interpret this as a very oblique biblical reference, an inversion of
Jacob's rescue from the well (Gn 37.28), but presumably the truly comical
aspect of the passage is the specification that the peasant lands in a *monastic*
dunghill.

Other Drinkers' and Gamblers' Masses

Although every drinkers' Mass drew on the stock comic images of the drink
world, some augmented their buffoonery with other types of parody. Pedantic
sermons are the subject of mockery in the *Collacio iocosa de diligendo Lieo* (A
merry text on beloved Wine), a thirteenth-century partial parody Mass from a
manuscript which also contains a ribald parody sermon.[34] The pseudopedantry
begins with an ironic assurance that the audience will be directed onto the path
of correct understanding; the preacher's doctrine is sound because it comes not
from inhuman stone but from the heart of a venerably carnal man.

> Moyses legem scriptam dedit populo Judaico et hoc tabulis lapideis, quia
> duri et lapides erant. Nos vero tenemus legem non in lapide scriptam, sed
> in tabulis cordis carnalibus inpressam secundum apostolum carnalia car-
> nalibus compensantes. (Lehmann 231)

> [Moses gave the written law to the Jewish people, and he did this on
> stone tablets, because they were hard and stony. We, truly, keep the law
> not written on stone but inscribed on the fleshly tablets of the heart, in
> accordance with the apostle, pairing carnal things with the carnal.]

The drink-evangelist takes as his text Jesus' commandment (in the evangelist's
version) "Diliges dominum Lieum ex toto corde tuo et ex toto ventre tuo et ex
omnibus visceribus tuis" [Love the Lord with thy whole heart and with thy
whole stomach and with all of thy innards]. This is an exclusively carnal
version of the original, which reads: "Diliges Dominum Deum tuum ex toto
corde tuo et ex tota anima tua et ex tota mente tua et ex tota virtute tua" [Love
the Lord thy God why thy whole heart and with thy whole soul and with thy

---

34. The *Collacio* is edited in Lehmann 231–32. The manuscript, Oxford, Bodleian Library
MS Add. A.44, also contains the cento-sermon *De cuiusdam claustralis dissolucionis et castracionis eventu* (edited in Lehmann 224–30).

whole mind and with thy whole strength] (Mc 12.30). The spiritual wellsprings of the love for God are translated into corporeal terms, and in the process the virtue vanishes entirely. Where the devout soul hungers for God and the spiritual nourishment of the host given in the Mass, the gluttonous soul hungers for Lieus and carnal satiation provided by the drink-liturgy. In support of God's approbation for drunkenness the mock preacher cites the example of Noah.

> Sit Noe benedictus a Domino, qui fecit ciphum et cannam, quoniam ipse primus plantavit vineam et inebriatus est et hec passus est pro nobis vobis relinquens exemplum, ut sequamini vestigia eius. (Lehmann 231)

> [May Noah be blessed by the Lord, who made the goblet and the cup, for he first planted the vine and became drunk, and he suffered these things for us to leave an example for you, so that we may follow in his footsteps.]

He then embarks on a gluttonous imitation of the pedantry of sermon-exegesis, examining word by word the commandment to love Lieus, a procedure which gives him occasion to emphasize the importance of drinking as much as possible. His ludicrous arguments are illustrated with biblical examples: in support of the veneration of wine, he notes that Jesus changed water into wine at Galilee and that Paul advocated wine for the stomach's sake. Finally the sermon turns to the subject of baptism; whereas John baptized with water, which engulfs the sinner, the drink-evangelist baptizes with wine, which the sinner engulfs. The preacher's zeal to baptize incessantly, until he obtains, as he says, the "remissio poculorum" [the remission of cups] leads him to repeat the engulfing until the ceremony resembles a series of toasts.

Although eating cannot boast as many comic consequences as drinking, parody Masses often depicted gluttons gorging themselves in between their drinking bouts. The lection from the *Leccio actuum potatorum* begins with the statement that "In principio creavit bibulus ciphum et canam" [In the beginning the drinker created the goblet and the cup] (Lehmann 241), and continues with a gluttonous nonsense sermon set at the wedding feast in Cana. The *Sequentia leti euuangelii secundum Lucium* (Sequences of the happy Gospel according to Lucius), a drinkers' Gospel of the fourteenth century, sets gluttony in the larger context of an inverted world, a world in which those who have, consume.

> . . . interrogavit eum unus dicens: "Magister dic, quid faciam et vitam iocundam possidebo?" At ille respondens ait: " . . . Comedite pinguia et

bibite multum. Unusquisque honus suum potabit [Gal 6.5: portabit], quia non in solo pane vivit homo. Et qui habet duas tunicas, det non habenti, sed tum: qui tenet, teneat, et qui potest capere capiat." (Lehmann 250)

[. . . one questioned him, saying, "Tell me, master, what must I do to possess a merry life?" And answering, he said: ". . . Eat rich foods and drink a great deal. Every man shall drink his own burden, because man does not live by bread alone. And he who has two coats, let him give to him who has none, but then: he who has, let him have, and who can take away, let him take."]

The *Officium lusorum* (Office of the gamblers), found in the thirteenth-century *Carmina Burana* manuscript, uses a different device: this brief Mass takes place in a gambling world in which all sinners fear and venerate the Die. As in the Christian world, in the gambling world the vagaries of fortune are difficult to predict, and much of the text is occupied with the dicers' fear of losing their clothes. The text's stark emphasis on these two things—dicing and clothing—recalls the soldiers' dice game at the foot of the cross, although in that game they hoped to win Christ's tunic rather than lose their own. The Die fills a quasi-malevolent position in the world of the *Officium lusorum,* and the text is filled with lamentation at his power to deprive his followers of their tunics. Even the Gospel reading reiterates this story, describing the appearance of the Decius to a doubting gambler who, because of his unbelief and an unlucky roll of the dice, lost all his money and fled naked. Unlike Bacchus, Decius is an oppressive god, and his disciples bewail their misfortunes unceasingly as they enact the rites of worship. The sense of oppression in the *Officium lusorum* is not unique to the gamblers' Mass; drinkers' Masses in general recognized the meager return obtained from worshiping Decius, and he is vilified nearly as much as drink is praised.

Other Liturgical Parody

Liturgical parody allowed medieval clerics to discuss their preoccupations in the language most familiar to them. In drinkers' Masses the subject of discussion was agreeable, but satirists also employed the language of the Mass to condemn the disagreeable. Sometimes this took the form of nonce parody, as in the following small joke, a parody of more conventional prayers, on dialectic:

. . . ut quidam ait: In dialectica sola non possidetur regnum dei. Haec dicentes, artes non negligendas, immo relegendas et intelligendas cen-

semus, ne hereticorum labefactemur versutiis, quas quidam idiota
catholicus formidans, dum cum dialectico confligeret, exclamavit: A
dialectica libera nos, domine.[35]

[. . . as a certain one said: The Kingdom of God is not obtained by
dialectic alone. In saying these things, we reckon the arts not insignificant but rather to be studied and understood, so that we are not weakened
by the strategems of heretics; when a certain ignorant Catholic, fearing
such strategems, contended with dialectic, he cried out: From dialectic
free us, Lord.]

Liturgical parody also expressed exasperation at religious groups, as ex-
emplifed by an antilitany litany, "A Litaniis Praedicatorum, libera nos,
Domine" [From the litanies of the preachers, deliver us, Lord];[36] at frustrating
political situations, as inscribed in a letter of the late eleventh century, from
Bishop Benzo of Alba, which culminates in a political prayer: "A felice Sicilia,
libera nos, Domine. / A Corsica et Sardinia, libera nos, Domine" [From happy
Sicily, deliver us, Lord. / From Corsica and Sardinia, deliver us, Lord]; and so
forth.[37]

These parodies represent the formulaic expression of disapproval; there is
no evidence that they circulated as independent texts. Two prayers for
deliverance do occur as self-sufficient works. The first is a catalog of the
author's dislikes couched in prayer form.

A cibo bis cocto,
A servo nimis docto,
A procuratore et advocato,
Ab amico reconciliato,
Ab auditore camere,
Libera me domine . . .[38]

---

35. This passage occurs in a commentary on the "Ecloga Theodoli," a Christian-pagan
dialogue; it is printed in R. B. C. Huygens, *Accessus ad Auctores: Bernard d'Utrecht, Conrad
d'Hirsau, Dialogus Super Auctores,* 2d ed. (Leiden, 1970), 28.

36. Printed in César Égasse Du Bouley, *Historia Universitatis Parisiensis III* (Paris, 1666),
276.

37. *MGH, Scriptorerum Germanicarum* 11:623.

38. This poem is quoted in Marks, "Parody," 286. Marks attributes the poem to "Wolfenbüttel
Guelf. 688 Helmst., fol. 242," but the librarians of the Herzog-August-Bibliothek in Wolfenbüttel
inform me that this manuscript has only forty-seven folios, and that they cannot locate the parody
in any other Wolfenbüttel manuscript.

[From warmed-over food,
From an overly educated servant,
From the proctor and the advocate,
From a newly reconciled friend,
From the auditor of the chamber,
Lord, deliver me . . .]

The second is something of a mock-litany tour de force, a substantial parodic roster which details the shortcomings of tavern food. The text, *In nomine infinite miserie* (In the name of infinite misery),[39] occurs in a single fifteenth-century manuscript. The form of the parody mimics a litany to Mary and the saints, with *Maria* transposed to *Biruaria* (beer house, tavern [the medieval Italian word was *birraria,* giving the modern form *birreria*]), and with various types of unpalatable food taking the place of the saints. Thus the text participates in the drink-world: the Biruaria, like Mary, is the vessel through which the object of worship is delivered to the sinner. However, the satirist spends little time envisioning the details of this world: he is principally concerned with disparaging the tavern food. The parody is essentially an elaborate repetition of a single joke, but the author shows skill in devising new characterizations of the vileness of the food. He uses increasingly longer phrases, culminating in extended catalogs of insulting supplication to the food served in the tavern.

Sancta chapra marcida, ora pro nobis.
Sancta capra magrissima, ora pro nobis.
Sancta capra fame mortua, ora pro nobis.
Sancta capra antiqua, ora pro nobis.
Sancta capra sine gladio mortua, ora pro nobis.
Sancta capra mater ircorum olentissima, ora pro nobis.
Omnes Sancte capre martires marcide dolorose et tristes, orate pro nobis.
Sancte bos antique, ora pro nobis.
Sancte bos qui lapidem fundamenti ad Sanctam reparatam portasti, ora
   pro nobis.
Sancte bos macilentissime, ora pro nobis.
Sancte bos sub iugo mortue, ora pro nobis.
Sancta vacha antiquissima, ora pro nobis.
Sancta vacha que genuisti bovem stantem prope presepe Kristi, ora pro
   nobis.

---

39. The mock litany *In nomine infinite miserie* is edited in Alfredo Straccali, *I Goliardi ovvero i clerici vagantes delle università medievali* (Florence, 1880), 91–94.

Sancta bufalla a lupis mortua, ora pro nobis.

Sancta bufalla super asino per perpetuam antiquitatem portata, ora pro nobis.

Sancta bufalla carnes tristes et durissime, orate pro nobis.

Omnes sancte carnes bovine et bufaline antiquissime et durissime, orate pro nobis.[40]

[Holy withered she-goat, pray for us.

Holy most scrawny she-goat, pray for us.

Holy she-goat, dead of starvation, pray for us.

Holy ancient she-goat, pray for us.

Holy she-goat, dead without a blade, pray for us.

Holy she-goat, most rank mother of goats, pray for us.

All holy martyr she-goats, withered, mournful, and sad, pray for us.

Holy ancient ox, pray for us.

Holy ox who carried the cornerstone to rebuild the Temple, pray for us.

Holy ox, most attenuated, pray for us.

Holy ox, dead in the yoke, pray for us.

Holy cow, most ancient one, pray for us.

Holy cow who gave birth to a cow who stood near the manger of Christ, pray for us.

Holy cow, killed by wolves, pray for us.

Holy cow, carried by an ass throughout deep antiquity, pray for us.

Holy cow, dismal and most tough of flesh, pray for us.

All holy flesh of cows and cattle, most ancient and most tough, pray for us.]

The text proceeds through several variations on this form ("te rogamus exaudi nos," "libera nos domine," and so forth) and ends with a mock Agnus Dei and prayers. Although this suggestion of a gluttons' Mass is intriguing, the parody is perhaps most interesting as a catalog of fifteenth-century tavern food: among the items disparaged are cheese, bread, gelatin, goose, pork, fish, and fried eggs.

Tristabitur iustus (The just man shall be saddened), an anti-Hussite parodic Mass of the fifteenth century, is of a different order of vituperation.[41] This acrimonious satire appears in three manuscripts; a fourth contains a related "Generatio de Wicleff" (Genealogy of Wyclif) and "Symbolum de Wicleff"

---

40. Straccali, *I Goliardi,* 91–92.

41. *Tristabitur iustus* is edited in Lehmann 217–23.

(Creed of Wyclif).[42] The parodist does not attempt to contend with the beliefs of the reformers but merely denounces them all as devils and followers of the Devil. He does this by setting a Mass within a Mass: the framing Mass, an office which denounces the Hussites, quotes at length from the supposed Mass of the Wycliffites, which is diabolical. Thus the framing Mass purports to be an entreaty for preservation from diabolical heretics. Special Masses in times of danger were customary, and at least one serious *Missa contra Hussitas* appeared in the fifteenth century.[43] Using the liturgical form to inveigh against the Hussites was an apt strategy on the part of the orthodox: instead of merely using the Mass to appeal to God, it became an aggressive denunciation of a group who claimed superior understanding of correct doctrine and liturgical forms. *Tristabitur iustus* claimed to portray the hidden content of the Hussites' new forms of worship, worship that served the Devil rather than God.

The text implicates the Hussites in satanic worship by associating Hus and Wyclif with Satan and quoting from a supposed office in which the Hussite faithful intone their devotion to Wyclif, their devil-leader. The creed typifies the text's approach.

Symbolum: Credo in Wykleph, ducem inferni, patronum Boemi, et in Hus filium eius unicum nequam nostrum, qui conceptus est ex spiritu Luciferi, natus ex matre eius et factus dyabolus incarnatus, equalis Wikleph secundum malam voluntatem et maior secundum eius persecu- cionem, regnans tempore desolacionis studii Pragensis, tempore quo Boemia a fide apostatavit; qui propter nos hereticos descendit ad inferna et non resurget a mortuis nec habebit vitam eternam. (Lehmann 220)

[Creed: I believe in Wyclif, duke of hell, protector of Bohemia, and in our Hus, his evil only-born son, who was conceived from the spirit of Lucifer, born from his mother and created the devil incarnate, equal to Wyclif in evil will and greater in his persecution, reigning at the time of the desolation of the learning of Prague; who according to us heretics descended into hell and will not rise from the dead nor have life eternal.]

Though the text is of considerable length, it has little to offer beyond this blanket vituperation. It suffers particularly from a confusion about its point of view, at times purporting to represent the Wycliffites, at times framing their

---

42. Munich, Bayerische Staatsbibliothek MS clm. 23833, fols. 114–15; these are unpublished.

43. Marks describes this Mass in "Parody," 323–24; it appears in Munich, Bayerische Staatsbibliothek MS clm. 21582 (a. 1460), fols. 265v–266 (unpublished).

words as if addressing an orthodox audience, and at times addressing the
Wycliffites directly. The text sacrifices subtlety in its eagerness to malign
Wyclif's followers, as in the offertory.

> Offertorium: Amen, amen, dico vobis. Maledictus a Deo, qui exasperat
> matrem suam; heresis, qua diabolo regenerati estis, mater vestra est.
> Exterminate mulierem extraneam, que Christianorum fides dicitur, tam-
> quam adulteram a cubilibus vestris, dicit Wykleph deus vester.
> (Lehmann 222)

> [Offertory: Amen, amen, I say unto you. Cursed unto God is he who
> provokes his mother; heresy is your mother, by which you are reborn
> through the Devil. Do away with that foreign woman who is called the
> faith of Christians, as though you were banishing an adulterous woman
> from your beds, says Wyclif, your god.]

Tristabitur iustus fails because it does not construct a coherent world in which
the orthodox worship of God finds its comic inverse, as occurs in drinking
parodies and money parodies. It appears that the author regarded the reformers
with such dislike that he could not restrict his satire to only the most comic
aspects of their errors.

The Cultural Context of Liturgical Parody

Parody Masses reveal a limited amount of information about their use and
performance. As is the case for medieval Latin parody in general, their language restricts their composition and enjoyment to those with a Latin education; this, combined with the fact that a detailed familiarity with the liturgy is
necessary to understand the humor of the genre, means that their circulation
was most probably confined to the clergy. The Mass form suggests oral performance, though only a single version—*Confitemini Dolio,* with its division of
the Mass between priest and deacon—preserves any indication of public performance within the text itself.

It has widely been assumed that parody Masses were composed for performance on Fools' Festivals, the days of merriment (and possibly of parody)
celebrated by the clergy shortly before or after New Years's Day.[44] Both the

---

44. The most comprehensive survey of the sources for Fools' Festivals is E. K. Chambers, *The
Medieval Stage,* 2 vols. (Oxford, 1903), 1:274–335. Bibliographies of primary and secondary

nature of the customs common to Fools' Festivals and the differences between individual festivals are complicated and problematic objects of study; the difficulties of assessing such usage are elaborated further in chapter 6. The subject will need a great deal more scholarship before the role of liturgical parody in Fools' Festivals can be ascertained. It is possible, however, to make some preliminary points on the relationship between the two. First, the parody Masses discussed in this chapter provide almost no evidence—in rubrics, in the text, or in manuscript context—that they belonged to Fools' Festivals. Of eighteen examples of liturgical parody, only two are explicitly associated with such a festival: the *Fallax evangelium secundum Lupum,* which situates itself at an Oxford festival of Misrule, and *Confitemini Dolio,* which, the copyist reports, was used at monastic feast days.[45] An association might also be posited for a collection of parodic material, some of which refers to a carnivalesque lord of epicures, compiled from diverse sources and found in a fifteenth-century manuscript from Venice. The material comprises a nonsense-sermon, a cento sermon, a Money-Gospel, a mock letter, and a mock confession, and so it does not in itself form a coherent parody Mass; its role in carnival is therefore more problematic.[46] Although this lack of evidence does not exclude any parody Mass from performance at Fools' Festivals, it does suggest that there is no cause to associate liturgical parody exclusively with Fools' Festivals: liturgical parody may well have been an entertainment for any occasion of merriment, as were drinking songs and ribald stories.

Paul Lehmann attempts to assign parody Masses a French origin on the grounds that the French universities of the eleventh and twelfth centuries provided fertile soil for such revelry.[47] He does acknowledge, however, that the majority of the surviving manuscripts have a German or German-Swiss

sources are also provided by Jacques Heers in *Fêtes des fous et carnavals* (Paris, 1983) and by Emmanuel Le Roy Ladurie in *Carnival in Romans: A People's Uprising at Romans 1579–1580,* trans. Mary Feeney (Harmondsworth, 1981).

45. The *Fallax evangelium* is edited in Wright and Halliwell, *Reliquiae Antiquae,* 2:58 (for fuller references see appendix 1). The rubric of *Confitemini Dolio* is reproduced in this chapter and in the edition in appendix 2, no. 11.

46. The contents of the manuscript (Venice, Biblioteca Nazionale Marciana MS it.XI.66) are listed in Maria Cristofari, *Il codice marciano it.XI,66* (Padua, 1937); the carnivalesque materials, on fols. 120r–121v of the manuscript, are listed on Cristofari's p. 34. These consist of the nonsense-cento-sermon *Sermo sententiosissimus* (edited in Appendix 2, no. 14), the satirical cento-sermon *Neglectio epistolae beati Paulisper* (edited by Novati; see appendix 1 for references), an abbreviated Money-Gospel (edited in chap. 5), and a *Littera quam scribit Carnisprivium* and *Confessio Carnisprivii* (the latter in Italian). The last two items are edited in Luigi Manzoni, *Libro di Carnevale dei secoli XV e XVI* (1881; reprint, Bologna, 1968), 235 and 237.

47. Lehmann discusses parody Masses on pp. 145–50 of *Die Parodie im Mittelalter.*

pedigree; other Masses unknown to him, such as *Confitemini Dolio,* are English in origin. This distribution casts further doubt on the supposition that liturgical parody was exclusively or even principally the domain of Fools' Festivals; such festivals were widely celebrated in France but were apparently less popular in England and German-speaking areas.

The longevity of the parody Mass also suggests that it was not confined to a single use or occasion. The form proved to be one of the most enduring types of medieval parody, with six surviving manuscripts copied in the sixteenth century and another in the seventeenth.[48] In the same period Fools' Festivals showed a sharp decline.[49] One of the reasons advanced for the disappearance of both practices was the more defensive attitude toward liturgy and orthodoxy assumed by the Catholic Church in the face of Protestantism. But there is no evidence in liturgical parody that the threat of the Reformation produced such a retrenchment: as the anti-Hussite pieces prove, some champions of the old order even used liturgical parody to vilify the new and unorthodox religious belief.

Apart from the problematic testimony of material pertaining to Fools' Festivals, there are few contemporary indications of the status of liturgical parody. Bernardino of Siena (1380–1444), a priest and Franciscan, later vicar general of the order's Strict Observance, composed a collection of sermons on dicers and drunkards, *Contra alearum ludos* (Against dice games), which refers to parody Masses.[50] Although not a parody itself, the invective borrows the form of drinkers' Masses.

Initium epistolae taliter nuntietur: Incipit epistola boni pabuli appositi ad ebrios. Canissimi: Ebrii estote et manducate etc. Graduale sit ex ludo gradatim ruere in peccata. Evangelium, quod bonum nuntium, scilicet

---

48. Many adaptations of medieval parodic forms also appeared in the Renaissance, where they were used to satirize different concerns. Most have not been published in modern editions; a number can be found in Caelius Secundus Curio's *Pasquillorum tomi duo* (Basel, 1544). Marks describes two representative adaptations of the parody-Mass form: an unpublished seventeenth-century anti-papal Pater Noster (Marks, "Parody," 201–2) and *Der Papisten handtbuechlein* (1548), a collection of antipapal mock prayers attributed to Luther, which concludes with a prayer almost identical to that appearing in a number of medieval parody Masses. The collection is printed by A. von Dommer, *Autotypen der Reformationzeit auf der Hamburger Stadtbibliothek* (Hamburg, 1881); the medieval example is no. 54, on Dommer's p. 12. The whole is discussed by Marks in "Parody," 285–86.

49. For an overview of the rise and decline of Fools' Festivals see Chambers, *The Medieval Stage.*

50. *S. Bernardini Senensis Ordinis Fratrum Minorum Opera Omnia,* 9 vols. (Florence, 1950–65), 2: sermo XLII, pp. 20–34.

pro nobis, interpretatur, sit cum dicitur a lusore: Perde; et socius, quasi clericus, dicit: Vinco. *Credo* sit in lusoribus credere numquam mori. . . . Communicatio sit denariorum imbursatio. Communionem annuntiare sit ad tabernam post ludum invitare. Postcommunio sit crapula et inebriatio.[51]

[The beginning of the epistle would be announced like this: Here begins the Epistle of Good Grub set before the Inebriates. Most foamy ones: Be drunk, and eat, etc. The gradual would be to go to ruin, gradually, from gambling into sin. The Gospel, which means good news, that is, for us, would be when the gambler says: Lose! and his companion, like a cleric, says: I win! The creed would be, among gamblers, to believe they will never die. . . . Communication would be the fulfillment of purses with coins. To announce Communion would be the invitation to the tavern after the game. Post Communion would be drunkenness and inebriation.]

This is a denunciation not of parody Masses but of those who drink and gamble to such excess that their obsession resembles a mock religion. Bernardino uses a device identical to that of drinkers' and gamblers' Masses themselves; the only difference is that he distances himself from such vice by providing a description of the practice rather than setting out the actual words of the sermon, and by putting his description in the mouth of the Devil. Thus although Bernardino is critical of drinkers and gamblers, he is sympathetic to the satirical possibilities of the parody Mass, sympathetic enough to adapt it to his own purposes. Such metaphorical invectives as this seem to have been a staple of sermon-writers.[52]

A second piece of testimony is provided by the rubric of a fragment of a parody-Mass in a manuscript written at Saint Gall.[53] The scribe, Kemly (b. 1417), notes at the conclusion of the Mass:

---

51. Ibid., 2:24. None of the surviving drinkers' or gamblers' Masses conforms exactly to Bernardino's citations, although many are similar; the closest text is the *Leccio actuum potatorum.*

52. A similar text by a Dominican is quoted in Owst, *Literature,* 394; and another more metaphorical treatment appears in the *Fasciculus morum:* see Wenzel, *Fasciculus morum,* VI.ii.55–64 (p. 630).

53. The Mass is printed in Lehmann 241, col. 2, as Z in the apparatus to *Confitemini Bacho;* the fragment is too short to ascertain whether it is genuinely a relative of *Confitemini Bacho.* The entire Mass originally occupied two folios (now lost) between the present folios 75v and 76r of Zurich, Zentralbibliothek MS C.101 (s. xv). A list of contents and the scribal rubric are printed by Jakob Werner, *Beiträge,* 160. The version of *Nemo* found in the same manuscript has never been edited; excerpts are printed as the Zurich *Nemo* in chapter 4.

Istud officium fuit quondam conpositum a quodam magistro magno in studio Parisiensi, cuius scolares et studentes tabernam et ludos frequentantes qui nullo modo poterant corrigi per lecturam optimorum librorum et ipsis convocatis legit eis ad presentiam (?) hoc officium, unde multi eorum correxerunt vitam suam et ad bonum statum pervenerunt. (Werner, *Beiträge,* 211)

[This office was composed once by a master great in studies in Paris, whose scholars and students frequented the tavern and gambling, and who would not take correction in any way from reading from the best books. Having gathered them together, he read to them . . . this office, whereupon many of them mended their ways and became worthy men.]

This surprising story seems to support Bernardino's view of the parody Mass as an instrument of reproof. But we may question whether the form was invariably used as a medium of morality rather than as entertainment. Though Kemly describes the Mass as correction for reprobates, he does not fail to transcribe it himself, as he also does with other undeniably frivolous material, such as the sermon on Nemo.

Liturgical parody, then, fulfilled two functions. It could serve as a celebration of the comic aspects of one's own sinning, a mild form of self-mockery. It could also be used as a means of condemning the offensive or immoral behavior of others; but even at its most vilificatory it is full of jokes, puns, and conceits, and it is clear that the satirists are not lampooning vice so earnestly that they fail to enjoy themselves.

CHAPTER 5

Humorous Centos

The cento is a new composition created by rearranging lines or passages from a well-known text or texts; the form had its origin in Classical antiquity and survived until the seventeenth century.[1] Since an appreciation of the centonist's skill demands an audience which can recall the original context of the lines, the cento presupposes a cultural or educational milieu which fostered detailed knowledge of certain canonical works. Accordingly, the late antique period saw centos of the poems of Virgil and Homer; in the Middle Ages, the Bible most often supplied the raw material for the centonist. Writers often employed the form to serve serious ends, but because absurd juxtapositions could result accidentally even in a serious cento, the technique obviously had rich potential for the parodist. Centonists of the Middle Ages, in particular, were quick to exploit these possibilities.

The Cento in Antiquity

Although there is evidence that Latin centos were composed in the Classical period itself, the earliest surviving example of the form dates from the late third century.[2] This is a tragedy constructed from lines of Virgil, the *Medea* of

---

1. The Latin word *cento* and its Greek cognate originally meant a patchwork cloth. The etymology of the term is outlined by Walter Belardi, "Nomi del centone nelle lingue indoeuropee," *Ricerche linguistiche* 4 (1958): 29–57. Of the few scholars who have written about the form in English, a number have retained the Latin plural, "centones"; I shall adopt the simpler form "centos."

2. The history of the cento in Classical antiquity is outlined in Giovanni Salanitro, *Osidio Geta: Medea,* Bibliotheca Athena 24 (Rome, 1981), 18–60; in F. Ermini, *Il centone di Proba e la poesia centonaria latina* (Rome, 1909), 19–55; and, on Late Latin centos, briefly in Angelo Di Berardino, ed., *The Golden Age of Latin Patristic Literature from the Council of Nicea to the Council of Chalcedon,* vol. 4 of *Patrology,* trans. Placid Solari (Westminister, Md., 1988), 269–73 (translated from the Italian *Patrologia,* vol. 3 [Turin, 1978]). The most extensive collections of centos are those of Octave Delepierre, *Tableau de la littérature du centon chez les anciens et chez les modernes,* 2 vols. (London, 1874–75), originally published as *Centoniana, ou Encyclopédie du centon,* 2 parts, Philobiblon Society Miscellanies 9–10 (London, 1866–68).

Hosidius Geta.[3] Perhaps the most notorious cento of the late antique period is Ausonius's *Cento nuptialis,* an epithalamium describing the delights of the wedding night in the language of Virgilian warfare. This licentious tour de force was written around 368 in response to a similarly bawdy cento (now lost) by the emperor Valentinian; it is noteworthy both because it is the earliest known humorous cento and because its preface contains a prescription of the rules of cento composition. According to Ausonius, a cento should be entirely composed of material taken from another context, and the units of borrowing should be strictly confined to half or whole lines. Comparing the cento to a puzzle called the *ostomachia,* in which different shapes of bone are arranged to form pictures, Ausonius relates:

> Hoc ergo centonis opusculum ut ille ludus tractatur, pari modo sensus diversi ut congruant, adoptiva quae sunt, ut cognata videantur, aliena ne interluceant: arcessita ne vim redarguant, densa ne supra modum pro-tuberent, hiulca ne pateant. quae si omnia ita tibi videbuntur, ut praecep-tum est, dices me composuisse centonem.[4]

> [And therefore this little work, the cento, is drawn together like that game, so that different meanings come together into a single form, and disparate things seem to be related, so that unrelated things let no light through the gaps: to prevent the far-fetched elements from being con-tradictory, the densely packed from standing out too much, the slack from gaping open. If these conditions seem fulfilled according to the rule, then you will say I have constructed a cento.]

Ausonius accompanies this comparison with detailed precepts for the construc-tion of a cento, but in fact he is describing an ideal, for in reality few centos conformed perfectly to these strictures.[5] Later, when centonists turned from the poets to the Bible for their source material, the rules appropriate to verse centos became irrelevant, and centonists had the freedom to excerpt passages of any length and even to connect these with phrases of their own making. Medieval authors of parodic centos also introduced puns into the narrative, thus doubly superimposing new meaning onto old forms.

---

3. The *Medea* is edited in Salanitro, *Osidio Geta;* and in Rosa Lamacchia, *Hosidii Getae Medea: Cento Vergilianus* (Leipzig, 1981).

4. The *Cento nuptialis* is edited in *Decimi Magni Ausonii Burdigalensis Opuscula,* ed. S. Prete (Leipzig, 1978), 159–69 (at 161, lines 43–47).

5. David F. Bright discusses the extent to which centonists conformed with these rules in "Theory and Practice in the Vergilian Cento," *Illinois Classical Studies* 9 (1984): 79–90.

The biblical centos of the Middle Ages were heir to a venerable tradition of cento writing. In the Classical and Late Latin periods, passages from Virgil were forged into a variety of literary genres; succeeding Christian authors sought to refashion Classical poetry into biblical narrative, and finally, in the Middle Ages proper, the Bible itself yielded the raw material for profane narrative. The advent of Christianity transformed the cento into a significant vehicle for religious truth, but the form was popular even before it acquired doctrinal value, as is evident from the wealth of Late Latin Virgilian centos. Their survival—as of many works of that era—has largely been a matter of chance: most extant examples appear in a single manuscript, the Codex Salmasianus, a poetic anthology assembled in the sixth century from older material.[6] The collection preserves twelve Virgilian centos, primarily rehearsing mythological legends, as their titles testify: *Narcissus, Hercules et Antaeus, Progne et Philomela,* and the *Iudicium Paridis.* Of the twelve, only one is Christian: a quasi-allegorical religious disquisition entitled *De ecclesia,* problematically attributed to one Mavortius.

The coming of Christianity lent a new ideological impetus to the writing of centos; the form was particularly suitable for Christian poets educated in the Classical tradition, who sought to accommodate the traditional forms of poetic expression to Christian themes. The cento was not the sole form to bear the weight of this aspiration: the impulse to reconcile Classical forms of literature to the new Christian subject matter was expressed in a variety of ways. In the most extreme cases it produced anachronistic reinterpretations of Classical works themselves, such as the medieval interpretation of Virgil's Fourth Eclogue as a prefiguration of Christ.[7] The desire to retain traditional poetic forms also gave rise to verse retellings of the Bible in epic form, such as Juvencus's *Evangelium libri quattuor* (ca. 330), Sedulius's *Carmen paschale* (fifth century), and Arator's *De actibus apostolorum* (544).[8]

---

6. A brief outline of the contents and history of the Codex Salmasianus can be found in the description by R. J. Tarrant in "Anthologia Latina," in *Texts and Transmission: A Survey of the Latin Classics,* ed. L. D. Reynolds (Oxford, 1983), 9–13. The contents of the manuscript are edited in F. Buecheler and A. Riese, *Anthologia Latina sive Poesis Latinae Supplementum,* 5 vols. (Leipzig, 1894–1926); the centos are printed in vol. 1, pp. 33–82. A new edition of the manuscript is in preparation by D. R. Shackleton Bailey, *Anthologia Latina;* the centos have not yet been published.

7. On this phenomenon see P. Courcelle, "Les exégèses chrétiennes de la quatrième Églogue," *Revue des études anciennes* 59 (1957): 294–319.

8. Juvencus is edited by J. Hümer in *CSEL* (1891), vol. 24; Sedulius by J. Hümer in *CSEL* (1885), vol. 10; and Arator by A. P. McKinlay in *CSEL* (1951), vol. 72. On the impulse to rewrite the Bible in epic form see Carl P. E. Springer, *The Gospel as Epic in Late Antiquity: The Paschale Carmen of Sedulius,* Supplements to Vigiliae Christianae 2 (Leiden, 1988).

Centos were the ideal expression of Christian veneration for traditional poetry: in this mode not only Virgil's verse form but his very words could be made to sing the praises of Christ. It was thus appropriate, if not inevitable, that a biblical epic should be attempted in cento form. This ambitious project was the undertaking of Faltonia Proba, an author of the 360s or 380s.[9] Proba's *Cento* surpassed other Late Latin biblical epics in scope, encompassing most of the important books of both the Old and New Testaments. This application of Virgilian phrasing to the complete span of biblical history found great favor in the Middle Ages. Both Boccaccio and Christine de Pizan, for example, praised Proba's efforts, and when Conrad Celtes wished to celebrate the newly re-discovered work of Hrothsvitha of Gandersheim in 1493, he did so by compar-ing Hrothsvitha to Proba.[10] The fame of the *Cento* is also attested to by its detractors: it was denounced as an apocryphal version of Scripture in the Gelasian Decree (a document most likely of the sixth century),[11] and the work drew fire from Jerome, who quoted Proba disparagingly in a letter to Paulinus of Nola.[12]

Proba was not alone, however, in her desire to explore Christian themes through reformulations of the Classical poets. The fifth century produced two further Christian centos of Virgil: *De verbi incarnatione,* a poem on the Cre-ation (attributed in the Middle Ages to Sedulius), and the *Versus ad gratiam domini,* an essay on the faith, in the form of an eclogue, by a certain Pomponius.[13]

The Middle Ages continued to employ the cento for both serious and hu-morous literature. In the former category were the *Quirinalia* of Metellus of

---

9. Proba's *Cento* is edited by K. Schenkl in *CSEL* (1888), 16.1:513–609. The text is reprinted with translation by E. A. Clark and D. F. Hatch, *The Golden Bough, the Oaken Cross: The Vergilian Cento of Faltonia Betitia Proba,* American Academy of Religion, Texts and Translations 5 (Chico, Calif., 1981).

10. Boccaccio, *De mulieribus claris,* ed. Vittorio Zaccaria (Milan, 1967), chap. 95. There is no modern edition of Christine de Pizan in the original French; for an English translation see Christine de Pizan, *The Book of the City of Ladies,* trans. Earl Jeffrey Richards (London, 1983), I.29.1 (pp. 65–67). For Conrad Celtes's verse on Proba see Edwin H. Zeydel, "The Reception of Hrotsvitha by the German Humanists after 1493," *Journal of English and Germanic Philology* 44 (1945): 239–49 (at 245). Zeydel has misunderstood Celtes's meaning, apparently never having heard of Proba; he does not capitalize her name, and the translation of the verse on p. 245 n. 38 translates *proba* as "the good Muse."

11. Ernst von Dobschütz, *Das decretum Gelasianum,* Texte und Untersuchungen zur Geschichte der altchristlichen Literatur, 3d ser., 8.iv (Leipzig, 1912), 52 n. 287.

12. Jerome *Epistula* 53, edited by I. Hilberg in *CSEL* (1910), 54:454.

13. *De verbi incarnatione* is edited by Buecheler in Buecheler and Riese, *Anthologia Latina,* 1: no. 16, pp. 56–61; and by K. Schenkl in *CSEL* (1888), 16.1: 615–20. The *Versus ad gratiam domini* is edited by Schenkl, ibid., 609–15.

Tegernsee (of the mid–twelfth century), which relied heavily on quotations from Horace.[14] The *Trivita studentium* of Goswyn Kempgyn of Nussia (ca. 1420–1483) was a cento of one of the medieval period's most important grammatical texts, the *Doctrinale* of Alexander de Villa Dei.[15] Centos could also be found in forms more appealing than these didactic texts, and narrative centos were among the most interesting examples of the genre. One early thirteenth-century cento, for instance, celebrates a woman's achievement in overcoming armed and murderous conspirators. This piece, entitled the *Canticum triumphale et gratiarum actionis ob incolumitatem Henrici Comitis, Annae Musnieri benefacto servatam,* describes an event in 1175 when a woman named Anne Musnier foiled the plot of three knights on their way to murder Henry, count of Champagne.[16] Because the incident is described entirely in biblical quotations, it takes on an air of scriptural solemnity and importance.

Ecce opus factum est in diebus nostris quod nemo credet cum narrabitur [Hab 1.5]. Irati tres milites voluerunt insurgere in dominum suum, et occidere eum [Est 2.21]. Sedentes in insidiis in occultis quasi leo in spelunca sua [Ps 9.30]. Erat autem mulier cui nomen Anna quae noverat regere familiam et gubernare domum [Tb 10.13]. Quae cum intellexisset cogitationes eorum et curas diligentius pervidisset [Est 12.2] . . . (Delepierre, *Tableau,* 1:149)

[Behold, for a work is done in your days which no man will believe when it shall be told. Three wrathful soldiers designed to rise up against their lord, and kill him. They are lying in wait in secret like a lion in his den. There was a woman named Anna who knew how to take care of the family and govern the house. And when she had understood their designs and had diligently searched into their projects . . .]

A similar technique was employed in the composition of medieval plainchant. Such chants were constructed by recombining lines from Scripture; the juxtaposition of passages from different books of the Bible was designed to

---

14. These are edited by Peter Christian Jakobsen, *Die Quirinalien des Metellus von Tegernsee,* Mittellateinische Studien und Texte 1 (Leiden and Cologne, 1965).

15. The *Trivita Studentium* is edited in M. Bernhard, *Goswin Kempgyn de Nussia, Trivita Studentium,* Münchener Beiträge zur Mediävistik und Renaissance-Forschung 26 (Munich, 1976). See also W. Maaz, "Zur Rezeption des Alexander v. Villa Dei im 15. Jahrhundert," *Mittellateinisches Jahrbuch* 16 (1981): 276–81.

16. It is printed in Delepierre, *Tableau,* 1:149–53.

bring typological parallels into focus.[17] Thus the practice made passages which were insignificant in isolation meaningful in combination, a technique which later satirical centonists were to use with great effect.

The cento technique was also used in *passiones,* vituperative condemnations of historical events narrated in the form of the Gospels.[18] Although these narratives do rearrange and distort biblical passages, their intent is not to inspire laughter but to invoke the authority of Scripture and suggest biblical parallels to contemporary events. To this extent they might be considered a distant relative of satire, but their polemic is rarely leavened with humor.

Humorous centos were most often parodies, since it was easy to take advantage of the effect of removing passages to an unfamiliar context. One of the few nonparodic examples is the *Ecbasis cuiusdam captivi* (The escape of a certain captive), probably composed in the tenth century. This satiric beast fable of roughly 1,200 lines uses some five hundred borrowings from Classical and Late Latin authors, primarily Horace, Prudentius and Virgil.[19] The antics of the animals appear more ludicrous when described in epic terms, but the *Ecbasis captivi* has such a strong personality of its own that the borrowings never make the narrative itself mere mock epic.

In parodic centos the relation between the original text and the parody is much closer: the effect of the work is a direct result of the contrast between the legitimate context of a passage and its new one. Because the original context of the passages must remain recognizable, the cento depends on an educational system or manuscript culture which can transmit and preserve the text of a work in an unvarying form. In the Middle Ages, of course, the most fixed, canonical, and therefore recognizable text was the Bible. The writing of centos in the Middle Ages, then, was effectively restricted to ecclesiastics, who profited from both a Latin education and a day-to-day familiarity with the Bible.

The nature and concerns of parodic centos reflect this clerical constituency. Most often these centos served as a vehicle for the kinds of satire common to reform-minded cleries, and in particular for satire against papal avarice and ecclesiastical venality. These concerns were voiced in a genus called the Money-Gospel, a short satirical narrative constructed out of passages from the Gospels. The classic example is the *Evangelium secundum marcas argenti*

---

17. On this technique of plainchant composition and the modern controversies surrounding it see Leo Treitler, "'Centonate Chant': *Übles Flickwerk* or *E pluribus unus?*" *Journal of the American Musicological Society* 28 (1975): 1–23.

18. Political *passiones* are discussed in Lehmann 85–92.

19. It is edited in Karl Strecker, *Ecbasis cuiusdam captivi per tropologiam* (1935; reprint, Hanover, 1956).

(The Gospel according to marks of silver), a brief satire which appeared in many guises and rewritings throughout the medieval period. Similar to this was an *evangelium* in which a student seeks to avoid repaying his creditors. A more elaborate money-cento, the *Garcineida,* exploited the works of Ovid, Horace, and Terence as well as the Bible; and a mock letter, the *Epistola notabilis de Pecunia,* propounded generalizations about the venality of the world in the personified voice of money.

The potential for absurdity inherent in the juxtaposition of different passages meant that the cento did not actually need a topic to generate humor. The cento technique was inherently funny, for instance, when applied randomly to the Bible. Thus simple fascination with a text which many knew by heart gave rise to the nonsense-cento, in which biblical quotations are strung together to produce an incoherent but humorous narrative. Unlike the Money-Gospel, the nonsense-cento has few ulterior motives: its appeal lies in the joy of misusing the conventions of biblical prose.

Other centos used biblical phrases and reminiscences to produce comedy of deflation, narrating salacious tales in biblical phrasing or wrongly applying scriptural quotations in unexpected and inappropriate contexts. Apart from the illicit thrill of distorting solemn biblical phrases into insults and racy stories, these centos derived their interest from subjects particularly appealing to clerics: ridicule of monks, nuns, and the entire hierarchy of the Church.

Money Centos

The later Middle Ages saw the love of money as a pervasive sin, one increasingly characteristic of the Church in general and papal administration in particular. Money-centos were only one reflection of medieval alarm about the growing reliance of the papal curia on fund-raising of all sorts. Much of this change in papal finance was the result of a more bureaucratic and centralized Roman administration, and some was actually occasioned by attempts at papal reform, but the dependence of the Church on money for whatever cause was repugnant to many reformers. In part this was a result of the conviction that reliance on money was inimical to Christian values of poverty and unworldliness, and in part a reflection of disquiet about the growing importance of money in the medieval economy generally.[20] In judging the morality of the

---

20. Venality satire and its relation to developments in papal finance are discussed by John A. Yunck in "Economic Conservatism, Papal Finance, and the Medieval Satires on Rome," *Mediaeval Studies* 23 (1961): 334–51, reprinted in *Change in Medieval Society,* ed. S. Thrupp (New York, 1964), 72–85; by Yunck in *Lady Meed;* and by Rodney M. Thomson in "Origins," 73–83.

Church's financial conduct the critic appealed to the ultimate exemplar of morality, the Bible. The money cento is a narrative application of this assessment: it describes the financial dealings of Rome in terms pirated from the Bible. The conclusion implicit in this practice is that modern usage makes a perversion of the biblical original. Thus in overlaying the exemplary sense of the Bible with a modern reading, these satirical squibs did not merely recount the disparity between biblical ideals and the modern world: in a literal sense they exemplified them.

The *Money-Gospel*

The Money-Gospel was the most popular parodic cento in the Middle Ages, and the inclusion of one version in the *Carmina Burana* has guaranteed its familiarity among modern scholars. But the medieval popularity of the work results in a modern editorial conundrum: like many other medieval Latin parodies, the piece exists in a wealth of versions, none of which is appreciably more correct or representative than any other. The edition of the *Lectio ewangelii secundum marcham argenti* printed in appendix 2 subordinates most versions to the reading of a single typical manuscript (V, of the fifteenth century). This is done purely in the interests of expediency: only the publication of all sixteen surviving copies side by side would do full justice to the skill and resourcefulness of medieval redactors. Thus the edition in appendix 2 may give the false impression that a single canonical version of the Money-Gospel exists. I shall attempt to counteract this effect by illustrating my account with passages from individual manuscripts.

In all there exist, then, sixteen copies of the Money-Gospel. The earliest surviving version, from the thirteenth-century *Carmina Burana* manuscript, bears the title *Evangelium secundum marcas argenti;* following Lehmann's taxonomy, this may be considered the "oldest" version.[21] The text was then expanded into a variety of similar versions; these have been edited as a single "intermediate" version, titled *Lectio ewangelii secundum marcham argenti,* in appendix 2.[22] In all, the intermediate version comprises twelve manuscripts, two of which have been lost and are known only from later printed editions; the

---

For an outline of antipapal venality satire in verse see Schüppert, *Kirchenkritik,* 75–90 ("Kurie und Papst"). For the changing role of money in medieval society see Lester K. Little, *Religious Poverty and the Profit Economy in Medieval Europe* (London, 1978).

21. This version is edited in Lehmann 183–84 and in Hilka, Schumann, et al., *Carmina Burana* 1: no. 44, p. 86.

22. Edited as "The Money Gospel: The 'Intermediate' Version" in appendix 2, no. 8. Lehmann's edition of the "intermediate" version is printed in Lehmann 184–85, but his text is incomplete and has no critical apparatus.

earliest manuscripts date from the late thirteenth or early fourteenth century, the latest from the fifteenth. Finally, the intermediate version was elaborated to produce a "youngest" version, surviving in a single manuscript; the text is four times as long as the original as found in the *Carmina Burana*.[23] In addition, two other very brief versions survive embedded in collections of parody Mass material.[24]

Most versions of the story concur in describing the efforts of a poor cleric and a wealthy bishop to gain an audience with the pope. This miniature drama takes place in a world in which money is the chief preoccupation of the pontiff and the papal curia. The pope asserts the primacy of money from the beginning by avowing that he will apply the test of wealth even to Christ himself.

In illo turbine: Dixit papa Romanis: "Cum venerit filius hominis ad sedem maiestatis nostre [Mt 25.31], tunc dicat hostiarius illi: 'Amice, ad quid venisti?' [Mt 26.50] Si autem perseveraverit pulsans [Lc 11.8] nichil dans vobis, proicite eum in tenebras exteriores, ubi erit fletus et stridor dentium" [Mt 8.12]. (*Lectio* MS V)

[In that maelstrom: The pope said to the Romans: "When the Son of man shall come to our seat of majesty, then let the doorkeeper say to him: 'Friend, whereto art thou come?' Yet if he shall continue knocking without giving you anything, cast him out into the exterior darkness, where shall be weeping and gnashing of teeth."]

Having established the principles by which this world operates, the story presents the case of a poor cleric turned away at the door of the curia because of his poverty. The pauper sells his possessions and returns with the pittance he has received for them, but the officials of the curia spurn him with the exclamation, "Et quid hec inter tantos?" [And what are these among so many?] (*Lectio* 17; Jo 6.9). The unsuccessful pauper is followed by a wealthy and simoniacal bishop, "impinguatus, dilatatus, incrassatus" [fat, ample, portly] (version F), who gains immediate entry to the curia, and who expresses his gratitude by distributing presents liberally. At this point in the story the pope is taken ill and is saved from death only by the bishop's application of a salve of gold and

---

23. The classification of the *Evangelium* into three main groups was determined by Lehmann, who prints the text in three editions in Lehmann 183–88.

24. One version is printed in Lehmann 249–50; the other is edited in this chapter.

silver. Inspired by the touch of the divine, the pope recites the money-beatitudes.

> Beati divites, quoniam ipsi saturabuntur. Beati tenentes, quoniam ipsi vacui non erunt. Beati qui esurient et sitiunt pecuniam, quoniam ipsorum est curia Romana. (*Lectio* MS B)

> [Blessed are the rich, for they shall be satisfied. Blessed are they that have, for they shall not be empty-handed. Blessed are they who hunger and thirst after money, for theirs is the curia of Rome.]

He concludes with a call to follow him on the path of extortion: "Exemplum enim dedi vobis, ut quemadmodum ego capio, ita vos capiatis" [For I have given you an example, that as I take, so you should take also] (*Lectio* 38–39; cf. Jo 13.15).

The setting depicted here is an inverted world in which money is the deity and the officials of the Church its most faithful disciples. Gold and silver serve as the evangelists, the earthly evangelists of money. Money has miraculous powers, as its cure of the pope demonstrates, and the possession of it is equated with righteousness: when the simoniacal bishop cures the pope with money, the cardinals exclaim: "Vere, homo iustus est iste" [Indeed, this is a just man] (*Lectio* 27; Lc 23.47). Accordingly, poverty, the converse of greed and wealth, is diabolical: when the lowly cleric seeks entrance despite his penury, the doorkeepers cry, "Vade retro, Sathanas!" [Get thee behind me, Satan!] (*Lectio* 11; Mc 8.33).

The cento form provides an ideal means to depict the inverted world because of its unique ability to highlight the disparity between the original context—the unworldliness exemplified in the Bible—and the new text, which describes contemporary depravity. In setting up a polarity between timelessness and temporality, the ideal world and the corrupt world, the Money-Gospel follows a scriptural model. The Bible uses similar images of polarity and reversal to depict the differences between the earthly and the heavenly kingdoms, declaring that the present world is an inversion of the world to come, when the lowly will be exalted and the proud and avaricious humbled. Jesus expounded this theme in the Gospels: "Sic erunt novissimi primi et primi novissimi" [So shall the last be first and the first last] (Mt 20.16; also Mt 19.30; Mc 10.31; Lc 13.30).

The Money-Gospel points up the hypocrisy of the Church's claims to anticipate this world in which the last shall be first. In the pope's world, claims the

Money Gospel, the first shall be first—an inversion of an inversion. The text merely describes the constellation of wealth and power as they exist in the temporal world, but couching this account in biblical language reveals the extent to which temporal priorities pervert the divine order. In accordance with this, the pope proclaims:

> Et sic salvatus est homo in die illa, unde erunt divites primi et pauperes novissimi. Quia quantum habes, tantum vales. (*Lectio* MSS L and D)

> [And thus the man was saved in that day, in which the rich shall be first and the poor last. For as much as you have, so much shall you prevail.]

> Quia ad habenti, dabitur. Ab eo autem qui non habet, expedit ut quidquid habet aufferatur ab eo. Qui habent, habeant, et qui non habent, ceci fiant. (*Lectio* MS B)

> [For to those who have, it shall be given. And from him who has not, it is fitting that what he has shall be taken from him. They who have, let them have, and they who have not, let them be blind.]

The pope reiterates the disparity between the money world and the Christian world as he applauds the venality of his cardinals: "Non inveni tantam fidem in Israel sicut in vobis" [I have not found so great faith in Israel as in you] (*Lectio* 36; Mt 8.10). His final call for imitation sets him at odds with Christ himself, as he echoes Christ's words: "Hoc habeatis in meam commemoracionem" [Do this for a commemoration of me] (*Lectio* 37–38; Lc 22.19). Clearly the choice is between *imitatio Christi* and *imitatio papae,* between loving God and loving Mammon.

Among medieval Latin parodies, the Money-Gospel is perhaps the best example of the way in which medieval scribes and redactors continually revised and rewrote informal literature. A survey of the representatives of the intermediate Money-Gospel demonstrates the formal and thematic possibilities for alterations to the text. On the simplest level this is just a matter of widespread rephrasing, in which the Money-Gospel forms an interesting counterpoint to the Bible itself: whereas the phrasing of the Bible was felt to be immutable and divinely ordained, this Gospel was the product of man and therefore infinitely changeable. The biblical quotations were subject to some tampering, but of course scribes were obliged to leave them recognizable for fear of effacing the biblical assocations which gave the cento meaning. Scribes exercised their creativity more readily on transitional passages, so that even insignificant phrases—such as *Cardinales dixerunt,* "The cardinals said"—are rarely the same from one manuscript to the next. This tinkering often takes the form of puns: *in illo turbine* (in that maelstrom) for *in illo tempore* (in that time); rather than *cardinales, carpinales* (graspers) or even *carpidanares.* In short, the biblical passages—which redactors must have known from memory—are preserved intact, but connecting passages are almost never transmitted verbatim. This pattern of variation is exactly what one would expect of a text transmitted orally.[25]

Where scribes sought to amplify the text, they did so chiefly by multiplying the number of biblical quotations. Three copies, for example, add a passage from Acts. In its original context the line describes Peter's escape from prison, guided by an angel: "Transeuntes autem primam et secundam custodiam, venerunt ad portam ferream quae ducit ad civitatem, quae ultro aperta est eis" [And passing through the first and the second ward, they came to the iron gate that leadeth to the city, which of itself opened to them] (Act 12.10). Thus the passage recounts Peter's rescue from an enclave of human wickedness; but in the Money-Gospel the bishop, conspicuously lacking in angelic aid, is trying to get *into* the enclave: "Transiens autem primam et secundam custodiam, venit ad portam ferream que non aperta est ei" [And passing through the first and the second ward, he came to the iron gate, which was not opened to him] (*Lectio* MS P, apparatus to line 24; similarly MSS I and F). Where in Peter's case the final liberation is effected by a messenger from God, in this instance only a salve of money applied to the ailing pope enables the bishop to reach his goal. Other manuscripts make other changes: the pope's beatitudes are frequently subject to playful elaboration, with additions such as "Beati divites, quoniam ipsi me videbunt. Beati nobis aliquid portantes, quoniam filii mei vocabuntur" [Blessed are the rich, for they shall see me. Blessed are they who bring me things, for they shall be called my sons] (*Lectio* MS G, apparatus to line 33).

Finally, alternative versions of the story itself also exist, showing that redactors were not hesitant to tamper with the plot when the occasion moved them. The Leipzig manuscript (L, followed by D, a direct copy) omits the pope's illness entirely and reduces the narrative to the contrasting attempts of the poor cleric and the rich bishop to obtain a papal audience. The two anoma-

---

25. Two versions of the Money-Gospel, however, were certainly copied from written texts. Manuscript D is a verbatim copy of L (with the addition of two scribal errors), and the texts also share an attribution to the same scribe or redactor, "Jo. Franck." Manuscript H contains errors which show the scribe was working from a written text; the most prominent of these is "violla" for the original's "mola."

lous manuscripts present even more attenuated versions. The first of these is a
sixteenth-century Munich manuscript containing parts of a parody Mass: a
Pater Noster parody, a single verse of a hymn parody ("Ave, color vini clari"),
and the abbreviated Money-Gospel.[26] A fifteenth-century manuscript from
Venice includes a very similar version of this abbreviated Money-Gospel as
part of a hodgepodge of liturgical parody (the rest unrelated to the materials in
the Munich manuscript). As this Venice Money-Gospel has never been edited,
I print it for ease of comparison.

Galero gratias. Dolus vobiscum. Et cum gemitu tuo. Frequentia studentis
evangelii secundum marcham argenti. Gloria tibi ducato auro.
    In illo turbamine: Dixit papa rapax carpinalibus aliisque rapacibus
suis: "Amen, dico vobis: si venerit ad nos filius hominis nihil habens,
dicite ei: 'Amice, ad quid venisti nihil habens?' At si ille perseveraverit
in pulsatione, proicite eum in tenebras exteriores, ibi erit fletus et stridor
dentium."
    Tunc venit quidam pauper ad eos, nihil habens, et ceperunt omnes una
voce clamare, dicentes: "Tolle, tolle, cruciffige [*sic*], crucifige eum, qui
nihil attulit." Tunc iste pauper ivit retro ostium et flevit amare.
    Tunc domini carpinales iverunt ad dominum papam et dixerunt ei:
"Domine, quid possidemus pecuniam?" Quibus dominus papa dixit:
"Beati possidentes, quoniam ipsi heriditabunt terram. Beati qui esuriunt
et sitiunt pecuniam, quoniam ipsi filii diaboli vocabuntur. Beati eritis
cum salutaverunt vos muneribus et donis amplis homines, et cum dixerunt omnes de vobis propter nomen pecuniarum. Gaudete et exultate in
illa die, quoniam merces et anima vestra sepulta est in thesaurorum
cofinio." (Venice, Biblioteca Nazionale Marciana MS it.IX.66, fols.
121r–120v [*sic*])

[Thanks be to the cap. Deceit be with you. And with thy groaning. The
assembly of the student of the Gospel according to the Mark of silver.
Glory to you, gold ducat.
    In that tumult: The greedy pope said to his graspers and other money-
grubbers: "Amen, I say unto you: if the Son of man comes to us with
nothing, say to him: 'Friend, wherefore art thou come with nothing?'
And if he shall continue knocking, cast him into the exterior darkness,
where shall be weeping and gnashing of teeth."

---

26. These are printed in Lehmann 249–50.

Then a pauper came to them with nothing, and all began to cry with
one voice, saying: "Raise him up, raise him up, crucify, crucify him, who
has brought nothing." Then the pauper went behind the door and wept
bitterly.

Then the lord graspers went to the lord pope and said unto him: "Lord,
what must we do to possess money?" To whom the lord pope said:
"Blessed are they who have, for they shall inherit the earth. Blessed are
they who hunger and thirst after money, for they shall be called the sons
of the Devil. You shall be blessed when men greet you with gifts and with
generous offerings, and when all speak of you after the name of money.
Rejoice and glory in that day, for reward and your soul are buried in the
casket of treasures."]

In this instance the narrative has been abbreviated to form part of a longer
sequence of texts. Conversely, the "youngest" version was expanded to nearly
three times the length of the intermediate version, forming the *Passio domini
nostri pape Romanorum secundum marcam argenti et auri* (The Passion of our
lord the pope of the Romans according to the mark of silver and gold).[27] The
plot and theme are essentially unchanged, except that the length of the piece
allows a greater antipapal bias. One of the noteworthy features of the text is its
further reversal of biblical inversion.

Dixit eis iterum sermonum hunc: "Donantibus quorum remiseritis peccata remittuntur et quorum retinueritis retenta sunt" [Jo 20.23]. Hoc dicto
dixerunt ad eum: "Quam bene dixit et fecit. Satishabentes implevit bonis
et esurientes dimisit inanes" [Lc 1.53]. (Lehmann 186)

[He told them this also: "The givers whose sins you shall forgive, they
are forgiven, and whose sins you shall retain, they are retained." This
spoken, he said unto him: "How well he spoke and acted! He hath filled
the rich with good things, and the hungry he hath sent away."]

The Students' Money-Gospel

The Money-Gospel had one derivative, a students' Money-Gospel, entitled the
Sanctum evangelium secundum marcam auri et argenti.[28] Two manuscripts of
this survive, both of the fifteenth century: one sets the story in Paris, the other
in Leipzig. The text is almost certainly the work of students themselves, and we

---

27. Printed in Lehmann 186–88.
28. The Students' Money-Gospel is edited in appendix 2, no. 9 below.

can even discern their names: the Paris version calls the students John and Philip, while the Leipzig version has replaced Philip with Peter. The original author clearly modeled his parody on the standard Money-Gospel: though the plot is different, the title is nearly identical and a number of quotations are used in unmistakably similar ways.

Students rather than professional churchmen are the protagonists of the work, but the setting of the piece remains the money-world: the object of veneration is not God but Mammon. The theme is dramatized through the afflictions of John, a student, who has borrowed money from two compatriots; the narrative concerns John's desolation before the impending time of restitution. The repayment of the debt is presented in terms of the Passion; the contents of John's purse must be sacrificed to pay for his sins. The author identifies John's anguish over the loss of his money with Jesus' ordeal in the garden of Gethsemane. This section has been taken almost verbatim from the Gospels, as the following comparison shows. The passage in its original context reads:

. . . et dixit discipulis suis: "Sedete hic donec vadam illuc et orem." . . . Tunc ait illis: "Tristis est anima mea usque ad mortem." . . . Et progressus pusillum, procidit in faciam suam orans et dicens: "Mi Pater, si possibile est, transeat a me calix iste. Verumtamen non sicut ego volo, sed sicut tu." Et reversus denuo invenit eos dormientes: erant enim oculi illorum ingravati. Et dicit Petro: "Sic non potuistis una hora vigilare mecum? Vigilate et orate ut non intretis in temptationem. Spiritus quidem promptus est, caro autem infirma." Iterum secundo abiit et oravit, dicens: "Pater mi, si non potest hic calix transire . . . fiat voluntas tua." . . . Tunc venit ad discipulos suos et dicit illis: "Dormite iam et requiescite. Ecce adpropinquavit hora et Filius hominis traditur in manus peccatorum." (Mt 26.36–45 conflated with Mc 14.40)

[. . . and then he said to his disciples: "Sit you here, till I go yonder and pray." . . . Then he saith to them: "My soul is sorrowful even unto death." . . . And going a little further he fell upon his face, praying and saying: "My father, if it be possible, let this cup pass from me. Nevertheless, not as I will but as thou wilt." And when he returned he found them again asleep, for their eyes were very heavy. And he saith to Peter: "What? Could you not wait one hour with me? Watch ye and pray that ye enter not into temptation. The spirit indeed is willing, but the flesh weak." Again the second time, he went and prayed, saying: "My father, if this cup may not pass away . . . thy will be done." . . . Then he cometh to his disciples and said to them: "Sleep now and take your rest. Behold the hour is at hand, and the Son of man shall be given into the hands of sinners."]

The Students' Money-Gospel parodies this passage as follows:

Iohannes autem ait illis: "Sedete hic donec vadam illuc et orem." Et acceptis tribus de sociis suis secreto ait illis: "Tristis est anima mea usque ad evacuacionem burse." Et flexis genibus oravit, dicens: "Pater, si fieri potest, transeant a me creditores isti." Et reversus ad cameram suam iterum invenit super debitis suis litigantes: erant enim pre inopia gravati. Et iterum abiit et oravit eundem sermonem dicens: "Pater, si fieri potest, transeant a me creditores isti. Digitus quidem ad computandum promptus est, bursa autem infirma." Deinde dixit denariis suis: "Non potestis una hora mecum manere? Exite iam ab archa mea et recedite. Venit enim hora in qua vos trademus in manibus creditorum meorum." (Students' Money-Gospel 48–57)

[John said to them: "Sit you here, till I go yonder and pray." And taking three of his friends aside he said in secret: "My soul is sorrowful unto the emptying of my purse." And, bending his knees, he prayed, saying: "My father, if it be possible, let these creditors pass from me." And returning to his room again he found men contending over his debts, for the weight of their poverty was very heavy. And again he went and prayed, saying: "My Father, if it be possible, let these creditors pass from me. The hands are quick to reckon, but the purse is weak." Then he said to his coins: "Could you not wait one hour with me? Go forth from my chest and depart. Behold the hour is at hand in which you shall be given into the hands of my creditors."]

The text puns on the spiritual debt of sin owed to God and the financial debt born of sin—of avarice—owed to man. The debt repaid by Christ for man need never be paid again, but mankind's debts are infinite, and his purse is never full. In contrast to Christ's sacrifice, the story of the students' Money-Gospel ends with the debt still outstanding: as the poverty-stricken student says, "Multi vero denarii sunt mandati, pauci vero transmissi," [For many coins are called, but few are given over] (64–65). Christ commanded his followers to render due payment to both God and earthly authority; the poor student has gone astray because he has confounded his spiritual debt with his material one.

The *Garcineida*

These money-satires are not altogether unsophisticated, but they are eclipsed in ingenuity, not to say in literary merit, by a longer money-cento, the *Tractatus Garsiae* (Little tract of Garcia), or *Garcineida*.[29] This five-part work, largely constructed from biblical, Classical, and liturgical quotations, describes a journey to Rome undertaken by two ecclesiastics, in which they give the relics of the pseudosaints Albinus ("White," therefore Silver) and Rufinus ("Red," therefore Gold) into the care of the pope. Like the Money-Gospels, the *Garcineida* ridicules papal and ecclesiastical cupidity; in addition rich imagery of greed enlivens the narrative, and the mock sermons parody the bombastic rhetoric of veneration.

The *Garcineida* is unusual in that we know something about its author and the circumstances of its composition.[30] The text is attributed in two manuscripts to one Garcia, though this name may merely be an extrapolation from the character Garcia in the text, a cynical observer of ecclesiastical hypocrisy and avarice. In one manuscript the author is described as a canon of Toledo, and the fact that the text originated in Toledo can be confirmed from other evidence. The story concerns the journey of the archbishop of Toledo, Grimoard (clearly a pseudonym for Bernard, a historical archbishop of Toledo) to Rome in the pontificate of Urban II (1088–99), to obtain the legateship of Aquitaine. The narrative is in fact a thinly disguised roman à clef, as the genuine Archbishop Bernard did make such a journey in 1099, obtaining the legateship of Aquitaine, as he does in the satire, as a result. This topicality dates the *Garcineida* to 1099 or shortly thereafter. Even if the name Garcia is not mistakenly borrowed from the story, it is very likely a pseudonym for the author, who most likely would not have wished to retail such easily recognizable caricatures under his own name. Attempts to ascertain the true identity of the satirist have been unconvincing.[31] The most recent editor of the text, Rodney M. Thomson, refers to the piece as *Tractatus Garsiae,* as recorded in the rubric of one manuscript, but María Rosa Lida de Malkiel adduces convinc-

---

29. It is edited in Rodney M. Thomson, *Tractatus Garsiae,* Textus Minores 46 (Leiden, 1973).

30. On these questions see Thomson, *Tractatus Garsiae,* 5–6; E. Sackur in *MGH, Scriptores Libelli de lite imperatorum et pontificum* (Hannover, 1946), 2:424; and María Rosa Lida de Malkiel, "La *Garcineida* de García Toledo," *Nueva revista de filología hispánica* 7 (1953): 246–58 (at 247–51).

31. For a survey of these attempts and of critical literature on the text see Lida de Malkiel, *Garcineida,* 248 n. 2. Thomson's text and apparatus cite a number of the borrowings used in the story, but these references must be supplemented by the exhaustive catalog of borrowings from the Bible, the liturgy, Caesar, Juvenal, Horace, Terence, Pliny, and others, supplied by Lida de Malkiel in *Garcineida,* 252–55 n. 6–8.

ing evidence that the satire was conceived as a miniature epic on the order of the *Aeneid* and is more properly referred to as the *Garcineida*.[32]

The *Garcineida* and the Money-Gospels depict the same world, an anti-universe in which Mammon has usurped the place of God. As a result of this displacement, ecclesiastical advancement is contingent on avarice; Rome is the center of this religion because greed there is greatest, and the pope is at the summit of the Church hierarchy because he is venality's most fervent disciple. Archbishop Grimoard's quest for the legateship is in fact a trial of his ability to conform to the values of this world. In accordance with these themes, laudatory encomiums to greed and money alternate with drinking bouts in which the archbishop's immoral fiber is put to the test.

The quest of the archbishop and his display of prowess are narrated in five parts. The first introduces Grimoard, his servant Garcia, the pope and the curia, and the circumstances of the archbishop's visit bearing the holy relics. The relics thus introduced, the second part consists of the lection for the translation of relics to papal care, a mock homily on Gold and Silver read by one of the cardinals. The third section resumes the narrative, briefly describing the translation of the relics by the pope's own hands to the shrine of St. Cupiditas. Then follows a sermon by the pope himself, uttered as he installs the remains of the martyrs in their new reliquaries—gold-embroidered purses—in which he exalts the powers and inspiration of the saints and calls for increased fervor in their veneration. The final section is composed entirely of dialogue, adapted from Terence, in which the participants spur each other on to greater heights of greed, accompanied by cynical asides from Garcia; and in which the archbishop, having proven himself a fervent disciple of avarice, gains his legateship.

The success of the text springs from its visualization of the details of the inverted money-world. In the Christian universe, religious dedication is expressed by self-denial coupled with the love of God. In the antiworld these values are transposed: self-denial is replaced by selfishness, which goes hand-in-hand with the love of money. In both worlds, relics—whether coins or the bones of saints—are the tangible signs of abstract virtues, the embodiment of value in the economy of holiness. They are easily portable, confer power on their possessor, and inspire veneration among worshipers. Most important, in the money-world the possession of the relics of Gold and Silver grants entrance to the inner sanctum of money-worship and the joys of perpetual consumption.

---

32. Lida de Malkiel, *Garcineida*.

One of the cardinals enumerates the power of the relics to cleanse their possessors of sin and transport them to the highest spheres of the Roman Church.

O quam preciosi martires Albinus atque Rufinus, O quam praedicandi, O quam laudabiles, quorum qui habent reliquias, continuo ex peccatoribus iustificantur, ex terrenis coelestes fiunt, ex impiis uertuntur in innocentes. Vidimus, uidimus simoniales, sacrilegos et suarum dissipatores ecclesiarum ad papam uenire pontifices, qui ob praedictorum reliquias martirum apostolica purgati benedictione, nullo irretiti crimine, nihil uetustatis habentes, noui et tamquam renati ad propria rediere. . . . Venite, uenite, simoniales archiepiscopi, episcopi, archidiaconi, abbates, decani, sed et priores, offerte Romano pontifici martires duos, per quos introitus patet in Romanam Ecclesiam. . . . Petite ergo per Albinum et accipietis, quaerite per Rufinum et inuenietis, pulsate per utrumque martirum et aperietur uobis. Omnis enim qui petit per Albinum accipit, qui quaerit per Rufinum, inuenit, et pulsanti per utrumque martirem aperietur. (*Garcineida* 79–87, 98–101, 103–7)[33]

[O how precious are the martyrs Gold and Silver! How much to be proclaimed! How greatly to be praised! Sinners who possess their relics are perpetually justified, made fit for heaven from being earthly, turned from impiety to innocence. We have seen, we have seen simoniac bishops, sacreligious, and dissipators of their churches, come to the pope, cleansed with the apostolic blessing on account of these martyrs' relics, no longer enmeshed in crime, not retaining any of their old blame, return home new and as if reborn. . . . Come, come, simoniac archbishops, bishops, archdeacons, abbots, deacons and priors, offer the Roman pontiff the two martyrs through whom is granted entry into the Roman Church. . . . Ask therefore through Silver, and you shall receive, seek through Gold and you shall find, knock through either martyr and it shall be opened unto you. For everyone that asketh through Silver receiveth, and he that seeketh through Gold findeth, and to him that knocketh through either martyr, it shall be opened.]

---

33. Line numbers of passages quoted refer to Thomson's edition, although Thomson calls the text the *Tractatus Garsiae* rather than the *Garcineida*. English translations are taken from Thomson's edition except where noted.

With the formula *Vidimus, uidimus,* "we have seen, we have seen," the speaker attempts to convey the immediacy of the saints' power, but in reality his assurances serve merely as firsthand testimony to ecclesiastical corruption.

As in the ideal Christian world, in the money-world inward virtue is manifest through outward signs. In the Christian universe the abjuration of worldliness takes the form of physical self-denial and the mortification of the flesh, practices that leave visible evidence on the individual. In the inverted world, the practice of religion takes the form of consumption; obesity and drunkenness are the outward signs of inward consumption. The spiritual negation of self is translated into the physical enlargement of self. Whereas the typical hagiography offers the reader a catalog of the saint's moral virtues but regards the saint's physical characteristics as irrelevant, the story of Grimoard emphasizes the physical aspect of its subject. Grimoard's spiritual qualities are never described, but his appearance marks him out as a man familiar with temptation. His most conspicuous quality is *gravitas,* a description at first deceptively spiritual; but in fact Grimoard's *gravitas* is entirely corporeal, being associated with *pinguitudo* and *rotunditas,* and the catalog of his merits begins with his ability to emulate the physical characteristics and habits of his superiors.

Vnde ignauiae, immo pudoris esse uidebatur, si tantae grauitatis persona, tam pinguis, tam rotunda, tam delectabilis suorum priuaretur dignitate praedecessorum. Ceterum licet plenis arrideret calicibus (erat enim fortis ad bibendum uinum), licet dies noctesque sterteret (uigilare enim non poterat), licet uentrem haberet pontificis (turgebat enim uenter extentus non modicum, utpote ubi salmo totus uno prandi, sepeliri consueuerat), . . . minime tamen Romanae Ecclesiae legatus haberetur, nisi preciosas supradictorum reliquias martirum Romano praesentaret pontifici. (*Garcineida* 15–23, 29–32)

[It seemed, on this account, a shame, a crime, that a person of such weight, so plump, so rotund, so delicate, should be denied the dignity held by his predecessors. But, for the rest, although he could drain a full bowl (for he was a brave wine-drinker), although he snored day and night (for he could not keep himself awake), although he had a true bishop's belly (his distended stomach protruded not a little, since he usually put away a whole salmon at a sitting), . . . yet he had no chance of becoming a legate of the Roman Church, unless he presented the Roman pontiff with the precious relics of these martyrs.]

The rites of money-worship consist of the celebration of avarice in its most physical manifestation, gluttony. The moral qualities of the members of the curia are discernible from their bulk. Garcia presents a telling view of the papal court, arrayed like an image of heaven in which God is surrounded by the four evangelists, but here the wine-bibbing pope is surrounded by four corpulent cardinals holding aloft a goblet (*Garcineida* 44–49). The rite of prayer is transposed into a drinking ceremony, each appeal for intercession becoming a toast.

Hortabantur eum cardinales, ut fortiter biberet, cumque sextarium totum pro salute mundi, pro redemptione animarum, pro infirmis et captiuis, pro fructibus terrae, pro pace, pro iter agentibus, pro nauigantibus, pro statu Romanae Ecclesiae omnino deuorasset, iamque turgente stomacho minus haurire potuisset, hortabantur item eum cardinales, ut temptaret saltem, et se post eum temptaturos promittebant, et, ne falsitatis arguerentur, temptabant. Verba enim sacerdotis aut uera aut sacrilega. (*Garcineida* 53–61)

[The cardinals urged him to drink up like a man; and when he had downed a full gallon for the salvation of the world, for the redemption of souls, for the infirm and captive, for the fruits of the earth, for peace, for travellers, for seafarers, and for the state of the Roman Church, until his swelling belly could take no more, they encouraged him to try a little more, promising to drink along with him; and, lest they be accused of falsehood, so they did. For a priest's words are either truth or sacrilege.]

Like cardinals in the Christian world, these cardinals prize the fulfillment of vows, but in this case their dedication to ideals means that they cannot refuse a drink. In the money-world, sobriety is sacrilege. The author is unstinting in his description of the trials the "pinguissimus papa" has undergone in the pursuit of gluttony.

. . . hiis occisionibus interemptus est, periculis lampredarum, periculis salmonum, periculis barrorum, periculis ex saturitate, periculis ex ebrietatibus, praeter illa, quae intrinsecus sunt instantia, Romani pontificis cotidiana sollicitudo omnium cupiditatum. (*Garcineida* 164–68)

[. . . with such wounds was he slain; he was faced with perils of lampreys, perils of salmon, perils of carp, perils from over-feeding, perils from over-drinking, not to mention those other things which threaten the inner man, the Roman pontiff's daily anxiety for all possible lusts.]

When the pope takes the money-relics in his own hands, physical contact with the embodiments of greed inspires him to dream of spreading the love of cupidity throughout the world. If the kingdom of heaven is nigh when the message of the Gospels has been spread to the entire earth, the kingdom of worldly satisfaction will be achieved when the entire earth is consumed.

Quid ergo? Indulgeamus uentri, satisfaciamus gulae! Scriptum est enim: "Si uolueritis et audieritis Vrbanum, bona terrae comeditis." Igitur, cardinales mei, deuorate salmones, comedite barros, absorbete percase, traicite delphines, haurite rumbos, frangite mugiles, exossate congros, incorporate uobis lampredas. Quid plura? Aera, mare, terram, flumina, fontes, stagna, lacus, riuos, omnia traicite, consumite, perfundite, deuorate, bibite, bibite, beati cardinales mei, uere beati, intelligitis enim super Albinum et Rufinum. Bibite, inquam, uinum aromatum, Massicum, Falernum, pigmentum, meracum, hyssopum, Aluntinum. Quid plura? Incorporate uobis omnes mellitas potationes. (*Garcineida* 319–32)

[What about it, then? Let us satisfy our stomachs, let us indulge our appetites! For it is written: "If ye be willing and obedient to Urban, ye shall eat the good of the land." Therefore, my cardinals, devour salmon, eat carp, fill yourselves on perch, gorge on dolphin, swallow down sturgeon, break open mussels, fillet congers, wrap yourselves around the lampreys. What more can I say? Bring everything that inhabits air, sea, land, rivers, springs, swamps, lakes, streams; consume them, swallow them down, devour them; drink, drink, my blessed cardinals, truly blessed, for you understand the use of Silver and Gold. Drink, I say, perfumed wine, Massican, Falernian, flavoured, unmixed, hysop, Aluntine. What more? Fill yourselves with every honeyed drink and nectarean liquor.]

Even the conventional prompts for the continuation of the sermon ("Quid plura?") become a call for more food, and creation is reduced to a series of items on a menu. In this imaginary apocalypse the world is consumed not by fire but, literally, by the gluttony of the pope's henchmen. The greedy mouths of the curia resemble the conventional medieval depiction of hell, in which the Devil's mouth gapes to engulf the sinners of the world. Here the sinners themselves open their mouths to swallow the world: in their cosmic consumption the curia have usurped the role of the Devil. Greedily anticipating the coming apocalypse, the pope calls for the future to be realized then and there.

Opulentia sit ubique, diabolus sit pauper, appareat qui uir si[e]t Vrbanus.
Videatur si ceruices habet Romanus pontifex, si habet foenum in cornu.
(*Garcineida* 333–36)

[Let opulence be everywhere, let the Devil be poor, and let Urban be seen as the man he is! Let us see if the Roman pontiff has a throat, if he has hay on his horns!][34]

Clearly the pope's *virtus* is dependent on his ability to starve the Devil into submission, an act which he hopes to accomplish by consuming the Devil's fodder himself. Urban's declamation takes the form of the hero's boast before battle, but even as he proclaims his prowess he reveals his true nature, likening himself to a bull without straw on his horns (in other words, with full use of his weapons). The head of the universal Church shows himself to be stupidly unaware that the possession of horns is a characteristic far more appropriate to the Devil than to the Roman pontiff.

The true nature of the ecclesiastical hierarchy is now apparent, and this information invites a new assessment of Grimoard's suitability to aspire to the status of his superiors. Grimoard's candidacy is promising, for his merits are visible: both his reputation and his stomach precede him. As in epic, we size up the hero through the eyes of an impartial observer.

Interea Iohannes Gaditanus Toletanum intuens, uidit eum pinguem, nitidum, lautum, rotundum, molarem, ponderosum, grauem, rigidum, cyclopem, corpore giganteo, pectore extento, uentre profundo, amplis renibus, largo interoculari, fronte obducta, uultu terribili, graui respectu, hirta cesarie, ceruicali pinguissimo. Itaque coram papa et cardinalibus assurgens exclamauit: "Dignus est tribus calicibus Toletanus iste." (*Garcineida* 385–92)

[Meanwhile John of Gaeta had been sizing up the archbishop of Toledo, noting that he was fat, oily, refined, rotund, heavy, ponderous, weighty, massive, cyclopean, a giant in body, broad-chested, deep-bellied, fat-

---

34. The latter part of this is my own translation, as Thomson's obscures the metaphor of the horns.

buttocked, his eyes set wide apart, with a jutting forehead, a ferocious countenance, commanding of respect, with a good shock of hair and a bull-neck. Rising to his feet, therefore, before the pope and cardinals, he exclaimed: "This Toledan deserves three bowls."]

That the final test and culmination of his career should be the proffering of a cup recalls Christ's ordeal in the Garden of Gethsemane, but here no hesitation is necessary: the cup is not one of sacrifice but of inebriation and worldly gain. The insatiable desire to nurture the flesh is even emphasized by the author's choice of vocabulary: he writes, "tres calices *incorporauit*" (*Garcineida* 422; also 325, 331). Like that of Christ, the archbishop's corporeality is essential to the story, but whereas Christ assumes his to atone for the weakness of others— for original sin brought about by an act of gluttony—Grimoard's sole aim is to increase his fleshiness.

The testing of Grimoard's ability to emulate the higher orders of the church is played out against the backdrop of Gospel metaphors of eating and drinking. The cardinal's words "Beati qui bene potant, qui bene sapiunt uina" [Blessed are they who drink well, who savour wine well] (*Garcineida* 409–10) recall both the beatitude of righteousness, "Beati qui esuriunt et sitiunt iustitiam, quoniam ipsi saturabuntur" [Blessed are they who hunger and thirst after justice, for they shall be satisfied] (Mt 5.6), and Mark 8.33: "Vade retro, Sathana, quoniam non sapis ea quae Dei sunt, sed quae sunt hominum" [Get thee behind me, Satan, because thou savourest not the things which are of God, but that are of men]. These self-satisfied clergymen have exchanged heaven for earth, having claimed satisfaction before they have achieved righteousness. Since their hunger and thirst are literal rather than spiritual, they are clearly unable to savor those things which belong to God; instead their appetite for earthly provender transforms them into figures of Satan.

The final conversation comes to a halt with a remark that sums up the extent to which self-denial and *imitatio Christi* are alien to the consumers: "*Iohannes:* 'Humanum est potare.' *Teucer:* 'Homines sumus'" [*John:* "To drink is human." *Teuzo:* "We are but men."] (479–80). Like the Money-Gospels, the *Garcineida* portrays earthly existence, represented by images of gross corporeality, as an inversion and degradation of the world of God. But although this earthly existence may seem more real and sensible than the intangible world of God, it is actually the present world which is an imperfect shadow and parody of the perfect world. The achievement of the *Garcineida*'s Urban, and of all who proselytize his understanding of the world, is to invert values to such an extent that this false world seems truer than the Christian order.

Ecce Vrbanus ponit lucem tenebras, ecce bonum in malum transfigurat;
ecce coruos in candorem uertit, ecce cignos in Ethiopas mutat, ecce
mortem uitae ascribit, ecce absinthium in mel transformat. (*Garcineida*
296–300)

[Behold, Urban calls darkness light; behold, he turns good into evil;
behold, he turns crows white; behold, he makes swans as Negroes;
behold, he proclaims death life; behold, he transforms wormwood into
honey.]

What is actually perishable and insubstantial—food, drink, and the body—he
exalts above the intangible but actually more real substance of religion: again,
in Urban's world, the first shall be first. This equation not only brings into focus
the differences between divine order and ecclesiastical order but also emphasizes the similarity between ecclesiastical order and diabolical order. Teucer's
final comment, "Homines sumus" [We are but men] acknowledges the tension
between different perspectives on human nature: on the one hand, it is quasi-
diabolical, because man, like the Devil, is a fallen and sinful part of God's
creation; on the other hand, by his very nature man cannot expect to emulate
the innocence of the angels. In feeding the flesh man is participating in the
corruptible nature of the transient world, but, after all, he must eat to sustain
itself. There is a thin line, in other words, between acknowledging the needs of
mortality and abusing them: we must deplore the abuse while acknowledging
the impulse as intrinsic to human nature.

Thus in the end the author is deliberately ambivalent about the gravity of
ecclesiastical avarice and gluttony. He depicts the highest ranks of the Church
as deplorably corrupt, but he chooses to expose them not in a vicious treatise
but with a humorous narrative. The pope and curia use all their human powers
to grasp, consume and corrupt; but in the end their powers are indeed only
human, and from the perspective of the true kingdom their behavior is merely a
joke.

Other Money-Centos

The personification of abstract concepts was one of the most common literary
practices of the medieval period, and personification allegory was a popular
means of conveying moral truth through fiction. In the most common variety,
personified virtues and vices exemplified the roles these qualities played in the
human world: most of the important allegories of the Middle Ages were of this
type, including Alan of Lille's *De planctu naturae,* Guillaume de Lorris's and

Jeun de Meun's *Roman de la Rose,* and William Langland's *Piers Plowman.* A less elaborate mode of personification merely credited impersonal forces with agency, independent of an allegorical framework: this is the conceit, for example, behind the abundant "Nummus" satire that occurs from the twelfth century onward. This personification is implicit in the Money-Gospels and the *Garcineida,* in which money appears as a deity. It was more explicit in other kinds of satire, which decried the power of such tyrants as Nummus ("Coin"), Munera ("Gifts"), Regina Pecunia ("Queen Money"), Aurum ("Gold"), Denarii ("Coins"), or Bursa ("Purse"). The poet Horace himself had spoken of Regina Pecunia, and the theme became so common, especially among mediocre poets, that modern scholars have suggested that "Nummus" satires may have been a set assignment for medieval schoolboys.[35]

Medieval money-personification is most commonly expressed in verse, but a single example does appear in the form of a parodic biblical cento. The parody masquerades as an imperial letter from the Empress Pecunia; because it echoes biblical quotations in which the Lord asserts his primacy, it again implies that in earthly eyes money has usurped the place of God. The text, entitled the *Epistola notabilis de Pecunia* (Notable letter from Money), is found in a single manuscript of the fourteenth century.[36] Its parody of the form of imperial letters contributes to its depiction of money as an important political force. The epistle form also recalls both the New Testament Epistles and the apocryphal letters on religion which circulated throughout the Middle Ages. One of the most popular of these was the Sunday Letter, a missive from Christ which had purportedly fallen from heaven in response to mankind's failure to keep the Sabbath holy.[37] Similar to this was the Charter of Christ, dedicated to mankind, which had supposedly been written by Christ on the cross in his own blood.[38] Both represented exhortation to moral behavior given greater force by attribution to a transcendent authority. The *Epistola notabilis de Pecunia* im-

---

35. The passage from Horace is found at *Epodes* 1.6.37. On "Nummus" texts as school assignments, see Yunck, *Lady Meed,* 183–84.

36. It is edited in Charles Homer Haskins, "Latin Literature under Frederick II," in *Studies in Medieval Culture* (Oxford, 1929), 124–47 (at 138–39).

37. The most comprehensive account of the Sunday Letter is that of Robert Priebsch, *Letter from Heaven on the Observance of the Lord's Day,* ed. W. E. Collinson and Arthur Closs (Oxford, 1936). For a more up-to-date account of one version of the Sunday Letter see Dorothy Whitelock, "Bishop Ecgred, Pehtred, and Niall," in *Ireland in Early Medieval Europe: Studies in Memory of Kathleen Hughes,* ed. Dorothy Whitelock, Rosamond McKitterick, and David Dumville (Cambridge, 1982), 47–68.

38. A Latin version is edited in Marvin L. Colker, "Anecdota Dublinensia," *Medievalia et Humanistica,* old series, 16 (1964): 39–55 (at 55); see also M. C. Spalding, *The Middle English Charters of Christ* (Bryn Mawr, 1914).

plies that avarice, too, is a transcendent force, a claim underlined by the fact
that Pecunia is speaking in the words of God. Like the Money-Gospels, the
Epistola declares that money's most fervent disciples are to be found in the
higher ranks of the church.

> Que maior leticia michi posset accidere quam ut cardinales michi colla
> subiciant et currant in odorem unguentorum meorum [Ct 4.10]? Levate
> in circuitu oculos vestros et videte [Is 60.4] quia . . . per me concutitur
> orbis terrarum et universi qui habitant in eo [Ps 23.1]. Et quis enarrabit
> potencias meas [Jb 38.37; Ps 105.2]? Michi gremium suum non claudit
> ecclesia, michi summus pontifex aperit sinus suos et quotiens ad eum
> accedere voluero totiens in sinu suo colliget et dextera illius amplex-
> abitur me [Ct 2.6, 8.3]. (Haskins, "Latin Literature," 138–39)

> [What greater happiness could come to me than cardinals submitting to
> me and going in the sweet smell of my ointments? Lift up your eyes
> about and see, for . . . through me the orb of the world is shaken, and all
> they that dwell therein. And who can declare my powers? The Church
> does not bar me from its lap; to me the highest pontiff opens his lap, and
> as much as I roll money to him, so much does he collect in his lap, and his
> right hand shall embrace me.]

The obeisance paid to the empress by the pope is particularly ironic in view of
the protracted medieval struggle for supremacy between the papacy and secular rulers. Despite his struggle for jurisdiction over temporal powers, implies
the text, the pope has lost his autonomy to the earthly tyrant he should be most
careful to defy.

The *Epistola notabilis de Pecunia* is the earliest, and perhaps the only,
extant medieval personification satire in letter form. A number of comparable
satires used related techniques less successfully. Despite its witty title, the
Neglectio epistolae beati Paulisper (Neglect of the letter of the blessed Little-
While)—with puns on *neglectio* (neglect), *lectio* (reading), *paulisper* (a little
while), and St. Paul—is a flat-footed mock sermon rebuking the Franciscans in
phrases gleaned from the Bible.[39] The work survives in a single copy, from the
fifteenth-century Venice manuscript which also contains the abbreviated
Money-Gospel (printed in full earlier in this chapter) and a nonsense-cento, the
Sermo sententiosissimus, discussed later in this chapter. The subtitle of the
Neglectio addresses the piece to Franciscans, but this connection is only nomi-

---

39. It is edited in Novati, "La parodia," 308–10.

nal; the vituperation in the text itself could apply equally to any religious group.

Although it uses the cento technique, the *Neglectio* is only marginally a parody, being more abusive than humorous. The beginning is typical of the whole.

> Fratres, gaudete in domino semper: iterum dico, gaudete [Phil 4.4], quia in stadio currentes bravium accepistis [1 Cor 9.24] et quod erat alienum pecuniae largitione arripuistis, propter quod immodestia vestra nota est omnibus hominibus [Phil 4.5]; quia non estis sub lege, sed spiritu ambitionis ducimini, dignitatem inhiantes, paupertatem, humilitatem, castitatem negligentes [Gal 5.18–19] . . . (Novati, "La parodia," 308)

> [Brothers, rejoice in the Lord always: again, I say, rejoice, for you who run in the race receive the prize, and you seize what belongs to another by lavishing money, for your conceit is known to all men; for you are not under the law, but are led by the spirit of ambition, eager for dignity, disregardful of poverty, humility, and modesty . . .]

As in parodic centos, biblical quotations appear out of context to give the piece greater force; but here the contrast between the original and the satirical context produces sarcasm rather than the more complicated form of parody.

The "Devil's Letter" resembled the *Epistola notabilis de Pecunia* in purporting to be a letter from a malign force; the genre is in effect an inversion of the Sunday Letter. Instead of condemning Christians for immorality, the Devil commends them for immorality.[40] Although the form is nominally that of an imperial letter, Devil's Letters were not primarily an imitative form, and like the *Neglectio* they were more vituperative, and in fact sarcastic, than humorous. Unlike the *Epistola* and the *Neglectio,* the greater part of a Devil's Letter is original prose, and the genre does qualify as part of the history of centos. Though Devil's Letters may have come into existence as early as the eleventh century, the most widely circulating version was composed in 1351, and the form enjoyed considerable popularity through the Renaissance.

---

40. The evolution and character of the genre is discussed in Helen C. Feng, "Devil's Letters: Their History and Significance in Church and Society, 1100–1500" (Ph.D. diss., Northwestern University, 1982). A more accessible guide to the form, citing Latin and Middle English examples, is Robert R. Raymo, "A Middle English Version of the *Epistola Luciferi ad Cleros,*" in *Medieval Literature and Civilization: Studies in Memory of G. N. Garmonsway,* ed. D. A. Pearsall and R. A. Waldron (London, 1969), 233–48. Devil's Letters are also discussed in Lehmann 58–70.

Nonsense-Centos

The nonsense-cento, like the Money-Gospel, recombines phrases and sentences from the Bible; but, unlike the Money-Gospel, the nonsense-cento does not actually tell any story but forms a continually interrupted and incoherent narrative. It is perhaps simplest to illustrate this method with an example:

Unde Rabanus in Actibus Apostolorum concedens ait: "Si esurierit inimicus tuus, appone ei lignum et lapidem. Si sitit, appones ei cinerem et sal [Rm 12.20; Prv 25.21]. In his duobus mandatis tota lex pendet et prophete [Mt 22.40]. Sed quid multitudine maius? Si pes tuus scandalizat te, abscinde eum et proiice abs te" [Mt 5.29 etc.]. At ille dixit: "Domine, non tantum pedes meos, sed et manus et caput" [Jo 13.9]. Et ecce Judas Machabeus [2 Mcc 5.27], qui cognominabatur Cayphas [Mt 26.3], ait ad servum suum: "Habetis aliquid quod manducetur?" [Lc 24.41]. At illi obtulerunt ei paraliticum iacentem in lecto [Mt 9.2], dicentes: "Ecce duo gladii hic" [Lc 22.38]. (*Sermo sententiossimus* [see app. 2])

[Whence Hrabanus in the Acts of the Apostles, agreeing, said: "If thy enemy be hungry, give him wood and a stone. If he thirst, thou givest him ashes and salt. On these two commandments dependeth the whole law and the prophets. But what is greater than a multitude? If thy foot scandalize thee, cut it off and cast it from thee." And he said: "Lord, not only my feet, but also my hands and head." And behold Judas Machabeus, who was called Caiphas, said to his servant: "Have you anything to eat?" And they brought to him one sick of the palsy lying in a bed, saying: "Behold, here are two swords."]

Seven biblical nonsense-narratives are extant, though the relationships between them suggest that many more were in circulation. The earliest surviving example dates from the eleventh century. This cento, *Eusebius dixit* (Eusebius said), displays all the traits of later nonsense-centos: quotations borrowed primarily from the narrative parts of the Bible; false citations of authority (in this case Eusebius; the passages attributed to him are actually biblical); and the deliberate choice of certain types of narrative elements—biblical introductions, transitions, and concluding formulas.[41] We would expect such famil-

---

41. *Eusebius dixit* is edited in Bernhard Bischoff, "Eine Bibelparodie (elftes bis zwölftes Jahrhundert)," in *Anecdota Novissima: Texte des vierten bis sechzehnten Jahrhunderts,* Quellen und Untersuchungen zur lateinischen Philologie des Mittelalters 7 (Stuttgart, 1984), 162–64.

iarity with the Bible to have its origin in a clerical setting, and there is possible corroboration of this in a passage referring to catechumens.

> Et iterum: "Quid aliud est quam Nortmannorum infestatio?" "Tace, perverse et insipiens. Non indignamini, fratres, quia dixit 'Nortmannorum,' 'caticuminorum' dicere debuerat." (Bischoff, "Eine Bibelparodie," 163)

> [And again: "What is this but a Norman invasion?" "Quiet, wayward and foolish one. Do not be offended, brothers, that he said 'Normans'; he should have said 'catechumens.' "]

The author's ridicule of catechumens may imply a familiarity with the species born of a professional ecclesiastical background.

In other respects *Eusebius dixit* is anomalous. It predates the other nonsense centos by a considerable margin, and though in technique it is identical, in wording and subject matter it is not actually related to other surviving examples. The remaining six specimens are all related to each other in varying degrees: each shares some text with another, though there are no passages common to all.

The nonsense-centos also share remarkable affinities with other parodies: many parody-writers appear to have had access to a common core of puns and ludicrous biblical combinations which turn up again and again. To cite one recurring motif, a certain lascivious compilation of biblical quotes was clearly in widespread circulation. The first element of the passage is drawn from the account of Rachel at the well in 3 Kings, the second from Jesus' description of the colt at the gate, the third from the number of souls to be saved as given in Revelation, and the last from a passage in Acts about the men at the Pentecost. This concatenation results in descriptions like the following:

> Erat puella pulchra facie [3 Rg 1.4] super quam nullus hominum sedit [Mc 11.2] nisi centum quadraginta quatuor millia [Apc 7.4] ex omni natione quae sub caelo est [Act 2.5]. (*Exhortatio catechistica Luteranorum*)

> [There was a damsel, comely of face, upon whom no man hath yet sat, except a hundred forty-four thousand out of every nation under heaven.]

Variants of the passage are found in three nonsense-centos as well as in otherwise unrelated Latin parodies, such as the mock litany *Preces famulae sacer-*

dotis and the cento-fabliau *De cuiusdam claustralis dissolucione et castra-cionis eventu,* both discussed below later in this chapter. This and other sub-stantial interrelations between these texts suggest that few parodies were com-posed in isolation: borrowing is so widespread that most redactors must have known at least one other example, and this implies a huge circulation of the form across Europe of which we can see only the most fragmentary remains.

After the appearance of *Eusebius dixit,* the earliest Latin nonsense-centos date from the fifteenth century. These are *Fratres mei dilectissimi* (My most dearly beloved brothers), from a manuscript of 1435 which also contains a life of Invicem; *Sermo sententiosissimus* (A most succinct sermon), found in a Venice manuscript among a hodgepodge of parody Mass material; and a third, the *Leccio libri ex nichilo* (Reading of the book from nothing), from a more coherently integrated parody Mass in a Munich manuscript.[42] Two further examples are found in Anton Husemann's satire collection of 1575; these are the *Lectio Danielis prophete* (Reading of the Prophet Daniel), which is very closely related to the *Leccio libri ex nichilo,* and the *Sermo de nihil* (Sermon of nothing), perhaps the cleverest and most satirical example of the form.[43] A seventh nonsense-cento, the *Exhortatio catechistica Luteranorum* (Catecheti-cal Sermon of the Lutherans), appears in a manuscript of the early seventeenth century.[44] Though this is quite late, the text is so closely related to the others, particularly to the *Sermo de nihil,* that it may well be a copy of a medieval work; at the least it is very like medieval examples.

Though Money-Gospels and money-satires are not primarily polemical, they are informed by a moral schema and participate, even in mock inversion, in a moral universe. The advantage of the cento form is that it can imply two moral systems simultaneously to this end. In some cases, as in Virgilian centos, the new narrative implies the supplanting of pagan mythology with Christian; the cento functions as a sort of literary palimpsest in which the outdated order is visibly overlaid with the new. In Money-Gospels the base text is more legible: though the temporal world has perverted the truths of the Bible, the text makes sense because each perverted quotation brings to mind the true reading.

---

42. *Fratres mei dilectissimi* and the *Sermo sententiosissimus* are edited in appendix 2, nos. 13 and 14. The *Leccio libri ex nichilo* is found in the parody Mass beginning "Epistola. Leccio actuum potatorum ad ebrios fratres" edited in Lehmann 241–47. The nonsense-cento itself begins: "Prophecia. Leccio libri ex nichilo in diebus nullius" and is printed in Lehmann, 241–42.

43. The *Lectio Danielis prophete* and the *Sermo de nihil* are edited in appendix 2 as nos. 15 and 16.

44. The *Exhortatio catechistica Luteranorum* is edited in appendix 2, no. 17.

Although a corrupt moral schema is presented to the reader, this new reading does not efface the old morality but reemphasizes it.

By contrast, the nonsense-cento does not involve itself in the criticism of mores or of priorities of proper readings. The practice of the form raises questions about the encoding of meaning and the process of interpretation, but the authors evince no moral position on these concerns: nonsense-centos are not satire but simply narrative at play.

Although the basic impulse to create nonsense-texts needs little justification, the authors invent various pretexts to account for the form. The *Sermo de nihil,* for instance, apes the convolutions of philosphical treatises concerning such abstract insubstantialities as *nihil,* "nothing," implying that to discuss questions of this sort ultimately produces nonsense. The *Exhortatio catechistica Luteranorum* puts the text in the mouths of the Lutherans, suggesting that unorthodox concepts of God make nonsense of the Bible and render religious understanding impossible. The *Lectio Danielis prophete* and the *Leccio libri ex nichilo* begin with drunkards' parodies of Genesis, rightfully observing that drunkenness produces incoherence, whether of the Bible or of anything else.

Nonsense-centos are a form of play especially appropriate to the Middle Ages, with its unfailing reverence for *auctoritas.* Unlike the Virgilian centos, however, nonsense-centos do not attempt to fashion an obsolete *auctoritas* into a new one; nor do they seek to subvert authority altogether by dismantling it. Rather, a fascination with authority attracted medieval writers to explore its limitations, to test the uses to which it could be put and to examine the way units of meaning could be combined to produce transcendent meaning. The Bible was eminently suitable for these purposes. It embodied the ultimate authority, and thus to analyze the Bible was essentially to analyze the limits of the concept of authority itself. It was universally recognizable: thus the author of the nonsense-cento was never in danger of being misunderstood to mean what he said. And it was also the ultimate locus of meaning, expressing the meaning of the universe and God's relation to humans. It was thus particularly appropriate to use the Bible to investigate the mechanics of meaning. God used literature as the vehicle for the expression of the divine nature and purposes: so it was of the greatest importance that the medieval scholar understand how literature was capable of expressing these truths, and to understand this, he had to understand the mechanics of literature itself—how narrative was capable of expressing meaning at all. In understanding the features necessary to literary expression scholars could distinguish between those things necessary to the content of the message and those that merely worked to facilitate human understanding—separating the grammar from the content of the discourse, in effect. In this way, the mechanics of the message could become transparent, and the true meaning of the Bible could be more clearly understood.

The authors of the nonsense-centos were playing with this question on a very simple level, in the realm of narrative. They investigate the question of how meaning is produced by isolating the smallest units of narrative and expression: the phrases that denote sequence, cause and effect, similarity and repetition. The text of the nonsense-cento functions as a catch-riddle of narrative: it evokes expectations of what is to follow but then disappoints them, thereby bringing into focus the function of the element itself. This practice sets up contradictions in the text—between what a formula should introduce and what it does introduce, between what a theme should imply and what it does imply, between coherence and nonsense. Although this is merely a playful exploration of the subject, the literal contradictions in Scripture were a source of concern to serious theologians. To cite a very few cases, Peter Abelard, in his *Sic et non,* grappled with the problem by contending that scriptural contradictions could be shown to be illusory: he championed the didactic value of apparent paradox, stating that it led to more careful inquiry, which could lead to the elucidation of truth.[45] In this spirit of inquiry compilations of contradictory passages were assembled by a number of scholars, among them Ivo of Chartres, Gratian, and Peter Lombard.[46] Angelom of Luxeuil, writing in the eighth century, held a similar view, prizing the truth that could be ascertained through the careful investigation of paradox so much that he classified paradox as one of the senses of Scripture, equal in value to the historical and allegorical senses.[47] Irreconcilable paradox, however—as verified by these nonsense-centos—ultimately destroys meaning rather than contributing to it. It was, after all, the careful examination of biblical inconsistencies in the nineteenth century which led to the first questioning of the historical truth of the Gospels.

On the simplest level nonsense-centos make a mockery of connecting words such as *autem,* "moreover," and *quia,* "because." In the following passage, for

---

45. *Sic et non* is edited by B. B. Boyer and R. McKeon (Chicago, 1976–) and in Migne, *PL,* 178: cols. 1329–1610.

46. Ivo of Chartres attempted to reconcile apparently contradictory authorities in his *Panormia,* in Migne, *PL,* 161: cols. 1037–1428. Gratian juxtaposed contradictory passages from canon law in the *Concordia discordantium canonum* (commonly known as the *Decretum*); see *Decretum Magistri Gratiani,* ed. E. Friedberg, 2d ed., Corpus Iuris Canonici 1 (1879; reprint, Graz, 1959). Peter Lombard tried to harmonize contradictory passages from authority in his *Sententiae;* the text is edited as *Magistri Petri Lombardi Sententiae in IV Libris Distinctae,* 2 vols., Spicilegium Bonaventurianum 4–5 (Grottaferrata, 1971–81).

47. *Enarrationes in libros regum,* in Migne, *PL* 115: cols. 243–552 (at col. 245).

instance, nearly every phrase is connected to another by such an element, but the logical connections implied by the semantic and grammatical ones are absent.

> Postquam autem Alexander percussit Darium [1 Mcc 1.1], stravit Abraham asinum suum [2 Sm 17.23], et ascendit in arborem sicomorum [Lc 19.4], et traxit rete in terram [Jo 21.11], plenum quadratis rusticis. Piscatores autem [Lc 5.2] calefaciebant se [Mc 14.54] ad glacies, ne forte tumulus fieret in [Mt 26.5] piscibus. Petrus autem tunica succinxit se [Jo 21.7], quia frigus erat [Jo 18.18], dixitque: "Vado piscari" [Jo 21.3]. Erat autem ibidem fenum multum in loco [Jo 6.10]. Rete autem eorum rumpebatur [Lc 5.6] prae multitudine piscium [Jo 21.6]. Et ait ad eum Dathan [cf. Nm 16.12]: "Unde venis, Sathan?" Qui ait: "Circuivi terram et perambulavi eam [Jb 1.7], et tota domus impleta est ex odore ung⟨u⟩enti [Jo 12.3], incipiens a Galilea usque huc" [Lc 23.5]. Hieroboam vero dixit servo suo [3 Rg 14.2]: "Amice, quomodo huc intrasti non habens ventrem nuptialem?"[Mt 22.12] (*Lectio Danielis prophete*)

> [Moreover, after Alexander overthrew Darius, Abraham saddled his ass, and climbed up into a sycamore tree, and drew the net to land, full of sturdy peasants. The fisherman, moreover, warmed themselves at the ice, lest perhaps there should be a tumult among the fish. But Peter girt himself with his coat, because it was cold, and said: "I go a-fishing." There was, moreover, much grass in the place. But their nets broke before the multitude of fishes. And Dathan said to him: "Whence comest thou, Satan?" He said: "I have gone around the earth, and walked through it, and the whole house is filled with the smell of ointment, from Galilee to this place." And Jeroboam, truly, said to his servant: "Friend, how camest thou hither without a wedding stomach?"]

The nonsense is tantalizing because it is not quite random. Both the connecting phrases and the grammatical structure urge the reader to identify meaning in the passage. This is further encouraged by the use of recurring motifs such as the cold and the fish. The image of fish, for example, recurs in a mystifying way: Abraham is described fishing (albeit from a sycamore tree); later Peter declares his intent to go fishing, which brings to mind his role as a fisher of men; and soon thereafter we hear that the nets hanging from the tree are in fact bulging with fish. We are beguiled into searching for internal logic by the recurrence of similar events, a narrative device that gives meaning to any story, and above all to the story of the Bible, in which repetition and similarity are the keystones of typological interpretation. But our attentiveness to such narrative cues is confounded by the essential randomness of the work.

Thus in nonsense-centos repetition and similarity fail to convey significance; similarly the expectations excited by introductory phrases are deflated by subsequent homely or grotesque images. Satan's travels through the world conclude with an observation on smell: "I have gone around the earth, and walked through it, and the whole house was filled with the smell of ointment." Biblical stories of conflict, death, and divine revelation disappear, and what plot there is revolves around food and the ludicrous injuries of the characters. Thus the *vestem nuptialem,* the garment required of the wedding-guest in Christ's parable, is transformed in the *Lectio Danielis* into a *ventrem nuptialem,* "wedding stomach," and biblical action is reduced to pratfalls and comically exaggerated violence.

Saul enim querebat David regem [1 Sm 23.14] et amputavit auriculam eius dextram [Lc 22.50] et pedem sinistrum [cf. Apc 10.2], et ait: "Amice, non facio tibi iniuriam [Mt 20.13]. Tolle quod tuum est, et vade" [Mt 20.14]. (*Lectio Danielis prophete*)

[And Saul sought David the king and cut off his right ear and his left foot, and said: "Friend, I do thee no injury. Take what is thine and go."]

In the following example the introductory phrases "non sum dignus ut" and "tantum dic verbo et" invoke the memory of the passage at Matthew 8.8, in which the man begs Jesus to heal his son, and so set up the expectation of important events to follow; but in fact here the man is only offering to get Jesus' dinner.

Dixitque Nathan: "Domine, non sum dignus ut intres coquinam meam, sed tantum dic verbo, et assabitur gallus meus" [Mt 8.8]. (*Lectio Danielis prophete*)

[And Nathan said: "Lord, I am not worthy that thou shouldst enter my kitchen: but only say the word and my rooster shall be roasted."]

This method of construction draws attention to the degree to which context determines meaning in conventional literature. The exploitation of grammatical features, misleading formulas, and meaningless repetition is joined by pointless emphasis on concrete details of orientation. The author establishes time and place with great precision, using phrases such as "Nabuchodonozor autem genuit Marcolphum in transmigratione Hiericho anno primo ante diluvium" [And Nebuchadnezzer begat Marcolph in the transmigration of Jericho in the first year before the flood] (*Sermo de nihil*). Similarly we are often given the parentage of the characters and details of their bynames. Finally, much of this is spuriously credited to authority: the *Vitae patrum,* Sallust, "Rabanus in Actibus Apostolorum" (Hrabanus in the Acts of the Apostles), "Galienus in cronica sua super Ioannem ad Ephesios" (Galienus in his chronicles on John to the Ephesians), "Galienus in canonica sua super Lucam" (Galienus in his canon on Luke), "Vergilius in Canticis" (Virgil in the Songs). The texts set out cues which should orient the events of the narrative in time and space, and authorities to assure the authenticity of the account, but all of these are specious. The stories are not in fact ordered in a way that allows us to understand them: there is time but no sequence; there is location but no context; there is meaningless similarity and pointless repetition; there is cause without effect and effect without cause. And finally, none of the authorities cited are responsible for the quotations credited to them. In short, it is irresponsible narrative. Nonsense-centos function as an exploration of the limits and effects of narrative mechanics: the mechanics are exposed by setting them working on their own and not in cooperation with each other. The result affirms that authority is useless without coherence, whether it is the authority of the Church Fathers, of narrative convention, or of grammatical construction.

One nonsense-cento, the *Sermo de nihil,* imposes a layer of irony on its basic nonsense-material. Its stated theme, nothing, echoes other inquiries on the subject, and its convolutions of argument and lack of coherence imply that all other studies of a nonsubject must be unprofitable. The *Sermo de nihil* explores the paradoxes involved in constructing a substantial argument about an insubstantiality and resolves the paradox by reducing the argument to nonsense. The sermon cites authorities, implying agreement and logical connection between their arguments, but acknowledges that by nature this argument is fruitless from its inception:

> Fratres, ex nihilo nihil fit [cf. Sap 2.2]. Nolumus enim vos ignorare de dormientibus [1 Th 4.13], et de verbo quod abbreviatum est [cf. Rm 9.28], licet onerosum mihi, vobis autem pernecessarium [Phil 3.1]. Ait enim Scriptura: "Quid superbis terra et cinis?" [Sir 10.9] Sed nihil mihi conscius sum [1 Cor 4.4]. Et quid nihil? Nihil enim habens, nihil conferre potest [cf. Mt 13.12]. Nihil ergo tuleritis in via [cf. 1 Tm 6.7]. Si enim

nihil tuleritis, nihil vobis deerit [cf. Ps 22.1]. Ubi enim nihil est interius, nihil fit exterius. Nam in curia Romana legitur de Floreno, quod sine ipso factum est nihil [Jo 1.3]. Et iterum, sine quo nihil est validum, nihil sanctum, ut legitur in Vitis Patrum. Unde Galienus in canonica sua super Lucam scribens ait: "Si esurit inimicus tuus [Prv 25.21], erue ei oculum [Mt 18.9]. Et si perseveraverit pulsans [Lc 11.8], erue ei et alterum [cf. Mt 5.39]. Qui enim ista fecerit, legem adimplevit." [Rm 13.8] . . . Unde dicit Alexander in Canticis Canticorum, "Si vis perfectus esse [Mt 19.21], vade et fac tu similiter" [Lc 10.37]. Sed quid multis moror? Ecce Judas Machabeus qui dicitur Caiphas [cf. 2 Mcc 5.27; Mt 26.14] dixit ad discipulos suos [Lc 12.22]: "Habetisne aliquid quod manducetur?" [Lc 24.41] Et obtulerunt ei paraliticum iacentem in lecto [Mt 9.2], dicentes: "Ecce duo gladii hic [Lc 22.38] et quatuor ordines mendicantium" [Ex 28.17]. Manducaverunt ergo, et saturati sunt nihil [cf. Ps 77.29]. (*Sermo de nihil*)

[Brothers, nothing is made from nothing. We will not have you remain ignorant concerning them that are asleep; and as for the word cut short, though it may be worrisome to me, to you it is necessary. For Scripture says: "Why is earth and ashes proud?" But I am aware of nothing on my part. And why nothing? For he who has nothing can contribute nothing. Therefore you will bring nothing into the way. For if you bring nothing, you will lack nothing. For where there is nothing within, there will be nothing without. For in the Roman curia we read of Florenus that without him nothing was made. And, again, without him nothing is valid, nothing holy, as we read in the *Lives of the Fathers*. Whence Galienus, writing in his canons on Luke, says: "If thy enemy be hungry, pluck out his eye. And if the knocking continues, pluck out his other also. Who does these things, fulfills the law.". . . Whence saith Alexander in the Song of Songs: "If thou wilt be perfect, go thou and do in like manner." But why should I delay in these many things? Behold Judas Macchabeus, who was called Caiphas, said to his disciples: "Have you anything to eat?" And they brought to him one sick of the palsy lying in bed, saying: "Behold, here are two swords and four orders of mendicants." Thereupon they ate, and they were satisfied with nothing.]

At this point the listener, too, has sampled the author's wisdom and *saturatus est nihil.* The author exploits the double meanings of the word in a way similar to the *Nemo* texts: in this sermon, as he says: "nihil est validum, nihil sanctum."

That he has accorded the subject enough importance to devote a sermon to it, however, does not mean that it is possible to make sense of the inquiry. To attempt to investigate nothing is literally a contradiction in terms. He drives this conclusion home at several points: "Nihil enim habens, nihil conferre potest" [For he who has nothing can contribute nothing]; "Ubi enim nihil est interius, nihil fit exterius" [For where there is nothing within, there will be nothing without]. The author acknowledges his own vacuousness in attempting to expound the subject of nothing: in the context of a nonsense-sermon the biblical profession of innocence, "nihil mihi conscius sum" [I am aware of nothing] (1 Cor 4.4), becomes merely a confession of his own mindlessness. This reduction from sense to ignorance is a paradigm of the operation of the entire sermon: abbreviated and robbed of context, each statement becomes a fool's utterance, signifying only that it signifies nothing.

The *Sermo de nihil* contains long stretches which are ultimately unresolvable.

> Intrante autem eo domum cuiusdam principis Phariseorum Sabbato man- ducare panem [Lc 14.1], invenit eos dormientes [Mt 26.40] prae timore [Mt 28.4], percussoque latere Petri excitavit eum, dicens [Act 12.7]: "Non potuistis una hora vigilare mecum? [Mc 14.37] Surge velociter et comede [Act 12.7, 10.13]. Grandis enim tibi restat via" [3 Rg 19.7]. Et invenit subcinericium panem [cf. Gn 18.6] ad caput suum [3 Rg 19.6], et dixit: "Quid hec inter tantos? [Jo 6.9] Epulari enim et gaudere oportet, quia filius meus perierat, et inventus est" [Lc 15.32, 24]. Comedit ergo volumen istud [cf. Ez 3.1], et factum est in ore eius tanquam cera li- quescens [Ez 3.3; cf. Apc 10.9]. Et amaricatus est venter eius [Apc 10.10]. (*Sermo de nihil*)

> [And, going into the house of one of the chiefs of the Pharisees on the Sabbath day, to eat bread, he found them asleep from fear, and he, striking Peter in the side, raised him up, saying: "Could thou not wait with me one hour? Arise quickly and eat. For thou hast yet a great way to go." And he found a hearth cake at his head and said: "But what are these among so many? But it is fit that we should make merry and be glad: for my son was dead, and is found." Thereupon he ate the book, and it was like wax melting in his mouth. And his stomach was upset.]

On the most literal level this makes a certain amount of sense, and if the text were considered in isolation it might be understood as nothing more than a corrupt version of an originally coherent narrative. But in fact every phrase reminds the listener or reader of its biblical context; the passage cannot be experienced without recognition of the contradictions between the discordant original contexts. The recurring theme invites the reader to make sense of the passage, but when readers apply all their powers of understanding to the text, they are frustrated by their knowledge of the original biblical context of each passage: thus the understanding of the narrative is ultimately undermined by the reader's efforts to make connections. The author brings this nonsense-narrative to a close with a simultaneous restatement of theme and acknowledgment of the fruitlessness of the reader's efforts: "Et sic in nihilum redit, quia antea nihil fuit" [And thus it returns to nothing, which was nothing before].

In sum, the nonsense-cento is a more sophisticated form of parody than it purports to be. Familiar with the analysis of scriptural content, the authors wished instead to draw attention to the mechanics of religious truth, to define and identify the minimum possible units of meaning, and to amuse themselves in testing their properties and limitations.

Other Parodic Centos

Medieval parodists and satirists found cento techniques useful in the imitation of other literary forms. A clever conflation of parodic types was achieved by one humorist in *De cuiusdam claustralis dissolucione et castracionis eventu* (The downfall and castration of a certain monk). The earliest manuscripts of this Latin prose fabliau appear in the thirteenth century; the story later appeared in a simplified version, the *Passio cuiusdam nigri monachi secundum luxuriam* (The passion of a black monk according to excess), apparently a product of the thirteenth century.[48]

On the simplest level this is a tale of a lecherous monk who meets a bad end, similar though not identical to many of the Old French fabliaux. On a deeper level the story parodies the conventions of romance. Despite its raciness, it is introduced as an admonitory sermon or stern exemplum; and, of course, it is

---

48. The older version, *De cuiusdam claustralis dissolucione et castracionis eventu,* is edited in Lehmann 224–30, from four manuscripts. The younger *Passio cuiusdam nigri monachi secundum luxuriam* has not been properly edited. A single manuscript is printed in Julius Feifalik, "Studien zur Geschichte der altböhmischen Literatur," *Sitzungsberichte der kaiserlichen Akademie der Wissenschaften in Wien,* philologisch-historische Classe 36 (1861): 119–91 (at 173–74). Lehmann lists seven manuscripts of the *Passio* on p. 231 of *Die Parodie im Mittelalter.* It should be noted that he locates one of these in "Graz Univ.-Bibl. Ms. II 260"; the correct reference is Graz, Universitätsbibliothek MS 620. Five additional manuscripts are listed by A. G. Rigg, *A History of Anglo-Latin Literature 1066–1422* (Cambridge, 1992), p. 358 n. 251.

constructed from biblical passages, clothing the subject matter in incongruously solemn garb.

Like romance, the story concerns a hero who seeks adventure and woos a maiden, but the story is perverse from the beginning, when a monk appears in the role of a knightly hero. The mock romance opens, appropriately, with the protagonist wandering the world, but where wandering is evidence of a standard romance hero's determination to try his mettle, it merely signifies waywardness on the part of a monk. In the life of the romance hero, wandering signals adventure; in the monastery it signals scandal. The monk's attempts to emulate the conventional hero soon go further astray. The romance hero inaugurates his adventure by confronting danger, but in place of this, our monastic hero meets a woman: the maiden to be rescued has become, for the monk, the danger to be faced. The encounter with the maiden invokes an abundance of description in the tradition of the blazon, but the author undermines each set phrase with an explanation of the woman's cosmetics and character.

> Crines eius crines Apollinis, sed tamen calamistro crispari studuit, de colore crocum consuluit; frons candore lilia figurat, sed tamen fido parum de tali lilio quo non regnat, cum cessat unctio . . . (*De eventu* 21–24)

> [Her tresses are the tresses of Apollo, except that she has taken care to curl them with a curling-iron, and gone to the crocus for their color. Her brow is like a lily in whiteness, but I think there is too little of that lily where she does not reach, where the ointment stops . . .]

Despite the woman's flaws, however, the care devoted to her description leads the audience to anticipate the rituals of courtly love. But the monk's response is abrupt and to the point: "Monachus vidit et invidit" [The monk saw and he coveted] (line 30). This is a blatantly carnal use of grammatical Platonism: seeing (*vidit*) is more than halfway to desiring (*invidit*). He woos the antiquated maiden with stock phrases of beguilement; she responds with a combination of token romance and hardheaded bargaining for cash.

> Que stetit et ait: "Quam dulcia faucibus meis eloquia tua super mel ori meo. Si dictis facta compenses, tuis obtemperabo mandatis nec renuntiabo muneribus." (*De eventu* 33–35)

[She stood and said: "How sweet the eloquence of your lips, like honey to my mouth. If your promises equal your deeds, I will submit to your request, and I will not refuse your presents."]

The hesitant give-and-take between the lovers of romance has become a matter-of-fact assessment of the terms of the deal. As in courtly love, the hero burns with love for a married woman; but as in fabliau, he obtains her favors with little trouble. "Quod petis, faciam" [What you ask, I will do], she says (43). If the woman can be described as "similitudo templi" [like a temple] (20), then, like his profane predecessors, he violates the temple.

This wandering monk is also placed in implicit contrast to members of other wandering orders, the friars, who were charged with poverty and preaching to bring the populace closer to God. The parody monk is certainly not poor, as his rich gifts to the woman attest, and he also fails to serve as an intermediary between God and sinners. On the contrary, the woman complains, "Religio tua abominatio est mihi et habitum hunc odivit anima mea" [Your faith is an abomination to me, and my soul loathes this habit] (59). Like a true romance hero, he defends his lady from that which she fears, soothing her: "Si religionem causaris, subiecta es michi et ego ponam me inter te et Deum" [If you oppose religion, be subject to me and I will place myself between you and God] (63). In the end, though, he reaps what he sows: the husband returns and decides to prevent recurrences by transforming the monk into a eunuch for God.

This cautionary tale would be a gruesome exemplum but for the relish with which the narrator relates it. He presents the story to his congregation as a warning, but in fact he is torn between revulsion at the horror of the tale and the urge to relay a juicy piece of scandal. Eventually, under the pretense of edification, scandal wins out.

Most religious parodies make use of the Bible to lend their trivial subject matter a mock grandiosity; biblical centos are the result of this parodic citation taken to extremes. To try to pattern anything after the Bible, whether life or fiction, is to be forced to confront the preposterous result, the degree to which profane life necessarily falls short of Holy Scripture. Biblical centos impose the pattern of heaven on daily life: earthly dramas seen from such an exalted perspective will inevitably appear trifling and comic. *De eventu* and its younger derivative, the *Passio monachi*, epitomize the debasement of the spiritual to the corporeal: when men like the lecherous monk imitate the Scriptures, they generate only carnal and laughable interpretations.

Other parodies expose the contrast between the earthly and the spiritual by juxtaposing biblical passages with nonbiblical formulas: these might be more properly called demicentos. Two of these survive—both counterfeit parts of the Mass which normally incorporate biblical passages. The *Metra de monachis carnalibus* (Verse on lustful monks), an antimonastic satire, mixes original hexameters with verses from the Psalms, mimicking the liturgical alteration of verse and response.[49] The text's division into quasi-independent units meant that enormous differences could develop between versions as scribes combined and rearranged passages to their liking. Accordingly, the *Metra de monachis carnalibus* exists in an assortment of versions, the fourteen surviving copies falling into three main groups. Manuscript studies show the text to have originated in England, later spreading to the Continent. The wide diffusion of the piece is unsurprising, given the apparent appetite for such works in the medieval period, but the specific provenance of the manuscripts is significant. The most recent editor of the *Metra,* A. G. Rigg, points out that of the seven English manuscripts, at least four come from monastic houses.[50] This is valuable evidence of antimonastic satire, and most likely for the composition of the genre as well. In no manuscript, moreover, is the *Metra* the sole satirical work; in fact two contain other parodies, one a parody Mass and the *Passio monachi,* and one a partial parody Mass and *De eventu.*[51] In the manuscript tradition of the *Metra de monachis carnalibus,* then, we can catch a glimpse of the rich satiric activity which took place at centers of learning, and we can even identify some of the perpetrators of antimonastic satire: the monks themselves.[52]

The earliest version of the *Metra,* the English version, is the most artistically coherent, forming a sarcastic paean to monastic gluttony.

1   Quis nescit, quam sit monachorum nobile vulgus?

—   In omnem terram exiuit sonus eorum et in fines orbis terre verba
       eorum [Ps 18.5]

2   Omnia consumunt nec eos possunt saciare

---

49. The *Metra de monachis carnalibus* is edited in A. G. Rigg, "'Metra de Monachis Carnalibus'—The Three Versions," *Mittellateinisches Jahrbuch* 15 (1980): 134–42 (at 135, 136–37, 139). The first of the versions printed in Rigg is a reprint of that edited in Lehmann 194–95.

50. Rigg, "Metra," 140.

51. The parody Mass and the *Passio* are found in London, British Library MS Harley 913 (Rigg's Hn), the partial Mass and *De eventu* in Oxford, Bodleian Library MS A.44 (Rigg's A), the "Bekynton Anthology." On the contents of the Bekynton Anthology see A. G. Rigg, *A History of Anglo-Latin Literature 1066–1422* (Cambridge, 1992), 152–53.

52. One manuscript (Oxford, Bodleian Library MS Digby 65) also contains a nonparodic verse reply to the *Metra:* on this see Rigg, *A History of Anglo-Latin Literature,* 231 and 237.

— Volucres celi et pisces maris, qui perambulant semitas maris [Ps 8.9]
3   Fercula multa petunt et longum tempus edendi;
— Ipsi vero dispergentur ad manducandum, si vero non fuerint saturati, murmurabunt, etc. [Ps 58.16]
4   Non curat socium, positas cum respicit escas
— Superbo oculo et insaciabili corde, cum hoc non edebam. [Ps 100.5] . . .
6   Gutture nil pingui preter mendacia promunt:
— Vana locuti sunt unusquisque ad proximum suum, labia dolosa in corde et corde locuti sunt [Ps 11.3] . . .

                                        (Rigg, "Metra," 136–37)

[1   Who does not know how noble a group of monks is?
— Their sound hath gone forth into all the earth; and their words unto the ends of the world.
2   They consume all things, nor is it possible to satisfy them
— The birds of the air, and the fishes of the sea that pass through the paths of the sea.
3   They seek many dishes and a long time to eat;
— They shall be scattered abroad to eat, and shall murmur if they be not filled.
4   He cares nothing for his companion when he awaits the serving of the meal
— With him that had a proud eye and an unsatiable heart, I would not eat. . . .
6   Nothing but lies issue forth from a fat throat:
— They have spoken vain things every one to his neighbor: with deceitful lips and with a double heart have they spoken . . .]

The denunciation continues, concluding with an anathema: "Fiat habitacio eorum deserta et in tabernacula non sit, qui inhabitet!" [May their dwelling place be a desolation and let no one dwell in their tents!] (Ps 68.26; Rigg, "Metra," 137). The Continental version, which does not appear until the fifteenth century, is similar but dilutes the glutton-imagery with invective of a more general sort.

The third version, the "Nun Adaptation," is potentially the most interesting by virtue of its connection with women. There is very little evidence for the contribution of women to medieval Latin satire generally, although so much of the corpus is anonymous that the possibility of substantial female participation cannot be definitively ruled out. In nonliterary parody, such as I discuss in this study, the depiction of women is confined to stereotyped figures, such as the quasi virgin of *De eventu* or the "puella pulchra facie" of nonsense-centos and other texts (though of course women play a much larger role in true fiction parody, such as mock romance). Nevertheless, where evidence is available it indicates that men, rather than women, were responsible for the production and enjoyment of nonliterary parody: men appear as the primary characters, as the audience implied by the many sermons beginning "Fratres," as authors where authors are named, and as scribes where scribes are named. The "Nun Adaptation" of the *Metra,* which is extant in two manuscripts, is the sole exception to male hegemony; yet, though the suggestion that nuns rewrote their own parodies is intriguing, the text itself is uninformative and unexceptional. The evils attributed to the nuns are very similar to those ascribed to monks in other versions of the *Metra,* with some allowances for the fluid nature of the text. The only difference is a lesser emphasis on gluttony as a vice and hence a greater emphasis on personal vanity; this may reflect the more ascetic character of medieval women's relationship to food.[53]

It is perilous to speculate on the precise authorship of the nuns' version, but one observation might be made. In so far as women have any role in nonliterary parody, they usually introduce sex into a work: this is the case in nonsense-centos, in *De eventu* and the *Passio monachi,* and in parody Masses. By contrast, the "Nun Adaptation" of the *Metra* is free of sexual innuendo. The relative propriety of the nuns' version may simply be a result of the fact that it is based on an original about monks; or its lack of lewd insinuation about women's sexual availability may also betoken a female redactor or audience.

The interests of the *Preces famulae sacerdotis* (Prayers of the priest's housekeeper), another demicento, are similar to those of the *Metra de monachis carnalibus,* except that the author has expanded his derision to take in the entire ecclesiastical hierarchy.[54] The text is found in three manuscripts (again with considerable variations), the oldest of the fifteenth century. The parody takes the form of a series of prayers, but where the petitioner usually seeks intercession for a catalog of the needy, here the supplicant brings down curses and invective on each in turn. In this the *Preces* represents the intersection of the cento with estates satire. The disparagement of the ranks and grades of the Church is put into the mouth of a priest's housekeeper, who presumably em-

---

53. This point is noted by Caroline Walker Bynum in *Holy Feast and Holy Fast: The Religious Significance of Food to Medieval Women* (Berkeley, 1987), 79.

54. The text is edited in Hans Walther, "Parodistische Gebete der Pfarrköchin in einer Züricher Handschrift," *Studi Medievali,* n.s., 4 (1931): 344–57 (at 349–55).

bodies the disillusionment of those familiar with the mundane realities of ecclesiastical life. A voice, presumably that of a priest, announces the subject of each prayer, and the housekeeper counters with a quotation from the Psalms. The technique is very similar to that of the *Metra de monachis carnalibus,* and the use of identical quotations suggests that the author of the *Preces* had the *Metra* as his model. The *Preces,* however, is not only much longer—one manuscript has sixty-four quotations, against the *Metra*'s ten or so—but much better realized. The quotations are by and large apposite to their subjects, and the satire is pleasingly mordant and cynical. The text begins with an indication of the scope of the work:

1)   Oremus pro omni gradu ecclesie!
Omnes declinaverunt, simul inutiles facti sunt: non est qui facit bonum, non est usque ad unum. [Ps 13.3]

(Walther, "Parodistische," 349)

[1]   Let us pray for every rank of the Church!
They are all gone astray, they are become unprofitable together: there is none that doth good, no, not one.]

The petition comprises chiefly the grades of the Church in order of hierarchy but also makes mention of a few of the secular estates, including the emperor ("Fiant filii eius orphani, ut uxor eius vidua" [May his children be fatherless, and his wife a widow], Ps 108.9), nobles, farmers, peasants, simpletons, gamblers, and even sinners ("Beatus populus, qui scit jubilationem" [Blessed is the people that knoweth jubilation], Ps 88.16). Not every biblical quotation is reproduced verbatim; some have undergone slight alteration to make them more appropriate. A case in point is the passage from Revelation 14.4 (a rare departure from the usual custom of borrowing from the Psalms). The correct quotation reads: "Hii sunt, qui cum mulieribus non sunt coinquinati: virgines enim sunt" [These are they who were not defiled with women: for they are virgins]. The parody shifts one crucial word.

10)   Pro canonicis.
Hii cum mulieribus sunt coinquinati: virgines enim non sunt.

(Walther, "Parodistische," 250)

[10]   For the canons.
These are they who were defiled with women: for they are not virgins.]

The author disparages all ranks equally and takes care to heap abuse on different orders of monks and friars, maligning the Carmelites, Augustinians, Franciscans, Cistercians, and Dominicans. Having begun with the pope and worked down through the ecclesiastical and temporal orders, the author finally reaches the lowest of all, Nummus, "Money," who is in fact the most powerful: "Adorabunt eum omnes reges terre et omnes gentes servient ei" [And all kings of the earth shall adore him: all nations shall serve him] (Ps 71.11). Thus the prayer closes with a blanket condemnation of all stations.

Although these prayers are attributed to the priest's housekeeper, a number of comments in the text make it clear that this is a late attribution and that the piece was originally meant to be spoken by men.

34)   Pro femineo sexu.
Delectationes eorum laetificaverunt animos nostros. [Ps 93.19]

60)   Pro femineo sexu.
Beatus vir, qui implevit desiderium suum ex ipsis: non confundetur in
    eternum. [Ps 126.5]

61)   Pro uxoribus nostris.
Currunt de gente in gentem et de populo ad populum, et intrabunt in
    regnum ullum. [Ps 104.13; Lc 18.24]

66)   Concubinis nostris.
Constitues super eas legislatorum, et ipse sunt judices nostri. [Ps 9.21;
    Mt 12.27]

                                   (Walther, "Parodistische," 351, 354)

[34)   For the feminine sex.
Their comforts have given joy to our souls.

60)   For the feminine sex.
Blessed is the man that hath filled the desire with them: he shall never be
    confounded.

61)   For our wives.
They shall pass from nation to nation, and from one kingdom to another
    people, and enter into any kingdom.

66)   For our concubines.

Appoint a lawgiver over them, and they shall be our judges.]

The piece is accompanied by two prayers satirical of peasants along with a cento description of the housekeeper herself, an exuberant elaboration of the familiar motif.

46)   Descriptio famulae sacerdotis.
Puella decora nimis virgoque pulcherrima [Gn 24.16], super quam nullus hominum sedit [Mc 11.2] nisi centum quadraginta quatuor milia [Apc 7.4] in die omnium sanctorum et in dominica palmarum turba multa et in vigilia ascensionis omnes gentes et in Donato septuaginta octo vel paulo plus et ibidem reliqui pene omnes et in simbolo Attanasii quicumque vult.
                              (Walther, "Parodistische," 352–53)

[46]   A description of the priest's housekeeper.
An exceedingly comely maid and a most beautiful virgin, upon which no man yet hath sat, except a hundred and forty-four thousand on the day of All Saints, and on Palm Sunday a great multitude, and in the vigil of the Ascension all peoples, and in Donatus seventy-eight or a little more, and likewise almost all the rest, and in the Athanasian Creed, whoever wants.]

The Uses of Parodic Centos

It is notoriously difficult to assess the way in which most forms of medieval literature reached their audience, and the same holds true for many types of parody. Parodic centos, however, are an exception to the general ambiguity surrounding issues of performance, simply because most show clear signs of having been written to be read aloud. Of the sixteen principal centos discussed in this chapter, a full thirteen take the form of sermons. The desire to frame the pieces for oral performance is evident in the variety of genres which have been given sermon tags to make them suitable for oration; as a result even the fabliaux, *De eventu* and the *Passio monachi,* are clothed in sermon rhetoric. The Money-Gospels are also conspicuous in this regard: although they could function simply as Gospel-parodies, they are uniformly presented as liturgical readings from the Gospels. This is obvious from the liturgical tags that surround many of the Gospel parodies themselves, ranging from the introduction inaugurating liturgical Gospel readings, *In illo tempore,* "in that time" (or its parody, *in illo turbine*), to simple invocations, such as *Gloria tibi Paschalis,* "the glory of Easter to you" (P), to elaborate liturgical preambles such as that in version F.

Evangelium Pasquilli olim Romani iam peregrini. Dolus vobiscum. Et comiti tuo. Frequentia falsi evangelii secundum archam auri et argenti. Gloria tibi auro et argento.

[The Gospel of Pasquil, formerly of Rome, now wandering. Fraud be with you. And with your comrade. The assembly of the false gospel according to the ark of Gold and Silver. Glory to thee, Gold and Silver.]

An even longer liturgical introduction distinguishes the Venice Money-Gospel quoted in full earlier in this chapter. The titles of Money-Gospels present further corroboration that their performance was intended to mirror the delivery of the Gospel in the divine office. In the Mass the Gospel reading falls under the title *Sequentia;* some parodies retain the term, while others present this as *Frequentia* (SF) or *Iustitia* (H). Finally, some announce the oral character of the piece outright, terming the work "Lectio." Similarly, though nonsense-centos parody biblical narrative, the narrative itself is framed as a sermon, making use of either sermon introductions, such as *Fratres mei* or sermon conclusions rounded off with *Amen* or *Dixi* (I have spoken) or both.

Of the three parodic centos which do not imitate the sermon, only the *Epistola de Pecunia* is not indisputably designed for oral performance. Like the Gospel readings, the *Metra de monachis carnalibus* and the *Preces famulae sacerdotis* parody parts of the liturgy, here verse-and-response and the litany. In these instances it is particularly unfortunate that no description of the performance survives. As in the case of parody Masses, the form of the texts suggests that performance was not the responsibility of a single actor before an audience but called for the participation of a number of players, possibly of the audience themselves. Despite these ambiguities, the public nature of parodic centos is clear; and from the fact that verbatim biblical knowledge is essential to the humor of the pieces we can infer that this public must have been constituted of the clergy. If the experience of cento parody was public and therefore communal, we can also rule out the idea that clerical enjoyment of religious humor was necessarily clandestine—a conclusion which may have wider implications for the place of humor in medieval religious culture.

CHAPTER 6

Religion and Humor in the Middle Ages

. . . il n'y a généralement aucune contradiction entre l'espirit chrétien, entre les
dévotions les plus sincères, et ces exubérances collectives, parfois de mauvais goût;
elles s'inscrivent dans un contexte beaucoup plus vaste et complexe.

—Jacques Heers, *Fêtes des fous et carnavals*

Risum fecit mihi Deus.

—Arras *Cena* 29.2

The later Middle Ages saw a wealth of exuberant religious humor, of which
parody formed a substantial part. In this concluding chapter I discuss questions
arising from this abundance of religious levity. The first of these is the contribution parody can make to the vexed question of the relationship betwen
religious humor and the medieval Church. In the course of this examination I
consider both modern and medieval theoretical views of humor, as well as the
tendency—not confined to the Middle Ages—of pundits to preach one thing
and practice another. I also examine the structure of much religious humor and
its relation to the structure of Christian belief, and I propose that these struc-
tural similarities made medieval parody less subversive than it often appears to
the modern eye. Finally, I outline a range of ways in which humor and religion
are related. In the discussion as a whole I hope to show that medieval humor
embodies a wide range of attitudes and that to limit the relation of religious
humor and the Church to a single configuration is to oversimplify the rich and
complex culture of the Middle Ages.

Medieval Latin parody can serve as a unique test case in attempting to
explore the relationship between medieval religion and humor. Religious parody was close to the heart of the Church: the evidence of authorship, the fact
that there is such a large body of the genre in Latin, and the familiarity with
Scripture, theology, and the Church required to appreciate the jokes suggest
that these texts were written by and for members of the clergy and were not
intended primarily, if at all, for lay consumption. These religious parodies play

specifically with the sacred texts and institutions of medieval Christianity and provoke us to ask what place we can assign such humor in the medieval Church and in medieval culture. Is it an aberration, the flippant or cynical product of fringe elements or malcontents? Is it a normal, though deplorable, reaction to the strict seriousness with which medieval religious life was conducted, tolerated as a safety valve that permitted the reimposition of rules and hierarchies in everyday life? Or are the number of surviving parodies, allied with other evidence of religious merrymaking and carnival, evidence of actual ecclesiastical tolerance of, or even sympathy for, merriment?

The analysis of the causes and motivations of humor and of the role of play in culture has been informed by a variety of literary, anthropological, and psychoanalytical perspectives. In the following sections, I outline modern theoretical debate on this subject, giving a brief account of the views of the most influential scholars in the field.

Humor as Folk Carnival and Carnival as Subversion

Mikhail Bakhtin's analysis of medieval carnival, found in its most complete form in his *Rabelais and His World,* has been seminal to the modern discussion of medieval humor and popular culture.[1] His identification of humor as an integral part of medieval tradition, rather than as a marginal aberration from a monolithically serious culture, has been important in calling attention to the diversity of medieval culture. Almost uniquely among critics of his time, Bakhtin understood medieval humor as a significant and socially valuable force. In attempting to identify the precise role of humor in culture, however, his analysis is grounded in Marxist tenets which do not do full justice to the complexities of the problem.

Bakhtin's definition of carnival embraces a wide variety of celebrations and practices "bearing the common traits of popular merriment" (*Rabelais and His*

---

1. Mikhail Bakhtin, *Rabelais and His World.* Bakhtin also expounds his theory of carnival in "From the Prehistory of Novelistic Discourse," in *The Dialogic Imagination: Four Essays,* ed. Michael Holquist, trans. Caryl Emerson and Michael Holquist, University of Texas Press Slavic Series 1 (Austin and London, 1981), 41–83, esp. 68–82. The literature on Bakhtin and Carnival is immense and largely positive; an important critical view is offered by Dietz-Rüdiger Moser, "Lachkultur des Mittelalters? Michael Bachtin und die Folgen seiner Theorie," *Euphorion: Zeitschrift für Literaturgeschichte* 84 (1990): 89–111. Moser's views are discussed by Aaron J. Gurjewitsch, "Bachtin und der Karneval. Zu Dietz-Rüdiger Moser: 'Lachkultur des Mittelalters? Michael Bachtin und die Folgen seiner Theorie,'" *Euphorion* 85 (1991): 423–29. (Gurjewitsch's views are also discussed later in this chapter under the name Aron Gurevich, the spelling under which Gurevich's writings have appeared in English.) A further synthesis is offered by Dietz-Rüdiger Moser, "Auf dem Weg zu neuen Mythen," *Euphorion* 85 (1991): 430–37.

World, 218). In *Rabelais and His World* he outlines three categories of behavior that constitute carnival: ritual spectacles, comic verbal compositions, and oaths and curses (5). Under the rubric of "ritual spectacles" Bakhtin cites carnivals, Fools' Festivals and the Feast of the Ass, the *risus paschalis* (the ritual joking permitted in church at Easter), Church feasts, mystery plays and *sotties,* agricultural festivals, and civil and social ceremonies. This is a broad list, and it is little wonder that he can find so much evidence of carnival in medieval culture if all of these things qualify. But in fact Bakhtin fails to specify the essential defining elements which consitute merriment. In practice, in Bakhtin's view, different types of carnival are not defined so much by similarity of form as by a shared evolutionary history and an identical role in class conflict.

All manifestations of carnival, according to Bakhtin, are the product of the lower classes or the folk in medieval culture and express limited but vital resistance to the social order that keeps them subjugated. His paradigm is thus based on a polarity between the solemn, oppressive upper classes and the merrymaking, rebellious lower classes. The cogency of Bakhtin's analysis depends on this dichotomy between "official," serious, formal culture and "unofficial," informal, often humorous, popular culture.

> All these forms of protocol and ritual based on laughter and consecrated by tradition . . . offered a completely different, nonofficial, extraecclesiastical and extrapolitical aspect of the world, of man, and of human relations; they built a second world and a second life outside officialdom. (Bakhtin, *Rabelais and His World,* 5–6)

In Bakhtin's view, the relegation of humor to the folk level was the result of a historical trend of class oppression. In remote antiquity, Bakhtin states, "preclass and prepolitical order," the serious and the comic were equally sacred (*Rabelais and His World,* 6). As the political structure of society evolved, the upper classes safeguarded the stability of the social order by putting strict limits on humor, which, Bakhtin implies, would otherwise foster irreverence and hence insubordination. As a result, humor and carnival were preserved only among the lowest and least powerful classes, who presented the least danger to the established order, and who were allowed to express levity only in strictly controlled ways.

Bakhtin thus equates seriousness with order and power, humor with disorder and subversion. To allow the oppressed classes to let off steam, those at the top of the hierarchy set aside times for licensed quasi subversion.

During the entire medieval period the Church and state were obliged to make concessions, large or small, to satisfy the marketplace. Throughout the year there were small scattered islands of time, strictly limited by the dates of feasts, when the world was permitted to emerge from the official routine but exclusively under the camouflage of laughter. (Bakhtin, *Rabelais and His World,* 90)

This structure can then be adduced to explain apparently anomalous combinations of official (ecclesiastical) and folk (humorous) culture, such as the medieval mystery plays: they represent an attempt to gather "the people" into the fold of ecclesiastical control by speaking to them in their own folk language.

This paradigm appears ill suited to Fools' Festivals, carnivalesque celebrations conducted by and for the clergy, an elite sector of society. Bakhtin overcomes this difficulty with the explanation that the lower clergy, excluded from positions of power or influence, fulfilled the role of the "common people" in the microcosm of the Church. In other words, Fools' Festivals shared so many of the characteristics of secular popular culture because they were the products of a corresponding irrepressible ecclesiastical popular culture.

The cornerstone of Bakhtin's polarity between official and unofficial culture is that humor was exclusive to the folk. But this contention is in blatant contradiction to the abundance of parody, satire, and humor in Latin, the language of the educated elite. Bakhtin's claim that such literature is the product of an oppressed cadre within the elite cannot withstand historical scrutiny. It is now known, for instance, that a number of the goliards, until recently thought to be the disaffected riffraff of the clergy, were among the prominent and influential members of the ecclesiastical establishment.[2]

Bakhtin's paradigm of the social position of humor is particularly ill founded with regard to medieval Latin parody. Like much literary humor, this was the work not only of the educated class but often of its most learned members. The point is so important that it is worth reiterating historical information on the authorship of Latin parody. Though most pieces were anonymous, some information can be gleaned about the authors of the texts merely by the character of the works themselves. They are unquestionably the products of a learned group of clerics, not only literate in Latin, but familiar with the Bible, and in many cases clearly students of biblical exegesis. Wide fields of reference, encompassing a range of Classical authors as well as the Church Fathers, show many authors to have been steeped in Latin learning. It should

---

2. Schüppert devotes considerable space to establishing the professions and social standing of a number of satirists and goliards in *Kirchenkritik,* 1–32.

also be noted that the scribes and redactors who contributed so much to the evolution of the tradition were among the best-educated of the clergy.

Not surprisingly, the names attached to parodies tend to belong to illustrious authors. This is not unambiguous evidence that these texts were chiefly composed by the great and famous. Parodies endowed with eminent origins were more likely to survive, and the possibility also exists that scribes assigned anonymous texts to famous authorities to increase their appeal. Nevertheless, it is noteworthy that a variety of eminent names are associated with a genre which modern thought holds in such disrepute. It is worth calling the roll of these authors and patrons once more. Predictably, it is the most didactic parodies that are most directly associated with august figures. Cyprian, presumed author of the *Cena Cypriani,* not only was a saint and martyr but was considered a father of the Church by later generations.The later rewritings of the *Cena* had no less eminent patronage. One of the most learned theologians of the early Middle Ages, Hrabanus Maurus, undertook a new version and dedicated it to Lothar II; the *Cena Azelini* was similarly dedicated to Henry III. The evidence for the *Cena Iohannis* is still more impressive: the poem was dedicated to Pope John VIII and performed at the imperial coronation of Charles the Bald. It was not just *Cena* texts that circulated in such august milieux. For example, the story of the inception of the sermon on Nemo assigns this text a background among the elite, the piece having been presented to Cardinal-deacon Caetani (later Pope Boniface VIII). Thus the texts originated not only among the learned, "official" classes but often among the highest ranks of those classes. These origins are a far cry from Bakhtin's folk milieu.

Bakhtin sees carnival as liberating: it represented the folk reclamation of part of the year to a vanished Utopian social structure, characterized by equality, freedom, and abundance. Although the official culture succeeded in containing carnival subversion and confining it to strictly limited periods, it was not able to abolish this folk rebellion altogether. Bakhtin's recognition of the Utopian qualities of carnival is illuminating, but his assertion that such merriment was tied to the Church calendar is not supported by the evidence. This view even runs contrary to Bakhtin's own definition of carnival, in which he specifies colorful oaths as one manifestation of the carnival spirit: these at least were independent of official celebrations. Similarly, each parody is a movable feast: unlike the Corpus Christi plays, most parodies were short enough and simple enough to have been everyday jokes, and there is no evidence that they were limited to specific occasions.

The assumption that humor was confined to certain periods apppointed by the Church leads Bakhtin to make claims unsubstantiated by historical evidence. For instance, on Hrabanus Maurus's *Cena nuptialis* Bakhtin states: "For Rabanus Maurus and his contemporaries the festive banquet justified such a playful handling of religious topics; at other times it would be considered sacrilege" (*Rabelais and His World,* 289). There is in fact no evidence that the *Cena nuptialis* was restricted to festive banquets. This conclusion is the result of a circular argument: because Bakhtin believes parodies were confined to feast days, he defines any time at which the *Cena Hrabani* was performed as a religious feast. At another point he qualifies this assertion, claiming only that "free laughter was related to feasts and to a certain extent limited by the time allotted to feast days" (89).

These suppositions spring from a conviction that merriment, as inherently subversive, had to be excluded from most aspects of medieval society; feast days were exceptional because they permitted indulgence in a proscribed state of mind. This paradigm, however, is based on a purely theoretical set of modern assumptions about humor. If we reversed our preconceptions and saw merriment as a common and unextraordinary component of medieval culture, feast days would represent not an indulgence of the forbidden but a celebration, evidence that the official powers favored this aspect of everyday life to such an extent that entire days were set aside for its observance. Bakhtin's failure to entertain this possibility is the result of an underlying political ideology which gives rise to a set of a priori assumptions. Since Bakhtin's time, critics have attempted to refine carnival theory to take greater account of the complicated dynamics of social reality.

Responses to Bakhtin's Theory of Carnival

One of the strengths of Bakhtin's approach is the position he accords medieval humor as an important component of the "unofficial" aspect of medieval culture. Bakhtin presents this in comparatively simple theoretical terms, seeing the relationship between the official and the nonofficial in terms of a dialectical model, which he designates dialogic.

The rise of semiotics and the study of symbolic orders has given critics a new theoretical vocabulary to describe the interaction of opposites in carnival. Terry Eagleton, for example, understands carnival not only as a ritual of subversion that calls the established hierarchy into question but as a deconstruction of the meaning that permits the establishment of any order. In a display of intellectual bravura presumably meant to echo the flamboyance of carnival, Eagleton describes this collapse of meaning.

. . . this liberation of the image into polyvalence has for Bakhtin the
name of carnival. In a riot of semiosis, carnival unhinges all transcenden-
tal signifiers and submits them to ridicule and relativism; by the "radical-
ism of humor" (Jean Paul), power structures are estranged through grotesque parody, "necessity" thrown into satirical question and objects
displaced or negated into their opposites. A ceaseless practice of travesty
and inversion (nose/phallus, face/buttocks, sacred/profane) rampages
throughout social life, deconstructing images, misreading texts and col-
lapsing binary oppositions into a mounting groundswell of ambiguity
into which all articulate discourse finally stutters and slides. Birth and
death, high and low, destruction and renewal are sent packing with their
tails in each other's mouths. Absolutely nothing escapes this great spasm
of satire: no signifier is too solemn to be blasphemously invaded, dis-
mantled and turned against itself. The grotesque is intrinsically double-
faced, an immense semiotic switchboard through which codes are read
backwards and messages scrambled into their antitheses.

Through this crude cackling of an ambivalently destructive and liber-
atory laughter emerges the shape of an equally negative and positive
phenomenon: utopia. Carnival is more than deconstruction: in rendering
existing power strucures alien and arbitrary, it releases the potential for a
golden age, a friendly world of "carnival truth" in which "man returns to
himself."[3]

Bakhtin believed that the folk celebration of carnival represented a last vestige
of the Utopian order, diminished but still preserved by the folk. Eagleton,
however, sees the yearning for a golden age thwarted by carnival's role as an
officially sanctioned pseudosubversion; carnival, in other words, ultimately
represents not disorder but the affirmation of order.

> Carnival, after all, is a *licensed* affair in every sense, a permissible
> rupture of hegemony, a contained popular blow-off as disturbing and
> relatively ineffectual as a revolutionary work of art. As Shakespeare's
> Olivia remarks, there is no slander in an allowed fool. (Eagleton, *Walter
> Benjamin,* 148)

Bakhtin's view of folk power is also contested by Umberto Eco, who
assigns the only real power to the official spheres that grant carnival license to

---

3. Terry Eagleton, *Walter Benjamin or Towards a Revolutionary Criticism* (London, 1981),
145–46.

operate. In Eco's view carnival and its literary counterpart, parody, always serve the interests of the ruling class, because any perversion of a model or norm ultimately acknowledges the preexistence of that norm.

> Thus the prerequisites of a "good" carnival are: (i) the law must be so pervasively and profoundly introjected as to be overwhelmingly present at the moment of its violation . . . (ii) the moment of carnivalization must be very short, and allowed only once a year (*semel in anno licet insanire*); an everlasting carnival does not work: an entire year of ritual observance is needed in order to make the transgression enjoyable. . . . In this sense, comedy and carnival are not instances of real transgressions: on the contrary, they represent paramount examples of law reinforcement. They remind us of the existence of the rule.[4]

Roger Sales agrees that carnival can affirm the established order.

> There were two reasons why the fizzy, dizzy carnival spirit did not necessarily undermine authority. First of all, it was licensed or sanctioned by the authorities themselves. They removed the stopper to stop the bottle being smashed altogether. The release of emotions and grievances made them easier to police in the long term. Second, although the world might appear to be turned upside down during the carnival season, the facts that Kings and Queens were chosen and crowned actually reaffirmed the *status quo*.[5]

Similar arguments are propounded by Michael Camille in his study of play in the margins of medieval art.[6]

The assumption that there can be no meaningful change in the power relations of different members of society without a complete dissolution of hierarchy is a legacy of the Marxist origins of carnival theory and contradicts the Christian doctrine of the millennium, when the temporal order will be overturned through an inversion of hierarchy. I return to this argument in my discussion of parodic inversion later in this chapter.

---

4. Umberto Eco, "The Frames of Comic 'Freedom,'" in *Carnival!*, ed. Thomas A. Sebeok and Marcia E. Erikson (Berlin, 1984), 1–9 (at 6). Eco does not cite the source of his Latin quotation.

5. Roger Sales, *English Literature in History 1780–1830: Pastoral and Politics* (London, 1983), 169.

6. Michael Camille, *Image on the Edge: The Margins of Medieval Art* (Cambridge, Mass., 1992).

Religious Humor as a Moral Force

Bakhtin and his followers interpreted carnival as a political force; other critics have seen medieval literary humor as a religious issue. The religious humor of the Middle Ages first came to the attention of modern scholars as it appeared in medieval drama, which almost without exception infuses religious legend with comedy. On the prevalence of the combination, Jarmila Veltrusky notes,

> apart from [the thirteenth-century *Le Garçon et l'aveugle*], the fragmentary English *Interludium de clerico et puella* and Adam de la Halle's *Jeu de la Feuillée* and *Jeu de Robin et Marion* virtually all the comic scenes recorded before the fifteenth century occur in plays of a more [or] less distinctly religious nature.[7]

It is noteworthy, too, that the plays which display only one of these elements are not religious plays without comic scenes but comic plays without religious scenes. According to our evidence, then, virtually all religious plays incorporated humor into their depiction of religious truth. Is this an accident of survival—an indication that the only comedy worth preserving was that with a redemptive religious aspect—or is it indicative of a wider relationship between humor and the practice of religion which has until now been most conspicuous in medieval drama?

To the modern mind, the humorous elements contained in religious drama are the most easily explicable type of medieval religious humor. The profanity of religious drama has been explained by recourse to the supposed vulgarity of the common people, the audience of the plays, who needed the sweetener of humor to make their religious medicine palatable. Even with this justification, however, many modern scholars have expressed great uneasiness about the seemliness of religious comedy and have attempted to excuse it by regarding it as an attempt to convey religious truth in covert ways.

A. P. Rossiter, in his study of early English drama, broke new ground in the analysis of religious humor by assigning it a part in the medieval ethos which also gave rise to Fools' Festivals.[8] Later critics sought a literary or didactic function in such humor. Carol Billman is hard-pressed to defend the glee with which the Roman soldiers carry out the Slaughter of the Innocents in religious

---

7. Jarmila F. Veltrusky, *A Sacred Farce from Medieval Bohemia: Mastickár*, Michigan Studies in the Humanities 6 (Ann Arbor, 1985), 285.

8. A. P. Rossiter, *English Drama from Early Times to the Elizabethans* (London, 1950).

drama, but she concludes by seeing it as a way of frightening the spectator
away from impiety.

> When he [the spectator] realized the irreverence of his fascination with
> the comic grotesque—and this would have been inevitable either during
> the serious moments of the mothers' lamentations or during the last quiet
> scene of Herod's death when noisy action and laughter exist only as
> haunting echoes—he would, I suggest, have been shocked by his be-
> haviour, which approached blasphemy, and thus both embarrassed and
> frightened into a stronger faith in the overriding Christian design.[9]

It is not clear here why the spectator would realize his laughter is irreverent. Is
the comedy not given implicit sanction by its presence in an orthodox religious
drama? If humor is truly blasphemous, thereby making a farce of the play,
would it not more likely have the effect of undercutting the mothers' sorrow in
the next scene? And would it not ultimately have the effect of weakening the
audience's distinction between acceptable and unacceptable irreverence? Billman's argument is special pleading, based not on an objective analysis of the
play but on an a priori conviction that humor in a religious context can easily
give rise to blasphemy.

The fullest exposition of the role of humor in religious literature appears in
V. A. Kolve's analysis of Corpus Christi drama, *The Play Called Corpus
Christi*.[10] Kolve initiated the true scholarly rehabilitation of religious humor,
collecting a number of medieval sources which defended the compatibility of
humor and religion and championed both the didactic and the recreational
benefits of entertainment. In particular he drew attention to the extent to which
humor was central to the moral complexion of the drama.

> Laughter was respectable in the Middle Ages partly because it could
> teach. Notwithstanding its value as entertainment, it seldom wholly ne-
> glected this other function, as even genres less obviously didactic than
> the cycle-plays can testify.[11]

The assertion that humor in the medieval period was primarily retailed in the
interests of Christian piety was a significant reversal of the prevailing view-

---

9. Carol Billman, "Grotesque Humor in Medieval Biblical Comedy," *American Benedictine
Review* 31 (1980): 406–17 (at 417).

10. V. A. Kolve, *The Play Called Corpus Christi* (Stanford, 1966), especially 124–44 (chap.
6, "Religious Laughter") and 145–74 (chap. 7, "The Invention of Comic Action").

11. Ibid., 129.

point. In support of the redeeming features of humor, Kolve observed that most of the medieval playwrights' expansions of biblical stories are humorous, and he illustrates this phenomemon with a discussion of two dramatic traditions founded on humorous extracanonical legends, the Noah plays and the Wakefield *Secunda Pastorum.*

Kolve has performed a valuable service in drawing attention to the plethora of unambiguously moral religious humor, but he does not question the assumption that subversion is latent in humor and can only be defused by unambiguously didactic aims. He goes to some lengths to dissociate Corpus Christi drama from less overtly moral religious festivities, and emphasizes the strictly reverent humor in the plays themselves. Although, as he notes, characters within the drama are often depicted jeering at sacred personages, they never escape without punishment. Moreover, the audience is invited to laugh only at the minor characters of Scripture, such as Joseph or Noah's wife, never at those central to Christianity, such as Mary or Christ himself. The Corpus Christi plays are in fact unusual in this regard, and their decorousness cannot be taken to mean that a more farcical presentation would necessarily constitute blasphemy. Veltrusky points out, for instance, that Continental drama assumes sufficient intimacy with religion to portray the holy characters, even Jesus, as buffoons, dolts, and ruffians.[12]

Carnival and Anthropological Studies of Inversion

The view that the structures which constitute religious humor are potentially disruptive finds parallels in other schools of critical thought. Theorists seeking to explore the ramifications of carnival have tried to associate it with basic structures of the mind, explaining the Utopian aspects of carnival according to the binary theory of cognition. This view holds that the basic mechanism of the mind's ability to analyze and classify lies in its ability to negate, to separate the objects of its thought into x and *not-x.* Carnival, a reversal of the established order, is *not-x,* a negation of the status quo. Since x and *not-x* cannot exist at the same time, it follows that the imposition of *not-x* is subversive of x. By this logic, inversion, then, is the structure of subversion.

To use an example pertinent to the medieval world, one very simple manifestation of binary classification is the *monde renversé,* a way of describing what is by means of depicting what is not.[13] This makes the *monde renversé* a

---

12. Veltrusky, *A Sacred Farce,* 297–304.
13. A broad outline of the history of the *monde renversé* has been undertaken by Curtius in

useful tool for social comment: the natural order can be emphasized by depicting a topsy-turvy world, and the imperfections of the world can be defined by constructing its opposite, a Utopia. The medieval topsy-turvy world is more familiar to modern scholars; it was, for instance, a popular theme for illustration in the margins of manuscripts.[14] But Utopia is also a *monde renversé,* a way of revealing imperfection by envisioning perfection. This is in fact Bakhtin's point about carnival: it is the ceremonial creation of a world, through the reversal of the established order, which reenacts a lost Utopia or anticipates a future one.

These theoretical views on the uses of duality and opposition have been a subject of inquiry on the practical level by scholars studying carnival and symbolic inversion in twentieth-century societies. Anthropologists have analyzed carnival/ritual rebellion in a variety of cultures and have arrived at no uniform equation: some studies have seen carnival as destabilizing and subversive, while others have found that it functions as a homeostatic mechanism in the service of the established order. One of the chief values of anthropological evidence, therefore, is its demonstration that there is no universal law of carnival, that at different times and in different societies carnival and symbolic inversion can serve a variety of functions.

Of most interest here are those studies which controvert Bakhtin's view that carnival is genuinely subversive and an exercise of political protest on the part of the oppressed.[15] Max Gluckman identified ritual rebellion as the guardian of the status quo in a number of East African tribal societies. In these cultures licensed protest coexists with an established power structure, but ritual rebellion does not serve as a pacifier that keeps potential revolution in check. Though such ceremonies defuse tension, the society is kept stable by other mechanisms which guarantee that ritual rebellion will remain benign. In societies with a secure power structure, then, these rituals serve a cathartic

---

European Literature, 94–98. Postmedieval images of the inverted world, much like those found in the margins of medieval manuscripts, are described and reproduced in David Kunzle, "World Upside Down: The Iconography of a European Broadsheet Type," in *The Reversible World: Symbolic Inversion in Art and Society,* ed. Barbara A. Babcock (Ithaca and London, 1978), 39–94; a succinct survey of the topic in psychological and anthropological thought has been undertaken by Barbara A. Babcock in her introduction to *The Reversible World,* 13–36. The theme in postmedieval English literature is discussed in Ian Donaldson, *The World Upside Down: Comedy from Jonson to Fielding* (Oxford, 1970).

14. A general selection of such illustrations is reproduced by L. M. C. Randall, *Images in the Margins of Gothic Manuscripts* (Berkeley and Los Angeles, 1966). A broader array of Renaissance examples appear as illustrations to Kunzle's "World Upside Down."

15. Studies of modern cultures in which carnival does embody genuine rebellion and serves as an agent of change are cited by Babcock in her introduction to *The Reversible World,* 23.

function, helping dissipate the stress of minor social discord. Gluckman explains:

> The acceptance of the established order as right and good, and even sacred, seems to allow unbridled excess, very rituals of rebellion, for the order itself keeps this rebellion within bounds. Hence to act the conflicts, whether directly or by inversion or in other symbolical form, emphasizes the social cohesion within which the conflicts exist. Every social system is a field of tension, full of ambivalence, of co-operation and contrasting struggle. This is true of relatively stationary—what I like to call *repetitive*—social systems as well as of systems which are changing and developing. In a repetitive system particular conflicts are settled not by alterations in the order of offices, but by changes in the persons occupying those offices.[16]

Later he again underlines the distinction between societies capable of harmless ritual rebellion and those for whom it may be subversive.

> . . . there is point to stressing that "ritual rebellion" can be enjoyed by tradition, as a social blessing, in repetitive social systems, but not in systems where revolution is possible. (Gluckman, "Rituals," 135)

Similar conclusions have emerged from Victor Turner's study of ritual role reversal across cultures, among them Ghana, village life in India, and the celebration of Halloween in the United States.[17] Like Gluckman, Turner sees role reversal as a ritual way of easing tensions between different social groups, and he defines such customs as important factors in *communitas,* the harmony of the entire group. Turner is most interested in role reversal and inversion as they appear in rites of passage, which serve as a means of freeing the subject from an old status and enabling him to assume a new. Of this transition stage Turner relates:

> It includes symbolic behaviour—especially symbols of reversal or inversion of things, relationships and processes secular—which represents the detachment of the ritual subjects (novices, candidates, neophtyes or "ini-

---

16. Max Gluckman, "Rituals of Rebellion in South-East Africa," in *Order and Rebellion in Tribal Africa* (London, 1963), 110–36 (at 127–28).

17. Victor Turner, "Humility and Hierarchy: The Liminality of Status Elevation and Reversal," in *The Ritual Process: Structure and Anti-Structure* (London, 1969), 166–203; and Turner, *From Ritual to Theatre: The Human Seriousness of Play* (New York, 1982).

tiands") from their previous social states. In the case of members of a society, it implies collectively moving from all that is socially and culturally involved in an agricultural season, or from a period of peace as against one of war, from plague to community health, from a previous socio-cultural state or condition, to a new state or condition, a new turn of the seasonal wheel.[18]

Turner also makes a significant observation often absent from studies of ritual reversal: that such inversion is enjoyable as well as socially rewarding to the performers.

> We have seen how . . . status reversal does not mean "anomie" but simply a new perspective from which to observe structure. Its topsy-turviness may even give a humorous warmth to this ritual viewpoint. If the liminality of life-crisis rites may be, perhaps audaciously, compared to tragedy—for both imply humbling, stripping, and pain—the liminality of status reversal may be compared to comedy, for both involve mockery and inversion, but not destruction, of structural rules and over-zealous adherents to them.[19]

A few historians have applied a similar rigorous cultural and contextual analysis to the study of carnival in past centuries.[20] Emmanuel Le Roy Ladurie's *Carnival in Romans* describes the structure of society and the cultural tensions which led to an uprising during a celebration of carnival in the French city of Romans in 1580.[21] Le Roy Ladurie sees the carnival form as a relic of the seasonal celebrations of an agrarian society, which became, in late sixteenth-century urban culture, an occasion for license and a breeding ground for class struggle. Satire and symbolic reversal were important components of the festival, but a detailed examination of the sources also reveals a perhaps unexpected plurality of contending groups and oppositions. Le Roy Ladurie discusses the role of carnival in this pluralistic social order.

---

18. Turner, *From Ritual to Theatre*, 24.

19. Turner, "Humility," 201.

20. See also Natalie Zemon Davis' "The Reasons of Misrule," in *Society and Culture in Early Modern France* (Cambridge, 1987), 97–123. Davis concludes that charivari in early modern urban culture in France served as a rite of passage and a way of letting off steam for unmarried young men.

21. Le Roy Ladurie's theory of carnival is outlined in *Carnival in Romans*, 283–99 (chap. 12, "The Winter Festival").

Carnival in Romans was never simply an opposition of old and young or rich and poor. Instead, as in Lyons or Italy, it represented a sort of comprehensive and poetic description of society, neighbourhoods, professions, age groups, the young, males, and so forth. Embracing so many elements made Carnival particularly apt as an instrument of *social change,* which was slow but undeniable in sixteenth-century towns successively shaken by the Renaissance, the Reformation, the Counter-Reformation. In other words Carnival was not merely a satirical and *purely temporary* reversal of the dual social order, finally intended to justify the status quo in an "objectively" conservative manner. It would be more accurate to say it was a satirical, lyrical, epic-learning experience for highly diversified groups. It was a way to action, perhaps modifying the society as a whole in the direction of social change and *possible progress.* (Le Roy Ladurie, *Carnival in Romans* 292), emphasis in original)

These historical and anthropological studies illuminate the variety of functions carnival can fulfill in society. Another category of scholarship seeks to describe similar phenomena in terms of individual or psychological motivation.

Play and the Psychological Health of the Individual

As early as Malinowski, students of humankind recognized that some social phenomena serve to maintain the well-being of the individual rather than that of the group. The role of humor, carnival, or play has since been analyzed from this perspective, and scholars of the field have sought to explain the universality of play and the motivation for it in the life of the individual.

Johan Huizinga's *Homo Ludens* was among the earliest attempts to rehabilitate play as an object of study.[22] Huizinga did not attempt to explore the function of play in the sphere in which it is usually located, the development of the child; instead he took a wider view, recognizing as a form of play the practices and customs of adult society which have no clear pragmatic or utilitarian goals. He noted that such activities shared a number of other characteristics, being confined to specific time and place, being performed according to rules, encouraging group cohesion, and very often being considered "not

---

22. Johan Huizinga, *Homo Ludens: A Study of the Play-Element in Culture,* trans. R. F. C. Hull (London, 1949).

real," or as participating in an alternative reality in some sense.[23] These characteristics are often shared with the sacred, as Huizinga noted, classifying the two as congruent expressions. Huizinga was among the first to recognize that play was not chiefly the property of children, and hence indicative of immaturity, but was one of the defining characteristics of the human being. Aristotle's definition of man as *risus capax* was hence carried into the modern age with Huizinga's *homo ludens*.

Subsequently Eugen Fink sought to analyze the psychological motivation behind the universal practice of play.

Play is an essential element of man's ontological makeup, a basic existential phenomenon—not the only such phenomenon, to be sure, but still a clearly identifiable and autonomous one that cannot be explained as deriving from other existential phenomena. . . . Play is not for the sake of a "final goal." . . . It is frequently said that play is "purposeless" or "undirected" activity. This is not the case. Considered as a whole it is purposive and each individual phase of play action has its own specific purpose, which is an integral part of the whole. But the *immanent* purpose of play is not subordinate to the ultimate purpose served by all other human activity. Play has only internal purpose, unrelated to anything external to itself. . . . In the autonomy of play action there appears a possibility of human timelessness in time. Time is then experienced, not as a precipitate rush of successive moments, but rather as the one full moment that is, so to speak, a glimpse of eternity.[24]

Fink's play, then, is psychological carnival, a brief experience of a timeless Utopia. We shall see that a similar timelessness is deliberately fostered by medieval examples of play.

Fink saw this psychological Utopia as an end in itself rather than as a response to external tensions. By contrast, Peter Stallybrass and Allon White see certain kinds of neurosis in the individual as the result of a failure to participate in liberating carnival rituals. In their study of the structures of personal rebellion, *The Politics and Poetics of Transgression,* they understand the symptoms of hysteria as the struggles of the psyche to enact the purging

---

23. The player's willingness and ability to signal the suspension of normal rules and social signals has been studied and discussed by Gregory Bateson, "A Theory of Play and Fantasy," in *Steps to an Ecology of Mind* (London, 1972), 177–93.

24. Eugen Fink, "The Oasis of Happiness: Toward an Ontology of Play," *Yale French Studies* 41 (1968): 19–29 (at 19, 21). This article is a translation of selections from Fink's book *Oase des Glücks: Gedanken zu einer Ontologie des Spiels* (Freiburg and Munich, 1957).

rituals of carnival, an opportunity which is no longer publicly available in the modern age.

> In the *Studies on Hysteria* many of the images and symbols which were once the focus of various pleasures in European carnival have become transformed into the morbid symptoms of private terror. Again and again these patients suffer acute attacks of disgust, literally vomiting out horrors and obsessions which look surprisingly like the rotted residue of traditional carnival practices. At the same time the patients seem to be reaching out, in their highly stylised gestures and discourses, towards a repertoire of carnival material as both expression and support. They attempt to mediate their terrors by enacting private, made-up carnivals. In the absence of social forms they attempt to produce their own by pastiche and parody in an effort to embody semiotically their distress.[25]

This analysis interprets carnival as exclusively purgative: there is no suggestion of celebration or entertainment. Where Fink saw play as the positive creation of happiness, Stallybrass and White see "personal carnival" as an escape from intolerable pressures.

Laura Kendrick uses similar theories in her attempt to analyze Chaucer's humor as psychological carnival.[26] This humor, she maintains, assures the smooth functioning of the psyche (whether that of Chaucer, of his medieval audience, or of modern readers) and hence the maintenance of social equilibrium in the face of hierarchical oppression. She interprets this inescapable oppression in Freudian terms, seeing the reader as the symbolic child and the agents of oppression as fathers who must be symbolically dethroned.

> . . . in the late Middle Ages, on festive occasions associated with seasonal change, and especially in the days leading up to and following the New Year, "youth" rebelled against the restrictions and censorship of age and authority and committed deliberately churlish, infantile, goliardic acts of interpretative parody or burlesque performance that, in effect, *desublimated the sacred texts and rites, unmasked the euphemisms, removed the verbal loincloths of exegesis, and exposed the revitalizing energy of infantile, egocentric desire.* (emphasis in original)[27]

---

25. Peter Stallybrass and Allon White, *The Politics and Poetics of Transgression* (London, 1986), 174.

26. Laura Kendrick, *Chaucerian Play: Comedy and Control in the* Canterbury Tales (Berkeley, 1988).

27. Ibid., 19.

Throughout her study Kendrick mechanically equates parody with subversion and finds inversion vital to this process.

> The logic—the medieval mentality—behind the structure of Chaucer's *Canterbury Tales* is a Carnivalesque one: the best way to stabilize a structure at dangerous points of necessary transition or change is to exteriorize tension at these points by destabilizing the structure symbolically in controlled and controlling play. . . . By putting the "bottom" symbolically "on top," by inverting the order of things, externalizing tension in playful contests contained within a limited field (such as the circular or rectangular world of the column capital), medieval builders and "makers" intended to relax temporarily the tension of subordination (the column's subordination to its load, the monks' rigid discipline) at pressure points or points of structural transition.[28]

Kendrick sees ritual destabilization in "many a medieval verbal edifice," even claiming that manuscript collections of lengthy serious works of literature are significantly strewn with shorter comic poems (*Chaucerian Play,* 158). Reduced to its essence, Kendrick's argument frames in goliardic, destabilizing, carnivalesque, psychological terms what has usually been known as comic relief.

Psychological explanations of play or carnival, then, frequently interpret these phenomena as a private form of subversion which helps to preserve the emotional health of the individual. Huizinga and Fink are unusual in defining play as intrinsically satisfying, without regard to any larger emotional or social benefit. Kendrick, by contrast, sees the humor of the *Canterbury Tales* as evidence that medieval individuals shared with modern individuals the need to gain control of their psychological world through subversive carnival.

Humor as Grotesque

Both literary and psychological investigations of medieval religious humor represent attempts to elucidate the aspect of medieval culture that is most alien from our own, the association of levity or flippancy with ideas we regard as inherently solemn, an association which modern society finds improper or profane. We have seen critics' efforts to resolve this difficulty by references to literary, anthropological, or psychological models of equilibrium, models which maintain that what looked like irreverence was actually a subtle way of temporarily destabilizing the social structure for ultimately utilitarian ends.

---

28. Ibid., 156–57.

Others have attempted to explain the apparent conundrum of the abundance of medieval religious humor by locating in medieval culture a completely alien *mentalité* which they term the grotesque.

The term *grotesque* derives from a word used to describe a certain school of sculpture and painting; it subsequently came to denote any incongruous constellation of high and low styles, particularly one which included an element of the repugnant. The view that this amalgamation of high and low, or of the sublime and the ridiculous, was one of the salient characteristics of medieval culture has informed the works of many scholars of the literature and culture of the Middle Ages—both those writing specifically about the phenomenon of the grotesque and those describing literature and humor of the period generally.[29]

Most recently Aron Gurevich has challenged Bakhtin's view of humor (manifested in carnival) as the defining characteristic of medieval folk culture, stating that the grotesque is a more accurate description of medieval attitudes.[30] Gurevich does not dispute Bakhtin's observations of the inversion and polarity inherent in medieval culture but attributes them to an inherently peculiar worldview.

> The exceptional character of this culture lies in the strange combination of opposite poles: heaven and earth, spirit and body, gloom and humor, life and death. Holiness can be seen as a fusion of lofty piety and primitive magic, of extreme self-denial and a pride in being the elect, of wordly detachment and greed, of mercy and cruelty. . . . Learning is glorified and ignoramuses are treated with scorn, and at the same time foolishness, poverty of spirit, even madness, are reckoned the surest way to salvation. Life and death, extreme opposites in any world-view, are reversible, and the border between them is penetrable: the dead return to the living, and people temporarily dead may visit the Other World for a while. . . .

These and other strange paradoxes in medieval Latin works are not marginal features but belong to the foundation of the culture that generated them. I have collected this material to demonstrate that paradox-

---

29. Important studies of the medieval grotesque include Thomas Wright, *A History of Caricature and the Grotesque* (London, 1875); Wolfgang Kayser, *The Grotesque in Art and Literature,* trans. Ulrich Weisstein (Bloomington, Ind., 1963); and Huizinga, *Waning of the Middle Ages,* 152–71 and passim. A cogent and useful study of the grotesque, with a good general critique of other treatments, is Neil Rhodes, *Elizabethan Grotesque* (London, 1980).

30. Aron Gurevich, *Medieval Popular Culture: Problems of Belief and Perception,* trans. János M. Bak and Paul A. Hollingsworth, Cambridge Studies in Oral and Literate Culture 14 (Cambridge, 1988), esp. 176–210 (chap. 6, "'High' and 'Low': The Medieval Grotesque").

icality, strangeness and contradiction were integral organic features of
the medieval mind. (Gurevich, *Medieval Popular Culture,* 135)

For Gurevich, the grotesque is epitomized in humanity's experience of religion, in which the elevated spirit of the divine comes into contact with the
base and corrupt nature of mankind. Medieval Latin religious parody would
seem to be the ideal incarnation of this combination; curiously, Gurevich
deliberately excludes it from his study on the grounds that humor is not the sole
manifestation of this polarity.

> Medieval grotesque is not an artistic device and not the fruit of the
> cultivated intention of the author. It is rather the norm for viewing the
> world. I exclude from consideration here explicit satire and parody. . . .
> Bakhtin indicates the enormous significance of grotesque in culture out-
> side the church, in carnival and farce, but he reduced it to the principle of
> laughter and comedy. By contrast, my material suggests the hypothesis
> that the grotesque was a style of medieval man's thinking in general,
> embracing the entire culture, beginning from the lower, folkloric level
> and continuing up to the level of official church culture. (Gurevich,
> *Medieval Popular Culture,* 208)

Unfortunately, Gurevich's discussion of the polarities of medieval culture is
undermined by his failure to see that his polarities of heaven/spirit/gloom
versus earth/body/humor are culture-specific rather than absolute. His labels of
"paradoxicality, strangeness and contradiction" are based on the assumptions
of the modern world. Medieval culture clearly considered many combinations
and juxtapositions unexceptional that we now think extraordinary. To term
these facts "strange," however, is to imply a moral hierarchy in which modern
values supersede the inferior and illogical views of medieval culture—a judgment that harkens back to characterizations of the Middle Ages as "childish."
The term *grotesque* may serve a useful function as a description of certain
constellations of phenomena, but it cannot serve as an explanation for them. To
use it as such is merely to reify an a priori category that inhers not in medieval
culture but in the perceptions of the modern scholar.

Inversion and Subversion in Religious Humor

Implicit in the interpretation of Gurevich, as in the arguments of most critics of
medieval humor, is an assumption about the social role of humor that should be

stated explicitly. The overwhelming critical attitude toward humor/carnival/ play is the idea that humor fosters irreverence and thus subversion and danger. In the secular world this danger is social revolution and the overthrow of hierarchies; in the ecclesiastical world its religious equivalent, blasphemy and godlessness.

The assumption that humor must be subversive and hence inimical to religion is not consonant with the evidence provided by medieval Latin parody. As scholars such as Kolve point out, humor clearly can be a moral force in medieval religious drama, and this capacity for moral value is also visible in religious parodies such as the *Cena Cypriani*. But rather than merely adducing examples which contradict conventional modern views about religious parody, it may be more useful to investigate the structure of the texts themselves. The inversion in religious humor has led many critics to relate it to the wider role of inversion in culture and in cognition. As this inversion is situated in religious humor, it is also vital to examine the role of inversion in religion and, finally, to explore the range of possible motivations for inversion and for humor generally.

Inversion and the substitution of one register for another are the foundations of medieval religious parody. Medieval parodic humor often practices comedy of debasement: it substitutes the literal for the allegorical, the physical for the spiritual, and the concrete for the abstract. This frequently takes the form of the literal-minded visualization of allegory or of spiritual metaphor. One of the most common images exploited in this way is that of feasting or eating. In the Bible eating serves as a metaphor for God's generosity and for the concepts of community and sharing. To envisage the exact details of such feasts, however, was to make the image vividly corporeal and hence laughable, a device parodists used in the many versions of the *Cena Cypriani,* in nonsense-centos, and in a number of other texts. Food was the *locus classicus* for comedy of debasement, and parodists were not alone in using kitchen humor. The same explicit association of inversion and a misplaced emphasis on food was used, for instance, by the author of the Old French *Aucassin et Nicolette,* in which the soldiers of the inverted world use cheeses and rotten apples as weapons, in the Old Irish *Aislinge Meic Conglinne,* in which the characters of the glutton kingdom row with bacon oars over a sea of cream, and in the Provençal and English stories of the food-glutted Land of Cockaigne.[31]

---

31. Mario Roques, ed., *Aucassin et Nicolette: Chantefable du XIIIe siècle,* 2d ed., Classiques français du moyen âge (Paris, 1980); Kuno Meyer, ed., *Aislinge Meic Conglinne* (London, 1892); on the Land of Cockaigne see J. Delumeau, *Mort de pays de Cocagne* (Paris, 1976). For an extensive bibliography of the *monde renversé* in art see O. Odenius, "Mundus Inversus," *Arv* 10

Other parodies substitute a base world and base values for the spiritual world and its values: this is the conceit of the drinkers' Masses, with their substitution of physical inebriation for spiritual elation. The mock litany *In nomine infinite miserie* combines the two forms of debasement, substituting tavern food for spiritual sustenance. The puns which are a staple of such parodies perform the same process in miniature, substituting words of low spiritual content for those of high—*potemus* for *oremus* and *Decius* for *Deus*. The inverted world of the Money-Gospel is another such substitution.

Religious parody might well be seen, then, as the epitome of medieval inversion. According to most critical models of inversion, these parodies must therefore be subversive or destabilizing, whether permanently or temporarily. Before accepting this model, however, we should examine the role of inversion in other aspects of medieval culture.

The religious archetype of inversion was the Bible, which expresses the dissimilarity between the temporal world and the heavenly kingdom by describing each as an inversion of the other. The medieval Church enjoined the faithful to anticipate and emulate this inversion on certain festivals. Jacques Heers notes that this was the original impetus of Fools' Festivals, initially a celebration of Christ's infancy, subsequently generalized first to the exaltation of children and then further to that of all the humble and meek.[32] This is an inversion of hierarchy after the pattern of Scripture, conforming with the beatitudes and Christ's statement that the last shall be first. As such it is not, in motivation, a subversion of the earthly order but a fulfillment of the divine.

This use of merriment might be called a millenarianism of laughter, and there is significant support for this doctrine in medieval theology. The Bible itself expressed different sentiments in different contexts. Scripture generally condemned temporal laughter but condoned spiritual joy and even earthly merriment as a prefiguration of spiritual felicity. Delight was an image of the spiritual joy that awaited the chosen in heaven.

> Ait illi dominus eius: "Euge, bone serve et fidelis, quia super pauca fuisti fidelis, super multa te constituam. Intra in gaudium domini tui." (Mt 25.21)

> [His lord said to him: "Well done, good and faithful servant: because thou hast been faithful over a few things, I will place thee over many things. Enter thou into the joy of the lord."]

(1954): 142–70.

32. Heers, *Fêtes des fous*, 136–41.

Amen, amen, dico vobis, quia plorabitis et flebitis vos, mundus autem gaudebit; vos autem contristabimini, sed tristitia vestra vertetur in gaudium. (Jo 16.20)

[Amen, amen I say to you, that you shall lament and weep, but the world shall rejoice; and you shall be made sorrowful, but your sorrow shall be turned into joy.]

Theologians agreed in identifying this as *gaudium spirituale,* the joy appropriate to the world to come. Gregory the Great describes millenarian laughter in his commentary on Job 8.21, "Donec impleatur risu os tuum et labia tua iubilo" [He will yet fill your mouth with laughter, and your lips with shouting].

Sanctorum risus post luctum. Jubilum. Os quippe justorum tunc risu replebitur, cum eorum corda, finitis peregrinationis fletibus, aeternae laetitiae exsultatione satiabuntur. De hoc risu discipulis Veritas dicit: *Mundus gaudebit, vos autem contristabimini; sed tristitia vestra vertetur in gaudium* [Jo 16.20]. Et rursum: *Videbo vos, et gaudebit cor vestrum, et gaudium vestrum nemo auferet a vobis* [Jn 16.22]. De hoc risu sanctae Ecclesiae Salomon ait: *Ridebit in die novissimo* [Prv 31.25].[33]

[*The laughter of the saints after the struggle. A shout of joy.* Certainly the mouths of the just will be filled with laughter when their hearts, the sorrow of the pilgrimage over, are suffused with the exultation of eternal joy. Of this laughter Truth says to the disciples: *The world shall rejoice, and you shall lament; but your sorrow shall be turned into joy.* And again: *I will see you again, and your heart shall rejoice, and your joy no man shall take from you.* Of this laughter Solomon says of the holy Church: *She will laugh in the times to come.*]

The theme likewise appears in Jerome's discussion of Zechariah 8.5, "Et plateae civitatis conplebuntur infantibus et puellis ludentibus in plateis eius" [And the streets of the city shall be filled with boys and girls playing in its streets].

Plateae quoque civitatis impleantur pueris puellisque ludentibus. Hoc autem fieri solet, quando securitas et profunda pax urbium est, ut gaud-

---

33. Gregory the Great, *Sancti Gregorii Magni Romani Pontificis Moralium Libri sive Expositio in librum b. Job,* 8.52, in Migne, *PL* 75: cols. 510–1162 (at col. 855).

ium civitatum, lusibus et choreis aetas lasciva concelebret. . . . Juxta quod scriptum est: *Exsultaverunt et laetatae sunt filiae Judae in omnibus judiciis tuis, Domine* [Ps 96.8]. Quae cum audierint ab Apostolo: *Gaudete, iterum dico gaudete* [Phil 4.4], mentis laetitiam gestu corporis indicabunt, et tripudiante saltatu, dicent cum David: *Saltabo et ludam in conspectu Domini* [2 Sm 6.22, Vetus Latina].[34]

[Let the streets of the city, also, be filled with boys and girls playing. This occurs when the city enjoys security and profound peace, so that the playful celebrate together the joy of the city with play and dancing. According to which it is written: *And the daughters of Judah rejoiced because of thy judgments, O Lord.* When they hear from the Apostle, *Rejoice in the Lord, again, I say, rejoice,* they shall reveal the joy of their spirits in bodily motion and, dancing, they shall say with David: *I will leap and play before the face of the Lord.*]

Other forms of religious literature reflect the same point of view. In the third-century *Passio sanctarum Perpetuae et Felicitatis,* Perpetua, imprisoned for her faith, has a vision of heaven in which she approaches the throne of God. The vision is described by Saturus, her catechist, in a way that demonstrates that the joy of the blessed on earth is a foretoken of the joy of heaven.

Et introeuntes cum admiratione stetimus ante thronum, et quattuor angeli sublevaverunt nos. . . . Et dixerunt nobis seniores: "Ite et ludite." Et dixi Perpetuae: "Habes quod vis." Et dixit mihi: "Deo gratias, ut, quomodo in carne hilaris fui, hilarior sim et hic modo."[35]

[And entering, we stood before the throne in wonder, and four angels raised us up. . . . And the elders said to us: "Go and play." And I said to Perpetua: "You have what you wish." And she said to me: "Thanks be to God that, as I was merry in the flesh, now I am even merrier here."]

The doctrine is found in a number of other medieval sources from all periods.[36] In the thirteenth-century vita of St. Vincent found in the *South English Legend-*

---

34. Jerome, *Comentariorum in Zachariam Prophetam ad exsuperium Tolosanum episcopum libri duo,* 8, in Migne, *PL* 25: cols. 1415–1542 (at cols. 1465–66).

35. C. I. M. I. van Beek, ed., *Passio Sanctarum Perpetuae et Felicitatis,* Florilegium Patristicum tam Veteris quam Medii Aevi Auctores Complectens 43 (Bonn, 1938), 42.

36. A number of examples are cited in Hugo Rahner, *Man at Play,* trans. Brian Battershaw and Edward Quinn (London, 1965).

ary, the saint laughs as he is tortured, his laughter signaling his disdain for earthly trials and his faith in the joys of the kingdom to come.[37] In the fifteenth century it appears in the Middle English didactic dialogue *Dives and Pauper.*

> PAUPER. Salomon seyth: Spes que differtur affligit animam, Prouer. xiii [12], the hope, the desyr & the longynge that is delayyd tormentyth the soule, for the mor that man or woman longyth aftir a thing the mor is his dishese til he hat his disyr & his longynge. But now is it so that the rest & the merthe & the ese & the welfare that God hat ordeynyd in the halyday is tokene of endeles reste, ioye & merthe & welfare in heuene blisse that we hopyn to han withoutyn ende, for there men shul halwyn withoutyn ende from alle maner trauayle & fro thout & care. And therfor, as Y seyde first, God wil that we thinken in the halyday of that reste, ioye and blysse that the halyday betokenyth and han it in thout, in desyr & in longynge & hope to come therto . . .[38]

Conventional critical models of inversion are founded on the image of official, "serious" society on a high register: the inverted world then reflects that image downward, transposing it to a low and degrading register. But scriptural inversion operates to elevate the earthly world by giving it a view of the perfect world to come. The present world is already in a low register: scriptural inversion cannot degrade it further but reflects it upward, turning men's thoughts away from the earthly city to the City of God. This is the effect of such inversions as those brought about by the Money-Gospel. It is not the satirist but the earthly world which substitutes money for God. The Money-Gospel demonstrates that the temporal world, with its perversion of divine order, is already the debased half of the dichotomy between spiritual and worldly: it exposes earthly weaknesses by holding them up to the pattern of the spiritual. The same equation is true of liturgical parody; here the authors implicate themselves in the sin as well.

The traditional uneasiness about humor has stemmed from the fact that it diminishes the figurative distance between those of low standing and those of

---

37. The text is edited in *The South English Legendary,* ed. Charlotte D'Evelyn and Anna J. Mill, Early English Text Society 235 (London, 1956), 25–31. The comic aspects of the text are discussed in Gregory M. Sadlek, "Laughter, Game, and Ambiguous Comedy in the *South English Legendary,*" *Studia Neophilologica* 64 (1991): 45–54. Sadlek sees St. Vincent's behavior as contributing to the story's entertainment value rather than as a foretaste of the joys of heaven.

38. *Dives and Pauper,* possibly the work of a Franciscan, was written between 1405 and 1410. It is edited in *Dives and Pauper,* ed. Priscilla Heath Barnum, 2 parts, Early English Text Society 275 and 280 (Oxford, 1976 and 1980); the quotation is found in part 1, III. xvii (pp. 294–95).

higher; to laugh at God is to relax one's fear of him. Unless accompanied by reverence and humility, this lessened distance may lead to defiance or blasphemy; yet not every instance of familiarity with God led to dangerous subversion. Humor is also a mark of intimacy, and in the willingness to play with sacred institutions, we see an ease with religion, a levity born of security. In this spirit the followers of St. Francis called themselves the *ioculatores dei* and *mundi moriones*. To play the fool for God is to acknowledge man's true place in the universe, to relax the pretense, born of excessive pride, that postlapsarian man can escape the follies and imperfections inherent in his earthly nature. Scriptural inversion makes it clear that the rejection of earthly stature and self-importance is vital to salvation.

> "Amen, dico vobis, quisque non receperit regnum Dei velut parvulus non intrabit in illud." (Mc 10.15)

> [Amen, I say to you, whosoever shall not receive the kingdom of God as one of these little ones shall not enter into it.]

> . . . respondens Iesus dixit: "Confiteor tibi, Pater Domine caeli et terrae, quia abscondisti haec a sapientibus et prudentibus, et revelasti ea parvulis." (Mt 11.25)

> [. . . Jesus answered and said: "I confess to thee, O Father, Lord of heaven and earth, because thou hast hid these things from the wise and prudent, and hast revealed them to little ones."]

In adopting this spirit of play, medieval people were not taking the role of children in the psychological or anthropological development of humankind but in the sight of the heavenly Father. In creating the *monde renversé* of parody and carnival, they situated themselves in the lower register, corresponding to their relation to God.

The sense of detachment inherent in laughter makes it an important medium for the elevation of the spirit. As Hazlitt says, "We laugh at what only disappoints our expectations in trifles."[39] We are able to regard the struggles of the temporal world as trifles only if we cultivate a sense of detachment from earthly matters—this is the laughter of detachment finally achieved by

---

39. William Hazlitt, "On Wit and Humour," in *Lectures on the English Comic Writers and Fugitive Writings,* with introductions by Arthur Johnston (1819; reprint, London and New York, 1963), 5–30 (at 5).

Chaucer's Troilus as he rises beyond the sphere of earth. Religious humor is a way of experiencing and cultivating this disengagement. In the mystery plays we, the audience, are spatially separated from the playing area which denotes "earth"; the sequence of biblical stories enacted before us creates the illusion of timelessness, and we are able to acquire an overview of history. From such a perspective the unfolding of the Christian plan is a grand Comedy, and this allows us to appreciate the miniature comedies enacted by the players. We are temporarily enabled to share God's perspective on evil and earthly tribulation. It is as if we are situated at the end of time, and so the laughter of the heavenly kingdom is available to us.

The inversion central to so much religious parody also fosters this perspective. The contrast between heaven and earth is highlighted by depicting the two as literal opposites: when the temporal order is defined as *not-x,* the heavenly kingdom, *x,* is brought to mind. Inversion also helps us make the transition between immersion in the temporal world and anticipation of the next. Victor Turner has shown that inversion is central to rites of transition, helping to divorce the subject from an old status and ready him or her for the new. Defining the world as *not-x* increases our detachment from it and focuses our attention on the world to come. Merriment through inversion, then, serves as a symbolic rite of passage from an earthly to a heavenly perspective and antici-pates the passage from one to the other at the end of time, when laughter will truly be appropriate.

These theological justifications did not mean that carousal of the clergy was intended as a spiritual exercise. The human mind simply has an appetite for humor, and medieval theories of recreation, outlined by Glending Olson, sup-plied the justification, rather than the motivation, for play.[40] The millenarian aspects of laughter assured that merriment involving the exaltation of the lowly and anticipated eschatological inversion (Fools' Festivals, the *risus paschalis,* religious parody) could be sanctioned by the Church.

Recent scholarship has done much to elucidate both the didactic role of medieval religious humor and the theories with which medieval commentators often defended recreation, but the systematic examination of medieval moral and theological literature has also produced a wealth of evidence that laughter and humor were frequently censured by "official" culture.[41] The sheer abun-

---

40. Glending Olson, *Literature as Recreation in the Later Middle Ages* (Ithaca, 1982).

41. For an exhaustive study of medieval official attitudes toward humor see Joachim Suchomski, *"Delectatio" und "Utilitas": Ein Beitrag zum Verständnis mittelalterlicher komischer Literatur,* Bibliotheca Germanica 18 (Bern, 1975). Suchomski finds pervasive, though not univer-sal, condemnation of humor on the part of religious authorities. Similar conclusions for monastic

dance of clerical levity, however, suggests that the right hand often disregarded what the left hand was doing.[42] To resolve these contradictions, thoughtful clerics often attempted to distinguish between proper and improper laughter, either employing the traditional distinctions between the two or devising their own. One example is that of Burchardus, a twelfth-century abbot of Bellevaux and author of the extraordinary *Apologia de barbis* (In defense of beards), a lighthearted yet purposeful romp through the biblical literature on beards.[43] Burchardus makes a distinction between the laughter of wisdom, which delights in the works of the Lord, and the laughter of foolishness, which ridicules creation.

> . . . alii rident cum iocunditate ad laudem et honorem et gloriam sapien-
> tiae, alii rident cum iocositate ad incrementum et propalationem stul-
> ticiae: iocundantur sapientes in risu et non irrident, stulti iocantur in risu
> et derident. Risit Sara de ludo sapientiae cum natura, cum sterilitati
> fecunditas promittebatur, sed Sara risit cum iocunditate et risum genuit
> iocunditatis filium, videlicet Ysaac, pro risu matris sic appellatum et
> interpretatum *risum* [Gn 18.12, 21.6]. Riserunt pueri stulti de calvitio
> Helisei et deriserunt calvum, dicentes: *Ascende, calve, ascende, calve!*
> Sed quia deriserunt opus naturae et operationem et ludum sapientiae, a
> duobus ursis strangulati sunt quotquot fuerunt qui calvum deriserunt [4
> Rg 2.24]. (*Apologia* 3.179–90 [p. 180 Huygens])

> [. . . some laugh with delight at the excellence and honor and glory of
> wisdom; others laugh with silliness at the growth and hawking of
> foolishness. The wise are made merry by laughter and do not jeer; the

---

culture have been reached by I. M. Resnick in " 'Risus Monasticus': Laughter and Medieval Monastic Culture," *Revue Bénédictine* 97 (1987): 90–100. A potpourri of opinions has been assembled by Curtius, *European Literature,* "Jest and Earnest in Medieval Literature," 417–35, esp. section 2, "The Church and Laughter," 420–22. The recreative and redemptive importance of play in medieval thought is discussed by Hugo Rahner, with a number of interesting quotations in support of his thesis, in *Man at Play.* The cultivation of devotion through the affective aspects of humor, particularly as this doctrine appears in the writings of Bernard of Clairvaux, is discussed, with references to primary and secondary literature, in Jean Leclerq, *The Love of Learning and the Desire for God: A Study of Monastic Culture,* trans. Catharine Misrahi (New York, 1982), 136–37 ("Monastic Humor").

42. Humor particularly found its way into sermons: examples and analysis are provided in Wenzel, "Joyous Art of Preaching"; and in Jeannine Horowitz and Sophia Menache, *L'humour en chaire: Le rire dans l'Église médiévale,* Histoire et Société 28 (Geneva, 1994).

43. Burchard of Bellevaux, *Apologia de barbis,* in *Apologiae Duae,* ed. R. B. C. Huygens, with an introduction by Giles Constable, Corpus Christianorum, Continuatio Mediaeualis 62 (Turnhout, 1985).

foolish are made silly by laughter and indulge in ridicule. Sarah laughed from the playing of wisdom with nature, when she, a sterile woman, received the promise of fertility. But Sarah laughed with delight and gave birth to laughter, the offspring of delight, that is, Isaac, which means "laughter," named thus from the laughter of his mother. The foolish boys laughed at the baldness of Elijah and ridiculed the bald man, saying: "Go up, you baldhead! Go up, you baldhead!" But because they mocked the work of nature and the working and merriment of wisdom, they were strangled by two bears, one bear for each of them who had ridiculed the bald man.]

Later Burchardus cites an example of divine inversion which provokes laughter.

Cum admiratione et iocunditate, non cum iocosa derisione ridendum est. In lucta Iacob cum angelo sapientia ludi sui spectaculum mirabile dedit ad ridendum, quia victus incolumis discessit et victor claudus factus est: cum auditis haec, nonne ridetis? Accepisse Iacob cum benedictione claudicationem de tali ludo sapientiae nonne ridetis? (*Apologia* III.1146–50 [p. 210 Huygens])

[It is fitting to laugh out of wonder and delight, not with joking derision. In the combat between Jacob and the angel, wisdom made his sport a wonderful spectacle, worthy of laughter, for the conquered one departed uninjured and the victor was made lame. When you hear these things, do you not laugh? Do you not laugh at Jacob, inflicted with lameness as a blessing, at such playfulness on the part of wisdom?]

Much of what was written about laughter in the Middle Ages springs from the pens of theologians whose experience of humorous literature cannot be determined. Burchardus, by contrast, is one of few clerics who both composed humor and discussed the nature of levity. The *Apologia* itself is full of drolleries—one chapter, for instance, is entitled "De differentia forcipis et rasorii dupliciter assignata sensu morali" (On the difference between the tweezers and the razor doubly taken in the moral sense)—and there is extensive discussion of the beards and general hairiness of biblical figures. Yet Burchardus's attitude, spelled out in a number of passages, is unfailingly benign rather than subversive. He takes as his emblem the text of Proverbs 8.29–31, a passage which explicitly links play and the divine.

Quando appendebat fundamenta terrae, cum eo eram cuncta componens
et delectabar per singulos dies ludens coram eo, omni tempore ludens in
orbe terrarum, et deliciae meae esse cum filiis hominum. (*Apologia*
3.164–69 [p. 179 Huygens])

[When he marked out the foundations of the earth, then I was beside him
and I was delighted daily, playing before him always, playing in the
sphere of the earth, and my delights were with the sons of men.]

Burchardus is unambivalent about the value of humor, but even those who
espouse more conservative views may falter in practice. The *Cronica* of Salimbene de Adam, written in the late thirteenth century, displays these contradictory elements in abundance. Salimbene is greatly concerned by the jokes of one
Brother Detesalve, who, for instance, when asked by a joker if he would like
anything beneath him, answered, "Yes, your wife." Salimbene discusses the
propriety of such witticisms at length and finally arrives at eight reasons for
their condemnation, supported by no fewer than seventy biblical quotations.
Despite this muster of authority, Salimbene exonerates Detesalve in the end.

Frater vero Deustesalvet, cuius occasione ista posuimus, excusari potest
multiplici ratione; non tamen verbum suum ducendum est in exemplum,
ut iterum dicatur ab aliquo. . . . Est autem prima ratio excusationis ipsius
quia *respondit stulto iuxta stultitiam suam, ne sibi sapiens esse videretur,*
Prover. XXVI. Secunda, quia non intendebat tantum dicere, quantum
verbum sonat, cum homo solatiosus esset. Ideo dicit Ecclesiasticus XIX:
*Est qui labitur lingua sua, sed non ex animo. Quis est enim qui non
deliquerit in lingua sua?* Ideo dicit Iacobus III: *Si quis in verbo non
offendit, hic perfectus est vir.* . . . .Tertia ratio est quia concivibus suis
locutus fuit, qui inde malum exemplum non habuerunt, cum sint homines
solatiosi et maximi truffatores.[44]

[Brother Detesalve can be excused, nevertheless, for more than one
reason, although his words should not be taken as a model to be used
again by anyone. . . . Here, however, is the first reason why he might be
excused, because he answered "a fool according to his folly, lest he
imagine himself to be wise," as Proverbs 26 [.5] says. The second reason

---

44. *Salimbene de Adam Cronica,* ed. Giuseppe Scalia, 2 vols. (Bari, 1966), 115. Translation
from *The Chronicle of Salimbene de Adam,* trans. Joseph L. Baird et al. (Binghamton, N.Y., 1986),
59.

is that he did not mean what he said literally, since he was a humorous and witty man. Thus Ecclesiasticus 19 [.16–17] reports: "There is one, that slippeth with the tongue, but not from his heart. For who is there that hath not offended with his tongue?" and James 3 [.2]: "If any man offend not in word, the same is a perfect man." . . . The third reason is that he spoke with his own fellow citizens, who did not, therefore, receive a bad example, since they themselves are witty men and great pranksters.]

Salimbene sanctions levity, then, when it is used to put down the foolish, when one is in company with other wits, and only if one is not serious, a condition which in effect declares that humor is its own excuse. One suspects that Salimbene is merely attempting to rationalize his own admiration for wit. Later he appends a fourth excuse which illustrates his confusion on the subject.

Unum vero pretereundum non est, quod Florentini non habent malum exemplum. . . . Hi, quadam vice audientes quod fratrer Iohannes de Vicentia ex Ordine Predicatorum, cuius supra fecimus mentionem, Florentiam ire volebat, dixerunt: "Pro Deo non veniat huc. Audivimus enim quod mortuos suscitat, et tot sumus, quod civitas nostra capere nos non potest." Et valde bene sonant verba Florentinorum in ydiomate suo.

Benedictus Deus, qui nos de hac materia expedivit! (*Salimbene de Adam Cronica,* 117)

[One thing that should not be passed over is that one cannot set a bad example for the Florentines. . . . Once, having heard that the Dominican whom we mentioned above, Brother John of Vincenza, wished to come to Florence, they said, "For God's sake, don't let him come here. We've heard that he raises the dead, and we are already so numerous that our city can't hold all of us." Yet it must be admitted that such words in the Florentine dialect have a splendid ring to them.

Blessed be the Lord, who has helped me through these matters! (trans. from Salimbene de Adam, *Chronicle,* trans. Baird et al., 61)

It might appear that Salimbene has gone through considerable agony wrestling with the question of whether to condemn some slight jokes, but in fact he appears to feel no compunction about proffering a great deal of wit himself. His discussion of Brother Detesalve's remark is followed by a long, approving section on Primas, and the chronicle as a whole cites an enormous quantity of goliardic literature. In these contradictions Salimbene's chronicle exemplifies clerical practice as a whole: although strictures against levity are plentiful, clerical merriment is rife.

Against the rigid precepts of the moralists we must set an additional suggestive phenomenon: the character of much medieval religious humor. I believe it is no accident that religious parody is often founded on humor of inversion— this is the type of humor that might be most easily countenanced by the church. Although the impetus for merrymaking was independent of religion, forms that came closest to the structures of religious devotion were more likely to receive official encouragement. Thus the form of religious humor was influenced by religious concerns, giving rise to a corpus which largely conforms with these ends. The modern scholar is apt to think that extant religious humor is that which escaped the notice of the church; ironically, it could be that many of these pieces survive precisely because their structure attracted the attention of the Church and earned them ecclesiastical sanction.

To sum up, humor and religion occurred in a variety of configurations in medieval culture. In didactic contexts, such as religious drama, humor sharpened the point of the lesson. In other contexts it might be blasphemous; or it might serve an affective function, drawing humans closer to the divine by giving a foretaste of divine joy and establishing an intimacy in which they could assume their true relationship with God. And finally, humor could be entirely amoral, an irreducible force indulged in for its own sake and bearing no relation to the religious or moral order. To impose a monofactorial scheme on these disparate phenomena is to deprive medieval culture of its full richness and diversity.

The Uses of Religious Humor in Literature

If we accept that the relationship of humor and religion occupies a spectrum of possible manifestations, we should be able to see these reflected in medieval religious humor. I shall survey the range of religious humor once more as it appears in the literature of the period, adducing examples from both parodic and nonparodic texts, as both exemplify a common range of configurations.

On the most didactic and moral level, humor played a part in the literary representation of religious truth. In many instances humor not only sweetens the pill of doctrine and exhortation but forms an essential part of the meaning of the text. The Arras *Cena* does this very effectively, with its clear depiction of the roles played by the guests in God's banquet. The clarity of the allegory is supported by the chronological ordering of the banqueters, by the correspondence of the projected three days of the feast to the three ages of human history, and by the correlation of each guest's role in the *Cena* to his role in the Bible. The power of the allegory is strengthened by the fact that there are no gratuitous jokes in the Arras *Cena*. Every action bears the weight of its counterpart in the Bible, and even the wordplay is central to the allegorical scheme. When Eve violates the *ius,* the law and the soup, the pun points up the fact that the first sin was a transgression born of gluttony. This single point of comic detail elucidates the appositeness of the feast image: the whole of humanity's earthly existence was touched off by an act of eating. The Arras *Cena* extends the profundity of wordplay to puns, suggesting that their association is not arbitrary but an expression of religious truth, a manifestation of grammatical Platonism.

Because humor often operates by emphasizing the difference between ideal and reality, it serves as an appropriate medium for conveying the contrast between the perfect world of God and the imperfect earthly world. This contrast is well articulated in a humorous manner in the Wakefield *Secunda Pastorum*.[45] In the main section of the play, a crooked shepherd steals a sheep and tries to conceal his theft by disguising it as an infant; the sheep is so ill suited for this role that at first the other shepherds mistake it for a deformed child. This ludicrous scenario presents a contrast to the end of the play, when the shepherds gather to see the real infant Jesus, the true Lamb of God, brought forth without sin. The initial degradation of the image of the Lamb of God is precisely what drives home the message of humankind's essential sinfulness and excessive pride. Similarly the behavior of the abusive soldiers in the York *Crucifixion Play* encourages the audience to regard them as fools; their folly is underlined by their unwittingly accurate statements on the situation of Christ. The degradation that produces humor also expresses humanity's relationship to God, and to present that degradation in its full humor inspires the laughter that comes from achieving a perspective on the value of earthly endeavor.

The paradox also unites humor and profundity. In the medieval period paradox was often understood as an example of God's powers, which miraculously allow a single thing to be composed of contradictory components. It was this understanding that led the Anglo-Saxon scholar Aldhelm to compose a series of paradoxical riddles on God's creation: in borrowing the literary form from Symphosius, whose riddles were simply amusements, Aldhelm recognized that the divine could be fittingly represented by expressing the transcen-

---

45. The *Secunda Pastorum* is edited in A. C. Cawley, *The Wakefield Pageants in the Towneley Cycle* (Manchester, 1958), 43–63.

dant reconciliation of contradictory elements.[46] The *Ioca monachorum,* a collection of scriptural riddles, apply the same strategy to the Bible and call attention to the paradoxical and miraculous in seemingly commonplace biblical events.[47] But because the structure of a paradox and a joke are so similar, the *Ioca* are entertaining as well as instructive. So well are the two effects integrated that it is impossible to say which is predominant: the text is both essentially amusing and essentially edifying.

These texts, and others like them, combine humor and a serious moral component. Far from being inimical to the text's moral import, the humor contributes to it in a vital way. Humor is useful to religion far beyond its ability to sweeten the pill of doctrine. The transformed awareness of multiple ways of seeing which produces humor also serves as a model for the relationship of God and humans.

In other works humor predominates over the religious elements; though a moral or didactic sense is present, the criticism is muted. Although we may laugh at the fool, we do not despise him. This less acerbic criticism coincides with the fact that in primarily humorous religious literature the audience's identification with the protagonists is greater. A comparison with more edificatory religious humor may illustrate this. In the York *Crucifixion Play* the behavior of the soldiers encourages the audience to perceive and laugh at the folly of the abusive posturing of the soldiers; watching them from the persepective of those who are not involved, the audience can say, with Jesus, "What thei wirke wotte thai noght" (line 261; Lc 23.34).[48] The audience attains God's perspective on humankind. But ultimately the spectators are human and have been reminded constantly by Christian teaching that their sins made Christ's sacrifice necessary. By this route the audience must come to realize that, although they temporarily share the perspective of God, their true counterparts are the soldiers who put Christ on the cross; that they inhabit the earthly realm of the human vice and folly displayed on stage.

In the *Crucifixion Play* the experience of recognizing one's own sin takes place gradually: at first the sinful characters in the play may seem to have nothing in common with the audience. In less didactic literature the author relies on the fact that the audience will recognize their folly immediately. The

---

46. Aldhelm's riddles are edited in "Aenigmata Aldhelmi," *Collectiones Aenigmatum Merovingicae Aetatis,* ed. F. Glone, Corpus Christianorum, Series Latina 133, no. 1 (Turnhout, 1968), 359–540.

47. The *Ioca* are edited in Walther Suchier, *Das mittellateinische Gespräch Adrian und Epictitus nebst verwandten Texten (Joca monachorum)* (Tübingen, 1955).

48. The play is edited in Richard Beadle, *The York Plays* (London, 1982), 215–23.

satirists lampoon the devotion with which clerics drink and gamble, a devotion so strong that it is as if they have elevated the wine and the dice to God's position. This is the conceit behind drinkers' and gamblers' Masses, which directly and unequivocally implicate the audience. Few members of the medieval audience would have recognized themselves immediately in the Roman soldiers of the *Crucifixion Play,* but the role of the ludicrous sinner at Mass was more familiar. The *Crucifixion Play* was directed at an audience; parody Masses were most likely performed *by* the audience. The words are assigned not to any specific other but to all Mass-goers. This gives the audience a much more direct experience of their complicity; but it also ensures that the self-criticism will not be too harsh. Rather, the recognition of their own habits makes the humor more immediate.

Finally, religious ideas, phrases, and images were exploited by humorists with no underlying moral or ideological motivation. In other words, religion was available, like any other motif or comic device, simply to enhance the comic impact of secular literature. One Middle English example is the poem "Alison," which plays on love conceits involved in the lover's worship of his lady.[49] The narrator, Alison, in love with the clerk Jankin, so mixes up the divine service and their love affair that the "Kyrie Eleison" of the Mass becomes "Kyrie Alison." This is religious grammatical Platonism with a vengeance. We see a similar scheme in the exploitation of clerics as figures of fun. The monk in *De cuiusdam claustralis et castracionis eventu* and the *Passio cuiusdam monachi* could just as well be a layman but for the additional comic effect of having the mishaps occur to a man of the cloth. The delight in seeing the ecclesiastics brought low resulted in the appearance of clerics in drinking literature as well. A desire to use religious themes and images also stimulated the use of the Bible in humorous compositions. The fabliaux *De eventu* and *Passio monachi* could well have been written without recourse to biblical passages, and the nonsense of nonsense-centos need not depend on biblical echoes for its effect, but parodists incorporated the Bible to enhance the comedy. Here it was not that humor was added to religious texts to sweeten the pill; rather, religion was added to humorous texts to sweeten the fun.

In medieval Latin parody, then, we can see the range of relationships between humor and religion visible in other medieval literature. In profoundly moral works, humor is subservient to (rather than inimical to) overriding didactic concerns. In other cases humor and piety are equal partners, each

---

49. The poem is edited in R. T. Davies, *Medieval English Lyrics: A Critical Anthology* (London, 1963), no. 73, pp. 162–63.

furnishing the text with important qualities. And finally, in many texts humor has the upper hand, employing religious images and conventions for entirely profane purposes. The plethora of didactic humorous works demonstrates that humor was not intrinsically subversive of ecclesiastical values and that it could even be a religious force in itself. But to concentrate on this aspect of humor, novel as it is to modern criticism, is to lose sight of the preponderant motivation behind the inclusion of humor in religious works and behind the practice of medieval humor and carnival in general. Whatever their theological or prophylactic justifications, writers and others employed humor because it is an irreducible pleasure, an amoral operation which is intrinsically gratifying.

The fundamental amorality of humor did endow it with a latent threat, the same threat that inhered in other forms and practices subject to humankind's corruptible nature. Thus while in one form humor could serve the interests of piety and anticipate the spiritual joy of heaven, in another it might be used as a weapon against the cardinal structures and beliefs of religion. Medieval literature, like medieval society, contained these contradictory forces. From a modern perspective, these apparent contradictions are especially visible in clerical culture: many men of religion are unequivocal in their assertions that frivolity was sinful and irreligious; but despite this professed disapproval, clerics employed levity abundantly for both moral and frivolous ends.

Appendices

Handlist of Medieval Latin Parody

This handlist includes medieval Latin parodies from the fifth to the fifteenth centuries, listing in addition a few related postmedieval texts and sixteenth-century works of probable earlier origin. Where other evidence is lacking, texts have been assigned the date of the earliest manuscript extant. Each entry gives both title and incipit. Spellings have been reproduced as they appear in the printed edition.

With this list I aim to catalog every medieval Latin parody known to me; the sheer number of such works precludes any attempt to discuss every one. Hence the previous chapters of this study examine a limited number of parodic traditions, and this handlist includes a number of parodies not covered in the text.

Parodies with Ecclesiastical Models

Parodies of Biblical Narrative

Eighth Century or Earlier

Cena Cypriani. "Quidam rex nomine Johel nuptias faciebat." Edited in Karl Strecker, "Iohannis Diaconi versiculi de Cena Cypriani," *MGH, Poetae,* 4.2: 857–900 (at 872–98); and in Christine Modesto, *Studien zur Cena Cypriani und zu deren Rezeption,* Classica Monacensia 3 (Tübingen, 1992), 14–29. Fifty-four MSS: earliest s. ix. An allegory parodying allegoresis and biblical exegesis, in which the characters of the Bible attend a wedding feast.

Ninth Century

Cena nuptialis (Cena Hrabani). "Quidam vir magnus et praepotens . . ." Edited in Christine Modesto, *Studien zur Cena Cypriani und zu deren Rezeption,* Classica Monacensia 3 (Tübingen, 1992), 132–56, using fifteen MSS. Additional copies exist in Paris, Bibliothèque Nationale MS lat. 3549, fols. 18r–22r; Oxford, Trinity College MS 39, fols. 138r–144v; and Grenoble, Bibliothèque Municipale MS 265, fols. 136r–138v. Eighteen MSS: earliest

s. x. Written 855–56. An expanded reworking of the *Cena Cypriani* by Hrabanus Maurus.

Cena Iohannis. "Quicumque cupitis saltantem / me Iohannem cernere . . ." Edited in Karl Strecker, "Iohannis Diaconi versiculi de Cena Cypriani," *MGH, Poetae,* 4.2: 857–900 (at 870–900); reprinted in Christine Modesto, *Studien zur Cena Cypriani und zu deren Rezeption,* Classica Monacensia 3 (Tübingen, 1992), 178–201. Written 876 or 877 by Iohannes Hymmonides (also known as Iohannes Diaconus). Eleven MSS: earliest s. x. A verse rewriting of the *Cena Cypriani.*

Tenth Century

Heriger, urbis Maguntiacensis. "Heriger, urbis Maguntiacensis / antistes, quondam vidit prophetam . . ." Edited in Karl Strecker, *Die Cambridger Lieder, MGH, Scriptores rerum Germanicarum* 40 (Berlin, 1926), 65–66, no. 24. Four MSS: earliest s. xi. Datable to the tenth century on internal evidence. A poem about a supposed vision in which several biblical characters preside at a meal; parodies visions as well as the *Cena Cypriani* tradition.

Eleventh Century

Cena Azelini. "Galileae rex inclitus / suis Johel est cognitus . . ." Edited in Christine Modesto, *Studien zur Cena Cypriani und zu deren Rezeption,* Classica Monacensia 3 (Tübingen, 1992), 220–30; two further verses in Claude de Saumaise, *Historiae Augustae Scriptores IV* (Paris, 1620), 397, 410, reprinted in Modesto 234–35. It is not clear if Saumaise used the now lost second half of the surviving exemplar or if he had another manuscript at his disposal. Hence one or two MSS: the longer MS is s. xii. Written in the early eleventh century by Azelinus of Reims. A verse redaction of the *Cena Cypriani.*

Twelfth Century

Prelibo necessarium (Arras *Cena*). "Prelibo necessarium / Prefationis titulum . . ." Edited in appendix 2, no. 1, and in Christine Modesto, *Studien zur Cena Cypriani und zu deren Rezeption,* Classica Monacensia 3 (Tübingen, 1992), 244–78. One MS: s. xii. A verse rewriting of the *Cena Cypriani* with many elaborations of the humor and allegory of the original.

Mock Saints' Lives

Thirteenth Century

Vita sanctissimi et gloriosissimi Neminis (Long *Nemo*). "Multifarie multisque modis, carissimi, loquebatur olim deus . . ." Edited in appendix 2, no. 2. Eight MSS: earliest s. xiii[2]. A sophisticated mock vita of the fictional saint Nemo, employing a range of biblical and Classical citations.

Fourteenth Century

Fuit vir in oriente (Combined *Nemo*). "Fuit vir in oriente nomine Nemo . . ." Edited in appendix 2, no. 5. One MS: s. xiv[ex]/xv[in]. A mock vita of Nemo, a combination of the Long and Short *Nemo*s, with some original elaboration.

Fifteenth Century

Sermo de sancto Nemine (Short *Nemo*). "Vir erat in oriente nomine Nemo . . ." Edited in appendix 2, no. 4. Seven MSS: earliest s. xv. A simple mock hagiography in the tradition of the *Vita Neminis*.

Recolendi patres (Cambridge *Nemo*). "Recolendi patres et domini, scriptura teste . . ." In Cambridge, Gonville and Caius MS 230/116, pp. 73–77 (old foliation 34r–36r). Quoted in chapter 3; otherwise unpublished. One MS: s. xv. A rewriting of the legend of Nemo using the framework of the Long *Nemo*.

Sermo de beatissimo Nemine (Zurich *Nemo*). "Benedictionem omnium gencium dedit illi . . ." In Zurich, Zentralbibliothek MS C.101, fols. 166v–167v. Quoted in chapter 3; otherwise unpublished. One MS: s. xv. An elaborate mock sermon on Nemo, distantly related to the long version.

Sermo non inelegans de sanctissimo fratre Invicem (Long *Invicem*). "Suscipite Invicem. Tharsensis ille noster Paulus . . ." Edited in appendix 2, no. 6. Three MSS: earliest s. xv. The deeds of a fictional character, Invicem, who is associated with St. Paul through deliberate misinterpretation of the word *invicem* in the text of the Pauline Epistles.

Suscipite Invicem (Short *Invicem*). "Suscipite Invicem. Ad Romanos xii. Notandum quod beatus Paulus habuit . . ." The Hamburg Recension is edited in appendix 2, no. 7; the Besançon Recension, which has a similar incipit, is quoted in chapter 3; otherwise unpublished. Two MSS: s. xv. A shorter version of the vita of Invicem.

Sixteenth Century

Sermo elegans (Abbreviated Long *Nemo*). "Multifarie multisque modis deus olim locutus est . . ." Edited in appendix 2, no. 3. One MS: s. xvi. An abbreviated rewriting of the *Vita Neminis.*

Liturgical Parody

Thirteenth Century

Collacio iocosa de diligendo Lieo. "De veteri testamento aliqua vobis . . ." Edited in Lehmann 231–32. One MS: s. xiii. A mock sermon for gluttons and drinkers.

Officium lusorum. "Lugeamus omnes in Decio . . ." Edited in Lehmann 247– 49; *Carmina Burana* no. 215, pp. 64–65. One MS: s. xiii. A gamblers' Mass.

Deus, qui nos potestate vini. Edited in Lehmann 125. Two MSS: s. xiii. A drinkers' prayer.

Parts of a Drinkers' Mass. "Ave color vini clari . . ." Edited in appendix 2, no. 12.1. "Fragments of Drinkers' Masses." One MS: s. xiii. A drinkers' hymn and prayer.

Dico pater noster. "Dico pater noster / pro conversis, ut eos ter . . ." Edited in Lehmann 195–97. One MS: s. xiii/xiv. A verse prayer comically incorporating the Pater Noster, ridiculing monastic lay brothers.

Fourteenth Century

Fallax euuangelium secundum Lupum. "Fraus tibi, Bache!" Edited by J. Gough Nichols in Thomas Wright and James Orchard Halliwell, *Reliquiae Antiquae,* 2 vols. (1841–43; reprint, New York, 1966), 2:58. One MS: s. xiv. A drinkers' Gospel relating to festivities at Oxford.

Sequencia leti evangelii secundum Luc⟨i⟩um. "In illo tempore: erat quidem Phariseus Lucius . . ." Edited in Lehmann 250. One MS: s. xiv. A drinkers' Gospel.

Fifteenth Century

Leccio actuum potatorum ad ebrios fratres. "Epistola. Leccio actuum potatorum ad ebrios fratres. In diebus miseriis . . ." Edited in Lehmann 241– 47. One MS: s. xv. A drinkers' Mass.

Confitemini Bacho. "Confitemini Bacho, quoniam bonus . . ." Edited in Lehmann 233–41, from three MSS; a fourth manuscript is edited in appendix 2, no. 10, as the *Missa potatorum.* Four MSS: s. xv. A drinkers' and gamblers' Mass.

Circumdederunt me lusores. "Circumdederunt me lusores et bibuli, latrones pincerne . . ." Edited in Julius Feifalik, "Studien zur Geschichte der alt-böhmischen Literatur," *Sitzungsberichte der kaiserlichen Akademie der Wissenschaften in Wien,* philosophisch-historische Classe 36 (1861): 119–91 (at 174–75). One MS: 1459. Parts of a drinkers' Mass.

Tristabitur iustus. "Tristabitur iustus et letabitur impius . . ." Edited in Lehmann 217–23. Three MSS: s. xv; variants of the genealogy and confession are also found in Munich, Bayerische Staatsbibliothek MS clm. 23833, fols. 14–15 (unpublished). An anti-Hussite Mass.

Quicumque vult salvus esse. Edited in W. Wattenbach, "Lateinische Reime des Mittelalters," *Anzeiger für Kunde der deutschen Vorzeit,* n.s., 18 (1871): cols. 130–31. One MS: 1459. A verse parody of the Athanasian Creed, satirizing avarice.

In nomine infinite miserie et sue follie miserrime. Edited in Alfredo Straccali, *I Goliardi ovvero i clerici vagantes delle università medievali* (Florence, 1880), 91–94. One MS: s. xv. A mock litany satirizing the poor provisions of a tavern.

Pour les buveurs. "Pour les buveurs. Ave color vini clari . . ." In Paris, Bibliothèque Nationale MS lat. 3528, fol. 119r; never edited. One MS: s. xv. A drinkers' hymn and prayer.

Sixteenth Century

Missa de potatoribus (in one MS under the title "Missa Gulloni"). "V. Introibo ad altare Bachi." Edited in Lehmann 233–41. Three MSS: s. xvi. A drinkers' Mass.

Potus noster. "Potus noster, qui es in cypho." Edited in Lehmann 249–50. One MS: s. xvi. Parts of a drinkers' Mass; includes a Money-Gospel.

Confitemini Dolio. "Sacerdos: Confitemini Dolio quoniam bonum." Edited in appendix 2, no. 11. One MS: s. xvi. A drinkers' Mass.

Exhortatio ad potandum perutilis. "Quicunque vult esse bonus frater . . ." Edited in appendix 2, no. 12.2, "Fragments of Drinkers' Masses." One MS: s. xvi. Parts of a drinkers' Mass.

Seventeenth Century

Parts of a Drinkers' Mass. "Potator quidam egregius / In laudem Bacchi . . ." Edited in appendix 2, no. 12.3, "Fragments of Drinkers' Masses." One MS: s. xvii. A drinkers' hymn and prayer.

Parts of a Drinkers' Mass. "Vinum bonum cum sapore . . ." Edited in Jakob Werner, *Beiträge zur Kunde der lateinischen Literatur des Mittelalters aus Handschriften gesammelt*, 2d ed. (Aarau, 1905), 211–12. One MS: s. xvi. A drinkers' hymn, verse and response, and prayers.

Parodic Centos

Eleventh Century

Garcineida (*Tractatus Garsiae*). "Quo tempore Urbanus Romanae Ecclesiae . . ." Edited and translated in Rodney M. Thomson, *Tractatus Garsiae*, Textus Minores 46 (Leiden, 1973); reprinted from an incomplete edition by Ricardo García-Villoslada, *La Poesia ritmica de los goliardos medievales* (Madrid, 1975), 311–16. Written ca. 1099. Four MSS: three s. xii. A set of five texts for the translation of the relics of the fictional saints Albinus (Silver) and Rufinus (Gold), including a mock homily and mock sermon, by a churchman of Toledo.

Eusebius dixit. "Eusebius dixit: 'Non comedetis ex eo crudum . . .'" Edited in Bernhard Bischoff, "Eine Bibelparodie (elftes bis zwölftes Jahrhundert)," in *Anecdota Novissima: Texte des vierten bis sechzehnten Jahrhunderts*, Quellen und Untersuchungen zur lateinischen Philologie des Mittelalters 7 (Stuttgart, 1984), 162–64. One MS: s. xi/xii. A nonsense cento with a mock biblical plot.

Thirteenth Century

Evangelium secundum marcas argenti. "In illo tempore: dixit papa Romanis: 'Cum venerit . . .'" Edited in Lehmann 183–84. One MS: s. xiii. The "oldest" version of the Money-Gospel, a biblical cento satirizing the greed of the Roman curia.

Lectio ewangelii secundum marcham argenti (Money-Gospel: "Intermediate" version). "In illo turbine: Dixit papa Romanis: 'Cum venerit . . .'" Edited in appendix 2, no. 8. Twelve MSS: earliest s. xiii/xiv. The "intermediate" version of the Money-Gospel, a biblical cento satirizing the avarice of the Roman curia, longer and more elaborate than the *Evangelium secundum marcas argenti*.

Metra de monachis carnalibus. "Quis nescit, quam sit monachorum . . ."; one version begins "Scire vis, quid sit monachrum . . ." Edited in A. George Rigg, "'Metra de Monachis Carnalibus'—The Three Versions," *Mittellateinisches Jahrbuch* 15 (1980): 134–42 (at 135, 136–37, 139). Fourteen

MSS (two of the nuns' version): earliest s. xiii[in]. Three versions of a satire, in part a cento, critical of monks (in one version altered to apply to nuns). *De cuiusdam claustralis dissolucione et castracionis eventu.* Edited in Lehmann 224–30. Four MSS: earliest. s. xiii. A Latin prose fabliau about a libertine monk, presented as a sermon, largely a cento.

Fourteenth Century

Epistola notabilis de Pecunia. "Pecunia Romanorum imperatrix et totius mundi semper augusta . . ." Edited in Charles Homer Haskins, "Latin Literature under Frederick II," in *Studies in Mediaeval Culture* (Oxford, 1929), 124–47 (at 138–39). One MS (date unavailable). A mock imperial letter as if from the "Empress Pecunia," largely a biblical cento satirizing avarice.

Fifteenth Century

Passio domini nostri pape Romanorum secundum marcam auri et argenti. "In illo tempore: Cum sero esset die una sabbatorum . . ." Edited in Lehmann 186–88. One MS: s. xv. (The additional manuscript cited by Lehmann on his p. 186 is not a copy of this text but of the *Lectio ewangelii secundum marcam argenti,* the "intermediate" version of the Money-Gospel.) The "youngest" version of the Money-Gospel, an elaborate biblical cento satirizing the avarice of the Roman curia.

Frequentia studentis evangelii secundum marcham argenti. "Galero gratias. Dolus vobiscum." Edited in chapter 5. One MS: s. xv. A brief Money-Gospel satirizing the avarice of the papal curia. Related to a Money-Gospel which forms part of a parody Mass found in a sixteenth-century manuscript, edited in Lehmann 249–50.

Sanctum ewangelium secundum marcam auri et argenti (Students' Money-Gospel). "Viro venerabili et discreto domino . . ." Edited in appendix 2, no. 9. Two MSS: s. xv. A biblical cento satirizing students' attitudes toward money.

Fratres mei dilectissimi. "Fratres mei dilectissimi, quod vobis pigrum est . . ." Edited in appendix 2, no. 13. One MS: s. xv. A nonsense-cento in the form of a sermon.

Sermo sententiosissimus. "Sermo sententiosissimus inclusione dignissimus domini Maphille catechumini ordinis spalentrinorum contra febrenses. Ex nihilo nihil fit . . ." Edited in appendix 2, no. 14. One MS: s. xv. A nonsense-cento in the form of a sermon.

Preces famulae sacerdotis. "Oremus pro omni gradu ecclesie!" Edited in Hans Walther, "Parodistische Gebete der Pfarrköchin in einer Züricher Handschrift," *Studi Medievali*, n.s., 4 (1931): 344–57 (at 349–55). Reprinted from a single MS by Ricardo García-Villoslada, *La Poesia ritmica de los goliardos medievales* (Madrid, 1975), 321–22. Three MSS: two s. xv. A parody prayer with affinities to estates satire: the text matches the ecclesiastical ranks and orders with biblical quotations which, out of context, have the effect of ridiculing the subjects.

Neglectio epistolae beati Paulisper. "Fratres, gaudete in domino semper . . ." Edited in Francesco Novati, "La parodia sacra nelle letterature moderne," in *Studi critici e letterari* (Turin, 1889), 177–310 (at 308–10). One MS: s. xv. A sarcastic sermon, in cento form, rebuking the Franciscans.

Passio cuiusdam nigri monachi secundum luxuriam. "In illis temporibus erat quidem monachus . . ." One version is printed by Julius Feifalik, "Studien zur Geschichte der altböhmischen Literatur," *Sitzungsberichte der kaiserlichen Akademie der Wissenschaften in Wien,* philosophisch-historische Classe 36 (1861): 119–91 (at 173–74). References to six other manuscripts are given by Lehmann on his p. 231: for his Graz, Universitätsbibliothek "Ms. II 260," read MS 620. Seven MSS: s. xv. A *passio* about a libertine monk, largely a cento; related to *De cuiusdam claustralis dissolucione et castracionis eventu* (cited earlier).

Sixteenth Century

Sermo plurimum utilis ex diuersis collectus de nihil (*Sermo de nihil*). "Fratres, ex nihilo nihil fit." Edited in appendix 2, no. 15. One MS: s. xvi. A nonsense-cento in the form of a sermon.

Lectio Danielis prophete. "Fratres, ex nihilo vobis timendum." Edited in appendix 2, no. 16. One MS: s. xvi. A nonsense-cento in the form of a sermon.

Seventeenth Century

Exhortatio catechistica Luteranorum. "Ex nihilo nihil fit. Fratres, Scriptura dicit . . ." Edited in appendix 2, no. 17. One MS: s. xvii. A nonsense-cento in the form of a sermon.

Miscellaneous Parodies with Ecclesiastical Models

Twelfth Century

Apocalypsis Goliae. "A tauro torrida lampade Cynthii . . ." Edited in Karl Strecker, *Die Apokalypse des Golias,* Texte zur Kulturgeschichte des Mittelalters 5 (Rome and Leipzig, 1928). Sixty-eight MSS: earliest s. xii/xiii. A parody of the Apocalypse of John, satirizing the orders and ranks of the clergy in turn.

Thirteenth Century

In nomine summe et indiuidue vanitatis. "Surianus diutina fatuorum fauente demencia . . ." Edited in Theodor Mayer, "Spicilegium von Urkunden aus der Zeit der österreichischen Babenberger-Fürsten," *Archiv für Kunde österreichischer Geschichts-Quellen* 6 (1851), 273–318 (at 316–18); reprinted and translated in Helen Waddell, *The Wandering Scholars* (London, 1927), 239–40. Reprinted in Ricardo García-Villoslada, *La Poesia ritmica de los goliardos medievales* (Madrid, 1975), 317, 319. Written 1209. One MS: A mock decree from the archprimate of wandering scholars, expressing sympathy for his flock, with reference to a specific Austrian church.

Grave gerimus. "Grave gerimus quod infra, ex parte dilecti filii . . ." In Besançon, Bibl. Mun. MS 592, fol. 6v; and Vienna, Österreichische Nationalbibl. MS 480, fol. 13rv. Unpublished. Two MSS: s. xiii. A mock papal decree in praise of wine.

Fifteenth Century

Monachus ethymologyce. "Morum oppressor, nequicie amator . . ." Edited in appendix 2, no. 18, "Parody Acrostics." Four MSS: s. xv. A parody of laudatory acrostics on *monachus.*

Nos Gorgias, ingurgitantium abbas. "Nos Gorgias, ingurgitantium abbas, bachantium antistes . . ." An excerpt is printed in *Histoire littéraire de la France,* 41 vols. (Paris, 1733–1981), 22:156; the rest is in Paris, Bibl. Nat. MS lat. 863, fols. 122v–124r, otherwise unpublished. One MS: s. xv. A gluttons' parody of an episcopal decree.

Sermo sew Dictamen contra abstinentiam sew ieiunium. "Si dimisero eos ieiunos, deficient in via." Edited in W. Wattenbach, "Historia Neminis," *Anzeiger für Kunde der deutschen Vorzeit,* N. F. 13 (1866): cols. 393–97. One MS: s. xv. A mock sermon demonstrating the folly of fasting by sophisticated use of the arguments of Aristotle and Boethius out of context.

Sixteenth Century

Flevit lepus parvulus. "Flevit lepus parvulus / Clamans altis vocibus . . ." Edited in Giuseppe Scalia, "Il 'Testamentum Asini' e il lamento della lepre," *Studi Medievali,* 3d ser., 3 (1962): 129–51 (at 143–44). Two MSS: s. xvi. A lament by a hare chased by dogs, parodying the Good Friday *Improperia,* and concluding with a brief mock will.

Of Uncertain Date

Cacologion pape secundum Satanam. "Liber generationis pape, filii diaboli . . ." Edited in Lehmann 257. Another version, beginning "Liber generationis Antichristi filii Diaboli," is printed in Caelius Secundus Curio, *Pasquillorum tomi duo* (Basel, 1544), 307–8, from an unknown manuscript. Mock genealogy attacking the pope for avarice and corruption, parodying the genealogy of Jesus at Matthew 1.1–17.

Parodies with Secular Models

Mock Grammars

Thirteenth Century

Scribere clericulis. "Scribere clericulis / paro novellis omnibus . . ." Edited in Lehmann 223–24. Two MSS: s. xiii. A bawdy parody of the *Doctrinale* of Alexander Villa Dei, a widely used schoolboy grammar of 1209, edited in D. Reichling, *Das Doctrinale der Alexander de Villa Dei,* Monumenta Germaniae Pedaegogica 12 (Berlin, 1893).

Fifteenth Century

Nummus que pars. "Nummus que pars est? Preposicio." Edited in Lehmann 190–92. Three MSS: s. xv. Money satire in the form of a grammar.

Rusticus que pars. "Rusticus que pars est? Nomen." One version is printed in Lehmann 197–98, though it is not collated with the version in Munich, Bayerische Staatsbibl. MS clm. 15602, which Lehmann mentions. A third version is printed in Hans Walther, "Parodistische Gebete der Pfarrköchin in einer Züricher Handschrift," *Studi Medievali,* n.s., 4 (1931): 344–57 (at 355–57). Lehmann's printed version, which differs from Walther's in having been altered to an anti-Semitic point of view, is attributed to Georius [*sic*] Prenperger of Vienna. Three MSS: s. xv. Satire of peasants; in the form of a grammar.

De Monachis. "Monachus que pars est? Nomen invidum . . ." Edited in Lehmann 192–94, from one MS; the other, Vienna, Österreichische Nationalbibl. MS 4120, fol. 39v, is unedited. Two MSS: one s. xv. Satire of monks; in the form of a grammar.

Nom. hic villanus. Printed in Lehmann 77, after Francesco Novati, *Carmina Medii Aevi* (Florence, 1883), 28 n. 2. One MS: s. xv. Satire of peasants; in the form of a grammatical paradigm.

Pidgin Latin

Thirteenth Century

Quondam fuit factus festus. "Quondam fuit factus festus / Et vocatus ad co-
mestus . . ." or a number of variations. Five manuscripts are edited by
Wilhelm Meyer, "Quondam fuit factus festus: Ein Gedicht in Spottlatein,"
*Nachrichten von der königlichen Gesellschaft der Wissenschaften zu Göt-
tingen,* philologisch-historische Klasse (1908), 406–26 (at 412–26); another
is edited by Alfredo Straccali, *I Goliardi ovvero i clerici vagantes delle
università medievali* (Florence, 1880), 86–90. There are also unedited versions in Poitiers, Bibliothèque Municipale MS 93, fols. 106v–107; Landau-
Finaly MS 209, fol. 23; Munich, Bayerische Staatsbibliothek MS clm.
19685, fols. 112r–113v; Oxford, Bodleian Library MS Add.C.296, fol.
158r; Bern, Burgerbibliothek MS 556, fol. 34rv; and Gdansk, Marien-
bibliothek F.239, fol. 131. Twelve MSS: earliest s. xiii. A poem in comically
bad Latin about a dispute at a monastic feast.

Fifteenth Century

Dominus Iohannes presbiter de mane missa villa de Caudatis. Edited in
Bernhard Bischoff, "Parodistischer Brief des Priesters Iohannes de Caudatis
(um 1470)," in *Anecdota Novissima: Texte des vierten bis sechzehnten Jahrhunderts,* Quellen und Untersuchungen zur lateinischen Philologie des Mittelalters 7 (Stuttgart, 1984), 167–68 (at 167; see also 292). One MS: s. xv. A
letter purporting to be from one priest to another, in comically bad Latin with
a number of puns on English words.

Of Uncertain Date

Sermo noster audiatis. "Sermo noster audiatis / quid petimus, faciatis . . ."
Edited in Wilhelm Meyer, "Das Gedicht: Sermo noster audiatis,"
*Nachrichten von der königlichen Gesellschaft der Wissenschaften zu Göt-
tingen,* philologisch-historische Klasse (1908), 426–29 (at 427–29). One
MS (date unavailable). A verse lamentation in comically bad Latin.

Miscellaneous Parodies with Secular Models

Eighth Century or Earlier

Parody of the *Lex Salica.* "Incipit totas malb. In nomine Dei patris . . ." Printed
in D'Arco Silvio Avalle, "Ancora sulla Parodia della 'Lex Salica,'" in
Miscellanea di Studi in onore di Alfredo Schiaffini, Rivista di cultura classica

e medieovale (Rome, 1965), 29–61. Reprinted in D'Arco Silvio Avalle, *Protostoria delle Lingue Romanze* (Turin, 1965), 363–414; and in Veikko Väänänen, *Introduction au latin vulgaire,* 3d ed. (Paris, 1981), 198–99. One MS: s. viii². A short parody of the *Lex Salica,* an early French law document.

Twelfth Century

Altercatio quorundam philosophorum. "Epicurus: Soli sunt athomi totius semina mundi." Printed in E. Dümmler, "Gedichte aus dem elften Jahrhundert," *Neues Archiv der Gesellschaft für ältere deutsche Geschichtskunde* 1 (1876): 175–85 (at 182); and in Stephan Endlicher, *Catalogus codicum philologicorum Latinorum Bibliothecae Palatinae Vindobonensis* (Vienna, 1836), 170. Also in Copenhagen, Kong. Bibl. MS Fabr. 81 8º, fol. 46rv; London, British Library MS Burney 216, fol. 103v; Trier, Dombibl. MS 93; Vorau, Chorherrenstift MS 33; Munich, Bayerische Staatsbibl. MS clm. 6911, fol. 128r; and Brussels, Bibliothèque Royale MS (old) 10615–10729. 7 MSS: earliest s. xi. A short verse parody of a philosophers' debate.

Thirteenth Century

Testamentum asini. "Rusticus dum asinum . . ." Edited in Giuseppe Scalia, "Il 'Testamentum Asini' e il lamento della lepre," *Studi Medievali,* 3d ser., 3 (1962): 129–51 (at 132–34, 135, 137). Eleven MSS, some with considerable variations: earliest s. xiii. A mock will, in verse, as if by a donkey.

Fourteenth Century

Fridericus XXXVIII. "Fridericus XXXVIII, divina ingratitudine Remalorum depilator . . ." Printed in Karl Hampe, "Reise nach England vom Juli 1895 bis Februar 1896. III," *Neues Archiv der Gesellschaft für ältere deutsche Geschichtskunde* 22 (1897): 607–99 (at 619–20). One MS: s. xiv. A mock imperial letter of Frederick II, equating him with the Antichrist.

Receptum pro stomacho s. Petri et reformatione totali eiusdem. "Recipe XXIV cardinales . . ." Printed in Lehmann 68, after Hermann von der Hardt, *Magnum Oecumenicum Constantiense Concilium,* 6 vols. (Frankfurt and Leipzig, 1697–1700), 1:499. One MS: s. xv. A mock recipe to rid the church of corrupt clergy.

Proprietates Anglicorum. "De animalibus Roucestriae existentibus, qualia quidem animalia . . ." Edited in Thomas Wright and James Orchard Halliwell, *Reliquiae Antiquae,* 2 vols. (1841–43; reprint, New York, 1966), 2:230–37. One MS: s. xv. A mock scientific treatise classifying the inhabitants of Rochester as a low form of life.

Transaetherius pater patrum. "Transaetherius pater patrum ac totius eccle-siasticae . . ." Printed in H. H. Henson, "Letters Relating to Oxford in the 14th Century, from Originals in the Public Record Office and British Museum," *Collectanea,* Oxford Historical Society, old series, 5 (Oxford, 1885), 1–56 (at 48–49). One MS (date unavailable). A mock decree from an Oxford University Lord of Misrule.

Of Uncertain Date

Salomon et Marcolfus. "Cum staret rex Salomon super solium David . . ." Edited in Walter Benary, *Salomon et Marcolfus,* Sammlung mittella-teinischer Texte 8 (Heidelberg, 1914), 1–51. Twenty-three MS: earliest s. xiv. Uncertain evidence for its existence from the sixth and tenth century; certainly extant in some form by the thirteenth century. A parody of wisdom dialogues, with Marcolf countering Solomon's wise platitudes in scurrilous language.

Appendix 2

Editions and Translations

The editions included in this appendix are as follows.

1. The Arras *Cena*
2. The Long *Nemo*
   First Appendix: Ciceronian Additions to the Heidelberg Manuscript (H)
   Second Appendix: The End of the Hamburg Manuscript Version (G)
   Third Appendix: The End of the Paris Manuscript Version (P)
3. The Abbreviated Long *Nemo*
4. The Short *Nemo*
5. The Combined *Nemo*
6. The Long *Invicem*
7. The Short *Invicem:* The Hamburg Recension
8. The Money-Gospel: The "Intermediate" Version
9. The Students' Money-Gospel
10. *Missa potatorum*
11. A Drinkers' Mass (*Confitemini Dolio*)
12. Fragments of Drinkers' Masses
13. *Fratres mei dilectissimi*
14. *Sermo sententiosissimus*
15. *Sermo de nihil*
16. *Lectio Danielis prophete*
17. *Exhortatio catechistica Luteranorum*
18. Parody Acrostics

The following signs are used in the editions in appendix 2 and in quotations appearing in the text.

⟨ ⟩   editorial addition
[ ]   editorial deletion
[?]   illegible word
(?)   illegible part of word
†   text corrupt

1. The Arras *Cena*

Manuscript: Arras, Bibliothèque Municipale MS 624 (olim 557), fols. 145v–148r. s. xiii[ex]. Provenance: Arras. Since this edition was prepared, the text has also been edited in Christine Modesto, *Studien zur Cena Cypriani und zu deren Rezeption,* Classica Monacensia 3 (Tübingen, 1992), 244–78.

1   Prelibo necessarium
     Prefationis titulum,
     Enarraturus mysticas
     Regis Iohelis nuptias.

2   Has primus in Carthagine
     Uir Ciprianus nomine,
     Honore pollens martyris,
     Scripsit recuruis digitis.

3   Post hunc Iohannes saltitans,
     Predictum uirum imitans,
     Sub una cena retulit,
     Ut primus ille cecinit.

4   Hos subsecutus Azelin
     Plura dilatans addidit
     Vnaque cena principem
     Henricum pauit cesarem.

5   Sed tribus sub temporibus
     Nos hanc ipsam distinguimus:
     Ante legem et sub ea
     Et sub moderna gratia.

6   Iohelem ergo dominum
     Intellige Christum Iesum,
     Vt sponsam eius unicam
     Accipias ecclesiam.

7   Tobiam namque sequimur   **7.1–4** Tb 8.4
     Priuantem se complexibus
     Tribus diebus, coniugem
     Dum uirgo seruat uirginem.

8   Quod ille fecit typice
Canamus nos ueridice,
Dantes diem pro tempore
Res possit ut subsistere.

9   Et ne causeris ordinem
Non imitantem seriem,
Erunt primi nouissimi,   **9.3–4** Mt 20.16; Mc 10.31; Lc 13.30
Nouissimi primarii.

10   Nam ad regales epulas
Si cunctas sedes ordinas
Cum temporis dispendio,
Ciborum fit perditio.

     Explicit prefatio. Incipit liber.

11   Facturus olim inclitas
Magnus Iohel rex nuptias;
Sub mane primo penetral
Luce noua clarificat.

12   Sexta die preueniens
Omnem uocauit hominem,
Vt ad incomparabiles
Delitias succederet.

13   In loco remotissimo,
Cunctis dehinc incognito,
Sedes amenas collocat
Dapesque partas commodat.

14   Necdum erat conuiuium
Per ordinem dispositum
Cum fauce furtim auida
Ius cene uirgo uiolat.

15   Qui aderant, consentiunt,
Participant edulium,
Et mente male conscia
Diffugiunt in latebras.

16   Vnde Iohelis principis
     Acerbis querimoniis
     Mersit omnes in lacrimas
     Rupta familiaritas.

17   Mox ab amenis sedibus
     Tristes reiecti longius
     Cum hispidis induuiis
     Querunt cibos in infimis.

18   Non ibi tanta dignitas
     Quanta prius, nec copia,
     Sed cum sudore manditur
     Quicquid labore queritur.

19   Nec inde uicta claudicat
     Regis beniuolentia,
     Immo largitur omnia
     Ad uictum necessaria.

20   Videres tamen miseros
     Luctari dampnaticios
     Cum spinis atque tribulis,
     Armatis ferro dexteris.

21   Tellurem fodit cernuus   **21.1–4** Gn 4.2
     Cain furore liuidus;
     Abel balantes sequitur
     Plectendus fratris manibus.

22   Pomis, herbis et glandibus
     Conuiua nouus uescitur
     Panisque sustentaculo,
     Nec carnes addit prandio.

23   Omnes escas mandibiles   **23.1–2** Gn 6.21–22
     Seruat Noe sagaciter,
     Vt natos cum coniugibus
     Quindenis alat mensibus.

24 Post hec, minutis uiribus,   **24.1–4** Gn 8.20
   Utuntur cuncti carnibus
   Quos cataclismo libera
   Archa feta pepererat.

25 Sacerdos hinc et rex Salem,   **25.1–4** Gn 14.18–20
   Honorans celi principem,
   Abre suscepit decimas
   Panem, uinum cui dederat.

26 Tum fide fretus Abraham
   Regis meretur gratiam,
   Per quem recuperabilis
   Fit amor pii principis.

27 In signum circumcisio   **27.1–2** Gn 17.10–14
   Iubetur e uestigio;
   Hinc omne iam conuiuium
   Gestit in maius gaudium.

28 Iam senex ridet Abraham,   **28.1** Gn 17.17
   Ridet Sara post ianuam: **28.2** Gn 18.10–12
   Risus uocatur Ysaac   **28.3–4** Gn 21.6
   Vter parens quod riserat.

29 Pater exclamat protinus,
   "Risum fecit mihi Deus.   **29.2–4** Gn 21.6
   Quicumque hoc audierit
   Mox conridebit sterili."

30 Cum ablactatus Ysaac,   **30.1–2** Gn 21.8
   Abraham cenam preparat;
   Grandeque fit tripudium
   Dum celebratur prandium.

31 At cetera cibaria
   Ne prepediret tarditas,
   Pentapolis succenditur,   **31.3** Gn 19.24–25
   Loth uxor sal efficitur.   **31.4** Gn 19.26

32	Centuplicatis frugibus				**32.1–2** Gn 26.12
	Receptis ex seminibus,
	Prebebat aquam Ysaac				**32.3–4** Gn 26.18
	De puteis quos foderat.

33	Post hec, regem Abimelech			**33.1–4** Gn 26.26–33
	Phicolque cum reficeret,
	Post Latitudinis aquam,
	Inuenit Habundantiam.

34	Ollam uidens famelicus,				**34.1–4** Gn 25.30–34
	Esurieque tabidus,
	Emit Edom lenticulas
	Uenditque primogenita.

35	Defert Ruben mandragoras,			**35.1–4** Gn 30.14–16
	Pulcra Rachel desiderat
	Et contra Lia murmurat,
	Sed lectus lites mitigat.

36	Iacob in monte Galaad				**36.1–4** Gn 31.52–54
	Cum Laban litat uictimas
	Cum structo prandet tumulo
	Iurato testimonio.

37	Pharao natalitium				**37.1–4** Gn 40.20–22
	Festiua cena praeditum
	Edentibus Egiptiis
	Pistore penso perficit.

38	Panem Ioseph promiserat,			**38.1** Gn 42.25, 44.1
	Sed postmodum inebriat			**38.2** Gn 43.34
	Patremque iubet fratribus			**38.3–4** Gn 45.9–13
	Ad se adduci comminus.

39	Tunc Israhelis populo				**39.1–2** Gn 45.9–46.7
	Gessen impletur gaudio,
	In cuius cerimoniis				**39.3–4** Gn 47.12
	Sic cena prima desinit.

40	Mactant quidem agniculos	**40.1** Ex 12.3–10
	Et dominus Egyptios,	**40.2** Ex 12.29
	Complentque leti prandium,	
	Egiptii iusticium.	**40.4** Ex 12.30
41	Hinc baptizati mystico	**41.1–2** Ex 14.21–29
	In maris rubri lauacro	
	Sub monte Sina denuo	**41.3–4** Ex 19
	Se preparant conuiuio.	
	Explicit liber primus. Incipit secundus.	
42	Iubente rege Moyses	**42.1–3** Nm 10.1–2
	Tubas procudit ductiles;	
	Argento clare bucinat	
	Atque cenam reciprocat.	**42.4** Nm 10.10
43	Hesterni cum succiduis	**43.1–4** Nm 11.1–25
	Totis se fundunt copiis	
	Sollicitus quos Moyses	
	Distribuit per ordines.	
44	Adam sede ficulnea	**44.1–2** Gn 3.7
	Cum Eua sedet socia,	
	Cain super manipulum,	**44.3** Gn 4.3
	Abel super agniculum.	**44.4** Gn 4.4
45	Archam supersedet Noe	**45.1** Gn 6.14
	Et Abraham sub ylice;	**45.2** Gn 18.8
	In monte Loth se collocat	**45.3** Gn 19.30
	Et super aram Ysaac.	**45.4** Gn 22.9
46	In hostio sedet Sara	**46.1** Gn 18.10
	Et Esau in pharetra,	**46.2** Gn 25.27
	Iacob in petra typica	**46.3** Gn 28.11
	Rachelque super idola.	**46.4** Gn 31.34
47	Fratres, uasa bellantia,	**47.1** Gn 49.5

	Sedent per muri gramina	**47.2** Gn 49.6
	Rubenque lectulo patris;	**47.3** Gn 35.22, 49.4
	Prede Iudas accubuit.	**47.4** Gn 49.9
48	Hinc Zabulon in nauibus	**48.1** Gn 49.13
	Et Ysachar super onus;	**48.2** Gn 49.14–15
	Cerasten Dan sedens premit	**48.3** Gn 49.17
	Et Gad uaginam gladii.	**48.4** Gn 49.19
49	Aser in farinario	**49.1** Gn 49.20
	Et Beniamin in sacculo	**49.2** Gn 44.12
	Et Neptalin in cathedra;	
	Sedet Ioseph in palea.	**49.4** Gn 41.22–36, 47–49, etc.
50	At Moyses in fiscina	**50.1** Ex 2.3, 5
	Et Pharao in tegula	
	Et Iosue in galea;	
	Achar sedet in regula.	**50.4** Jos 7.20–26, 22.20
51	Sedet super coccum Raab	**51.1** Jos 2.18
	Et super utrem Sisara,	**51.2** Jdc 4.19
	Eglon super cenaculum	**51.3** Jdc 3.20
	Et Iahel super malleum.	**51.4** Jdc 4.21
52	Super lagenam Gedeon,	**52.1** Jdc 7.16
	Super columpnam et Samson,	**52.2** Jdc 16.25–30
	Super molam Abimelech,	**52.3** Jdc 9.53
	Iepte super fulcrum sedet.	
53	Ruth vero super stipulam	**53.1** Rt 2.2
	Helique super sellulam,	**53.2** 1 Sm 4.13
	Super lebetem Finees,	**53.3** 1 Sm 2.14
	Super tridentem Opfni sedet.	**53.4** 1 Sm 2.13
54	In scopulo tunc Ionathas,	**54.1** 1 Sm 14.4–5
	Super capram sedet Nabal	**54.2** 1 Sm 25.2–3
	Et super currum Absalon	**54.3** 1 Sm 15.1
	Et super mulam Salomon.	**54.4** 3 Rg 1.33
55	Dauid rex super tympanum	**55.1** 2 Sm 6.5

Et Roboam super iugum;   **55.2** 3 Rg 12.4–14
Cancellis et Ochozias   **55.3–4** 4 Rg 1.2
Inde casurus sederat.

56   Helias axe flammeo,   **56.1** 4 Rg 2.11
     Heliseus in aratro;   **56.2** 3 Rg 19.19
     In dupla ueste Giezi,   **56.3** 4 Rg 5.22–23
     Ezechias in scriniis.   **56.4** 2 Par 30.1; Is 38.9

57   In torculari Ysaias,   **57.1** Is 5.2
     In horologio Achatz;   **57.2** 4 Rg 20.11; Is 38.8
     Super leonem Danihel   **57.3** Dn 6.7–24
     Et super canem Hiezabel. **57.4** 3 Rg 21.23; 4 Rg 9.3

58   Tobias super feretrum   **58.1** Tb 14.11?
     Et proles super thalamum; **58.2** Tb 8.1–4
     Super pannos Hieremias   **58.3** Jr 38.11–12
     Ianas sedet sub hedera.   **58.4** Jon 4.6–10

59   Anna super monticulum,   **59.1** Tb 11.5
     Iosias super solium,   **59.2** 4 Rg 21.26–22.1; 2 Par 33.25–34
     Susanna super pixidem,
     Et Saul super fornicem.   **59.4** 1 Sm 15.12

60   Ihezechiel in latere,   **60.1** Ez 4.1
     Prostibulo tunc Osee;   **60.2** Os 1.2
     In trulla cementarii   **60.3–4** Am 7.7–8
     Amos sedens accubuit.

61   Micheas genu complicat;
     In rupe sedet Abdias,   **61.2** Abd 3
     Iohel ollam carboneam   **61.3** Jl 2.6
     Cum Naum habet cathedram.

62   Facit domum bidentium   **62.1–2** So 2.6
     Sophonias cliotedrum,
     Aggeus sedet in tripoda,
     Super borith Malachias.   **62.4** Mal 3.2

63   At Abacuc presepium   **63.1–3** Dn 14.32–35

Miratus animalium,
Fenum super molle sedet
Pauensque typum preuidet.   **63.4** Hab 3.16

64   Sedet curuli krisio   **64.1–2** Za 4.2
     Zacharias candelabro,
     Et toruus in uestibulo   **64.3–4** Est 5.11, 7.7?
     Assuerus arboreo.

65   Hester super cubiculum,   **65.1** Est 2.16
     Aman super patibulum,   **65.2** Est 7.10
     Mardocheus in gradibus,   **65.3** Est 2.19, 21, etc.?
     Et Achior in restibus.   **65.4** Jdt 6.9

66   Holofernis super thronum   **66.1** Jdt 10.19?
     Et Iudith super gladium,   **66.2** Jdt 13.8–10
     Super cunas Elisabeth,   **66.3** Lc 1.24
     Scabello Iohannes sedet.

67   Lazarus super tumulum,   **67.1** Jo 11.17, 38
     Balaam super asinum,   **67.2** Nm 22.21–30
     Lapisque super puteum   **67.3–4** Jo 4.6
     Fessum fouet bonum Iesum.

68   In littore Petrus sedet   **68.1** Mt 4.18; Mc 1.16, Lc 5.1–3; Jo 21.7–9
     Et sub ficu Nathanahel,   **68.2** Jo 1.48
     Post Zachariam reliqui
     Cuncti carent subselliis.

69   At Iob in sterquilinio   **69.1–2** Jb 2.8
     Sedet audito nuntio
     Sabei quod irruerant   **69.3–4** Jb 1.15
     Predamque sibi tulerant.

70   Rex interim conqueritur
     Quod frustra Iob affligitur.   **70.2** Jb 2.3
     In hostem dat imperia
     Ne iustus uir deficiat.

71   Tunc Cain prendit sarculum   **71.1** Gn 4.2

	Et Noe dolatorium,	**71.2** Gn 6.14–16
	Nemroth sumit uenabulum;	**71.3** Gn 10.9
	Lot timens clausit hostium.	**71.4** Gn 19.6
72	Trecentos hinc uernaculos	**72.1–2** Gn 14.14
	Armat Abram in emulos;	
	Tubal inuadit martulum	**72.3** Gn 4.22
	Et Ysaac fossorium.	
73	Esau tollit pharetram	**73.1** Gn 25.27
	Et Iacob petram lympidam,	**73.2** Gn 28.10–11, 18–19
	Rotabulum rapit Ioseph,	**73.3** Gn 43.31–34?
	Securim et Abimelech.	**73.4** Jdc 9.48
74	Virgam uibrauit Moyses	**74.1** Ex 7.17–20, 17.5–6, Nm 20.11
	Et pugionem Finees;	**74.2** Nm 25.7
	Iosue leuat clipeum	**74.3** Jos 8.18
	At Aoth stringit capulum.	**74.4** Jdc 3.21–22
75	Samgar prehendit uomerem,	**75.1** Jdc 3.31
	Samson maxillam uindicem,	**75.2** Jdc 15.15
	Iahel clauim et malleum,	**75.3** Jdc 4.21
	Ensem Barach sanguineum.	**75.4** Jdc 4.16
76	Fundam Dauid et lapidem	**76.1** 1 Sm 17.40
	Saulque furens cuspidem;	**76.2** 1 Sm 18.10–11
	Sagittas poscit Ionathas	**76.3–4** 1 Sm 20.36–37, 1 Sm 19.9–10
	Trans puerum quas iecerat.	
77	Rapit Ioab tres lanceas	**77.1** 4 Rg 13.18?
	Et Abner hastam baiulat,	**77.2** 2 Sm 2.23
	Eleazar cum gladio,	**77.3** 2 Sm 23.9–10
	Ruit Ioas cum iaculo.	**77.4** 4 Rg 13.18
78	Rex ponti fugit Arioth	**78.1–4** Gn 14.1–10?
	Fugit et Chodorlaomor;	
	Rex gentium fugit Thadal	
	At Amraphel rex Fennaar.	
79	Fugit Bersa, fugit Bara,	**79.1** Gn 14.2, 10

Fugit Agar, fugit Thamar,	**79.2** Agar: Gn 16.6
Fugit Senna et Semeber,	**79.3** Gn 14.2, 10
Fugit et Adonisedech.	**79.4** Jos 10.1, 11

80	Fugit Ohan, fugit Faran	**80.1** Jos 10.3, 11
	Et puer fugit Ioathan,	**80.2** Jdc 9.21
	Iaphie fugit et Dabir,	**80.3** Jos 10.3, 11
	Sisara fugit et Iabin.	**80.4** Sisara: Jdc 4.15

81	Tunc fugit Adonibezech,	**81.1** Jdc 1.6
	Fugit Oreb fugitque Zeb,	**81.2** Jdc 7.21, 25
	Fugit Zebe, fugit Gaal,	**81.3** Jdc 8.12, 9.39–41
	Iobab fugit et Salmana.	**81.4** 3 Rg 2.28; Jdc 8.5, 10–12

82	Fugit Ioram et Benadab	**82.1** 4 Rg 9.23; 3 Rg 20.20, 29–31?
	Et Sedechias et Ahab	**82.2** 4 Rg 25.4, Jr 39.4, 52.8; 3 Rg
	Et Aazias rex fugit;	22.34
	Fugit Syrus Sennacherib.	**82.4** 4 Rg 19.36; Is 37.37

83	Fugit Razon, fugit Adad,	**83.1** Razon: 3 Rg 11.23, Adad: 3 Rg 11.17
	Adramelech et Sarasar,	**83.2** 4 Rg 19.37; Is 37.38
	Ieroboam et Ismahel,	**83.3** 3 Rg 11.40
	Ledit fuga Mifiboseth.	**83.4** 2 Sm 4.4

84	Fugit Soba, fugit Roob,	**84.1–2** 2 Sm 10.8, 13
	Maacha fugit et Istob,	
	Fugit Soba proles Bocri,	**84.3** 2 Sm 20.2
	Helias fugit de Thesbi.	**84.4** 3 Rg 17.1, 19.3

85	Arcum Hieu corripuit,	**85.1** 4 Rg 9.24
	Abimelech fedus petit,	**85.2** Gn 21.27, 32
	Salomon bella temperat,	**85.3** 3 Rg 4.24–25
	Recepit Iob duplicia.	**85.4** Jb 42.10

86	Nutu regis sedilia	
	Reposcunt omnes pristina	
	Circum supraque Moyses	**86.3–4** Ex 26.1–6
	Cortinas tendit nexiles.	

87 Addit passim preterea
   Egyptia tentoria;
   Dein ministri properant
   Et ministrantes cursitant.

88 Primus minister pestifer   **88.1–4** Gn 3.1–6
   Apponit pomum coluber;
   Adam cum Eua coniuge
   Accelerat comedere.

89 Cain de terre frugibus   **89.1** Gn 4.3
   Et lac Abel de ouibus,   **89.2** Gn 4.4
   Noe de botris uinee;   **89.3** Gn 9.20–21
   Gustat Abram de uolucre.   **89.4** Gn 15.9

90 De panibus Loth, saturo   **90.1** Gn 19.3
   Mandit Sara de uitulo;   **90.2** Gn 18.7–8?
   Isaac pro cerui carnibus   **90.3–4** Gn 27.1–25
   Hedum uorauit nescius.

91 Esau rufa coctio   **91.1–2** Gn 25.30, 34
   Ventrem repleuit oppido;
   Seruatur ius ad poculum   **91.3–4** Jdc 6.19?
   Sumatur ut post prandium.

92 Frumentum, uinum, oleum,   **92.1–2** Gn 27.27
   Capit Iacob potissimum;
   Gaudet Rachel mandragoris   **92.3–4** Gn 30.14–16
   Sub nocte lecto uenditis.

93 Mandit Ioseph amigdalas   **93.1–2** Gn 43.11
   Pater Iacob quas miserat,
   Et carduos est Ysacar;   **93.3** Gn 49.14?
   Dan equi mordet ungulas.   **93.4** Gn 49.17

94 Moyses agno uescitur
   Lactucis cum agrestibus;
   Nuces manducat Aaron,   **94.3** Nm 17.8
   Iosue botrum de Ebron.   **94.4** Nm 13.23

95 Lac degustabat Sisara,	**95.1** Jdc 4.19
Crassus Eglon est pinguia,	**95.2** Jdc 3.17
Necnon de ramni fructibus	**95.3–4** Jdc 9.6, 14.15
Abimelech reficitur.	
96 Samson manducat de fauo;	**96.1–2** Jdc 14.8–9
Manue datur portio;	
Ruth panem ordeaceum,	**96.3** Rt 2.14
Noemi cruste reliquum.	**96.4** Rt 2.18
97 Melle ieiunus Ionathas	**97.1–2** 1 Sm 14.27
Edictum patris uiolat;	
Amon sorbitiunculas	**97.3** 2 Sm 13.6
Panes Dauid sanctos uorat.	**97.4** 1 Sm 21.3–6
98 Celi captabat uictimas;	
Diuisit partes Helchana.	**98.2** 1 Sm 1.4
Armum reseruat Samuhel,	**98.3–4** 1 Sm 9.23–24
Rodit Saul sollempniter.	
99 Salomon prandit bubalum,	**99.1** 1 Rg 4.23
Ozias idolotitum,	**99.2** 4 Rg 15.4
Cum carne panem Helias,	**99.3** 3 Rg 17.6
Heliseus colothintidas.	**99.4** 4 Rg 4.38–41
100 Hedum balantem Tobias	**100.1–2** Tb 2.20–21
Furtum timescens ruminat;	
Est Sophonias trepidus	**100.3–4** So 2.14
Coruum de liminaribus.	
101 Danihel coch⟨l⟩earium	**101.1–4** Dn 14.32–38
Sumens cauat alueolum,	
Ad os crebro ducens manum	
De pleno reddit uacuum.	
102 Tres pueri legumina	**102.1** Dn 1.12
Et Ysaias olera;	
In fimo panem decoquit	**102.3–4** Ez 4.12–15
Hiezechiel et comedit.	

103	Est uitulum conterritus	**103.1** 1 Sm 28.24–25
	Saul phitone spiritu;	**103.2** 1 Sm 28.8, 20
	Iudith maducat caseum	**103.3–4** Jdt 10.5
	Panem quoque sollicitum.	

104	Cupiuit micas Lazarus;	**104.1–2** Lc 16.20–21
	Dives negauit impius.	
	Anna producit lacrimas,	**104.3** Tb 7.19
	Isaac dolorem temperat.	**104.4** Gn 24.67

105	Interea plenissime	**105.1–4** Nm 7.10–82
	Cibis succedunt epule	
	Cum reges atque principes	
	Profundunt escas largitur.	

106	Cum Naason Nathanael	**106.1–4** Nm 7.17–41
	Et Heliab gerunt dapes,	
	Cum Helisur Salamihel	
	Dant uictum liberaliter.	

107	Heliasaph, Helisama,	**107.1–4** Nm 7.42–77
	Gamalihel et Abibas,	
	Adiezel et Phegihel	
	Mensas complent alacriter,	

108	Cum ipsis duodecimus	**108.1–2** Nm 7.78–82
	Adira, Henna filius;	
	In tribubus duodecim	
	Hi duces et clarissimi	

109	Tradunt boues duodecim,	**109.1–4** Nm 7.87
	Arietes duodecim,	
	Agnos, hyrcos duodecim,	
	Que cuncta flamma sorbuit.	

110	Sed hec ipsi restituunt	**110.1–4** Nm 7.87–88
	In duplum et in quincuplum	
	Vt hostia pacifica	
	Pacificet conuiuia.	

111 Uiginti quattuor boues,   **111.1–4** Nm 7.88
     Sexaginta arietes,
     Et hyrcos cum agniculis
     Dant totidem in epulis.

112 Salomon boum hostias   **112.1–4** 3 Rg 8.63; 2 Par 7.5
     Viginti duo milia
     Arietumque uictimas
     Centum uiginti milia,

113 Iustus Asa nobiliter   **113.1–4** 2 Par 15.11
     Rex septingentos dat boues,
     Super septenis milibus
     Impensis arietibus.

114 At Ezechias inclitus   **114.1–4** 2 Par 29.21
     Tauros cum arietibus,
     Agnos cum hyrcis olidis
     Septem in primis obtulit.

115 Deuotus offert denuo   **115.1–2** 1 Par 29.32
     Agnos ducentos numero,
     Sexcenta boum somata   **115.3–4** 2 Par 29.33
     Ouesque tria milia.

116 Septuaginta deinceps   **116.1–4** 2 Par 29.32
     Tauros, centum arietes,
     Ducentos agnos integra
     Profert beniuolentia.

117 Idem cum suis postea   **117.1–4** 2 Par 30.24
     Dat tauros duo milia,
     Oues quoque de pascua
     Decem et septem milia.

118 Iosias totis uiribus   **118.1–4** 2 Par 35.18
     Insistit uictualibus,
     Par uoluntate regibus
     Euo se precedentibus.

119   Gregis triginta milia,   **119.1–4** 2 Par 35.7
       Armenti tria milia
       Cibariis adnumerat
       Ad regis magni fercula.

120   Helchias atque Ieihel   **120.1–4** 2 Par 35.8
       Et Zacharias principes,
       Balantum duo milia
       Atque sexcentum capita,

121   Boues trecentos perinde   **121.1–4** 2 Par 35.8–9
       Attribuunt spontanee.
       Et Leuitarum proceres
       Quingentos offerunt boues;

122   At uero quinque milia   **122.1–2** 2 Par 35.9
       Superaddentes pecora
       Pinguedine et adipe
       Latebras implent anime.

123   Nulla sit estimatio
       In tam magno conuiuio
       Vbique quanta largitas
       Exundet complens prandia!

124   Quicumque subintroeunt
       Et conferunt et comedunt,
       Et nemo discumbentium
       Sentit dolorem dentium.

125   Iosias ossa proicit,   **125.1** 4 Rg 23.16
       Hiezechiel recolligit,   **125.2** Ez 37.7
       Tobias mestus sepelit,   **125.3** Tb 2.3–6
       Ornat Symon pyramidis.   **125.4** 1 Mcc 9.19?

126   Flagranti desiderio
       Tunc omnis illa contio
       Vinum ardenter postulat,
       Siti coquente guttura.

127   Mox Dauid surgit et Ioseph,
      Dantes scyphos uelociter;
      Iahel coaptat phialas,   **127.3** Jdc 4.19
      Architriclinus ydrias.   **127.4** Jo 2.6–8

128   Naason et Nathanahel   **128.1–4** Nm 7.10–82
      Decemque sui suppares
      Rumpunt moras et irruunt
      Vinoque uasa deferunt.

129   Cum phyalis turibula   **129.1–4** Nm 7.12–20
      Tollunt simul argentea;
      Ex auro mortariola
      Prensant singuli singula.

130   Vasa Cyrus adnumerat   **130.1–4** 1 Esr 1.7
      Que de Syon adtulerat
      Crudus Nabugodonosor,
      Malis malo deterior;

131   Auri triginta phialas,   **131.1–4** 1 Esr 1.9–10
      Mille dehinc argenteas,
      Triginta scyphos aureos,
      Quadringentos argenteos.

132   Tum mille uasa cetera   **132.1–4** 1 Esr 1.10–11
      Manu recenset libera
      Ad summam inter omnia
      Consignat quinque milia.

133   De quadringentis numerum   **133.1–4** 1 Esr 1.11
      Super expleuit integrum
      Vt regis ministeria
      Ornaret opulentia.

134   Rex autem promtuaria
      Pandi iubet ditissima
      Bachique plura genera
      Propinari per fercula.

135 Pincerne mox prosiliunt,
     Crateras, cados rapiunt,
     Sine mensura conuehunt
     Et indiscrete tribuunt.

136 Noe Tharsinum amphora,   **136.1** Gn 9.20–21?
     Abram Albanum phiala,
     Scypho Ioseph Amineum,   **136.3** Gn 43.34?
     Iob bibit orca Creticum.

137 Melchisidec Argitium,   **137.1** Gn 14.18?
     Pharao Mareothidum,   **137.2** Gn 40.11?
     Crudus Nabudonosor
     Merum pitissat ex Bosor.

138 Musto bachatur Heliu
     Et leporalio Saul;   **138.2** 1 Sm 16.20
     Phalernum potat Balthasar,   **138.3** Dn 5.1–4?
     Fit temulentus Benadab.   **138.4** 3 Rg 20.16?

139 Galenum Ruben patera,
     Abel rubrum fidelia,
     Bumasticum petit Sichem,
     Sternutat L⟨o⟩th ad calicem. **139.4** Gn 19.33–35?

140 Vrna lieum rex Hela   **140.1–2** 3 Rg 16.9–10
     Mox moriturus in Tersa,
     Ioab rubente uasculo
     Suranum mortariolo

141 Vtre Florentinum Agar   **141.1** Gn 21.14–19?
     Rebecca clarum ydria,   **141.2** Gn 24.15?
     Lagena rufum Gedeon,
     Flascone Rhodium Eglon.

142 Oua Surrentinum Edom,
     Gemma Phaneum Salomon,
     Semmetim pneum situla,
     Laxa gamum Cham gabata.

143   Dan glaucum acetabulo,
       Iaphet Lageum urceo,
       Iudith Leneum cyato,   **143.3** Jdt 10.5?
       Hester Campanum poculo.

144   Cratere Holofernea   **144.1–2** Jdt 12.20?
       Cum defruto stat dextera;
       Tobias gutto Rethicum,
       Vitro Dauid Methimneum.

145   Cis Massicum seriola,
       Ruth Tmolium cum patina,   **145.2** Rt 2.9, 14?
       Nemroth ampulla Thasium,
       Golias conca turbidum.

146   Sappam Iacob dat Ysaac,   **146.1** Gn 27.25
       Hinc Esau flens murmurat,   **146.2** Gn 27.34
       Rebecca plaudit, conscia   **146.3–4** Gn 27.5–17
       Iacob de fraudulentia.

147   Thubal Gazetum bacceo,
       Carenum Zeb oenophoro,   **147.2** Jdc 7.25?
       Obba Petrus luctificum,
       Sed circa gallicinium.   **147.4** Mt 26.74; Mc 14.72; Lc 22.60;
                                      Jo 18.27

148   Andreas bibit limpidum,
       Maria honorarium,
       Pasum Iesus cum calice,   **148.3–4** Mt 27.34; Mc 15.36; Jo 29.30
       Spreta fellis acredine.

149   Cain et Iudas cantharo
       Mergunt foeces in stomacho;
       Exclamat uirgo uirginum   **149.3–4** Jo 2.3
       Deesse uini poculum.

150   Nam quia dudum deerat,
       Iahannes aquam biberat;
       Aquis replentur ydrie   **150.3–4** Jo 2.7–10
       Fiuntque uinum nobile.

151	Architriclynus labia Primus tinguit in phiala; "Seruasti," ait protinus, "Vinum bonum usque adhuc."	**151.1–4** Jo 2.8–10
152	Latrinas fabricat Hieu, Uentrem premens purgat Saul, Crassus Eglon se stercorat, Naaman septies lauat.	**152.1** 4 Rg 10.27 **152.2** 1 Sm 24.4 **152.3** Jdc 3.22 **152.4** 4 Rg 5.14
153	In Ioseph ardet domina, Annon accumbens constuprat, Pregnans Agar intumuit, Gemens Rebecca parcurit.	**153.1** Gn 39.7 **153.2** 2 Sm 13.14 **153.3** Gn 16.4 **153.4** Gn 25.22–26
154	Ruben cum Bala cubitat Stratumque patris maculat; Ionas iratus imminet, Rex Niniuita penitet.	**154.1–2** Gn 35.22, 49.4 **154.3-4** Jon 3.4–6
155	Cum Loth cubant et filie Sepulto patre calice, Vadit Ioseph in carcerem Propter notam culpabilem.	**155.1–2** Gn 19.30–35 **155.3–4** Gn 39.7–20
156	At Dauid sciphum inuolat, Abner furantem increpat, Beniamin sacco baiulat, Augur Ioseph recuperat.	**156.1** 1 Sm 26.12 **156.3** Gn 44.2 **156.4** Gn 44.12, 15
157	Ofni carnes rapuerat Et Finees consenserat, Nihil gustarat Moyses, Manducat totum Danihel.	**157.1–2** 1 Sm 2.12–14 **157.3** Ex 34.28 **157.4** Dn 14.38
158	Fur regulam tollit Achan Nam coccinum sublegerat; Arguitur furto Iacob; Vinclis artatur Achior.	**158.1–2** Jos 7.21 **158.3** Gn 27.35, 31.30 **158.4** Jdt 6.9

159	Obtutus Dauid inicit,	**159.1** 2 Sm 11.2
	Assuerus incaluit,	**159.2** Est 2.17?
	Nudat Noe uirilia,	**159.3** Gn 9.20–21
	Bersabee fit succuba.	**159.4** 2 Sm 11.3–4?

160	Tristatur tunc Zorobabel,	**160.1** Agg 1.12
	Arcum tetendit Hismahel,	**160.2** Gn 21.20
	Et per fenestram rex Ioas	**160.3–4** 4 Rg 13.16–17
	Sagittam dat in Arabas.	

23.1 escas] escans *MS* 65.4 Et] E *MS* 71.1 sarculum] sacculum *MS*
87.4 Et] E *MS* 129.1 phyalis turibula] phyalas acibula *MS*
129.4 Prensant] prensentant *MS* 137.4 pitissat] pitasset *MS*
146.4 fraudulentia] fraulentia *MS* 155.4 Propter] Preter *MS*
156.1 sciphum] si ciphum *MS*

The Arras *Cena:* Translation

1 I shall sample the introduction, an essential piece of writing, as I set out to tell of the mystical nuptials of Joel the king.
2 These nuptials a man in Carthage, Cyprian by name, mighty with the honor of martyrdom, first wrote about with fingers bent.
3 After him dancing John, imitating the aforementioned man, with the example of the one feast, repeated what the first man sang.
4 Following them, Azelinus, amplifying it, added more things, and with a single feast fed Prince Henry the emperor.
5 But we divide this feast itself into three periods: before the law, under it, and in the modern period of grace.
6 Therefore understand the lord Joel as Jesus Christ, so that you interpret his only bride as the Church.
7 We may follow the example of Tobias, depriving himself of embraces for three days while he, a virgin, preserves his bride as a virgin.
8 What he did as a type let us present as actual deeds, using a single day to represent each period so that the thing may have a firm basis.
9 And lest you object that the arrangement does not follow the correct order, "the first shall be last, the last first."
10 For if you order all the seats at the royal feasts, with a corresponding waste of time, it makes a ruin of the food.

The end of the preface. The book begins.

11 Once the great king Joel was about to make a celebrated marriage. In the first dawning he made the innermost recesses shine with a new light.

12 Coming first, on the sixth day, he called all men to succeed to incomparable delights.

13 In a most remote place, unknown to everyone thereafter, he arranges pleasant seats and furnishes a prepared feast.

14 And not yet had the feast been arranged in order when secretly, with eager jaws, the virgin assaults the soup (law) of the meal.

15 Those who were there, join in and share the food. Then, their minds conscious of evil, they disperse into the hiding places.

16 And so the broken companionship of the lord Joel plunged everyone into tears with bitter lamentation.

17 Then the sad outcasts, banished far from their comfortable seats, with rough clothes seek food from the earth.

18 There is not such dignity as there was before, nor is there such plenty; instead what is sought after with toil is eaten with sweat.

19 But the benevolence of the king is not vanquished nor does it waver; rather, he provides abundantly everything necessary for sustenance.

20 You might see, however, the wretched condemned ones, fighting spines and thorns, their right hands armed with iron.

21 Cain, livid with furious rage, bending over the ground, digs the earth; Abel, soon to be struck down at the hands of his brother, follows the sheep.

22 A new guest eats apples, plants, acorns, and the sustenance of bread, and does not bring meat to the feast.

23 Noah wisely saves up all edible things so that he might feed his sons and their wives for fifteen months.

24 After these events, with strength diminished, they all make use of the meats of creatures to which the fertile ark, free from the flood, had given birth.

25 Thereupon the priest and king of Salem, honoring the Lord of heaven, took a tithe from Abram, to whom he gave bread and wine.

26 Then Abraham—through whom the love of the pious lord is recovered— relying on faith, earned the king's grace.

27 Circumcision is ordered at that point as a sign, whereupon the entire feast now exults in greater joy.

28 Now elderly Abraham laughs; Sarah laughs behind the door. Isaac is called "laughter" because both his parents had laughed.

29 The father exclaims straightaway, "God made laughter for me. Whoever hears this will soon laugh with the sterile one."

30 When Isaac is weaned, Abraham prepares a feast; and there is great joy when the meal is celebrated.

31 And lest lateness spoil the rest of the food, Pentapolis is set on fire, Lot's wife is made into salt.

32 With fruit, produced from seeds, increased a hundredfold, Isaac provided water from the wells he dug.

33 After that, when he refreshed King Abimelech and Phicol, and after the water of the well of "Latitude," he found the well of "Abundance."

34 Seeing a pot, famished and wasting with hunger, Edom buys lentils and sells his birthrights.

35 Reuben delivers mandrakes, pretty Rachel longs for them, and Leah mutters against her; but the bed soothes the contention.

36 Jacob sacrifices victims with Laban when they dine on Mount Galeed, the mound constructed, the testimony sworn.

37 Pharaoh held a birthday party, furnishing a festive banquet for the feasting Egyptians, the baker having been hanged.

38 Joseph had given a promise of bread, but he soon makes his brothers drunk and orders them to bring his father to him.

39 Then Goshen is filled with joy by the people of Israel; in their ceremonies the first feast thus ends.

40 They slay little lambs and the Lord slays the Egyptians; and they fulfill the feast happily; the Egyptians complete their mourning.

41 Thence baptized by the mystic font of the Red Sea, they prepare themselves under Mount Sinai, anew, for the feast.

The first book ends. The second begins.

42 At the king's orders, Moses produces hammered trumpets. He sounds out clearly with the horn and reconvenes the feast.

43 The men of yesterday, with all their failing troops, spread themselves out. Moses carefully distributes them in order.

44 Adam, with a chair of fig wood, sits with Eve, his companion; Cain sits on a sheaf, Abel on a little lamb.

45 Noah sits on an ark and Abraham under an ilex; Lot places himself on a mountain and Isaac on an altar.

46 Sarah sits in the doorway and Esau on a quiver, Jacob on a figurative rock and Rachel on idols.

47 The brothers, vessels of war, sit among the grasses of the wall, and Reuben in his father's little bed; Judah lies down on prey.

48 Then Zebulon in boats and Isachar on a load; Dan, sitting down, puts his weight on a snake, and Gad on the sheath of a sword.

49 Asher sits in meal and Benjamin on a small sack, Nephtalin on a throne; Joseph sits in chaff.

50 And Moses sits in a small basket, Pharaoh on a roof tile, Joshua on a helmet, Achar on a rule.

51 Raab sits on scarlet and Sisera on a bag, Eglon in the upper room and Jahel on a hammer.

52 Gideon sits on a flask and Samson on a column, Abimelech on a millstone, Japhthah on a couch.

53 Ruth, truly, sits on a stalk, and Eli on a little chair, Phineas on a cauldron; Ophni sits on a three-pronged fork.

54 Then Jonathan sits on a rock, Nabal on a she-goat, and Absolon on a chariot, Solomon on a she-mule.

55 David the king on a tambourine and Rehoboam on a yoke; and Ahaziah on lattices, about to fall from where he had been sitting.

56 Elijah sits on a fiery chariot, Heliseus on a plough, Gehazi on a pair of garments, Ezechias on a writing box.

57 Isaiah sits on a winepress, Ahaz on a clock, Daniel on a lion, and Jezebel on a dog.

58 Tobias sits on a bier and his son on a marriage bed, Jeremiah on rags and Jonah under ivy.

59 Anna sits on a little mountain, Josiah on a throne, Susanna on a small box, Saul on an arch.

60 Ezekiel on a tile, then Hosea with a prostitute; Amos, sitting, reclined on a plumb line.

61 Micheas folds his knees, Obadiah sits on a rock; Joel has a jar to sit on and Nahum has a throne.

62 Sophonias makes a sheep pen his folding chair; Aggeus sits on a three-legged stool and Malachias on soapwort.

63 And Habakkuk, amazed at the pen of animals, sits on soft straw and, quaking, foresees a prefiguration.

64 Zacharias, with a golden candlestick, sits on a curule chair; Ahasuerus sits, furious, in the shady courtyard.

65 Esther sits in a bedchamber, Haman on a gallows, Mardocheus on steps, and Achior on ropes.

66 Holofernes sits on a throne and Judith on a sword, Elizabeth on a cradle and John on a footstool.

67 Lazarus sits on a grave-mound, Balaam on an ass, and a stone on a well warms good Jesus, who is weary.

68 Peter sits on the shore and Nathaniel under a fig tree. After Zacharias all the rest lack seats.

69 And Job sits on a dung-hill, having heard the messenger's news that the Sabeans had invaded and taken booty.

70 The king meanwhile laments because Job had been afflicted wrongly. He gives power over the enemy, lest a just man be weakened.

71 Then Cain takes a hoe and Noah a carpenter's tool; Nimrod takes a hunting spear. Fearful Lot closes the door.

72 Then Abram arms three hundred household slaves against the enemy. Tubal takes a small hammer and Isaac a dagger.

73 Esau takes up a quiver and Jacob a gleaming rock; Joseph seizes a cooking fork and Abimelech an axe.

74 Moses brandishes a stick and Phineas a dagger; Joshua raises a shield and Ehud draws a sword hilt.

75 Samgar takes hold of a plowshare, Samson an avenging jawbone, Jahel a nail and hammer, Barach a bloody sword.

76 David takes a sling and a stone and mad Saul a spear; Jonathan asks for the arrows he had shot past the boy.

77 Joab takes three lances and Abner carries a spear; Eleazar has a sword, Joash rushes forward with a dart.

78 Arioch, the king of the sea, flees, and Chedorlaomer flees also; Tidal, king of the people, flees, and Amraphel, king of Senaar.

79 Bersa flees, Bara flees, Agar flees, Thamar flees, Senna flees and Sameber, and Adonisedech flees.

80 Ohan flees, Faran flees, and the boy Jonathan flees, Japhia flees and Dabir flees, Sisara flees and Iabin.

81 Next Adonibezech flees, Oreb flees and Zeb flees, Zebee flees and Gaal flees, Iobab flees and Salmana.

82 Ioram flees and Benadab, and Sedechias and Ahab, and Aazias the king flees. The Syrian Sennacherib flees.

83 Razan flees, Adad flees, Adramelech and Sarasar, Ieroboam and Ismaael flee. Flight injures Mifiboseth.

84 Saba flees, Roob flees, Maacha flees, and Istob, Seba the son of Bocri flees, Helias of Thesbi flees.

85 Hieu seizes a bow, Abimelech requests a treaty. Solomon refrains from war, Job received twofold.

86 All claim their former seats by the command of the king, and Moses stretches woven curtains over and around.

87 He adds, furthermore, Egyptian tents all around; then helpers hurry and servers run here and there.

88 The first attendant, the deadly serpent, serves an apple; Adam with Eve, his wife, makes haste to eat.

89 Cain eats of the fruits of the earth, Abel sheep's milk, and Noah from the grapes of the vine; Abram samples a fowl.

90 Lot eats bread loaves; Sarah chews on the fatted calf; Isaac, unawares, devoured kid in mistake for venison.

91 A red stew quickly filled Esau's stomach. The broth is kept for the cup so it can be taken after the meal.

92 Jacob takes the best fruits, wine, and oil. Rachel rejoices in mandrakes, sold for a bed in the night.

93 Joseph nibbles almonds which his father Jacob had sent, and Ysacar eats thistles. Dan gnaws on the hooves of a horse.

94 Moses feeds on lamb with field lettuces; Aaron chews nuts, Joshua a grape from Hebron.

95 Sisara gulped milk, stout Eglon eats fats, and Abimelech is refreshed by the fruits of the thornbush.

96 Samson eats from a honeycomb; a section is given to Manoah. Ruth eats barley bread, Naomi, the rest of the crust.

97 Hungry Jonathan violates the command of his father with honey. Amon takes little draughts, David devors the holy bread.

98 Celi caught animals for sacrifice, Helchana divided the parts, Samuel keeps back the shoulder of the animal, Saul gnaws solemnly.

99 Solomon eats gazelle, Ozias a sacrifice, Helias bread with meat, Heliseus a colocynth.

100 Tobias, fearful, chews the theft, a bleating kid; anxious Sophonias eats a raven from the threshold.

101 Daniel, taking a spoon, empties the tray; bringing a hand frequently to his mouth, he returns the full tray empty.

102 The three boys eat pulses, Isaiah vegetables; Ezechiel boils the bread in dung and eats.

103 Saul, terrified by a python spirit, eats veal; Judith munches on cheese and troubled bread.

104 Lazarus wanted crumbs; the impious rich man refused. Anna came forth with tears, Isaac restrained sadness.

105 Meanwhile very full platters of food follow, when kings and rulers cause the fare to flow bountifully.

106 Naason with Nathaniel and Heliab bear forth the feast, Helisur and Sal-
amihel distribute the food liberally.

107 Helisaph, Helisama, Gamalihel and Abibas, Adiezel and Phegihel fill the
tables speedily.

108 With these is the twelfth, Ahira son of Enan. In twelve tribes these leaders
and most illustrious ones

109 Hand over twelve cows, twelve rams, twelve sheep and goats, all of which
the flame swallowed.

110 But these same men restore these numbers twofold and five, so that the
peaceful victim may make the feast peaceful.

111 They give at the feast twenty-four cows, sixty rams, and just as many
goats and lambs.

112 Solomon gives twenty-two thousand cows as sacrifices and 120,000 rams
as sacrifices.

113 Just Asa, the king, nobly gives seven hundred cows in addition to seven
thousand rams.

114 And renowned Ezechias offered bulls and rams, sheep with odorous
goats, seven in the beginning.

115 Devoted, he gives in offering anew two hundred lambs in number, six
hundred head of cattle and three thousand sheep.

116 And then he offers seventy bulls, one hundred rams, two hundred sheep,
with full generosity.

117 Afterward he also, with his men, gives two thousand bulls and seventeen
thousand sheep from pasture.

118 Josias, with all his strength, devotes himself to the provisions, equal in
enthusiasm to the kings preceding him in time.

119 He counts out as rations thirty thousand of the flock, three thousand of the
herd, for the dishes of the great king.

120 The rulers Hilkiah, Jehiel, and Zacharias give 2,600 head of sheep.

121 In like manner they give three hundred cows willingly, and the chiefs of
the Levites offer five hundred cows.

122 And truly with five hundred head added in addition, they fill the soul's
insides with richness and fat.

123 Let there be no reckoning, in such a large banquet, of how much generosity flows out, filling the feast!

124 Anyone who enters both joins in and feasts, and no one of the seated has
any oral complaint.

125 Josiah throws the bones away, Ezechiel gathers them up again, unhappy
Tobias buries them, Simon furnishes them with monuments.

126 Then with burning desire all that assembly demands wine ardently, thirst parching their throats.

127 Soon David and Joseph rise, dispensing vessels speedily; Jahel prepares pitchers, the master of the feast wine jugs.

128 Naason and Nathaniel and ten of their fellows end the delay and hurry in; they offer vessels for wine.

129 They take silver turibles together with cups; each one of them takes one gold dipper.

130 Cyrus counts out the vessels which cruel Nebechudnezzar—worse than bad men in his evil—had brought from Jerusalem:

131 thirty-one vessels of gold, and after this a thousand silver ones; thirty gold goblets, four hundred of silver.

132 Then he counts out a thousand other vessels with a free hand. As the total of all of them, he gives five thousand.

133 With four hundred he fulfills the complete number so that the opulence may adorn the service of the king.

134 The king orders the richest storerooms to be opened, and many kinds of wine to be dispensed with the dishes.

135 The waiters soon leap up; they seize jugs and jars, bring them in without measure, and distribute them freely.

136 Noah drinks Tharsinian wine from an amphora, Abram Alban wine from a saucer, Joseph white wine from a cup, Job Cretan wine from a butt.

137 Melchisidec drinks Argethian wine, Pharaoh Mareotic wine, cruel Nebechudnezzar spits pure wine from Bosor.

138 Heliu revels with must, Saul with leporalius, Balthazar drinks Falernian wine, Benadab gets drunk.

139 Ruben drinks Calenan wine from a bowl, Abel red wine from an earthen pot, Sichem seeks Bumastic wine, Lot sneezes at the cup.

140 King Hela drinks wine from an urn, soon to die in Tersa; Joab drinks Suranum wine from a small dipper, a red vessel.

141 Agar drinks Florentinian wine from a wine skin, Rebecca clear wine from a water jug, Gideon red wine from a lagena, Eglon Rhodian wine from a flask.

142 Edom Surrentine wine from an egg, Solomon Phanaean wine from a gem cup, Semmetim *pneum* from an urn, Ham *gamum* from a spacious vessel.

143 Dan sparkling wine from a goblet, Japhet Egyptian wine from a pitcher, Judith Bacchic wine from a measure, Hester Campanian wine from a tankard.

144 The right hand of Holofernes has a crater of boiled must; Tobias drinks Rhaetian wine from a cruet, David Methymnan wine from a glass.

145 Cis drinks Massic wine in a small jar, Ruth Tmolian wine from a dish, Nimrod Thasian wine from a vessel, Goliath muddy wine from a shell.

146 Jacob gives Isaac must; hence Esau, crying, laments. Rebecca applauds, knowing Jacob's deceitfulness.

147 Tubal drinks Gaza wine from a Bacchic cup, Zeb sweet wine from a wine holder, Peter doleful wine from a decanter, but around cockcrow.

148 Andrew drinks clear wine, Mary the honorary wine, Jesus raisin wine from a cup, having refused the bitterness of gall.

149 Cain and Judas with a tankard submerge the dregs in their stomach; the virgin of virgins exclaims that the goblet of wine is lacking.

150 Because something had been missing for some time, John had drunk water. Jugs are filled with water and are made into noble wine.

151 First the master of the feast wets his lips with a jug. "You have kept," he says straightaway, "the good wine until now."

152 Hieu makes latrines; Saul, pressing his stomach, purges himself; stout Eglon soils himself; Naaman washes seven times.

153 The mistress is ardent for Joseph; Annon, lying down, debauches. Pregnant Agar swells up; groaning Rebecca gives birth.

154 Reuben lies down with Bala and stains the covers of his father, angry Jonah threatens, the king of Nineveh repents.

155 And Lot's daughters lie with him, their father being buried with wine. Joseph went into jail by reason of certain guilt.

156 But David steals a cup, Abner blames a thief, Benjamin carries it in a sack, Joseph recovers it as if by magic.

157 Ophni had seized the meat and Phineas had agreed. Moses had tasted nothing, Daniel chewed everything.

158 The thief Achan steals the rule, for he had secretly carried off scarlet. Jacob is accused of theft; Achior is bound with chains.

159 David casts a glance, Assuerus grows hot, Noah bares his genitals, Bersheba becomes a strumpet.

160 Then Zorababel grows sad, Ismael drew his bow, and through the window Joas the king shoots an arrow toward the Arabs.

2. The Long *Nemo*

Manuscripts

O   Oxford, Bodleian Library MS Selden supra 74, fols. 10rv, 12r–13v. s. xiii[2]. Previously edited by P. Meyer in Anatole de Montaiglon and James de Rothschild, eds., *Recueil de poésies françoises,* 13 vols. (Paris, 1855–78), 11:314–20.

V   Vatican, Biblioteca Apostolica Vaticana MS lat. 2040, fols. 72v–74v. s. xiv[ex]. Not previously edited.

M   Munich, Bayerische Staatsbibliothek MS clm. 12034, fols. 140r–142r. a. 1404. Not previously edited.

A   Oxford, Bodleian Library MS Add. A. 365, fols. 10v–13r. s. xv[in]. Not previously edited.

L   London, British Library MS Royal 12.D.III, fols. 158r–160v. s. xv[in]. Not previously edited.

G   Hamburg, Staats- und Universitätsbibliothek MS Petri 22, fol. 261rv. a. 1435. Not previously edited.

H   Heidelberg, Universitätsbibliothek MS Pal. germ. 314, fols. 100v–102r. a. 1443–47. Previously edited in W. Wattenbach, "Historia Neminis," *Anzeiger für Kunde der deutschen Vorzeit,* N. F. 13 (1866): cols. 361–67 (at cols. 362–67).

P   Paris, Bibliothèque Nationale MS lat. 3127, fols. 159va–161ra. s. xv. Not previously edited.

The text as edited represents the Second Recension of the Long *Nemo,* of which manuscripts V, A, L, and H give the fullest text. V serves as the base text in this edition. G is a derivative of the Second Recension: the most idiosyncratic parts of this version are printed as the second appendix to the Long *Nemo.* The First Recension (represented by manuscripts O and M) is not edited separately; the variant readings of O and M are recorded in the apparatus in the same way as those of the other manuscripts. P is a derivative of the First Recension: most of this text is printed as the third appendix to the Long *Nemo.*

Incipit vita sanctissimi et gloriosissimi Neminis.

Multifarie multisque modis, karissimi, loquebatur olim deus per prophetas, qui, velut in enigmate et quasi sub nebulosa voce, unigenitum dei filium, pro redimendis laborantibus in tenebris et in umbra mortis sedentibus, pre-

5   conizarunt venturum. Novissimis autem diebus per suam sanctam scripturam palam loquitur, et beatissimum et gloriosissimum Neminem ut sibi comparem, ante secula genitum, humano tamen generi hactenus (peccatis exigentibus) incognitum fore predicat, enucleat et testatur. Sed ipsemet salvator noster et dominus, cui semper proprium est misereri et qui suos nunquam deserit in-

10   adiutos, suo sanguine proprio redempti populi misertus est, et ab oculis nostris remota penitus vetusta caligine thesaurum huius gloriosissimi Neminis tam celebrem nobis dignatus est aperire, ut ipsum usque nunc damnifere nobis absconditum intueri deinceps oculata fide salubrius valeamus.

Beatus igitur Nemo iste contemporaneus dei patris et in essentia precipue

15   consimilis filio, velut nec creatus nec genitus sed procedens in sacra pagina reperitur, in qua plene dictum est per psalmistam dicentem: *Dies formabuntur et Nemo in eis.* Cui postea merito tanta crevit auctoritas ut, ac si terrena respuens, ad celorum culmina volatu mirabili pervolavit, sicut legitur: *Nemo ascendit in celum.* Et hoc idem testatur dominus, dicens: *Nemo potest venire ad*

20   *me.*

Qui, dum celum ascenderet, ut dictum est, deitatem puram et integram et insimul trinitatem vidit ibidem sanctissimus Nemo, sicut legitur: *Nemo deum vidit.* Quod deum vidisset iste Nemo, evangelium protestatur, sicut legitur: *Nemo novit filium,* et alibi: *Nemo loquens in spiritu sancto.* Quia enim ipsum

25   viderat cum patre et filio, securus loquebatur, nam qui vidit, testimonium perhibuit.

Deinde, rediens de celo, iste virtuosus et potentissimus Nemo tanta audacia et securitate claruit et illuxit ita quod dum Iudei maledicti, Ihesum capere venientes, non essent ausi eum invadere, solus iste audacissimus Nemo, qui

30   cum eis aderat, cepit eum, sicut legitur: *Et Nemo misit in illum manus.*

Princeps autem Iudeorum, Nichodemus nomine, potentiam istius gloriosis-simi Neminis referens, ait: *Rabi, Nemo potest hec signa facere que tu facis.* Et licet Nichodemus, ut dictum est, istum beatissimum potentem profiteatur, et merito multo potentior probatur alibi per scripturam, nam ipse solus poten-

35   tissimus Nemo domino nostro Ihesu Christo contrariari potest, sicut legitur: *Deus claudit et Nemo aperit, deus aperit et Nemo claudit.*

Beatus etiam Iob, hoc attestans, deum alloquitur, inter multa sic proferens de eius potestate: *Cum sit Nemo qui de manu tua possit eruere.* Et quod nulli concessum est, solus iste benedictus Nemo potest, nam de ipso legitur: *Nemo*

40   *potest duobus dominis servire,* et alibi: *Utiliter servit Nemo duobus heris.*

Ipsemet vero dominus noster Ihesus Christus, de potentia istius gloriosis-simi Neminis suos alloquens discipulos, ait: *Et gaudium vestrum Nemo tollet a vobis.* Sciens autem Neminem potentissimum inter omnes et non miremini,

karissimi, si hoc dixit de discipulis suis Ihesus Christus, cum de se ipso gravius
45 fateatur, dicens: *Nemo tollit a me animam meam.* Et, si tanta virtute consistit
iste sanctissimus Nemo, non est mirum cum ipse incarnari et nasci voluit in hoc
mundo, velut Christus, ex illustri prosapia generari, sicut legitur in Ecclesiastico: *Nemo enim ex regibus aliud nativitatis habet initium.* Est etiam de
genere Ihesu Christi, ut habeatis, nam de nomine sancti Iohannis baptiste in
50 evangelio quereretur, responsum est: *Nemo est in cognatione tua.*

Fuit enim valens miles et strenuus, sicut legitur: *Nemo militans.* De sua vero
probitate et securitate dicitur: *Nemo securus.* Merito quidem securus dicitur
cum naturam superet in virtute, ut hic: *Quod natura negat, Nemo feliciter
audet,* et iterum de eodem: *Quod natura dedit, Nemo tollere potest.*

55 Sua vero militia, ut moderni milites, non est usus, qui, ad modum allecium
recentium pro quibus habendis a venditoribus prius solvitur precium, sunt
venales, et non pro honore, immo verius, quod verecundor dicere, precio
plerumque letiferis pestibus se exponunt. Sed isti gloriosissimo Nemini placuit
penitus et nunc placet (ob ipsius grandes divicias et redditus quibus precellit
60 viventes ceteros) militare, officium sumptibus propriis exercere, sicut legitur:
Nemo tenetur propriis stipendiis militare.

Verum quia potentes dudum strenui et sublimes in litterali dogmate eruditi
pre ceteris anhelabant, idcirco beatus iste Nemo miles, a genere quo processit
nolens modis aliquibus deviare, litteras didicit et sapientissimus proinde factus
65 est, sicut legitur: *Nemo propheta.* Prophetiam autem suam et suum dogma
generale, quod multis vigiliis acquisivit, ut moderni clerici non consumpsit, qui
ob aliud non curant addiscere, nisi ut solum pecuniam cumulent pecunie et
pinguibus ditentur prebendis, et ob hoc, omissis liberalibus scientiis, solummodo facultates petunt lucrativas, sed prorsus quibuslibet sumptibus contagiis
70 solus iste Nemo sanctissimus celestia contemplatus est, sicut legitur: *Nemo
sine crimine vivit,* et alibi: *Nemo ex omni parte beatus.* Et iterum dicitur:
Maiorem caritatem Nemo habet. Et quod maiorem caritatem Nemo habeat
clamat sancta mater ecclesia, ubi dicitur: *Ecce quomodo moritur iustus, et
Nemo percipit corde,* et iterum: *Viri iusti tolluntur et Nemo considerat.*

75 Nunc autem videre potestis, karissimi, compassionem istius gloriosissimi
Neminis qualiter compassus est Christo morienti, ubi dicitur: *Ecce quomodo
moritur iustus,* et qui etiam misertus est pauperis illius, ad cuius preces civitas
obsessa a potente Nemine extitit liberata, sicut scriptum est: *Et Nemo recordatus est pauperis illius.*

80 Insuper vos habetis quod solus iste sanctissimus Nemo absque vera confessione et sine iniuncta sibi penitentia salutari in tremendo magno dei iudicio
salvus erit, prout in sacra pagina planius declaratur, dicendo sic: *Nemo absque*

vera confessione et sine penitentia salvabitur. Summus etiam inter omnes
possessores possessor fuit iste ditissimus Nemo, et est, nam ipsum deum ali-
85   quando possidet, et amittit hunc eundem et quandocumque sibi placet ut in
quadam auctoritate dicit beatus Augustinus: *Nemo amittit te deus nisi qui te
dimittit.* Item iste firmissimus Nemo solus est qui ista terrena potest diligere et
ipsemet firmus esse, ut in quadam auctoritate dicit beatus Gregorius, dicendo
sic: *Nemo valet ista mobilia diligere et ipse immobilis stare.* Item iste doc-
90   tissimus Nemo tanta scientia preclaret, ita quod per sui discretionem scit illud
quod homo vivens nequit scire, prout in Ecclesiastico legitur: *Nemo scit utrum
amore dei vel odio dignus sit.*

Et quod iste peritissimus Nemo liberalibus scientiis sit edoctus, vos habetis,
nam adeo sciebat arismetricam, ita quod turbam magnam quam Iohannes in
95   Apocalypsi viderat, solus iste Nemo potuit numerare, ut legitur: *Et vidi turbam
magnam quam dinumerare Nemo poterat.* Et iterum ibidem dicitur de eius
dignitate et scientia, dicendo sic: *Et Nemo fuit dignus aperire librum et solvere
signacula eius.* De eo etiam illucide testatur Priscianus quod ei fuit similis in
grammatica et socius, dicendo sic in maiore volumine: *Neminem inveni so-
100   cium.* Fuit etiam astronomus, sicut legitur: *Nemo observat lunam.*

Nunc autem videre potestis, karissimi, quantis fulget meritis Nemo iste
sanctissimus, quanta sit eius scientia, et inde quanto prosequi debeat ab omnibus laude et gloria, puris affectibus et honore. Cum ipse cui omnia vivunt et
quem laudant archangeli istum sanctum Neminem benedictum per secula adeo
105   puro dilexit amore, ita quod dum suos per mundum misisset apostolos, precepit
eis ut cum Nemine beatissimo obviarent, ipsum salutarent et eidem visiones et
secreta eius tanquam suo secretario fiducius aperirent, sicut scriptum est:
Neminem per viam salutaveritis, et alibi: *Visionem quam vidistis Nemini dixeritis.* Curato etiam de lepra dixit: *Vade, Nemini dixeris.*

110   Quid plura? Non solum per suos discipulos dominus noster Ihesus Christus
istum sanctum Neminem venerari voluit, sed ipsemet personaliter eum dignatus est honorare. Nam dum Iudei in verbis dominum capere cuperent, et
mulierem in adulterio deprehensam coram eo adducerent, ipse, cui nihil absconditum est, discretionem, scientiam et valorem dilecti sui Neminis ag-
115   noscens, plenarie in beati Neminis reverentia et honore dictam mulierem accusatam per eum renuit iudicare, dicens: *Mulier, ubi sunt qui te accusant?
Nemo te condemnavit?* Que respondit: *Nemo, domine.* Audiens hoc dominus,
nolens falcem mittere in messem alienam, dictam mulierem remisit ad sanctum
Neminem, dicens: *Nec ego te condempnabo.*

120   Considerabat enim dominus eius statui et persone esse deferendum, et voluit tunc suo deferre magistro, nam alibi dicitur de eius magisterio ipse *Nemo*

propheta et doctor. Cum autem Christus loqueretur cum Samaritana ad fontem, et alii discipuli non essent ausi ei dicere verbum, velut magister bonus Ihesum reprehendit, sicut legitur: *Nemo tamen dixit, "Quid queris?" aut "Quid lo-*
25 *queris cum ea?"* Item nolens Nemo quod Ihesus per viam erraret, interrogabat eum quo esset iturus, sicut legitur: *Nemo tamen dixit, "Quo vadis?"* Item cum dominus manifestaret se discipulis suis, Nemo audebat eum interrogare quis esset, cum alii discipuli non essent ausi, sicut legitur: *Nemo dixit, "Tu quis es?"*
De magisterio vero discreti Neminis plenius habetur in parte illa evangelii
30 ubi de lege contendebat dominus cum Iudeis, dicens: *Nonne Moyses dedit vobis legem? Et Nemo ex vobis facit legem?* Insuper tanta fulsit patientia et humilitate iste sanctissmus Nemo ita quod iuxta verbum apostolicum, *Qui non laborat non manducet,* et alibi in psalmo, *Labores manuum tuarum quia manducabis,* voluit propriis manibus laborare, et non solum in secularibus sa-
35 tagebat, ut Martha, sed in divinis habuit curam ut Maria, unde de primo dicitur de Martha: *Nemo mittens manum ad aratrum,* et tanquam contemplativus et orthodoxus surgebat quantum ad secundum scilicet de Maria ad matutinas et nocte dieque sacriste et cantoris officium faciebat, ut hic: *Nemo accendit lucernam;* cantoris officium ut hic: *Nemo poterat dicere canticum.*
40 Tanti vero cordis et animi fuit iste sanctissimus Nemo quod non solum toto conamine laborabat, sed etiam ociosos una secum conducere et laborare volebat, ut in evangelio dicitur ociosis, *Cur hic statis tota die ociosi?* Responsum est ab eisdem: *Quia Nemo nos conduxit.*
Verbum autem domini dicentis *Frange esurienti panem tuum* non oblitus,
45 elemosinas faciebat, unde cum pauper Lazarus in evangelio elimosinam peteret et saturari cupiens de micis que cadebant de mensa divitis, solus iste Nemo sanctissimus compassionis intuitu erogabat eidem, ut habetur ibidem: *Et Nemo illi dabat.*
Per predicta igitur, karissimi, in parte plane videre potestis formationem,
50 essentiam, potentiam, audaciam, incarnationem, nobilitatem, militiam, probitatem, securitatem, scientiam, doctrinam, dignitatem, firmitatem, immobilitatem, sanctitatem, gratiam, honorem, felicitatem, beatitudinem, reverentiam, castitatem, verecundiam, fortitudinem, largitatem, compassionem, patientiam, bonitatem, pietatem, immutabilitatem, humilitatem et caritatem
55 istius gloriosissimi Neminis, iuxta quod in sacra pagina scriptum est de eodem. Que omnia summi pontifices amore dei nostri (cuius vicarii sunt in terris modernis temporibus) ponderantes, istum sanctissimum Neminem cum deo perpetualiter regnaturum et domino potentissimo coeternum, sicut scriptum est: *Nemo semper regnaturus,* et alibi: *Nemo est qui semper vivat,* eundem
60 Neminem, quem omnipotens deus in celis beari voluit, in terris dotari cum

magnis favoribus decreverunt, unde in utroque iure tantum est quod sibi conceditur quod absque bigamie nota possit matrimonium contrahere libere, sicut
legitur: *Nemini permittitur binas habere uxores.*

    Potest etiam iste sanctus Nemo corpora sanctorum alienare et vendere, sicut
165   legitur: *Nemo martires distrahat,* et alibi: *Nemo mercetur.* Potest etiam
iudiciaecclesiastica dirimere, sicut legitur: *Nemo contempnat ecclesiastica
iudicia.* Preterea vos habetis quod inter diversos religiosos tam intra quam
extra claustra solus iste Nemo potentissimus post completorium loquendi lib-
eram habeat potestatem, prout in beati Benedicti et aliorum diversorum
religiosorum
170 regula continetur, dicendo sic: *Post completorium Nemo loquatur.* Et ultra
manifeste habetis quod in omnibus privilegiis et concessionibus summorum
pontificum, voluntas beatissimi et gloriosissimi Neminis excipitur, prout in fine
litterarum suarum plenius annotatur, ubi dicunt: *Presentis autem nostre concessionis paginam Nemini liceat infringere.* Reges autem et principes
175 quoscumque in suis consiliis recipiunt, iurare et promittere faciunt sub hac
forma supradicta, inter alia vero que ad iuramentum fidelitatis pertinent, additur sic: *Tu iurabis secreta et concilia domini nostri tenere et Nemini revelare.*

    Absit ergo ab humanis creaturis potentiam, laudem et gloriam patroni nostri
beatissimi et gloriosissimi Neminis in aliquo per bilingues denigrari, qui su-
180 perni dei ire resistere potest, sicut legitur, Iob ix: *Deus cuius ire Nemo resistere
potest,* et iterum Iob xii: *Si destruxit deus, Nemo est qui edificat,* et Sapientie
xv: *Nemo poterit se similem deo fingere.* Et in Ecclesiastico dicitur: *Nemo
vincit deum,* et iterum Iob xviii: *Ipse solus sanctus est deus, et Nemo potest eum
corrigere.* Et Mathei xiii: *Nemo enim potestatem habet facere et agere omne
185 quidem et movere castra.* Nonne etiam Marcus qui ore dominico loquebatur:
*Occurit e monumentis homo in spiritu inmundo, neque catenis quisquam potuit
eum ligare, et Nemo poterat eum domare.*

    Quid plura? Certe nec penna nec calamus cum ambabus manibus illius
scribe velociter scribentis, de quo loquitur citharista, ad laudem et gloriam
190 patroni nostri beatissimi et gloriosissimi Neminis non competent lucidandam,
cum de eius immutabilitate et constancia dicit Iob xv: *Nemo immutabilis, nec
celi sunt mundi in conspectu eius.* Fugiat ergo omnis hostis iniquus beatissimi
et gloriosissimi Neminis patroni nostri, et deleatur de libro viventium et cum
iustis non scribatur, nec sit ulterius eius memoria super terram, qui glorioso
195 operi nostro recalcitrare nititur, et corda fidelium nostrorum suis falsis suggestionibus nuperime credidit subornare. Quod autem fugere debeant infideles
beatissimi et gloriossimi Neminis patroni nostri sic probatur, Levitici vi:

Fugietis Nemine sequente, et iterum in eodem capitulo: *Inimicis audebat Nemo resistere.* De hoc etiam scriptum est clarius in Proverbiis xxviii: *Fugit impius*
200 Nemine persequente.

Estote igitur viri fortes in agone, velut doctor noster Nemo, et robusti. Et certamen illius qui nullis falsis probationibus nec scripturis subsistit non recusetis subire. Reservamus etiam in nostri pectoris scrinio ad laudem et gloriam patroni nostri beatissimi Neminis et suorum tot et tantas auctoritates
205 tam divinas canonicasve quam civiles cum infinitis sanctorum sanctionibus patrum, philosophicis insuper et naturalibus argumentis.

Infinitis autem virtutibus pollet et laudibus Nemo iste sanctissimus, quas, ne vos tedeat audire, et, quod absit, alicuius vestrum prolixitatis materia animum torqueat, et que pia mente de isto beatissimo Nemine patrono nostro in nostro
210 sermone presenti cepistis, inutili volatu non transeant, sed ut in muro lapis, vestris in domino cordibus perpetuo maneant commendata, ad presens sub silencio decrevimus pertransire. Ad cuius beatitudinem et gloriam qui sine fine vivit et regnat nos et vos pervenire concedat per omnia secula seculorum. Amen.

16–17 Ps 138.16   18–19 Jo 3.13   19–20 Jo 6.44   22–23 Jo 1.18   24 Mt 11.27; 1 Cor 12.3   30 Jo 7.30   32 Jo 3.2   36 Apc 3.7   38 Jb 10.7   39–40 Mt 6.24   40 Walther, *Proverbia,* no. 32734   42–43 Jo 16.22   45 Jo 10.18   48 Sap 7.5   50 Lc 1.61   51 2 Tm 2.4   52 Augustine *Confessions* 10. 32   55 On herrings compared to clerics, cf. J. A. Herbert, *Catalogue of Romances in the Department of Manuscripts in the British Museum,* vol. 3 (London, 1910), 560, no. 7 (Frederic C. Tubach, *Index exemplorum: A Handbook of Medieval Religious Tales,* FF Communications 86, no. 204 [Helsinki, 1969], no. 2586).   61 1 Cor 9.7   65 Lc 4.24   70–71 "Nemo sine crimine vivit": *Disticha Catonis* 1.5; Walther, *Proverbia,* no. 16447. "Nemo ex omni parte beatus": Walther, *Proverbia,* no. 16343   72 Jo 15.13   73–74 Matins for Easter Sunday   74 Matins for Easter Sunday   78–79 Ecl 9.15   91–92 Ecl 9.1   95–96 Apc 7.9   97–98 Apc 5.4, 9   108 Lc 10.4   108–9 Mt 17.9   109 Mc 1.44   116–19 Jo 8.10–11   124–25 Jo 4.27   126 Jo 16.5   128 Jo 21.12   131–32 Jo 7.19   133–34 2 Th 3.10   134–35 Ps 127.2   137 Lc 9.62   139–40 Lc 11.33   140 Apc 14.3   143–44 Mt 20.7   145 Is 58.7   148–49 Lc 16.21   160 Ecl 9.4   181–82 Jb 9.13   182 Jb 12.14   183 Sap 15.16   184–85 cf. Ecl 7.14: "considere opera Dei quod nemo possit corrigere"   187–88 Mc 5.4   192–93 Jb 15.15   199 Lv 26.17   199–200 Lv 26.37   200–201 Prv 28.1

1 *No title in OMGH.* Incipit prologus de vita vel gestis beatissimi et gloriosissimi
Neminis *A*   Incipit prologus de vita et gestis beatissimi et gloriosi Neminis et de
miraculis eius etc. *L*   Sequitur sermo de Nemo *P*   2 Multifarie] Multifariam *P*
karissimi] *om. MP*   loquebatur olim deus] olim deus loquebatur *G*   deus olim
loquebatur *P*   olim] *om. O*   3 velut] quasi *G*   et quasi sub] quam *M*   et
quasi *OP*   nebulosa] *om. V*   nebulose *P*   voce] *om. MP*   4 laborantibus]
laborantes *G*   laborantibus . . . preconizarunt] *om. M*   in²] *om. OM*
preconizarunt] preconizaverunt *O*   *om. M*   sedentibus] sedentes *G*   venturum]
om. O   5 Novissimus] Novissime *MP*   autem] vero *M*   *post* diebus *add.* istis *MP*
sanctam] sacram *MGHAL*   6 palam loquitur] loquitur palam *V*   loquitur]
alloquitur *O*   loquebatur *P*   et beatissimum et gloriosissimum Neminem] beatum
Nemonem et *M*   et gloriosum beatissimumque *H*   beatissimum Neminem et *P*   et²]
ac *V*   et gloriosissimum] *om. O*   ut] velut *AL   om. G*   comparem] compare
V   post comparem *add.* et *MP*   7 secula] seculam *P*   genitum] unigenitum *M*
post genitum *add.* penes illud prophete: Dies formabuntur et Nemo in eis, scilicet prius
erat, psalmo 138 ipsius David prophete *H*   tamen] enim *G*   hactenus] *om. M*
post peccatis *add.* eorum *G*   8 fore] fere *O*   enucleat] *om. MP   post* Sed *add.* et
MALH   ipsemet] ipse *G*   salvator noster] noster salvator *M*   salvator *AL*   et
dominus] *om. GP*   9 cui] cuius *P*   suos nunquam] nunquam suos *O*   semper]
om. P   proprium est misereri] misereri proprium est *P*   misereri est proprium et
parcere *V*   proprium] *om. G*   et qui suos] *om. G*   deserit] deserens *G*
inadiutos] inauditos *M   om. PG*   10 suo] sui *OM*   suo . . . et] misertus populi
quem[?] sanguine redemit *G*   suo sanguine proprio] suo pretioso sanguine *V*   ad
vitam suo proprio sanguine *P*   sanguine . . . populi] populi proprio sanguine
redempti *M*   11 remota penitus] penitus ammota *M*   pulsa penitus *P*   vetusta]
vetustatis *MG   om. P*   huius gloriosissimi Neminis] huiusmodi *O*   nobis *MP   post*
gloriosissimi *add.* ac beatissimi *G*   12 nobis¹] *om. MHP*   largiri *G*   dignatus est
aperire] misericorditer reservare *P   post* est *add.* nobis *H*   aperire] feliciter
reservare *O*   misericorditer reservare *M   om. G*   ut] et *M*   usque . . . nobis]
nobis usque nunc damnifere *P*   usque] *om. G*   damnifere nobis] nobis damnifere
O   nobis *G*   13 oculata] celerata *O*   culta *V*   ecclesiastica *MP*   occulta *AG*   14
beatus] beatissimus *G*   igitur] ergo *M*   Nemo iste] Nemo *O*   iste Nemo *MP*
contemporaneous] temporaneus *V*   coetporaneo *corr.* coetporaneus *M*   essentia]
esse *M*   15 consimilis] similis *P   post* filio *add.* et in origine maxime spiritui sancto
conformis, utpote *P*   velut] *om. AL*   nec¹] non *O*   genitus] procedens
VALH   procedens] genitus *VH*   formatus *AL*   16 reperitur] invenitur *M*   in
. . . dicentem] unde in psalmo legitur *P*   in . . . eis] et ubi supra psalmo 138 *H*
plene] plane *GA*   psalmistam dicentem] prophetam sic *O*   per prophetam *M*
psalmistam *G*   17 *post* eis *add.* psalmo 138 *P*   Cui] Qui *O*   cuius *MGP*
merito tanto] tanto merito *OP*   in tanto *M*   tanta *G*   crevit] erat *G*   ut] *om. P*
ac si] quasi *M*   quod quasi *P*   si] *G*   18 respuens] dispiciens *M*   respueret *P*
celorum culmina] ad celos *M*   volatu mirabili] mirabili volatu *G*   pervolavit]

volavit *M*   sicut legitur] ut hic *OM*   secundum evangelium beati Iohannis 3°
capitulo *P*   *post* legitur *add.* Et *G*   in evangelio *H*   *post* Nemo *add.* inquit *P*   19 Et]
om. G   Et . . . dicens] unde Iohannes sexto in persona dei dicit *H*   unde et dominus
testatur Iohannis 8° dicens *P*   potest venire] venit *OMGHP*   21 Qui] Unde *H*
dum] cum *M*   priusquam *P*   celum] *om. G*   ascenderet] ascenderat *PH*   ut
dictum est] *om. MHP*   et²] *om. O*   ac *AL*   et insimul trinitatem] *om. P*   22
insimul] simul *MAL*   *post* insimul *add.* et *O*   sanctam et individuam *ALH*   ibidem
. . . Nemo] *om. GP*   ibidem, ut inquit Damascenus, et Iohannis primo dicitur *H*
sanctissimus] sanctus *OM*   sanctissimus . . . legitur] in Iohannis 4°, unde Iohannis
primo *P*   sicut] quod nunquam alius facere potuit, ut *O*   quod nullus alius potuit
facere, ut *M*   Nemo deum vidit] Deum Nemo vidit *MP*   Deum Nemo vidit unquam,
id est aliquo tempore *H*   Nemo vidit deum *GAL*   23 *post* vidit *add.* Et *MH*   Quod
. . . legitur] Item *G*   quod filium viderit, testatur evangelium Math. 11, Mar. 10 *H*
Quod . . . perhibuit] quod tam alius nunquam potuit facere, sed et ipse novit filium
solus, Mathei xi. Quippe nam ipse Nemo est locutus in spiritu sancto, secundum quod
scribitur primo ad eorum 12 *P*   deum] *om. AL*   vidisset iste Nemo] Nemo vidisset
M   iste Nemo] Nemo sanctissimus *V*   sanctissimum *AL*   protestatur] attestatur
M   sicut legitur] ubi dicitur: Nemo novit patrem, et iterum *O*   ibi *M*   24 *post*
filium *add.* in evangelio *G*   et alibi] Item *G*   vel alibi *L*   loquens] loquitur *O*
quia enim] sed quia *O*   cum *M*   ipsum] *om. GH*   25 viderat] videt *O*   vidisset
M   viderat ipsum *H*   cum patre et filio] *om. G*   securus] securius *GHL*   nam
. . . perhibuit] *om. OM*   vidit] *om. G*   27 deinde] deinceps *M*   rediens de celo]
de celo rediens *P*   de] a *V*   *om. H*   celo] celis *O*   *om. H*   iste] *om. M*
virtuosus] virtuosissimus *G*   audacia et] audacie *AL*   28 securitate] bonitate *O*
virtute *P*   et illuxit] *om. GP*   ita] *om. OMGP*   dum] cum *M*   Iudei
maledicti] maledicti Iudei *OGP*   Ihesum . . . invadere] qui venerant ad capiendum
Christum non audientes in ipsum ponere manum *P*   29 eum] ipsum *OM*   *om. VH*
post invadere *add.* sed *O*   iste audacissimus] *om. OMP*   autem *G*   audacissimus
Nemo] Nemo audacissimus *H*   30 cum eis] (?)peris *M*   eis *G*   aderat] venerat
P   cepit] ceperit *M*   sicut legitur] ut legitur sic *O*   ut legitur *GM*   ut dicitur
Iohannis septimo et octavo *H*   ut ibidem legitur Iohannis 7° *P*   Et] *om. MGH*
misit in illum] in eum misit *M*   misit] posuit *OP*   illum] eum *OVHP*   manus]
manum *L*   31 *For the first addition to H see the First Appendix to the Long Version,*
below. For the continuation of P see the Third Appendix to the Long Version, below.
autem] vero *ALG*   etiam *H*   Iudeorum] sacerdotum *V*   nomine] reserans *G post*
nomine *add.* qui venit ad Ihesum nocte *AL*   istius] ipsius *VM*   huius *G*
gloriosissimi] *om. M*   32 Neminis] Nemini *O*   Nemonis *M*   *om. AL*   referens]
reserans *VMH*   *om. G*   *post* referens *add.* alibi *M*   ait] dixit *G*   ait ad Ihesum *H*
Rabi] *om. MH*   potest . . . facere] facit hec signa *H*   potest facere hec signa *AL*
Et . . . legitur] Probatur et potentior aliis per scripturam quod solus Nemo deo
contrariari potest, unde *H*   33 licet] *om. M*   *post* Nichodemus *add.* iste *VM*   ut
dictum est] *om. O*   istum] gloriosum *G*   beatissimum] beatum Neminem *O*

beatum Nemonem *M*   Neminem *G*   ac potentissimum Nemine *L*   sanctum ac
potentissimum Neminem *A*   potentem] potente *AL*   profiteatur] perfiteatur *L*
cognoscens *M*   et merito] *om. G*   34 multo potentior] potentie cum in multo *O*
potencior quam dominus un multis *M*   multo enim potentior *G*   probatur alibi per
scripturam] per scripturam probatur *MG*   *post* probatur *add.* et *V*   alibi] locis *M*
nam] cum *G*   ipse] iste *OL*   potentissimus] *om. OMG*   35 Nemo] *om. G*
Ihesu Christo] *om. G*   contrariari] contrariare *O*   contraire *M*   potest] potens est
M   videatur *G*   sicut] ut *OM*   cum *G*   et patens est sicut *AL*   legitur] dicitur
G   36 deus aperit . . . claudit] *om. M*   37 Beatus] [?] beatus *G*   Beatus . . .
potestate] Hoc attestatur Iob deum alloquens, Iob 30 *H*   etiam] enim *O*   autem *M*
om. G   Iob] in *V*   hoc] *om. L*   hoc . . . alloquitur] *om. G*   attestans]
attestatur *M*   attestatus *L*   alloquitur] cum loquitur *M*   colloquitur *AL*   sic
proferens] *om. G*   38 de eius potestate] *om. OM*   sit] si *V*   manu] potestate
H   Et] *om. M*   38 quod . . . heris] *om. M*   *post* nulli *add.* [?] *V*   39 solus . . .
legitur] videlicet servire duobus dominis, huic Nemini concessum fuit, ut in evangelio
dicitur *H*   solus iste] iste solus *O*   iste *G*   benedictus] *om. O*   beatissimus *G*
post Nemo *add.* facere *O*   de ipso] ipse *O*   legitur] *om. O*   40 et] unde *O*
alibi] poeta *H*   Utiliter] *om. G*   heris] dominis. Item Nemo potest deo servire et
mamone *G*   41 Ipsemet . . . discipulos] Ostensum est quod benedictus Nemo solus
multo potest, nam propter audaciam suam dominus alloquens suos *M*   Ipsemet vero]
Ipsemet *V*   Ipse vero *G*   Et ipsemet *H*   dominus . . . Ihesus] *om. H*   istius
gloriosissimi] et audacia ipsius *O*   huius *G*   illius *H*   gloriosissimi] *om. H*   42
Neminis . . . ait] dicit ad discipulos *G*   Neminis alloquens discipulos suos inquit *H*
Et] *om. GH*   tollet] auferet *V*   tollat *M*   tollit *G*   a vobis] *om. G*   43 Sciens
. . . omnes] *om. OM*   Sciens . . . dicens] Neque mirentur discipuli de hoc, cum et
Christus de se ipso dicat Iohannis decimo *H*   Neminem] Nemine *A*   autem] hunc
venerabilissimum *G*   et non miremini] ergo nulli mirum, fratres *G*   miremini]
miremur *O*   44 dixit] dixerit *O*   de] *om. M*   de . . . Christus] Ihesus discipulis
suis *O*   Ihesus Christus] Ihesus *M*   *om. ALG*   se] *om. O*   45 tollit] tollat
M   a me animam meam] animam meam a me *GH*   Et] *om. V*   Sed quid *H*   si]
quod *AL*   consistit] consistat *ALH*   46 iste sanctissimus] sanctus iste *O*   iste
sanctus *M*   iste beatissimus *VG*   non est mirum] nimirum etiam *G*   ipse incarnari
et] *om. G*   voluit] voluerit *MV*   47 velut] secundum *MV*   ex] et *O*   et ex
M   generari] generi *O*   *om. AL*   nascetur *G*   sicut] ut *OM*   in Ecclesiastico]
om. MG   Ecclesiastici quinto *H*   48 enim] *om. G*   regibus] regalibus *M*
habet initium] initium sumpsit *M*   habuit initium *V*   aliud] *om. OMALG*   aliud
nativitatis] *om. AL*   Est] et *AL*   Est etiam] Fuit Nemo *M*   Fuit etiam *G*   etiam]
etenim *O*   enim *V*   de genere] ex cognatione *G*   49 Christi] Christe *M*   *post*
Christi *add.* et Marie, que fuit de stirpe regia *H*   ut habeatis] habetis *O*   *om. VH*
post nam *add.* dum *O*   ut . . . evangelio] nam, ut habetis in ewangelio domini, dum
de natione beati Iohannis *M*   ut . . . est] et Iohannis vii *G*   nam] nam dum *O*
dum *V*   nam cum *H*   sancti] sancto *L*   *om. H*   in evangelio] *om. H*   50

quereretur] queritur *AL*   *post* est[1] *add.* Luce primo *H*   et *AL*   est . . . tua] in
cognatione *V*   est de congregacione tua qui vocetur hoc nomine *H*   tua] sua *O*
51 *For the continuation of G see the second appendix to the Long* Nemo   Fuit] Item
ipse fuit *M*   enim] etiam *VH*   sicut legitur] ut hic *OM*   unde apostolus *H*   Nemo
. . . dicitur] *om. M*   Nemo militans] Nemo militat propriis stipendiis *H*   De . . .
dicitur] Securus eciam fuit propter eius probitatem, ut dicitur *H*   vero] etiam *O*
52 dicitur] scribitur *V*   quidem] enim *O*   enim est *M*   dicitur] *om. M*
naturam] natura *V*   superet] superat *M*   Quod . . . eodem] *om. V*   Quod . . .
audet] Quod natura dedit, Nemo tollere potest *L*   Quod] Quot *M*   54 audet] audit
M   audeat *A*   *post* eodem *add.* poeta *H*   Quod . . . potest] Quod natura negat, Nemo
feliciter audeat *L*   Nemo tollere] tollere Nemo *AH*   55 Sua . . . penitus et (lines
55–59)] Sua namque militia *M*   moderni] *om. AL*   qui] que *O*   allecium]
athletum *V*   alicium *L*   56 *post* precium *add.* quam recepitur *O*   *post* sunt *add.*
enim *O*   58 exponunt] imponunt *O*   Sed . . . penitus] immo sibi *O*
gloriosissimo Nemini] glorioso Nemini militi *V*   Nemini glorioso militi *H*   60
ceteros] ceteris *O*   exercere] deviare *L*   sicut] ut *O*   *post* legitur *add.* ad Cor.
nono *H*   61 stipendiis] sumptibus *O*   62 Verum quia] Vero quod *V*   potentes
dudum] dudum potentes *OM*   potentes *V*   in litterali] et litterali *O*   illiterati *M*
eruditi] erudiri *MH*   *om. AL*   63 anhelabant] avolabant *O*   beatus iste] beatus *M*
iste beatissimus *A*   beatissimus *L*   Nemo miles] miles Nemo *O*   processit]
precessit *M*   *post* processit *add.* ut dicimus *O*   64 nolens] volens *O*   deviare]
obviare *M*   deviare aut declinare *H*   proinde] inde *AL*   65 sicut] ut *OM*
legitur] *om. V*   sicut . . . propheta] propheta namque extitit in patria sua, ut dicitur
Luce quarto: Nemo est acceptus propheta in patria *H*   *post* propheta *add.* Vere propheta
est iste sanctus Nemo, ut annotatur plenius per scripturam, ubi de futura die Iudicii
loquitur dicens: De die autem et hora Nemo scit *O*   est in patria sua *M*   suum
dogma] dogma suum *M*   66 generale] gratiale *OA*   quod] que *A*   quo *L*   *post*
multis *add.* suis *M*   vigiliis acquisivit] acquisivit vigiliis *AL*   *post* vigiliis *add.* curis
et studiis sibi *OM*   acquisivit] pavit adquirere *O*   curavit acquirere *M*   67 ob] *om.*
O   ad *M*   curant] curavit *A*   addiscere] addicere *O*   discere *H*   ut solum]
solum ut *OH*   solummodo ut *M*   solum *AL*   pecuniam] *om. H*   cumulent
pecunie] pecunie cumulent *O*   accumulent *MAL*   cumulent peccuniam et peccunia
H   et] ut *M*   68 *post* ditentur *add.* beneficiis et *M*   et . . . scientiis] *om. M*
omissis] amissis *AL*   liberalibus scientiis] artibus liberalibus *O*   *post* scientiis *add.*
qui *V*   solummodo facultates petunt] petunt facultates solummodo *OM*   facultates
solummodo petunt *H*   facultates assumunt solomodo *AL*   69 lucrativas] lucraturas
V   prorsus . . . celestia] ipse spretis prorsus quibuslibet *M*   sumptibus] spretis
OH   70 solus iste] iste solus *O*   sanctissimus] *om. OH*   *post* est *add.* et vitam
innocentem a crimine duxit *H*   sicut] ut *OM*   71 et alibi] *om. M*   et iterum *O*
post beatus *add.* Unde tanta patientia ab adversariis mala sustinendo fuit, usque se ipsos
emendarent, unde Cor. 7: Capite nos. Neminem lesimus, Neminem corrumpimus,
Neminem circumvenimus *H* (*See first appendix to the Long* Nemo *for the continuation*

of this variant reading in H.) Et] ut *M* iterum] alibi *OM* dicitur] *om. V*
72 Maiorem . . . Nemo] Nemo maiorem caritatem *M* habet . . . Nemo] *om. V* Et
. . . habeat] habet *M* Nemo habeat] habeat sanctus iste Nemo *O* Nemo habet
AL 73 sancta] sanctissima nostra *O* ubi dicitur] *om. M* dicitur] dicit *OH*
et] *om. AL* et cetera et *H* 74 *post* iterum *add.* ibidem *O* vicem[?] *M* 75 Nunc
. . . karissimi] Modo videte *O* Modo videtis *M* compassionem] passionem *O*
gloriosissimi] gloriosi *O* 76 Neminis] Nemonis *M* qualiter] qui *M*
compassus] passus *O om. V* est] fuit *V post* Christo *add.* in cruce *M*
morienti] moriente *O* ubi . . . iustus] et sanctis eius beatis *O* et sanctis eius *M*
ubi] ut *L post* ubi *add.* supra *H* 77 *Post* iustus *add.* et cetera. Et sanctis eius beatis,
ubi dicitur: Viri iusti tolluntur et cetera *HV* et] *om. OMV* ubi supra *H* pauperis
illius] illius pauperis *O* preces] sapientiam *M* civitas 78 obsessa] obsessa civitas
O civitas possessa *M* aliquis obsessa *H* a] et *H* Nemine] *om. OM* sicut]
om. O secundum *M* Et] *om. M* 79 pauperis illius] illius pauperis *OM* 80
Insuper . . . dignus sit (lines 80–92)] *om. OM* vos] *om. H* solus] *om. H*
sanctissimus Nemo] Nemo sanctissimus *V post* Nemo *add.* solus *H* 81 et sine sibi
iniuncta] sine iniuncta sibi *AL* magno] *om. H* magni *AL* dei] diei *AL* 82
pagina] scriptura *AL* planius] clarius *H* plenius *AL* sic] *om. H* 83
salvabitur] salvabvabitur [*sic*] *A* Summus] Sed unus *V* inter . . . fuit] possessor
fuit inter omnes possessores *V* 84 iste] *om. L* ditissimus] sanctissimus *AL*
85 et¹] *om. V* hunc] huius *L* et²] *om. HV* et hoc *AL* 86 *post* Augustinus
add. dicens sic *V* nisi . . . dimittit] *om. AL* 87 firmissimus] stabilissimus *H*
est] *om. AL* potest] possit *V* 88 ut] prout *AL post* quadam *add.* alia *V*
dicendo sic] *om. H* sic dicendo *AL* 89 ipse] ipsemet *AL* Item . . . dignus sit]
om. AL iste] *om. V* 90 scit] sit *V* 91 homo] Nemo *V* prout] ut *H post*
legitur *add.* quinto *H* 92 dignus sit] sit dignus *V* 93 peritissimus] sanctissimus
OM doctissimus *VAL* liberalibus . . . edoctus] non tantum liberalibus doctus sit
O in liberalibus doctus sit *M* vos] *om. M* vos habetis] claret *H* 94 ita] *om.*
OM magnam] *om. M post* quam *add.* sanctus *M* Iohannes . . . viderat] vidit
Iohannes in Apochalipsim *V* Iohannes viderat in Apocalipsi *H* Iohannes evangelista
viderat in Pathmos insula *AL* 95 solus . . . poterat] ipse sanctus Nemo dinumerare
poterat *O* ipse Nemo dinumerare poterat *M* solus iste] iste solus beatissimus et
doctissimus *L post* iste *add.* peritissimus *V* ut] sicut *VAL post* legitur *add.* in
Apocalipsi *AL* 96 magnam] *om. L* dinumerare Nemo] Nemo dinumerare *V*
Et] ut *M* iterum] *om. MAL* dicitur . . . dicendo sic] dicitur et de eius sapientia dicitur
M Apocalipsis de eius dignitate dicitur *H* dicitur] legitur *OM* 97 dignitate et]
om. O dogmate et *AL* dicendo sic] ut dicitur *O* Et] *om. OM* 98 signacula]
signaculum *M* eo] eodem *OM* etiam illucide] *om. OM* etiam lucide *H post*
testatur *add.* lucide *O* Priscianus] scriptura *M* Precianus *A* quod . . .
volumine] dicens *O om. M* quod . . . socius] *om. AL* similis] consimilis *H*
99 socius] socium *V* dicendo . . . volumine] dicit, dicendo sic in maiori volumine
V cum dicit in maiori volumine *H* in maiori volumine dicendo sic *L* in maiore

volumine dicendo sic *A*   Neminem] Nemonem *M*   *post* inveni *add.* michi *H*   100
etiam] enim *A*   sicut legitur] ut hic *OM*   observat] servat *M*   *post* lunam *add.*
Quomodo eciam fuerit conpositor legum et magnus in musica, vide in alio Nemine in
appollogis Cyrilli *H (See first appendix to the Long* Nemo *for the continuation of this
variant reading in H.)*   101 Nunc . . . potestis] Modo potestis videre fratres *M*
autem] *om. O*   modo *H*   fulget] fulgeat *M*   meritis] misteriis *OM*   Nemo iste
sanctissimus] sanctus iste *O*   sanctis istis *M*   iste sanctissimus Nemo *AL*   102
quanta] et quanta *O*   sit] scit *V*   inde] *om. O*   pro *M*   in *VAL*   quanto] quantis
M   ab . . . gloria] in laude et gloria ab omnibus *AL*   103 omnibus] eius *M*
puris] *om. V   post* ipse *add.* sit *M*   104 quem] *om. M   post* laudant *add.* angeli et *O*
archangeli] angeli *V*   sanctum] *om. OM*   sanctissimum *V*   sanctum et *AL*
Neminem] Nemonem *M*   105 dilexit] dilectum *M*   ita] *om. O*   sui gl[?] *M*
dum] cum *AL*   apostolos] discipulos *M   om. AL*   precepit eis] voluit et precepit
ipsis *OM*   106 Nemine beatissimo] beatissimo Nemine *O*   beatissimo Nemone
M   106 ipsum salutarent] salutarent ipsum *O   post* salutarent *add.* sicut dicitur in
evangelio: Neminem per viam salutaveritis. Et insuper precepit dominus *H*   et] ut
H   et . . . scriptum est] dicentes *M*   eidem] eorum *O*   107 eius] eidem *O*
tanquam . . . secretario] *om. O*   fiducius] fiducialiter *H*   sicut] ut *O   post* est *add.*
Luce quarto *H*   108 Neminem] Nemonem *M*   Neminem . . . alibi] *om. H*   per
viam salutaveritis] salutaveritis per viam *O*   et alibi] item salvum[?] dixeritis in hac
vita [?] ut eorum visiones et secreta fiducialiter ei aperirent, prout scriptum est *M*
Visionem . . . dixeritis] Nemini dixeritis visionem vestram *O*   Nemoni dixeritis
visionem hanc *M*   Nemini dixeritis visionem hanc *H*   109 Curato] Mandato *M*   A
Christo curato *H*   etiam] *om. H   post* lepra *add.* in evangelio *O*   dixit] inquit ad
eum Christus *H   post* dixit *add.* illi *O*   dominus in ewangelio *M*   Vade] Vide *O*
110 Quid] Et quid *O*   Non . . . Christus] Dominus noster Ihesus Christus per suos
discipulos *AL*   discipulos] apostolos *M*   dominus noster] *om. OM*   noster
Ihesus Christus] *om. H*   111 sanctum] beatissimum *O*   istum . . . voluit] venerari
beatissimum Neminem *M*   voluit] *om. O*   sed . . . honorare] *om. AL*
personaliter eum] *om. M*   eum] ipsum *O*   dignatus est honorare] dignatus est
venerari *V*   venerari dignatus est *H*   112 *post* est *add.* eum *M*   dum] cum *M*
post dum *add.* vagabundi *O*   [?] *M*   Iudei in verbis] in verbis Iudei *V   post* Iudei
add. ut *OM*   in verbis dominum] dominum in verbis *M*   dominum] deum *O   om.*
V   eum *AL*   capere cuperent] caperent *OMAL*   et] *om. OM*   113 in adulterio
deprehensam] accusatam de adulterio *O*   de adulterio accusatam *M*   coram eo
adducerent] ducerent coram eo *O*   adducerent coram eo *M   post* adducerent *add.*
Iohannis octavo *H*   ipse] *om. O*   ipse Christus *H*   nihil] nullus *M*
absconditum est] est absconditum *M*   114 est] *om. L*   dilecti] *om. M*
agnoscens] cognoscens *V*   115 plenarie] *om. M*   Neminis] Nemonis *M*
reverentia] reverentiam *OMV*   honore] honorem *OMV*   accusatam] *om. O*
116 *post* eum *add.* accusatam *O*   Mulier] *om. O*   ubi sunt] quis est *AL*
accusant] condempnavit *M*   accusavit *L*   117 Nemo . . . respondit] Cui illa

respondit *O*   Respondens ipsa *M*   hoc] hec *O*   dominus] deus *M*   *post* dominus
add. consideravit et unde quod forum huiusmodi non pertinebat ad eum *O*
considerabat unde quod forum huiusmodi non pertinebat ad eum *M*   118 *post* nolens
add. utpote iudex iuridicus et fidelis *O*   utpote iudex veridicus *M*   mittere] suam
ponere *O*   suam mittere *MV*   alienam] alteram *M*   sanctum] *om. OM*   119
post condempnabo *add.* Vade, amplius noli peccare *M*   120 eius . . . deferendum et]
quod deferendum erat statui et persone *O*   quod deferendum est statui et persone *M*
eius] omnes *AL*   statui et] status *AL*   deferendum] differendas *AL*   et] *om.*
O   voluit] volens *M*   noluit *V*   121 suo deferre magistro] deferre suo magistro
O   differe suo magisterio *A*   differe suo magistro *L*   alibi . . . magisterio] alias
OM   eius] suo *V*   ipse] *om. H*   *post* magisterio *add.* scilicet *V*   122 propheta]
prophetandi magister *O*   propheta dei et magister *M*   Cum . . . fontem] eundem
Ihesum Christum, dum loqueretur ad fontem cum Samaritana muliere *O*   eundem
dominum nostrum Ihesum Christum dum loqueretur ad fontem cum muliere Samaritana
M   loqueretur] loquebatur *AL*   cum Samaritana] ad Samaritanam *H*   ad
fontem] cum fonte, Iohannis 8 *H*   123 alii] astantes *O*   astantas *M*   essent . . . ei]
erant ausi sibi *OM*   *post* discipuli *add.* eius circumquaque *O*   essent] fuerunt *AL*
dicere verbum] verbum dicere *M*   *post* verbum *add.* reprehendit et *O*   reprehendit ipse
M   Nemo *H*   magister bonus] bonus magister *OM*   Ihesum reprehendit] et
diligens, discipulum suum castigavit *O*   et diligens, discipulum castigavit *M*   124
sicut legitur] prout legitur sic *O*   prout legitur *M*   dicens ibidem *H*   tamen] *om. M*
autem *V*   causam *AL*   125 Item . . . Tu quis es] Et alibi, testante domino, dixit sibi
doctor iste, ubi dicebat dominus: Vado ad eum qui me misit, et Nemo interrogat me: Quo
vadis? Quia noluit beatus iste Nemo quod dominus deviaret eundo. Et alibi legitur dum
dominus manifestaret se discipulis suis: Et Nemo audebat interrogare eum: Tu quis es?
O   Et alibi, testatante domino, dixit sibi doctor ipsius ubi dominus dicebat: Vado ad
eum qui me misit et Nemo interrogat me: Quo vadis? Quia noluit ut deus erraret eundo.
Alibi legitur dum deus manifestavit se discipulis suis et Nemo audebat eum interrogare:
Tu quis es? *M*   *post* nolens *add.* iste prudens et pius *V*   iste prudentissimus *AL*
Ihesus] Iohannes *H*   interrogabat] interrogavit *V*   126 Quo . . . Nemo dixit] *om.*
AL   127 *post* suis *add.* iste audax *V*   Iohannis 21 *H*   128 sicut legitur] *om. H*
post Nemo *add.* tamen *H*   129 De magisterio vero] [?]io siquidem predicti *O*   De
magisterio siquidem beati *M*   De magistro vero *V*   discreti] *om. M*   istius *H*   huius
discreti *AL*   Neminis] Nemonis *M*   plenius] planius *H*   parte illa] illa parte *O*
parte *H*   *post* evangelii *add.* Iohannis septimo *H*   130 de . . . dominus] dominus de
lege contendebat *M*   de lege] *om. V*   dominus] *om. VHAL*   *post* Iudeis *add.*
domino *L*   dominus *A*   Nonne . . . Et] *om. AL*   131 ex vobis] *om. OM*
patientia] potentia *MAL*   132 iste sanctissimus] sanctus iste *O*   sanctus *M*   iste
. . . ita] *om. H*   ita] *om. OM*   Nemo] *om. AL*   iuxta] *om. O*   apostolicum]
propheticum *OM*   *post* apostolicum *add.* scilicet *AL*   133 laborat] laboret *V*   in
psalmo] *om. OM*   quia] *om. OM*   *post* manducabis *add.* beatus es et [?] *M*   etc.
H   134 et] beatus Nemo *M*   sed *O*   in secularibus satagebat] satagebat

secularibus negociis *O*   in temporalibus negotiis *M*   135 ut] sicut *O*   velut *M*
etiam in] etiam *O*   in *AL*   habuit curam] *om. O*   ut] sicut *O*   Maria]
Magdalena *H*   unde . . . de Maria] *om. AL*   unde . . . Martha] prout legitur *O*   ut
legitur *M*   *post* dicitur *add.* scilicet *V*   136 mittens] mittet *V*   ad] a *M   post*
aratrum *add.* etc. *H*   tanquam] alibi ut *O*   [?] [?] et alibi ut *M*   contemplativus]
contemplarius *V*   137 orthodoxus] verus orthodoxus *O*   quantum . . . Maria] *om.*
OM   Maria] Magdalena *H*   138 cantoris] canstoris *M   om. AL*   *O om.*
AL   et] *om. AL   post* officium *add.* humiliter *OMH*   faciebat] *om. V*   faciebat
. . . officium] *om. V*   ut hic] sacriste officium ut hic *H*   139 cantoris officium ut
hic] ut iterum *O*   Item Nemo [?] *M*   cantoris] cantorum *AL   post* Nemo *add.* [?] *M*
post canticum: *For reading of H here see first appendix to the Long* Nemo   140
Tanti] Tantique *OM*   vero] *om. OM*   et animi] et animi est et *O*   est et *M*   iste
sanctissimus] iste sanctus *O*   sanctus iste *M*   iste fortissimus *VH   post* Nemo *add.*
quod *AL*   toto] *om. O*   tanto *AL*   141 laborabat] laborare cupiebat *OM*   142 in
. . . ociosi] legitur *M*   Cur] Quid *M*   hic . . . die] ita tota die statis *O*   statis tota
die *M*   statis hic tota die *AL*   143 ab eisdem] per eosdem *O*   per eos *M*   ab eis
V   Quia] *om. M*   144 *post* domini *add.* non est oblitus iste sanctus *O*   non oblitus
est sanctus iste Nemo *M   post* dicentis *add.* scilicet *V*   non . . . faciebat] preceptum
ipsius adimplevit *O*   preceptum ewangelicum adimplevit *M*   145 unde cum] Nam
dum *O*   Nam cum *M*   Lazarus] *om. OM*   in evangelio] *om. MH*   elemosinam]
om. AL   elemosinam . . . divitis] cupiens saturari de micis que cadebant de mensa
divitis elemosinam peteret *OM*   146 solus] et solus *O   om. AL*   147 Nemo
sanctissimus] sanctus Nemo *OM*   sanctissimus Nemo *AL   post* sanctissimus *add.* et
largissimus *V*   compassionis intuitu] compassus *O*   compassionem intuitu *M*
habetur ibidem] habetis *O*   habetis in ewangelio *M*   ibidem habetur *H*   148 illi
dabat] dabat illi *V*   149 Per predicta igitur] Similiter ergo *O*   igitur] ergo *M   post*
karissimi *add.* predicta *O*   in parte plane] plene in parte illa *M*   plane] plena *O*
om. V   formationem] *om. OM*   150 nobilitatem . . . securitatem] genus *O   om.*
M   audaciam, incarnationem] incarnationem, audaciam *M*   incarnationem . . .
humilitatem] securitatem, nobilitatem, miliciam, probitatem, doctrinam, scienciam,
dignitatem, sanctitatem, gloriositatem, virtuositam, laudem, honorem, reverenciam,
verecundiam, castitatem, providentiam, beatitudinem, felicitatem, compassionem,
obedienciam, pacienciam, prudenciam, iusticiam, fortitudinem, temporanciam,
largitatem, coeternitatem, sempiternam, perpetualitatem, stabilitatem, immobilitatem,
humilitatem, corroboracionem, fidem, spem *AL*   militiam] milicie *H*   151
doctrinam . . . patientia] *om. OM   post* dignitatem *add.* conpassionem *H*   scientiam,
doctrinam] doctrinam, scientiam *H*   152 sanctitatem . . . humilitatem] patientiam,
obedientiam, honorem, reverentiam, dilectionem, sanctitatem, felicitatem, gloriam,
verecundiam, immutabilitatem, constantiam, fidem, spem *H*   154 pietatem,
immutabilitatem] honorem *O*   et honorem *M*   et] *om. M*   155 Neminis] Nemonis
M   scriptum est] scripture *M*   156 Que] quod *O*   qua *L*   quia *A*   omnia]
omnes *AL*   amore] a morte *AL*   dei nostri] domini *OM*   vicarii sunt] sunt

vicarii *M*   157 *post* ponderantes *add.* et considerantes *OM*   istum] ipsum *O*   *om.*
M   sanctissimum] beatissimum *OM*   sanctum *H*   Neminem] Nemonem *M*
cum deo] *om. OM*   158 domino] deo *O*   *om. M*   dominum *A*   potentissimo]
potentissimum *MAL*   sicut scriptum est] ut legitur *OM*   159 regnaturus]
duraturus *OM*   vivat] vivit *M*   160 Neminem] Nemonem *M*   deus] dominus
O   omnipotens deus] dominus omnipotens *AL*   celis] celo *M*   beari]
beatificari *M*   voluit] voluit voluit *M   om. AL*   dotari] doctores *OM*   cum
magnis] con(?)fgnis *M*   161 magnis] dignis *O*   decreverunt] decrevit *AL*
unde] ut *O*   ut quod *M*   tantum] prohibitum *M*   decretum *H*   est quod] *om. O*
est *M*   sibi] ei *H*   162 quod] ut *OM   om. AL*   bigamie] bigamia *M*   nota]
om. M   possit . . . libere] libere possit contrahere cum duabus *O*   possit contrahere
libere cum duabus *M*   possit] possit in *V   om. AL*   sicut legitur] ut hic *OM*
163 binas habere uxores] habere binas uxores *O*   duas uxores habere *M*   164 etiam]
etenim *O*   iste sanctus] sanctus iste *OH*   iste sanctos *M*   iste sanctissimus *L*
Nemo] *om. OVH*   corpora . . . vendere] bona ecclesiastica vendere et sanctorum
corpora alienare *O*   bona ecclesiastica et sanctorum corpora alienere et vendere   et]
vel *AL*   sicut legitur] ut scriptum est *OM*   secundum scriptum est *M*   165 et alibi]
om. O   Nemo mercetur] mercens dictabat [?] *M*   Potest . . . legitur] Item *M*
iudicia] iura *VH*   iudicia ecclesiastica] ecclesiastica iudicia *OAL*   166 dirimere]
contempnere *AL*   167 Preterea . . . loquatur (lines 167–70)] *om. OM*   religiosos]
om. V   intra . . . claustra] extra claustra quam infra claustra *V*   infra claustra quam
extra *AL*   168 Nemo potentissimus] sanctissimus Nemo *AL*   169 habeat] habet
AL   et . . . regula] regula et aliorum religiosorum diversorum *AL*   religiosorum]
om. H   170 completorium] completorum *A*   171 manifeste] manifesta *M*   et]
om. OM   post concessionibus *add.* et indulgenciis *O*   indulgenciis *M*   summorum
pontificum] quas concedunt summi pontifices *OM*   172 beatissimi et gloriosissimi]
semper beati *O*   beati *M*   gloriosissimi et beatissimi *H*   et] ac *V*   Neminis]
Nemonis *M   post* excipitur *add.* semper *MAL*   prout] ut *OM*   173 litterarum
suarum] suarum litterarum *O*   plenius] planius *HAL*   annotatur] annotatum est
AL   dicunt] dicunt sic *M*   dicitur *H   post* nostre *add.* et *AL*   concessionis]
concossionis *M*   174 paginam] pagninem *M   om. AL*   Reges . . . revelare (lines
174–77)] *om. O*   175 in . . . recipiunt] recipiunt in suis consiliis ad p(?) fiduciam
quam de ista beato Nemone generalem habere dinoscimus *M*   promittere] permittere
A   sub] in *M*   176 supradicta] *om. M*   vero] *om. AL*   ad iuramentum] in
iuramento *M*   pertinent] pertinet *MH*   additur] adicitur *M*   177 et] *om. AL*
consilia] consiliam *M*   nostri] mei *MH   post* nostri *add.* secrete *V*   firmiter
HAL   178 Absit . . . argumentis (lines 178–206)] *om. OM*   Absit] *om. AL*
179 beatissimi et gloriosissimi] *om. AL*   180 *post* bilingues *add.* liceat Nemini *L*   liceat
Nemine *A*   superni] superne *H*   180 *post* potest *add.* et potens est et factus similis
creatori *V*   et factus est similis creatori *H*   et potens est *AL   post* ix *add.* capitulo ubi
dicitur *AL*   Deus cuius] Dei *AL*   Nemo resistere] resistere Nemo *HAL*   181
iterum] *om. AL*   destruxit] destruxerit *H*   182 *post* xv *add.*

ubi dicitur sic de eius potestate *AL*   poterit] potest *AL*   in Ecclesiastico]
Ecclesiastici *H*   dicitur] *om. AL*   183 sanctus] factus *H*   est] et *A*   potest
eum corrigere] eum corrigere potest *H*   184 *post* xiii *add.* ubi eciam dicitur de eius
potestate, dicendo sic *AL*   potestatem habet] habet potestatem *V*   et[2]] vel *L*
agere] corrigere *AL*   185 quidem et] quod est *AL*   etiam] enim *AL* *post*
loquebatur *add.* ait *HAL*   186 Occurit] Qui currit *AL*   e] et *AL*   monumentis]
monumento *H* *post* inmundo *add.* et sequitur *VAL* *post* catenis *add.* iam *H*
quisquam] quis *AL*   187 domare] dogmare *V*   188 penna nec calamus] calamus
nec penna *AL*   cum] nec *AL*   189 velociter] velocis *L* *post* scribentis *add.*
scribere valeat *AL* *post* citharista *add.* ista *V*   190 patroni] patronis *AL*
beatissimi et] *om. H*   et] ac *V*   competent] competeret *H*   191 et] *om. V*
dicit] dicat *HAL*   xv] xxv *VA*   192 sunt] fient *AL*   eius] *om. V*   Fugiat]
Pereat *AL*   beatissimi] sanctissimi *V*   193 *post* et *add.* nomen eius *AL* *post* nostri
add. constanciam *H* *post* deleatur *add.* eciam *H*   de] ex *V*   194 scribatur]
probatur *V*   super] desuper *V*   glorioso] gloriosissimo *AL*   196 nuperime
credidit] autumnat *H*   Quod] quo *L*   que *A*   autem] ante *L*   debeant] debeat
AL *post* infideles *add.* inimici *AL*   197 et gloriosissimi] *om. H*   Neminis] *om.*
V *post* nostri *add.* potenciam et audaciam *H*   sic] sicut *AL*   Levitici] Levitico
AL   198 Fugietis] Fugiens *AL*   Nemine] Neminem *V*   sequente] persequente
V   sequentis *A* *post* capitulo *add.* dicitur *AL*   audebat] audeat *AL*   199 De . . .
persequente] *om. V*   200 persequente] sequente *AL*   201 Et] *om. AL*   202
nullis] nulli *AL*   recusetis] recusantes *AL*   203 Reservamus] Reservemus *H*
in . . . tot et] *om. AL*   nostri pectoris] nostris pectoribus *V* *post* beatissimi *add.* et
gloriosissimo *V*   auctoritates] auctores *AL*   205 divinas] divines *L*
canonicasve] canonicas *V*   civiles] civilas *V*   infinitis] in cunctis *V*   207
autem] aut *VAL* *post* autem *add.* aliis *OM*   pollet] posset *H*   pollet et laudibus]
et laudibus pollet *M*   Nemo iste sanctissimus] iste sanctus Nemo *O*   iste sanctos
Nemo *M*   sanctissimus Nemo iste preconizari *H*   208 tedeat audire] audire tedeat
O   ne vos] omne nos *M*   nec nos *AL*   alicuius] aliquorum *OM* *post*
prolixitatis *add.* cuius *OM*   materia] materie *OMAL*   209 torqueat] torpeant *O*
perturbet *M*   que] qui *AL*   mente] *om. O*   de isto] vitam et gesta istius *AL*
beatissimo Nemine] beato Nemone *M*   sanctissimo Nemine *H*   beatissimi Neminis
AL *post* beatissimo *add.* et gloriosissimo *V*   patrono nostro] *om. OM*   patroni
nostri *AL*   in nostro] *om. M*   210 sermone presenti] presentis sermone *M*
presenti sermone *HAL*   presenti] *om. O*   inutili] *om. M*   transeant] recedant
M *post* sed *add.* maneant *O*   in muro lapis] mura lapides *M*   muro lapides *AL*
211 vestris . . . maneant] cordibus *O*   vestris] verbis *V*   perpetuo] *om. M*
commendata] comedata *V*   212 decrevimus] *om. O*   cuius] eius *O*
beatitudinem] benedictum *M*   qui . . . vos] nos *M*   213 qui vivit sine fine et regnat
in secula seculorum *M*   vivit] bibit *H*   et vos] vosque *H*   per . . . seculorum]
om. O   secula seculorum] pocula poculorum. Explicit vita beatissimi et gloriosissimi
Neminis *V*   pocula poculorum *H*   214 Amen] *om. H*

In top margin of MS A, fol. 12v.

Nemo portabat dyadema. [?] Mathei viii.
Nemo in spiritu dei loquens dicit Anathema Ihesu. Ad Corinth.
Nemo potest dicere dominus Ihesus.

First Appendix: Ciceronian additions to the Heidelberg manuscript (H)

Following line 29, ". . . *in illum manus.*]"

Similiter flagiciosissimus Verres, qui predonibus captis vita reservatis cives Romanos securi percussit, quemquam neque timebat adversarium nullumque habuit excepto Nemine, ut Tullius in oratione contra Verrem testatur, dicens ad Verrem: *Inimicum habebas Neminem.* [*Ver* 5.74]

Following line 71 (in apparatus), ". . . *Neminem circumvenimus.*"

Et Tullius in Verrem: *A principio ita sim versatus, ut defenderem multos, leserim Neminem, subito hunc mutata voluntate descenderim.*

Following line 100 (in apparatus), ". . . *Cyrilli.*"

Et ideo Tullius ipsum Neminem maiorem se fatetur, cum in principio oracionis in Verrem inquit: *Et in hac causa profecto Neminem preponendum michi esse actorem putabit.*

Following line 139, ". . . *dicere canticum.*"

Magnus orator et reorum defensor erat, unde Tullius oracione tercia de Verre inquit: *Ne quem Nemo actione defendere ausus esset, eum ego bis accusare non possem.* [*Ver* 1.31]

Second Appendix: The end of the Hamburg manuscript version (G)

Following line 50, ". . . *in cognatione tua.*"

Fuit miles strenuus, unde et *Nemo militans.* Est etiam potens super naturam, unde: *Quod natura negat, Nemo donare potest.* Propterea etiam valde securus est in omnibus, unde: *Nemo securius,*

Fuit etiam propheta magnus et sapiens, unde: *Nemo propheta acceptus est.* Super afflictos [afflicbes *MS*] legitur fuisse valde compatiens, unde: *Maiorem caritatem Nemo habet.* Item: *Ecce quomodo moritur iustus et Nemo considerat; Viri iusti tolluntur et Nemo percipit corde.*

In hoc enim patet quomodo compassus est Christo et sanctis eius. Item solus iste beatus Nemo est qui potest ista terrena delere et solus permanere, unde: *Nemo potest ista mobilia delere et ipse immobilis stare.* Iste etiam sanctus Nemo scit que nullus hominum scire potest, unde Gregorius: *Nemo scit utrum amore dei vel odio dignus sit.*

De sanctitate vel secreta scientia eius dicitur in Apocalipsi: *Vidi turbam magnam quam Nemo dinumerare poterat.* Item ibidem: *Nemo fuit dignus aperire librum et solvere signacula eius.* Fuit etiam iste sanctus Nemo sapientissimus in artibus, unde Priscianus: *Neminem inveni similem.* Item fuit custos et rector planetarum, unde: *Nemo observabat lunam.*

Sed et nunc videndum quantum fulget meritis tamen namque dilectus est a deo ut dum suos per mundum misisset apostolos, precepit eis ut cum beatissimo Nemine obviarent, ipsum salutarent et eidem visiones et secreta tamque secretario suo funditus revelarent, sicut legitur: *Neminem per viam salutaveritis,* et alibi: *Nemini dixeritis visionem hanc.* Curata lepra, precepit dominus: *Vade, Nemini dixeris.*

Dominus etiam noster Ihesus Christus hunc sanctum personaliter honorare voluit, nam cum Iudei mulierem adulteram adducerent, Christus, cui nihil est absconditum, discretionem et sapientiam dilecti sui cognoscens, plenarie dictam in presentia dicti beati Neminis accusatam et dampnatam ipsam rennuit iudicare. Interrogans tamen eam ob honorem et reverentiam beati Neminis quis eam condempnasset, que respondit: *Nemo, domine.* Dominus autem nolens mittere falcem in messem alteram, dixit: *Nec ego te condempnabo.*

Insuper beatissimus Nemo magna humilitate et patientia circumfultus ut iuxta verba prophetica vatum [?], unde: *Qui laborat, manducat,* et alibi: *Labores manuum quia manducabis,* unde non solum in secularibus sicut Martha satagebat, sed etiam in spiritualibus ut Magdalena. Exemplum primum de Martha: *Nemo tendit manum ad aratrum.* Etiam ut contemplativus et orthodoxus unde nocte et die sacriste et cantoris officium faciebat [sacriste], ut ibi: *Nemo accendit lucernam;* ut ibi: *Nemo poterat dicere canticum.*

Third Appendix: The end of the Paris manuscript version (P)

Following line 29, ". . . *in illum manus.*"

Sed et Nichodemus, princeps Iudeorum, de potencia huius beatissimi Neminis sic dicit: *Rabi, Nemo potest hec signa facere que tu facis,* Iohannis 3. Et non solum ex testimonio Nichodemi, sed ex pluribus aliis sacre scripture locis comprobatur iste beatus Nemo fuisse potentissimus, nam ipse solus deo resistit, ut scribitur Apocalypsis quinto: *Deus claudit et Nemo aperit, deus aperit et Nemo claudit.*

Et beatus Iob inter alia quibus deum alloquitur ait: *Nemo est qui de manu tua possit eruere,* Iob 10. Ostensum est igitur quod solus iste Nemo multa potest, nam per audaciam suam et invincibilem potenciam dominus alloquens discipulos: *Et gaudium vestrum Nemo tollit a vobis,* Iohannes. Ibidem quid mirum nam de ipso conqueritur dominus gravius, dicens: *Nemo tollit a me animam meam,* Iohannis ix. Sed unde ei tanta audacia vel potentia procul dubio quia ex illustri prosapia et de stirpe regia natus est et originem traxit, nam scribitur Sapientie septimo quod *Et Nemo ex regibus habet inicium.* Et tanta strenuitate claruit quod ad regiam potestatem sublimatus est, unde scribitur in Machabeis: *Nemo portabit dyadema,* primi Machabeorum viii. Unde angelus, volens ostendere nobilitatem Christi quantum ad eius genetricem dicit ad Helizabeth cognatam matris Ihesu: *Nemo,* inquit, *est in cognatione tua,* Luce primo, et ideo quia ab ipso denominatur tota parentela Christi.

Tamquam a dignitate, mirum non est quod deo resistere potuit, unde Iob 9: *Deus cuius ire Nemo resistere potest,* et idem dicitur de deo quod *Ipse solus est qui facit omnia, et Nemo potest corrigere.* Ymo: *Si destruxerit deus, Nemo est qui edificet,* Iob 12°, secundum quod dicit beatus Petrus, et ideo non incongrue, de primo dicitur in Ecclesiastico quod: *Nemo vincit eum,* Ecclesiastici 48. Et in libro Sapientie ubi agitur de ipso deo, dicitur quod *Nemo sibi similis poterit eum frangere.* Et ideo merito dicitur omnipotens, unde in libro Machabeorum dicitur quod *Nemo habebit potentiam agere.* Nonne etiam Marchus qui ore dominico loquebatur, testans de ipso, dicens: *Occurrit de monumentis homo in spiritu inmundo qui domicilium habebat in monumentis et neque cathenis iam quicquid poterat eum ligare, qui eum sepe compedibus et cathenis vinctus, dirupisset cathenas et compedes confregisset; Nemo poterat eum domare,* Marci quarto.

Quia igitur sic potens fuit, aptus fuit militie. Et ideo Paulus dicit de eo: *Nemo militans.* De sua autem probitate et securitate scribitur alibi quod *Nemo securus.* Quippe cum naturam superet in virtute, ut dicit poeta: *Quod natura dedit, Nemo tollere potest,* et iterum de eodem: *Quod natura negat, Nemo feliciter audet.*

Et iterum Lucas dicit de eo quod *Nemo maior in natis mulierum,* Luce primo. Unde quia singularis tam in natura sua quam in virtute, et in omni perfectione fuit. Ideo singularem modum habuit militandi, nam de ipso solo dicitur quod *Nemo tenetur propriis sumptibus militare.*

Verum quia dudum nobiles et spectabiles genere hanelabant in litterali dignitate pre ceteris erudiri, idcirco beatus iste Nemo a genere quo processit, nolens aliquibus deviare, litteras didiscit, et sic super omnes coetaneos suos profecit, quod tandem propheta effectus est, unde in evangelio Luce quarto capitulo dicitur: *Nemo propheta.* Quam sine fictione didiscit et sine invidia communicavit et gratis ne in aliquo reprehendi posset, et ideo legitur de eo quod *Nemo sine crimine vivit.* Unde sicut fuit perfectus in vita, fuit etiam in gloria, quia scribitur in quodam loco de eo quod *Nemo ex omni parte beatus.* Fuit etiam iste beatissimus Nemo perfectus in caritate, ymo perfectior ceteris in actibus, quia Iohannis 14° scribitur de eo quod *Maiorem caritatem Nemo habet.* Unde propter suam maiorem caritatem et compassionem clamat ecclesia: *Ecce quomodo moritur iustus et Nemo percipit,* et iterum: *Viri sancti tolluntur et Nemo considerat.* Videte compassionem istius gloriosissimi Neminis, quomodo compassus est in cruce Christo morienti, et etiam sanctis eius migrantibus de hoc mundo fuit igitur caritate plenus.

Sed numquid fuit in scientia perfectus utique quia adeo unde scivit arismetricam, quod illam innumeram multitudinem quam vidit Iohannes, *Nemo dinumerare poterat,* Apocalypsis septimo. Fuit etiam bonus grammaticus, sicut lucide testatur Priscianus de eo: *Neminem,* inquit, *inveni socium.* Fuit item procul dubio doctus astronomus, sicut de ipso alibi scribitur: *Nemo observat lunam.* Et quia sic undecumque fuit scientia illuminatus iste gloriosus Nemo, ideo ipse solus fuit dignus aperire librum quem Iohannes in Apocalypsi viderat clausum et signatum vii sigillis, unde legitur de eo quod *Nemo fuit dignus aperire librum.* Quantis ergo preconiis debet ab omnibus terrigenis venerari, cum ipse sit cui omnia vivunt et quem laudent angeli!

Tantis honoribus ipsum sublimaverat deus quod precepit discipulis suis quod si beato Nemini obviarent, ipsum salutarent et visiones et secreta sui fiducialiter revelarent eidem, ut ibidem Luce 10: *Neminem,* inquit, *per viam salutaveritis,* et iterum Mathei 17: *Nemini dixeritis visionem.* Sed et curato de lepra hoc idem precepit, unde inquit Mathei 8°: *Nemini dixeris.*

Quid plura? Certe ne hoc parum videatur, quod a discipulis Christi ipsemet Christus personaliter ipsum voluit honorare. Nam mulierem adulteram noluit condemnare, quia ipsam beatus Nemo condemnaverat, volens in hoc deferre ei, et sciens quod non pertinebat ad ipsum, unde cum interrogata fuisset a salvatore, si aliquis condemnasset eam, et ipsa[m] respondisset: *Nemo, domine,* dixit: *Et ego te non condemnabo,* Iohannis 8, quia [?] noluit ponere falcem in messem alienam, considerans quod deferendum est statui et persone, nam non decet discipulum contraire sententie magistri sui, sed potius contrario. Nam ad magistrum pertinet corrigere et castigare discipulum et ipsum instruere, quod legitur unde fecisse iste sanctus Nemo. Nam dum Christus loqueretur ad fontem cum muliere Samaritana, et discipuli astantes non auderent ei dicere verbum, iste gloriosus Nemo castigavit eum, unde legitur ibi sic: *Nemo tamen dicit ei "Quid queris?" aut "Quid loqueris cum ea?,"* Iohannis 4°. Et alibi quando dominus dicebat discipulis suis, *Vado ad eum qui me misit,* iste interrogavit eum de via sua: *Nemo,* inquit, *interrogat me, "Quo vadis?,"* Iohannis 16, quia certe noluit quod deus erraret in via.

De magisterio autem suo habetur plenius in illa parte evangelii ubi semper Iudei contendebant de lege cum domino: *Nonne,* inquit dominus, *Moyses dedit vobis legem, et Nemo facit eam?* , Iohannis 7°. Ergo fuit imperator cuius est statuere legem. Et quamvis fuerit supra legem utpote conditor legis, legitimi subditus fuit, quia non venit solvere legem sed adimplere. Et ideo quia scriptum est in psalmo: *Labores manuum tuarum manducabis,* psalmo 28, et secundo ad Thessalonicenses tertio: *Qui non laborat non manducet,* voluit beatus Nemo propriis laborare manibus non solum in spiritualibus sicut Maria, verum etiam in media [?] velut Martha, unde scribitur de eo quod *Nemo mittens manum ad aratrum,* Luce 9°. Et iterum fuit adeo contemplativus et devotus quod surgebat ad matutinas et nocte dieque officium sacriste et etiam cantoris diligenter exequebatur, unde legitur de eo, Luce xi, quod *Nemo accendit lucernam,* et Apocalipsis 14°: *Nemo poterat dicere canticum.*

Et quando occupabatur exteriori opere, ordinaverat quod alii vacarent contemplationis ocio vice sua, unde quando isti requirebantur, *Cur tota die starent ociosi?* responderunt: *Nemo nos conduxit* (Mathei 20). Et priusquam aliquid excercitio manuum suarum acquisiverat, libere hoc idem pauperibus erogabat, unde scribitur de eo quod quando pauper ille cupiebat saturari de micis que cadebant de mensa divitis et non potuit obtinere, tunc *Nemo ei dabat,* Luce 16.

Factum itaque quod in utraque vita activa, unde videlicet et contemplativa fuit perfectus, ob cuius reverentiam et auctoritatem Romani pontifices obtemperant eidem, et etiam imperatores, quia quod in utroque iure cautum est concedunt ei, unde absque bigamine [*sic*] nota potest licite contrahere matrimonium cum duabus uxoribus, ut ibi: *Nemini permittatur duas uxores habere.*

Potest etiam iste sanctus bona ecclesiastica et sanctorum corpora vendere et alienare, sicut scriptum est: *Nemo martires distrahat; Nemo mercetur.* Potest etiam iura ecclesiastica dirimere, ut ibi: *Nemo condempnet ecclesiastica iudicia.* Sed et in omnibus beneficiis, privilegiis, confessionibus et indulgentiis quas concedunt summi pontifices, voluntas sancti Neminis semper excipitur, secundum quod in fine suarum litterarum plenius annotatur, ubi dicunt: *Presentis autem concessionis paginam Nemini liceat infringere.* Reges etiam et principes, quando aliquos in suum ministerium assumunt vel in officium constituunt, ob plenam fiduciam quam de isto beatissimo Nemini gerunt, compellunt ipsos iurare et promittere: faciunt sub hac forma inter alia que ad iuramentum fidelitatis pertinent; additur sic: *Tu iurabis secreta consilia domini tenere et Nemini revelare.*

His itaque et pluribus ymo infinitis aliis conditionibus hominis et optimis fulget iste beatissimus Nemo, qui ante mundum cepit esse, et eius vita caret morte, nam scribitur Ecclesiastae quinto quod *Nemo est qui semper vivat.* Ad quod vivere nos perducat qui sine fine vivit et regnat. Amen.

The Long *Nemo:* Translation

Here begins the life of the most holy and most glorious Nobody.

At sundry times and in divers manners, dearly beloved, God spoke in times past through the prophets, who, as if in riddles and an obscure voice, foretold the coming of the only-begotten son of God for the redemption of those who labor in darkness and sit in the shadow of death. In the last days, however, he speaks openly through his holy Scripture, and foretells, explicates, and bears witness to the most blessed and glorious Nobody as similar to himself, begotten before the ages, yet unknown to humankind until now by reason of our sins.

But our own Savior and Lord himself, who is always merciful, and who never leaves his own helpless, showed pity to the people redeemed by his own blood, and with the ancient darkness wholly removed from our eyes, he has deigned to reveal to us the treasure, so renowned, of this most glorious Nobody, that we may be able to see him (hidden to us, damnably, until now) more soundly thereafter, with the eye of faith.

This blessed Nobody, therefore, is found to be contemporaneous with God the Father, and in essence particularly like the Son, as he was neither created nor begotten but proceeds forth in Holy Scripture, in which it is set forth fully by the psalmist, who says: *Days shall be formed, and Nobody in them.* To whom, afterward, such authority justly accrued, with such great merit, that as if spurning earthly things, he ascended to the heights of heaven in miraculous flight, as it is read: *Nobody ascended into heaven.* And the Lord himself testifies to this, saying: *Nobody can come to me.*

When this most holy Nobody ascended into heaven, as it is said, he saw the pure and complete and at the same time threefold Godhead himself, as it is read: *Nobody hath seen God.* That this Nobody had seen God the Gospel gives witness, as it is read: *Nobody knoweth the Son,* and elsewhere: *Nobody speaking to the Holy Spirit.* Because, indeed, he had seen him together with the Father and the Son, he spoke fearlessly, for he who saw, bore witness.

Thence, returning from the heavens, this virtuous and most powerful Nobody shone forth with such daring and fearlessness and was so resplendent that when the accursed Jews, coming to seize Jesus, did not dare to attack him, only this most daring Nobody, who had been there with them, took hold of him, as it is read: *And Nobody laid hands on him.*

The ruler of the Jews, moreover, Nicodemus by name, referring to the power of this most glorious Nobody, said: *Rabbi, Nobody can do these signs which thou dost.* And although Nicodemus may profess this most blessed power, as it is said, he is also rightly shown to be more powerful by far elsewhere in Scripture, for only this most powerful Nobody can contradict Jesus Christ our Lord, as it is read: *God shutteth and Nobody openeth, God openeth and Nobody shutteth.*

The blessed Job, also, testifying to this, spoke to God, among many things referring to his power like this: *Whereas there is Nobody that can deliver out of thy hand.* And what is allowed to no one, only this blessed Nobody can do, for it is read of him: *Nobody can serve two masters,* and elsewhere: *Nobody serves two masters usefully.*

Indeed, our Lord Jesus Christ himself, speaking to his disciples of the power of this most glorious Nobody, said: *And your joy Nobody shall take from you.* And you should not be amazed, dearly beloved, if Jesus Christ, knowing that Nobody is the most powerful of all, said this to his disciples when he confessed about himself most solemnly, saying: *Nobody taketh my soul away from me.* And, if this most holy Nobody embodies such virtue, it is no wonder that he wanted to be incarnated and born into this world, like Christ, begotten of an illustrious lineage, as it is read in Ecclesiasticus: *For Nobody has his birth from kings.* He is also of the lineage of Jesus Christ, as you may see, for in the Gospel the name of St. John the Baptist is asked, and the answer is: *Nobody is in thy kindred.*

He was indeed a mighty and vigorous soldier, as it is read: *Nobody being a soldier.* Of his honesty and security, indeed, it is said: *Nobody is secure.* He is called secure deservedly, since he surpasses nature in virtue, as this: *What Nature forbids, Nobody dares successfully,* and again about the same: *What Nature has given, Nobody may take away.*

He did not profit by his military service in the way of modern soldiers, who, like fresh herring for which the price must be paid before it can be obtained from the fishmonger, are up for sale, and not for honor, but rather, more truly, I blush to say, they offered themselves up for a price, for the most part, to deadly dangers. But it pleased this most glorious Nobody greatly, and still does please him (on account of his great wealth and and the returns by which he excelled over other living men), to serve as a soldier and to perform his duties at his own expense, as it is read: *Nobody is forced to serve as a soldier at his own expense.*

In truth, because the powerful, formerly strong and lofty and learned in literal dogma above all others, were now gasping, for that reason this blessed Nobody the soldier, not wanting, because of the kind from which he came, to go astray in any way, learned letters and accordingly became most wise, as it is read: *Nobody, a prophet.* But he did not squander his powers of prophecy and his wide learning, which he acquired through much study, in the manner of modern clerics, who, in pursuit of a certain other thing, do not care to increase their learning unless they can add money to money and be enriched by hefty allowances; and because of that, disregarding the liberal arts, they pursue only the lucrative faculties. But as they have certainly taken on all manner of impurities, this most holy Nobody alone has regarded the heavenly things, as it is read: *Nobody lives without fault,* and elsewhere: *Nobody is blessed in every way.* And again it is said: *Nobody has greater love.* And that Nobody has greater love the holy mother Church proclaims, as it is said: *Behold how the just man dies, and Nobody feels it in his heart,* and again: *Just men are destroyed and Nobody takes heed.*

Now, moreover, you may see, dearly beloved, the compassion of this most glorious Nobody, as he was merciful to the dying Christ, as it is said: *Behold how the just man dies.* And he was also merciful to the poor man at whose prayers the city beseiged by the mighty Nobody was liberated, as it is written: *Nobody remembered that poor man.*

You may see, moreover, that only this most holy Nobody will be saved in the fearful great judgment of God without true confession and without health-giving penance imposed on him, as it is declared plainly in holy writ, saying thus: *Nobody will be saved without true confession and without penance.* This most wealthy Nobody was also the greatest owner among all owners, and remains so, for he possesses God himself at times, and loses him also whenever he likes, as blessed Augustine says in a certain book of authority: *Nobody loses you, God, unless he renounces you.* Likewise this most steadfast Nobody alone can love earthly things and remain steadfast himself, as the blessed Gregory says in a certain book of authority, saying this: *Nobody is strong enough to love these inconstant things and remain constant himself.* Likewise this most learned Nobody was so illustrious in the greatness of his knowledge that through his discernment he knows that which no living man can know, as it is read in Ecclesiasticus: *Nobody knoweth whether he be worthy of love or hatred.*

And you may see also that this most accomplished Nobody was educated in the liberal fields of knowledge, for he knew arithmetic, so that the great multitude that John had seen in Revelations, only this holy Nobody could count up, as it is read: *And I saw a great multitude which Nobody could number.* And again the same is said of his worthiness and knowledge, in saying thus: *And Nobody was found worthy to open the book and to open the seals thereof.* Of him also Priscian testifies clearly that he was similar to himself in grammatical knowledge, and a friend, as he says thus in the *Ars maior: I found Nobody my friend.* He was also an astronomer, as it is read: *Nobody observes the moon.*

But now you can see, dearly beloved, how greatly this most holy Nobody shines through his merit, how great is his knowledge, and therefore how much he should be attended by praise and glory, the purest affection and honor, from everyone. Since he for whom all things live, and whom the archangels praise, loved this holy Nobody, blessed through the ages, with such a pure love that when he sent his apostles through the world, he commanded them that when they met the most blessed Nobody along the way they should greet him and reveal to him the visions and secret things just as if to their secretary, with great confidence, as it is written: *Salute Nobody by the way,* and elsewhere: *Tell the vision which you have seen to Nobody.* He also said to the man cured of leprosy: *Go, tell this to Nobody.*

What further? Our Lord Jesus Christ did not want this holy Nobody to be revered solely through his disciples, but deigned to honor him personally. For when the Jews wished to ensnare the Lord in words, and brought the woman taken in adultery before him, he to whom nothing is hidden, recognizing the discernment, wisdom, and valor of his beloved Nobody, refused to judge the aforesaid woman accused by him, full of reverence and honor for the blessed Nobody, saying: *Woman, where are they who hath accused thee? Hath Nobody condemned thee?* She replied: *Nobody, Lord.* Hearing this, the Lord, not wanting to ply his sickle in another man's field, conceded the aforesaid woman to the holy Nobody, saying: *Neither will I condemn thee.*

For the Lord considered him venerable in estate and in his person, and wanted therefore to defer to his master, for elsewhere we read about his learning that this *Nobody is a prophet and learned man.* But when Christ spoke with the Samaritan woman at the well, and the other disciples did not dare to say a word to him, he rebuked Jesus like a good master, as it is read: *Yet Nobody said: "What seekest thou?" or "Why talkest thou with her?"* In addition, Nobody, not wanting Jesus to go astray along the way, asked him where he was going, as it is read: *Yet Nobody said: "Whither goest thou?"* Likewise, when the Lord showed himself to his disciples, Nobody dared to ask him who he was, while the other disciples did not dare, as it is read: *Nobody said: "Who art thou?"*

Of the learning of the distinguished Nobody, indeed, there is much set out fully in that part of the Gospel in which the Lord contended with the Jews about the law, saying: *Did not Moses give you the law? And among you Nobody maketh the law?* Moreover, this most holy Nobody was so illustrious in such patience and humility that, according to the words of the apostle—*Who will not work shall not eat,* and in another place in the Psalms, *The labors of your hands that you shall eat*—he wanted to labor with his own hands. And not only did he toil in worldly things, like Martha, but he also attended to divine things, like Mary. Whence of the first it is said of Martha: *Nobody putteth his hand to the plow.* And as he arose from bed like a contemplative and an officer of the church, so he performed the office of sacristan and cantor day and night like the second, that is, Mary at matins, as in: *Nobody lighteth a lantern;* the office of cantor as in: *Nobody could say the canticle.*

Indeed, this most holy Nobody was of such a heart and mind that not only did he labor with great effort, but also he wished to hire the idle and to work together with them, as it is said to the idle in the Gospel: *Why stand you here all the day, idle?* The answer from them is: *Because Nobody hath hired us.*

Remembering, moreover, the words of the Lord, *Break your bread to the hungry,* he gave alms, so that when Lazarus, the poor man in the Gospel, asked for alms and wanted to be filled with the crumbs which fell from the table of the rich man, only this most holy Nobody gave him a look of compassion, as we read: *And Nobody gave to him.*

By the above, dearly beloved, you can see distinctly to some extent the form, essence, power, daring, incarnation, nobility, military valor, honesty, security, knowledge, learning, dignity, steadfastness, fixity, holiness, grace, honor, felicity, blessedness, reverence, chastity, modesty, strength, generosity, compassion, patience, goodness, piety, stability, humility, and charity of this most glorious Nobody, according to that which is written in Holy Scripture about him. Weighing up all these things, the highest pontiffs, through the love of our God (whose representatives they are on earth in these times), decreed that this most holy Nobody will reign with God eternally and is coeternal with our most powerful Lord, as it is written: *Nobody will reign forever,* and elsewhere: *There is Nobody who lives forever,* and that this same Nobody, whom omnipotent God wanted to be blessed in heaven, should be endowed with great favors on earth. Whence in both laws he is granted so much that without any charge of bigamy he is allowed to enter into wedlock freely, as it is read: *Nobody is permitted to have two wives.*

This holy Nobody may also alienate and sell the bodies of the saints, as it is read: *Nobody may divide the martyrs,* and elsewhere: *Nobody may carry on trade.* He can also frustrate ecclesiastical judgment, as it is read: *Nobody may condemn ecclesiastical judgment.* Besides this you may see that only this most powerful Nobody has the power of speaking freely after compline among various men of religion, both within and outside the cloister, as it is held in the rule of the blessed Benedict and of various other religious men, saying thus: *After compline Nobody may speak.* And, further, you may see clearly that in all privileges and concessions of the highest pontiffs, the desire of the most blessed and most glorious Nobody is excepted, as it is noted fully at the end of their letters, where they say: *And Nobody is allowed to infringe upon the contents of our present concession.* And whoever the kings and princes receive in their counsel, they make them swear and promise in that form described above. Among other things which pertain to the swearing of fidelity is added this: *You will swear to keep the secrets and the counsel of our lord and reveal them to Nobody.*

May everyone refrain from disparaging with deceitful tongues in any way the power, excellence, and glory of our patron, the most blessed and most glorious Nobody, who is able to withstand the wrath of God on high, as it is read, Job 9: *God, whose wrath Nobody can resist,* and again Job 12: *If he pull down, Nobody can build up,* and Wisdom 15: *Nobody can make a god like to himself.* And Ecclesiasticus says: *Nobody conquers God,* and again Job 18: *He alone is holy God, and Nobody can correct him.* And Matthew 13: *For Nobody has the power to make and to drive everything and even to change position.* Is it not Mark, also, who spoke with the mouth of the Lord: *There ran out of the monuments a man with an unclean spirit, nor could anyone bind him with chains, and Nobody could tame him.*

What further? Certainly neither the quill nor the reed pen, with both hands of the scribe writing furiously, of which the harpist speaks, are sufficient to express the excellence and glory of our patron, the most blessed and most glorious Nobody, when Job 15 says of his immutability and constancy: *Nobody is unchangeable, and the heavens are not pure in his sight.* Therefore let every wicked enemy of our patron, the most blessed and glorious Nobody, take flight, and let him be blotted out from the Book of the Living and not be inscribed among the just; nor let his memory remain on earth who strives to reject our glorious work, and who not long ago thought to seduce the hearts of our faithful with deceitful promptings. And that those unfaithful to our patron, the most blessed and most glorious Nobody, ought to take flight is shown thus, Leviticus 6: *You shall flee with Nobody pursuing you,* and again in the same chapter: *Nobody shall dare to resist the enemies.* Of this it is also written clearly in Proverbs 28: *The wicked man fleeth when Nobody pursueth.*

Therefore be brave men in the fight, like our teacher Nobody, and strong. And may you not refuse to enter into the struggle of him who stands firm through no false proof or scripture. Let us lay up in the coffer of our heart, for the praise and glory of our patron, the most blessed Nobody, the testimony of so many and such great authorities, divine and canonical as well as civil, with unending confirmation from the holy Fathers, and, what is more, with arguments from philosophy and nature.

This most holy Nobody is valiant in countless virtues and excellence, which we have decided to pass over in silence for now, lest it tire you to hear it, and lest, God forbid, the amount of wordiness torment the mind of any one of you;

and so that these things which you have received with a pious mind about the most blessed Nobody, our patron, in our present sermon, do not pass away in useless flight, but remain a treasure in your hearts perpetually in the Lord, like a stone in a wall. May he who lives and reigns eternally grant that you and we may attain his glory and blessedness, world without end. Amen.

3. The Abbreviated Long *Nemo*

Manuscript: Munich, Bayerische Staatsbibliothek MS clm. 10751, fols. 180r–
187r. a. 1575. Not previously edited.

Sermo cum primis elegans de sancto Nemine
Multifarie multisque modis deus olim locutus est patribus in prophetis, qui in
enigmate nubilosaque voce unigenitum dei filium pro redemendis hominibus
in tenebris umbraque mortis sedentibus condixerant. Alloquitur idem
5   novissimis diebus, hocque palam per scripturam Neminem beatissimum, ante
secula genitum, humano generi hactenus (exigentibus peccatis) incognitum:
magnificavit dominus Neminem sanctum in multis mirabilibus.

Beatus igitur Nemo patri contemporaneus, filio in essentia consimilis, non
factus nec genitus sed procedens, ut spiritus sanctus, in sacro reperitur eloquio,
10 ubi per prophetam dicitur: *Dies formabuntur et Nemo in eis.* Cui tanta in brevi
accrevit authoritas ut, terram respuens, celorum culmina mirabiliter pervolaret,
nam sequitur: *Nemo ascendit in celum.* Hoc et ipsa veritas contestatur, dicens:
Nemo venit ad me.

Celum denique conscendens, deitatem illam divinissimam simul et tri-
15 nitatem integram et perfectam oculis ei licuit contueri, omnibus mortalibus
negatum, quia dicitur: *Deum Nemo vidit.* Visionis huius veritatem evangelista
clarius describens ait: *Nemo novit patrem;* item *Nemo novit filium;* et alibi:
Nemo loquens in spiritu sancto, quia ipsum vidit cum patre et filio.

Princeps denique Iudeorum, Nicodemus nomine, potentiam Neminis invic-
20 tissimi domino nostro referens, ait: *Nemo potest hec signa facere que tu facis.*
Et quanquam Nicodemus Neminem fateatur potentem, scripture sacre testi-
moniis Christo domino potentior invenitur, nam solus Nemo sanctus omnipotenti domino contrariari audet, unde scribitur: *Deus aperit, Nemo claudit,* item:
Deus claudit, Nemo aperit.

25 Insuper Iob potentie Neminis illius magnitudinem animo secum revolvens,
deum alloquitur: *Cum sit Nemo,* ait, *qui de manu tua possit eruere.*

Salvator noster tandem Christus, cognita audacia et potentia Neminis, alloquens discipulos suos, dicit: *Gaudium vestrum Nemo tollet a vobis.* Nec mirum
si Christus dixerit discipulis suis, Neminem eos praestito promissoque pri
30 vaturum gaudio, cum de se ipso veritas ipsissima rem fateatur graviorem,
Nemo, inquiens, *a me tollet animam meam.* Concessum est etiam Nemini,
potestque id quod omnibus est negatum, quia ipse potest duobus dominis
servire, unde metrista: *Utiliter servit dominis Nemoque duobus.* Tante virtutis,
potentie simul et audacie cum sit, non est mirum si in mundo parem Christo

35 incarnationem, nativitatem, prosapiamque voluerit habere. De nativitate
Neminis sic scriptum habemus: *Nemo ex regibus nativitatem habet et initium.*
Est enim de genere Christi, dum enim de nomine quereretur Iohannis, responsum est: *Nemo est de cognatione tua.*
    Fuit Nemo ille sanctissimus miles strenuus et invicte potentie, nam legitur:
40 *Nemo securus in omnibus.* Dicitur securus quia naturam superat in virtute,
unde poeta: *Quod natura negat, Nemo presumere tentat.* Item: *Quod natura
dedit, tollere Nemo potest.* Militia vero Neminis invictissimi longe est
gloriosior aliis militibus propter stipendia militantibus. Nemo non sic, nam de
eo habemus scriptum: *Nemo tenetur propriis stipendiis militare.*
45   Mirificus hic Nemo literas novit, sapiens fuit, sed et propheta extitit. Verum
doctrinam et prophetiam suam non modernorum more in luxu, mundi vanitate
peccatisque, consumpsit, sed in puritate vite ambulans, deque virtute in virtutem progrediens, ad virtutis culmen apicemque devenit, unde dicitur: *Nemo
sine crimine vivit.* Item: *Nemo ex omni parte beatus.* Item compassivus fuit,
50 magnitudinem compassionis ecclesia rememorans: *Ecce,* ait, *quomodo moritur
iustus, et Nemo percipit corde.* Et ibidem: *Viri iusti tolluntur et Nemo
considerat.*
    Modo, charissimi, ad oculum videtis compassionem eius, qualiter morienti
Christo sanctisque illius sit compassus. Quoties cum hoc etiam misericordie
55 estuaverit visceribus sacro id prodente eloquio dignoscimus, cum dicatur:
Nemo recordatus est pauperum. Pauperis etiam illius evangelici, qui ante
ianuam divitis existens cupiebat saturari de micis que cadebant de divitis
mensa—oblitus hic ab omnibus, *Nemo illi dabat.* Virtute etiam dilectionis dei
videlicet et proximi quantum resplenduerit, preque omnibus mortalibus quan-
60 tum in dilectione profecerit, veritatis patet testimonio, dum dicitur: *Maiorem
dilectionem Nemo habet.*
    Dies tempusque me deficiet, si virtutes omnes Neminis sanctissimi ma-
nifestare voluero, cum non in multis, verum in omnibus virtutibus perfectus
non tantum, sed et perfectissimus, extiterit. In liberalibus artibus disertus et
65 eruditus, nam dicitur: *Nemo novit omnia.* In arithmetica celebris et doctus, quia
turbam illam magnam et innumerabilem quam Iohannes vidit in Apocalipsi,
Nemo dinumerare poterat. Fuit Nemo ille sanctus secretorum celestium cognitor, dignusque celestia secreta intelligere et pervidere. Dicitur enim: *Nemo
dignus fuit aperire librum et solvere signacula eius.* Fuit etiam astronomus,
70 quia dicitur: *Nemo lunam observat.*
    Iam si iubet, dilectissimi in domino, videre potestis Nemo quantis fulgeat
mysteriis, quantisque charismatibus virtutum et signorum superemineat, cum
ipse cui omnia vivunt, quemque nullum latet secretum et quem angeli pariter et

archangeli laudant, quam pure et sincere Neminem dilexerit sanctissimum.
75   Nam cum apostolos suos mundum mitteret per universum, serio quam potuit,
eis praecepit ut videlicet cum obviarent Nemini ipsum salutarent, visiones
quoque et secreta sua eidem fiducialiter aperirent, dicens: *Neminem per viam*
salutaveritis. Et iterum: *Nemini dixeritis visionem quam vidistis.* Omnipotens
deus qui occultorum est cognitor, cordium et cogitationum rimator, et quem
80   nullum latet secretum, cum magni aliquid egit in carne mortali constitutus,
ilico voluit quo illud Nemini intimaretur, unde cum leprosum pristine red-
didisset sanitati, *Vade,* ait, *Nemini dixeris.*

Sed quid plura? Cum non solum per discipulos suos, sed per semetipsum
Christus benedictus Neminem sanctum voluerit honorare, nam cum vagabundi
85   Iudei mulierculam in adulterio deprehensam Christo iudicandam adducerent,
mulierem accusatam absque dilecti sui Neminis discretione simul et iudicio
iudicare renuit, dicens: *Mulier, ubi sunt qui te accusabant?* At illa: *Nemo,*
domine. Audiens hec mire magneque reverentie dominus, quia Nemo eam
accusaret, falcem nolens mittere in alienam messem, *Si Nemo te condemnavit,*
90   ait, *mulier, neque ego te condemnabo. Vade.*

Videte, charissimi fratres, quam magne authoritatis quanteque potentie
Nemo sanctus fuerit. Non enim tantum propheta verum et doctor et magister
nostri salvatoris sacro adstipulante eloquio fuisse refertur, nam cum Christus
ad fontem cum Samaritana loqueretur, et astantes discipuli eius non essent ausi
95   ei dicere verbum, Nemo tanquam magister idoneus Christum ut discipulum
negligentem etiam durius quo potuit redarguit, cum dicitur: *Nemo tamen dixit,*
"Quid queris?" aut "Quid loqueris cum illa?" Etiam cum quadam vice
dominus discipulis suis dixisset, *Vado ad eum qui me misit,* Nemo dignoscere
volens iter quo pergeret, interrogavit eum, dicens: *Quo vadis?* Noluit idem
100 Nemo beatissimus quod dominus eundo erraret, aut mali quid pateretur. Inde
est quod cum dominus ad mare discipulis piscantibus non cognosceretur,
Nemo eum interrogavit, inquiens: *Tu quis es?*

De magisterio vero Neminis plenius habetur in lectione illa evangelica ubi
dum dominus de lege contendebat cum Iudeis, dicens: *Nonne Moises dedit*
105 *vobis legem?* subditur: *Nemo tamen fecit legem.* Ecce prefertur Moisi Nemo,
propter magisterium eius. Tantus ei legis divine implende inerat fervor, ut non
modo ei legem scire sufficeret, verum legem implere summo satageret conatu.
Nam cum scriptum iuxta Pauli verbum sciret, *qui non laborat non manducet,* et
alibi, *labores manuum tuarum quia manducabis,* propriis manibus gravissimos
110 quosque perfecit labores, quemadmodum scribitur: *Nemo mittens manum suam*
ad aratrum. In laboribus et secularibus negotiis licet continue ut altera Martha
exercitaretur, illam tamen partem que optima veritatis testimonio perhibetur,

contemplationem et orationem cum Magdalena iugiter in exercitio usuque habuit. De vigilantia eius in contemplationem et oratione scribitur: *Nemo sem-*
115   *per orat.* Hoc etiam quasi in consuetudinem duxit, et pro laudabili exercitamento habuit, quia semper de nocte surrexit, et ad matutinas ivit, iuxta illud: *Nemo accendit lucernam.* Et devote non solum oravit, imo dulcissime etiam cantavit, iuxta illud in Apocalipsi: *Nemo poterat dicere canticum.*

Tanti etiam fervoris in laborando fuit, quod non solum ipse solus laborabat,
120   sed etiam otiosos et non laborantes ad laborandum hortaretur. Patet hoc quia cum paterfamilias increparet ocio torpentes nonnullos, dicens: *Quid hic statis tota die otiosi?* responderunt: *Nemo nos conduxit.*

Omni laude dignissimus ille Nemo omnipotenti consimilis in eternitate finem non habebit; de eo enim legitur: *Nemo semper duraturus.* Et item: *Nemo*
125   *est qui semper vivit.* Eundem sanctissimum Neminem deus in terris etiam privilegiavit. In utroque enim iure canonico et civili nulli licet habere duas uxores, sibi tamen permittitur absque nota bigamie, unde legitur: *Nemini permittitur binas habere uxores.*

Potest etiam bona ecclesiastica alienare et vendere corpora sanctorum, iuxta
130   illud: *Nemo contemnat ecclesiastica iudicia.* Item potest infringere bullas papales, unde in concessionibus privilegiisque papalibus semper ponitur in fine: *Presentem nostre concessionis paginam Neminem liceat infringere,* eique ausu contrario contraire. Item reges et principes, cum quosdam in consiliarios recipiunt, ob pleniorem fiduciam eos iurare faciunt, ubi Nemo excipitur. Sed quod
135   maius est, tante probitatis Nemo sanctus dignoscitur quod etiam principes hoc quodammodo mandare videntur consiliariis suis ut secreta eorum tenere et Nemini debeant revelare. Videte, charissimi, quomodo ei omnia principum consilia sunt revelanda.

Infinitus igitur Nemo pollet virtutibus, sed ne prolixitas nauseam segni
140   generet auditori, neve inutili volatu narrata de eo pertranseant, finiendus noster est sermo. Ut audita de illo vestris in cordibus perpetuo maneant, et nunquam in oblivionem vobis veniant, id obnixe efflagitamus. Ceteras eius virtutes ad presens sub silentio preterire decrevimus. Ad cuius tamen beatitudinem et gloriam ille nos perducat, qui sine fine vivit et regnat in secula seculorum.
145   Amen.

65 doctus] doctis *MS*

4. The Short *Nemo*

Manuscripts

A   Lost exemplar of a printed pamphlet; the pamphlet is now pp. 152r–154v of
      Augsburg, Staats- und Stadtbibliothek rar 58 (olim D.L. 388). The pamphlet
      dates from 1505–10. Edited in Johannes Bolte, "Die Legende vom heiligen
      Niemand," *Alemannia* 16 (1888): 193–201 (at 200–201). Reprinted by Otto
      Clemen, "Zu Huttens Nemo," *Theologische Studien und Kritiken* 79 (1906):
      308–12. This edition has been done anew from the pamphlet.

B   Brno, Statní Oblastní Archív MS E 6 Benedictins of Rajhrad H e 19 [*sic*]
      (olim Raigern MS i.I), fols. 140r–141r. s. xv. Not previously published.

F   St. Florian, Stiftsbibliothek MS XI.619, fols. 83v–84r. s. xv. Not previously
      published.

G   Berlin, Staatsbibliothek MS boruss. fol. 720, fol. 479v. a. 1448. Not pre-
      viously published.

M   Munich, Bayerische Staatsbibliothek MS clm. 903, fol. 113v. a. 1420–57.
      Cited in part by an anonymous scholar in "Nemo," *Anzeiger für Kunde der
      deutschen Vorzeit,* N. F. 17 (1870): cols. 51–52; otherwise not previously
      published.

S   Salzburg, Bibliothek der Erzabtei St. Peter MS b.V.15, fols. 230v–232r. s. xv.
      Not previously published.

V   Vienna, Österreichische Nationalbibliothek MS lat. 3282, fols. 5v–7v. s. xv.
      Previously edited in W. Wattenbach, "Nemo vir perfectus," *Anzeiger für
      Kunde der deutschen Vorzeit,* N. F. 14 (1867): cols. 205–7.

The base text used in this edition is B.

Sermo de sancto Nemine

Vir erat in oriente nomine Nemo, et erat vir ille ut alter Iob inter omnes
orientales. Magnus namque erat sanctus iste Nemo in genere et prosapia,
magnus in potentia, magnus in scientia, magnus in clementia et in compas-
5   sione, magnus in honore et reverentia, et magnus in audacia. Et hec omnia per
sacram scripturam comprobantur.

       Primo dico quod magnus fuit iste sanctus Nemo in genere et prosapia,
similis Ade, qui nec creatus nec genitus sed formatus, secundum quod habetur
per prophetam dicentem: *Dies formabuntur et Nemo in eis.* Fuit etiam de
10   genere militari, secundum illud apostoli: *Nemo militans deo.* Ymo fuit nobilis
miles qui propriis, non alienis, stipendiis militavit, secundum illud apostoli:
Nemo tenetur propriis stipendiis militare. Et fuit de genere non qualicunque

sed regali, Ecclesiastici quinto: *Nemo ex regibus sumpsit exordium.* Et fuit de
cognatione virginis gloriose, eo quod fuit de stirpe regia et de cognatione
15 sancte Elizabeth, Luce primo: *Nemo est in cognatione tua.* Nec solum fuit de
stirpe regia sed cum ipso deo eternaliter legitur semper regnaturus, Ecclesiastes
undecimo: *Nemo semper regnaturus.*
     Secundo iste Nemo fuit magnus in potentia. Nam aperit id quod deus
claudit, iuxta illud: *Deus claudit et Nemo aperit.* Item de manu dei audacter
20 eripit, Iob xxix: *Cum sit Nemo qui de manu tua possit eruere.* Item edificat
quod deus destruit, Iob: *Si deus destruit Nemo est qui edificat.* Item ipsum
deum superat et vincit, Ecclesiastici quinto: *Nemo vincit deum.* Propterea signa
que deus facit ipse facere potest si voluerit, sicut dicit Nicodemus in evangelio:
Nemo potest hec signa facere que tu facis. Item gaudium ab apostolis potenter
25 tollit, unde Iohannes: *Gaudium vestrum Nemo tollet a vobis.* Ymo quod magis
est, animam Christi rapit, Iohannes: *Animam meam Nemo tollit a me.* Item sicut
nullus potest duobus dominis servire, ipse servit utiliter, iuxta illud poeticum:
Utiliter servit Nemo duobus heris, et in evangelio: *Nemo potest duobus dominis
servire.*
30   Tertio iste Nemo fuit magnus in scientia. Scivit enim an amore vel odio sit
dignus, iuxta illud: *Nemo scit utrum amore vel odio sit dignus.* Fuit etiam
magnus in grammatica, Prisciano se conformans, ipso attestante: *Neminem
inveni mihi socium.* Fuit magnus in arismetrica, iuxta illud Apocalipsis: *Nemo
poterat numerare turbam hanc.* Fuit magnus in musica, in Apocalipsi: *Nemo
35 poterat dicere canticum.* Fuit etiam magnus propheta, secundum illud Mathei:
Nemo propheta acceptus est in patria sua.
     Item fuit magnus in clementia et in compassione. Primum signum fuit
compassionis quia Christo fuit compassus in cruce, unde in evangelio: *Ecce
quomodo moritur iustus et Nemo considerat.* Etiam martiribus fuit compassus
40 pro Christo morientibus, iuxta illud: *Viri iusti tolluntur et Nemo considerat nec
percipit corde.* Item Lazaro mendicanti fuit compassus, qui petebat saturari de
micis que cadebant de mensa, et *Nemo illi dabat.* Item filio prodigo compassus
fuit, qui cupiebat ventrem suum saturare de siliquis quas porci manducabant, et
Nemo illi dabat. Fuit etiam pauperum consolator, unde Ecclesiastae decimo:
45 *Verti me ad alia et vidi calumpnias que sub sole geruntur, et consolatorem
Neminem inveni.*
     Etiam fuit magnus in vita contemplativa, deo et sanctis servitia impen-
dendo, iuxta illud: *Nemo accendit lucernam suam.* Etiam fuit magnus in vita
activa, iuxta illud: *Nemo mittens manum ad aratrum.*
50   Item ut anime eius dignitatem concludam breviloquio, fuit sanctus iste
Nemo quem singulari honore honoravit dominus per suos discipulos saluta-

tiones suas sibi transmittendi cum dixit: *Neminem per viam salutaveritis.* Fuit etiam magnus consiliarius domini, iuxta illud: *Nemini dixeritis visionem hanc.* Etiam ex speciali honore conceditur sibi ut possit cum duabus contrahere
55 matrimonium, iuxta dictum decreti: *Nemini licet habere duas uxores.*

Fuit iste sanctus Nemo magnus in audacia. Cum Iudei non essent ausi manum mittere in Iesum, ipse autem audacter irruit in eum et ligavit eum, iuxta illud: *Et Nemo in eum misit manus.* Et finaliter iste Nemo sanctus accusavit mulierem in adulterio deprehensam, iuxta illud dictum domini: *Mulier, ubi sunt*
60 *qui te accusabant?* Respondit: *Nemo, domine.* Item ut omnem eius dignitatem concludam, iste homo videns vana huius mundi, conscendit ad celestia, iuxta illud evangeliste: *Nemo ascendit in celum.* Quod nobis patrare dignetur. Amen.

On the bottom margin of MS S, fol. 231r.

Fuit autem tante fortitudinis ille Nemo quod mordebat nullum in sacco, de quo loyci ponunt exemplum, scilicet *Nullus et Nemo mordent se in sacco.*

Following line 55, ". . . *duas uxores,*" in MS S.

Patet etiam eius magnificentia quanta sit in ecclesia ad quod aliis prohibetur, sibi permittitur. Dicit enim canon quod nullus aput civilem iudicem debeat episcopum aut clericum accusare, sed Nemo habet hoc facere, unde dicit decretum: *Nemo episcopum aut clericos reliquos aput iudicem secularem accusare presummat.* Ymo habet per se ipsum excommunicare absque cause probacionis, unde dicit canon: *Nemo episcopus, Nemo presbiter excommunicet aliquem antequam causa probetur.* Ex hiis claret ipsum etiam sacerdotali ymo episcopali dignitate sublimatum.

2–3 Jb 1.1–3   9 Ps 138.16   10 2 Tim 2.4   12 1 Cor 9.7: "Quis militat suis stipendiis umquam?"   13 Sap 7.5: "Nemo enim ex regibus aliud habuit nativitatis initium."   15 Lc 1.61: "Nemo est in cognatione tua, qui vocetur hoc nomine."   19 Apc 3.7; Jb 12.14   20 Jb 10.7   21 Jb 12.14   24 Jo 3.2   25 Jo 16.22   26 Jo 10.17–18: ". . . Ego pono animam meam. . . . nemo tollit eam a me."   28 Walther, *Proverbia,* no. 32734   29–30 Mt 6.24; Lc 16.13   31 Ecl 9.1   33–34 Apc 7.9   34–35 Apc 14.3   36 Lc 4.24   39–40 Matins for Easter Sunday   41–42 Matins for Easter Sunday   43 Lc 16.21   45 Lc 15.16   46–47 Ecl 4.1: "Verti me ad alia et vidi calumpnias quae sub sole geruntur et lacrimas innocentum et

consolatorem neminem." 49 Lc 11.33 50 Lc 9.62 53 Lc 10.4 54 Mt
17.9 59 Jo 7.44 60–61 Jo 8.10–11 63 Jo 3.13

1 Sermo pauperis Henrici de sancto Nemine cum preservativo regimine eiusdem ab
epidimia. Figura Neminis quia Nemo in ea depictus. *A* Vita Sancti Nemonis. Si non
credis, tunc palpa. *B* Sermo de sancto Nemine *F* Vita Nemonis *crossed out, then*
added: Sermo de sancto Nemine *G* Quantus, quis, qualis fuerit Nemo *M*
Sequitur relatio de quodam sancto cuius nomen erat Nemo. *In margin:* Illa relatio est
scripta propter solacium, non propter veritatem. *S* Nemo vir perfectus *V* 2 vir
erat] vir quidam erat *AF* erat vir *G* oriente] oriente cui *G* terra *A* erat vir ille]
hic erat *F* iste vir erat *G* erat ille vir *M* *post* Iob *add.* magnus *S* *post* omnes *add.*
enim *F* 3 namque . . . Nemo] ymo maximus et sanctus *F* sanctus iste] vir iste
G ille *M* sanctus . . . magnus] *om. S* Nemo . . . prosapia] magnus in sapia
G 4 *post* potentia *add.* magnus in audacia *G* scientia] clementia *F*
clementia] scientia *F* et in compassione] *om. AFGM* 5 magnus[1]] *om. F* in[1]]
om. B reverentia] re *M* et[2]] *om. AFS* et magnus in audacia] *om. M*
magnus . . . comprobantur] *om. G* *post* audacia *add.* et magnus in gloria *FS* per
sacram scripturam] in sacra pagina *A* 6 comprobantur] approbavit *M* probantur *S*
aprobando *V* 7 Primo dico] Primo et principaliter *B* Primo et principaliter dico
FV Dixi primo *G* quod] quam *A* quod . . . Nemo] iste Nemo fuit magnus
BV quod magnus sanctus fuit iste Nemo *F* magnus erat *M* magnus fuit iste
sanctus Nemo *S* in] a *V* *post* prosapia *add.* et etiam *A* etiam *F* etiam fuit *M* et
V 8 similis Ade] *om. S* qui] quia *MS* *post* qui *add.* fuit *V* *post* genitus *add.*
dicitur *ASF* *post* formatus *add.* fuit *G* secundum . . . dicentem] iuxta prophetam
dicentem *G* unde propheta *M* habetur per] per *A* habemus per *F* aperte habemus
per *S* habemus *V* 9 dicentem] dicitur psalmo centesimo tricesimo octavo A
Fuit] Erat *G* etiam] autem *S* 10 genere] progenere *M* secundum illud
apostoli] unde apostolus *GM* ut illud in Apocalipsi *V* *post* apostoli *add.* ii. ad
Thimoth. ii *A* Nemo militans deo] *om. G* Ymo] *om. AM* fuit] fuit etiam
AM erat *FG* nobilis] nobiliter *G* nobiles *S* 11 qui] quia *M* propriis . . .
militavit] propriis stipendiis militavit, non alienis *A* propriis stipendiis, non alienis,
militavit *F* non alienis sed propriis militavit stipendiis *G* propriis stipendiis militavit
M non alienis sed propriis stipendiis militavit *S* secundum illud apostoli] unde
iterum apostolus primo ad Corintheos ix *A* unde iterum apostoli *F* *om. GS* unde
apostolus *M* unde illud apostoli *V* 12 militare] militari *AV* militare deo *F*
militavit *corr.* militare *M* Et] Item *AG* *om. F* Etiam *MV* fuit] erat *G* Fuit
etiam *F* Et . . . quinto] Et non solum militari, ymo regie fuit prosapie, secundum
illud Ecclesiastae *S* 13 *post* sed *add.* de genere *G* Ecclesiastici] Sapientie *A*
quinto] vii *A* ii *G* *om. M* regibus] regalibus *AF* Et fuit] Fuit etiam *AF* Etiam
erat *G* Fuit *M* Et fuit insuper *S* Etiam fuit *V* de] ex genere seu *A* 14
cognatione] natione *BG* virginis . . . quod] gloriose virginis Marie que *F*
virginis gloriose] beate virginis *S* *post* gloriose *add.* sancte Marie *M* eo quod] quia

A et *G*   que *MS*   fuit . . . regia] de stirpe regia fuit *S*   et] eo quod *AM*   vel etiam
S   et de] eo quod esset *F*   15 sancte] *om. AMSV*   beate *F   post* Elizabeth *add.*
unde *F*   in] de *AGM   post* tua *add.* qui vocetur hoc nomine *AFMS*   Nec] Et non
G   Nec . . . fuit] Et constat [quod beata virgo de *crossed out*] Nemo [?] *F*   fuit]
om. G.   16 *post* regia *add.* secundum carnem sanctus Nemo *A*   fuit secundum
carnem *F*   secundum carnem *MS*   sed] sed etiam *A*   sed legitur *M*   ymo *S*
ipso] *om. AFGM*   eternaliter] sempiterno *A*   eterno *F*   eternaliter . . . Nemo]
sicut ex fine patebit *S*   legitur semper] semper *F om. GM*   semper legitur *V*
Ecclesiastes] Ecclesiastici *F*   17 undecimo] quarto *F   om. M*   Nemo] *om. S.*
post semper *add.* est *MS   post* regnaturus *add.* Invenitur etiam in primo parte doct[?]:
Nemo sanctus homoque, et etiam in Cathone: Nemo sine crimine vivit. Quare(?) et
sanctissimus aff[?] legitur etiam de muliere apprehensi in adulterio, Iohannis octavo:
Cuius te condempnavit?   Mulier: Nemo, domine. Quod etiam alibi loc[?]: Maiorem
caritatem Nemo habet *F*   et omne de primo *G*   Secundo] Dixi secundo *G*   iste
. . . magnus] dico quod magnus fuit iste sanctus Nemo *AF*   quod iste vir Nemo erat
magnus *G*   dico magnus fuit ille Nemo *M*   dico sanctus iste Nemo fuit magnus *S*
Nam] ut patet *A*   ut *F*   nam ipse *G*   ut patet aperte *M*   quia *V*   Nam . . . Nemo
aperit] Quod deus claudit, Nemo aperit *M*   Nam . . . illud] Patet in Apocalipsi, ubi
dicitur *S*   id] Nemo *A*   enim *F   om. GV*   iuxta . . . aperit] *om. A*   19 Deus . . .
aperit] Si deus aperit Nemo claudit *G   post* aperit *add.* et e converso *MV   post* Item
add. animam *V*   de . . . audacter] ipse audacter de manu dei *G*   audacter]
audaciter *A*   20 eripit] eruit *AFG*   eripuit *M*   Iob xxix] unde Iob x *A*   unde Iob
19 *F*   unde Iob ii *G*   Iob quinto *M*   unde in Iob dicitur deo *S*   Cum] *om. A   post*
Item *add.* ipse *G*   21 Iob] unde iterum Iob xii *A*   iterum Iob *F   unde Iob G*   unde
iterum Iob *S*   destruit[2]] destruet *B*   edificat] edificet *B*   Item ipsum] Ymo quod
magnus est, ipse *G*   Item . . . vincit deum] *om. V*   ipsum . . . vincit] superat et
vincit deum *M*   22 superat et vincit] vincit *G*   vincit et superat *B*   quinto] ii *G*
om. M   vincit deum] deum vincit *G   post* deum *add.* Vixit etiam sanctissimus Nemo
sine omni crimine, ut patet per Cathonem: Nemo sine crimine vivit *A   post* deum *add.*
Item *G   post* Propterea *add* hec *F*   signa] dicitur *A   om. M*   23 que deus facit]
quod deus facit *A*   quod deus fecit *M*   facit deus que *S*   que deus fecit *V*   ipse]
sanctus Nemo *A*   ipse sanctus Nemo *F*   ipse Nemo *M*   Nemo *S*   facere potest]
potest facere *S*   si voluerit] si voluit *G   om. S*   sicut dicit] unde *FMV*   sicut
. . . evangelio] unde dixit sanctus Nicodemus aperte in evangelio Iohannis iiii *A*   sicut
dicit Nicodemus in evangelio Iohannis *G*   unde et Iohannis 3° capitulo dicitur *S   post*
evangelio *add.* Rabi *M*   24 hec signa facere] facere hec signa *A*   signa] signum
B   post facis *add.* Item ipsum deum superat et vincit, Ecclesiastici quinto: Nemo vincit
deum *V* ab . . . tollit] tollit ab apostolis *G*   25 tollit] rapit *AFS*   eripit *M*
Iohannes] Iohannis iiii dicitur *A*   Iohannes in evangelio *FV   om. G*   Matheus in
evangelio *M*   in evangelio Iohannis *S   post* Gaudium *add.* domini *V*   vestrum]
vestre *M*   Ymo] Item *F*   quod magis est] *om. AG*   quod maius est *FM*   quod
maximum est, etiam *S*   26 Christi rapit] tollit a Christo *A*   pro Christo rapit *B*   a

Christo tollit *FS* Christi tollit *M* Christo rapit *V* Iohannes] unde iterum Iohannis
vi *A* unde iterum in evangelio *F* Iohannis *B* iuxta illud *G* unde idem Iohannes
loquitur, ymo potius Christus per Iohannem *S* unde Iohannes in evangelio *V* tollit]
tollet *GMS* Item . . . *servire*] et omne de secundo *G* sicut . . . utiliter] duobus
dominis utiliter servire potest *F* sicut . . . heris] duobus dominis utiliter servit *A*
sicut . . . servire] perutiliter servit duobus dominis *M* duobus dominis utiliter servit *S*
duobus dominis, quod nullus potest servire *V* 27 ipse . . . evangelio] unde in
evangelio *M* poeticum] evangelii *F* iuxta poeticum *S* 28 Utiliter . . .
evangelio] *om. F* servit Nemo] Nemo servit *V* et] ut *A* *post* evangelio *add.*
Mathei habetur *A* 30 Tertio] Dixi tertio *G* Tertio dico *MSV* Tertio . . . magnus]
Tertio dico quod magnus sanctus fuit iste Nemo *F* iste . . . magnus] magnus fuit iste
sanctus Nemo *A* quod iste vir Nemo erat magnus *G* magnus fuit ille Nemo *MS* in
scientia] sanctus *BV* in audacia *G* iustitia *M* *post* scientia *add.* nam *G* enim] *om.*
GV an] utrum *AMV* an . . . illud] utrum amore dei vel odio dignus fuit, quod
aliquis alius scire non potuit, Ecclesiastici 5° *F* amore vel odio] odio vel amore *G*
post amore *add.* dei *AFM* vel] an *V* sit dignus] dignus fuit *AM* dignus fuerit *F*
dignus esset *G* dignus sit *V* 31 iuxta illud] unde dicitur *A* unde *G* iuxta illud
Ecclesiastae *S* iuxta . . . dignus] *om. MV* Nemo . . . dignus] Nemo scire potest
utrum amore vel odio dignus sit *S* utrum] an *AG* sit dignus] dignus est *A*
dignus sit *G* Fuit] Item ipse erat *G* *om. M* Et fuit *V* etiam] *om. V* 32 in
grammatica] *om. G* se conformans] conformis *AFM* conformans se *GV* similis
S ipso attestante] existendo Prisciano attestante *A* unde Priscianus *F* ipso
attestante *G* Prisciano attestante, qui ait *M* qui dicit *S* 33 inveni mihi] mihi inveni
B Fuit] Fuit etiam *AFMS* Item erat *G* iuxta illud Apocalipsis] secundum illud
Apocalipsis *A* secundum illud Apocalipsi *F* unde in Apocalipsi ii *G* apostolus *M*
unde in Apocalipsi *S* secundum illud Apocalipsis *V* Nemo . . . hanc] Vidi turbam
quam dinumerare Nemo poterat *M* Vidi turbam magnam quam dinumerare Nemo
poterat *S* 34 numerare] dinumerare *V* numerare . . . hanc] turbam numerare
F hanc] *om. AV* Fuit] Fuit etiam *AFM* Item erat *G* Fuit magnus in musica]
Et fuit magnus musicus *S* in Apocalipsi] unde iterum Apocalipsis *A* secundum
illud in Apocalipsi *F* in Apocalipsi prophetis *G* apostolus *M* ut iterum habetur in
Apocalipsi *S* Apocalipsi *V* *ante* Nemo *add.* et *S* 35 poterat] potest *A* *post* dicere
add. seu cantare *A* *post* canticum *add.* gaudium *G* Fuit etiam] Item erat *G* Fuit
M propheta] prophetia *M* in prophetia *V* secundum illud Mathei] secundum
illud *A* iuxta illud *G* unde *M* unde in evangelio *S* unde Matheus *V* 36 est] *om.*
B acceptus est . . . sua] acceptus in patria acceptus [*sic*] *F* in patria sua] in
propria sua patria *A* *om. M* 37 Item . . . *corde*] *om. F* Item . . . Item Lazaro]
om. G Item] Quarto dico quod *A* Sanctus denique Nemo *S* fuit magnus]
magnus fuit iste Nemo *A* erat magnus *G* in clementia et in compassione] in
compassione *A* in clementia et compassione *G* in compassione et clementia *S* *post*
compassione *add.* domini *A* nam *GS* Primum . . . evangelio] iuxta illud
Ecclesiastici *A* summe compassus est Christo, iuxta illud *S* fuit] erat *G* fuit

compassionis] sue compassione erat *G*   38 quia] qui *V   post* cruce *add.* moriturus
G   morienti *V*   in evangelio] unde Ecclesiastes *G*   illud Ecclesiastae *V*   Ecce]
om. A   Ecce quomodo] Quoniam *GV*   considerat] percipit corde *AS*   percipit
corde, considerat *G*   39 Etiam martiribus fuit] Item martiribus etiam *A*   Item
compatiebatur cum martiribus *G*   Etiam sanctis martiribus *S*   40 pro Christo
morientibus] est *A*   Christi valde compassus est *S*   iuxta illud] unde dicit apostolus
G   unde ibidem *S   om. V*   tolluntur] coluntur *A*   ] *om. A*   considerat nec] *om.*
V   nec percipit corde] *om. AGS*   41 Item] *om. S*   Item . . . mendicanti fuit
compassus] Fuit magnus in largitate, sicut legitur de Lasaro mendicante *F*   Lazaro
. . . compassus] magnus fuit in largitate, sicut in evangelio legitur de Lazaro *A*   erat
compassus Lazaro mendicanti *G*   fuit magnus in largitate, unde Nemo de Lazaro *M*
fuit etiam magnus in largitate, sicut in evangelio de Lazaro legitur de Lazaro *S*   fuit
compassus] compassus fuit *V*   qui] que *B*   petebat] cupiebat *AGMS*   peciebat
ventrem suum *B*   peciebat *V*   petebat saturari] cupiens saturare suum ventrem *F*
42 cadebant] cadebat *FM   post* mensa *add.* divitis *FGMS*   Item] Legitur etiam de
F   Item . . . dabat] *om. V*   Item . . . aratrum] *om. AM*   Fuit etiam in vita activa
operarios ociosos ad labores conducendo, iuxta illud: Nemo lucernam accendit suam
S   filio . . . fuit] erat compassus filio prodigo *G*   compassus fuit] *om. F*   43
cupiebat . . . saturare] cupiens saturare ventrem suum *F*   cupiebat saturari *G*   44
Fuit . . . inveni] *om. G*   Fuit . . . aratrum] *om. F*   etiam] et *V*   47 Etiam fuit]
Item erat *G   post* magnus *add.* quia *B*   contemplativa] contemplativus *B*   sua,
primo in vita contemplativa, unde quia *G*   contemplatoria *V*   sanctis servitia]
dibus(?) sanctis suis servitium *G*   impendendo] impendebat *G*   48 Etiam fuit
magnus] Secundo *G*   Etiam magnus *V*   49 illud] dictum apostoli *G*   manum]
manus *V*   50 Item ut anime eius] Ut eius *A*   ut [?] [?] *G*   Item etiam eius *M*   Item
. . . dignitatem] Ut ergo omnis eius dignitatis *F*   Item . . . breviloquio] *om. S   post*
dignitatem *add.* anime eius *G*   concludam] collaudem *A*   concludam sub *BS*
breviloquio] *om. G*   fuit sanctus iste Nemo] sanctus Nemo *A*   iste sanctissimus
Nemo fuit *F*   ille vir Nemo erat sub breviloquio et varitate *G*   sanctus igitur Nemo fuit
M   sanctus insuper Nemo fuit magnus *S*   fuit iste sanctus Nemo *V*   51 quem] ita
dignus quod *V*   quem . . . dixit] fuit singulari honore et reverentia dignus. Nam
honoravit eum dominus tanquam amicum specialem sibi transmittendo suas
salutationes, secundum quod in evangelio legitur *A*   magnus singulari honore et
reverentia honoravit N. eum dominus tamquam specialem amicum suum per discipulos
suos sibi transmittendo suas salutaciones, unde in evangelio *F*   item dominus singulari
honore honoravit eum, cum per discipulos suos salutari eum mandavit, cum dixit *G*
speciali honore et reverentia honoratus a deo per discipulos ipsum salutando, unde in
evangelio Lucus *M*   singulari honore et et [*sic*] reverentia honoravit cum dominus eum
deus tamquam specialem amicum suum per discipulos suos sibi transmittendo
salutationes, iuxta illud *S   post* honoravit *add.* eum *V*   salutaciones suas] suas
salutaciones *V*   52 transmittendi] transmittendo *V*   cum dixit] ut in evangelio

V   per viam salutaveritis] salutaveritis in via *G*   *post* salutaveritis *add*. Item fuit
magnus in vita activa, iuxta illud: Nemo mittens manum suam ad aratrum suam.
Similiter et in vita contemplativa fuit perfectus sicut deum intueri possit, iuxta illud:
Nemo vidit deum *S*   Fuit etiam] Item erat *G*   Fuit namque *M*   Fuit *V*   53
magnus] intimus *AFS*   *om*. *M*   iuxta illud] secundum quod legitur de
transfiguratione domini in evangelio *A*   sicut legitur de transfiguratione domini *F*
unde *G*   unde in evangelio Lucus legitur de transfiguratione in evangelio *M*   secundum
quod legitur in evangelio de transfiguratione domini *S*   ut ibi *V*   hanc] *om*. *MS*
54 Etiam] Item *AG*   Erat etiam *F*   *om*. *M*   ex] de *F*   honore] gratia, honore et
reverentia *A*   *om*. *BV*   honore et reverentia ideo *F*   privilegio et honore *G*   honore et
reverentia *M*   ut] quod *G*   *om*. *M*   possit . . . matrimonium] possit contrahere
matrimonium cum duabus *A*   cum duabus possit contrahere matrimonium *FV*   potest
contrahere matrimonium cum duabus *G*   cum duabus licet contrahere matrimonium
M   cum] ad *S*   55 iuxta] *om*. *M*   dictum decreti] illud decretum *AS*   illud
decreti *F*   dictum apostoli *G*   unde decretum *M*   illud *V*   56 Fuit . . . magnus] Item
sanctus Nemo fuit etiam magnus *A*   Fuit etiam magnus *F*   Item magnus erat *G*
sanctus ille Nemo magnus fuit *M*   Sanctus denique Nemo fuit magnus *S*   Fuit iste
Nemo magnus *V*   *post* audacia *add*. quia *GM*   Cum . . . ligavit eum] *om*. *A*   *post*
Cum *add*. ipsi *F*   enim *S*   essent ausi] audebant *M*   57 manum mittere] inmittere
manus *B*   manus mittere *FM*   mittere manum *G*   mittere manus *S*   Iesum] Iesum
Christe *B*   ille *M*   ipse . . . ligavit eum] ipse cepit *F*   autem . . . eum] audacter
irruit *G*   cepit eum *M*   Nemo hoc fecit *S*   ligavit eum] ligavit *M*   sepelevit *V*
iuxta illud] unde *GM*   secundum illud evangelium *S*   *om*. *V*   58 Et[1]] *om*. *FGMS*
in eum misit manus] misit manum in Iesum *A*   misit in illum manus *F*   misit manum
suam in eum *G*   misit in illum manum *M*   misit in eum manus *V*   Et finaliter] in fine
AMV   *om*. *G*   Et finaliter . . . domini] Et mulierem in adulterio deprehensam ipse
condempnavit, sicut legitur in evangelio quod Christus eam interrogat *S*   Et finaliter
. . . homo] In fine, sanctus Nemo *F*   iste] ipse *G*   iste . . . concludam] *om*.
AM   Nemo sanctus] sanctus Nemo *V*   *om*. *G*   59 deprehensam] comprehensam
corr. deprehensam *G*   reprehensam *V*   dictum domini] cum dixit dominus *G*   ubi
. . . accusabant] Nemo te condempnabit? *S*   60 accusabant] accusant *G*
Respondit] et respondit *G*   illa ait *S*   Item . . . concludam] *om*. *S*   ut] ymo *G*
eius dignitatem] dignitatem eius *G*   61 iste homo videns] iste sanctus Nemo videns
A   vir iste Nemo videns *G*   videns ille sanctus Nemo *M*   denique ipse sanctus Nemo,
proficiens virtutibus, videns *S*   homo] sanctus Nemo *V*   vana] una *A*   omnia *GS*
bona *V*   *post* mundi *add*. relinquens terrestria et *A*   relinquens terrestria *FM*   esse
vana et inutilia *G*   vana esse, relinquens ecclesia *S*   conscendit ad] conscendit *AS*
ascendit in *G*   ascendit *M*   ad] *om*. *AF*   celestia] celum *G*   iuxta] secundum
GS   62 illud] *om*. *GV*   evangeliste] *om*. *A*   apostolum Iohannem qui dicit *G*
evangelium *SV*   nobis] et nobis *A*   vobis *V*   patrare] prestare *A*   *post* dignetur
add. qui plus dat quam sibi prebetur per omnia secula seculorum *A*   qui plus dat quam

sibi datur per infinita secula seculorum *F* qui plus dat quam sibi prebetur *M*   Quod
. . . Amen] Et [ymo?] ascensio domini nostri Iesu Christi perducat nos una cum
Neminem in vitam eternam. P. D. *G*   Ideo ipsum in speciali veneratione habeamus ut
nobis impetret ea que possidet cum gloria. Amen. *S*   Amen] *om. BM*

The Short *Nemo:* Translation

The Sermon on Saint Nobody

There was a man in the East named Nobody, and that man was like another Job
among all the people of the East. For this holy Nobody was great in race and
lineage, great in power, great in knowledge, great in mercy and compassion,
great in honor and reverence, and great in daring. And all of these things are
confirmed in Holy Scripture.

First, I say that this holy Nobody was great in race and lineage, like Adam,
who was neither created nor begotten but formed, as it is said by the prophet:
The days will be formed and Nobody in them. He was also of a military lineage,
according to the saying of the apostle: *Nobody being a soldier to God.* Rather
he was a noble soldier who served at his own expense, not that of another,
according to the saying of the apostle: *Nobody serveth as a soldier at his own
expense.* And he was of a race of no other kind than royal, Ecclesiasticus 5:
Nobody took his birth from kings. And he was of the kindred of the glorious
virgin, for he was from royal stock and kin to Saint Elizabeth, Luke 1: *Nobody
is in thy kindred.* Nor was he only of royal stock, but it is read that he will reign
eternally with God himself, Ecclesiastes 11: *Nobody will reign forever.*

Second, this Nobody was great in power. For he opens that which God
closes, according to that: *God shutteth and Nobody openeth.* Likewise he can
snatch away boldly from the hand of God, Job 29: *Whereas there is Nobody
that can deliver out of thy hand.* He also builds up what God destroys, Job: *If
God pulls down, there is Nobody that can build up.* Likewise he overcomes and
conquers God himself, Ecclesiasticus 5: *Nobody conquers God.* Therefore
those signs which God performed he is able to do if he likes, as Nicodemus
says in the Gospel: *Nobody can do these signs which thou dost.* Likewise he
forcefully takes joy from the apostles, whence John: *Your joy Nobody shall
take from you.* Indeed, what is more, he steals away the soul of Christ, John:
Nobody taketh my soul away from me. Likewise, just as no one is able to serve
two masters, this one is useful in service, according to the poet: *Nobody serves
two masters usefully,* and in the Gospel: *Nobody can serve two masters.*

Third, this Nobody was great in knowledge. For he knew whether he deserved love or hatred, according to the passage: *Nobody knoweth whether he be worthy of love or hatred.* He was also great in grammar, emulating Priscian, with that man as witness: *I found Nobody my friend.* He was great in arithmetic, according to Revelations: *Nobody could number that multitude.* He was great in music, in Revelations: *Nobody could say the canticle.* He was also a great prophet, according to Matthew: *Nobody is accepted as a prophet in his own country.*

He was also great in mercy and in compassion. The first mark of compassion was that he was merciful to Christ on the cross, whence in the Gospel: *Behold how the just man dies and Nobody takes heed.* In addition he was merciful to the martyrs dying for Christ, according to the passage: *Just men are destroyed and Nobody is concerned nor feels it in his heart.* Likewise he was merciful to Lazarus the beggar, who asked to be filled with the crumbs which fell from the table, and *Nobody did give him.* He was also merciful to the prodigal son, who wanted to fill his stomach with the husks which the swine ate, and *Nobody gave unto him.* He was also the comfort of the poor, whence Ecclesiastes 11: *I turned myself to other things, and I saw the oppressions that are done under the sun, and I found Nobody a comforter.*

He was also great in the contemplative life, giving service to God and the saints, according to the passage: *Nobody lighteth his lamp.* He was also great in the active life, according to the passage: *Nobody putteth his hand to the plough.*

In addition, so that I may conclude with brevity on the worthiness of his soul, it was this holy Nobody whom the Lord honored with a singular honor, sending his greetings to him through his disciples when he said: *Salute Nobody by the way.* He was also a great counselor of the Lord, according to the passage: *Tell this vision to Nobody.* In addition it was granted to him, as a special honor, that he might enter into wedlock with two women, according to the decree: *Nobody is permitted to have two wives.*

This holy Nobody was great in daring. When the Jews did not dare to lay a hand on Jesus, he, by contrast, ran to him and put him in bonds, according to the passage: *Nobody laid hands on him.* And finally this holy Nobody accused the woman taken in adultery, according to the words of the Lord: *Woman, where are they that hath accused thee?* She answered: *Nobody, Lord.* And also, so I may bring the account of his dignity to a conclusion, this man, seeing the vanities of this world, ascended to the heavens, according to the words of the evangelist: *Nobody ascended into heaven.* Which may he deign to bring about for us. Amen.

On the bottom margin of MS S, fol. 231r.

> This Nobody was, moreover, of such great strength that he bit no one in the balls, about which the logicians have a saying, that is, *No one and Nobody bite themselves in the balls.*

Following line 57, ". . . two wives," in MS S.

> His magnificence in the church is evident in that what is forbidden to others is permitted to him. For the canon says that no one may accuse a bishop or cleric in civil judgment, but Nobody may do this, whence the decree says: *Nobody may presume to accuse a bishop or other cleric in secular judgment.* What is more, he may excommunicate that one without reason of proof, whence the canon says: *Nobody as a bishop, Nobody as a priest may excommunicate anyone until cause is shown.* From these things he shows himself exalted as well to a priestly, or rather an episcopal, dignity.

5. The Combined *Nemo*

Manuscript: The "Sterzing Miscellany," formerly in the Vitipeno (Sterzing) Stadtarchiv (no MS number), fols. 11r–12v. s. xiv^ex/xv^in. The manuscript is now lost; it was published in facsimile in Eugen Thurnher, Manfred Zimmermann, et al., *Die Sterzinger Miszellaneen-Handschrift,* Litterae, Göppinger Beiträge zur Textgeschichte 61 (Göppingen, 1979). This version of *Nemo* has not been previously edited.

Fuit vir in oriente nomine Nemo, et fuit vir ille ut alter Iob magnus inter omnes orientales. Magnus fuit namque in genere et prosapia, magnus in potentia, magnus in scientia, magnus in compassione et clementia, magnus in perfectione multimoda, magnus ⟨in⟩ honore et reverentia, magnus in audacia, magnus
5 ⟨in⟩ gloria e⟨t⟩ felicitate. Hec omnia probantur per sacram scripturam.

    Primo sanctus iste Nemo fuit magnus in genere et prosapia. Fuit Nemo de genere militari, secundum epistolam ad Ephesios: *Nemo militans deo.* Fuit Nemo nobilis miles qui propriis stipendiis, non alienis, militavit, secundum illam epistolam: *Nemo tenetur propriis stipendiis militare.* Et fuit de genere
10 militari non qualicumque sed regali, unde Ecclesiastes: *Nemo ex regalibus nativitatis sumpsit exordium.* Fuit etiam de cognatione virginis gloriose que fuit de stirpe regali, quia fuit de cognatione Elizabeth, secundum Lucam: *Nemo est de cognacione tua.* Et constat quod beata virgo Maria et Elizabeth de duabus sororibus fuerunt. Nec solum fuit de genere regali secundum carnem,
15 sed cum Christo deo eterno legitur semper regnaturus, Ecclesiastes: *Nemo semper regnat.* Et quia de stirpe regia est ortus et cum deo semper regnaturus, dici potest *rex magnus super omnem terram.*

    Secundo iste sanctus Nemo fuit magnus in potentia. Et hoc patet: *Aperit Nemo quod deus claudit,* secundum Apocalipsim, *Deus claudit et Nemo aperit.*
20 Item de manu dei audacter eruit, Iob: *Nemo est qui de manu tua possit eruere.* Item ire dei viriliter resistit, Iob: *Deus cuius ire Nemo potest resistere.* Item edificat quod deus destruit, Iob: *Si deus destruit Nemo est qui edificat.* Item ipsum deum superat et vincit, Ecclesiastes: *Nemo vincit deum.* Propterea signa que fecit deus potest sanctus Nemo facere si voluerit, Iohannes: *Rabi, Nemo*
25 *potest hec signa facere que tu facis.* Item gaudium ab apostolis potenter rapit, ut hec: *Gaudium vestrum Nemo tollet a vobis.* Imo, quod maius est, animam a Christo violenter tollit, secundum illud: *Animam meam Nemo tollit a me.* Item duobus dominis Nemo potest uteliter servire, iuxta poetam: *Uteliter servit Nemo duobus heris,* et in ewangelio: *Nemo potest duobus dominis servire.* Item
30 cursum naturalem divinit, iuxta poetam: *Quod Natura divinit, Nemo feliciter*

audet. Propterea potest dici iste sanctus Nemo in psalmo: *Magnus es tu et faciens mirabilia.*

Tertio iste sanctus Nemo fuit magnus in scientia. Scit Nemo sanctus utrum amore dei vel odio dignus fuit, quod nullus hominum umquam facere potuit,

35 iuxta illud Sapientie: *Nemo scire potuit utrum amore vel odio dignus sit.* Item fuit magnus in grammatica. †Spiritus suus cum paulo foris existendo prius testando,† qui ait: *Neminem inveni socium.* Item magnus in arismetrica ut hec in Apocalipsi: *Nemo poterat dinumerare turbam.* Item magnus in musica, Apocalipsis: *Nemo poterat dicere canticum.* Item fuit magnus in lege Mosaica,

40 non solum illam speculando sed etiam aperte faciendo, Iohannes: *Nemo ex vobis facit legem.* Item fuit magnus in lege ewangelica, misteria dominica reserando, Apocalipsis: *Nemo poterat aperire librum.* Item fuit magnus in hac lege futura predicando ⟨et⟩ prophetando, iuxta illud Mathei: *Nemo propheta acceptus est in patria.* Et quoniam qui fecerit et docuerit hinc magnus vo-

45 cabitur in regno celorum, et iste sanctus Nemo utrumque fecit quod sit magnus in regno celorum, iuxta illud Mathei, *Vere, qui fecerit et docuit sic magnus vocabitur in regno celorum.*

Quarto fuit iste Nemo magnus in compassione et clementia. Solus namque fuit iste sanctus compassus Lazaro mendicanti, iuxta illud: *Nemo illi dabat.*

50 Solus ipse misertus est pauperis ad cuius preces civitas obsessa fuit liberata, Ecclesiastes: *Nemo recordatus a paupere illius.* Item summe compassus est Christo morienti, Ecclesiastes v: *Quomodo moritur iustus et Nemo considerat.* Item summe compassus est martiribus propter Christum passis, Ecclesiastes: *Viri iusti tolluntur et Nemo considerat ⟨nec⟩ percipit corde.* Propter istam

55 compassionem Lazarus mendicans et pauper et Christus moriens et quilibet martires dicere possunt de isto sancto iuxta psalmistam: *Quia ⟨misericordia⟩ tua magna est super me.*

Quinto iste sanctus Nemo fuit magnus in perfectione multimoda. Fuit Nemo activus ut Martha manum ad aratrum mittendo, iuxta ewangelium: *Nemo mit-*

60 *tens manum ad aratrum.* Et non solum fuit activus ad aratrum mittendo, unde et otiosos ad laborem conducendo ut in Matheo: *Nemo nos conduxit.* Fuit etiam contemplativus ut Maria officium sacriste faciendo, iuxta illud: *Nemo lucernam accendat.* Et propter hanc perfectionem multimodam, potest dici de eo quod dicitur de I[a]saac, Genesis: *Ibat proficiens et succrescens et vehementer*

65 *effectus est magnus.*

Sexto, iste sanctus fuit magnus singulari honore et reverentia. Honoravit ipsum deus tamquam specialem amicum suum per discipulos suos eum salutando in ewangelio: *Neminem salutaveritis per viam.* Item secreta sua tamquam secretario suo sibi reserando in ewangelio: *Nemini dixeritis visionem*

70   *hanc.* Item honoravit eum dominus sanctum suum approbando, unde cum
dominus mulierem deprehensam in adulterio condempnasset, iuxta illud:
"Nemo te condempnavit?" Mulier: *"Nemo, domine." "Nec ego te condempnabo."* Item ex speciali reverentia conceditur sibi ut possit contrahere
cum duabus sive bigamus esse, iuxta illud decretalem: *Nemini licet habere*
75   *duas uxores.* Conceditur sibi etiam a iure ut possit corpora sanctorum alienare,
iuxta illud decretum: *Nemo transferat.* Item potest bona ecclesiastica vendere,
iuxta illud decretum: *Nemo mercedem accipiet.* Iura ecclesiastica potest
dirimere, iuxta decretum: *Nemo condempnat ecclesiastica iudicia.* Et
quomodo sanctus Nemo [multiplici decreta] legitur a domino honoratus fuisse,
80   possit dicere domino de isto sancto illud psalmista⟨e⟩: *Gloriam et magnum*
decorem posuisti super eum.

      Septimo, sanctus Nemo fuit magnus in audacia. Ipse enim solus fuit ausus
mittere manum in Iesum cum Iudei non essent ausi, Iohannes: *Nemo misit in*
eum manus. Item cum dominus loqueretur cum muliere [. . .] Samaritana, iste
85   sanctus Nemo ausus fuit solus dicere *"Quid queris?"* vel *"Quid loqueris?,"*
Iohannes: *Nemo [n] ausus fuit dicere "Quid loqueris cum ea?"* Item cum
dominus manifestaret se discipulis suis, solus Nemo ausus fuit eum interrogare
quis esset, secundum illud: *Nemo tamen ⟨ausus⟩ fuit dicere, "Tu quis es?"* Item
cum dominus iret ad patrem, iste solus ausus fuit eum interrogare quo iret
90   Iohannes: *Vado ad eum qui me misit et Nemo interrogat, "Quo vadis?"* Item
hostibus publicis nudus et inermis ausus est obviare, iuxta illud: *Nemo nudus*
debeat contendere et inermis hostibus obviare. Et propter hec potest dici sanctus iste *magnus coram domino et plus quam magnus manus in ipsum*
dimittendo.

95   Octavo et ultimo, iste sanctus Nemo ⟨fuit⟩ magnus ⟨in⟩ gloria et felicitate
eterna. Exemplo namque salvatoris nostri, terrena relinquens, celestia conscendit, Iohannes: *Nemo ascendit in celum.* Hoc idem testatur deus pater dicens:
Nemo venit ad me. Ibi autem habuit ipsius dei visionem, Iohannes: *Nemo vidit*
eum, sed etiam ipsius filii dei cognicionem, iuxta illud: *Nemo novit dei filium.*
100 Hunc autem habere visionem dei et filii dei est, Iohannes: *Hec est vita eterna ut*
Nemo cognoscat te verum ⟨deum⟩ et quem misisti Christum. Si ergo sanctus iste
hoc utrumque ⟨videret⟩, ut dictum est, constat istum sanctum Neminem totaliter esse beatum, iuxta illud: *Nemo ex omni parte beatus.*

      Potest ergo dici qualiter iste sanctus Nemo fuit magnus ⟨in⟩ genere et
105 ⟨pro⟩sapia, scientia et clementia, perfectione multimoda, honore et reverentia,
audacia et gloria et felicitate eterna, unde potest dici de eo illud psalmum:
Magna est gloria eius in salutari tuo. Et hec omnia tot et tantis auctorita⟨ti⟩bus
que credibilia scripta sunt nimis comprobantur. Rogemus ergo sanctum istum

Neminem ut per precium suarum instanciam in presenti consequamur gratiam
110   et in futuro gloriam, ad quam nos perducat Iesus Christus dominus noster qui
est benedictus in secula seculorum. Amen.

Additions in margin:

> Item eternaliter vivat e⟨t⟩ non moritur, Ecclesiastes ix: *Nemo est qui
> semper vivat.* [Ecl 9.4]

> Item pecuniam concessam pro [. . .] exsolvat [. . .] est et *Nemo reddet ei
> pecuniam.*

> Item sancta dei et dies Iudicii ma⟨n⟩ifestum per eum fecit, Mathei 24: *De
> die autem illa et hora Nemo scit neque angeli.* [Mt 24.36]

> Item solus ausus fuit tenere hominem obsessum in monumento quem
> nusquam potuit domare nec ligare cathenis et vinculis, Marce quinto:
> *Nemo poterat eum domare.* [Mc 5.4]

1–2 Jb 1.1, 3   7 2 Tm 2.4   9 1 Cor 9.7: "Quis militat suis stipendiis
umquam?"   10–11 Sap 7.5: "Nemo enim ex regibus aliud habuit nativitatis
initium."   12–13 Lc 1.61   18 Ps 46.3   19–20 Apc 3.7   20 Jb 10.7:
"Cum sit nemo qui de manu tua possit eruere."   21 Jb 9.13   22 Jb
12.14   24–25 Jo 3.2   26 Jo 16.22   27 Jo 10.17–18   28–29 Walther,
Proverbia, no. 32734   29 Mt 6.24; Lc 16.13   31–32 Ps 85.10   35 Ecl 9.1
38 Apc 7.9   39 Apc 14.3   40–41 Jo 7.19   42 Apc 5.3   43–44 Mt
13.57; Lc 4.24   46–47 Mt 5.19: "qui fecerit et docuit hic magnus vocabitur in
regno celorum."   49 Lc 16.21   51 Ecl 9.15: "et nullus deinceps recordatus est
hominis illius pauperis."   52 Matins of Holy Sunday   54 Matins of Holy
Sunday   56–57 Ps 85.13   59–60 Lc 9.62   61 Mt 20.7   62–63 Lc
11.33   64–65 Gn 26.13   68 Lc 10.4   69–70 Mt 17.9   72–73 Jo 8.10–
11   80–81 Ps 20.6   83–84 Jo 7.30   85 Jo 4.27   86 Jo 4.27   88 Jo
21.12: "Et nemo audebat discentium interrogare eum, 'Tu quis es?'"   90 Jo
16.5   91–92 Ex 32.25: "Videns ergo Moses populum quod esset nudatus,
spoliaverat enim eum Aaron propter ignominiam sordis, et inter hostes nudum
constituerat."   97 Jo 3.13   98 Jo 6.44   98–99 Jo 1.18; Hbr 12.14; 1 Jo
4.12   99 Mt 11.27   100–101 Jo 17.3   107 Ps 20.6

2 orientales] orgntales *MS*   3 perfectione] profectione *MS*   24 Iohannes]
Iohannis *MS*   40 solum illam] illa solum *MS*   53 passis] passus *MS*   69
sibi] se *MS*

The Combined *Nemo:* Translation

There was a man in the East named Nobody, and that man was like another Job, great among all the people of the East. For he was great in race and lineage, great in power, great in knowledge, great in compassion and mercy, great in manifold perfection, great in honor and reverence, great in daring, great in glory and felicity. All these things are shown in Holy Scripture.

First, this holy Nobody was great in race and lineage. Nobody was of a military lineage, according to the Epistle to the Ephesians: *Nobody being a soldier to God.* Nobody was a noble soldier who served at his own expense, not that of another, according to the epistle: *Nobody serveth as a soldier at his own expense.* And he was of a race of no other kind than royal, whence Ecclesiastes: *Nobody took his beginning from royal birth.* He was also of the kindred of the glorious virgin, who was of royal stock, for he was kin to Elizabeth, according to Luke: *Nobody is in thy kindred.* And it is agreed that the blessed Virgin Mary and Elizabeth were the children of two sisters. Nor was he only of royal stock in the flesh, but we read that he will reign forever with Christ the eternal God, Ecclesiastes: *Nobody will reign forever.* And because he arose from royal stock and will reign with God forever, he can be called *a great king over all the earth.*

Second, this holy Nobody was great in power. And this is clear: *Nobody shutteth what God openeth,* according to Revelations, *God shutteth and Nobody openeth.* Likewise he can boldly pluck away from the hand of God, Job: *There is Nobody who can deliver out of thy hand.* In addition he can withstand the wrath of God like a man, Job: *God whose wrath Nobody can resist.* He also builds up what God destroys, Job: *If God pulls down, there is Nobody that can build up.* Likewise he overcomes and conquers God himself, Ecclesiastes: *Nobody conquers God.* Therefore the signs which God made, he is able to do if he likes, John: *Rabbi, Nobody can do those signs which thou dost.* Likewise he forcibly steals joy from the apostles, as in these words: *Your joy Nobody shall take from you.* Indeed, what is more, he takes the soul of Christ: *Nobody taketh my soul away from me.* Likewise Nobody can usefully serve two masters, according to the poet: *Nobody serves two masters usefully,* and in the Gospel: *Nobody can serve two masters.* He also foresees the course of nature, according to the poet: *What Nature foresees, Nobody dares successfully.* Therefore this holy Nobody can be described in the psalm: *Thou art great and thou dost wonderful things.*

Third, this holy Nobody was great in knowledge. The holy Nobody knew whether he was worthy of God's love or of hatred, which no man was ever able to do, according to the saying in Wisdom: *Nobody was able to know whether he be worthy of love or hatred.* He was also great in grammar [. . .], who said: *I found Nobody my friend.* Likewise he was great in arithmetic, as in Revelations: *Nobody could number that multitude.* He was also great in music, Revelations: *Nobody could say the canticle.* In addition he was great in Mosaic law, not only in study but also in creating it openly, John: *Nobody among you makes the law.* Likewise he was great in the law of the Gospels, disclosing the divine mysteries, Revelations: *Nobody was able to open the book.* He was also great in foretelling and prophesying in the law to come, according to the saying of Matthew: *Nobody is accepted as a prophet in his own country.* And since he who does and teaches henceforth shall be called great in the heavenly kingdom, and this holy Nobody did both because he is great in the heavenly kingdom, according to the passage in Matthew, *Truly, he that did and taught thus shall be called great in the heavenly kingdom.*

Fourth, this holy Nobody was great in compassion and mercy. For only this holy Nobody was merciful to Lazarus the beggar, according to the passage: *Nobody gave to him.* He alone was merciful to the poor man at whose prayers the beseiged city was liberated, Ecclesiastes: *Nobody remembered that pauper.* Likewise he was exceedingly merciful to the dying Christ, Ecclesiastes 5: *How the just man dies and Nobody takes heed!* He was also exceedingly merciful to the martyrs who suffered for Christ, Ecclesiastes: *Just men are destroyed and Nobody is concerned nor feels it in his heart.* Because of this compassion the beggar and pauper Lazarus and the dying Christ and the martyrs can say of the saint as it is said in the psalm: *For great is thy mercy toward me.*

Fifth, this holy Nobody was great in manifold perfection. Nobody was active, like Martha, in putting his hand to the plough, according to the Gospel: *Nobody putteth his hand to the plough.* And he was not active merely in putting his hand to the plough, but also in leading the idle to labor, as in Matthew: *Nobody hath hired us.* He was also contemplative, like Mary, in performing the office of sacristan, according to the passage: *Nobody lighteth a lamp.* And because of that manifold perfection, it could be said of him as it was said of Isaac, Genesis: *He prospered and grew successful and became exceedingly great.*

Sixth, this saint was great in singular honor and reverence. God honored him as his special friend by greeting him through his disciples in the Gospel: *Salute Nobody by the way,* and also by revealing his secrets to him in the Gospel, as if to his secretary: *Tell this vision to Nobody.* The Lord also honored his saint through approval, whence the Lord had condemned the woman taken in adultery, according to the passage: *"Hath Nobody condemned thee?"* The woman: *"Nobody, Lord." "Neither do I condemn thee."* It was also given to him, out of a special reverence, to be able to marry two women, or to be a bigamist, according to the decree: *Nobody may have two wives.* It was also given to him in law that he might remove the bodies of the saints, according to the decree: *Nobody may transfer.* Likewise he can sell ecclesiastical goods, according to the decree: *Nobody will take a reward.* He can sunder ecclesiastical law, according to the decree: *Nobody may condemn ecclesiastical judgment.* And as [in many decrees] Saint Nobody is seen to have been honored by the Lord, the passage of the psalmist might be said to the Lord about this saint: *Glory and great honor thou hast bestowed upon him.*

Seventh, Saint Nobody was great in daring. For he alone dared to lay a hand on Jesus when the Jews did not dare, John: *Nobody laid hands on him.* Likewise when the Lord was speaking with the [. . .] Samaritan woman, this holy Nobody alone dared to say *"What seekest thou?"* or *"Why speakest thou?"*— John: *Nobody dared to say: "Why speakest thou with her?"* And when the Lord showed himself to his disciples, only Nobody dared to ask him who he was, according to the passage: *Nobody dared to say: "Who art thou?"* Likewise when the Lord went to the Father, he alone dared to ask him where he was going, John: *I go to him that sent me and Nobody asketh: "Whither goest thou?"* Likewise he dared to withstand public enemies naked and unarmed, according to the passage: *Nobody may fight naked and withstand enemies unarmed.* And because of these things the saint can be said to be *great before the Lord and more than great in giving forth his hands to him.*

Eighth and last, this holy Nobody was great in glory and eternal felicity. For after the example of our Savior, leaving earthly things behind, he ascended to heavenly ones, John: *Nobody ascended into heaven.* God the Father testifies to the same thing, saying: *Nobody came to me.* And there he had a vision of God himself, John: *Nobody hath seen God,* but also knowledge of God the Son, according to the passage: *Nobody knoweth the son of God.* To have this vision of God and the Son, moreover, is from God, John: *This is eternal life, that Nobody may know thee, the only true God, and Christ, whom thou hast sent.* If therefore this saint saw both of these, as it is said, then it is clear that this holy Nobody is wholly blessed, according to the saying: *Nobody is blessed in every way.*

It can be told, therefore, in what way this holy Nobody was great in race and lineage, knowledge and mercy, manifold perfection, honor and reverence, daring and glory and eternal felicity, whence it can be said of him according to the psalm: *His glory is great through thy help.* And all these things are shown greatly by so many and such authorities, which are credible written things. Therefore let us ask this holy Nobody that through the the constancy of his

prayers we may attain grace and glory in the time to come, to which may Jesus
Christ our Lord lead us, he who is blessed, world without end. Amen.

Additions in margin:

Also he may live eternally and not die, Ecclesiastes 9: *There is Nobody
who lives forever.*

Also [. . .] money returned [. . .] he paid [. . .] and *Nobody repays him
money.*

Also he made manifest through him the holy day of God and of Judgment, Matthew 24: *But of that day and hour Nobody knoweth, and not
the angels.*

Also he alone dared to seize the man besieged in the tomb, whom at no
time could he subdue nor tie up with fetters or chains, Mark 5: *Nobody
could subdue him.*

6. The Long *Invicem*

Manuscript: Munich, Bayerische Staatsbibliothek MS clm. 10751, fols. 192v–195r. a. 1575. Previously edited in W. Wattenbach, "Geistliche Scherze des Mittelalters III," *Anzeiger für Kunde der deutschen Vorzeit,* N. F. 15 (1868): cols. 38–41. This edition has been prepared anew from the manuscript; biblical references are original to this edition.

Sermo non inelegans de sanctissimo fratre Invicem
Suscipite Invicem.

Tharsensis ille noster Paulus quendam habens discipulum Invicem nuncupatum, intime sibi dilectum, quem cubiebat tradere religioni, ut seculi spretis
5   vanitatibus, religiose vivere deoque famulari assuesceret. Id quidam, conditiones ipsius primo, deinde religionis religiosorumque considerantes insolitam consuetudinem, Paulo dissuaserunt, dicentes quia religiosi scandalizare et tradere Invicem deberent. *Multi,* aiunt, *scandalizabuntur et Invicem tradent.* Ad hec quoque odium et tyrannidem quorundam religiosorum mente tenus re-
10   memorantes dixerunt: *Odio habebunt Invicem.*

    Paulus nihilominus sperans faustiora salutique viciniora de religione et religiosis, etiam quia ob Pauli amorem chariorem habere deberent eundem discipulum, voluit ut religionem intraret. Scripsit ergo ad prefatos religiosos orans et obsecrans pro eo, primo pro susceptione eius ad habitum, inquiens:
15   *Suscipite Invicem,* deinde instanter pro Invicem deprecatur eos, ut sibi mansueti, benigni et favorabiles esse debeant, dicens: *Estote Invicem benigni et misericordes.* Ne etiam inopiam patiatur ibidem, vult ut munera donaque ei conferant: *Donantes,* ait, *Invicem sicut Christus donavit vobis.* In Apocalipsi quoque: *Munera mittite Invicem.* Pusillanimitatem quoque eius, quae multos in
20   religione deicit, considerans, hortatur eos quibus commissus in religione fuerat, ut ipsum dulcibus consolarentur verbis, *Consolamini Invicem,* aiens, *in verbis.* Etiam ut non solum ipsum consolarentur eos admonuit, sed ut etiam ad meliora promoverent et edificarent consolando, ipsos expetiit: *Consolamini Invicem et edificate.*

25   Tertio rogavit ut sibi reverentiam exhiberent, *Subiecti estote Invicem,* aiens, *in timore Christi,* et alibi: *Superiores [sic] Invicem arbitrantes.* Quarto beatus Paulus rogavit ut bona frequenter ei impenderent, scribens de eo: *Hospitales Invicem.* Postremo ne eum in aliquo molestarent, sed ut sincere et humaniter absque dolo in omnibus secum agerent, id quo melius potuit, eis in mandato
30   dedit, *Nolite,* inquiens, *fraudari Invicem.* Volens interea etiam beatus Paulus ipsum Invicem honeste conversari inter fratres ⟨et⟩ in omni benignitate et

modestia iugiter proficere, seriosus ut potuit, ei dixit: *Quod bonum est, sectamini Invicem.*

Deinde beatus Paulus, recedens ab eo, ob vehementem dilectionem quam
35   erga discipulum habuit, ei in oblivionem nunquam venit, imo quoties predicavit semper memor ipsius existens, a fidelibus orationes pro eo fieri expetiit, *Orate,* inquiens, *pro Invicem.* Insuper in omnibus scriptis suis ipsum fratribus commendavit: *Hec mando,* scribens, *vobis, ut diligatis Invicem.* Item: *Si dilexeritis Invicem, deus in vobis manet.*

40   Monachi nihilominus petitionem Pauli spernentes, ei insidias paraverunt, dicentes ad alterutrum: *Consideremus Invicem in provocationem.* Dictumque est beato Paulo quod prefatum Invicem male tractarent: *Facta est dissensio ut discederent ab Invicem.* Tandem his auditis Paulus venit ad visitandam domum istam, et intrans ianuam audiensque murmura eorum, dixit eis illud Luce 24:
45   *Qui sunt hi sermones quos confertis ad Invicem?* Surrexitque unus ex monachis; accusavit eum quia suspectus esset de mulieribus, Marci 16: *Mulieres dixerunt ad Invicem.* Alter accusavit eum de homicidio, Actuum 28: *Dicebant ad Invicem, "Utique homicida es."* Volueruntque quod deberet occidi, Mathei 21: *Dixerunt ad Invicem, "Hic est heres: venite occidamus eum."*

50   Abbas monasterii, sibi metuens de proditione sui, ait ad fratres: "Certa relatione hausi, *quia unus vestrum tradet me." His auditis aspiciebant ad Invicem.* Tunc Invicem graviter cepit murmurare, quem Paulus paterne admonuit, dicens: *Nolite murmurare Invicem.* Ultimus accusavit eum de furto; his auditis beatus Paulus rogavit Invicem ut ei veritatem diceret et non men-
55   tiretur, Colossenses 3: *Nolite mentiri Invicem.*

Invicem vero omnia ei obiecta ab accusatoribus negavit, addiditque quod male tractaretur in monasterio, et nulla cura haberetur de eo. Tunc denuo Paulus, ingrediens domum illam, voluit ut omnes emuli Invicem cum accusatoribus eius expellerentur, Danielis illud inquiens: *Separate eos ab In-*
60   *vicem procul.* Ipsi hec audientes, penitentiam agentes *dixerunt ad Invicem: Merito hec patimur, quia peccavimus in fratrem nostrum.* Beatus Paulus concordando eos, dixit glorie esse magne talem habere socium in monasterio, dicens eis: *Gloriam ab Invicem accepistis.* Voluit etiam quod honorem ei impenderent, Romanos 12: *Honore Invicem prevenientes.*

65   Addiditque beatus Paulus quod sibi deservire deberent in omni charitate, Galatas 5: *Charitate servite Invicem.* Ad quod quidam de fratribus dixerunt se non bene posse ei deservire, quia semper post alios veniret. Respondit beatus Paulus huiusmodi proferentibus, dicens: *Cum veneritis ad manducandum, Invicem expectate.* Statim quidam ex eis dixerunt quod interdum remaneret ex
70   toto, nec veniret. Quibus Paulus ait quod interdum esset supportandus ab eis,

Ephesios 4: *Supportantes Invicem in charitate.*

In fine idem beatus Paulus instanter rogavit pro Invicem, imo precepit et mandavit, quo eum diligerent, *Hoc est,* inquiens, *mandatum meum, ut diligatis Invicem.* Item: *In hoc cognoscent homines quod mei discipuli estis, si dilec-*
75 *tionem habueritis ad Invicem.* Quo id tandem commodius fieret strictiusque observaretur erga Invicem, dona, libertates, privilegia domui isti simul et fratribus contulit plurima, *Nemini,* dicens, *quicquam debeatis, nisi ut Invicem diligatis.* Discedens ab eis, beatus Paulus visitata domo et monasterio, pacif-icatis omnibus, obnixe rogavit dominum ut donaret eis animum ad hec obser-
80 vanda promptum, *Vos autem,* inquiens, *deus multiplicet, et abundare faciat charitatem vestram in Invicem.* Quod nobis prestare dignetur Jesus Christus dominus noster. Amen.

8 Mt 24.10   10 Mt 24.10   15 Rm 15.7   16–17 Eph 4.32   18 Col 3.13   19 Apc 11.10   21–22 1 Th 4.18   23–24 1 Th 5.11   25–26 Eph 5.21   26 Phil 2.3   27–28 1 Pt 4.9   30 1 Cor 7.5   32–33 1 Th 5.15   37 Jac 5.16   38 Jo 15.17   38–39 1 Jo 4.19   41 Hbr 10.24   42– 43 Act 15.39   45 Lc 24.17   46–47 Mc 16.1, 3   47–48 Act 28.4   49 Mc 12.7   51–52 Jo 13.21–22   53 Jo 6.43   55 Col 3.9   59–60 Dn 13.51   60–61 Gn 42.21   63 Jo 5.44   64 Rm 12.10   66 Gal 5.3   68– 69 1 Cor 11.33   71 Eph 4.1   73–74 Jo 15.12   74–75 Jo 13.35   77–78 Rm 13.8   80–81 1 Th 3.12

The Long *Invicem:* Translation

A Not Inelegant Sermon on the Most Holy Brother One-Another
Receive One-Another.

Our Paul of Tarsus had a certain disciple named One-Another, deeply beloved by him, whom he desired to give over to religion so that, spurning the vanities of the secular world, he might become accustomed to living in a religious manner and to serving God. Thereupon certain people, reflecting on first his status and then the unusual customs of religion and religious men, argued against Paul, saying that the religious brothers would scandalize and betray One-Another: *Many,* they said, *shall be scandalized and shall betray One-Another.* In addition to these things, recalling to mind the hatred and tyranny of certain men of religion, they said: *They will hate One-Another.*

Nevertheless Paul wanted him to enter religion, hoping for a most favorable outcome, and one most favorable to salvation, from religion and the men of religion, and hoping as well that they would accept him as a disciple out of devoted love for Paul. He wrote therefore to the aforementioned men of religion, praying and making entreaties for him, first of all for his acceptance into the religious life, saying: *Receive One-Another.* And then he beseeched them earnestly on behalf of One-Another to be friendly, mild, and kind to him, saying: *Be ye friendly and merciful to One-Another.* In addition, so that he might not suffer any need, he wanted them to bestow gifts and presents on him: *Giving,* he said, *to One-Another as Christ has given to you.* In Revelations, also: *Giving gifts to One-Another.* Considering his fearfulness, as well, which put off many in religion, he ordered them to whom he had been committed in religion to console him with kind words, saying: *Comfort One-Another in words.* Also he commanded them not only to console him but also to move him to better things and to edify him by consolation, demanding of them: *Comfort One-Another and edify One-Another.*

Third, he asked them to show him reverence, saying: *Be subject to One-Another in the fear of Christ,* and elsewhere: *Judging One-Another superior.* Fourth, the blessed Paul asked them to confer good things upon him often, writing of him: *Granting hospitality toward One-Another.* Last, so that they would not molest him in any way, but behave honestly and with humanity toward him in all things, without guile, he gave them a commandment, saying: *Do not defraud One-Another.* In addition the blessed Paul, wanting One-Another to live honestly among the brethren and to prosper in all kindness continually, as earnestly as he could, said to him: *Toward that which is good, follow, One-Another.*

Thereafter the blessed Paul, departing from them, by reason of the zealous love he bore toward his disciple, did not ever forget him, but rather whenever he preached, remaining mindful of him always, he desired the faithful to say prayers for him, saying: *Pray for One-Another.* In addition he commended him to the brethren in all his writings, writing: *This is my commandment, that you love One-Another.* Likewise: *If you love One-Another, God will remain in you.*

But the monks, rejecting Paul's request, laid traps for him, saying to each other: *Let us consider One-Another in provocation.* And the blessed Paul was told that they treated the aforesaid One-Another badly: *There arose a dissension so that they parted from One-Another.* Finally, hearing these things, Paul came to visit the house, and coming through the door, and hearing their murmuring, he spoke the words of Luke 24: *What are these discourses that you hold with One-Another?* And one of the monks arose; he accused him of suspicious behavior with women, Mark 16: *The women spoke to One-Another.* Another accused him of murder, Acts 28: *They said to One-Another, "Undoubtedly you are a murderer."* And they wanted him to be put to death, Matthew 21: *They said to One-Another, "This is the heir: come, let us kill him."*

The abbot of the monastery, fearing for himself because of that one's treachery, said to the brothers: "I have gathered from a trustworthy report *that one of you shall betray me." Hearing this, they looked at One-Another.* Then he began to murmur vehemently against One-Another, and Paul reprimanded him in a fatherly fashion, saying: *Murmur not at One-Another.* Last, he accused him of theft; hearing this, the blessed Paul asked One-Another to tell him the truth and not to lie, Colossians 3: *Tell, One-Another, no lies.*

One-Another, indeed, denied all the complaints about him from his accusers, and added that they had treated him badly in the monastery and had no concern for him. Then Paul, coming into the house again, wanted all those jealous of One-Another to be expelled along with the accusers, citing the passage from Daniel: *Separate them far from One-Another.* Hearing these things, performing penance, *they said to One-Another: We deserve to suffer these things, because we have sinned against our brother.* The blessed Paul, agreeing with them, said it was a great glory to have such a companion in the monastery, saying to them: *You receive glory from One-Another.* In addition he wished them to do him honor, Romans 12: *With honor coming before One-Another.*

And the blessed Paul added that they should serve him devotedly in great charity, Galatians 5: *With charity serve One-Another.* At which certain of the brothers said that they were not able to serve him well, for he always arrived after them. The blessed Paul gave an answer to the waiters of this kind, saying: *When you come together to eat, wait for One-Another.* Straightaway certain of them said that from time to time he remained behind them all, nor did he come. To these Paul said that from time to time he should be supported by them, Ephesians 4: *Supporting One-Another in charity.*

Last, on behalf of One-Another the blessed Paul himself made an earnest request—or rather, ordered and commanded—that they love him, saying: *This is my commandment, that you love One-Another.* Likewise: *By this shall all men know that you are my disciples, if you have love for One-Another.* So that this might be done most fittingly and observed most strictly toward One-Another, he bestowed many gifts, liberties, and privileges to that house and to the brothers, saying: *Owe no man anything, but to love One-Another.* Departing from them, his visit to the house and the monastery complete, having restored peace to everyone, the blessed Paul asked the Lord earnestly to give them hearts ready to observe these things, saying: *May the Lord multiply you and make you abound in your charity to One-Another.* Which may our Lord Jesus Christ deign to bestow upon us. Amen.

7. The Short *Invicem:* The Hamburg Recension

Manuscript: Hamburg, Staats- und Universitätsbibliothek MS Petri 22, fol.
260rv. a. 1435. Not previously edited.

Suscipite Invicem. Ad Romanos xii. Notandum quod beatus Paulus habuit
quendam discipulum valde discretum quem tradere voluit religioni, ut ibi deo
ministraret et a mundi naufragio servaretur, quique Invicem vocabatur. Considerantes autem fratres monasterii quod monasterium intrare volebat, modum
5   et gestum predicti Invicem desuaserunt beato Paulo, dicentes illud Mathei xiiii:
Odio habuerunt Invicem ut Invicem traderent. Et quia in tali monasterio habun-
davit iniquitas et refriguit caritas multorum, nichilominus sperans beatus
Paulus quod amore ipsius gratum eum haberent, volens quod retineretur, scrip-
sit verba proposita: *Suscipite Invicem.* Quod et scriptum est. Et rogavit eos ut
10   familiares et mansueti sibi essent, ad Ephesios iiii: *Estote Invicem mansueti et*
misericordes.
    Secundo rogavit eos ut consolacionem ei facerent, 1 ad Tessalonicenses v:
Consolamini et edificate Invicem. Tertio rogavit eos ut ei reverentiam exhiberent, ad Ephesios v: *Subditi estote Invicem in timore Christi,* ad Philip-
15   penses ii: *Superiorem Invicem arbitrantes.* Quarto rogavit eos beatus Paulus ut
sibi bonas recreaciones facerent, ad Philippenses ii: *Hospitales estote Invicem*
sine murmuratione. Quinto rogavit eos ut de muneribus et de peculiis sibi
curiales essent, Apocalipsis iiii: *Munera mittent Invicem.* Postmodum decescit
ab eis beatus Paulus nec prefatum discipulum suum oblivioni dedit, ymo
20   quandocumque predicabat pro eo orationes fieri ab ecclesia [ad] sollicite pro-
curavit, Iacob v: *Orate pro Invicem ut salvemini.* Item quandocumque nuntium
habebat semper eum salutabat, 1 ad Corinthios xii: *Salutate Invicem.* Item sepe
ipsum fratribus et amicis per litteras commendavit, Iohannis xv: *Hec mando*
vobis, ut diligatis Invicem.
25   Postea dictum est beato Petro quod fratres monasterii Invicem male tractarent, ad Ghalatas v: *Invicem adversantes, Invicem provocantes, Invicem in-*
videntes. Hiis auditis, beatus Paulus perturbatus venit ad visitandum eos, et
cum intrasset, dixit illud Luce xxiii: *Qui sunt hii sermones quos confertis ad*
Invicem? Tunc surrexit unus qui accusabat eum de suspecto consortio
30   mulierum, eo quod ⟨cum⟩ eo secrete loquerentur, Marci xvi: *Mulieres loque-*
bantur ad Invicem. Postea surrexit unus accusans eum de homicidio, Actuum
xxiiii: *Dicebant ad Invicem, "Utique homicida est homo hic."*
    Sed beatus Paulus quantum potuit ab hiis omnibus eum excusavit. Videntes
autem fratres quod nichil proficerent adversus eum, nec sic possent eum

35 deprehendere, voluerunt eum occulte occidere, Mathei xxi: *Dixerunt ad In-*
vicem, "Venite occidamus eum." Beatus autem Paulus eripuit eum de manibus
eorum, sciens quod per invidiam tradidissent eum. Propterea *dixerunt ad In-*
vicem, "Merito hec patimur, quia peccamus in fratrem nostrum," Genesis xlii.
Tunc surrexit frater unus et eum gravi prodicione accusavit, Iohannis xiiii:
40 *"Unus ex vobis me tradet." Et aspiciebant ad Invicem.* Sed cum non invenissent causam mortis, facta est discordia inter eos, Actuum xv: *Facta est dissen-*
cio inter eos ut discederunt ab Invicem.

Hiis auditis, beatus Paulus vocavit Invicem ad portam, rogans ut de omnibus sibi diceret veritatem, ad Colossenses iiii: *Nolite mentiri Invicem.* Qui
45 omnia negavit et dixit quod male tractaretur, nec fieret sibi aliquo genere ob
rogatum beati Pauli.

Beatus vero Paulus intrans capitulum cum illis, precepit omnes illos eici qui
Invicem accusarunt, eo quod dolose egissent contra eum, Danielis xiii: *Sepa-*
rate eos ab Invicem procul. Ceteris vero dixit beatus Paulus: "Magna quidem
50 gloria vobis est talem habere fratrem, Iohannis v: *gloriam ad Invicem acci-*
pientes. Ideo bonam societatem cum eo tenentes, eundem honorate, ad Romanos xii: *honore Invicem prevenientes,* scilicet ei servite in caritate, ad
Ghalatas v: *Per caritatem spiritus servite Invicem."*

Quidam autem ex ipsis volentes se iustificare, ceperunt se excusare, di-
55 centes quod non commodose possent ei servire, eo quod semper ad mensam
esset ultimus. Quibus dixit beatus Paulus illud ad Corinthios iiii: *Venientes ad*
manducandum, Invicem expectate. Invicem vero se excusans dixit se fore
infirmum et sic non posse cito venire. Tunc beatus Paulus dixit quod deberent
eum habere supportatum in modico, iuxta illud ad Ephesios iiii: *Supportantes*
60 *Invicem in caritate.*

Hiis itaque gestis, precepit beatus Paulus districte ut eum diligerent,
Iohannis xv: *Hoc est preceptum meum, ut diligatis Invicem.* Secundo precepit
eis ne ei inviderent et morderent: *Si Invicem mordetis et comeditis, videte ne*
Invicem consumamini. Tertio fecit eis salubrem repromissionem, scilicet muta-
65 tionem de omnibus debitis et obligatis, ut Invicem diligerent, ad Romanos xiii:
Nemini quicquam debeatis, sed ut Invicem diligatis. Quarto, blandis oblocu-
tionibus eos ad dilectionem Invicem insitavit, Iohannis xii: *In hoc cognoscunt*
homines quia mei discipuli estis, si dilectionem habueritis ad Invicem.

Tunc beatus Paulus, volens discedere, consolabatur Invicem, dicens illud ad
70 Tessalonicenses ii: *Consolamini Invicem in verbis istis.* Et sic beatus Paulus
recessit ab eis rogans dominum ut daret eis ista fideliter observare, ad
Tessalonicenses iiii: *Vobis autem multiplicet et habundare facit caritatem In-*
vicem. Quam caritatem vobis prestare dignetur. Amen.

1 Rm 15.7   6 Mt 24.10   7 Mt 24.12   9 Rm 15.7   10–11 Eph
4.32   13 1 Th 5.11   14 Eph 5.21   15 Phil 2.3   16–17 1 Pt
4.9   18 Apc 11.10   21 Jac 5.16   22 Rm 16.16; 1 Cor 16.20; 2 Cor
13.12; 1 Pt 5.14   23–24 Jo 13.34   26 Gal 5.26   28–29 Lc
24.17   30–31 Mc 16.1, 3   32 Act 28.4   35–36 Mc 12.7   37–38
Gn 42.21   40 Jo 13.21–22   41–42 Act 15.39   44 Col 3.9   48–
49 Dn 13.51   50–51 Jo 5.44   52 Rm 12.10   53 Gal 5.13   56–57
1 Cor 11.33   59–60 Eph 4.2   62 Jo 13.34   63–64 Gal 5.15   66
Rm 13.8   67–68 Jo 13.35   70 1 Th 5.11   72–73 1 Th 3.12

The Short *Invicem:* The Hamburg Recension, Translation

Receive One-Another. Romans 12. It is worthy of note that the blessed Paul had a certain disciple, very distinguished, whom he wished to give over to religion, so that there he might serve God and be saved from the shipwreck of this world, and who was called One-Another. But the monastic brothers, contemplating the fact that he wanted to enter the monastery, argued to the blessed Paul against the ways and deeds of the aforesaid One-Another, citing Matthew 14: *They hated One-Another so that they betrayed One-Another.* And since in such a monastery iniquity abounded and the charity of many had grown cold, the blessed Paul, hoping nevertheless that they would show him favor out of love for himself, wanting him to be accepted, wrote the words set forth: *Receive One-Another.* And this was written down. And he asked them to be friendly and gentle with him, Ephesians 4: *Be ye friendly and merciful to One-Another.*

Second, he asked them to give comfort to him, 1 Thessalonians 5: *Comfort and edify One-Another.* Third, he asked them to show reverence to him, Ephesians 5: *Be subject to One-Another in the fear of Christ,* Philippians 2: *Judging One-Another superior.* Fourth, the blessed Paul asked them to provide agreeable recreation for him, Philippians 2: *Showing hospitality toward One-Another without murmuring.* Fifth, he asked them to be courteous with gifts and goods for him, Revelations 4: *Send gifts to One-Another.* Shortly thereafter the blessed Paul left them, but he did not forget the aforementioned One-Another, but rather, whenever he preached he thoughtfully had prayers said for him by the church, James 5: *Pray for One-Another, that you may be saved.* Likewise whenever he had a message he gave greetings to One-Another, 1 Corinthians 12: *Greet One-Another.* Likewise he always commended him to his brethren and friends in letters, John 15: *I give a commandment unto you, that you love One-Another.*

Afterward the blessed Paul was told that the brothers of the monastery treated One-Another badly, Galatians 5: *Opposing One-Another, provoking One-Another, envying One-Another.* Hearing these things, the blessed Paul, troubled, came to visit them, and when he came in, he spoke the words of Luke 23: *What are these discourses that you hold with One-Another?* Then one rose up who accused him of suspicious association with women, because they spoke secretly with him, Mark 16: *The women spoke to One-Another.* Afterward one rose up accusing him of murder, Acts 24: *They said to One-Another, "Undoubtedly this man is a murderer."*

But the blessed Paul excused him of these things as much as he could. The brothers, however, seeing that they could prevail against him not at all, nor could they thwart him in this way, wanted to kill him secretly, Matthew 21: *They said to One-Another, "Come, let us kill him."* But the blessed Paul snatched him from their hands, knowing that they had betrayed him through jealousy. Because of this *they said to One-Another, "We deserve to suffer these things, because we have sinned against our brother,"* Genesis 42. Then one brother rose up and accused him of great treachery, John 14: *"One of you shall betray me." And they looked at One-Another.* But when they did not find a means of death, dissension arose among them, Acts 15: *And there arose a dissension so that they departed from One-Another.*

Hearing these things, the blessed Paul called One-Another to the door, asking him to tell him the truth about all these things, Colossians 4: *Tell, One-Another, no lies.* He denied everything and said that they treated him badly, nor was he treated in any way as the blessed Paul had requested.

The blessed Paul, truly, entering the chapter with them, ordered everyone who had accused One-Another expelled, because they had acted deviously against him, Daniel 13: *Separate them far from One-Another.* To the others, truly, the blessed Paul said: "Great, certainly, is the glory to you in having such a brother, John 5: *Receiving glory from One-Another.* Therefore, keeping good company with him, honor him, Romans 12: *With honor preventing One-Another,* that is, serve him in charity, Galatians 5: *By charity of the spirit serve One-Another.*"

But a certain one of them, wanting to justify himself, began to make excuses for himself, saying that they could not serve him easily because he was always the last one to the table. To whom the blessed Paul said the words of Corinthians 4: *When you come together to eat, wait for One-Another.* But One-Another, excusing himself, said that he was feeble and thus he could not come quickly. Then the blessed Paul said that they should give him a little support, according to the words of Ephesians 4: *Supporting One-Another in charity.*

And so, these things done, the blessed Paul ordered them strictly to love him, John 15: *This is my commandment, that you love One-Another.* Second, he gave them orders so that they should not envy and backbite him: *If you bite and devour One-Another, take heed you be not consumed by One-Another.* Third, he made them a beneficial promise in return, that is, the exchange of all debts and obligations, so that they would love One-Another, Romans 13: *Owe no man anything, but to love One-Another.* Fourth, he urged them to the love of One-Another with flattering contradictions, John 12: *By this shall all men know that you are my disciples, if you have love for One-Another.*

Then the blessed Paul, wishing to depart, comforted One-Another, saying the words of Thessalonians 2: *Comfort One-Another in these words.* And thus the blessed Paul went away from them, asking the Lord to grant them these things to observe faithfully, Thessalonians 4: *May the Lord multiply you and make you abound in charity toward One-Another.* Which charity may he deign to bestow upon you. Amen.

8. The Money-Gospel: The "Intermediate" Version

Manuscripts

I   Ivrea, Biblioteca Capitolare MS 80, fols. 114v–115r. s. xiii/xiv. Not previously edited.

H   London, British Library MS Harley 3678, fol. 97v. s. xiii/xiv. Edited in E. Dümmler, "Verse und Satire auf Rom," *Neues Archiv der Gesellschaft für ältere deutsche Geschichtskunde* 23 (1898): 204–12 (at 209–12, Dümmler's L). This collation has been done anew from the manuscript, with some readings (noted) taken from Dümmler's edition where the text has been effaced since Dümmler's time.

V   Vatican, Biblioteca Apostolica Vaticana MS Ottobon. 1472, fol. 51rv. s. xiv^{in}. Previously edited in E. Dümmler, "Verse und Satire auf Rom," *Neues Archiv der Gesellschaft für ältere deutsche Geschichtskunde* 23 (1898):204–12 (at 209–12, Dümmler's R).

W   Vienna, Österreichische Nationalbibliothek MS 4459, fol. 106rv. s. xv^{in}. Not previously edited.

B   Besançon, Bibliothèque Municipale MS 592, fols. 5v–6v. s. xv^{med}. Collated in Lehmann 184–85 (variants not noted). Collated anew for this edition.

L   Leipzig, Universitätsbibliothek MS 176, fol. 17v. s. xv. Previously printed in Hermann von der Hardt, *Magnum Oecumenicum Constantiense Concilium,* 6 vols. (Frankfurt and Leipzig, 1697–1700), 1:498–99.

M   Munich, Bayerische Staatsbibliothek MS clm. 952, fols. 15r–16r. s. xv. Previously collated in Lehmann 184–85 (variants not noted).

P   Paris, Bibliothèque Nationale MS lat. 3195, fol. 17r. s. xv. Previously collated in Lehmann 184–85 (variants not noted).

S   Schlägl, Stiftsbibliothek MS 232, fols. 21v–22r. s. xv. Previously collated in Lehmann 184–85 (variants not noted).

D   Berlin, Deutsche Staatsbibliothek MS boruss. fol. 720, fol. 16v. a. 1448. A copy of L. Not previously edited.

F   Lost manuscript of unknown date from Freiburg: printed in Caelius Secundus Curio, *Pasquillorum tomi duo* (Basel, 1544), 302–5, from which this collation is taken.

G   Lost manuscript of unknown date from Breslau: printed in Wilhelm Gundlach, *Heldenlieder der deutschen Kaizerzeit,* 3 vols. (Innsbruck, 1899), 3:797–99, from which this collation is taken. Gundlach's edition is reprinted from a work which he cites, on his p. 796, as " 'Von Schlesien vor und seit dem Jahr 1740' II (Freiburg 1785), 370–372." I have not been able to locate this earlier edition.

Francesco Novati, "La parodia sacra nelle letterature moderne," in *Studi critici e letterari* (Turin, 1989), 195, states that there is a copy of this text in Venice, St. Mark "XI.120," fol. 49r. However, the librarians of the Biblioteca Nazionale Marciana report that there is no text resembling this in MS lat.XI.120, MS it.XI.120, MS lat.IX.120, or MS it.IX.120.

The text in Venice, Bibl. Marc. MS it.XI.66 (wrongly cited in Lehmann 184 as "cl.XI.66"), which Lehmann notes as containing this Money-Gospel, actually contains the related Money-Gospel from the parody Mass which Lehmann prints on his pp. 249–50.

Lehmann 184 also cites a lost manuscript, Fr, "verschollene Grundlage des Druckes von 1815." However, the only edition printed in 1815 listed in Lehmann's bibliography of editions (Lehmann 184) is that printed by "J. C. von Fichard im Frankfurtischen Archiv f. ä. deutsche Literatur und Geschichte. III (1815) S. 215ff.," which Lehmann identifies as manuscript F, that earlier printed by Curio in *Pasquillorum tomi duo.* I have not been able to locate Fichard's edition to see whether this is indeed a reprint of F or truly represents another lost manuscript.

These twelve manuscripts of the Money-Gospel, although virtually identical in plot, are so different in phrasing that collating them into a single edition can only be justified on the grounds that to print all twelve separately would try the reader's patience too greatly. The base text for this edition is a version of V, with its most unusual idiosyncrasies relegated to the apparatus.

Some of the biblical references cited have been taken from Lehmann 185; Jill Mann, "Satiric Subject and Satiric Object in Goliardic Literature," *Mittellateinisches Jahrbuch* 15 (1980): 63–86 (at 75–76); and Rodney M. Thomson, "The Origins of Latin Satire in Twelfth Century Europe," *Mittellateinisches Jahrbuch* 13 (1978): 73–83 (at 78–79).

Lectio ewangelii secundum marcham argenti

In illo turbine: Dixit papa Romanis: "Cum venerit filius hominis ad sedem maiestatis nostre, tunc dicat hostiarius illi: 'Amice, ad quid venisti?' Si autem perseveraverit pulsans nihil dans vobis, proicite eum in tenebras exteriores, ibi
5   erit fletus et stridor dentium." Cardinales dixerunt: "Ad quid faciendo pecuniam possidebimus?" Papa respondit: "In lege scriptum est. Quomodo legis? 'Dilige aurum et argentum ex toto corde tuo et ex tota anima tua et divitem sicut te ipsum.' Hoc fac et vives."

Tunc venit quidam clericus ab episcopo suo iniuste oppressus, qui non
10   potuit intrare ante illum, quia pauper erat. Hostiarii vero veniebant et percutie

bant eum, dicentes: "Vade retro, Sathanas, quia non sapis ea que nummi sapiunt." Pauper autem ille clamabat, dicens: "Miseremini mei, miseremini mei,
saltem vos hostiarii domini pape, quia manus paupertatis tetigit me." At illi
dixerunt: "Paupertas tua tecum sit in perditionem; non intrabis donec red-
15   dideris novissimum quadrantem." Pauper ille abiit et vendidit omnia que
habuit. Primo dedit ostiariis et postea cardinalibus. At illi accipientes dixerunt:
"Et quid hec inter tantos?" Et eiecerunt eum foras et egressus flevit amare.

    Tunc venit ad curiam quidam episcopus pinguis, simonialis, qui per sedi-
tionem fecerat homicidium, et erat valde dives. Cardinales hec audientes dix-
20   erunt: "Benedictus qui venit in nomine auri et argenti." Episcopus ille apertis
thesauris suis primo dedit ostiariis, postea cardinalibus. Camerarius et can-
cellarius arbitrati sunt quod plus essent accepturi. Dedit enim unicuique decem
talenta.

    Papa autem infirmabatur usque ad mortem. Audiens episcopus ille quod
25   dominus papa infirmaretur, misit ei electuarium auri et argenti. Statimque
sanus factus est homo et dedit gloriam auro et argento, et osculatus est eum,
dicens: "Amice, bene venisti." Cardinales dixerunt: "Vere, homo iustus est
iste." Papa respondit: "Amen, amen, dico vobis, quodcumque petierit in nomine meo, fiat ei."

30   Papa autem sedens pro tribunali in loco qui dicitur Avaritia, id est Calvarie
locus, dixit cardinalibus: "Beati divites, quoniam ipsi saturabuntur. Beati tenentes, quoniam ipsi vacui non erunt. Beati qui habent pecuniam, quoniam
ipsorum est curia Romana. Ve illi qui non habet, expedit ut mola asinaria
suspendatur in collo eius et demergatur in profundum maris. Videte ne quis vos
35   seducat inanibus verbis. Quicumque vobis pecuniam dare voluerit, hic ad nos
introducite." Cardinales dixerunt: "Hec omnia servavimus a iuventute nostra."
Papa respondit: "Non inveni tantem fidem in Israel sicut in vobis. Hoc habeatis
in meam commemoracionem. Exemplum enim dedi vobis, ut quemadmodum
ego capio, ita et vos capiatis."

2–3 Mt 25.31   3 Mt 26.50   3–4 Lc 11.8   4–5 Mt 8.12, 22.13,
25.30   6–8 Lc 10.26–28   10 cf. Nm 27.17   10–11 Lc 22.63–64   11–
12 Mc 8.33   12–13 Jb 19.21   14 Act 8.20   14–15 Mt 5.26   15–16 Mt
13.46   16–17 Jo 6.9   17 Jo 9.34; Mt 26.75; Lc 22.62   18–19 Mc
15.7   20 Mt 21.9   20–21 Mt 2.11   21–22 Mt 20.10   22 Mt
25.15   24 Phil 2.27   25–26 Jo 5.9   26 Jo 9.24   26 Mt 26.49   27–28
Lc 23.47   28–29 Jo 14.12–13   30–31 Jo 19.13, 17   31 Mt 5.6   31–33
Mt 5.3–10   33–34 Mt 18.6   34–35 Mt 24.4; Mc 13.5; Eph 5.6   36 Mc
10.20   37 Mt 8.10   37–38 Lc 22.19   38–39 Jo 13.15

1 Lectio . . . argenti] Quodam ewangelium notabile secundum marcham argenti. Sequencia veri ewangelii secundum marcham argenti. Gloria tibi minime. *I* [Iustitia domini pape secund *Dümmler*]um marcham argenti *H* Passio domini nostri pape secundum marcam auri et argenti *W* *om. B* Passio in Romana curia secundum aurum et argentum *LD* Dolus vobiscum. Et cum gemitu tuo. Sequentia [?]tis evangelii secundum marcham argenti. Gloria tibi auro. *M* Gloria tibi Pascalis *P* Frequentia falsi evangelii secundum marcam argenti *S* Evangelium Pasquilli olim Romani iam peregrini. Dolus vobiscum. Et comiti tuo. Frequentia falsi evangelii secundum archam auri et argenti. Gloria tibi auro et argento. *F* Passio domini pape secundum marcam auri et argenti *G* 2 turbine] tempore *F* Dixit] iusit dominus *H* dixit dominus *LD* Romanis] Romanus *IV* Romanis discipulis suis *W* cardinalibus suis *LD* rapax carpidanaribus suis *M* ad Romanos *S* rapax carpinalibus suis *F* Romanus discipulis suis *G* Cum] Quando *LD* venerit] venit *LD* hominis] hominum *G* ad] in *H* ante *M* 3 *post* maiestatis *add.* .i. tempestatis *P* nostre] vestre *LD* nostre et pulsaverit ad ostium *G* tunc] *om. IPSF* tunc . . . illi] dicite ei *LD* tunc . . . venisti] *om. M* dicat] dic *W* hostiarius] hostiarie *W* illi] ei *B* ad quid] bene *H* Si autem] Si ille *I* Si *H* Et si *WSG* Et si quis *B* Si pauper *M* At ille si *P* Si autem perseveraverit] At ille diu morans et *LD* et si pertransierit *F* autem] *om. HSG* pauper *M* 4 pulsans] *om. WBLMD* pulsans et *P* paup⟨er⟩ *S* dans] donans *S* dans ligatis manibus et pedibus *F* vobis] *om. ILDF* nobis *WBMPG* proicite] eice *I* proice *W* eiicite *LD* *post* eum *add.* foras *LMD* in] ad *LD* tenebras] tenebris *H* exteriores] *om. I* inferiores *P* ibi] ubi *IHBMSG* ibi . . . dentium] *om. LPDF* 5 erit] est *WG* stridor] tridor *I* Cardinales] Tunc cardinalis *I* Carpinales *WF* Cardinales vero *LD* Carpidanares *M* dixerunt] dixit ei *I* dixerunt ei *P* vero dixerunt ei *F* Ad] *om. H* Domine, ad *B* Domine *S* Magister *PF* Ad . . . possidebimus] Magister, dic quid faciam ut plenitudinem peccunie possideam [?] *I* quid faciamus ut pecuniam possideamus *LD* Domine, ad quam pecuniam possidebimus *M* faciendo] faciendum *VG* pecuniam possidebimus] possidebimus peccuniam *F* 6 possidebimus] possidendo *P* *post* possidemus *add.* Non licet eam mittere in corbanam, quia precium sanitatis *V* Papa respondit] Dominus papa vero dixit *LD* Quibus papa respondit *M* Ille vero respondit *F* *post* respondit *add.* id est in prevaricatam legis *P* In . . . est] *om. LD* In . . . legis] *om. MSD* *post* lege *add.* quid *IHP* tua *B* Quomodo legis] *om. WF* quam modo vobis dixi *G* legis] scriptum est *V* legitis, nonne scriptum est *LD* 7 Dilige] Diliges *ILD* Diligite *MSF* tuo] vestro *MSF* et ex tota anima tua] *om. LD* anima] mente *M* tua] sua et ex totis visceribus tuis *B* vestra *MSF* divitem . . . ipsum] et divitias ex tota anima vestra sicut vosmet ipsos *M* et pecuniam sicut vosmet ipsos *F* 8 te ipsum] vos ipsos *S* Hoc] Sic *B* Hoc . . . vives] Et hoc facite in meam commemorationem, et vivetis in eternum *LD* Et sic faciatis et vivetis *M* Sic facietis et vivetis *S* Hoc facite et vivatis. Hoc enim mandatum do vobis, ut quemadmodum ego facio, sic ut vos

faciatis *F*   fac et] [faciens *Dümmler*] *H* *post* vives *add.* scilicet in inferno *P*
9 Tunc] et hymno dicto *M*   Et adhuc eo loquente *G*   venit] veniens ad curiam
I   venit ad curiam *PF*   quidam] pauper *LD*   quidam pauper *IWG*   *post* clericus
add pauper *S*   valde pauper *F*   ad curiam Romanam *LD*   ab . . . oppressus] in
veste oppressus ab episcopo suo *H*   iniuste a beneficio suo oppressus *V*   manifeste
oppressus ab episcopo suo *W*   qui oppressus erat ab episcopo suo *LD*   iniuste
oppressus ab episcopo suo *P*   qui oppressus ab episcopo suo, vero Israelita in quo
dolus inventus non erat *F*   oppressus ab episcopo suo et stetit ad ostium pulsans
G   iniuste oppressus] pressus *S*   qui] et *WPSG om. MF*   qui . . . sapiunt]
et dixerunt famuli: "Amice, ad quid venisti?" *I*   qui . . . clamabat] et clamavit
voce magna *LD*   non . . . illum] voluit intrare ante papam et non poterat *B*
cupiens intrare ad dominum papam et non potuit *M*   volebat intrare ad papam et
non potuit *S*   non poterat at intrare ad papam *F*   10 potuit] poterat *P*   ante] ad
H   pauper] pauperrimus *F*   *post* erat *add.* valde *V*   Ostiarius vero venit et
interrogavit eum, dicens: "Amice, ad quid venisti?" Ille autem respondit: "Ut videam
voluntatem domini et visitem templum ejus, et narrabo ei mirabilia et ab inimicis
meis salvus ero." Respondens ostiarius dixit illi: "Quid vis mihi dare, ut eas cito ante
papam?" Pauper contristatus animo et inclinato capite respondit: "Aurum et
argentum non est mecum" *G*   Hostiarii] Sed et hostiarii *P*   Tunc hostiarii *F*
Hoc audito quam plures ostiarii *G*   Et hostiarii *S*   Hostiarii . . . sapiunt] *om.*
H   vero] autem *V   om. MG*   vero . . . eum] percussiebant ipsum et clamabant
voce magna *B*   percutiebant eum dicentes *S*   percusserunt eum dicentes *F*
veniebant] *om. M*   (?)debant *P*   venerunt *G*   percutiebant] illudentes *V*   11
eum dicentes] ei dicebant *V*   Vade] Vade, vade *M*   quia . . . sapiunt] quoniam
non sapis quia pauper es, non licet enim in conspectu dei nostri papae quenquam
vacuum apparere *F*   non sapis ea] nescis *WG*   nescis ea *M*   sapis ea *S*   que]
quam bene *G*   *post* que *add.* [?] *B*   nummi] nummique *B*   indumenti *S*
sapiunt] sunt *MSP*   [sunt *crossed out*] sapiunt *V*   12 Pauper . . . dicens]
Respondit ei dicens *I*   At ille clamavit *H*   Pauper ille clamabat *WF*   Pauper ille
altissima voce clamabat, dicens *B*   Pauper vero clericus clamabat dicens *M*   At ille
[?] mag(?) clamabat *P*   Pauper clamabat *S*   Ille pauper clamavit *G*   mei,
miseremini mei] *om. G*   mei[2] *om. LDF*   13 saltem] *om. M*   vos] [vos
Dümmler] *H*   vos . . . pape] domini hostiarii mei *M*   vos hostiarii *S*   hostiarii]
amici mei [mei *crossed out*] *I*   amici mei *WG*   domini] *om. F*   domini pape]
om. G   manus paupertatis] paupertatis onus *LD*   onus paupertatis *M*   *post* me
add. peto ut subveniatis paupertati mee et miseremini *LD*   At illi dixerunt]
Clamaverunt omnes dicentes: "Vade *I*   Hostiarii clamabant hoc *B*   At illi
responderunt *M*   Fortunatus dixit ei *P*   Hostiarii dixerunt *S*   At illi dixere *F*   Illi
vero dixerunt *G*   14 *post* dixerunt *add.* Quid ad nos *LMSDG*   tua tecum sit]
[tua sit tec *crossed out*] etc. *S*   tecum sit] sit tecum *LDG*   perditionem]
perditione *HMP*   non] non enim *M*   tu non *S*   non . . . quadrantem] *om.*
LD   intrabis] introibis in gaudium domini pape *I*   reddideris] reddideris usque

ad *I*   reddas *WPS*   solveris *F*   dederis *G*   15 novissimum] ultimum *B*   *post*
quadrantem *add.* Et non potuit introire ad dominum papam quia pauper erat. Et
ostiarii venientes et perciscientes [*sic*] eum dicentes: "Vade retro, Sathanas, quia non
sapis ea que sapiunt nummi" *I*   Pauper ille] *om. I*   Pauper vero clericus *H*   Tunc
pauper ille *V*   Et confestim abivit pauper clericus *M*   Pauper *S*   Pauper autem ille
F   Pauper . . . habuit] Tunc vero pauper clericus ivit ad forum et vendidit
tunicam, pellicium, pallium, gladium et capucium *LD*   abiit] abiit autem clericus
ille *I   om. M*   vendidit] vendit *S*   omnia] capam et tunicam et omnia *I*
omnia bona sua *WM*   capam suam et tunicam suam *P*   universa *SG*   que habuit]
om. P   16 habuit] habebat *MF*   possidebat *G   post* habuit *add* Postea reversus
ad curiam *V*   et iterum venit *B*   Et reversus est statim ad curiam *M*   Deinde
rediens *F*   et reversus est ad palatium *G*   Primo] et *I*   Et primo *W*   et reversus
est ad palatium et primo *G*   Primo . . . cardinalibus] Et apertis thesauris suis
primum hostiariis, camerariis et carpidanaribus dedit *M*   Primo dedit eis
cardinalibus, cancellariis et hostiariis *S*   Postea dedit pecuniam hostiariis *P*   Dedit
pecuniam hostiariis *F*   dedit ostiariis et] hostiariis dedit *H*   ostiariis]
cardinalibus *LD*   ostiario *G*   et] *om. VG*   et postea cardibalibus] *om. I*
secundo ministris, tertio vero hostiariis *LD*   postea] tunc *B*   cardinalibus]
carpinalibus *W*   At . . . dixerunt] Dixerunt ostiarii *I*   At illi dixerunt *H*   At illi
recipientes dixerunt *W*   At illi accipientes dedignati sunt dicentes *BS*   At illi
dixerunt *LD*   Illi autem carpientes dedignati sunt et dixerunt *M*   At illi accipientes
dixerunt *P*   At illi dixere *F*   At illi recipientes cum indignatione dixerunt *G   post*
illi *add.* hoc *V*   17 Et] *om. BMF* Sed *P*   quid hec] hec quid sunt *HBPS*   hec
quid erunt *V*   Quid *M*   quae sunt haec *G   post* hec *add.* est *I*   tantos] tot *G*
Et eiecerunt] Statim deeiecerunt *B*   Et proicierunt eum agitantes caputia sua *M*   Et
eiece⟨run⟩t *S*   eijciebant *F*   eum] illum *G*   eum foras] *om. M*   foras] folris
H   et egressus . . . amare] *om. IPF*   et ille egressus flevit amare *B*   et ille
regressus foras flevit amare *M*   et flevit amare *S*   egressus pauper flevit amare
G   egressus] *om. LD   post* egressus *add.* foras *W   post* amare *add.* Dominus
papa vero dixit: "Non introibis gaudium domini tui donec tradideris ultimum
quadrantem" *LD*   18 Tunc venit] Convenit *V*   Facta autem contentione quadam
WG   Tunc venit paulopost *F*   Tunc . . . quidam] Post multum vero temporis
venit dives *LD*   Et post pusillum venit quidam *M*   ad curiam] *om. HWBLSDG*
autem *V*   quidam] *om. LDG*   episcopus] clericus *I*   pinguis, simonialis]
simonias, incrassatus, inpingatus, dilatatus *I*   impinguatus, incrassatus, dilatatus
LD   pinguis valde et dives *M*   symonialis *P*   symoniacus *S*   symoniacus,
impinguatus, dilatatus, incrassatus *F*   pinguis et simoniacus, incrassatus et delegatus
G   qui . . . dives] propter seditionem quandam quam fecerat *M*   per] pro *B*
in *P*   per seditionem] *om. LD*   19 fecerat homicidium] homicidium fecerat
HLF   quoddam homicidium fecerat *B*   quandam fecit homicidium *G   post*
homicidium *add.* ad sedem apostolicam accessit *WG*   erat valde dives] erat hic
dives valde *I*   et cum eo turba multa *LD*   erat dives valde *HP*   Cardinales . . .

argenti] *om. WG*   Cardinales hec audientes] Quem videntes carpidanares gavisi
sunt clamantes *M*   Carpinales autem clamaverunt cum viderunt eum *F*   hec
audientes] *om. H*   hoc audientes *B*   vero audientes *LD*   audientes *S*   dixerunt]
clamabant voce magna, dicentes: "Osana! *I*   quod episcopus venerat, occurrerunt ei
[ei *om. D*], dicentes et clamantes *LD*   dicentes *MF*   clamabant, dicentes *P*
Benedictus . . . capiatis (line 20 to end)] "Advenisti desiderabilis, quem
expectabamus in bursis nostris." Tunc episcopus misit eis copiam auri et argenti. At
illi dixerunt: "Hic homo iustus et sanctus est, sicut ceteri qui spem non habent."
Dominus papa vero dixit: "Amice, ascende superius et erit tibi triplo melius." Et sic
salvatus est homo in die illa, unde erunt divites primi et pauperes novissimi. Quia
quantum habes, tantum vales. Et si nichil habueris, in gaudium huiusmodi non
intrabis. Jo. Franck h. *LD*   20 venit] venis *H*   *post* nomine *add* domini *VM*
[domini *crossed out S*]   auri et argenti] aurum et argentum deferens *M*
Episcopus] clericus *I*   At *BM*   Tunc episcopus *F*   Episcopus ille] *om. WG*
Episcopus . . . suis] Tunc ille aperuit thesauros suos *S*   apertis] apertisque
WG   21 primo] *om. I*   primum *P*   dedit . . . cardinalibus] pecuniam in [?]
ostiariis, postea cardinalibus munera preciosa, vestes speciosasque, mulos et mulas,
equos et equas *I*   hostiariis dedit, postea cardinalibus, camerario ac et canzellerio
dedit, et letati sunt valde *H*   hostiariis, secundo carpinalibus munera praeciosa et
vestes praeciosas obtulit, et camerariis et cancellariis *F*   cardinalibus]
carpinalibus *G*   *post* cardinalibus *add.* At illi recipientes [recipientes *om. G*]
dixerunt: "Benedictus qui venit in nomine auri et argenti" *WG*   postea
cardinalibus] camerariis, carpidanaribus *M*   et postea cardinalibus munera preciosa,
equos et equas, mulos et mulas *P*   cancellariis, cardinalibus *S*   Camerarius]
Camerarii *I*   Camerarius autem *PG*   Camerarius et cancellarius] camerariis et
cancellariis et *B*   Qui carpientes *M*   At ille accipientes *S*   et *F*   Camerarius . . .
talenta] *om. H*   cancellarius] cancellarii *I*   castellanus *G*   22 quod . . .
accepturi] inter se donaque dedit ei episcopus dives *B*   *post* accepturi *add.* et
dixerunt ei: "Amice, ascende superius, quia exaudita est petitio tua usque ad tertium
celum" *I*   Dedit enim] Tunc autem clericus, volens iustificare se ipsum, dedit *I*
Dedit *B*   Ille autem vollens iustificare se ipsum, dedit *P*   At ille volens se
iustificare, dedit *F*   Dedit tamen *G*   Dedit . . . talenta] *om. MS*   unicuique]
utrique *B*   uni *G*   *om. F*   decem] xi *I*   23 *post* talenta *add.* alii autem quinque,
alii vero unum *G*   24 Papa autem infirmabatur] Audiens hec dominus papa
infirmatus est *I*   Referatis utique ianuis, introduxerunt eum summo pontifici, qui
tunc infirmabatur *M*   Audiens hoc papa infirmabatur *P*   autem] vero *HG*
usque ad mortem] *om. WMG*   *post* mortem *add.* Transiens autem clericus ille
primam et secundam custodiam, venit ad portam ferream que non ulterior aperta est
ei, nam papa infirmabatur *I*   Transiens autem primam et secundam custodiam, venit
ad portam feream que non aperta est ei, nam papa infirmabatur *P*   Audiens]
Sciens autem *WG*   Audiens autem *VP*   Audiens . . . homo] Et oblato ei per
episcopum electuario auri ⟨et⟩ argenti, pontifex sanatus est statim in illa hora *M*

Audiens hoc papa, qui ad mortem infirmabatur, laetatus est valde, et conversus ad carpinales, ait illis: "Amen, amen, dico vobis, non memini tantem fidem in Israel et omni Iudea." Transit primam et secundam custodiam, venit ad portam quae ultro aperta est ei, videns autem episcopus quod papa infirmabatur ad mortem, ad lectum eius aurum et argentum misit, et statim liberatus est homo *F* episcopus] hec clericus *I* episcopus ille] ille episcopus *HB* autem idem episcopus *S* ille] *om. WG* quod . . . infirmaretur] *om. S* 25 dominus papa] *om. I* papa *WPG* infirmaretur] infirmabatur *IWB* ei] *om. S* electuarium . . . argenti] domino electuaria, scilicet aurum et argentum, aurum ad purgandum, argentum ad mitigandum. Et cum tetigit papa aurum et argentum *I* aurum et argentum *H* electum argentum et aurum nimis *V* electuarium et fortativum, scilicet aurum et argentum *F* *post* electuarium *add.* eum *S* Statimque sanus factus] Dedit gloriam auro et sanatus *W* Et statim sanus factus *B* At ille recipiens dedit gloriam viro, et statim sanatus *G* Statimque . . . argento] *om. S* 26 sanus] *om. HV* factus] effectus *P* *post* homo *add.* ille, at ait illi: "Lucerna pedibus meis aurum tuum et [?] meis" *I* et] Surgens *I* Et surgens *PF om. G* et . . . argento] *om. WG* et argento] *om. IP* eum] ipsum *H* episcopum *V* eum, papa *WG* eundem episcopum *BS* eum dominum episcopum *M* 27 *post* amice *add.* mei(?) *I* bene venisti] ad quid venisti? Fiat voluntas tua. Amen, dico tibi, quodcumque petieris in nomine meo, hoc faciam *V* bene veneris *M* venisti bene *S* bene huc venisti *F* Cardinales] Carpinales *WF* Et cardinales *B* Carpidanares vero *M* dixerunt] clamaverunt de hoc *I* clamabant *B* dicebant *M* vero unanimiter et concorditer dixerunt *F* Vere . . . iste] Iste iustus est *I* Vere, iste homo iustus est *H* Vere, vere homo iustus erat iste *W* Vere, iste homo iustus est *B* Domine, hic homo vere iustus est *M* Vere, iustus est homo iste *P* Vere, hic homo iustus est *SF* Vere, vere, homo justus est ille *G* 28 *post* iste *add.* nam est manus domini cum illo *V* Papa] Et papa *F* Papa . . . vobis] *om. I* Papa . . . ei] *om. P* Amen . . . vobis] *om. HF* Amen, dico vobis *MS* quodcumque] quicumque *HS* quidcumque *W* quod, quidquid *M* si quid *F* quicquid *G* *post* petierit *add.* homo iste *G* 29 meo] nostro *I* auri et argenti *F* fiat] fiet *WG* [?] fiat *S* ei] illi *I* 30 Papa] Tunc *IF* Papa autem] Et *M* autem] *om.* *IBF* vero *P* autem . . . tribunali] vero sedit *H* qui] quod *B* qui . . . locus] cupiditatis *I* qui Avaritiae locus dicitur *G* Avaritia] Cavarie *H* Calvarie *W* Philargaritha *F* id . . . locus] *om. PS* quod est interpretatur Avaricia *F* Calvarie] Avariae *W* 31 dixit] dicebat *IPF* dicit *W* cardinalibus] enim papa carpinalibus *W* carpidanaribus suis *M* carpinalibus suis *F* cardinalibus suis *G* Beati . . . saturabuntur] *om. WMG* Beati . . . erunt] *om. HS* Beati . . . habent] Beati donantes, et qui possident *F* ipsi] *om. M* ipsi . . . ipsi] *om.* *I* 32 *post* erunt *add.* Beati divites, quoniam saturabuntur *M* scilicet de sulfure et procella *P* habent] esuriunt et sitiunt *IBPS* amant *H* exhauriunt *M* 33 *post* Romana *add.* Beati divites, quoniam ipsi me videbunt. Beati nobis aliquid portantes, quoniam filii mei vocabuntur *G* Ve . . . habent] Qui habent, habeant. Qui non

habent, ceci fiant. Et *M* *post* Ve *add.* homini *I* autem *BS* Ve illi] Et *F* illi]
illis *WSG* habet] habent quoniam *H* habent *WSG* *post* habet *add.* quia omni
habenti dabitur, et qui non habet, id quod habet auferetur ab eo *V* id quod habet
auferetur ab eo, induatur, sicut diploide, confusione, et sit vobis sicut ethnicus et
publicanus *F* pecuniam *WG* expedit ut] *om.* *WG* *post* expedit *add.* ei *I* illi
H enim homini non habenti *V* enim *S* enim ei *F* mola] violla *H* mola
asinaria suspendatur] suspendatur mola asinaria *IWPSG* suspendatur eis mola
asinaria *M* 34 in collo eius] *om.* *MS* ad collum eius *F* collo] colla *G* eius]
eorum *WG* demergatur] demergantur *WM* proijctatur *F* in²] ad *F*
profundum] profundis *S* fundum *G* maris] marium. Quia ad habenti dabitur; ab
eo autem qui non habet, expedit ut quidquid habet aufferatur ab eo. Qui habent,
habeant, et qui non habent, ceci fiant. O vos discipuli mei *B* maris. Qui habent,
habeant, et qui non habent, ceci fiant *S* maris. Et iterum *F* Videte . . .
introducite] *om.* *WMS* 35 inanibus verbis] *om.* *IF* vanis verbis *B* qui non
pecuniam deditur *P* *post* verbis *add.* suis. Qui habent, habeant, et qui non habent,
ceci fiant. Et *H* Qui habent, habeant, et qui non habent, ceci fiant *V* Quicumque
. . . introducite] Introducite ipsum ad nos, ut qui habent, habeant, et qui non habent,
ceci fiant *P* *om.* *G* vobis . . . voluerit] vobis pecuniam dederit *I* voluerit vobis
dare pecuniam *H* voluerat dare pecuniam *B* vult pecuniam dare *F* hic] hunc
IHB *om.* *F* nos introducite] vos hunc introducite. Viri qui habent que [*sic*] et qui
non habent, ceci fiant *I* nos introducatur *V* vos introducite *B* nos eum
introducite, et qui eam habet, obtinebit quodcumque petit, et qui non habent,
anathema sit *F* 36 Cardinales] Carpinales *WF* Carpidanares *M* *om.* *S*
dixerunt] clamaverunt: "Magister *I* *om.* *S* autem dixerunt *F* responderunt *G*
Hec] Hoc *V* Domine, hoc *BS* Omnia hec *M* Magister *P* omnia] autem
VWM totum *BS* ab] av *H* servavimus] observavimus *I* servabimus
MG servavimus . . . nostra] a iuventute nostra servavimus *H* servavimus usque
nunc a iuventute *V* in cordibus nostris *M* servabimus tota virtute nostra *F* a
iuventute nostra] *om.* *G* nostra] *om.* *S* 37 Papa respondit] Audiens hec papa
admiratus est valde, dicens: "In veritate dico vobis *IP* Papa autem respondit eis
M Audiens hoc papa miratus est valde, dicens *F* *post* respondit *add.* Amen, amen,
dico vobis *WBSF* Amen, dico vobis *M* Papa . . . vobis] *om.* *H* Non . . .
vobis] Amen, amen *G* inveni] memini *F* tantem] tantam *I* fidem]
fiduciam *IW* Israel] Isre *S* Hierusalem *F* sicut] quantam *VF* sicut in
vobis] *om.* *IBMPS* *post* vobis *add.* et videte ne quis vos seducat ina nibus verbis
W Hoc . . . commemoracionem] *om.* *BS* Hoc] Hec *IWG* Hoc autem *H*
Hoc enim *F* *post* Hoc *add.* autem *H* enim *F* habeatis] facite *IPF* 38
meam] *om.* *HV* auri *F* commemoracionem] *om.* *H* dedi] do *IBM* dedi ego
H relinquo *F* ut] et *H* *om.* *M* 39 capio] capiam *V* rapui *WG* carpio *M*
faciam *P* facio *F* ita] [ita *Dümmler*] *H* *om.* *B* sic *F* capiatis] rapiatis
WG similiter capiatis *B* carpiatis *M* faciatis *P* faciatis et rapiatis *F* *post*
capiatis *add.* a modo et usque in sempiternum. Amen. *I* [Regnet domino *Dümmler*]

aurum et argentum, cui est honor et dignatio in [curia Romana et Anagina in seculo *Dümmler*] seculorum. Amen *H*   Te deum *V*   etc. etc. *W*   Laus tibi auro. Curia Romana non vult oves sine lana *M*   Deo gratias. Amen et ideo *P*   Gloria tibi auro et argento *F*

The "Intermediate" Money-Gospel: Translation

Reading of the Gospel according to the Mark of Silver

In that maelstrom: The pope said to the Romans: "When the Son of man shall come to our seat of majesty, then let the doorkeeper say to him: 'Friend, whereto art thou come?' Yet if he shall continue knocking without giving you anything, cast him into the exterior darkness, where shall be weeping and gnashing of teeth." The cardinals said: "What shall we do to obtain money?" The pope answered: "It is written in the law. How readest thou? Thou shalt love gold and silver with thy whole heart and with thy whole soul and the rich man as thyself. This do, and thou shalt live."

Then a certain cleric, unjustly oppressed by his bishop, came and could not enter before him, for he was a poor man. The doorkeepers, indeed, came and struck him, saying: "Get thou behind, Satan, because thou savorest not the things that are of money." But the poor man cried out, saying: "Have pity on me, have pity on me at least, you the doorkeepers of the lord pope, because the hand of poverty hath touched me." But they said: "Thy poverty be with thee in perdition; thou shall not enter till thou repay the last farthing." The poor man went and sold all that he had. First he gave to the doorkeepers and afterward to the cardinals. But they, taking, said: "And what are these among so many?" And they cast him out, and he wept bitterly.

Then a certain fat, simoniacal bishop came to the curia, who in the sedition had committed murder, and he was very rich. The cardinals, hearing these things, said: "Blessed is he that cometh in the name of gold and silver." The bishop, opening his treasures, first gave to the doorkeepers, then to the cardinals. The chamberlains and the chancellors thought they should receive more. For he gave everyone ten talents.

The pope, moreover, was sick nigh unto death. The bishop, hearing that the lord pope was sick, sent him a salve of gold and silver. And immediately the man was made whole and gave glory to gold and to silver, and kissed him, saying: "Friend, thou art well come." The cardinals said: "Indeed, this was a just man." The pope answered: "Amen, amen, I say to you, whatever he shall ask in my name, let it be done for him."

This pope, moreover, sitting for the tribunal in the place that is called Avarice, that is the place of Calvary, said to the cardinals: "Blessed are the rich, for they shall be satisfied. Blessed are they that have, for they shall not be empty-handed. Blessed are they that have money, for theirs is the curia of Rome. Woe unto him that does not have it; let a millstone be hanged about his neck and let him be drowned in the depth of the sea. Take heed that no man seduce you with empty words. Whoever wishes to give you money, lead him in to us." The cardinals said: "All these things we have observed from our youth." The pope answered: "I have not found so great faith in Israel as in you. Do this in commemoration of me. For I have given you an example, that as I take, so should you take also."

9. The Students' Money-Gospel

Manuscripts

B   Besançon, Bibliothèque Municipale MS 592, fols. 10v–11v. s. xv^med.
       Previously edited in Lehmann 251–52.
M   Munich, Bayerische Staatsbibliothek MS clm. 14654, fol. 239rv. s. xv.
       Never edited.

Some of the biblical references cited in this edition are taken from Lehmann's
edition of the Besançon manuscript.

Viro venerabili et discreto domino B. archipresbitero dilecto fratri suo
Iohannes frater eius Parisius studens in artibus salutem et fraternam dilectionem. Quia iam vobis primo, secundo et tercio secretas transmisi epistolas,
quibus fidem adhibere non curastis, sicut per rei evidenciam expertus sum, ideo
5   ewangelium, quod anunciare et predicare debetis, mitto vobis in hunc modum.
     Inicium sancti ewangelii secundum marcam auri et argenti.
     In illo tempore: Erat Iohannes Parisius studens in artibus sine peccunia.
Propter quod erat sollicitus et turbatus circa plurima et, elevatis oculis in
celum, dixit ad Ihesum: "Domine, non est tibi cure quod frater meus relinquit
10   me Parisius sine denariis studere? Dic ergo illi ut me adiuvet." Et respondens
illi Ihesus ait: "Porro denarii Parisius studentibus sunt necessarii." Et ait Simon
Petrus intra se: "Si frater Iohannes esset propheta, sciret profecto que et quanta
necessitas Parisiensis scolaris occupat."
     Factum est quod quidam compatriote sui Iohannes et Philippus quandam
15   summam peccunie sibi concessissent et tempus restitucionis eiusdem iam diu
elapsum fuisset. Illi in arcto positi valde mane una sabbatorum venerunt ad
hospicium dicti Iohannis orto iam sole et, suam volentes recipere peccuniam,
ad hostium camere sue pulsabant ad invicem dicentes: "Rabi, aperi nobis!" At
ille respondens ait: "Amen, amen, dico vobis, quousque venerunt deniarii mei,
20   nescio vos." At illi magis clamabant dicentes: "Aperi nobis!" Et recordatus est
Iohannes quod tempore necessitatis sibi subvenerant, aperiens hostium intro-
duxit illos et ait: "Quid existis in desertum videre hominem mollibus vestitum?
Ecce, qui mollibus vestiuntur intus non sunt." Videntes autem hominem sedentem in camera sua coopertum tenui tunica obstupuerunt. Qui dixit illis:
25   "Nolite expavescere! Hominem queritis opulentem, diviciis repletum. Recessit, non est hic. Hic est locus in quo non est recondita peccunia. Euntes ergo
renunciabitis sociis vestris et Philippo, quia ad domum Iudeorum cum vades,
precedam eos. Ibi me videbunt, sicut dixi eis."

Et sedens docebat illos, dicens: "Beati misericordes, quoniam ipsi mis-
30 ericordiam consequentur. Et beati qui non exasperant debitores suos neque
molestant, quoniam cicius eius debita persolventur. Miseremini ergo mei, miseremini saltem, vos amici mei, quia bursa vacua tetigit me. Ecce enim quod
pelli mee, iam diu est, non adhesit nisi tunica, et derelicta sunt tantummodo duo
lintheamina circa lumbos meos. Non turbetur propter hoc cor vestrum neque
35 formidet. Cotidie enim vado et venio ad vos. Et quicquid vobis debeo, ego
recognosco et debitum meum contra me est semper. Scio tamen quod nuncius
meus vivit et in brevi reversurus est, et rursus circumdabor pelle mea, et tunc
restituetur unicuique vestrum quod suum est. Ite ergo, nunciate fratribus vestris
que audistis et vidistis."

40 Contigit autem quod cum quidam nuncius eidem Iohanni attulisset quandam summam peccunie, ecce turba et qui vocaba⟨n⟩tur Philippus et Iohannes
venerunt ad eum, dicentes: "Ave, Raby, redde quod debes. Audivimus enim
quod bursa tua, que vomuerat, pregnans est." Videns autem Iohannes quod
instanter debita sua repeterent, cepit mestus esse. Erat autem multum feni in
45 camera Iohannis, et ait sociis suis: "Facite creditores meos discumbere!" Et
discubuerunt viri vero quasi milia milia. Et cum discubuissent, ceperunt inter
se super debitis suis litigare. Iohannes autem ait illis: "Sedete hic donec vadam
illuc et orem." Et acceptis tribus de sociis suis secreto ait illis: "Tristis est
anima mea usque ad evacuacionem burse." Et flexis genibus oravit, dicens:
50 "Pater, si fieri potest, transeant a me creditores isti." Et reversus ad cameram
suam iterum invenit super debitis suis litigantes: erant enim pre inopia gravati.
Et iterum abiit et oravit eundem sermonem, dicens: "Pater, si fieri potest,
transeant a me creditores isti. Digitus quidem ad computandum promptus est,
bursa autem infirma." Deinde dixit denariis suis: "Non potestis una hora
55 mecum manere? Exite iam ab archa mea et recedite. Venit enim hora in qua vos
trademus in manibus creditorum meorum." Et proiecta pecunia ait illis: "Ac-
cipite ex hac omnes!"

Tunc orta est contencio inter illos cui eorum prior deberet fieri solucio. Et
extenderunt tunicam Iohannis super archam ipsius ut iacerent sortes, ut
60 adimpleretur quod scriptum est: "Super vestem meam miserunt sortem." Cum
autem soluti fuissent, ait sociis suis: "Colligite dispersos, ne pereant." Et
impleverunt duodecim loculos, ita vacui remanserunt. De residuo autem debito
ait debitoribus suis: "Pacientiam habete in me et omnia reddam vobis. Multi
vero denarii sunt mandati, pauci vero transmissi."

8 Lc 10.41; Dt 4.19   9–10 Lc 10.40   10–11 Lc 10.42   12–13 Lc
7.39   15 Act 3.21   16–18 Mc 16.2–3   18–20 Lc 13.25; Mt 25.11–

12   21 Sir 29.2   22–23 Mt 11.7–8   23–26 Mc 16.5–6   26–28 Mc
16.7   29–31 Mt 5.7, etc.   31–32 Jb 19.21   32–34 Jb 19.20   34–35 Jo
14.27–28   35–36 Jb 19.25   36–38 Jb 19.25–26   38–39 Mt 28.10   41
Lc 1.60   42 Mt 26.49   44–46 Jo 6.10   44 Mt 26.37   47–48 Mt
26.36   47–56 cf. Mc 14.34–41   48–50 Mt 26.37–39   50–52 Mt 26.43–
44; Mc 14.40   52–53 Mt 26.39   53–54 Mt 26.41   54 Mt 26.40; Mc
14.37   55–56 Mt 26.45   56–57 cf. Lc 22.17   59–60 Jo 19.24   60–62
Jo 6.12   63 Mt 18.26   63–64 Mt 20.16

1 Viro . . . modum (lines 1–5)] *om. M*   6 auri et] *om. M*   7 Parisius . . .
artibus] studens Lipczensis *M*   8 quod erat] *om. M*   circa] erat quoque ei
miseria *M*   in celum] *om. M*   9 non est] sunt *M*   10 me Parisius] hic in
Lipczensis *M*   studere] *om M*   Et . . . Porro] Dixit ergo dominus: "Quanti
M   11 Parisius] *om. M*   sunt necessarii] necessarii sunt *M*   Et ait] Dixit
etiam *M*   12 intra] inter *M*   profecto] utique *M*   quanta] tanta *B*   13
Parisiensis . . . occupat] occupat in Lipczensis studentes *M*   14 Factum] Et
factum *M*   compatriote sui] sui compatriote *M*   Philippus] Petrus eidem
Iohannem *M*   15 summam . . . concessissent] peccuniam mutasset *M*
eiusdem] *om. M*   16 Illi . . . positi] *om. M*   venerunt] *om. M*   17 *post*
Iohannis *add.* venerunt *M*   volentes recipere] volens repetere *M*   18 hostium]
hospicium *M*   camere sue] sue camere *M*   ad invicem] *om. M*   At] Quibus
M   19 respondens . . . mei] dixit: "Non intermitto vos. Quousque denarii mei
venerunt ad mei, amen, amen, dico vobis *M*   20 vos] vobis *M*   At] Ad *M*
est] cum *M*   21 tempore . . . subvenerunt] homine [?] ei subvenerunt *M*
hostium] hospicium *M*   22 illos et ait] eos et dixit illis *M*   Quid] Quoniam hic
M   desertum] deserto *M*   23 Videntes . . . camera] Et videns eum sedens in
catheta [*sic*] *M*   24 Qui . . . Recessit] Quibus ille dixit: "Quod adhuc existis in
deserto videre hominem mollibus vestitum? Ecce, queritur obpulentum et denariis
M   26 non . . . peccunia] peccunia non est abscondita *M*   Euntes ergo] Sed ite
M   27 renunciabitis] renuntietis *M*   Philippo] Pet⟨r⟩o *M*   cum . . . eos]
precedet vos cum libris et meis vadis [*sic*] *M*   28 Ibi me videbunt] ubi me
videbitis *M*   eis] vobis *M*   29 docebat illos] docebit eos *M*   ipsi] *om. M*
31 cicius] *om. M*   eius] eis *M*   *post* debita *add.* scito *M*   ergo] autem *M*
32 saltem, vos amici] vos socii mei, saltem *M*   Ecce] et *M*   33 pelli] pellie
M   est] *om. M*   *post* nisi *add* tenuis *M*   34 propter hoc] propterea *M*   35
venio] veniam *M*   vobis debeo ego] tenero[?] *M*   36 recognosco] cognosco
vobis *M*   tamen] enim *M*   37 vivit et] veniet *M*   est et rursus] et quoniam
reverso *M*   pelle] veste *M*   38 vestrum] *om. M*   nunciate . . . que]
renuntietis sociis vestris et Pet⟨r⟩o quem *M*   39 *post* vidistis *add.* Ad illi moti
continue recesserunt. Subsequenti autem brevi temporis [?] *M*   40 autem] *om.*
M   cum] *om. M*   eidem Iohannem attulisset] attulisset eidem Iohannem *M*
quandam summam peccunie] peccunie quendam [*sic*] summam et *M*   41 *post*

turba *add.* multa *M*   Philippus] Petrus *M*   42 venerunt ad eum] ad eum
venerunt *M*   43 que vomuerat] intumerat *M*   est] *om M*   Videns . . .
Iohannis et] Cum ergo audierit quod dicta instanter repeterent *M*   46 viri . . . Et]
in illa hora *M*   *post* cum *add.* autem *M*   ceperunt] inceperunt *M*   47 super]
sub *M*   Iohannes autem] Tunc *M*   hic donec] *om. M*   48 de] *om. M*
suis secreto] *om. M*   49 oravit] *om. M*   50 creditores . . . creditores] debitores
M   53 quidem ad computandum] autem *M*   *post* est *add.* ad numerandum
M   54 Deinde . . . manere] Tunc conversus ad denarios suos ait illis *B*   55
archa mea] bursa *M*   56 manibus] manus *M*   Et . . . ait] Erat apud proximum
Pascha dies [?] quantibus illis et ipsis discumbentibus dixit *M*   57 *post* hac *add.*
moneta *M*   58 Tunc orta] Et tunc eorum facta *M*   illos] eos *M*   prior] prior
eorum *B*   *om. M*   fieri] maius *M*   59 extenderunt] extendentes *M*
iacerent] iaceret *M*   60 adimpleretur] impleretur *M*   scriptum] dictum *crossed*
out, scriptum *added above B*   Super] Et super *M*   Cum] Et cum *M*   61
soluti] sic sit[?] *M*   sociis suis] illis *M*   Colligite dispersos ne] Tollite denarios
et *M*   62 *post* impleverunt *add.* de moneta *M*   vacui] quod loculi vacue *M*
debito . . . suis] debite rogabant debitores suos, dicens: "Consummatum est de bursa
totum." Et inclinato capite, bursa exspiravit. Tunc ait illis *M*   63 omnia . . .
vobis] ego dum possum reddam vobis que debeo *M*   64 vero] enim *M*
mandati] promissi *M*   transmissi] translegati *M*

The Students' Money-Gospel: Translation

To the venerable man and distinguished lord B., an archpriest beloved to his
brother, his brother John, a student of the arts in Paris, sends greetings and
brotherly affection. Because I have now sent private letters to you once, twice,
and three times, by which you have not taken pains to adhere to the faith, as I
have learned through evidence of the matter, I therefore send you in this way a
gospel which you ought to proclaim and preach.

The beginning of the holy gospel according to the mark of gold and silver.

In that time: John was a student of the arts in Paris without any money.
Because of this he was full of care and troubled about many things, and, with
eyes lifted to heaven, he said to Jesus: "Lord, hast thou no care that my brother
leaves me to study in Paris without any money? Speak to him therefore, that he
may help me." And Jesus, answering him, said: "Indeed, money is necessary to
students in Paris." And Simon Peter spoke within himself: "If Brother John
were a prophet, he would surely know what and how great a need falls to a
scholar in Paris."

It happened that a certain John and Philip, fellow countrymen to him, had
given him a certain sum of money, and the time of its restitution had already
elapsed. In dire straits, very early in the morning on the Sabbath, they came to

the lodging of the said John, the sun being now risen, desiring to receive their money. They knocked at the door of his chamber, saying to one another: "Lord, open to us!" But he, answering, said: "Amen, amen, I say unto you, until my money has come, I know you not." But they cried out all the more, saying, "Open to us!" And John remembered that they had helped him in his time of need. Opening the door, he brought them in and said: "What went you out into the desert to see, a man clothed in soft garments? Behold, those who are clothed in soft garments are not inside." But seeing the man sitting in his chamber clothed in a thin robe, they were astonished. He said to them: "Be not affrighted! You seek the rich man, abundant in wealth. He is departed, he is not here. This is a place where no money is hidden. Go, therefore; tell your friends and Philip that when you go to the house of the Jews, I will go before them. There they shall see me, as I told them."

And sitting, he taught them, saying: "Blessed are the merciful, for they shall obtain mercy. And blessed are they who do not provoke their debtors, nor trouble them, for the debts of such a one will be paid more quickly. Have pity on me, at least have pity on me, you my friends, for an empty purse has touched me. For behold, a long time now nothing but a thin garment has cleaved to my skin, and only two cloths are left about my loins. Let not your heart be troubled, neither let it be afraid. For every day I go away and I come unto you. Whatever I owe you, I remember, and my debt is always against me. Nevertheless I know my messenger is alive and shortly will return, and I shall be encompassed by my skin, and then he shall pay back to each of you whatever is his. Go, therefore: tell thy brethren what you have heard and seen."

But it happened that, when a messenger had brought John a certain sum of money, behold, a crowd, and the men named Philip and John came to him, saying: "Hail, Rabbi, return what you owe. For we have heard that your purse, which had vomited, is swollen." But John, seeing that they sought their debts urgently, began to grow sorrowful. And there was much interest in John's chamber. And he said to his companions: "Make my creditors sit down!" And the men sat down, indeed unto a thousand thousand men. And when they had sat down, they began to quarrel among themselves over his debts. But John said to them: "Sit you here, while I go yonder and pray." And taking three of his friends aside he said in secret: "My soul is sorrowful unto the emptying of my purse." And, bending his knees, he prayed, saying: "My father, if it be possible, let these creditors pass from me." And returning to his room again he found men contending over his debts, for the weight of their poverty was very heavy. And again he went and prayed, saying: "My Father, if it be possible, let these creditors pass from me. The hands are quick to reckon, but the purse is weak."

Then he said to his coins: "Could you not wait one hour with me? Go forth from my chest and depart. Behold the hour is at hand in which you shall be given into the hands of my creditors." And holding out the money, he said to them: "Take, all of you, from this!"

Then there arose a dispute among them about which of them should receive the first payment. And they stretched John's garment out upon his coffer, that they might cast lots, that what is written might be fulfilled: "Upon my garment they cast lots." And when they were broken up, he said to his companions: "Gather up the fragments that remain, lest they be lost." And they filled twelve baskets, so they remained empty. Concerning the remaining debt, he said to his creditors: "Have patience with me, and I will pay you all. For many coins are called forth, but few are given over."

10. *Missa potatorum*

Manuscript: Wolfenbüttel, Herzog-August-Bibliothek MS Guelph 32.16 Aug. fol., fols. 488r–489v. s. xv. The *Missa potatorum* is a variant of the Mass printed in Lehmann 233–41, col. 2, beginning "Confitemini Bacho . . ." The version printed here has not previously been collated.

Incipit missa potatorum.

Confitemini deo Bacho quoniam bonus, quoniam in ciphis et amphoris est potacio eius. Et ego reus et indignus potator peccavi nimis in vita mea, potando, ludendo, decimum non dando, filium dei periurando, vestimenta mea perdendo. Mea culpa, mea maxima culpa. Ideo precor vos fratres potatores ut bibatis pro me potatore, ad Dolium Deumque Bachum, ut miser⟨e⟩atur mei.

Misereatur tui mellipotens Bachus, et ducat te in bonam tabernam, et faciat perdere vestimenta tua, et liberet te ab oculis et dentibus, et pedibus et manibus, et idem Bachus qui est afflictio spiritus, qui bibit et potat, ducat te ab patibulum. Stramen.

Introitus. Luge⟨a⟩mus omnes in Dolio, diem mestum ululantes sub errore[m] Decii, de cuius iactacione plagunt miseri et periurant filium Dei.
Versus.

> Beati qui habitant in tabernacula tua, Bache,
> In pocula poculorum laudabunt te.
> Gloriae nullae sint michi
> Dum in bursa nihil habui.

Dolus vobiscum. Et cum gemitu tuo.
Potemus ciphum plenum.

Collecta. Qui tres quadratos decios sexaginta tribus oculis ornasti, presta, quesumus, ut omnes qui vestimentorum suorum pondere graventur, quadrati Decii de iacta[i]cione denudentur, per Dolium nostrum ciphum et Bachum, qui tecum bibit et sternit per omnia pocula poculorum. Stramen.

Epistola. Lectio actuum potatorum beati Bachi ad Ebrios. In diebus illis multitudo potatorum erat in taberna, quorum corpora nuda, tunicae autem nullae, nec omnium illorum quicunque assidebant, suum aliquid esse dicebant, sed erant illis communia. Et qui differebat premia, faciebat et prelia ante conspectum potatorum. Et erat quidam claudus nomine Trijmbir, lectorum pessimus. In poculo orationem dabat lusoribus et potatoribus ad ludendum prout vestes valebant.

Graduale. Iacta cogitatum Decio, et te decipiat, faciatque te perdere omnia vestimenta tua. A Dolio factum est istud, et mirabile in bursis nostris, ideoque raro salvi erimus.

Allelujua. Rorate ciphi desuper, et terra pluat mustum, et germinet potacionem. Alleluia.

Sequencia.

Vinum bonum cum sapore
Bibit abbas cum priore
Et conventus de peiore
    Bibit cum tristicia.

Ave felix creatura
Quam produxit vitis pura.
Omnis mens pro te secura
    Stat in vini poculo.

O quam felix in colore!
O quam placens es in ore!
Dulce quoque in sapore,
    Dulce lingue vinculum. [viaculum *MS*]

Felix venter quem nutrabis,
Felix lingua quam lavabis
Et beata Madefala
    O te Bache labia.

Supplicamus: hic abunda;
Omnis turba sit fecunda.
Sit cum voce non iucunda
    Personemus gaudia.

Monachorum grex devotus,
Cleris omnis, raro totus,
Bibunt ad aequatos potus
    Et nunc et in secula.

Dolus vobiscum. Ut superius [superum *MS*].
Evangelium.

Sequencia falsi [falsae *MS*] evangelii secundum Bachum.

O fraus tibi, rustice.

In illo turbine: Potatores loquebantur ad invicem: "Transeamus usque ad tabernam ut videamus si verum sit quod dictum est de pleno Dolio." Et venerunt festinantes et invenerunt tabernarium ante ostium sedentem, ac mensam paratam, et tres talos in disco. Videntes autem Bachum, cognoverunt quod dictum fuerat de Decio illo. Tabernaria autem cogitat in corde suo quantum vestes illorum valebant. Potatores stupefacti sunt valde, et diviserunt vestimenta sua. Et reversi sunt potatores in regionem suam, glorificantes Bachum et maledicentes Decium.

Dolus vobiscum. Et cum gemitu tuo.

Potemus.

Offertorium. O Bache fortissime, potatorum deus, qui de sapientibus stultos facis, ac de bonis malos, veni ad inebriandum nos, iam noli tardare.

Praefacio.

Per omnia pocula poculorum. Stramen.

Dolus vobiscum. Et cum gemitu tuo.

Rursum corda habemus ad Bachum.

Gratias agamus deo Bacho. Merum et mustum est.

Nos igitur debemus gratias agere, et in taberna bonum vinum bibere, laudare, benedicere et predicare, quod fodiunt miseri rustici, quod bibunt reverendi domini clerici, quod frequenter petunt, pro quod magna prelia veniunt in populo, pro quod sicientes potant, pro quod clamant rustici, pro quod letantur miseri, pro quod psallant clerici, qui non cessant clamare quotidie, cum inebriati fuerint, una voce dicentes:

Sanctus quantus, sanctus quantus, dominus Bachus. Pleni sunt ciphi et mensa gloria tua. Os[i]anna in excelsis. Maledictus qui bibit quod vestes suos amittit. O ve, ve, clamat in excelsis.

Per omnia pocula poculorum. Stramen.

Ploremus. Preceptis domini hospitis movemur ut de vino bono audemus [audiamus *MS*] bibere. Pater Bache qui es in ciphis, multiplicetur vinum tuum. Fiat tempestas tua sicut in Decio et in taberna. Vinum bonum ad bibendum da nobis hodie, et dimitte nobis pocula nostra sicut et nos dimittimus potatoribus nostris. Et ne nos inducas in sobrietatem, sed libera nos a vomitu. Stramen.

Per omnia pocula poculorum. Stramen.

Fraus, O rustici, sit semper vobiscum. Et cum gemitu tuo.

Agnus Bachi qui tollis pignora nostra, da potacionem nobis.

Agnus Bachi qui tollis pignora nostra, da potacionem nobis.

Agnus Bachi qui habes gaudia mundi, dona nobis potum.

Communio. Venite filii Bachi, percipite maerum, quod vobis paratum est ab origini vitis.

Dolus vobiscum. Et cum gemitu tuo.

Potemus.

Collecta. Deus qui perpetuam discordiam inter rusticos et clericos semi-nasti, qui multitudinem rusticorum ad servicium clericorum et dominorum percepisti, da nobis, queso, domine, de laboribus rusticorum laute vivere et illorum uxoribus et filiabus honeste uti, et semper de eorum mortalitate gaud-ere. Per dolium nostrum verumque Bachum qui tecum bibit et sternit per omnia pocula poculorum. Stramen.

Dolus vobiscum. Et cum gemitu tuo.

Rogemus pro vineis et illorum cultoribus, pro plenis Doliis et non pro vacuis, pro cunctis potatoribus et vivis et defunctis. Stramen.

Indulgenciam omnium, numerorum dissolucionem membrorum, amis-sionem omnium vestimentorum, membrorum corruptionem, ac aliorum bonorum prodicionem mittat vobis miser ac discors Bachus.

Ita, mensa musto vinoque plena.

Deo Bacho triplex correpta.

Et maledictio patris Bachi ut filiorum eius et spiritus corrupti descendat per os in membra vestra et pocula poculorum. Stramen.

Missa potatorum: Translation

Here begins the drinkers' Mass.

We confess to the god Bacchus because he is good, because his drink is in cups and goblets. And I, a sinner and unworthy drinker, have sinned exceed-ingly in my life in drinking, gaming, not giving tithes, swearing falsely to the Son of God, losing my clothes. Through my fault, through my most grievous fault. Therefore I beseech you, brother drinkers, to drink for me, an imbiber, to the Cask and God Bacchus, that he may have mercy on me.

May the honey-potent Bacchus have mercy on thee, and lead thee into the good tavern, and make thee lose thy clothing, and free thee from thine eyes and teeth, and feet and hands, and may that same Bacchus who is the affliction of the spirit, who drinks and guzzles, lead thee to the gibbet. Straw.

Introit. Let us lament in the Cask, bewailing a mournful day in the error of the Die, at whose rolling the wretched complain and perjure the son of God.

Verse.

Blessed are they who live in your tavernacle, Bacchus,
They shall praise thee, cups without end.
No glory is mine
When I have nothing in my purse.

Deceit be with you. And with thy groaning.
Let us drink the full cup.

Collect. Thou who didst adorn three four-square dice with sixty-three spots, assure, we entreat, that all who are burdened with the weight of their clothes shall be denuded by the casting of the four-square Die, through the Cask our vessel and Bacchus, who drinks and sneezes with thee, cups without end. Straw.

Epistle. The reading of the acts of the drinkers of the blessed Bacchus to the Inebriates. In those days: there was a multitude of drinkers in the tavern, whose bodies were naked, without any garments, nor did any of all of them that sat together call anything his own, but everything was common to them. And he who bore away the reward also instigated a battle before the face of the drinkers. And there was a certain lame man named Trijmbir, the worst of readers. In his prayer to the cup, he contributed to the gamblers and drinkers, for their game, just as much as their clothes were worth.

Gradual. Cast a thought to the Die, and he shall ensnare thee, and make thee lose all thy clothes. By the Cask this is done, and it is wonderful in our purses, and therefore seldom shall we be saved.

Hallelujah. Drop down dew, ye goblets, from above, and let the earth rain must, and produce drink. Hallelujah.

Sequence.

Good wine with savor
The abbot drinks with the prior,
And the monastery from the worse wine
          Drinks with sadness.

Hail, happy creature
Which the pure vine produced.
Every mind rests secure for thee
          In the cup of wine.

O how happy in color!
O how pleasing thou art in the mouth!

And sweet in savor,
    Sweet chain of the tongue.

Happy stomach which thou nourishest,
Happy tongue which thou washest
And happy Madefala lips
    O thou Bacchus.

We entreat: be overflowing here.
May every crowd be fruitful.
Let us proclaim joy
    With a cheerless voice.

A devoted crowd of monks,
Every cleric, seldom all,
Drink drinks to their peers,
    Now and forever.

Fraud be with you. As above.
Gospel.
The sequence of the false Gospel according to Bacchus.
O deceit be with you, peasant.
In that tempest: The drinkers spoke to one another: "Let us go over to the tavern and see if it is true which is said of the full Cask." And they came with haste and found the tavern keeper sitting before the door, and the table laid, and three dice in the dish. But seeing Bacchus, they knew what had been said of that Die. And the barmaid pondered in her heart how much their clothes were worth. The drinkers wondered exceedingly, and divided their garments. And the drinkers returned to their country, glorifying Bacchus and cursing the Die.
Fraud be with you. And with thy groaning.
Let us drink.
Offertory. O Bacchus most steadfast, lord of drinkers, who makest fools of the wise and bad of the good, come to inebriate us, and do not delay.
Preface.

Cups without end. Straw.
Fraud be with you. And with thy groaning.
Contrary hearts we have toward Bacchus.
We give thanks to the lord Bacchus. Neat and must is it.

We should therefore give thanks, and in the tavern we should drink, praise, bless, and commend good wine, which the wretched peasants cultivate, which the reverend lord clerics drink, which they frequently demand, by which great rewards come to the people, with which the thirsty drink, for which the peasants clamor, by which the wretched are made happy, for which the clerics, who sing incessantly every day when drunk, say the psalms, crying with one voice:

How holy, how holy, Lord Bacchus. Full are the goblets, and thy table is glory. Hosanna in the highest. Cursed be he who loses his clothes. O woe, woe, he cries out on high.

Cups without end. Straw.

Let us wail. We are moved by the bidding of the Lord our host to dare to drink the good wine. Father Bacchus who art in cups, increased be thy wine. Thy turmoil be done in the Die as it is in the tavern. Give us this day good wine to drink, and send forth our cups to us as we send them forth to our fellow drinkers. And lead us not into sobriety, but deliver us from vomit. Straw.

Cups without end. Straw.

Fraud, O peasants, be with you forever. And with thy groaning.

Lamb of Bacchus, who takest away the things we have pawned, grant drink to us.

Lamb of Bacchus, who takest away the things we have pawned, grant drink to us.

Lamb of Bacchus, who possessest the joys of the world, give us a drink.

Communion. Come, sons of Bacchus, take the wine [*also* inheritance] which has been prepared for you since the sprouting of the vine.

Fraud be with you. And with thy groaning.

Let us drink.

Collect. God, who hast sown perpetual discord between peasants and clerics, and who hast gathered a host of peasants into the service of the clerics and lords, grant us, we entreat, O Lord, that we may live luxuriously off their labors, and that we may use their wives and daughters properly, and always rejoice at their demise. By our Cask, the true Bacchus, who drinks and sneezes with thee, cups without end. Straw.

Fraud be with you. And with thy groaning.

Let us make entreaties for the vines and their cultivators, for full Casks and not for empty ones, and for all drinkers, living and dead. Straw.

May wretched and tempestuous Bacchus grant you an indulgence in everything, the weakening of all your limbs, the loss of your clothes, the defilement of your body, and the arrival [*also* betrayal] of other good things.

Go, the table is full of wine and must.

By Bacchus, the god three times lifted up.

And may the curse of Father Bacchus and his sons and the holey [*sic*] spirit descend through your mouth and into your limbs, cups without end. Straw.

11. A Drinkers' Mass (*Confitemini Dolio*)

Manuscript: Munich, Bayerische Staatsbibliothek MS cgm. 4379, fols. 88r–90v. s. xvi. Some passages from this text are reproduced in Antony Marks, "The Parody of Liturgical and Biblical Texts in Germany in the Sixteenth and Seventeenth Centuries" (Ph.D. diss., University of Cambridge, 1970), 320–22; otherwise it has never been edited.

Een Boeck gevonden in Engelant in een Abdie tussen Norwits en Londen in den Jaere 1535 also Conick Hendrick de achste alle de Cloosters ruyneerde ende alle de Monicken ende Bagynen ten Lande uytdreef, waermede de vorsehen Monicken der Abdye op feestdaegen haere recreatie mede Hielden.

Sacerdos: Confitemini Dolio quoniam bonum.

Diaconus: Quoniam in taberna misericordia eius.

Sac: Confiteor Dolio, regi Baccho et omnibus schyphis eius a nobis acceptis, quia ego potator potavi nimis in stando, sedendo, videndo, vigilando, ludendo, et ad schyphum inclinando, vestimentaque mea perdendo: mea crapula, mea crapula, mea maxima crapula. Ideo precor vos, solemnes potatores et manducatores, devote orare pro me.

Diac: Misereatur vestri ventripotens Bacchus.

Sac: Et permittat te perdere omnia vestimenta et sensu⟨m⟩, liberetque te ab oculis et dentibus tuis, et perducat te ad plenam tabernam.

Diac: Stramen.

Sac: Adiutorium nostrum in nomine Dolii et Bacchi.

Diac: Qui fecit scyphum et tabernam.

Officium Missae

Sac: Lugeamus omnes in Dolio, diem maestum ululantes sub honore quadrato Decii, de cuius potatione gaudent miseri.

Psalmus

Diac: Beati qui habitant in domo Dolii: in pocula poculorum laudabunt te.

Sac: Ploremus. Ventripotens deus qui tres quadratos decios sexaginta tribus oculis mirabiliter illuminasti, concede propitius ut omnes qui vestimentorum suorum pondere pergravantur quadrati Decii iactatione liberentur, tu qui incessanter bibis et potas, per omnia pocula poculorum.

Diac: Stramen.

Epistolae Textus
Lectio libri paterae ad Ebrios

Sac: In diebus illis: Dixit tabernarius ad potatores: "Omnes sitientes venite ad tabernas, et qui non habetis argentum, properate et vendite vestimenta vestra, ac date tabernario et vos habebitis thesaurum in schyphis, nam qui perdit in taberna vestimenta sua, in somnis inveniet ea."

Diac: Iactate cogitatum tuum in Decio et ipse te deducet ad Dolium. Cum inebriter clamavi et potus exaudivit me. Allernebria, allernebria.

Sac: Video tabernam apertam et scyphum positum a dextris Dolii.

Meum est propositum in taberna mori
Et vinum apponere sitienti ori,
Ut dicant cum venerint angelorum chori:
"Deus sit propitius huic potatori."

Magis quam ecclesiam diligo tabernam:
Illam nullo tempore sprevi neque spernam
Donec fratres grisei veniant Falernam,
Ut cantent cum ebriis requiem aeternam.

Potatores singuli semper sunt benigni,
Iam senes quam iuvenes adsedentes igni;
Crucientur rustici qui non sunt tam digni
Ut potare valeant vinum boni ligni.

Vini mirabilia nolo pertransire:
Vinum facit vetulas leviter salire
Et ditescit pauperes, claudos facit ire,
Mutos ad facundiam et surdos audire.

Vinum super omnia bonum eligamus,
Nam purga[n]mus vitia cum vina potamus.
Dum vini sit copia fortiter bibamus;
In schyphorum gloriam te Deum laudamus.

Diac: Stramen.

Evangelium

Sac: Doleo vobiscum.

Diac: Et cum genitu tuo.

Sac: Frequentia falsati evangelii secundum Marcolfum.

Diac: Horreo vobis rustici.

Sac: In illo tempore: Potatores loquebantur ad invicem, dicentes: "Transeamus usque ad tabernam, et videamus si verum sit quod dictum est a Dolio illo." Et festinantes venerunt et invenerunt tabernam apertam ac mensam ornatam et Decios appositos super mensam. Cum autem intrassent, de claro cognoverunt verum esse quod dictum erat de Dolio. Et tabernarius cogitabat in corde suo eorum vestes nihil valere. Potatores vero diviserunt vestimenta sua, glorificantes Dolium et maledicentes Decios.

Diac: Decii pravitas.

Sac: Dolio vobiscum.

Diac: Et cum genitu tuo.

Sac: Ploremus.

Offertorium

O fortissime Bacche qui dulcis es in ore nostro et sapor vini ad inebriandum nos, dilexisti iniustitiam, et odisti sobrietatem, propterea te destruet Decius tuus. Allernebria, per omnia pocula poculorum.

Diac: Stramen.

Sac: Doleo vobiscum.

Diac: Et cum genitu tuo.

Sac: Sursum colla.

Diac: Habemus ad Dolium.

Sac: Gratias agamus Dolio et deo Baccho.

Diac: Vinum et mustum est.

Praefatio

Sac: Vinum et mustum iniquum est damnare Bacchoque iustum est gratias agere, qui est inferni ventripotens patronus per vinum et Dolium nostrum, qui propter vini donationem bibentibus clarus apparuit et, ipsis potantibus, est elevatus in schyphis, ut nos ebrietatis suae tribuerit participes. Et rideo cum miseris, nudis, miserrimisque potatoribus impietate ludentibus vinumque sine fine bibentibus:

Planctus, planctus, planctus, decies, Decius Astaroth. Pleni sunt schyphi et patera tua. Maledictus qui venit in nomine Decii, perditio quoque in Deciis per omnia pocula poculorum.

Diac: Stramen.

Sac: Ploremus.

Oratio

Pater Bacche qui es in schyphis, sanctificetur bonum vinum. Adveniat damnum tuum. Fiat tempestas tua sicut in schypho sic etiam in taberna. Potum nostrum da nobis hodie. Et dimitte nobis pocula nostra, sicut et nos dimittimus compotatoribus nostris. Et sic nos inducas in ebrietatem, sed ne libera nos a vino.

Diac: Stramen.

Sac: Per omnia pocula poculorum.

Diac: Stramen.

Sac: Pax schyphi vobiscum.

Diac: Et cum genitu tuo.

Sac: Manus Decii, qui tollis pocula scyhphi, da nos bibere.

Diac: Vos qui secuti estis Decium, sedebitis super duodecim sedes gustantes lagenas vini, dicit Decius.

Sac: Doleo vobiscum.

Diac: Et cum genitu tuo.

Sac: Ploremus. Deus qui multitudinem laicorum ad congregationem spiritualium vino madidorum pervenire fecisti, concede propitius ut de eorum laboribus vivamus in terris, et de eorum uxoribus, filiabus ac domicellis ad cordis oblectationem diu perfrui mereamur, per ipsum Dolium nostrum.

Diac: Stramen.

Sac: Doleo vobiscum.

Diac: Et cum genitu tuo.

Sac: Benedicamus Dolio.

Diac: Decii pravitas.

Sac: Ite, missa est.

Finis

A Drinkers' Mass: Translation

A book found in England in an abbey between Norwich and London in the year 1535, when King Henry VIII destroyed all the monasteries and drove all the monks and beguines out of the country, which the aforementioned monks of the abbey used for their recreation on feast days.

Priest: We confess to the Cask because he is good.

Deacon: Because his mercy is in the tavern.

Priest: I confess to the Cask, to King Bacchus and to all his cups taken up by us, that I, a drinker, have drunk exceedingly while standing, sitting, watching, waking, gambling, and inclining toward the cup, and in losing my clothes, through my drunkenness, through my drunkenness, through my most extreme drunkenness. Therefore I beseech you, solemn drinkers and diners, to pray devoutly for me.

Deacon: May stomach-potent Bacchus have mercy on you.

Priest: And allow thee to lose all thy clothes and thy sense, and free thee from thine eyes and teeth, and bring thee into the full tavern.

Deacon: Straw.

Priest: Our help is in the name of the Cask and of Bacchus.

Deacon: Who made the goblet and the tavern.

Office of the Mass

Priest: Let us all lament in the Cask, bewailing a mournful day in four-square honor of the Die, at whose drinking the wretched rejoice.

Psalm

Deacon: Blessed are they who live in the house of the Cask: they shall praise thee, cups without end.

Priest: Let us wail. Stomach-potent God who didst wondrously adorn three four-square dice with sixty-three spots, grant most favorably that all who are burdened by the weight of their clothes shall be set free by the tossing of the four-square Die, thou who drinkest and imbibest without ceasing, cups without end.

Deacon: Straw.

Text of the Epistle
Reading of the book of the vessel to the Inebriates

Priest: In those days: The tavern keeper said to the drinkers: "All you that thirst, come to the tavern, and you that have no money, make haste and sell your clothes, and give to the tavern keeper, and you shall have treasure in the cups, for he that loses his clothes in the tavern shall find them in his dreams."

Deacon: Cast thy thought to the Die and he shall lead thee away to the Cask. When I called out drunkenly the drink also hath heard me. Halledrunken, halledrunken.

Priest: I see the tavern open and the goblet set on the right hand of the Cask.

> It is my intention to die in the tavern
> And to put wine near the mouth of the thirsty
> So that when the chorus of angels comes, they will say,
> "God be merciful to this drinker."
>
> More than the church, I love the tavern:
> At no time have I spurned it, nor shall I
> Until the Greyfriars come with Falernian wine
> To sing eternal rest with the drunkards.
>
> Drinkers are always kindly, every one,
> The old ones like the young ones sitting by the fire;
> May those peasants be tormented who are not worthy
>   enough
> To drink wine from good vines.
>
> The miracles of wine I shall not overlook:
> Wine makes old women leap lightly
> And enriches paupers, makes the lame walk,
> Makes mutes eloquent and the deaf hear.
>
> Let us choose good wine above all things,
> For we purge vices when we drink wine.
> When there's a lot of wine, we may drink deeply;
> In the glory of goblets we praise thee, Lord.

Deacon: Straw.

The Gospel

Priest: Fraud be with you.
Deacon: And with thy begetting.
Priest: The frequency of the false Gospel according to Marcolph.
Deacon: I tremble at you, peasants.
Priest: In that time: The drinkers spoke to one another, saying: "Let us go over to the tavern, and let us see if it is true which is said of that Cask." And they came with haste and they found the tavern open, and the table laid, and Dice set on the table. And when they came in,

they knew clearly that what was said of the Cask was true. And the tavern keeper pondered in his heart that their clothes were worth nothing. But the drinkers divided their garments, glorifying the Cask and cursing the Dice.

Deacon: The depravity of the Die.

Priest: Fraud be with you.

Deacon: And with thy begetting.

Priest: Let us wail.

Offertory

O most steadfast Bacchus who art sweet in our mouth, and the savor of wine to make us drunk, thou hast loved injustice and hated sobriety, and therefore thy Die is the ruin of thee. Halledrunken, cups without end.

Deacon: Straw.

Priest: Fraud be with you.

Deacon: And with thy begetting.

Priest: Necks on high.

Deacon: We have for the Cask.

Priest: We give thanks to the Cask and the lord Bacchus.

Deacon: Wine and must it is.

Preface

Priest: It is wicked wine and must to condemn and just to give thanks unto Bacchus, who is the stomach-potent defender of the infernal depths through wine and our Cask; who, on account of the bringing of the wine, appeared clear to the drinkers and, as they drank, was lifted up in goblets, so that he might make us partakers of his drunkenness. And I laugh with the wretched, the unclothed, and the most wretched drinkers, with impiety in gaming and imbibing wine without end:

Moaning, moaning, moaning, times ten, Die of Astaroth. Full are thy cups and thy vessel. Accursed is he that cometh in the name of the Die, and perdition in the Dice, cups without end.

Deacon: Straw.

Priest: Let us wail.

Prayer

Father Bacchus who art in cups, hallowed be good wine. Thy ruination come. Thy turmoil be done in the cup as it is in the tavern. Give us this day our daily drink. And send forth our cups to us as we send forth to our fellow drinkers. And lead us not into drunkenness, but do not deliver us from wine.

Deacon: Straw.

Priest: Cups without end.

Deacon: Straw.

Priest: Peace of the goblet be with you.

Deacon: And with thy begetting.

Priest: Hand of the Die, who takest away by the cups of the goblet, give us a drink.

Deacon: You who have followed the Die, you shall sit on twelve seats tasting tankards of wine, saith the Die.

Priest: Fraud be with you.

Deacon: And with thy begetting.

Priest: Let us wail. God who hast brought a multitude of laymen to the congregation of drunkards inspirited with wine, graciously grant that we may live off the labors of those who work the soil, and off their wives, and may we be worthy to enjoy their daughters and servant girls to the full, to the delight of the heart, through him our Cask.

Deacon: Straw.

Priest: Fraud be with you.

Deacon: And with thy begetting.

Priest: Let us bless the Cask.

Deacon: The depravity of the Die.

Priest: Go, the mass is finished.

End

12. Fragments of Drinkers' Masses

1

Manuscript: Munich, Bayerische Staatsbibliothek MS clm. 23108, fol. 138r. s. xiii. The prayer is printed in Lehmann 125; the remainder has never before been published.

Ave, color vini clari,
Ave, sapor sine pa⟨ri⟩,
Tua nos letificari
     Dignetur potencia.

O quam fragrans [flagrans *MS*] in odore,
O quam placens in colore,
O quam placidum in ore,
     Dulce linguae vinculum.

O quam felix creatura
Quam produxit vitis pura;
Omnis mensa sit secura
     De tui praesentia.

Felix venter quem intrabis,
Felix guttur quod rigabis,
Felix os quod tu lavabis,
     O beata labia.

Ergo vinum collaudemus,
Potatores exaltemus,
Non-potan⟨tes c⟩onfundemus
     Per eterna secula.

Vivat ⟨in eternum⟩ qui dat nobis ⟨vinum F⟩alernum

Deus qui non potestate [potestati *MS*] vini vel fortitudine nostri hodierna die multorum capita dolere fecisti, concede ut quorum cenali potacione capita ledantur matitudinali reiteracione recurentur. Per eundum ciphum et Bachum qui nos dignetur perducere ad eandem ebrietatem. Amen.

"Ave color vini clari": Walther, *Initia*, no. 1901

2

Manuscript: Munich, Bayerische Staatsbibliothek MS clm. 10751, fols. 204v–205v. a. 1575. Previously published in W. Wattenbach, "Geistliche Scherze des Mittelalters IV," *Anzeiger für Kunde der deutschen Vorzeit,* N. F. 15 (1868): cols. 134–36 (at cols. 134–35). The two prayers, the Pater Noster, and the final verse were printed in Lehmann 233–41, in his apparatus, col. 1, as manuscript M.

Exhortatio ad potandum perutilis

Quicunque vult esse bonus frater,
Bibat semel, bis, ter, quater,
Bibat semel et secundo
Donec nihil sit in fundo.
Bibat hera, bibat herus,
Nemo ad potandum sit serus.
Pro rege   vinum bibendum sine lege,
Pro papa   vinum bibendum sine aqua.
Hec fides potatica,
Sociorum spes unica.
Qui bene non potaverit
Bonus frater esse non poterit.
Rhense vinum   det nobis auxilium divinum.

Versiculus.
Collecta.
Oremus. Deus qui multitudine vini multorum capita dolere fecisti, tribue, quaesumus, ut qui serotina potatione leduntur, eadem matutinali refocillatione recreentur. Per Bachum Dominum nostrum etc. Stramen.
Oremus. Deus qui multitudine virtuteque vini et cerevisie capita hominum turbari, atque dura Thebeorum ossa mollificari fecisti, tribue nobis virtutem et fortitudinem, ut qui serotina potatione ledimur, alterius diei repotatione curemur. P. D. B. etc.
Sequentia vini.

Vinum bonum et suave
Bibat abbas cum priore

Et conventus de peiore
      Bibit cum tristicia.

Felix es⟨t⟩ qui te plantavit
Et te vinum nuncupavit.
Per te mundum satiavit
      Divina potentia.

Ave felix creatura
Quam produxit vitis pura!
Omnis mens⟨a⟩ sit iocunda
      In tua presentia.

O quam placens in colore!
O quam fragrans in odore!
O quam sapidum in ore,
      Conferens eloquia.

Felix venter quem intrabis,
Felix os quod tu rigabis,
Felix est quem satiabis
      Et beata labia.

Ave color vini clari,
Ave sapor sine [vini *MS*] pari,
Tua nos inebriari
      Digneris potentia.

Monachorum grex devotus,
Omnis mundus, clerus totus
Bibat ad equales haustus
      Te nunc et in secula.

Ergo vinum collaudemus,
Potatores exaltemus,
Non-potantes confundemus
      Ad inferni supplicia.

Pater Noster. Potus noster qui es in cypho, glorificetur nomen tuum. Adveniet potestas tua sicut in scala et in vitro. Panem pistum et album da nobis hodie et conpotatoribus nostris. Et ne nos inducas in tabernam malam, sed libera nos ab illa semper. Stramen.

Gratiarum actio

Christe tibi gratias
Qui nos abunde satias
De bonis rusticorum
Contra voluntatem eorum.

"Quicumque vult . . .": Walther, *Initia,* no. 15761   "Vinum bonum et suave": Walther, *Initia,* no. 20366

3

Manuscript: Munich, Bayerische Staatsbibliothek MS clm. 11963, fol. 341v. a. 1609–16. Never published.

Potator quidam egregius
In laudem Bacchi hos recitat versus

Meum est propositum in taberna mori
Et vinum appositum sitienti ori
Ut dicant cum venerint ebriorum chori,
"Deus sit propitius huic potatori."

Potatores incliti semper sunt benigni,
Tam senes quam iuvenes ab aeterno igni.
Cruciantur rustici ut sint magis digni
Gustare ut valeant haustum boni vini.

Fertur in conviviis vinus, vina, vinum.
Masculinum displicet, placet faemininum,
Sed in neutro genere vinum e⟨s⟩t amoenum:
Loqui facit clericos optimum latinum.

Vini mirabilia

Vini mirabilia nolo pertransire:
Vinum facit vetulas leviter salire,
Ditescit et pauperes, claudos facit ire,
Mutis dat eloquium et surdis audire.

Ultimo capitulo diligam tabernam:
Illam nullo tempore sprevi neque spernam,
Donec Bacchi milites venientes audiam,
Cantantes pro ebriis pulchram canti[c]lenam.

Adiuva nos, dulcissime Bache, ut haustum boni vini gustare digni efficiamur.
O valde potens et fortissime Bache, qui assiduis potationibus multorum capita
dolere fecisti, concede propitius ut nos qui seratina potatione gravamur,
matutina repotatione sanitatem recuperare valeamus. Per eundem Bachum qui
bibit et potat per pocula poculorum etc.

"Meum est propositum" (adapted from the "Archpoet's Confession"): Walther, *Initia*,
no. 10989   "Vini mirabilia": Walther, *Initia*, no. 20363

Fragments of Drinkers' Masses: Translations

1

Hail, color of clear wine,
Hail, savor without equal,
May your power deem us worthy
    To be merry.

O how aromatic in fragrance!
O how delightful in color!
O how soothing in the mouth,
    Sweet chain of the tongue.

O how happy the creation
Which the pure vine brought forth,
Let every table be secure
    In your presence.

Happy stomach which you enter,
Happy throat which you wet,
Happy mouth which you bathe,
    O blessed lips.

Therefore let's praise wine together,
Let us exalt drinkers,

We will confound the nondrinkers,
World without end.

May he live eternally who gives us Falernian wine.

God, who hast made the heads of many to throb this present day not through the strength of the wine or through our fortitude, grant that those whose heads are afflicted by the evening's wine may be reinvigorated by their morning dose. Through the cup and Bacchus; may he deign to bring us to drunkenness. Amen.

2

A very useful exhortation to the drink
Whoever wants to be a good brother,
Let him drink once, twice, thrice, four times,
Let him drink once and a second time
Until nothing remains in the bottom.
Let the lady drink, let the lord drink,
Let no one be late for the drinking.
For the king, drink wine lawlessly,
For the pope, drink wine without water.
This is the drinking faith,
Sole hope of the companions.
Who will not drink well
Cannot be a worthy brother.
May Rhenian wine grant us divine aid.

Versicle.
Collect.
Let us pray. God who hast made the heads of many to throb through an abundance of wine, grant, we entreat, that those who are afflicted by the evening drink may be revived by the morning refreshment. Through Bacchus our Lord etc. Straw.

Let us pray. God who hast made the heads of men to spin through the abundance and power of wine and of beer, and who hast softened the hard bones of the Thebans, grant us virtue and strength, that he who is afflicted by drink in the evening may be cured by drinking again the next day.

The sequence of wine.

Good wine with savor
May the abbot drink with the prior,
And the monastery drinks worse
   With sadness.

Happy is he who planted you
And who named you wine.
Through you divine power
   Fills the world.

Hail, happy creation
Which the pure vine brought forth!
May every table be delightful
   In your presence.

O how pleasing in color!
O how aromatic in fragrance!
O how delectable in the mouth,
   Bestowing eloquence.

Happy stomach which you enter,
Happy mouth which you wet,
Happy is he whom you fill,
   And blessed lips.

Hail, color of clear wine,
Hail, flavor without equal,
May your power deem us worthy
   To be drunken.

May a devoted throng of monks,
All the world, every cleric,
Drink a drink to his peers,
   Now and forever.

Therefore let's praise wine together,
Let us exalt drinkers,
Let us confound nondrinkers
   To infernal torment.

Our Father. Our drink who art in goblet, glorified be thy name. Thy power come on the stairs as in the glass. Give us and our fellow drinkers this day our bread baked and white. And lead us not into the bad tavern, but deliver us from it forever. Straw.

The act of thanksgiving

Thanks to thee, O Christ,
Who fillest us abundantly
With the goods of the peasants
Against their will.

3

A certain extraordinary drinker
Recites these verses in praise of Bacchus
It is my intention to die in the tavern
And wine will be near the mouth of the thirsty
So that when the chorus of drunkards comes, they will say,
"God be merciful to this drinker."

Celebrated drinkers are always kindly,
The old ones, like the young ones, from eternal fire.
The peasants are tormented so that they'll be more worthy
To have a taste, so they'll deserve a drink of good wine.

In to the guests is brought masculine, feminine, neuter wine.
The masculine is distasteful, the feminine pleasing,
But in the neuter gender wine is delightful:
It makes clerics speak the best Latin.

The miracles of wine
The miracles of wine I shall not overlook:
Wine makes old women leap lightly
And enriches paupers, makes the lame walk,
Gives eloquence to the dumb and hearing to the deaf.

In the last chapter, I shall love the tavern:
At no time have I spurned it, nor shall I
Until I hear the soldiers of Bacchus coming,

Singing a lovely hymn for the drunkards.

Help us, O Bacchus most sweet, that we may be made worthy to taste a draught of good wine.

O very powerful and most steadfast Bacchus, who hast made the heads of many to throb through continuous drinking, grant us most favorably that we who are weighed down by the evening's drinking may regain our health in the drink of the morning. Through Bacchus who drinks and imbibes, cups without end, etc.

13. *Fratres mei dilectissimi*

Manuscript: Hamburg, Staats- und Universitätsbibliothek MS Petri 22, fols. 259v–260r. a. 1435. Not previously edited.

Fratres mei dilectissimi,	
quod vobis pigrum est, michi autem	Phil 3.1
necessarium.	
Ait enim Scriptura:	
"Pane et aqua vita beata."	cf. Sir 29.28
Unde Salustius:	
"Si videris fratrem tuum esurientem,	cf. Prv 25.21; Rm 12.20; Mt 18.8
erue sibi oculum,	cf. Mt 5.30; Nm 16.14; Mt 18.9
et si perseveraverit,	Lc 11.8
erue sibi et reliquum.	
Quicumque ita fecerit,	
legem implebit."	Rm 13.8
Unde Virgilius in Canticis:	
"Si esurierit amicus tuus, appone sibi	Prv 25.21; cf. Rm 12.20
lapides; si sitit, sal et cineres.	
In hiis duobus mandatis tota lex perit et	Mt 22.40
prophete."	
Unde Oracius:	
"Qui facit hec, morietur aeternum."	cf. Jo 11.26
Sed quid plura?	
Iudas qui cognominatur Barsabas	Act 15.22
ait servo suo:	
"Amice, habesne quod manducetur?"	Lc 24.41
Qui ait: "Domine, ecce duo gladii hic	Lc 22.38
et quinque lapides.	
Sed hec quid inter tantos?"	Jo 6.9
Deinde navigantes	
super arborem sicomorum	Lc 19.4
traxerunt rethe ad terram plenum mag-	Jo 21.11
nis	
lapidibus et centum quadratis rusticis.	
Et cum	
tanti essent, non est scissum rethe.	
Et cum surrexisset ventus,	cf. Ps 106.25

sederunt	
ut calefacerent se ad glaciem	Mc 14.54
et esca[.] erat.	cf. Mt 3.4
Venit enim	
Nabuzardem princeps	4 Rg 25.8
totorum	
et dedit uni ex eis alapam, dicens:	Jo 19.3; cf. Jo 18.22
"Amice, quomodo huc intrasti non habens	Mt 22.12
vestem nuptialem?"	
Qui ait: "Domine,	
unde me nosti?"	Jo 1.48
Dicit ei Nathanael:	Jo 1.48
"Unde venis,	
Bathuel?"	Gn 22.23
Respondit ei Samuel:	
"Redde rationem villicationis tue.	Lc 16.2
Non enim heres erit filius ancille cum filio	Gal 4.30; cf. Gn 21.10
libere."	
Tunc Herodes clam vocatis magis.	Mt 2.7
Querunt discipuli eius, dicentes:	
"Vox quidem, vox Iacob, sed manus sunt Esau."	Gn 27.22
Et qui missi fuerant, erant ex Phariseis.	Jo 1.24
At illi nichil horum intellexerunt.	Lc 18.34
Hec autem eo cogitante	Mt 1.20
nuntiaverunt ei quod filius eius viveret.	Jo 4.51
Et postulans pugillarem scripsit, dicens:	Lc 1.63
"Non novi hominem."	Mt 26.72
Litigabant ergo Iudei, dicentes:	Jo 6.53
"Vinum non habent."	Jo 2.3
Et ceciderunt [..] cathene de manibus eius.	Act 12.7
Cumque intueretur in celum euntem illum,	Act 1.10
ecce duo Magi venerunt Iherosolimam, dicentes:	Mt 2.1
"Saule, Saule, quid me persequeris?"	Act 9.4, 22.7, 26.14

Respondens autem centurio ait:	Mt 8.8
"Vade ad natatoria Siloe	Jo 9.11
et non vocaberis ultra Iacob, sed Israhel	Gn 35.10
erit nomen tuum."	
Dixit autem Maria ad angelum:	Lc 1.34
"Vado piscari.	Jo 21.3
Modicum et non videbitis me.	Jo 16.16
Ecce creditor venit ut tollat filios meos	4 Rg 4.1
ad	
serviendum sibi."	
Estimabat autem se visum videre.	Act 12.9
Igitur	
qui quererant,	Mt 2.20; Ex 4.19, etc.
murmurabant, dicentes:	Lc 19.7, etc.
"Mulier, magna est fides tua.	Mt 15.28
Mitte gladium tuum in vaginam.	Jo 18.11
Tu autem et filii tui venite de reliquo."	
Et factum est. Dum	
mutuo loquerentur, ecce, sompniator	Gn 37.19
venit,	
et que parate erant, intraverunt cum eo	Mt 25.10
ad nuptias.	
Egressus autem Sathan a facie domini.	Jb 2.7, 1.12
Tunc surrexerunt omnes virgines ille,	Mt 25.7
dicentes:	
"Quid hic statis tota die ociosi?"	Mt 20.6
Qui responderunt:	
"Mulier nefas, quid petis?	cf. Est 5.6; Jo 20.15
Tolle grabatum tuum	Jo 5.8
usquequo ebria eris:	1 Sm 1.14
vade, Anania, et quere Saulum,	cf. Act 9.10–11
et tibi dabo gentes heriditatem tuam."	Ps 2.8
Qui ait:	
"Domine, Babilon non vidi et lacum	Dn 14.34
nescio.	
Sed mitte Lazarum ut intinguat ex-	Lc 16.24
tremum digiti	
sui in aqua ut refrigerat lingwam	
meam."	

Qui comederunt Iacob et locum eius desolaverunt.	Ps 78.7
Cumque sublevasset oculos eius	Jo 6.5
viso Petro resedit.	Act 9.40
Cecus autem clamabat, dicens:	cf. Mt 9.27, 20.30
"In Belzebut principe demoniorum eicit demonia."	Lc 11.15; Mt 9.34, 12.24
Et respondens dixit: "Nequaquam; sed vocabatur	Lc 1.60
Iohannes."	
Et factus est repente de celo sonus.	Act 2.2
Et adduxerant azinam et pullum, filium subiugalis.	Mt 21.5, 7
Et impleverunt ambas naviculas ut pene mergerentur.	Lc 5.7
Porro in lacu erant leones septem.	Dn 14.31
Et no⟨n⟩ erat eis infans eo quod Elizabeth	Lc 1.7
erat sterilis.	
Extrahentes autem eum de lacu,	cf. Jer 38.13
optulerunt ei partem piscis assi et favum mellis.	Lc 24.42
Stans autem publicanus orabat,	cf. Lc 24.42
dicens:	
"Assatum est. Iam versa et manduca.	
Date michi de piscibus quos prendidistis."	Jo 21.10
Indignatus Naaman dixit:	cf. 4 Rg 5.17
"Vade, Sathanas."	Mt 4.10
Et illi optulerunt ei denarium.	Mt 22.19
Comedit ergo et bibit	3 Rg 19.6
et amplius non vidit.	Act 8.39; cf. 4 Rg 2.12
Qui	
in se reversus dixit:	Lc 15.17
"Comedite et bibite et inebriamini	Ct 5.1
ut filii lucis sitis,"	Jo 12.36
dicit dominus.	

Fratres mei dilectissimi: Translation

My most dearly beloved brothers, that which to you is wearisome is nevertheless necessary to me. For Scripture says: "By bread and water is life blessed." Whence Salust: "If thou see thy brother hungry, pluck out his eye, and if he shall continue, pluck out the other from him also. Whosoever does so fulfills the law." Whence Virgil in the Songs: "If thy friend be hungry, give him stones; if he thirst, salt and ashes. On these two commandments perisheth the whole law and the prophets." Whence Horace: "He who doeth these things shall die for ever." But what further? Judas, who was surnamed Barsabas, said to his servant: "Friend, have you anything to eat?" He said: "Lord, behold, here are two swords and five stones. But what are these among so many?" Then, as they were sailing upon a sycamore tree, they drew the net to land, full of great stones and a hundred sturdy peasants. And although there were so many, the net was not broken. And when the wind had risen, they sat, that they might warm themselves at the ice, and that was food. But Nabuzardan, the leader of all peoples, came and gave a blow to one of them, saying: "Friend, how camest thou hither not having a wedding garment?" Who said: "Lord, whence knowest thou me?" Nathaniel saith to him: "Whence comest thou, Bathuel?" Samuel answered him: "Give an account of thy stewardship. For the son of the bondswoman shall not be heir with the son of the free woman." Then Herod privately calling the wise men [*sic*]. His disciples inquired, saying: "The voice indeed is the voice of Jacob, but the hands are the hands of Esau." And they that were sent were of the Pharisees. But they understood none of these things. But while he thought on these things, they brought word to him that his son lived. And demanding a writing table, he wrote, saying: "I know not the man." The Jews quarreled, therefore, saying: "They have no wine." And the chains fell [. . .] off from his hands. And while they were watching him going up to heaven, behold, there came two wise men to Jerusalem, saying: "Saul, Saul, why persecutest thou me?" And the centurion, making answer, said: "Go to the pool of Siloe and thou shall not be called any more Jacob, but Israel shall be thy name." And Mary said to the angel: "I go a-fishing. A little while, and you shall not see me. Behold the creditor is come to take away my sons to serve him." But he thought he saw a vision. Therefore they that sought murmured, saying: "O woman, great is thy faith. Put up thy sword into the sheath [*vaginam*]. But come, thou and thy sons, away from the rest." And it was done. While they spoke to one another, behold, the dreamer cometh, and they that were ready went in with him to the marriage. But Satan went forth from the presence of the Lord. Then all those virgins arose, saying: "Why stand you here all the day idle?" They answered: "Evil woman, what seekest thou? Take up thy bed till thou art drunk. Go, Ananias, and seek Saul, and I will give thee the Gentiles for thy inheritance." Who said: "Lord, I never saw Babylon, nor do I know the den. But send Lazarus, that he may dip the tip of his finger in water to cool my tongue." Who have devoured Jacob, and have laid waste his place. And when he had lifted up his eyes, seeing Peter, he sat up. But a blind man was crying out, saying: "He casteth out devils by Beelzebub, the prince of devils." And he, answering, said: "Not so, but he shall be called John." And suddenly there came a sound from heaven. And they brought an ass and a colt, the foal of her that is used to the yoke. And they filled both the ships so that they were almost sinking. And in the den there were seven lions. And they had no son, for Elizabeth was barren. But drawing him out of the den, they offered him a piece of a broiled fish and a honeycomb. But there stood a publican who was praying, saying: "It is cooked. Now turn and eat. Bring me of the fishes which you have caught." Offended, Naman said: "Begone, Satan." And they offered him a penny. Therefore he ate and drank and he saw no more. Who, returning to himself, said: "Eat and drink and be inebriated that you may be the children of the light," saith the Lord.

14. *Sermo sententiosissimus*

Manuscript: Venice, Bibliotheca Nazionale Marciana MS it.XI.66, fol. 120rv. s. xv. Not previously edited.

Sermo sententiosissimus inclusione dignissimus domini Maphille cathecumini ordinis spalentrinorum contra febrenses.

Ex nihilo nihil fit, et nihil inde venit.	
Papa Rabani capitulo nullo, folio corrupto.	
Patres et fratres mei, nolo vos ignorare	
de verbo quod abbreviatum est.	cf. Rm 9.28
Licet nobis pigrum sit, mihi autem necessarium.	Phil 3.1
Ait enim Scriptura:	
"Lapis et terra vita beata."	cf. Sir 29.28
Sed quia nihil mihi conscius sum, nihil inde venit.	1 Cor 4.4
Nihil tuleritis,	
nihil mihi deest.	cf. Ps 22.1; 1 Cor 1.7; Tit 3.13
In curia Romana legitur de Floreno, quia sine ipso factum est nihil.	Jo 1.3
Sine quo nihil validum, nihil sanctum, sicut legitur in Vitis Patrum.	
Unde Galienus in cronica sua super Joannem ad Ephesios scribens ait:	
"Si videris fratrem tuum necessitatem habere, erue sibi oculum.	1 Jo 3.17
Et si perseveraverit [pulsans *crossed out*] usque infinem pulsans, aufer et reliquum.	Lc 11.8 (variant); cf. Acts 12.16
Quicumque ista fecerit, legem implebit."	Gal 6.2

Unde Rabanus in Actibus Apostolorum concedens ait:

"Si esurierit inimicus tuus, appone   Rm 12.20; Prv 25.21
ei lignum et lapidem.

Si sitit, appones ei cinerem et sal.

In his duobus mandatis tota lex pen-   Mt 22.40
det et prophete.

Sed quid multitudine maius?

Si pes tuus scandalizat te, abscinde   cf. Mt 5.29, 18.9; Mc 9.46
eum et proiice abs te."

At ille dixit: "Domine, non tantum   Jo 13.9
pedes meos, sed et

manus et caput."

Et ecce Judas Machabeus,   2 Mcc 5.27

qui cognominabatur Cayphas,   Mt 26.3

ait ad servum suum:

"Habetis aliquid quod manducetur?"   Lc 24.41

At illi obtulerunt ei paraliticum   Mt 9.2

iacentem in lecto, dicentes:

"Ecce duo gladii hic."   Lc 22.38

Manducaverunt ergo et saturati sunt.   Mc 8.8

Veniente autem sponso   cf. Mt 25.10

venit quidam Hyeroboan nomine, et

dedit ei alapam,   Jo 19.3; cf. Jo 18.22

dicens:

"Amice, ad quid venisti?"   Mt 26.50

Dicit ei Nicodemus: "Quomodo pos-   Jo 3.9
sunt hec fieri?

Numquid custos fratris mei sum   Gn 4.9
ego?"

Dicit enim ei Natanael: Jo 1.46

"Redde rationem vilicationis tue.   Lc 16.2

Non enim erit heres filius ancille   Gn 21.10; Gal 4.30
cum filio libere."

At ille dixit centurioni:

"Mentiris, quia filius tuus mortuus   3 Rg 3.22
est. Meus autem

vivit."

Et qui missi fuerant erant ex Pha- riseis.	Jo 1.24
Piscatores autem ascendebant et la- vabant retia sua	Lc 5.2
super montes Armenie.	Gn 8.4
Et nihil horum intelexerunt.	Lc 18.34
Hoc autem eo cogitante	
servi eius occurrerunt et dixerunt	cf. Jo 4.51
ei quod filius suus viveret.	cf. Jo 4.50
Et postulans pugilarem scripsit, dicens: "Johannes	Lc 1.63
est nomen eius."	
Et ceciderunt cathene de manibus eius.	Act 12.7
Et velum templi s⟨c⟩issum est	Mt 27.51; Mc 15.38; Lc 23.45
a planta pedis usque ad verticem montis.	
Transeuntes autem primam et secun- dam custodiam,	Act 12.10
invenit eum orantem et dicentem:	
"Quid hic statis tota die ociosi?"	Mt 20.6
At ille dixit:	
"Mitte te deorsum."	Mt 4.6
Et ille respondit:	
"Vado piscari."	Jo 21.3
Exclamante autem voce sua,	
venerunt due mulieres ad regem Sa- lomonem.	3 Rg 3.16
Interogaverunt eum: "Tu quis es?"	Jo 1.19; cf. Mt 22.23; Lc 20.27
Et accusaverunt eum in multis,	Mc 15.3
maxime autem ad domesticos fidei.	Gal 6.10
Videns autem quia placeret Judeis,	Act 12.3
ascendit in arborem sicomorum.	Lc 19.4
Et cum cepisset mergi, clamavit voce magna, dicens:	Mt 14.30
"Sicio."	Jo 19.28
Et iterum responderunt: "Jam hos- tium meum clausum	Lc 11.7

est,

et filii mei non comparent.	Gn 37.30
Ite pocius ad vendentes et emite vobis." Dum	Mt 25.9–10

autem irent emere, venit

regina austri; a finibus illis egressa est	Mt 12.42
aurire aquam.	cf. Gn 24.11, 13, 43; Ex 2.16; 1 Sm 9.11
Erat enim pulcra valde decoraque facie	1 Sm 16.12; 3 Rg 1.4; Est 2.7
super quam nullus hominum con-cubuerat	cf. Mc 11.2; Lc 19.30
nisi illa centum quadraginta quattuor millia	Apc 7.4; Apc 14.1, 3
ex omni tribu que sub celo est.	Act 2.5
Et osculans eum ait:	cf. Mt 26.49; Mc 14.45
"Quid adhuc egemus testibus?"	Mt 26.65
Et facti sunt amici Herode et Pilatus in illa die.	Lc 23.12
Intravit autem domum cuiusdam principis Phariseorum	Lc 14.1

sabbato manducare panem.

Et invenit eum dormientem	Mt 26.40, 43; Mc 14.37, 40

prae tristicia

percussoque latere eius excitavit, dicens:	Act 12.7
"Surge et comede.	Act 10.13, 12.7
Grandis enim tibi restat via."	3 Rg 19.7
Et inclinans caput suum,	cf. Jo 19.30
vidit subcinericium panem	cf. Gn 18.6; Ex 12.39; Jdc 7.13; 3 Rg 19.6

et ait:

"Quid hoc inter tantos?	Jo 6.9

Multum

enim epulari et gaudere oportet:	Lc 15.32
Filius meus perierat et inventus est!"	Lc 15.24

Comedit ergo et bibit,

et factum est in ore eius tamquam cera liquescens	Ez 3.3; cf. Apc 10.9
in medio ventris eius.	
Et ambulavit in fortitudine cibi illius quadraginta	3 Rg 19.8
diebus et quadraginta noctibus	
ab hora sexta usque ad horam nonam.	Mt 27.45; Mc 15.33; Lc 23.44
Clamavit voce magna, dicens:	Mc 15.34; cf. Mt 27.46
"Saule, Saule, quid me persequeris?"	Act 9.4, 22.7, 26.14
At ille dixit: "Patientiam habe in me et ego omnia	Mt 18.26
reddam tibi."	
Et dixit ei in visu: "Ananias,	Act 9.10
numquid canis ego sum, quia venis ad me cum	1 Sm 17.43
baculo?"	
Non enim coutuntur Iudei cum Samaritanis.	Jo 4.9
Et dixit ad eum: "Quid ergo fecisti nobis sic?	Lc 2.48
Ego et pater tuus dolentes quaerebamus te.	Lc 2.48
Non enim ex dernario convenisti mecum?"	Mt 20.13
Et vox de terra audita est,	cf. Ct 2.12; Mt 2.18
dicens:	
"Nihil tibi et iusto illi.	
Tolle grabatum tuum et ambula	Jo 5.8
quia maledicta terra quae non novit legem."	Jo 7.49
Unde Galienus in Topicis:	
"Legem pone mihi, domine.	
Nonne duo passeres veneunt di[s]pondio?"	Lc 12.6
Et iterum:	
"Quid de vestimento solliciti estis?"	Mt 6.28
Extraxerunt autem illum de cisterno	Gn 37.28

per capillos capitis sui,
sicut dicit Lepoches in Paradoxis:
"Eripe me de luto ut non intingar."   Ps 68.15
Apertisque oculis nihil videbat. Ad   Act 9.8
    manus autem illum
trahentes,
introduxerunt eum in lacum leonum.   Dan 6.16
Et cepit pulmentum suum deditque   cf. Gn 27.17–18
    puero suo, dicens:
"Vade te, amplius noli peccare."   Jo 8.11, 5.14
Et amplius non vidit eum eunuchus.
Et sic in nihilum reditum est,
quid nihil nobis concedat
qui percussit primogenita Agypti ab   Ex 12.12; cf. Ex 12.29, 13.15; Nm
    homine   3.13, 8.17
usque ad pecus.
Dixi.

Sermo sententiossimus: Translation

A most succinct sermon, most worthy of inclusion, of the Lord Maphilla, a catechumen of the order of *spalentrini,* against the *febrenses.*

Nothing is made from nothing, and therefore nothing comes. The pope, in no chapter of Hrabanus, on a corrupt page. My fathers and brothers, I do not wish you to be ignorant about the word which has been cut short. Though it may be wearisome to you, it is, however, necessary to me. For Scripture says: "The blessed life is stone and earth." For since I am conscious of nothing on my part, nothing comes of it. You have borne nothing, nothing is wanting to me. In the Roman curia we read of Florenus, because without him nothing is made. Without whom nothing is valid, nothing holy, as it is read in the Lives of the Fathers. From which Galienus in his chronicle on John, writing to the Ephesians, said: "If thou see thy brother in need, pluck out his eye. And if he shall continue knocking till the end, take away the other also. Whosoever does these things shall fulfill the law." Whence Hrabanus in the Acts of the Apostles, agreeing, said: "If thy enemy be hungry, give him wood and a stone. If he thirst, thou givest him ashes and salt. On these two commandments dependeth the whole law and the prophets. But what is greater than a multitude? If thy foot scandalize thee, cut it off and cast it from thee." And he said: "Lord, not only my feet, but also my hands and head." And behold Judas Machabeus, who was called Caiphas, said to his servant: "Have you anything to eat?" And they brought to him one sick of the palsy lying in a bed, saying: "Behold, here are two swords." Therefore they did eat and were filled. But when the bridegroom came, there came a certain one named Jeroboam, and he gave him a blow, saying: "Friend, whereto art thou come?" Nicodemus saith to him: "How can these things be done? Am I my brother's keeper?" And Nathaniel saith to him: "Give an account of thy stewardship. For the son of the bondwoman shall not be heir with the son of the free woman." But he said to the centurion: "It is not as thou sayest, because thy son is dead, but mine is alive." And they that were sent were of the Pharisees. But the fishermen were gone out of them and were washing their nets upon the mountains of Armenia. And they understood none of these things. But while he was thinking this, his servants met him and told him that his son lived. And demanding a writing table, he wrote, saying: "John is his name." And the chains fell off from his hands. And the veil of the temple was rent from the sole of the foot even unto the head of the mountain. And passing through the first and second ward, he found him praying and saying: "Why stand you here all the day idle?" But he said: "Cast thyself down." And he answered: "I go a-fishing." But, with his voice crying out, there came two women to king Solomon. They asked him: "Who art thou?" And they accused him in many things, but especially to those who are of the household of the faith. And seeing that it pleased the Jews, he climbed up into a sycamore tree. And when he had begun to sink, he cried out with a loud voice, saying: "I thirst." And they responded a second time: "My door is now shut, and my sons do not appear. But go ye rather to them that sell and buy for yourselves." Now whilst they went to buy, the queen of the south came; she was come out from the ends of the earth to draw water. Now she was exceeding fair and of a comely face, upon whom no man hath yet lain except those hundred and forty-four thousand out of every nation under heaven. And kissing him, she said: "What further need have we of witnesses?" And Herod and Pilate were made friends that same day. But he went into the house of one of the chiefs of the Pharisees, on the Sabbath day, to eat bread. And he found him asleep on account of sadness, and striking his side, he raised him up, saying: "Arise and eat. For thou hast yet a great way to go." And bowing his head, he saw a hearth cake and said: "What is this among so many? For it is fit to make merry and be glad. My son was lost and is found!" Therefore he ate and drank, and in his mouth it was sweet as honey melting in the midst of his stomach. And he walked in the strength of that food forty days and forty nights, from the sixth hour until the ninth hour. He cried with a loud voice, saying: "Saul, Saul, why persecutest thou me?" But he said: "Have patience with me and I will pay thee all." And he said to him in a vision: "Ananias, am I a dog, that thou comest to me with a staff?" For the Jews do not communicate with the Samaritans. And he said to him: "Why hast thou done so to us? Thy father and I have sought thee sorrowing. Didst thou not agree with me for a penny?" And a voice was heard from the earth, saying: "It is nothing for thee and the just one. Take up thy bed and walk, because this earth, that knoweth not the law, is accursed." From which Galienus in the Topics: "Place the law in me, Lord. Are not two sparrows sold for two farthings?" And again: "For raiment why are you solicitous?" But they drew him out of the pit by the hair of his head, just as Lepoches says in the Paradoxes: "Draw me out of the mire, that I may not stick fast." And when his eyes were opened, he saw nothing. But they, leading him by the hands, cast him into the den of the lions. And he took his food and gave it to his son, saying: "Go, and now sin no more." And the eunuch saw him no more. And thus it is returned to nothing, which nothing may he grant to us, he who killed the firstborn of Egypt, both man and beast. I have spoken.

15. *Sermo de nihil*

Manuscript: Munich, Bayerische Staatsbibliothek MS clm. 10571, fols. 196v–201r. a. 1575. Previously edited in W. Wattenbach, "Geistliche Scherze des Mittelalters I," *Anzeiger für Kunde der deutschen Vorzeit,* N. F. 14 (1867): cols. 342–44. Biblical references are original to this edition.

Sermo alius plurimum utilis ex diversis collectus. De Nihil.

Fratres,	
ex nihilo nihil fit.	cf. Sap 2.2
Nolumus enim vos ignorare de dormientibus,	1 Th 4.13
et de verbo quod abbreviatum est,	cf. Rm 9.28
licet onerosum mihi, vobis autem pernecessarium.	Phil 3.1
Ait enim Scriptura:	
"Quid superbis terra et cinis?"	Sir 10.9
Sed	
nihil mihi conscius sum.	1 Cor 4.4
Et quid nihil?	
Nihil enim habens, nihil conferre potest.	cf. Mt 13.12, 25.29; Mc 4.25; Lc 8.18, 19.26
Nihil ergo tuleritis in via.	cf. 1 Tm 6.7
Si enim nihil tuleritis,	
nihil vobis deerit.	cf. Ps 22.1; 1 Cor 1.7; Tit 3.13
Ubi enim nihil est interius, nihil fit exterius.	
Nam in curia Romana legitur de Floreno,	
quod sine ipso factum est nihil.	Jo 1.3
Et iterum, sine quo nihil est validum, nihil	
sanctum, ut legitur in Vitis Patrum. Unde	
Galienus in canonica sua super Lucam	
scribens ait:	
"Si esurit inimicus tuus,	Prv 25.21; Rm 12.20

erue ei oculum.	Mt 18.9
Et si perseveraverit pulsans,	Lc 11.8
erue ei et alterum.	cf. Mt 5.39
Qui enim ista fecerit,	
legem adimplevit."	Rm 13.8
Cui Rabanus concordans Extra de Largitate,	
capitulo nihil, "Quicquam ulli dederis":	
"Si sitit inimicus tuus, appone ei	Rm 12.20
ligna et lapides,	cf. 1 Sm 5.11
inquiens:	
'Dic ut lapides isti panes fiant.'	Mt 4.3
Si infirmatur inimicus tuus,	cf. Rm 14.21
appone ei lapides et sal.	
So hefft he de gerichte all.	
In his duobus mandatis universa lex pendet	Mt 22.40
et prophete."	
Unde dicit Alexander in Canticis Canticorum:	
"Si vis perfectus esse,	Mt 19.21
vade et fac tu similiter."	Lc 10.37
Sed quid multis moror?	
Ecce Judas Machabeus qui dicitur Caiphas	cf. 2 Mcc 5.27; Mt 26.14
dixit ad discipulos suos:	Lc 12.22
"Habetisne aliquid quod man- ducetur?"	Lc 24.41
Et obtulerunt ei paraliticum ia- centem in lecto,	Mt 9.2
dicentes:	
"Ecce duo gladii hic	Lc 22.38
et quatuor ordines mendicantium."	Ex 28.17; cf. Ex 39.10
Manducaverunt ergo, et saturati sunt nihil.	cf. Ps 77.29; Mc 8.8
Veniente autem sponso,	
accessit Hieroboam	
et dedit ei alapam,	Jo 19.3; cf. Jo 18.22

dicens:

"Amice, ad quid venisti?"	Mt 26.50
Respondit Nicodemus: "Quomodo possunt hec fieri?	Jo 3.9
Nunquid custos fratris mei ego sum?"	Gn 4.9
Et dixit ei Nathanael:	Jo 1.46
"Redde rationem villicationis tue.	Lc 16.2
Non enim erit heres filius ancille sum filio libere."	Gal 4.30; cf. Gn 21.10
Et illa e contrario dixit: "Mentiris.	3 Rg 3.22
Filius tuus mortuus est, et meus vivit."	
Et qui missi erant, erant ex Phariseis.	Jo 1.24
Piscatores autem descenderant ut lavarent retia	Lc 5.2
sua super montes Armenie.	Gn 8.4
Et quidem horum nihil intellexerunt.	Lc 18.34
Hec autem eo cogitante,	
servi eius occurrerunt ei et dixerunt: "Filius tuus vivit."	Jo 4.51
Et postulans pugillarem, scripsit: "Joannes est	Lc 1.63
nomen eius."	
Et ceciderunt cathene de manibus eius.	Act 12.7
Et velum templi scissum est	Mt 27.51; Mc 15.38; Lc 23.45
ab homine usque ad pecus.	Ex 12.12
Transiens autem primam et secundam custodiam,	Act 12.10
venerunt due mulieres meretrices ad regem	3 Rg 3.16
Salomonem,	
et interrogaverunt eum: "Tu quis es?"	Jo 1.19; cf. Mt 22.23; Lc 20.27
Et accusaverunt eum in multis,	Mc 15.3
maxime in domesticis fidei.	Gal 6.10
Videns autem quia placeret Judeis,	Act 12.3

ascendit in arborem sicomorum.	Lc 19.4
Et cum cepisset mergi, clamabat dicens:	Mt 14.30
"Domine, salvum fac regem."	Ps 19.10
Et respondens de intus ait: "Jam os-tium	Lc 11.7
clausum est,	
et puer non comparet.	Gn 37.30
Ite potius ad vendentes et emite vobis." Cum autem	Mt 25.9–10
irent emere, venit	
regina austri a finibus illis egressa	Mt 12.42
haurire aquam.	cf. Gn 24.11, 13, 43; Ex 2.16; 1 Sm 9.11
Erat autem puella pulchra facie decoraque	1 Sm 16.12; 3 Rg 1.4; Est 2.7
aspectu,	
supra quam nullus hominum sedit, nisi	Mc 11.2; cf. Lc 19.30
centum quadraginta quatuor millia	Apc 7.4, 14.3
ex omni natione quae sub celo est.	Act 2.5
Et osculatus est eam	Gn 29.11
et dixit:	
"Quid adhuc egemus testibus?	Mt 26.65
Ipsi enim vidistis et audistis."	
Et facti sunt amici Herodes et Pil-atus in illa die.	Lc 23.12
Intrante autem eo domum cuiusdam principis	Lc 14.1
Phariseorum Sabbato manducare panem,	
invenit eos dormientes	Mt 26.40, 43; Mc 14.37, 40
prae timore,	Mt 28.4
percussoque latere Petri excitavit eum, dicens:	Act 12.7
"Non potuistis una hora vigilare mecum?	Mc 14.37
Surge velociter et comede.	Act 12.7, 10.13; 3 Rg 19.7
Grandis enim tibi restat via."	3 Rg 19.7

Et invenit subcinericium panem	cf. Gn 18.6; Ex 12.39; Jdc 7.13; 3 Rg 19.6
ad caput suum,	3 Rg 19.6
et dixit:	
"Quid hec inter tantos?	Jo 6.9
Epulari enim et gaudere oportet, quia filius meus	Lc 15.32, 24
perierat, et inventus est."	
Comedit ergo volumen istud,	cf. Ez 3.1
et factum est in ore eius tanquam cera	Ez 3.3; cf. Apc 10.9
liquescens.	
Et amaricatus est venter eius.	Apc 10.10
Ambulavitque in fortitudine cibi illius	3 Rg 19.8
quadraginta diebus et quadraginta noctibus	
ab hora sexta usque ad horam nonam.	Mt 27.45; Mc 15.33; Lc 23.44
Et circa horam nonam exclamavit voce magna,	Mt 27.46; Mc 15.34
dicens:	
"Saule, Saule, quid me persequeris?"	Act 9.4, 22.7, 26.14
Et ait: "Patientiam habe in me, et omnia tibi	Mt 18.26
reddam."	
Dixitque:	
"Nec mihi nec tibi sit puer, sed dividatur."	3 Rg 3.26
Cumque intuerentur in celum euntem illum,	Act 1.10
ecce Magi ab oriente venerunt, dicentes:	Mt 2.1–2
"Ubi enim est Abel frater tuus?"	Gn 4.9
Respondit: "Nescio.	
Numquid canis ego sum, quod venis ad me cum	1 Sm 17.43
baculo?"	

Non enim coutuntur Judei Sa-	Jo 4.9
maritanis.	
Et ille dixit ad eum:	
"Ego et pater tuus dolentes	Lc 2.48
quaerebamus te.	
Nonne ex denario diurno convenisti	Mt 20.13
mecum?	
Multa habeo vobis dicere, sed non	Jo 16.12
potestis	
portare modo.	
Quia	
si pes tuus scandalizat te, abscinde	cf. Mt 5.29, 18.9; Mc 9.46
eum et	
proiice abs te."	
Dixit autem Petrus: "Domine, non	Jo 13.9
tantum pedes,	
sed et manus et caput."	
Et percussit eum in posteriora	cf. Ps 77.66
et amputavit auriculam eius dex-	Lc 22.50; cf. Mt 26.51; Mc 14.47
tram.	
Dixitque:	
"Amice, non facio tibi iniuriam.	Mt 20.13
Tolle quod tuum est, et vade	Mt 20.14
in pace."	
Scriptum est enim:	
"Qui petit, accipit, et qui querit, in-	Mt 7.7; Lc 11.9
venit, et	
pulsanti aperietur."	
Et adduxerunt mulierem in adulterio	Jo 8.3
deprehensam, et statuerunt eam in	
medio,	
dictumque est eis: "Quoniam vidua	Mc 12.43; cf. Lc 21.3
hec pauper	
plus omnibus misit, qui miserunt in	
gazophilacium,	
maledicta enim terra	cf. Gn 3.17
quae	
non profert fructum."	cf. Lv 26.20

Ideo dicit Samuel in libro de
    Aminadab:

"Nonne duo passeres veneunt dipon-   Lc 12.6
    dio?

Et de vestimentis quid solliciti   Mt 6.28
    estis?"

Et extraxerunt eum de cisterna   Gn 37.28
per capillos

apertisque oculis nihil videbat. Ad   Act 9.8
    manus
autem trahentes introduxerunt
ad locum sanctum.

Notum autem factum est Judeis,   Act 19.17
quia

proximum erat Pascha, dies festus   Jo 6.4; cf. Jo 11.55
    Judeorum.

Querebant ergo eum   Jo 10.39

in die solemnitatis et letitie.   cf. 1 Esr 6.22; 2 Par 30.21

Et cum non invenissent eum,   cf. Gn 38.20; Mc 1.37; Jo 6.25

sciscitati sunt ubi Christus   Mt 2.4
    nasceretur,

dicentes: "Ubi est qui natus est rex   Mt 2.2
    Judeorum?"

Dixit autem Judas Machabeus   2 Mcc 5.27

cui nomen Cleophas: Lc 24.18

"Tu solus peregrinus es in
    Hierusalem, et
hec ignoras?

Ecce locus ubi posuerent eum."   Mc 16.6

Nabuchodonozor autem genuit Mar-   cf. Mt 1.1–16
    colphum

in transmigratione Hiericho

anno primo ante diluvium.   cf. Mt 24.38

Et erat inclitus in omni domo patris   Gn 34.19
    sui.

Fratres autem eius oderant eum   Gn 37.4

quia non erat ei locus in diversorio.   Lc 2.7

Veniens autem unus eorum dixit: cf. Mt 19.16

"Villam emi."

Qui omnes dixerunt:

"Exploratores estis ut enim videretis   Gn 42.9

infirmiora terre venistis."

Et spuit in faciem eius, dicens: Dt 25.9

"Vade, et amplius noli peccare."   Jo 8.11

Et amplius eum non vidit eunuchus.   Act 8.39

Et sic in nihilum redit, quod antea

   nihil fuit.

Quod nihil omnibus nobis concedat,

qui percussit primogenita Aegipti   Ex 12.12; cf. Ex 12.29; Nm 3.13,

                                 8.17

ab aquilone et mari.   Ps 106.3

Amen.

Sermo de nihil: Translation

Another exceedingly useful sermon gathered together from diverse places. Of Nothing.

Brothers, nothing is made from nothing. We will not have you remain ignorant concerning them that are asleep; and as for the word cut short, though it may be worrisome to me, to you it is necessary. For Scripture says: "Why is earth and ashes proud?" But I am aware of nothing on my part. And why nothing? For he who has nothing can contribute nothing. Therefore you will bring nothing into the way. For if you bring nothing, you will lack nothing. For where there is nothing within, there will be nothing without. For in the Roman curia we read of Florenus that without him nothing was made. And, again, without him nothing is valid, nothing holy, as we read in the Lives of the Fathers. Whence Galienus, writing in his canons on Luke, says: "If thy enemy be hungry, pluck out his eye. And if the knocking continues, pluck out his other also. Who does these things, fulfills the law." Hrabanus, agreeing with the Decretal "On Alms-giving," in the nothing-chapter "Thou shalt give anything to any": "If thy enemy be thirsty, bring him wood and stones, saying 'Command that these stones be made bread.' If thy enemy be enfeebled, give him stones and salt. So he lifts up all the dishes. On these two commandments dependeth the whole law and the prophets." Whence saith Alexander in the Song of Songs: "If thou wilt be perfect, go thou and do in like manner." But why should I delay in these many things? Behold Judas Machabeus, who was called Caiphas, said to his disciples: "Have you anything to eat?" And they brought to him one sick of the palsy lying in bed, saying: "Behold, here are two swords and four orders of mendicants." Thereupon they ate, and they were satisfied with nothing. But when the bridegroom came, he approached Jeroboam and gave him a blow, saying: "Friend, whereto art thou come?" Nicodemus answered: "How can these things be done? Am I my brother's keeper?" And Nathanael said to him: "Give an account of thy stewardship. For the son of the bondwoman shall not be heir with the son of the free woman." And the other woman answered to the contrary: "It is not as thou sayest. Thy son is dead, and mine is alive." And they that were sent were of the Pharisees. But the fishermen were gone out of them and were washing their nets upon the mountains of Armenia. And indeed they understood none of these things. But while he was contemplating these things, his servants met him and said: "Thy son liveth." And demanding a writing table, he wrote: "John is his name." And the chains fell off from his hands. And the veil of the temple was rent, both man and beast. And passing through the first and the second ward, there came two women that were harlots to king Solomon, and they questioned him: "Who art thou?" And they accused him in many things, especially to those who are of the household of the faith. And seeing that it pleased the Jews, he climbed up into a sycamore tree. And when he had begun to sink, he cried out, saying: "Lord, save the king." And he, answering from within, said: "The door is now shut, and the boy doth not appear. Go ye rather to them that sell and buy for yourselves." But whilst they went to buy, the queen of the south came from the ends of the earth to draw water. Now she was a damsel, exceedingly fair and of a comely face, on whom no man hath yet sat, except a hundred and forty-four thousand out of every nation under heaven. And he kissed her and said: "What further need have ye of witnesses? For you yourselves have seen and heard." And Herod and Pilate were made friends that same day. And, going into the house of one of the chiefs of the Pharisees on the Sabbath day, to eat bread, he found them asleep from fear, and he, striking Peter in the side, raised him up, saying: "Could thou not wait with me one hour? Arise quickly and eat. For thou hast yet a long way to go." And he found a hearth cake at his head and said: "But what are these among so many? But it is fit that we should make merry and be glad: for my son was dead, and is found." Thereupon he ate the book, and it was like wax melting in his mouth. And his stomach was upset. And he walked in the strength of that food forty days and forty nights, from the sixth hour to the ninth hour. And about the ninth hour, he cried with a loud voice, saying: "Saul, Saul, why persecutest thou me?" And he said: "Have patience with me and I will pay thee all." And he said: "Let the boy be neither mine nor thine, but divide him." And while they were watching him going up to heaven, behold, there came wise men from the east, saying: "Where is thy brother Abel?" He answered: "I know not. Am I a dog, that thou comest to me with a staff?" For the Jews do not communicate with Samaritans. And he said to him: "Thy father and I have sought thee sorrowing. Didst thou not agree with me for one day for a penny? I have yet many things to say to you: but you cannot bear them now. Wherefore, if thy foot scandalize thee, cut it off and cast it from thee." But Peter said: "Lord, not only my feet, but also my hands and head." And he smote him on the hinder parts and cut off his right ear. And he said: "Friend, I do thee no wrong. Take what is thine and go in peace." For it is written: "He who seeks, receives, and he who asks, finds, and by knocking it is opened." And they brought a woman taken in adultery, and they set her in the middle, and it was said to them: "Since this poor widow hath cast in more than they who have cast into the treasury, cursed is the earth, which yields no fruit." Therefore Samuel saith in the Book of Aminadab: "Are not sparrows sold for two farthings? And of your raiment why are you solicitous?" And they drew him out of the pit by the hair, and when his eyes were opened, he saw nothing. But they, leading him by the hands, brought him to the holy place. And this became known to the Jews, that Pasch, the festival day of the Jews, was near at hand. Therefore they sought him on a day of solemnity and joy. And since they had not found him, they inquired where Christ should be born, saying: "Where is he that is born king of the Jews?" But Judas Machabeus, whose name was Cleophas, said: "Thou alone hast sojourned to Jerusalem, and art ignorant of these things? Behold the place where they laid him." And Nebuchadnezzar begat Marcolph in the transmigration of Jericho in the first year before the flood. And he was the greatest in all his father's house. But his brethren hated him, because there was no room for him at the inn. But one of them came and said: "I bought the farm." They all said, "You are spies, as you are come to view the weaker parts of the land." And he spit in his face, saying: "Go, and sin no more." And the eunuch saw him no more. And thus it returns to nothing, which was nothing before. Which nothing may he grant to all of us, he who killed the firstborn of Egypt by wind and sea. Amen.

16. *Lectio Danielis prophete*

Manuscript: Munich, Bayerische Staatsbibliothek MS clm. 10751, fols. 201r–204v. a. 1575. Previously edited in W. Wattenbach, "Geistliche Scherze des Mittelalters II," *Anzeiger für Kunde der deutschen Vorzeit,* N. F. 15 (1868): cols. 9–11. Biblical references are original to this edition.

Lectio Danielis prophete

Fratres,	
ex nihilo vobis timendum est,	cf. Is 41.24; cf. Sap 2.2; 2 Mcc 7.28
quoniam quidem in principio deus	Gn 1.1
plasmator hominum postquam fecit hominem,	
nolens eundem siti et inedia deperire,	
ilico creavit Cyphum et Cannam. Cyphus	Gn 1.1–2
autem erat inanis, et Canna erat vacua.	
Et spiritus potatoris ferebatur super Cannam.	Gn 1.2
Viditque potator quod vinum esset bonum,	Gn 1.12
et dixit:	
"Rorate, Cyphi, desuper, et Canna pluat mustum;	Is 45.8
aperiatur Cyphus, et inebriet potatorem."	
Ceteri omnes dicebant:	
"Vos sitientes venite ad tabernam,	Is 55.1; cf. Jo 7.37
et qui non habent panes, vendant tunicas suas et	Lc 22.36
emant gladios."	
Scriptum est enim:	
"Si esurit inimicus tuus, appone ei ferrum et	Prv 25.21; cf. Rm 12.20
lapides. Si sitit, silices da ei bibere.	
Lapis enim et sal est vita hominis.	

In his quoque duobus tota lex pendet et	Mt 22.40
prophete."	
Et Bohemi mortui sunt.	
Et occiderunt multos, et effugi ego solus,	Jb 1.15
ut nunciarem vobis,	
quia cecus natus est,	Jo 9.19–20
unde dicit Vergilius in Canticis Canticorum:	
"Si videris fratrem tuum necesse habere,	1 Jo 3.17
erue ei oculum, et proiice abs te.	Mt 18.9; cf. Mt 5.29
Et si perseveraverit pulsans,	Lc 11.8 (variant)
erue ei et alterum."	cf. Mt 5.39
Judas autem Machabeus,	2 Mcc 5.27
qui dicitur Scariot,	Mt 26.3, 14
dixit discipulis suis:	Mt 16.24
"Habetis aliquid quod manducetur?"	Lc 24.41
At illi dixerunt:	
"Domine, ecce duo gladii hic."	Lc 22.38
Ait ille: "Satis est."	
Et manducaverunt, et saturati sunt nimis.	Ps 77.29
Et ambulaverunt in fortitutine cibi illius	3 Rg 19.8
in Dothaim.	Gn 37.17
Postquam autem Alexander percussit Darium,	1 Mcc 1.1
stravit Abraham asinum suum,	2 Sm 17.23; cf. 3 Rg 2.40
et ascendit in arborem sicomorum,	Lc 19.4
et traxit rete in terram, plenum quadratis rusticis.	Jo 21.11
Piscatores autem	Lc 5.2
calefaciebant se ad glacies,	Mc 14.54
ne forte tumultus fieret in piscibus.	Mt 26.5; Mc 14.2
Petrus autem tunica succinxit se,	Jo 21.7
quia frigus erat,	Jo 18.18
dixitque:	

"Vado piscari."	Jo 21.3
Erat autem ibidem fenum multum in loco.	Jo 6.10
Rete autem eorum rumpebatur	Lc 5.6
pre multitudine piscium.	Jo 21.6
Et ait ad eum Dathan:	cf. Nm 16.12, etc.
"Unde venis, Sathan?" Qui ait: "Circuivi	Jb 1.7
terram et perambulavi eam,	
et tota domus impleta est ex odore ung⟨u⟩enti,	Jo 12.3
incipiens a Galilea usque huc."	Lc 23.5
Hieroboam vero dixit servo suo:	3 Rg 14.2
"Amice, quomodo huc intrasti non habens	Mt 22.12
ventrem nuptialem?"	
At ille dedit ei alapam,	Jo 19.3; cf. Jo 18.22
dicens: "Domine,	
unde me nosti?"	Jo 1.48
Saul enim querebat David regem	1 Sm 23.14
et amputavit auriculam eius dextram	Lc 22.50; cf. Mt 26.51; Mc 14.47
et pedem sinistrum,	cf. Apc 10.2
et ait:	
"Amice, non facio tibi iniuriam.	Mt 20.13
Tolle quod tuum est, et vade."	Mt 20.14
At ille gaudens abiit, et	
narravit omnibus quanta fecisset sibi bona.	cf. Lc 8.39
Et laqueo se suspendit.	Mt 27.5
Laban autem genuit Nabuchodonozor	cf. Mt 1.1–16
in transmigratione Babilonis.	Mt 1.11
Dixitque Nathan:	
"Domine, non sum dignus ut intres coquinam	Mt 8.8; cf. Lc 7.6
meam,	
sed tantum dic verbo, et assabitur gallus meus."	Mt 8.8
Et statim auca cantavit.	cf. Mt 26.74; Mc 14.72; Lc 22.60

Tunc Beelzebub

erat eiiciens demonium, et illud erat   Lc 11.14
    mutum.

Et illi non poterant resistere   Act 6.10
    sapientie et spiritui

qui loquebatur.

Videntes autem discipuli quod multa   Gn 6.5
    esset malitia

super terram,

dixerunt ei:

"Videamus an Helias veniat ad   Mc 15.36; cf. Mt 27.49
    deponendum eum."

Cumque irent,

invenerunt Symonem quendam   Lc 23.26
    venientem de via,

et sciscitati sunt ab eo ubi Christus   Mt 2.4
    nasceretur.

At ille ait:

"Viam trium dierum ibimus in   Ex 5.3
    solitudine."

Non enim sciebat quid loqueretur.   Mc 9.5

Euntes itaque in civitatem que   Lc 7.11
    vocatur Naim,

et factum est mane et vespere una   Gn 1.5, 8, 13, 19, etc.
    Sabbatorum.

Venit Jesus ianuis clausis,   Jo 20.26

ubi erant discipuli clausi.   Jo 20.19

Pre timore autem eius exterriti sunt   Mt 28.4
    custodes,

ita ut preses miraretur vehementer.   Mt 27.14

Jesus autem videns malitiam eorum   cf. Gn 6.5

dixit per similitudinem: Lc 8.4

"Nunquid non dixi vobis: nolite   Gn 42.22
    peccare in

puerum?

Scio enim quod Jesum queritis.   Mt 28.5

Alleluia."

Accedens autem unus ex discipulis   Mt 19.16; Jo 6.8, 12.4
    eius dixit:

"Magister, scimus quia verax es.	Mt 22.16; cf. Mc 12.14
Dic ergo ut lapides isti panes fiant."	Mt 4.3
Respondens huic ait:	
"Quid mihi et tibi est, mulier?	Jo 2.4
Nescis quia in his que patris mei	Lc 2.49
sunt oportet me	
esse?	
Dico autem vobis quod a modo non	Lc 13.35; cf. Jo 16.17
videbitis me	
donec ponam inimicos meos	Ps 109.1
scabellum pedum	
meorum."	
Pharisei autem inierunt consilium	Mt 22.15, 27.1
adversus Jesum, dicentes:	
"Eamus in Dothaim,	Gn 37.17
sed non in die festo."	Mt 26.5; Mc 14.2
Perrexerunt ergo	
et invenerunt sicut predixerat eis	Lc 22.13
Jesus,	
et paraverunt Pascha.	Mc 14.16; Lc 22.13; Mt 26.19
Thomas igitur, unus ex illis qui	Jo 20.24; cf. Jo 21.2
dicitur Bibulus,	
non erat cum eis	
quando	
manducaverunt Pascha.	Jo 18.28
Venit ergo Thomas, et ait:	
"Jeiuno bis in Sabbato	Lc 18.12
et ter in sexta feria comedo."	
At illi dixerunt: "Blasphemat."	Mt 9.3; cf. Mt 26.65
Quid vobis videtur?	
Tunc ait rex:	
"Ligatis pedibus et non manibus,	cf. Mt 22.13
mittite eum in	
cellarium iuxta lagenam plenam."	
Et erit potus posterior maior priori.	cf. Lc 9.48
Tu autem potum fac nos infundere	
totum, ut fratres	
nostri omnes de potu inebrientur.	
Amen.	

Lectio Danielis prophete: Translation

The Reading of the Prophet Daniel

Brothers, you should be afraid of nothing, since indeed in the beginning God the creator of men, after he made man, not wanting him to perish from thirst and fasting, straightaway created the Goblet and the Cup. But the Goblet was empty, and the Cup was a void. And the spirit of the drinker moved over the Cup. And the drinker saw that the wine was good, and said: "Drop down dew, ye Goblets, from above, and let the Cup rain must; let the Goblet be opened, and make the drinker drunk." All the rest were saying: "All you that thirst, come to the tavern, and they that have not bread, let them sell their coats and buy swords." For it is written: "If thy enemy be hungry, give him iron and stones. If he thirst, give him stones to drink. For the life of man is stone and salt. And on these two commandments dependeth the whole law and the prophets." And the Bohemians died. And they slew many, and I alone escaped to tell you, because he was born blind, whence Virgil saith in the Song of Songs: "If thou seest thy brother in need, pluck his eye from him, and cast it from thee. And if the knocking continues, pluck out the other from him also." Judas Machabeus, moreover, who was called Escariot, said to his disciples: "Have you anything to eat?" And they said: "Lord, behold, here are two swords." And he said: "It is enough." And they did eat, and were filled exceedingly. And they walked in the strength of that food in Dothain. Moreover, after Alexander overthrew Darius, Abraham saddled his ass, and climbed up into a sycamore tree, and drew the net to land, full of sturdy peasants. The fishermen, moreover, warmed themselves at the ice, lest perhaps there should be a tumult among the fish. But Peter girt himself with his coat, because it was cold, and said: "I go a-fishing." There was, moreover, much grass in the place. But their nets broke before the multitude of fishes. And Dathan said to him: "Whence comest thou, Satan?" He said: "I have gone around the earth, and walked through it, and the whole house is filled with the smell of ointment, from Galilee to this place." And Jeroboam, truly, said to his servant: "Friend, how camest thou hither without a wedding stomach?" And he gave him a blow, saying: "Lord, whence knowest thou me?" And Saul sought David the king and cut off his right ear and his left foot, and said: "Friend, I do thee no injury. Take what is thine and go." And he departed rejoicing, and told everyone what great things he had done to himself. And he hanged himself with a halter. Laban, moreover, begat Nebuchadnezzar in the transmigration of Babylon. And Nathan said: "Lord, I am not worthy that thou shouldst enter my kitchen: but only say the word and my rooster shall be roasted." And immediately the cock crew. Then Beelzebub was casting out a devil: and the same was dumb. And they were not able to resist the wisdom and the spirit that spoke. But the disciples, seeing that wickedness was great upon the earth, said to him: "Let us see if Elijah has come to take him down." And when they went, they found one Simon coming from the way, and they inquired of him where Christ should be born. And he said: "We shall go three days' journey into the wilderness." For he knew not what he said. And they going [*sic*] into a city that is called Naim, and it was one Sabbath, a morning and an evening. Jesus came, the door being shut, where the disciples were enclosed. And for fear of him, the guards were struck with terror, so that the governor wondered exceedingly. But Jesus, seeing their wickedness, spoke by a similitude: "Did I not say to you: Do not sin against the boy? For I know that you seek Jesus. Alleluiah." But one of his disciples, coming to him, said: "Master, we know that thou art a true speaker. Therefore, command that these stones be made bread." Answering this one, he said: "What is that to me and to thee, woman? Did you not know that I must be about my father's business? And I say to you that, from now on, you shall not see me until I make my enemies my footstool." Then the Pharisees consulted among themselves against Jesus, saying: "Let us go to Dothain, but not on the feasting day." Therefore they went and found as Jesus had said to them and made ready the Pasch. Therefore one of them, Thomas, who is called the Drinker, was not with them when they ate the Pasch. Therefore Thomas came and said: "I fast twice on the Sabbath and I eat three times on Friday." But they said: "He blasphemeth." How does it seem to you? Then the king said: "Bind his feet but not his hands, cast him into the storeroom by the full flagon." And the drink that comes after shall be greater than the one that comes before. But thou, make us to pour out all the drink, that all our brothers may be drunk from the drink. Amen.

17. *Exhortatio catechistica Luteranorum*

Manuscript: Munich, Bayerische Staatsbibliothek MS clm. 11963, fol. 342rv.
a. 1609–16. Not previously edited.

Exhortatio catechistica Luteranorum. Ex F. Naas

Ex nihilo nihil fit. Fratres, Scriptura
dicit:

"Si videris fratrem tuum	1 Jo 3.17
necessitatem habentem,	
erue sibi oculum dextrum,	Mt 5.29; cf. Mt 18.9
et si perseveraverit pulsans,	Lc 11.8 (variant)
aufer ei et sinistrum,"	
et reliqua.	
Porro si esurierit inimicus tuus,	Prv 25.21; cf. Rm 12.20
appone ei lapides et ligna,	
dicens:	
"Dic ut lapides isti panes fiant."	Mt 4.3
In his duobus mandatis universa lex	Mt 22.40
pendet	
et prophetae.	
Unde Gallienus in sua canonica	
super Lucam,	
scribens ad Ephesios:	
"Vade et fac tu similiter."	Lc 10.37
Sed quid multum moror?	
Et ecce Judas Machabeus	2 Mcc 5.27
qui dicitur Caiphas	Mt 26.3
dixit ad discipulos suos:	Lc 12.22, etc.
"Habetisne aliquid quod	Lc 24.41
manducetur?"	
Et obtulerunt ei Paraclitum,	Mt 9.2
dicentes:	
"Ecce duo gladii hic."	Lc 22.38
Manducaverunt igitur et saturati sunt	Ps 77.29; cf. Mc 8.8
nihil.	
Veniente vero sponso	cf. Mt 25.5
dedit ei alapam dicens:	Jo 19.3; cf. Jo 18.22
"Amice, ad quid venisti?"	Mt 26.50

Respondit Nicodemus et ait:	Jo 3.9
"Nunquid custos fratris mei sum?"	Gn 4.9
Dicit ei Nathanel:	Jo 1.46
"Redde rationem villicationis tuae.	Lc 16.2
Non enim erit haeres filius cum filia liberae."	Gn 21.10; cf. Gal 4.30
Et illa e contrario dixit, "Mentiris.	3 Rg 3.22
Filius tuus mortuus est."	3 Rg 3.22, 23
Et qui missi fuerant erant ex Phariseis.	Jo 1.24
Piscatores autem descenderant ut lavarent retia sua	Lc 5.2
super montes Armeniae.	Gn 8.4
Et cum coepissent mergi, clamabant dicens:	Mt 14.30
"Domine, salvum fac regem,"	cf. Mt 14.30
et de intus respondit: "Iam," inquit, "ostium	Lc 11.7
meum clausum est	
et puer non comparet."	Gn 37.30
Cum autem irent emere, venit regina	Mt 25.10
austri a finibus illis egresa	
haurire aquas.	cf. Gn 24.11, 13, 43; Ex 2.16; 1 Sm 9.11
Erat puella pulchra facie	3 Rg 1.4; 1 Sm 16.12; Est 2.7
super quam nullus hominum sedit,	Mc 11.2; cf. Lc 19.30
nisi centum quadraginta quatuor millia	Apc 7.4; cf. 14.3
ex omni natione quae sub caelo est.	Act 2.5
Quid [Quis *MS*] adhuc egemus testibus?	Mt 26.65
Et invenit eos dormientes	Mt 26.40, 43; Mc 14.37, 40
prae timore	Mt 28.4
percussoque latere Petri dicens:	Act 12.7
"Non potuisti una hora vigilare mecum?	Mt 26.40; Mc 14.37
Surge velociter et comede."	Act 10.13, 12.7
Et invenit subcinericium panem,	cf. Gn 18.6; Ex 12.39; Jdc 7.13

et dixit:

"Quid haec inter tantos?"	Jo 6.9
Multum	
enim epulari oportet et gaudere, quia	Lc 15.32; cf. Lc 15.24
filius prodigus inventus est.	
Comedit igitur volumen illud,	Ez 3.3
et factum est in ore eius tanquam	Ez 3.3; cf. Apc 10.9
cera liquescens,	
et ambulavit in fortitudine cibi illius	3 Rg 19.8
quadraginta diebus et quadraginta	
noctibus	
ab hora sexta usque ab horam	Mt 27.45; cf. Mc 15.33; Lc 23.44
nonam.	
Et circa horam nonam clamabat,	Mt 27.46
dicens:	
"Saule, Saule, quid me credis?"	cf. Act 9.4, 22.7, 26.14
Et dixit:	
"Nec mihi nec tibi, sed dividatur."	3 Rg 3.26
Cumque intuerentur in caelum,	Act 1.10
ecce Magi.	Mt 2.1
Habeo vobis dicere, sed non potestis	Jo 16.12
sequi modo.	
Si igitur pes tuus scandalizat te,	Mt 18.8; cf. Mc 9.44
ascinde eum et	
proiice abs te.	
Dixit autem Petrus: "Non tantum	Jo 13.9
pedes sed et manus	
et caput."	
Et percussit eos in posteriora,	cf. Ps 77.66
et amputavit ei auriculam dexteram,	Jo 18.10; cf. Mt 26.51; Mc 14.47
dicens:	
"Non facio tibi iniuriam.	Mt 20.13
Tolle quod tuum est et vade."	Mt 20.14
Apertisque oculis nihil videbat	Act 9.8
cogitque.	
Pulmentum dedit patri suo, dicens:	cf. Gn 27.17
"Vade et noli amplius peccare."	Jo 8.11
Et amplius eum non vidit eunuchus,	Act 8.39
et evanuit ab oculis eorum,	Lc 24.31

et ita in nihilum rediit, quod ante
   nihil erat.
Hoc nihil nobis concedat,
qui percussit primogenita ab homine   Ex 12.12; cf. Ex 12.29; Nm 3.13,
   usque ad pecus.   41, 8.17
Amen etc.

Exhortatio catechistica Luteranorum: Translation

Catechetical Sermon of the Lutherans. From F. Naas

Nothing is made from nothing. Brothers, Scripture saith: "If you see thy brother in need, pluck out his right eye, and if the knocking continues, take the left from him also," and the rest. Further, if thy enemy be hungry, give him stones and wood, saying: "Command that these stones be made bread." On these two commandments dependeth the whole law and the prophets. From which Galienus in his canons on Luke, writing to the Ephesians: "Go, and do thou in like manner." But why do I delay so long? And behold Judas Machabeus, who is called Caiphas, said to his disciples: "Have you anything to eat?" And they brought to him the Paraclete, saying: "Behold, here are two swords." So they did eat, and were filled with nothing. But when the bridegroom came, he gave him a blow, saying: "Friend, whereto art thou come?" Nicodemus answered and said: "Am I my brother's keeper?" Nathaniel saith to him: "Give an account of thy stewardship. For the son of the bondwoman shall not be heir with the son of the free woman." And the other woman answered to the contrary: "It is not as thou sayest. Thy child is dead." And they that were sent were of the Pharisees. But the fishermen were gone out of them and were washing their nets upon the mountains of Armenia. And when they had begun to sink, they cried out, saying: "O Lord, save the king," and from within he answered: "Now," he said, "my door is shut and the boy doth not appear." Now whilst they went to buy, the queen of the south came from the ends to draw water. She was a damsel comely of face, upon whom no man hath yet sat, except a hundred and forty-four thousand out of every nation under heaven. What further need have we of witnesses? And he found them asleep for fear, and struck Peter on the side, saying: "Could you not watch one hour with me? Arise quickly and eat." And he found a hearth cake, and said: "What are these among so many?" For it is fit to make merry and be glad, because the prodigal son is found. Therefore he ate that book, and it was made in his mouth as if it were honey melting, and he walked in the strength of that food forty days and forty nights, from the sixth hour until the ninth hour. And about the ninth hour, he cried out: "Saul, Saul, why believest thou me?" And he said: "Neither mine nor thine, but divide it." And while they were looking up to heaven, behold, wise men. I have to speak to you, but you cannot follow now. Therefore, if thy foot scandalize thee, cut it off and cast it from thee. But Peter said: "Not only the feet, but also the hands and the head." And he smote them on the hinder parts, and cut off his right ear, saying: "I do thee no injury. Take what is thine and go." And when his eyes were opened, he saw and knew nothing. He gave the food to his father, saying: "Go, and sin no more." And the eunuch saw him no more. And their eyes were opened. And thus it returned to nothing, which was nothing before. May he grant this nothing to us, he who killed the firstborn, both man and beast. Amen etc.

18. Parody Acrostics

The acrostic was no mere game in the Middle Ages; there was often felt to be
an elemental affinity between a phrase or series of words and the acrostic that
could be constructed from them. So, for instance, in accordance with Adam's
creation from earthly matter, his name was supposed to have been derived from
the four points of the compass. Augustine explains the derivation in this
manner:

> Quia et ipse Adam . . . orbem terrarum significat secundum graecam
> linguam. Quattuor enim litterae sunt A, D, A et M. Sicut autem Graeci
> loquuntur, quattuor orbis partes has in capite litteras habent, !Ανατολην
> dicunt orientem; Δυσιν, occidentem; !Αρκτον, aquilonem; Μεσημβριαν,
> meridiem: habes, Adam. Ipse ergo Adam toto orbe terrarum sparsus est.[1]

> [For also *Adam* . . . means the sphere of the earth in the Greek language.
> For the four letters are *A, D, A,* and *M.* And as the Greeks say them, the
> four parts of the world begin with these letters. By *Anatolen* they indicate
> east; *Dusin* west; *Arkon* north, *Mesembrian* south: you get *Adam.* This
> Adam, therefore, covers the whole sphere of the earth.]

Similar formulas were devised to interpret other religious names.[2] Langland's
Piers Plowman cites the acrostical interpretation of *deus,* an interpretation
which also circulated independently. Langland stresses the reverence in which
such interpretations were held.

> For *Deus dicitur quasi dans eternam vitam suis, hoc est fidelibus; Et
> alibi, si ambulauero in medio vmbre mortis.*

---

1. Augustine, *Enarrationes in Psalmos,* ed. E. Dekkers and J. Fraipont, 3 vols., Corpus
Christianorum, Series Latina 38–40 (Turnhout, 1956), XXXIX, chap. 95, sec. 15, p. 1352. On the
acrostic naming of Adam see Gerald Bonner, "Adam," in *Augustinus Lexikon,* ed. Cornelius
Mayer, (Basel and Stuttgart, 1986–), 1: cols. 63–87 (at cols. 67–68); Émile Turdeanu, "Dieu créa
l'homme de huit éléments et tira son nom des quatres coins du monde," *Revue des études
roumaines* 13–14 (1974): 163–94; and Charles D. Wright, "Apocryphal Lore and Insular Tradition
in St Gall, Stiftsbibliothek MS 908," in *Irland und die Christenheit: Ireland and Christendom.
Bibelstudien und Mission: The Bible and the Mission,* ed. Próinéas Ní Chatháin and Michael
Richter (Stuttgart, 1987), 124–45 (at 139–42).

2. On the range of these, and for an account of medieval acrostic poems generally, see Dag
Norberg, *Introduction à l'étude de la versification médiévale,* Studia Latina Stockholmiensia 5
(Stockholm, 1958), 53–57; and Patrick S. Diehl, *The Medieval European Religious Lyric: An Ars
Poetica* (Berkeley, 1985), 116–18.

The glose grauteþ vpon þat vers a greet mede to truþe.[3]

[For *Deus* is like "Gives eternal life to his own," that is, to his faithful;
and elsewhere, "If I walk in the midst of the shadow of death."
The gloss upon that verse gives a great reward to truth.]

The name *Iesus* or *Ihesus* was subject to similar explanations. One of these
appeared in rhymed verse.

*I*ocunditas merentium.
*E*ternitas credencium.
*S*anitas languencium.
*U*tilitas confitencium.
*S*alvator in se sperancium.[4]

[Merriment of the worthy.
Eternity for believers.
Health of the weak.
Blessing of those who confess.
Savior of those believing in him.]

In one manuscript this is followed by an acrostic poem on *Maria* and another
on *Salve*.[5] Such an acrostic could introduce a lengthy disquisition on the
qualities of the subject: a speech on death in a preacher's handbook, for
instance, is prefaced by an acrostic interpretation of *mors*.

Unde est sciendum quod in isto verbo "mors" sunt quatuor littere core-
spondentes quatuor verbis et proprietatibus mortis cuiuslibet hominis.
Nam pro ista littera M hec proposicio corespondet: Mors est mirum

---

3. Langland, *Piers Plowman,*, Passus XII, pp. 291–94. The acrostic appears independently as
"Ethimologie aliquorum nominum per litteras vel sillabas: *Deus: Dans Eternam Vitam Suis,*" in
Paris, Bibliothèque Nationale MS lat. 3464 (a. 1458), 134v, printed in *Bibliothèque Nationale,*
5:462.

4. Printed in M. R. James, *A Descriptive Catalogue of the Manuscripts in the Library of
Gonville and Caius College,* 2 vols. and suppl. (Cambridge, 1907), 1:19, from Cambridge, Gon-
ville and Caius College MS 25/4 (s. xvi^ex), fol. 259r. An alternative version spelled the name with
an *H* as the second letter, giving the line "*H*ereditas indigentium." The poem is listed in Walther,
Initia, as no. 9868, with two manuscripts cited. In addition the *Iesus* acrostic is found in Paris, Bibl.
Nat. MS lat. 3528 (s. xv), fol. 79v.

5. These are contained in the Cambridge manuscript cited in n. 4 to this section of app. 2; they
are printed in James, *Catalogue,* 1:19.

speculum; secundo pro ista littera O corespondet hec proposicio: Mors est orologium; tercio pro ista littera R corespondet hec proposicio: Mors est raptor [rapiens]; quarto pro ista littera S corespondet hec proposicio: Mors est sitator circuiens.[6]

[Because of all these things we must know that in the word *Mors*, "death," there are four letters which stand for four words and the qualities of anyone's death. To the letter *M* corresponds the following sentence: Death is a marvelous mirror. Second, to the letter *O:* Death is a clock. Third, to the letter *R:* Death is a raping robber. And fourth, to the letter *S:* Death is a summoner on his circuit.]

Secular names, too, were given acrostic explanations. In a fifteenth-century manuscript *Willelmus* is expressed in acrostic form.

*V*ir *v*alidus, *i*ustus, *l*argus, *l*iberalis, *e*lectus,
*L*umine *m*undatus, *v*irtute *s*antificatus.[7]

[Powerful man, just, generous, bountiful, distinguished,
Bathed in light, sanctified by virtue.]

The exercise can also be critical of its subject: Walter Map played on this tradition in his comments on the avarice of Rome.

. . . quos ut Roma uidit uestibus et auro lucides, innata statim exarsit auaricia. Nec mirum; hoc enim nomen Roma ex auaricie sueque diffinicionis formatur principiis, fit enim ex R et O et M et A et diffinicio cum ipsa, *radix omnium malorum auaricia.*[8]

[. . . and when Rome beheld them glittering in raiment and gold, its native covetousness was straightaway kindled. No wonder, for this very name of *Rome* is made up out of the first letters of avarice and the definition of it; it is composed of R.O.M.A., and the definition goes with it—Radix Omnium Malorum Avaricia (The love of money is the root of all evil).]

6. Wenzel, *Fasciculus morum* 101–2. Translation by Wenzel.

7. Quoted in A. G. Rigg, *A Glastonbury Miscellany of the Fifteenth Century* (Oxford, 1968), 83.

8. Walter Map, *De nugis curialium* (c. 1182–83), ed. and trans. M. R. James, rev. C. N. L. Brooke and R. A. B. Mynors (Oxford, 1983), 68. Translation from James et al.

There was also at least one parody acrostic, lampooning the serious acrostics on *monachus* which circulated widely from at least the thirteenth century. A representative version of the serious acrostic reads:

M. Miles fortis contra demones in pugnacione,
O. Obediens cunctis sine simulacione,
N. Nichil habens proprium in absconsione,
A. Amans Deum firmiter pura intencione,
C. Custodiens se ipsum ab omni pollucione,
H. Humilis semper in simplici conversacione,
V. Verax in sermonibus et locucione,
S. Simplex ut columba in omni stacione,
    Et ita est verus monachus.[9]

[M. A soldier steadfast in the struggle against demons,
O. Obedient to all without feigning,
N. Hiding nothing of his own away,
A. Loving God steadfastly with pure devotion,
C. Keeping himself safe from every pollution,
H. Always humble in simple conversation,
V. Truthful in speech and talking,
S. Simple as a dove in every rank,
    And thus a true monk behaves.]

There were a number of variations of this cloying poem, ranging from "Miles contra daemonem fortis, / Obediens, humilis . . ."[10] to "Miles strenuus in omni temptatione."[11] In some cases the acrostic form is emphasized by the method of narration: "Per M miles contra daemonem fortis, per O obediens, hu-

---

9. Printed in Henry Martin, *Catalogue des manuscrits de la Bibliothèque de l'Arsenal,* 9 vols. (Paris, 1885–94), 2:95, from Paris, Bibliothèque de l'Arsenal MS 775 (s. xiv), fol. 26. Walther, *Initia,* no. 11008, lists this and five other manuscripts under the heading "Miles Christi fortis contra demonum impugnationem." To these may be added another variant, "Miles fortis contra daemonem in pugnatione," in Cologne, Historisches Archiv MS G. B. 4º 37 (s. xv¹), fol. 120, as well as those cited in notes 10–13 to this section of app. 2.

10. Paris, Bibliothèque Nationale MS lat. 3343 (s. xv), fol. 165. Similar is "Miles fortis contra dyabolum" in Paris, Bibl. Nat. MS lat. 3528 (a. 1470), fol. 79v, a manuscript that also contains the *Iesus* acrostic described above. These two manuscripts are not listed by Walther.

11. Walther, *Initia,* no. 11015. Walther cites six manuscripts; to these should be added Paris, Bibl. Nat. MS lat. 2851³, fol. 92v (the acrostic is s. xiii); Munich, Bayerische Staatsbibl. MS clm. 18551 (s. xv), fol. 290r; Vatican, Bibl. Apost. Vat. MS Reg. lat. 349 (s. xv¹), fol. 9rv; and Gdansk, Marienbibl. MS F.254 (s. xivⁿ), fol. 108 and MS Q.12, fol. 325. (The librarians of the Biblioteka Gdanska inform me that unfortunately this last manuscript has been lost.)

milis . . ."[12] At times a notice, such as "Monachus sic definitur secundum etymologiam nominis" [*Monachus* is defined like this according to the etymology of the word] is appended.[13]

The parody of this acrostic is much simpler but retains most of these features: the narration as acrostic, the explanation, and the implicit claim to a true understanding of the monastic character. The text is found, with minor variations, in four manuscripts of the early fifteenth century. The Erfurt version reads:

Monachus litteraliter ethymolizatur: per M morum, per O oppressor, per N nequicie, per A amator, per C cultor, per H herisis [*sic*], per V veritatis, per S spoliator; dicitur enim monachus quasi morum oppressor, nequicie amator, cultor heresis, veritatum spoliator.[14]

[*Monachus* (monk) etymologized according to the letter: for *M*, of morals, for *O* oppressor, for *N* of wickedness, for *A* lover, for *C* cultivator, for *H* of heresy, for *V* of truths, for *S* a despoiler: so *monachus* is like oppressor of morals, lover of wickedness, cultivator of heresy, despoiler of truths.]

Other versions are simpler. A manuscript now in Prague reads:

Monachus ethymologyce: morum oppressor, nequicie amator, cultor heresis, virtutum spoliator.[15]

A Salzburg manuscript is almost identical.

Mors [*sic*] oppressor, nequicie amator, cultor heresis, virtutum spoliator.[16]

---

12. Paris, Bibl. Nat. MS lat. 3343 (noted in n. 8 to this section of app. 2).

13. Paris, Bibl. Nat. MS lat. 2845 (s. xiv), fol. 170v. This manuscript is listed in Walther, *Initia,* no. 11015, where he mistakenly assigns the verse to fol. 190.

14. Erfurt, Wissenschaftliche Bibliothek MS Amplon. Duodez 13a (a. 1408–11); printed in Wilhelm Schum, *Beschreibendes Verzeichniss der Amplonianischen Handschrift-Sammlung zu Erfurt* (Berlin, 1887), 770, no. 8.

15. Printed in A. Podlaha, *Soupis Rukopisu Knihovny Metropolitní Kapitoly Prazské,* 2 vols. (Prague, 1910–1922), 2:495, from Prague, Metrop. Bibl. MS 1614 (a. 1397–1443), fol. 189v.

16. Printed in Hans Walther, "Beiträge zur Kentnnis der mittellateinischen Literatur (aus Handschriften süddeutscher und österreichischer Bibliotheken)," *Zentralblatt für Bibliothekswesen* 49 (1932): 270–83 (at 277), from Salzburg, Öffentliche Studienbibl. MS 8.F.68 (s. xv), (no folio given).

One compiler clearly understood the laudatory acrostic as a catalog of virtues to aspire to and the satiric version as a dire warning; he copies out the serious acrostic with the heading "Monachus Christi" and the parody with the notation "Monachus dyaboli."[17] It was more probably the self-righteousness of the original which provoked the parody, however; and the scribe of the Prague manuscript concurred with the satirical spirit enough to append an antimonastic jingle.

Sit tibi consultum, monachum non dilige multum,
Foris eum pota, ne uxor sit sibi nota.[18]

[If you're asked, don't favor a monk overmuch;
Give him a drink outdoors, so he doesn't spot your wife.]

17. Gdansk, Marienbibl. MS Q.12, fol. 325, described in Otto Günther, *Die Handschiften der Kirchenbibliothek von St. Marien in Danzig* (Gdansk, 1921), 482. This is the manuscript that has been lost (see n. 11 to this section of app. 2).

18. Printed in Podlaha, *Soupis,* 495. Walther, *Initia,* no. 18338. Podlaha notes another copy of this verse (without the acrostic) in Prague, Metrop. Bibl. MS 1618, fol. 83rv; this has not been noted by Walther.

Bibliography

Abelard, Peter. *Expositio symboli quod dicitur Apostolorum.* In *Patrologiae [Latinae] Cursus Copletus,* ed. J.-P. Migne, *PL* 178; cols. 617–30.

———. *Sic et non.* Ed. B. B. Boyer and R. McKeon. Chicago, 1976-.

———. *Sic et non.* In *Patrologiae [Latinae] Cursus Completus,* ed. J.-P. Migne, *PL* 178; cols. 1329–1610.

Acta Sanctorum quotquot toto orbe coluntur. Ed. Jean Bolland et al. Antwerp and Brussels, 1643–.

Aldhelm. "Aenigmata Aldhelmi." In *Collectiones Aenigmatum Merovingicae Aetatis,* Ed. F. Glorie. Corpus Christianorum, Series Latina 133, no. 1, pp. 359–540. Turnhout, 1968.

Ambrose. *De mysteriis liber unus.* In *Patrologiae [Latinae] Cursus Completus,* ed. J.-P. Migne, *PL* 16; cols. 389–410.

Angelom of Luxeuil. *Enarrationes in libros regum.* In *Patrologiae [Latinae] Cursus Completus,* ed. J.-P. Migne, *PL* 115; cols. 243–552.

Arator. *De actibus apostolorum.* Ed. A. P. McKinlay. In *Corpus Scriptorum Ecclesiasticorum Latinorum,* 72: Vienna, 1951.

Arnaldi, G. "Giovanni Immonide e la cultura a Roma al tempo di Giovanni VIII." *Bulletino dell'Istituto storico italiano per il medio evo e Archivio Muratoriano* 68 (1956): 33–89.

Augustine. *Enarrationes in Psalmos.* Ed. E. Dekkers and J. Fraipont. 3 vols. Corpus Christianorum, Series Latina 38–40. Turnhout, 1956.

Augustinus Lexikon. Ed. Cornelius Mayer. Basel and Stuttgart, 1986–.

Ausonius. *Decimi Magni Ausonii Burdigalensis Opuscula.* Ed. S. Prete. Leipzig, 1978.

Avalle, D'Arco Silvio. "Ancora Sulla Parodia della 'Lex Salica.'" In *Miscellanea di Studi in onore di Alfredo Schiaffini,* Rivista di cultura classica e medieovale, 29–61. Rome, 1965.

———. *Protostoria delle Linguae Romanze.* Turin, 1965.

Babcock, Barbara A. Introduction, to *The Reversible World: Symbolic Inversion in Art and Society,* ed. Barbara Babcock. Ithaca and London, 1978.

Baesecke, Georg. *Der Vocabularius Sti. Galli in der angelsächsischen Mission.* Halle, 1933.

Bakhtin, Mikhail. "From the Prehistory of Novelistic Discourse." In *The Dialogic Imagination: Four Essays,* ed. Michael Holquist, trans. Caryl Emerson and Michael Holquist, University of Texas Press Slavic Series 1, pp. 41–83. Austin and London, 1981.

———. *Rabelais and His World.* Trans. Helene Iswolsky. Cambridge, Mass., 1968.

Bardy, Gustave. "Remarques critiques sur une liste des saints de France." *Revue d'histore de l'église de France* 31 (1945): 219–36.

Bartholomaeis, Vincenzo de. *Origini della poesia drammatica italiana.* 2d ed. Nuova biblioteca Italiana 7. Turin, 1952.

Bateson, Gregory. "A Theory of Play and Fantasy." In *Steps to an Ecology of Mind,* 177–93. London, 1972.

Beadle, Richard. *The York Plays.* London, 1982.

Beek, C. I. M. I. van. *Passio Sanctarum Perpetuae et Felicitatis.* Florilegium Patristicum tam Veteris quam Medii Aevi Auctores Complectens 43. Bonn, 1938.

Belardi, Walter. "Nomi del centone nelle lingue indoeuropee." *Ricerche linguistiche* 4 (1958): 29–57.

Benary, Walter. *Salomon et Marcolfus.* Sammlung mittellateinischer Texte 8. Heidelberg, 1914.

Benzinger, Josef. *Invectiva in Romam: Romkritik im Mittelalter vom 9. bis zum 12. Jahrhundert.* Historische Studien 404. Lübeck and Hamburg, 1968.

Bernardino of Siena. *S. Bernardini Senensis Ordinis Fratrum Minorum Opera Omnia.* 9 vols. Florence, 1950–65.

Bernhard, M. *Goswyn Kempgyn de Nussia, Trivita Studentium.* Münchener Beiträge zur Mediävistik und Renaissance-Forschung 26. Munich, 1976.

Bezzenberger, Heinrich Ernst. *Fridankes Bescheidenheit.* Halle, 1872.

Bibliothèque Nationale: Catalogue général des manuscrits latins. 6 vols. Paris, 1939–75.

Billman, Carol. "Grotesque Humor in Medieval Biblical Comedy." *American Benedictine Review* 31 (1980): 406–17.

Bischoff, Bernhard. "Eine Bibelparodie (elftes bis zwölftes Jahrhundert)." In *Anecdota Novissima: Texte des vierten bis sechzehnten Jahrhunderts,* Quellen und Untersuchungen zur lateinischen Philologie des Mittelalters 7, pp. 162–64. Stuttgart, 1984.

———. "Parodistischer Brief des Priesters Iohannes de Caudatis (um 1470)." In *Anecdota Novissima: Texte des vierten bis sechzehnten Jahrhunderts,* Quellen und Untersuchungen zur lateinischen Philologie des Mittelalters 7, pp. 167–68. Stuttgart, 1984.

Blake, N. F. *The English Language in Medieval Literature.* London and New York, 1979.

Boase, T. S. R. *Boniface VIII.* London, 1933.

Boccaccio. *De mulieribus claris.* Ed. Vittorio Zaccaria. Milan, 1967.

Bolte, Johannes. "Die Legende vom heiligen Niemand." *Alemannia* 16 (1888): 193–201.

———. "Vom heiligen Niemand." *Alemannia* 18 (1890): 131–34.

———. "Von S. Niemand." *Alemannia* 17 (1889): 151.

Bonner, Gerald. "Adam." In *Augustinus Lexikon,* ed. Cornelius Mayer, 1: cols. 63–87. Basel and Stuttgart, 1986–.

Booth, Wayne C. *A Rhetoric of Irony.* Chicago, 1974.

Bouley, César Égasse du. *Historia Universitatis Parisiensis III.* Paris, 1666.

Brentano, Robert. *Rome Before Avignon: A Social History of Thirteenth-Century Rome.* Berkeley and Los Angeles, 1990.

Brewer, H. "Über den Heptateuchdichter Cyprian und die Caena Cypriani." *Zeitschift für katholische Theologie* 28 (1904): 92–115.

Brians, Paul E. "Medieval Literary Parody." Ph.D. diss., Indiana University, 1968.

Bright, David F. "Theory and Practice in the Vergilian Cento." *Illinois Classical Studies* 9 (1984): 79–90.

Buecheler, F., and A. Riese. *Anthologia Latina sive Poesis Latinae Supplementum.* 5 vols. Leipzig, 1894–1926.

Burchard of Bellevaux. *Apologia de barbis.* In *Apologiae Duae,* ed. R. B. C. Huygens, with an introduction by Giles Constable, Corpus Christianorum, Continuatio Mediaeualis 62. Turnhout, 1985.

Bynum, Caroline Walker. "'And Woman His Humanity': Female Imagery in the Religious Writing of the Later Middle Ages." In *Gender and Religion: On the Complexity of Symbols,* ed. Caroline Walker Bynum et al., 257–88. Boston, 1986.

———. *Holy Feast and Holy Fast: The Religious Significance of Food to Medieval Women.* Berkeley, 1987.

Camille, Michael. *Image on the Edge: The Margins of Medieval Art.* Cambridge, Mass., 1992.

Carroll, Lewis. *The Penguin Complete Lewis Carroll.* Ed. Alexander Woollcott. Harmondsworth, 1982.

Caro Baroja, Julio. *El carnaval.* Madrid, 1965.

Castan, Auguste. *Catalogue général des manuscrits des bibliothèques publiques de France: Départements* 32. Paris, 1897.

Cawley, A. C. *The Wakefield Pageants in the Towneley Cycle.* Manchester, 1958.

Chambers, E. K. *The Medieval Stage.* 2 vols. Oxford, 1903.

Chavasse, Claude. *The Bride of Christ: An Enquiry into the Nuptial Element in Early Christianity.* London, 1940.

Christine de Pizan. *The Book of the City of Ladies.* Trans. Earl Jeffrey Richards. London, 1983.

Clark, E. A., and D. F. Hatch. *The Golden Bough, the Oaken Cross: The Vergilian Cento of Faltonia Betitia Proba.* American Academy of Religion, Texts and Translations 5. Chico, Calif., 1981.

Clemen, Otto. "Zu Huttens Nemo." *Theologische Studien und Kritiken* 79 (1906): 308–12.

Cohn, Norman R. C. *The Pursuit of the Millennium: Revolutionary Millenarians and Mystical Anarchists of the Middle Ages.* Rev. ed. London, 1970.

Colie, Rosalie Littell. *Paradoxica Epidemica: The Renaissance Tradition of Paradox.* Princeton, 1966.

Colker, Marvin L. "Anecdota Dublinensia." *Medievalia et Humanistica,* old series, 16 (1964): 39–55.

Colledge, Edmund, and J. C. Marler. "Céphalogie, a Recurring Theme in Classical and Medieval Lore." *Traditio* 37 (1981): 411–26.

Coulton, G. G. *From St. Francis to Dante: Translations from the Chronicle of the Franciscan Salimbene (1221–88).* 2d ed. 1907. Reprint, Philadelphia, 1972.

Courcelle, P. "Les exégèses chrétiennes de la quatrième Églogue." *Revue des études anciennes* 59 (1957): 294–319.

Crapelet, Georges Adrien. *Proverbes et dictons populaires.* Paris, 1831.

Cristofari, Maria. *Il codice marciano it.XI,66.* Padua, 1937.

Croce, Giulio Cesare. *Le sottilissime astuzie di Bertoldo: Le piacevoli e ridicolose simplicità di Bertoldino.* Turin, 1978.

Cross, James E., and Thomas D. Hill. *The* Prose Solomon and Saturn *and* Adrian and Ritheus. McMaster Old English Studies and Texts 1. Toronto, 1982.

Curio, Caelius Secundus. *Pasquillorum tomi duo.* Basel, 1544.

Curtius, Ernst Robert. *European Literature and the Latin Middle Ages.* Trans. Willard R. Trask. 1953. Reprint, London, 1979.

Dane, Joseph A. *Parody: Critical Concepts versus Literary Practices, Aristophanes to Sterne.* Norman, Okla., and London, 1988.

Daniélou, Jean. "Les repas de la Bible et leur signification." *La Maison-Dieu* 18 (1949): 7–33.

Davies, R. T. *Medieval English Lyrics: A Critical Anthology.* London, 1963.

Davis, Natalie Zemon. "The Reasons of Misrule." In *Society and Culture in Early Modern France,* 97–123. Cambridge, 1987.

De verbi incarnatione. Ed. F. Buecheler and A. Riese. In *Anthologia Latina sive Poesis Latinae Supplementum,* 5 vols. 1: no. 16, pp. 56–61. Leipzig, 1894–1926.

Delepierre, Octave. *Tableau de la littérature du centon chez les anciens et chez les modernes.* 2 vols. London, 1874–75. Originally published as *Centoniana, ou Encyclopédie du centon,* 2 parts, Philobiblon Society Miscellanies 9–10 (London, 1866–68).

Delisle, Léopold. *Rouleaux des morts du IXe au XVe siècle.* Paris, 1866.

Delumeau, J. *Mort de pays de Cocagne.* Paris, 1976.

Denifle, Heinrich. "Ursprung der Historia des Nemo." *Archiv für Literatur- und Kirchen-Geschichte des Mittelalters* 4 (1888): 330–48.

Devos, Paul. "Le mystérieux épisode finale de la *Vita Gregorii* de Jean Diacre: Formose et sa fuite de Rome." *Analecta Bollandiana* 82 (1964): 355–81.

Di Berardino, Angelo, ed. *The Golden Age of Latin Patristic Literature from the Council of Nicea to the Council of Chalcedon.* Vol. 4 of *Patrology.* Trans. Placid Solari. Westminster, Md., 1988.

Diehl, Patrick S. *The Medieval European Religious Lyric: An Ars Poetica.* Berkeley, 1985.

Dives and Pauper. Ed. Priscilla Heath Barnum. 2 parts. Early English Text Society 275 and 280. Oxford, 1976 and 1980.

Dobschütz, Ernst von. *Das Decretum Gelasianum.* Texte und Untersuchungen zur Geschichte der altchristlichen Literatur, 3d ser., 8.iv. Leipzig, 1912.

Dommer, A. von. *Autotypen der Reformationzeit auf der Hamburger Stadtbibliothek.* Hamburg, 1881.

Donaldson, Ian. *The World Upside Down: Comedy from Jonson to Fielding.* Oxford, 1970.

Dreves, G. M., ed. *Analecta Hymnica Medii Aevi.* 58 vols. in 30. Leipzig, 1886–72.

Duckett, Eleanor. *Death and Life in the Tenth Century.* Ann Arbor, 1967.

du Méril, Édélestand. *Poésies populaires latines du moyen âge.* Paris, 1847.

Dümmler, E. "Gedichte aus dem elften Jahrhundert." *Neues Archiv der Gesellschaft für ältere deutsche Geschichtskunde* 1 (1876): 175–85.

————. "Verse und Satire auf Rom." *Neues Archiv der Gesellschaft für ältere deutsche Geschichtskunde* 23 (1898): 204–12.

Eagleton, Terry. *Walter Benjamin or Towards a Revolutionary Criticism.* London, 1981.

Eco, Umberto. "The Frames of Comic 'Freedom.'" In *Carnival!,* ed. Thomas A. Sebeok and Marcia E. Erikson, 1–9. Berlin, 1984.

Ehrmann, Jacques. "Homo Ludens Revisited." *Yale French Studies* 41 (1968): 31–57.

Endlicher, Stephan. *Catalogus codicum philologicorum Latinorum Bibliotecae Palatinae Vindobonensis.* Vienna, 1836.

Ermini, F. *Il centone di Proba e la poesia centonaria latina.* Rome, 1909.

Feifalik, Julius. "Studien zur Geschichte der altböhmischen Literatur." *Sitzungsberichte der kaiserlichen Akademie der Wissenschaften in Wien,* philologisch-historische Classe 36 (1861): 119–91.

Feng, Helen C. "Devil's Letters: Their History and Significance in Church and Society, 1100–1500." Ph.D. diss., Northwestern University, 1982.

Fink, Eugen, *Oase des Glücks: Gedanken zu einer Ontologie des Spiels.* Freiburg and Munich, 1957.

————. "The Oasis of Happiness: Toward an Ontology of Play." *Yale French Studies* 41 (1968): 19–29.

Fischer, B., ed. *Novae Concordantiae Bibliorum Sacrorum iuxta Vulgatam Versionem Critice Editam.* 5 vols. Stuttgart, 1977.

Flint, Valerie I. J. "The *Historia Regum Brittaniae* of Geoffrey of Monmouth: Parody and Its Purpose. A Suggestion." *Speculum* 54 (1979): 447–68.

Fluck, Hans. "Der risus paschalis." *Archiv für Religionswissenschaft* 31 (1934): 188–212.

Förster, Max. "Adams Erschaffung und Namengebung." *Archiv für Religionswissenschaft* 11 (1908): 477–529.

Franceschini, Ezio. "Il teatro postcarolingio." In *I problemi comuni dell'Europa postcarolingia,* 295–312. Spoleto, 1955.

Freeman, Rosemary. "Parody as a Literary Form: George Herbert and Wilfred Owen." *Essays in Criticism* 13 (1963): 307–22.

García-Villoslada, Ricardo. *La Poesia ritmica de los goliardos medievales.* Madrid, 1975.

Geoffrey of Monmouth. *The* Historia regum Brittaniae *of Geoffrey of Monmouth.* Ed. Anton Griscom. London and New York, 1929.

Gilman, Sander L. *The Parodic Sermon in European Perspective.* Wiesbaden, 1974.

Gluckman, Max. "Rituals of Rebellion in South-East Africa." In *Order and Rebellion in Tribal Africa,* 110–36. London, 1963.

Golopentia-Eretescu, Sanda. "Grammaire de la parodie." *Cahiers de linguistique théorique et appliquée* 6 (1969): 167–81.

Gratian. *Decretum Magistri Gratiani.* Ed. E. Friedberg. 2d ed., Corpus Iuris Canonici 1. 1879. Reprint, Graz, 1959.

Gray, Nick. "The Clemency of Cobblers: A Reading of 'Glutton's Confession' in *Piers Plowman.*" *Leeds Studies in English,* n.s., 17 (1986): 61–75.

Gregory the Great. *Sancti Gregorii Magni Romani pontifici moralium libri sive Expositio in librum b. Job.* ed. J.-P. Migne, *PL* 75: col.s 510–1162.

Gundlach, Wilhelm. *Heldenlieder der deutschen Kaiserzeit.* 3 vols. Innsbruck, 1899.

Günther, Otto. *Die Handschriften der Kirchenbibliothek von St. Marien in Danzig.* Gdansk, 1921.

Gurevich, Aron. *Medieval Popular Culture: Problems of Belief and Perception.* Trans. János M. Bak and Paul A. Hollingsworth. Cambridge Studies in Oral and Literature Culture 14. Cambridge, 1988.

——. [as Gurjewitsch, Aaron J.]. "Bachtin und der Karneval Zu Dietz-Rüdiger Moser: 'Lachkultur des Mittelalters? Michael Bachtin und die Folgen seiner Theorie.'" *Euphorion: Zeitschrift für Literaturgeschichte* 85 (1991): 423–29.

Hagen, Hermann. "Eine Nachahmung von Cyprian's Gastmahl durch Hrabanus Maurus." *Zeitschrift für wissenschaftliche Theologie* 27 (1883): 164–87.

Hampe, Karl. "Reise nach England vom Juli 1895 bis Februar 1896. III." *Neues Archiv der Gesellschaft für ältere deutsche Geschichtskunde* 22 (1897): 607–99.

Hardt, Hermann von der. *Magnum Oecumenicum Constantiense Concilium.* 6 vols. Frankfurt and Leipzig, 1696–1700.

Harnack, Adolf. "Drei wenig beachtete Cyprianische Schriften und die 'Acta Pauli.'" *Texte und Untersuchungen zur Geschichte der altchristlichen Literatur,* N. F. 4, 3b. Leipzig, 1899.

Hartmann, W. *Salomon und Markolf.* Halle, 1934.

Haskins, Charles Homer. "Latin Literature under Frederick II." In *Studies in Mediaeval Culture,* 124–47. Oxford, 1929.

Hass, W. *Studien zum Heptateuchendichter Cyprian mit Beiträgen zu den vorhieronymianischen Bibelübersetzungen.* Berlin, 1912.

Hauréau, B. *Initia Operum Scriptorum Latinorum Medii Potissimum Aevi.* 8 vols. Turnhout, n.d.

Hazlitt, William. "On Wit and Humour." In *Lectures on the English Comic Writers and Fugitive Writings,* with introductions by Arthur Johnston, 5–30. 1819. Reprint, London and New York, 1963.

Heers, Jacques. *Fêtes des fous et carnavals.* Paris, 1983.

——. *Fêtes, jeux et joutes dans les sociétés d'Occident à la fin du moyen âge.* Montreal, 1971.

——. *Fêtes, jeux et joutes dans les sociétés médiévales d'Occident.* 2d ed. Montreal, 1982.

Hempel, Wido. "Parodie, Travestie und Pastiche: Zur Geschichte von Wort und Sache." *Germanisch-romanische Monatsschrift,* 46 (N.F. 15) (1965): 150–76.

Henryson, Robert. *The Poems of Robert Henryson.* Ed. Denton Fox. Oxford, 1981.

——. *Robert Henryson: Poems.* Ed. Charles Elliot. 2d ed. Oxford, 1974.

Henson, H. H. "Letters Relating to Oxford in the 14th Century, from Originals in the Public Record Office and British Museum." *Collectanea,* Oxford Historical Society, old series, 5, 1–56. Oxford, 1885.

Herbert, J. A. *Catalogue of Romances in the Department of Manuscripts in the British Museum.* Vol. 3. London, 1910.

Highet, Gilbert. *The Anatomy of Satire.* Princeton and London, 1962.

Hilka, Alfons, Otto Schumann, et al., eds. *Carmina Burana.* 3 vols. Heidelberg, 1930–71.

Histoire littéraire de la France. 41 vols. Paris, 1733–1981.

Hofmann, C. "Ueber die lateinischen Sequenzen." *Sitzungsberichte der philosophisch-philologischen und historischen Classe der k. b. Akademie der Wissenschaften zu München* 2 (1872): 454–60.

Hone, William. *The Three Trials of William Hone.* With introduction and notes by W. Tegg. London, 1876.

Horowitz, Jeannine, and Sophia Menache. *L'humour en chaire: Le rire dans l'Église médiévale.* Histoire et Société 28. Geneva, 1994.

Householder, F. W., Jr. "Parodia." *Classical Philology* 39 (1944): 1–9.

Huizinga, Johan. *Homo Ludens: A Study of the Play-Element in Culture.* Trans. R. F. C. Hull. London, 1949.

———. *The Waning of the Middle Ages.* Trans. F. Hopman. 1924. Reprint, Harmondsworth, 1975.

Hutcheon, Linda. "Authorized Transgression: The Paradox of Parody." In *Le singe à la porte: Vers une théorie de la parodie.* New York, 1984.

———. *A Theory of Parody: The Teachings of Twentieth-Century Art Forms.* New York and London, 1985.

Huygens, R. B. C. *Accessus ad Auctores: Bernard d'Utrecht, Conrad d'Hirsau, Dialogus Super Auctores.* 2d ed. Leiden, 1970.

Ilvonen, Eero. *Parodies de thèmes pieux dans la poésie française du moyen âge.* Paris, 1914.

Ivo of Chartres. *Panormia.* Ed. J.-P. Migne, *PL* 161: cols. 1037–1428.

Jakobsen, Peter Christian. *Die Quirinalien des Metellus von Tegernsee.* Mittellateinische Studien und Texte 1. Leiden and Cologne, 1965.

James, M. R. *A Descriptive Catalogue of the Manuscripts in the Library of Gonville and Caius College.* 2 vols. and suppl. Cambridge, 1907.

Jerome. *Commentariorum in Zachariam prophetam ad exsuperium Tolosanum episcopum libri duo.* Ed. J.-P. Migne, *PL* 25: cols. 1415–1542.

———. *Epistulae.* Ed. I. Hilberg. In *Corpus Scriptorum Ecclesiasticorum Latinorum,* 54. Vienna, 1910.

Juvencus. *Evangelium libri quattuor.* Ed J. Hümer. In *Corpus Scriptorum Ecclesiasticorum Latinorum,* 24. Vienna, 1891.

Kaijser, Dick. "Het laatmiddeleeuwse spotsermoen." *Spektator* 13 (1983–84): 105–27.

Kayser, Wolfgang. *The Grotesque in Art and Literature.* Trans. Ulrich Weisstein. Bloomington, Ind., 1963.

Keith-Spiegel, P. "Early Conceptions of Humor: Varieties and Issues." In *The Psychology of Humor: Theoretical Perspectives and Empirical Issues,* ed. Jeffrey H. Goldstein and Paul E. McGhee, 3–39. New York and London, 1972.

Kemble, J. M. *The Dialogue of Salomon and Saturnus.* London, 1848.

Kempgyn, Goswin. *Goswin Kempgyn de Nussia: Trivita Studentium.* Ed. M. Bernhard. Münchener Beiträge zur Mediävistik und Renaissance-Forschungen 26. Munich, 1976.

Kendrick, Laura. *Chaucerian Play: Comedy and Control in the* Canterbury Tales. Berkeley, 1988.

Kern, Edith. "The Importance of Not Being Earnest: Modern-Medieval." *Symposium* 38 (1984): 13–27.

Kiremidjian, G. D. *A Study of Modern Parody: James Joyce's* Ulysses, *Thomas Mann's* Doktor Faustus. New York and London, 1985.

Kitchin, George. *A Survey of Burlesque and Parody in English.* Edinburgh, 1931.

Koller, Hermann. "Die Parodie." *Glotta* 35 (1956): 17–32.

Kolve, V. A. *The Play Called Corpus Christi.* Stanford, 1966.

Koopmans, Jelle. *Quatre sermons joyeux.* Geneva, 1984.

―――. *Recueil de sermons joyeux.* Textes littéraires français 362. Geneva, 1988.

Koopmans, Jelle, and Paul Verhuyck. "Quelques sources et parallèles des sermons joyeux français des XVe et XVIe siècles." *Neophilologus* 70 (1986): 168–84.

―――. *Sermon joyeux et truanderie (Villon―Nemo―Ulespiègle).* Faux Titre 29. Amsterdam, 1987.

Krassold, Lorenz. *Dr. Theodorich Morung: Der Vorbote der Reformation in Franken.* 2 parts. Bayreuth, 1877.

Kunzle, David. "World Upside Down: The Iconography of a European Broadsheet Type." In *The Reversible World: Symbolic Inversion in Art and Society,* ed. Barbara A. Babcock, 39–94. Ithaca and London, 1978.

Lamacchia, Rosa. *Hosidii Getae Medea: Cento Virgilianus.* Leipzig, 1981.

Langland, William. *Piers Plowman: The B Version.* Ed. George Kane and E. Talbot Donaldson. London, 1975.

Lapôtre, Arthur. "La 'Cena Cypriani' et ses énigmes." *Recherches de science religieuse* 3 (1912): 497–596.

―――. "Le Souper de Jean Diacre." *Mélanges d'archéologie et d'histoire* 21 (1901): 305–85.

Le Roy Ladurie, Emmanuel. *Carnival in Romans: A People's Uprising at Romans 1579–1580.* Trans. Mary Feeney. Harmondsworth, 1981.

Leclerq, Jean. *The Love of Learning and the Desire for God: A Study of Monastic Culture.* Trans. Catharine Misrahi. New York, 1982.

Lehmann, Paul. *Die Parodie im Mittelalter.* 1st ed., Munich, 1922. 2d ed., Stuttgart, 1963.

―――. *Parodistische Texte.* Munich, 1923.

Lejeune, Rita. "Hagiographie et grivoiserie: À propos d'un Dit de Gautier le Leu." *Romance Philology* 12 (1958): 355–65.

Lelièvre, F. J. "The Basis of Ancient Parody." *Greece and Rome,* 2d ser., 1 (1954): 66–81.

Lerch, David. "Zur Geschichte der Auslegung des Hoheliedes." *Zeitschrift für Theologie und Kirche* 54 (1957): 257–77.

Lexikon für Theologie und Kirche. Ed. Josef Hofer and Karl Rahner. 2d ed. 10 vols. Freiburg, 1957–67.

Lida de Malkiel, María Rosa. "La *Garcineida* de García Toledo." *Nueva revista de filología hispánica* 7 (1953): 246–58.

Little, Lester K. *Religious Poverty and the Profit Economy in Medieval Europe.* London, 1978.

Lombard, Peter. *Magistri Petri Lombardi Sententiae in IV Libris Distinctae.* 2 vols. Spicilegium Bonaventurianum 4–5. Grottaferrata, 1971–81.

Longfellow, Henry Wadsworth. *The Poetical Works of Henry Wadsworth Longfellow.* 6 vols. New York, 1966.

Lowe, E. A. *The Bobbio Missal: A Gallican Mass-Book (MS. Paris Lat. 13246).* 3 vols. Henry Bradshaw Society 53, 58, and 61. London, 1917–24.

———. *Codices Latini Antiquiores.* 12 vols. Oxford, 1934–72.

Maaz, W. "Zur Rezeption des Alexander v. Villa Dei im 15. Jahrhundert." *Mittellateinisches Jahrbuch* 16 (1981): 276–81.

MacAlister, R. A. S. *The Secret Languages of Ireland.* Cambridge, 1937.

Manitius, Max. *Geschichte der lateinischen Literatur des Mittelalters.* 3 vols. 1911–31. Reprint, Munich, 1965–73.

Mann, Jill. "Satiric Subject and Satiric Object in Goliardic Literature." *Mittellateinisches Jahrbuch* 15 (1980): 63–86.

Manzoni, Luigi. *Libro di carnevale dei secoli XV e XVI.* 1881. Reprint, Bologna, 1968.

Map, Walter. *De nugis curialium.* Ed. and trans. M. R. James. Rev. C. N. L. Brooke and R. A. B. Mynors. Oxford, 1983.

Marks, Anthony. "The Parody of Liturgical and Biblical Texts in Germany in the Sixteenth and Seventeenth Centuries." Ph.D. diss., University of Cambridge, 1970.

Martin, Henry. Catalogue des manuscrits de la Bibliothèque de l'Arsenal. 9 vols. Paris, 1885–94.

Mayer, Theodor. "Spicilegium von Urkunden aus der Zeit der österreichischen Babenberger-Fürsten." *Archiv für Kunde österreichischer Geschichts-Quellen* 6 (1851): 273–318.

Ménard, P. *Le rire et le sourire dans le roman courtois (1150–1250).* Geneva, 1969.

Menner, Robert J. *The Poetical Dialogues of Solomon and Saturn.* Modern Language Association of America Monograph Series 13. New York and London, 1941.

Méon, Dominique Martin. *Nouveau recueil de fabliaux et contes inédits des poètes français des XIIe, XIIIe, XIVe et XVe siècles.* 2 vols. Paris, 1823.

Merceron, Jacques E. *Dictionnaire des saints burlesques et imaginaires français.* Paris, forthcoming.

Meyer, Kuno. *Aislinge Meic Conglinne.* London, 1892.

Meyer, Wilhelm. "Das Gedicht: Sermo noster audiatis." *Nachrichten von der königlichen Gesellschaft der Wissenschaften zu Göttingen,* philologisch-historische Klasse (1908): 426–29.

———. "Quondam fuit factum festus: Ein Gedicht in Spottlatein." *Nachrichten von der königlichen Gesellschaft der Wissenschaften zu Göttingen,* philologisch-historische Klasse (1908): 406–26.

Modesto, Christine. *Studien zur Cena Cypriani und zu deren Rezeption.* Classica Monacensia 3. Tübingen, 1992.

Monaci, Ernesto. "Per la storia della *Schola cantorum* lateranense." *Archivio della R. Società Romana di storia patria* 20 (1897): 451–63.

Montaiglon, Anatole de, and Gaston Raynaud. *Recueil général et complet des fabliaux des XIIIe et XIVe siècles.* 6 vols. Paris, 1872–90.

Montaiglon, Anatole de, and James de Rothschild, ed. *Recueil de poésies françoises.* 13 vols. Paris, 1855–78.

Morin, G. "Un critique en liturgie au XIIe siècle. Le traité inédit d'Hervé de Bourgdieu. *De correctione quarundam lectionum.*" *Revue Bénédictine* 24 (1907): 36–61.

———. Review of "La 'Cena Cypriani' et ses énigmes," by Arthur Lapôtre. *Revue Bénédictine* 30 (1913): 472–73.

Moser, Dietz-Rüdiger. "Auf dem Weg zu neuen Mythen." *Euphorion: Zeitschrift für Literaturgeschichte* 84 (1991): 430–37.

———. "Lachkulter des Mittelalters ? Michael Bachtin und die Folgen seiner Theorie." *Euphorion: Zeitschrift für Literaturgeschichte* 84 (1990): 89–111.

"Nemo." *Anzeiger für Kunde der deutschen Vorzeit,* N. F. 17 (1870): cols. 51–52.

Noomen, Willem, and Nico van den Boogaard. *Nouveau Recueil complet des fabliaux.* Assen, 1983–.

Norberg, Dag. *Introduction à l'étude de la versification médiévale.* Studia Latina Stockholmiensia 5. Stockholm, 1958.

Novati, Francesco. *Carmina Medii Aevi.* Florence, 1883.

———. "La parodia sacra nelle letterature moderne." In *Studi critici e letterari,* 177–310. Turin, 1889.

Odenius, O. "Mundus Inversus." *Arv* 10 (1954): 142–70.

Ohly, F. *Hohelied-Studien.* Wiesbaden, 1958.

Olson, Glending. *Literature as Recreation in the Later Middle Ages.* Ithaca, 1982.

Origen. *In canticum canticorum.* ed. J.-P. Migne, *Patrologia Graeca,* 13: cols. 35–198.

———. *Origenes Werke.* Ed. W. A. Baehrens. Die griechischen christlichen Schriftsteller der ersten drei Jahrhunderte 8. Leipzig, 1925.

Orlandi, Giovanni. *Rielaborazioni medievali della "Cena Cypriani."* Centro di Studi sul Teatro medioevale e rinascimentale. Rome, 1978.

Owst, G. R. *Literature and Pulpit in Medieval England.* 2d ed. 1933. Reprint, Oxford, 1961.

Oxford Classical Dictionary. Ed. N. G. L. Hammond and H. H. Scullard. 2d ed. Oxford, 1970.

Oxford Dictionary of the Christian Church. Ed. F. L. Cross and E. A. Livingstone. 2d ed. London, 1974.

Peiper, Leo Rudolf. *Cypriani Galli Poetae Heptateuchos.* In *Corpus Scriptorum Ecclesiasticorum Latinorum,* 23: Vienna, 1891.

Picot, Émile. "Le monologue dramatique dans l'ancien théâtre français." *Romania* 15 (1886): 358–422.

Piper, Paul. *Die Schriften Notkers und seiner Schule.* 3 vols. Freiburg, 1882–83.

Podlaha, A. *Soupis Rukopisu Knihovny Metropolitní Kapitoly Prazské.* 2 vols. Prague, 1910–22.

Pomponius. *Versus ad gratiam domini.* Ed. K. Schenkl. In *Corpus Scriptorum Ecclesiasticorum Latinorum,* 16.1: 615–20. Vienna, 1888.

Priebsch, Robert. *Letter from Heaven on the Observance of the Lord's Day.* Ed. W. E. Collinson and Arthur Closs. Oxford, 1936.

Proba, Faltonia. *Probae Cento.* Ed. K. Schenkl, In *Corpus Scriptorum Ecclesiasticorum Latinorum,* 16.1: 513–609. Vienna, 1888.

Rädle, Fidel. "Zu den Bedingungen der Parodie in der lateinischen Literatur des hohen Mittelalters." In *Literaturparodie in Antike und Mittelalter,* ed. Wolfram Ax and Reinhold F. Glei, 171–85. Trier, 1993.

Rahner, Hugo. *Man at Play.* Trans. Brian Battershaw and Edward Quinn. London, 1965.

Randall, L. M. C. *Images in the Margins of Gothic Manuscripts.* Berkeley and Los Angeles, 1966.

Raymo, Robert R. "A Middle English Version of the *Epistola Luciferiad Cleros.*" In *Medieval Literature and Civilization: Studies in Memory of G. N. Garmonsway,* ed. D. A. Pearsall and R. A. Waldron, 233–48. London, 1969.

Reau, Louis. "Du role des mots et des images dans la formation des légendes hagiographiques." *Mémoires de la Société Nationale des Antiquaires de France,* 8th ser., 8 (1934): 145–68.

Reichling, D. *Das Doctrinale der Alexander de Villa Dei.* Monumenta Germaniae Pedaegogica 12. Berlin, 1893.

Resnick, I. M. "'Risus Monasticus': Laughter and Medieval Monastic Culture." *Revue Bénédictine* 97 (1987): 90–100.

Reynolds, Roger E. *The Ordinals of Christ from their Origins to the Twelfth Century.* Beiträge zur Geschichte und Quellenkunde des Mittelalters 7. Berlin and New York, 1978.

Rhodes, Neil. *Elizabethan Grotesque.* London, 1980.

Ribner, Irving, and George Lyman Kittredge. *The Complete Works of Shakespeare.* Waltham, Mass., and Toronto, 1971.

Riewald, J. G. "Parody as Criticism." *Neophilologus* 50 (1966): 125–48.

Rigg, A. G. *A Glastonburg Miscellany of the Fifteenth Century.* Oxford, 1968.

———. *A History of Anglo-Latin Literature 1066–1422.* Cambridge, 1992.

———. "'Metra de Monachis Carnalibus'—The Three Versions." *Mittellateinisches Jahrbuch* 15 (1980), 134–42.

Rönsch, Hermann. "Einiges zur Erläuterung der Caena Hrabani Mauri." *Zeitschrift für wissenschaftliche Theologie* 27 (1883): 344–49.

Roques, Mario. *Aucassin et Nicolette: Chantefable du XIIIe siècle.* 2d ed. Classiques français du moyen âge. Paris, 1980.

Rose, Margaret. "Defining Parody." *Southern Review* 13 (1980): 5–20.

———. *Parody: Ancient, Modern, and Post-Modern.* Cambridge and New York, 1993.

———. *Parody/Meta-Fiction: An Analysis of Parody as a Critical Mirror to the Writing and Reception of Fiction.* London, 1979.

Rossiter, A. P. *English Drama from Early Times to the Elizabethans.* London, 1950.

Sadlek, Gregory M. "Laughter, Game, and Ambiguous Comedy in the *South English Legendary.*" *Studia Neophilologica* 64 (1991): 45–54.

Salanitro, Giovanni. *Osidio Geta: Medea.* Bibliotheca Athena 24. Rome, 1981.

Sales, Roger. *English Literature in History 1780–1830: Pastoral and Politics.* London, 1983.

Salimbene de Adam. *The Chronicle of Salimbene de Adam.* Trans. Joseph L. Baird et al. Binghamton, N.Y., 1986.

———. *Salimbene de Adam Cronica.* Ed. Giuseppe Scalia. 2 vols. Bari, 1966.

Saumaise, Claude de. *Historiae Augustae Scriptores IV.* Paris, 1620.

Scalia, Giuseppe. "Il 'Testamentum Asini' e il lamento della lepre." *Studi Medievali,* 3d ser., 3 (1962): 129–51.

Schmitt, J.-C. *The Holy Greyhound: Guinefort, Healer of Children since the Thirteenth Century.* Trans. M. Thom. Cambridge, 1982.

Schultz, Thomas R. "A Cognitive-Developmental Analysis of Humour." In *Humour and Laughter: Theory, Research, and Applications,* ed. Antony J. Chapman and Hugh C. Foot, 11–36. London, 1976.

Schum, Wilhelm. *Beschreibendes Verzeichniss der Amplonianischen Handschrift-Sammlung zu Erfurt.* Berlin, 1887.

Schüppert, Helga. *Kirchenkritik in der lateinischen Lyrik des 12. und 13. Jahrhunderts.* Medium Aevum, Philologische Studien 23. Munich, 1972.

Sedulius. *Carmen paschale.* Ed. J. Hümer. In *Corpus Scriptorum Ecclesiasticorum Latinorum,* 10. Vienna, 1885.

Shackleton Bailey, D. R., ed. *Anthologia Latina.* Stuttgart, 1982–.

———. "Three Pieces from the 'Latin Anthology.'" Harvard Studies in Classical Philology 84 (1980): 177–217.

The South English Legendary. Ed. Charlotte D'Evelyn and Anna J. Mill. Early English Text Society 235. London, 1956.

Spalding, M. C. *The Middle English Charters of Christ.* Bryn Mawr, 1914.

Springer, Carl P. E. *The Gospel as Epic in Late Antiquity: The Paschale Carmen of Sedulius.* Supplements to Vigiliae Christianae 2. Leiden, 1988.

Stallybrass, Peter, and Allon White. *The Politics and Poetics of Transgression.* London, 1986.

Stegmüller, Friedrich. *Repertorium Biblicum Medii Aevi.* 11 vols. Madrid, 1940–80.

Stone, Christopher. *Parody.* London, 1915.

Straccali, Alfredo. *I Goliardi ovvero i clerici vagantes delle università medievali.* Florence, 1880.

Strecker, Karl. *Die Apokalypse des Golias.* Texte zur Kulturgeschichte des Mittelalters 5. Rome and Leipzig, 1928.

———. *Die Cambridger Lieder. MGH, Scriptores Rerum Germanicarum* 40. Berlin, 1926.

———. "Die *Cena Cypriani* und ihr Bibeltext." *Zeitschift für wissenschaftliche Theologie,* 54 (N. F. 19) (1912): 61–78.

———. *Ecbasis cuiusdam captivi per tropologiam.* 1935. Reprint, Hanover, 1956.

———. "Iohannis Diaconi versiculi de cena Cypriani." In *MGH, Betae Latini Aevi Carolini,* 4.2: 857–900. Berlin, 1923.

Stroh, Norman A. "Parodic Activity." Ph.D. diss., University of Nebraska at Lincoln, 1975.

Suchier, Walter. *Das mittellateinische Gespräch Adrian und Epictitus mebst verwandten Texten (Joca monachorum).* Tübingen, 1955.

Suchomski, Joachim. *"Delectatio" und "Utilitas": Ein Beitrag zum Verständnis mittelalterlicher komischer Literatur.* Bibliotheca Germanica 18. Bern, 1975.

Suls, J. M. "A Two-Stage Model for the Appreciation of Jokes and Cartoons: An Information-Processing Analysis." In *The Psychology of Humor: Theoretical Perspectives and Empirical Issues,* ed. Jeffrey H. Goldstein and Paul E. McGhee, 81–100. New York and London, 1972.

Symons, Arthur, ed. *A Book of Parodies.* London, n.d. (*c.* 1908).

Tatlock, J. S. P. "Mediaeval Laughter." *Speculum* 21 (1946): 289–94.

Tarrant, R. J. "Anthologia Latina." In *Texts and Transmission: A Survey of the Latin Classics,* ed. L. D. Reynolds, 9–13. Oxford, 1983.

Thomson, Clive, and Alain Pagès, eds. *Dire la Parodie: Colloque de Cerisy.* American University Studies, series 2, Romance Languages and Literature 91. New York, 1989.

Thomson, Rodney M. "The Origins of Latin Satire in Twelfth Century Europe," *Mittellateinisches Jahrbuch* 13 (1978): 73–83.

———. *Tractatus Garsiae.* Textus Minores 46. Leiden, 1973.

Thurnher, Eugen, Manfred Zimmermann, et al. *Die Sterzinger Miszellaneen-Handschrift.* Litterae, Göppinger Beiträge zur Textgeschichte 61. Göppingen, 1979.

Travis, Peter W. *Dramatic Design in the Chester Cycles.* Chicago, 1982.

Treitler, Leo. "'Centonate' Chant: *Übles Flickwerk* or *E pluribus unus?*" *Journal of the American Musicological Society* 28 (1975): 1–23.

Tubach, Frederic C. *Index Exemplorum: A Handbook of Medieval Religious Tales.* FF Communications 86, no. 204. Helsinki, 1969.

Turdeanu, Émile. "Dieu créa l'homme de huit éléments et tira son nom des quatres coins du monde." *Revue des études Roumaines* 13–14 (1974): 163–94.

Turner, Victor. *From Ritual to Theatre: The Human Seriousness of Play.* New York, 1982.

———. "Humility and Hierarchy: The Liminality of Status Elevation and Reversal." In *The Ritual Process: Structure and Anti-Structure.* London, 1969.

Ungureanu, Marie. *La bourgeoisie naissante: Societé et littérature bourgeoises d'Arras aux XIIe et XIIIe siècles.* Mémoires de la Commission des Monuments Historiques du Pas-de-Calais 8¹. Arras, 1955.

Väänänen, Veikko. *Introduction au latin vulgaire.* 3d ed. Paris, 1981.

Veltrusky, Jarmila F. *A Sacred Farce from Medieval Bohemia: Mastickár.* Michigan Studies in the Humanities 6. Ann Arbor, 1985.

Virgilius Maro Grammaticus. *Virgilio Marone Grammatico: Epitomi ed Epistole.* Ed. G. Polara. Trans. L. Caruso. Nuovo Medioevo 9. Naples, 1979.

Viscardi, Antonio. *Le origini.* Storia letteraria d'Italia 1. Milan, 1939.

Vuillard, P. *Le Cantique des Cantiques d'après la tradition juive.* Paris, 1925.

Waddell, Helen. *The Wandering Scholars.* London, 1927.

Walther, Hans. "Beiträge zur Kenntniss der mittellateinischen Literatur (aus Handschriften süddeutscher und österreichischer Bibliotheken)." *Zentralblatt für Bibliothekswesen* 49 (1932): 270–83.

———. *Initia carminum ac versuum medii aevi posterioris Latinorum: Alphabetisches Verzeichnis der Versanfänge mittellateinischer Dichtungen.* Carmina medii aevi posterioris Latina 1. Göttingen, 1959.

———. "Parodistische Gebete der Pfarrköchin in einer Züricher Handschrift." *Studi Medievali,* n.s., 4 (1931): 344–57.

———. *Proverbia sententiaeque Latinitatis medii aevi: Lateinische Sprichwörter und Sentenzen des Mittelalters in alphabetischer Anordnung.* 9 vols. Carmina medii aevi posterioris Latina 2. Göttingen, 1963–86.

———. *Das Streitgedicht in der lateinischen Literatur des Mittelalters.* Quellen und Untersuchungen zur lateinischen Philologie des Mittelalters 2. Munich, 1920.

———. "Zur lateinischen Parodie des Mittelalters." *Zeitschrift für deutsches Altertum* 84 (1952–53): 265–73.

Wardroper, John. *The Demaundes Joyous.* London, 1971.

Watenphul, Heinrich, and Heinrich Krefeld. *Die Gedichte des Archipoeta.* Heidelberg, 1958.

Wattenbach, W. "Das Fest des Abts von Gloucester." *Anzeiger für Kunde der deutschen Vorzeit,* N. F. 28 (1881): cols. 121–28.

———. "Historia Neminis." *Anzeiger für Kunde der deutschen Vorzeit,* N. F. 13 (1866): cols. 393–97.

———. "Geistliche Scherze des Mittelalters I." *Anzeiger für Kunde der deutschen Vorzeit,* N. F. 14 (1867): cols. 342–44.

———. "Geistliche Scherze des Mittelalters II." *Anzeiger für Kunde der deutschen Vorzeit,* N. F. 15 (1867): cols. 9–11.

———. "Geistliche Scherze des Mittelalters III." *Anzeiger für Kunde der deutschen Vorzeit,* N. F. 15 (1867): cols. 38–41.

———. "Geistliche Scherze des Mittelalters IV." *Anzeiger für Kunde der deutschen Vorzeit,* N. F. 15 (1868): cols. 134–36.

———. "Lateinische Reime des Mittelalters." *Anzeiger für Kunde der deutschen Vorzeit,* N. F. 18 (1871): cols. 130–31.

———. "Nemo vir perfectus." *Anzeiger für Kunde der deutschen Vorzeit,* N. F. 14 (1867): cols. 205–7.

Wehrli, Max. "Christliches Lachen, christliche Komik?" In *From Wolfram and Petrarch to Goethe and Grass: Studies in Literature in Honour of Leonard Forster,* ed. D. H. Green, L. P. Johnson, and Dieter Wuttke, Saecula Spiritalia 5, pp. 17–31. Baden-Baden, 1982.

Wenzel, Siegfried. "The Joyous Art of Preaching; or, The Preacher and the Fabliau." *Anglia* 97 (1979): 304–25.

———, ed. and trans. *Fasciculus morum: A Fourteenth-Century Preacher's Handbook.* University Park, Pa., and London, 1989.

Werner, Jakob. *Beiträge zur Kunde der lateinischen Literatur des Mittelalters aus Handschriften gesammelt.* 2d ed. Aarau, 1905.

Weymann, Karl. *Beiträge zur Geschichte der christlich-lateinischen Poesie.* Munich, 1926.

Whitelock, Dorothy. "Bishop Ecgred, Pehtred, and Niall." In *Ireland in Early Medieval Europe: Studies in Memory of Kathleen Hughes,* ed. Dorothy Whitelock, Rosamond McKitterick, and David Dumville, 47–68. Cambridge, 1982.

Wilmanns, W. "Ein Fragebüchlein aus dem neunten Jahrhundert." *Zeitschrift für deutsches Alterthum,* n.s., 3 (1872): 166–80.

Wilmart, André. "Le prologue d'Hervé de Bourgdieu pour son commentaire de la *Cena Cypriani.*" *Revue Bénédictine* 35 (1923): 255–63.

Wright, Charles D. "Apocryphal Lore and Insular Tradition in St Gall, Stiftsbibliothek MS 903." In *Irland und die Christenheit: Bibelstudien und Mission,* ed. Próinséas Ní Chatháin and Michael Richter, 124–45. Stuttgart, 1987.

Wright, Thomas. *A History of Caricature and the Grotesque.* London, 1875.

———. *The Latin Poems Commonly Attributed to Walter Mapes.* London, 1841.

Wright, Thomas, and James Orchard Halliwell. *Reliquiae Antiquae.* 2 vols. 1841–43. Reprint, New York, 1966.

Wuttke, H. *Die Kosmographie des Istrier Aithikos.* Leipzig, 1853.

Yunck, John A. "Economic Conservativism, Papal Finance, and the Medieval Satires on Rome." *Mediaeval Studies* 23 (1961): 334–51. Reprinted in *Change in Medieval Society,* ed. S. Thrupp (New York, 1964).

———. *The Lineage of Lady Meed: The Development of Mediaeval Venality Satire.*

University of Notre Dame Publications in Mediaeval Studies 17. Notre Dame, Ind., 1963.

Ysengrimus: Text with Translation, Commentary and Introduction. Ed. Jill Mann. Mittellateinische Studien und Texte 12. Leiden and New York, 1987.

Zaranka, William. *Brand-X Poetry: A Parady [sic] Anthology.* London, 1984.

Zeno of Verona. *Zenonis Veronensis Tractatus.* Ed. B. Löfstedt. Corpus Christianorum, Series Latina 22. Turnhout, 1971.

Zeydel, Edwin H. "The Reception of Hrotsvitha by the German Humanists after 1493." *Journal of English and Germanic Philology* 44 (1945): 239–49.

Ziegelbauer, Magnoald. *Historia rei litterariae ordinis S. Benedicti.* 4 vols. 1754. Reprint, Farnborough, 1967.

Zimmerman, M. "Controversies on *Le Jeu de la Feuillée.*" *Studia Neophilologica* 39 (1967): 229–43.

Index of Manuscripts

General Index

DATE DUE

MAR 2 2 1997	

UPI 261-2505 G   PRINTED IN U.S.A.